W9-BEH-634

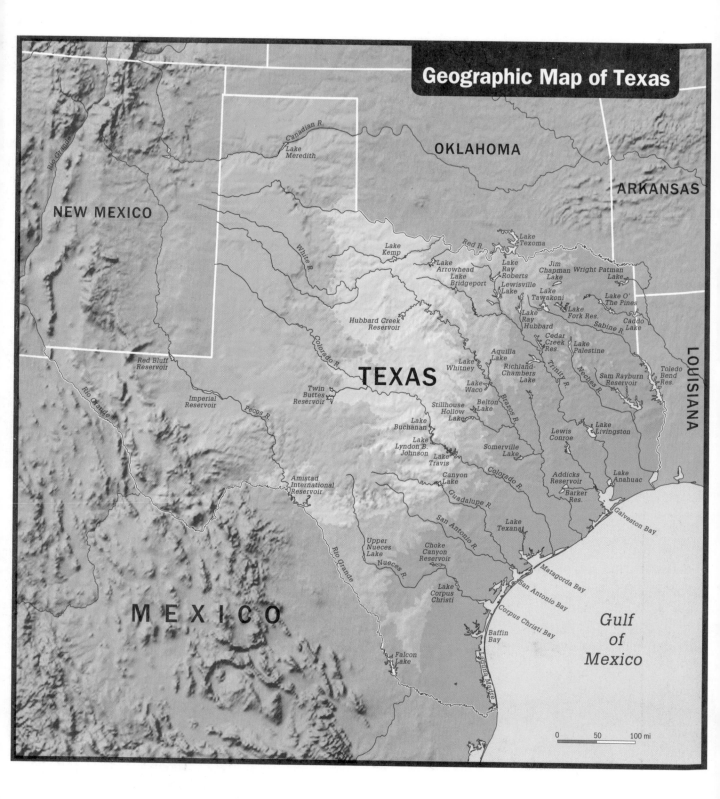

Geographic Map of Texas

OKLAHOMA

ARKANSAS

NEW MEXICO

LOUISIANA

TEXAS

MEXICO

Gulf of Mexico

Rio Grande

Canadian R.
Lake Meredith

Red R.

Lake Texoma

Lake Kemp

White R.

Lake Arrowhead
Lake Bridgeport

Lake Ray Roberts
Lewisville Lake

Jim Chapman Lake

Wright Patman Lake

Lake Tawakoni

Lake O' The Pines

Lake Fork Res.

Hubbard Creek Reservoir

Colorado R.

Lake Ray Hubbard

Sabine R.

Caddo Lake

Cedar Creek Res.

Aquilla Lake

Lake Palestine

Red Bluff Reservoir

Lake Whitney

Richland-Chambers Lake

Trinity R.

Neches R.

Sam Rayburn Reservoir

Toledo Bend Res.

Lake Waco

Twin Buttes Reservoir

Imperial Reservoir

Pecos R.

Stillhouse Hollow Lake

Belton Lake

Brazos R.

Lake Buchanan

Lake Lyndon B. Johnson

Somerville Lake

Lewis Conroe

Lake Livingston

Lake Travis

Canyon Lake

Colorado R.

Addicks Reservoir

Lake Anahuac

Rio Grande

Amistad International Reservoir

Guadalupe R.

Barker Res.

San Antonio R.

Lake Texana

Galveston Bay

Upper Nueces Lake

Choke Canyon Reservoir

Nueces R.

Matagorda Bay

San Antonio Bay

Lake Corpus Christi

Corpus Christi Bay

Baffin Bay

Falcon Lake

Laguna Madre

0   50   100 mi

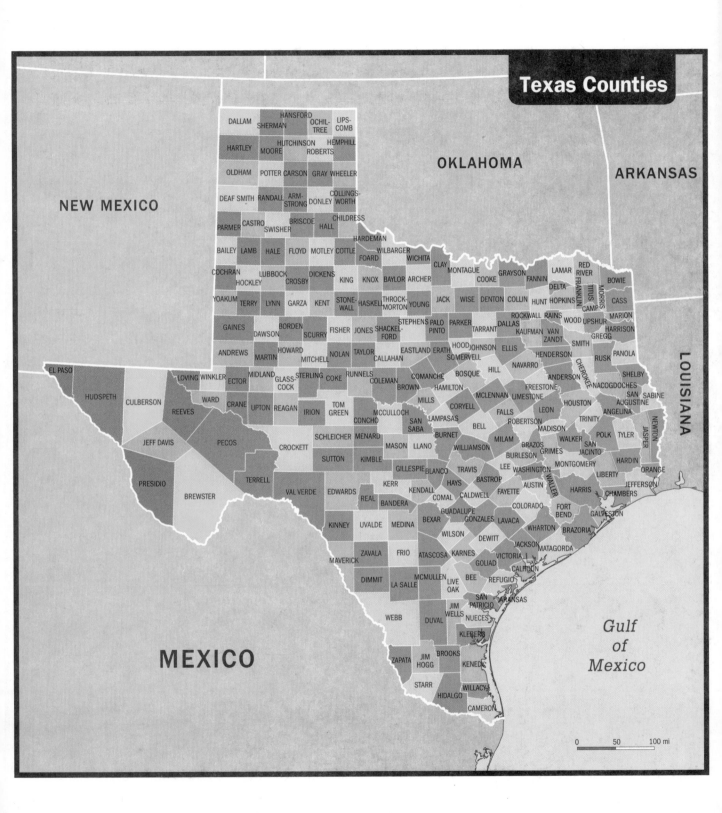

Texas Counties

Governing Texas

Governing Texas

Anthony Champagne
UNIVERSITY OF TEXAS AT DALLAS

Edward J. Harpham
UNIVERSITY OF TEXAS AT DALLAS

 W. W. NORTON & COMPANY
NEW YORK   LONDON

W. W. Norton & Company has been independent since its founding in 1923, when William Warder Norton and Mary D. Herter Norton first published lectures delivered at the People's Institute, the adult education division of New York City's Cooper Union. The firm soon expanded its program beyond the Institute, publishing books by celebrated academics from America and abroad. By mid-century, the two major pillars of Norton's publishing program—trade books and college texts—were firmly established. In the 1950s, the Norton family transferred control of the company to its employees, and today—with a staff of four hundred and a comparable number of trade, college, and professional titles published each year—W. W. Norton & Company stands as the largest and oldest publishing house owned wholly by its employees.

Copyright © 2013
All rights reserved.
Printed in the United States of America.
First Edition

Editor: Ann Shin
Associate Editor: Jake Schindel
Associate Editor, Ancillaries: Lorraine Klimowich
Manuscript Editor: Ellen Lohman
Project Editor: Christine D'Antonio
Electronic Media Editor: Peter Lesser
Editorial Assistant: Sarah Wolf
Editorial Assistant, Media: Jennifer Barnhardt
Marketing Manager, Political Science: Sasha Levitt
Associate Director of Production, College: Benjamin Reynolds
Photo Editor: Stephanie Romeo
Photo Researcher: Elyse Rieder
Permissions Manager: Megan Jackson
Text Design: Lissi Sigillo and Chris Welch
Information Graphics Design: Kiss Me I'm Polish LLC, New York
Art Director: Hope Miller Goodell
Composition: Jouve International—Brattleboro, VT
Manufacturing: R.R. Donnelley & Sons—Jefferson City, MO

Library of Congress Cataloging-in-Publication Data has been applied for.

ISBN 978-0-393-92035-2

W. W. Norton & Company, Inc., 500 Fifth Avenue, New York, N. Y. 10110
www.wwnorton.com

W. W. Norton & Company Ltd., Castle House, 75/76 Wells Street, London W1T 3QT

1 2 3 4 5 6 7 8 9 0

contents

4 ● Political Parties in Texas   105

5 ● Elections in Texas   133

6 ● Interest Groups and Lobbying   161

7 ● The Texas Legislature   181

9 ● The Texas Judiciary 247

10 ● Crime and Corrections Policy 279

13 ● Local Government in Texas   379

preface

Our goal in this text is to offer readers a broad understanding of the factors that are reshaping political processes and institutions in the Lone Star State in the first two decades of the twenty-first century. We are particularly concerned with explaining how the principles underlying constitutional government in Texas are being reworked in the face of new political, economic, and demographic changes. By supplementing our institutional analysis with concrete examples from everyday political life in Texas, we hope to show the reader that politics and government in Texas are not only important to their lives but endlessly fascinating as well.

Features of the Text and Accompanying Resources

Another, related goal of the book is to provide students with extensive pedagogical support throughout each chapter. In every chapter, several features engage students' interest and help them master the learning objectives for the topic.

- **Chapter Goals** appear at the start of the chapter and then recur at the start of the relevant sections throughout the chapter to create a more focused, active reading experience.

- **Extensive end-of-chapter review sections organized around Chapter Goals** include section outlines, practice quiz questions, key terms, and Recommended Websites, as well as information about related online resources. Students have everything they need to master the material in each section of the chapter.

- **Who Are Texans? infographics** engage visually oriented students with a "statistical snapshot" of the state related to each chapter's topic. These features help students grasp the political implications of demographic, political, economic, and regional diversity in Texas and compare Texas to other states. Critical-thinking questions in each Who Are Texans? box, related exercises on the StudySpace website, and slides in the instructor PowerPoints give students a chance to compare their own views and experiences and consider the political implications.

- **You Decide boxes in every chapter** address controversial issues in Texas politics that students care about. These boxes encourage students to think beyond their knee-jerk reactions and consider all sides of the debate.

- **What Government Does and Why It Matters chapter introductions** draw students into the chapter by showing them why they should care about the chapter's topic.

Governing Texas is accompanied by an extensive set of support materials including a free and open student StudySpace website (wwnorton.com/studyspace), free online coursepacks, a standard testbank, a Texas SLO Assessment Test Bank, an instructor's manual, and lecture and art PowerPoints.

About the Authors

Over the past 25 years, we have worked together on a number of books that have studied various aspects of government and political life in Texas. We come to the study of Texas politics and government from two very different backgrounds.

Anthony Champagne was born in Louisiana as the French surname suggests. His mother's family, however, were pioneer farmers and ranchers in Hopkins County, Texas. It was growing up with Louisiana and Texas connections that gave him a life-long interest in politics. When he moved to the University of Texas at Dallas in 1979, he immediately visited the Sam Rayburn Library in Bonham. Sam Rayburn was one of the Texas's most influential political figures. He was elected to the U.S. House of Representatives in 1912 and served until his death in 1961. During that time, he was chairman of one of the most influential committees of the House, was Majority Leader, Speaker, and Minority Leader of the House. He is responsible for much of the major legislation in the New Deal and for his key role in the politics of the Truman, Eisenhower, and early Kennedy Administrations. A chance meeting at the Sam Rayburn Library with H. G. Dulaney, Sam Rayburn's secretary for 10 years, led to the opportunity to do over 130 oral histories with persons associated with Sam Rayburn. As a result, Champagne was completely hooked on studying Texas politics. He was particularly interested in the transformation of the state from an overwhelmingly Democratic state to a Republican bulwark. And, he was interested in how Texas changed from being a key partner with the national government in the cooperative federalism of the New Deal period to a state whose leaders are frequent critics of national power today. Political change in the state from the Sam Rayburn era to today is a key research focus of his.

Edward Harpham, in contrast, was born in Montreal to second generation Canadian parents who immigrated to the United States soon after his birth. His family's migration over the last 100 years from Sheffield to Toronto (1919) to Delaware (1952) to Texas (1978) and the industries that employed the family (auto service industry, chemical industry, and academia) mirror the demographic changes that have reshaped much of the population movement in the United States and Texas throughout the twentieth century. Trained as a political theorist with a deep interest in political economy, Harpham's move to Texas sparked an interest in how economic changes in the late twentieth century were changing the contours of the state's traditional political life in new and unexpected ways. At the heart of his work lies an abiding interest on the role that ideas play in shaping the growth and development of political institutions and public policies in the modern information age.

acknowledgments

We are grateful for the suggestions that we have received from many thoughtful and experienced government instructors across the state. For their input on the plan and execution of this book, we thank:

Jason Abbott, Hill College
Lee Almaguer Midland College
Marcos Arandia, North Lake College
Ellen Baik, University of Texas–Pan American
Robert Ballinger, South Texas College
Annie Johnson Benifield, Lone Star College–Tomball
David Birch, Lone Star College–Tomball
Robin Marshall Bittick, Sam Houston State University
Patrick Brandt, University of Texas at Dallas
Gary Brown, Lone Star College–Montgomery
Lee Brown, Blinn College
Jonathan Buckstead, McLennan Community College
Daniel Bunye, South Plains College
James V. Calvi, West Texas A&M University
Michael Campenni, McLennan Community College
Max Choudary, Northeast Lakeview College
Mark Cichock, University of Texas at Arlington
Adrian Clark, Del Mar College
Tracy Cook, Central Texas College
Cassandra Cookson, Lee College
Leland M. Coxe, University of Texas at Brownsville
Rosalyn Crain, Houston Community College–Northwest
Sandra K. Creech, Temple College
Kevin Davis, North Central Texas College
Steve Davis, Lone Star College–Kingwood
Henry Dietz, University of Texas at Austin
Brian Dille, Odessa College
Douglas Dow, University of Texas at Dallas
Jeremy Duff, Midwestern State University
David Edwards, University of Texas at Austin
Matthew Eshbaugh-Soha, University of North Texas
Lou Ann Everett, Trinity Valley Community College
Victoria Farrar-Myers, University of Texas at Arlington
Ben Fraser, San Jacinto College
Joey Fults, Kilgore College

David Garrison, Collin College
Terry Gilmour, Midland College
Randy Givens, Blinn College
Donna Godwin, Trinity Valley Community College
Larry Gonzalez, Houston Community College–Southwest
Paul Gottemoller, Del Mar College
Kenneth L. Grasso, Texas State University
Heidi Jo Green, Lone Star College–CyFair
Sara Gubala, Lamar University
Yolanda Hake, South Texas College
Jeff Harmon, University of Texas at San Antonio
Tiffany Harper, Collin County Community College
Billy Hathorn, Laredo Community College
Ahad Hayaud-Din, Brookhaven College
Virginia Haysley, Lone Star College–Tomball
Tom Heiting, Odessa College
Kevin Holton, South Texas College
Taofang Huang, University of Texas at Austin
Casey Hubble, McLennan Community College
Glen Hunt, Austin Community College
Tammy Johannessen, Austin Community College
Doris J. Jones, Tarrant County College
Joseph Jozwiak, Texas A&M Corpus Christi
Christy Woodward Kaupert, San Antonio College
David Kennedy, Lone Star College–Montgomery
Edward Korzetz, Lee College
Melinda Kovacs, Sam Houston State University
Heidi Lange, Houston Community College–Southwest
Boyd Lanier, Lamar University
James Lantrip, South Texas College
David Lektzian, Texas Tech University
Raymond Lew, Houston Community College–Central
Bob Little, Brookhaven College
Robert Locander, Lone Star College–North Harris
Nicholas Long, St. Edward's University

George Lyon, El Paso Community College
Lynne Manganaro, Texas A&M International University
Sharon Manna, North Lake College
Bobby J. Martinez, Northwest Vista College
Mike McConachie, Collin College
Elizabeth McLane, Wharton County Junior College
Phil McMahan, Collin College
Eddie Meaders, University of North Texas
Banks Miller, University of Texas at Dallas
Eric Miller, Blinn College
Patrick Moore, Richland College
Sherri Mora, Texas State University–San Marcos
Dana Morales, Lone Star College–Montgomery
Amy Moreland, Sul Ross State University
Rick Moser, Kilgore College
Mark R. Murray, South Texas College
James Myers, Odessa College
Sugumaran Narayanan, Midwestern State University
Jalal Nejad, Northwest Vista College
Timothy Nokken, Texas Tech University
James Norris, Texas A &M International University
John Osterman, San Jacinto College
Cissie Owen, Lamar University
David Putz, Lone Star College Kingwood
Himanshin Raizada, Lamar University
Prudencio E. Ramirez, San Jacinto College
John Raulston, Kilgore College
Daniel Regalado, Odessa College
Darrial Reynolds, South Texas College
Donna Rhea, Houston Community College–Northwest
Laurie Robertstad, Navarro College

Mario Salas, University of Texas at San Antonio
Larry Salazar, McLennan Community College
Michael Sanchez, San Antonio College
Raymond Sandoval, Richland College
Gilbert Schorlemmer, Blinn College
Mark Shomaker, Blinn College
Dennis Simon, Southern Methodist University
Shannon Sinegal, Temple College
Brian William Smith, St. Edward's University
Michael Smith, South Plains College
Thomas E. Sowers II, Lamar University
John Speer, Houston Community College
Jim Startin, University of Texas at San Antonio
Andrew Teas, Houston Community College–Northwest
John Theis, Lone Star College Kingwood
Sean Theriault, University of Texas at Austin
John Todd, University of North Texas
Delaina Toothman, Texas State University
Steven Tran, Houston Community College
Homer D. Trevino, McLennan Community College
Christopher Turner, Laredo Community College
Ronald W. Vardy, University of Houston
Linda Veazey, Midwestern State University
Albert Waite, Central Texas College
David Watson, Sul Ross State University
Clay Wiegand, Cisco College
Neal Wise, St. Edward's University
Kathryn Yates, Richland College
Michael Young, Trinity Valley Community College
Tyler Young, Collin College
Rogerio J. Zapata, South Texas College

We also thank Jason Casellas, of the University of Texas at Austin, for his contributions to the book. Jason developed Chapters 4 and 5 on parties and elections, bringing a current perspective and important insights to these topics. We thank the following University of Texas at Dallas students for their assistance: Lisa Holmes, Josh Payne, Ali Charania, Alan Roderick, and Basel Musharbash.

At W.W. Norton, Ann Shin provided editorial guidance throughout the process of developing and publishing the book. Project editor Christine D'Antonio and editorial assitant Sarah Wolf kept everything organized. Developmental editor Gabe White and copy editor Ellen Lohman helped polish the text. Production manager Ben Reynolds made sure we ended up with a high-quality book, right on schedule. Emedia editor Peter Lesser and associate emedia editor Lorraine Klimowich worked with the authors of the accompanying resources to develop useful tools for students and instructors. Our sincere thanks to all of them.

Anthony Champagne
Edward J. Harpham

December 2012

Governing Texas

In some ways, state-level politics in Texas resembles national politics, but in other ways Texas's political culture is quite distinctive.

1

The Political Culture, People, and Economy of Texas

WHAT GOVERNMENT DOES AND WHY IT MATTERS Certain myths define Texas—and Texans—in the popular imagination. The cowboy who challenges both Native American and Mexican rule, the rancher and farmer who cherish their economic independence, the wildcatter who is willing to risk everything for one more roll of the dice, and the independent entrepreneur who fears the needless intrusion of government into his life—such are the myths about Texans. But the reality of the people of Texas is a far cry from the myths.

Texas today is not only the second-largest state in the Union, comprising more than 261,000 square miles; it is also the second most populous state. Texas has a rapidly expanding population of more than 25 million people that is becoming more and more diverse. Anglos constitute a little more than 45 percent of the population, while people of Hispanic descent constititue more than 37 percent. Just fewer than 12 percent of the population are African American, and 3.8 percent are of Asian descent. Eighty-eight percent live in urban areas, with many of them involved in an economy that is driven by the twin engines of high-tech industry and globalization. More than a quarter of the population have a bachelor's degree. On the whole, Texans are young, with 27.3 percent under the age of 18 and 10.3 percent over the age of 65.

Texas today is a political community that is dominated by the Republican Party. The Democratic Party of Vice President John Nance Garner (1868–1967), Speaker of the House Sam Rayburn (1882–1961), President Lyndon Johnson (1908–73), and Lieutenant Governor Bob Bullock (1929–99) no longer controls the key political offices in the state. Texas politics and government are largely controlled by a Republican Party led by such individuals as President George W. Bush (b. 1946), Governor Rick Perry (b. 1950), and Texas Speaker of the House Joe Straus (b. 1959). In recent years, the Texas Republican Party has advocated increasingly conservative political positions on a variety of social and economic issues, including abortion, birth control, gay marriage, immigration, and lower taxes. Conservatives in the Republican Party in Texas have been revitalized at the grassroots level by the Tea Party movement. Tea Party supporters have pushed Texas Republicans further to the right by melding a cultural conservatism on issues like abortion and gay rights to an anti-Washington rhetoric that calls for lower taxes, less government spending and regulation, and a balanced budget.

A new myth has emerged about the people of Texas: that they are business-savvy conservatives who reject government interference in the economy but want a government that protects "traditional" values such as the family and marriage. As with many myths, there is some truth to this one. But the reality of Texas, its people, and its politics is much more complex. Republicans may control the short- and near-term political agenda of the state, but their long-term dominance in politics and government is by no means certain. Long-term demographic pressures appear to favor the Democrats. The future of the state and its people will be determined in large part by the struggle between an assertive Republican majority and a resurgent Democratic minority as both try to address the various political, economic, and demographic challenges facing the state.

chaptergoals

- **Describe the defining characteristics of political culture in Texas** (pages 5–7)

- **Identify the major geographic regions in Texas** (pages 7–9)

- **Trace the evolution of Texas's economy** (pages 9–20)

- **Explain how the population of Texas has changed over time** (pages 20–26)

- **Describe the shift from a rural society to an urban one in Texas** (pages 27–32)

Texas Political Culture

Describe the defining characteristics of political culture in Texas

Studies of Texas politics often begin with a discussion of the **political culture** of the state. Though the concept is somewhat open ended, states do often exhibit a distinctive culture that is the "product of their entire history." Presumably the political culture of a state has an effect on how people participate in politics and how individuals and institutions interact.[1] Daniel Elazar has created a classification scheme for state political cultures that is used widely. He uses the concepts of moralistic, individualistic, and traditionalistic to describe such cultures. These three state political cultures are contemporary manifestations of the ethnic, socioreligious, and socioeconomic differences that existed among the original thirteen colonies.[2]

According to Elazar, **moralistic political cultures** were rooted in New England, where Puritans and other religious groups sought to create the Good Society. In such a culture, politics is the concern of everyone and government is expected to be interventionist in promoting the public good and in advancing the public welfare. Citizen participation in politics is viewed as positive; people are encouraged to pursue the public good in civic activities.

Individualistic political cultures, on the other hand, originated in the middle states, where Americans sought material wealth and personal freedom through commercial activities. A state with an individualistic political culture generally places a low value on citizen participation in politics. Politics is a matter for professionals rather than for citizens, and the role of government is strictly limited. Government's role is to ensure stability so that individuals can pursue their own interests.

Traditionalistic political culture developed initially in the South, reflecting the values of the slave plantation economy and its successor, the Jim Crow era. Rooted in preindustrial values that emphasize social hierarchy and close interpersonal, often familial, relations among people, traditional culture is concerned with the preservation of tradition and the existing social order. In such states, public participation is limited and government is run by an established **elite**. Public policies disproportionately benefit the interests of those elites.

States can, of course, have cultures that combine these concepts. One book classified Colorado, for example, as having a "moralistic" political culture. California was classified as having a "moralistic individualistic" political culture and New York an "individualistic moralistic" culture. New Jersey was classified as "individualistic" and Georgia "traditionalistic." Florida and Kentucky were seen as "traditionalistic individualistic."

Often Texas is categorized as having a "traditionalistic individualistic" political culture.[3] Taxes are kept low, and social services are minimized. Political elites, such as business leaders, have a major voice in how the state is run. In spite of the difficulty in measuring the concept of political culture in any empirical way, it is a concept widely regarded as useful in explaining fundamental beliefs about the state and the role of state government.

Yet, the political culture of a state can change over time. Texas is undergoing dramatic changes, including some change in its political culture. It is also difficult to classify the political culture of a state as large and as diverse as Texas in any one category. In fact, Texas has many different political cultures or subcultures within its borders.[4] These people of Texas reside in a state that is larger in area than the

political culture broadly shared values, beliefs, and attitudes about how the government should function and politics should operate. American political culture emphasizes the values of liberty, equality, and democracy

moralistic political culture the belief that government should be active in promoting the public good and that citizens should participate in politics and civic activities to ensure that good

individualistic political culture the belief that government should limit its role to providing order in society, so that citizens can pursue their economic self-interests

traditionalistic political culture the belief that government should be dominated by political elites and guided by tradition

elite a small group of people that dominates the political process

The Lone Star is the symbol of Texas and reflects its individualistic political culture.

for critical analysis

How would one describe Texas political culture? What patterns of Texas politics reflect its political culture?

combined area of the 15 smallest states. Texarkana, in the far northeastern corner of the state, is actually closer to Chicago than it is to El Paso. El Paso is closer to the Pacific Ocean than it is to the eastern boundary of Texas, and the eastern boundary is closer to the Atlantic Ocean than it is to El Paso. One can drive in a straight line for over 800 miles without leaving Texas—almost the same distance as from New York City to St. Louis.

Three long-lasting patterns in Texas politics seem to indicate a "traditionalistic individualistic" state political culture. These patterns relate to a domination of the state by political elites interested in limited government with low taxes and few social services. It is also the case that at least some of these characteristics of state politics are undergoing rapid change. These three patterns of state politics are described below.

The One-Party State

For over 100 years, Texas was dominated by the Democratic Party. Winning the Democratic Party primary was tantamount to winning the general election. As we will see in later chapters, this pattern no longer holds. During the 1990s, substantial competition emerged between the parties for control of the state legislature. Following redistricting in 2002, the Republicans secured a 7-vote majority in the state Senate and a 24-vote majority in the state House. Between 2002 and 2012, all major statewide elected offices were controlled by Republicans. The question today is not whether the political culture of Texas will continue to be defined by a powerful Democratic Party, but how that culture will be redefined by two forces: a powerful Republican Party in most suburban and rural areas and a resurgent Democratic Party in Texas's most urban counties.

Provincialism

provincialism a narrow, limited, and self-interested view of the world

A second pattern that once defined Texas political culture is **provincialism**, a narrow view of the world that is often associated with rural values and Jeffersonian notions of limited government. The result often was an intolerance of diversity and a notion of the public interest that dismissed social services and expenditures for education. Some of the more popular politicians in Texas have stressed corn pone, intolerance, and a narrow worldview rather than policies that might offer advantages to the state as it competes with other states and with other nations. Like the one-party Democratic state, Texas provincialism has faded as a defining feature of the political culture. The growing influence of minorities, women, and gays in state politics and the ongoing urbanization of the state have undercut provincialism.

Business Dominance

A third, continuing pattern that has helped define Texas's political culture is its longtime dominance by business. Labor unions are rare in Texas except in the oil-refinery areas around Beaumont–Port Arthur. Other groups that might offer an alternative to a business perspective, such as consumer interests, are poorly organized and poorly funded. Business groups are major players in Texas politics, in terms of campaign contributions, organized interest groups, and lobbyists.

This chapter will investigate the economic, social, and demographic changes that transformed Texas's political culture during the twentieth century. These changes shook Texas government and politics in the 1990s and have continued to shape them in the second decade of the twenty-first century.

Ties between business and political leaders in Texas have always been strong. Here, Governor Rick Perry appears with Ralph Babb, the chief executive of Comerica Bank, to announce that Comerica would move its corporate headquarters to Dallas.

● The Land

> **Identify the major geographic regions in Texas**

Much of Texas's history has been shaped by the relationship forged between its people and the land. Texas is the second-largest state in size, next to Alaska, comprising 267,000 square miles. The longest straight-line distance across the state from north to south is 801 miles; the longest east–west distance is 773 miles. To put this into perspective, the east–west distance from New York City to Chicago is 821 miles, cutting across five different states. The north–south distance between New York City and Charleston, South Carolina, is 763 miles, cutting across six different states.

Distances alone do not tell the whole story of the diverse geography found in Texas. There are four distinct physical regions in Texas: the Gulf Coastal Plains, the Interior Lowlands, the Great Plains, and the Basin and Range Province (Figure 1.1).[5]

The Gulf Coastal Plains

The Gulf Coastal Plains extend from the Louisiana border and the Gulf of Mexico, along the Rio Grande up to Del Rio, and northward to the line of the Balcones Fault and Escarpment. As one moves westward, the climate becomes increasingly arid. Forests become less frequent as post oak trees dominate the landscape until they too are replaced by the prairies and brushlands of central Texas.

The eastern portion of the Gulf Coastal Plains—so-called east Texas—is characterized by hilly surfaces covered by forests of pine and hardwoods. Almost all of

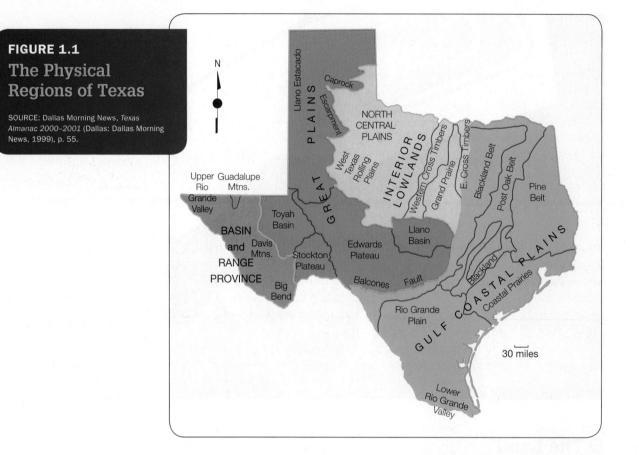

FIGURE 1.1

The Physical Regions of Texas

SOURCE: Dallas Morning News, *Texas Almanac 2000–2001* (Dallas: Dallas Morning News, 1999), p. 55.

Texas's timber production takes place here. It is also the home of some of Texas's most famous oilfields. To the west is the Blackland Belt. A rolling prairie soil made the Blackland Belt a prime farming area during the late nineteenth and early twentieth centuries. It was a major center of cotton production in Texas. Today it is the most densely populated area of the state and has a diversified manufacturing base.

The Coastal Prairies around Houston and Beaumont were the center for the post–World War II industrial boom, particularly in the petrochemical industry. Winter-vegetable and fruit production plays a major role in the Lower Rio Grande Valley, while livestock is important in the Rio Grande Plain, an area that receives less than 24 inches of rainfall on average every year and during the summer months experiences rapid evaporation.

The Interior Lowlands

The Interior Lowlands are an extension of the interior lowlands that run down from Canada. They are bordered by the Balcones Escarpment on the east and south and the Caprock Escarpment on the west. Beginning to the west of Fort Worth, the eastern edge of the Interior Lowlands has predominantly an agricultural economy and a rural population. The western portion, meanwhile, rises from 750 to 2,000 feet in elevation. The West Texas Rolling Plains contain much level, cultivable land and are home to a large cattle-raising industry. Many of the state's largest ranches are located here.

The Great Plains

Pushing down into northwest Texas from the Rocky Mountains to the Balcones Fault, the Great Plains define the terrain in much of western Texas, rising from 2,700 feet in the east to more than 4,000 feet along the New Mexico border. The major city on the northern plains is Amarillo. Ranching and petroleum production dominate the economy. The southern plains economy centers on agriculture and cotton production, with Lubbock as the major city. Large-scale irrigation from underwater reservoirs, particularly the Ogallala Aquifer, has played a major role in the economic development of this region. A major concern of policy makers is that pumping out of the aquifer exceeds replenishment, raising questions of the viability of basing future growth on the irrigation practices of the past.[6]

for critical analysis

How has the diverse geography of Texas affected its development?

The Basin and Range Province

The fourth geographic region in Texas is the Basin and Range Province. Here one finds Texas's true mountains in the Guadalupe Range along the border with New Mexico, which includes Guadalupe Peak (8,749 feet) and El Capitan (8,085 feet). To the southeast is Big Bend country, so named because the Rio Grande River surrounds it on three sides as the river makes its southward swing. Rainfall and population are sparse in this region.

● Economic Change in Texas

Trace the evolution of Texas's economy

The famous twentieth-century economist Joseph Schumpeter characterized the capitalist economic system as being a process of "creative destruction."[7] By this he meant that capitalism was an economic system that underwent periodic waves of transformation fueled by technological innovations in production and distribution. These waves of technological transformation were put into place by entrepreneurs who had visions of new ways to produce and distribute goods and services and who were willing to act on those visions. The capitalist process of creative destruction not only creates a new economic and social world; it destroys old ones. The world of railroads, steam, and steel transformed American economic and social life by nationalizing the market and making new opportunities available to businesses and individuals during the late nineteenth century. It also destroyed the local markets that had defined rural American communities since the Founding. Similarly, the technological innovation tied to gasoline combustion engines, electricity, and radio restructured the American economy again in the 1920s, leaving in its wake a society and economy that would never be the same.

Schumpeter's theory of creative destruction provides a useful way to think about the economic changes that have shaped and reshaped the Texas economy since the days of the Republic. Three great waves of technological change have helped define and redefine the Texas political economy over the last 150 years. The first centered on the production of cotton and cattle and their distribution by an extensive railroad system. The second grew out of the oil industry. The third and most recent is tied to the development of the high-tech digital economy.

Cotton

Cotton is one of the oldest crops grown in Texas.[8] Missions in San Antonio in the eighteenth century are reported to have produced several thousand pounds of cotton annually, which were spun and woven by local artisans. Serious cultivation of cotton began in 1821 with the arrival of Anglo Americans. Political independence, statehood, and the ongoing removal of the Native American "threat" in the years before the Civil War promoted the development of the cotton industry. By the mid-nineteenth century, cotton production in Texas soared, placing Texas eighth among the top cotton-producing states in the Union. Although production fell in the years following the Civil War, by 1869 it had begun to pick up again. By 1880, Texas led all states in the production of cotton in most years.

A number of technological breakthroughs further stimulated the cotton industry in Texas. In the 1870s, barbed wire was introduced, enabling farmers to cordon off their lands and protect their cash crop from grazing cattle. Second, the building of railroads brought Texas farmers into a national market. Finally, a newly designed plow made it easier to dig up the prairie soil and significantly increase farm productivity.

Throughout the 1870s, immigrants from the Deep South and Europe flooded the prairies of Texas to farm cotton. Most of these newly arrived Texans became tenant farmers or sharecroppers. Tenants lived on farms owned by landowners, providing their own animals, tools, and seed. They generally received two-thirds of the final value of the cotton grown on the farm, while the landlords received the other third. Sharecroppers furnished only their labor but received only one-half of the value of the final product. Almost half of the state farmers were tenants by the turn of the century.[9]

Two important consequences resulted from the tenant and sharecropping system. First, it condemned many rural Texans to lives of social and economic dependency. The notorious "crop-lien" system was developed to extend credit to farmers in exchange for liens on their crops. The result often was to trap farmers in a debt

During the late nineteenth century, in most years Texas produced more cotton than any other state. But although one-quarter of the cotton produced in the United States still comes from Texas, the importance of the cotton industry to the state's economy has declined since the 1920s. This photo shows land and machinery used to farm cotton.

cycle from which they could not escape. Second, the tenant and sharecropping system helped fuel radical political discontent in rural areas, sparking both the Grange and Populist movements. These movements played a major role in defining the style of Texas politics throughout much of the late nineteenth and early twentieth centuries.

Cotton production cycled up and down as farmers experienced a series of crises and opportunities during the late nineteenth and early twentieth centuries, ranging from destructive boll weevils to an increased demand brought on by World War I to a collapse in prices following the war. Although some sharecroppers returned to the farm during the Great Depression in the 1930s, the general decline of the cotton culture continued after World War II. The production of cotton also shifted from east and central Texas to the High Plains and Rio Grande Valley.[10]

Cattle Ranching

The history of ranching and the cattle industry parallels that of cotton in many ways.[11] The origins of ranching and the cattle industry extend back to the late seventeenth century, when the Spanish brought livestock to the region to feed their missionaries, soldiers, and civilians. Ranching offered immigrants an attractive alternative to farming during the periods of Mexican and Republican rule. In the 1830s, traffic in cattle was limited to local areas. This began to change as cattle drives and railroads began opening up new markets in the East.

Following the Civil War, the cattle industry took off, expanding throughout the state. As with cotton, the invention of barbed wire helped close off the lands used for grazing. By the end of the nineteenth century, ranch lands had been transformed from open range to fenced pasturing. As a result, conflicts over land often broke out between large and small ranchers, as well as between ranchers and farmers. As cattle raising became a more specialized and efficient business, periodic conflicts broke out between employers and employees. Throughout the twentieth century, ranching remained a cyclical industry, struggling when national and international prices collapsed and thriving during upturns in the economy.

Cattle ranching is another of Texas's dominant industries. The most famous ranch in Texas is the King Ranch, shown here in 1950. Currently covering almost 1,300 square miles, it is larger than the state of Rhode Island.

Ranching and cotton production remain important industries in the state, although increasingly dominated by big agribusiness companies. As in the past, in 2010 Texas continued to lead the nation in livestock production. Similarly, it leads all other states in cotton production. Approximately one-quarter of the total cotton production in the United States comes from Texas. In 2008, the annual cotton crop was 4.6 million bales, down from a peak in 2005 of 8.4 million bales. The decline was in large part caused by a severe drought. However, after two years of low production, cotton production dramatically increased to 8.05 million bales in 2010.[12]

Neither cotton production nor ranching drives the Texas political economy as in the past. The number of people making a living from agriculture has dropped significantly over the last 50 years as agribusiness has pushed out the family farm and ranch. In 1940, 23 percent of the population worked on farms and ranches. Another 17 percent were suppliers to farms and ranches or helped assemble, process, or distribute agricultural products. Currently, fewer than 2 percent of the population live on farms and ranches, with an additional 15 percent of the population providing support, processing, or distribution services to agriculture in Texas.

A new set of technological breakthroughs challenged the nineteenth-century dominance of cotton and cattle in the early twentieth century. These breakthroughs focused not on what grew on the land, but on what lay beneath it.

Oil in the Texas Economy

Oil was first sighted in the mid-seventeenth century by Spanish explorers.[13] There was no market or demand for the product, and nothing was done to develop this natural resource. Over a century later, encouraged by a growing demand for petroleum products following the Civil War, a scattering of entrepreneurs dug wells, although they were not commercially viable. The first economically significant oil discovery in Texas was in 1894 in Navarro County near Corsicana. By 1898, the state's first oil refinery was operating at the site. Although production peaked in 1900, the economic viability of oil production had been proven.

What catapulted Texas into the era of oil and gas was the discovery at Spindletop on January 10, 1901. Located three miles south of Beaumont along the Gulf Coast, the Spindletop discovery produced Texas's first oil boom. The success of Spindletop encouraged large numbers of speculators and entrepreneurs to try their luck in the new business. Within three years, three major oilfields had been discovered within 150 miles of Spindletop.

Oil fever spread throughout Texas over the next decade. In north central Texas, major discoveries took place at Brownwood, Petrolia, and Wichita Falls. In the teens, major discoveries were made in Wichita County, Limestone County near Mexia, and once again in Navarro County. In 1921, oil was found in the Panhandle, and by the end of the decade major oilfields were being developed all across the state. The biggest oilfield in the state was found in October 1930 in east Texas. As Mary G. Ramos notes, "By the time the East Texas field was developed, Texas's economy was powered not by agriculture, but by petroleum."[14]

The oil and gas industry transformed the social and economic fabric of Texas in a number of important ways. By providing cheap oil and gas, the industry made possible a new industrial revolution in twentieth-century America that was fueled by hydrocarbons. Cheap oil provided a new fuel for transportation and manufacturing. Railroads and steamships were able to convert from coal to oil. Manufacturing plants and farms were able to operate more efficiently with a new, cheap source of energy, encouraging individuals to migrate to cities away from farms. Automobile production was encouraged, as was the building of roads. The Interstate Highway System that was built during the 1950s and 1960s changed fundamentally the transportation patterns that shaped the movements of people and goods in Texas. The triangle formed by I-35 from San Antonio to Dallas–Fort Worth, I-45 from Dallas–Fort Worth to Houston, and I-10 from Houston to San Antonio became the heartland of the Texas economy and the location of an increasing percentage of the state's population (see Figure 1.2).

The oil and gas industry also sparked a rapid industrialization of the Gulf Coast region. Among the companies developing the Gulf Coast oilfields were Gulf Oil, Sun Oil, Magnolia Petroleum, the Texas Company (later Texaco), and Humble Oil (which later became Esso, then Exxon, and finally ExxonMobil). The refineries, pipelines, and export facilities laid the foundations for the large-scale industrialization that would take place along the Gulf Coast in the Houston–Beaumont–Port Arthur region. By 1929 in Harris County, for example, 27 percent of all manufacturing employees worked in refineries. By 1940, the capacity of all the refineries had increased fourfold.[15] The petrochemical industry continued to flourish throughout the 1960s when demand for its products grew at the rate of 10 percent a year.

One important effect of the oil and gas boom in Texas was the development of a new rhythm to economic life in the state. There had been a natural pace to the economy when it was tied to the production of cotton and cattle. Prices of products could rise and fall, bringing prosperity or gloom to local economies. But there was

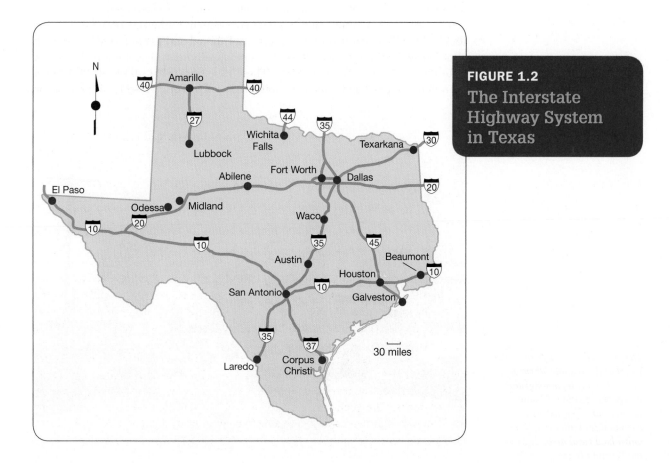

FIGURE 1.2

The Interstate Highway System in Texas

a bond between the land and the people and the communities that formed around them. Oil and gas, on the other hand, introduced a boom-and-bust mentality that carried over into the communities that sprang up around oil and gas discoveries. Rural areas were often unprepared for the population explosion that followed an oil or gas strike. Housing was often inadequate or nonexistent. Schools quickly became overcrowded. General living conditions were poor as people sought to "make it big." The irony of the oil and gas business was that a major discovery that brought large amounts of new oil and gas to market could lead to a sudden collapse in prices. Prosperous economic times could quickly turn into local depressions. And when particular fields were tapped out, boom towns could quickly become ghost towns.

The oil and gas industry also transformed government and the role that it played in the economy. Following the Civil War, a series of attempts to regulate the railroads had largely failed. In 1890, after considerable controversy fueled by Populist anti-railroad sentiment, a constitutional amendment was passed to create an agency to regulate the railroads, the Texas Railroad Commission. This regulatory agency was extended in 1917 to regulate energy. The Railroad Commission was empowered to see that petroleum pipelines were "common carriers" (that they transported all producers' oil and gas) and to promote well-spacing rules. In an attempt to bring stability to world oil prices brought on by the glut of oil on world markets in the 1930s, the commission won the authority to prorate oil and determine how much every oil well in Texas might produce. Through the late 1960s, the Texas Railroad Commission was one of the most important regulatory bodies in the nation. It was also one of the few democratically elected agencies.

Helping to expand the power of state government in the economy through the Railroad Commission was only one effect of the oil and gas industry in Texas. It also had an important fiscal effect on state government. Beginning in 1905, the state collected oil-production taxes. These rose from $101,403 in 1906 to over $1 million in 1919 and almost $6 million in 1929. For 2010–11, oil production

The oil industry transformed the social and economic fabric of Texas, leading to, among other things, the creation of boom towns—hastily constructed communities built around the oilfields in rural areas such as the Permian Basin.

The Keystone XL Pipeline and Competing Interests

The oil and gas industry has long been an important economic engine in Texas. In southeast Texas, many Texans work in the oil and gas business. Most of the oil comes from the Gulf of Mexico and the Middle East, but in recent years, because of global political unrest, some American politicians and other business leaders have argued that we should focus on domestic sources of energy rather than the Middle East and Venezuela. Many environmental activists, however, argue that Americans should seek alternative sources of energy, including solar, wind, and other green options in order to minimize pollution and preserve the planet. The controversy over the Keystone XL pipeline highlights the trade-offs between energy independence and environmental stewardship.

In 2011, TransCanada, a Canadian oil exploration company, announced plans to extend a pipeline to carry unrefined oil from Alberta to Houston and Port Arthur, Texas. The Keystone XL pipeline, as it is called, would extend from Canada to Texas through Nebraska and some other midwestern states. Its cost is estimated at $7 billion, but proponents say that the economic benefits would outweigh the initial investment. Nebraska has expressed concerns that the pipeline might negatively affect the Ogalalla aquifer, a key source of drinking water for the state and the region. While Republican Nebraska governor Dave Heineman supports the pipeline in principle, he made efforts to divert the construction of the pipeline so that it would not be built along the sensitive aquifer.

Proponents of extending the pipeline argue that it would create more domestic capacity and therefore reduce America's dependence on foreign oil. They also argue that the extension would create at least 20,000 new jobs,

a possibility particularly important during a recession and high unemployment. They also argue that obtaining oil from Canada, a political ally, would significantly lessen the United States' reliance on political adversaries such as Iran or Venezuela. They also suggest that because of tension in the Middle East, oil prices are volatile, and this project would keep supplies of oil more consistent, thus stabilizing prices. Canadian prime minister Stephen Harper has put pressure on the United States by suggesting that he would sell the oil to China if the United States did not permit the pipeline extension.

Opponents argue that the pipeline is a possible environmental hazard that could pose problems for the environment along the route and beyond. Air quality, water, and wildlife along the route might be adversely affected should a spill or other calamity take place. Environmentalists also fear that the pipeline might not withstand certain earthquakes that might be possible along the route, which includes a zone of seismic activity. In addition to these concerns, environmentalists argue that increased use of gasoline leads to more greenhouse gas emissions, climate change, and potential environmental damage.

Republicans in Congress pressed President Obama to make a decision regarding the pipeline early in 2012. Obama delayed his decision for a year in order to consider some of the concerns brought up by environmentalists, many of whom are his strongest political supporters. Republicans accused the president of pandering to his base for their support in the November 2012 election, but Democrats made the same claim about Republicans who used the issue to appeal to unemployed Americans in difficult economic times. The U.S. Department of State was tasked to decide whether the pipeline's extension was in the national interest. This is a complicated job because there are both clear costs and clear benefits to this proposal. The Keystone XL pipeline is a powerful recent example of the conflict between industry and environmental activists in political debate.

critical thinking questions

1. Is compromise possible on the Keystone XL pipeline? If so, how might both sides come to an agreement?

2. Under what conditions do you think environmentalists would support the pipeline's extension? Under what conditions do you think TransCanada would address some of the major environmental concerns?

taxes, or severance taxes, contributed $1.8 billion to the state budget. Natural gas production taxes added another $2 billion to the state budget.[16]

Much like the state coffers, higher education in Texas has benefited from the oil and gas industry. What many thought was worthless land at the time had been set aside by the state constitution of 1876 and the state legislature in 1883 to support higher education (the Permanent University Fund). As luck would have it, oil was discovered in the West Texas Permian Basin in 1923 on university lands. Soon 17 wells were producing oil on university lands, sparking a building boom at the University of Texas. In 1931, the income of the Permanent University Fund was split between the University of Texas at Austin and Texas A&M University, with the former receiving two-thirds and the latter one-third. In 1984, the income was opened up to all University of Texas and Texas A&M schools. Along with the royalties from other natural resources on university land, oil and gas royalties created one of the largest university endowments in the world. In August 2010, the net asset value of the Permanent University Fund was calculated to be $10.725 billion.[17]

The oil and gas industry had one other effect on life in Texas that is worth noting. Fortunes were made in the industry that paved the way for an expansion of private philanthropy that would have a major influence in shaping Texas's culture. Among the most famous of these were the Meadows Foundations, established in 1948 to promote programs in health, education, visual arts, social services, and historical preservation. The Sid W. Richardson Foundation was founded in 1947 and supported health and education programs, as well as the development of the arts in Fort Worth. The Bass Performance Hall, which opened in May 1998, was funded by the Bass brothers, grandnephews of the independent oilman Sid Richardson.

One can trace the rise and decline of the oil and gas industry in Texas through production figures (see Table 1.1). In the early decades of the twenty-first century,

for critical analysis

During the 1980s, the price of oil fell from almost $35 a barrel to $10 a barrel, bringing Texas's economy close to collapse. To what extent has the economy of Texas changed so that devastation in one industry will not have the catastrophic effect that the failure of the oil industry did in the 1980s?

TABLE 1.1

Oil Production in Texas

YEAR	CRUDE OIL PRODUCTION IN THOUSANDS OF BARRELS	AVERAGE PRICE PER BARREL
1915	24,943	$0.52
1945	751,045	$1.21
1955	1,002,480	$2.93
1965	932,810	$3.01
1975	1,185,683	$12.21
1980	931,078	$37.42
1985	830,597	$26.92
1990	645,941	$23.19
1995	511,962	$16.75
2000	398,678	$27.39
2005	344,226	$50.04
2010	356,911	$71.21
2011	393,880	$87.04

SOURCE: Texas Railroad Commission and "Historical Crude Oil Prices," InflationData.com.

oil and gas remained significant industries in the Texas economy. New technologies such as horizontal drilling and fracking raise the possibility of a new boom era of oil and gas production in Texas. Nevertheless, new industries and technologies have come to assume significant roles in plotting the state's economic future. Among the most important of these was the burgeoning high-tech industry.

The Emergence of the High-Tech Digital Economy

The movement out of the era of oil and gas and into that of high tech was not an easy one.[18] World oil prices rose in 1981 to almost $35 per barrel. At the time, oil-related businesses accounted for 26 percent of the gross state product. From 1971 to 1981, the average rate of economic growth was 4.4 percent. Fueled by a booming oil-based economy and a rapidly increasing population, real estate prices shot up in urban areas such as Houston and Dallas. Projections were made that as oil prices rose, perhaps to $70 or $80 per barrel on the world market, future prosperity was inevitable. Indeed, there was some talk that Texas's oil-driven economy had become recession-proof. Such talk proved to be premature, to say the least.

World oil prices began to collapse in 1982, bottoming out on March 31, 1986, at $10 per barrel. Other sectors of the economy began to suffer as the price of oil fell. Real estate deals fell through, and construction projects slowed and then shut down. Speculators defaulted on their loans, and banks began to fail. Throughout the 1980s, 370 banks went under in Texas. At the same time, the state went through two major recessions, one in 1982 and another in 1986–87. The average annual economic growth slowed to 1.7 percent, the worst since World War II.

Texas emerged from the economic malaise of the 1980s with a transformed state economy. Though remaining an important sector in the economy, the oil and gas business was no longer the primary driving force. By 1992, the production of oil had fallen to 642 million barrels worth only $11.8 billion. Production continued to fall until 2000 to just under 349 million barrels worth a little over

In the 1990s, Texas emerged as a leader in high-tech industries. Here, a Texas Instruments employee oversees the production of silicon wafers in the company's Dallas semiconductor plant.

$10 billion. Over 146,000 jobs had been lost in the oil industry throughout the 1980s. By the early 1990s, oil accounted for only about 12 percent of the gross state product.

In contrast to the 1980s, the 1990s were a period of rapid growth. Unlike early periods of speculative booms, such as the 1970s, the economy's growth was grounded in a rapidly diversifying economy. At the heart of this boom was a fast-growing manufacturing sector tied to high tech. In the 1990s, Texas went from seventh in the nation in total manufacturing employment to second. By 2008, 13 percent of the $160.8 billion gross state product came from manufacturing.[19]

Two metropolitan areas stand out as national centers for the rapidly evolving high-tech industry. The Austin–San Marcos metropolitan area has become a production center for computer chips, personal computers, and other related computer hardware. Seven of the area's largest employers are part of the computer or semiconductor industry. The Dallas metropolitan area, particularly north of the city, is the home of a number of important electronic and electronic-equipment companies.

NAFTA

Texas's place in national and international markets has been shaped by its central location, its border with Mexico, and its sophisticated transportation infrastructure. There are 306,404 miles of highways in Texas (the most in the nation) along with 45 railroads operating on 10,405 rail miles (the most in the nation). There are 12 deep-water ports in Texas, including the Port of Houston, which was ranked second nationally for total trade and thirteenth globally for total cargo volume. The Dallas–Fort Worth International Airport and the George Bush Intercontinental in Houston ranked high on the list of the world's busiest airports and were major hubs for both national and international travel. Over 3.2 million trucks, 31.5 million personal vehicles, and 17.1 million people crossed the Texas-Mexico border in 2010.[20]

One defining feature of the Texas economy in the 1990s and 2000s was the **North American Free Trade Agreement (NAFTA)**. Signed on December 17, 1992, by Prime Minister Brian Mulroney of Canada, President Carlos Salinas de Gortari of Mexico, and President George H. W. Bush of the United States, NAFTA sought to create a free-trade zone in North America that was the largest of its kind in the world. Considerable controversy surrounded the passage of NAFTA, with many groups arguing that free trade would hurt U.S. workers and companies because of the cheap labor available in Mexico. An important milestone in the agreement was reached on October 19, 2001, when Mexican trucks were finally allowed to cross over into the United States with goods for U.S. markets. Despite NAFTA provisions, Mexican trucks had been banned in the United States for almost 20 years because of strong labor union opposition and concerns over safety.

After 20 years, it appears that the trade agreement has had both negative and positive impacts on Texas. A 2011 study by the Economic Policy Institute calculated that almost 683,000 jobs had been lost in the United States because of NAFTA. The study estimated that three-fifths of these jobs were in the manufacturing sector. Over 55,000 of these displaced jobs came from Texas.[21] U.S. workers generally lost their jobs because of the stiffer competition from low-wage businesses in Mexico or because plants had been relocated to Mexico. (Under federal law such workers are entitled to additional unemployment compensation.)

North American Free Trade Agreement (NAFTA) trade treaty among the United States, Canada, and Mexico to lower and eliminate tariffs among the three countries

The signing of NAFTA in 1992 created a free-trade zone in North America. Although many Texas workers were adversely affected by the availability of cheaper labor in Mexico, NAFTA appears to have had a beneficial effect on the state's economy as a whole. Here, President George H. W. Bush stands between President Carlos Salinas de Gortari of Mexico and Prime Minister Brian Mulroney of Canada at the signing ceremony.

Although there were some losers in the movement toward free trade with Mexico and Canada, there were also big winners. According to a Texas Public Policy Foundation report, conservative estimates are that Texas increased exports to Canada and Mexico by over $10 billion in the first five years of NAFTA. Of the 32 industries in Texas that export to Mexico, 24 had double-digit gains. Meanwhile, 27 of the 31 industries that exported to Canada showed gains as well. Studies by the Department of Commerce and the Council of the Americas put the total number of jobs added to Texas's economy by NAFTA at 190,000 or higher. The following statistics from 2010 put the importance of Texas's international trade, particularly with Mexico and Canada, into perspective:[22]

- Texas exports totaled $207 billion, a $38.7 billion increase from 2007, with 16.2 percent of all U.S. exports originating in Texas.
- The North American market (Mexico and Canada) was the destination for 44.2 percent of these exports.
- Mexico was the top importer of Texas exports at almost $79.0 billion.
- Canada's imports from Texas totaled $13.0 billion.

For the past 20 years, the information age and the global economy have transformed the Texas economic landscape. It is impossible to say exactly how these forces will continue to change Texas over the next 20 years, or which companies will become the Texacos or ExxonMobils of the information age. We can say, however, that it will be an economy as different from that of the oil and gas era as the oil and gas era was from the era of cotton and cattle.

Texas in the Great Recession

In December 2007, the nation entered what some have called "the Great Recession," a time of chronic economic problems that drew analogies to the Great Depression of the 1930s. A speculative bubble in the housing market fueled by

Texas was not hit as hard as other states by the recession that started in 2007 and deepened in 2008. However, some Texans—including these Tea Party protesters—were alarmed by the massive spending involved in the national government's stimulus efforts.

cheap credit and poor business practices culminated in a credit crisis that brought some of America's largest banks and investment houses to their knees. Only the massive intrusion of the Federal Reserve System into credit markets in the fall of 2008 prevented the banking system from melting down. The Federal Reserve reported that between November 2007 and March 2009, 86 percent of American industries cut back production. The GNP dropped 1.7 percent and household net worth fell $11 trillion or 18 percent during the recession.[23]

Compared with the rest of the nation, Texas weathered the Great Recession relatively well. The housing market declined much less severely in Texas than in the rest of the nation. Most of Texas did not experience the surge in real estate values found in other states like California, Nevada, Florida, and Arizona. While foreclosure rates throughout the country increased sixfold between 2005 and 2009, in Texas they rose only marginally. Texas's banking industry also appeared to have weathered the storm better than its counterparts in other states. Article XVI of the Texas Constitution, as amended in 1997, forbids consumers from using home-equity loans for credit that exceeds 80 percent of the mortgage, and this probably provided a cushion against the credit crunch.[24]

Texas was one of the last states to enter the Great Recession and seems likely to be one of the first to exit. In 2010, Texas led the nation with 209,800 jobs added to the state's economy, and unemployment in Texas stood well below the national rate. Housing starts and exports were also up, as were other leading economic indicators in the state. However, Texas faces huge budget shortfalls that have no easy solution. A diversified economy has helped Texas weather the economic storm to a considerable degree, but there are no guarantees that the Great Recession is over.[25]

● The People: Texas Demography

> **Explain how the population of Texas has changed over time**

The population in Texas has grown rapidly since the early days of the Republic. In 1850, the population stood at a little more than 210,000 people, more than one-quarter of whom were African American slaves. Texas in 1850 also was an overwhelmingly rural state. Only 4 percent of the population lived in urban areas. By 1900 the population had increased to more than 3 million people, with 83 percent continuing to live in rural areas. The 1980s began as boom years for population growth, with increases running between 2.9 percent and 1.6 percent per year from 1980 through 1986. With the collapse of oil prices, however, population growth slowed significantly between 1987 and 1989 to less than 1 percent.[26]

With a recovering economy, however, population growth surged forward in the 1990s (see Table 1.2). In 1990, 17 million people resided in the state. By 2010, the number of people was estimated to be 25.1 million. Forty-five percent of the population were non-Hispanic white in 2009, down from 61 percent in 1990.

TABLE 1.2

The Changing Face of Texas, 1850–2010

	1850	1900	1950	1990	2010
Population	213,000	3,050,000	7,710,000	17,000,000	25,146,000
Anglo	72%	80%	87%	61%	47%
African American	28%	20%	13%	12%	11%
Hispanic	NA	NA	NA	25%	37%
Other	NA	NA	NA	2%	5%

NA=not available

SOURCES: *Statistical Abstract of the United States: 1994* (Washington, DC: U.S. Department of Commerce, Bureau of the Census, 1994); Dallas Morning News, *Texas Almanac 2004–2005* (Dallas: Dallas Morning News, 2004), p. 10; 2010 U.S. Census.

Eleven percent were African American. Thirty-eight percent were Hispanic, up from 25 percent in 1990.

Three factors account for the population growth in Texas: natural increase due to the difference between births and deaths; international immigration, particularly from Mexico; and domestic immigration from other states. The makeup of the growth in population shifted in significant ways over the course of the decade. In 1991, almost two-thirds of population growth was accounted for by natural increases. A little more than 20 percent was due to international immigration, while less than 14 percent was due to domestic immigration. By 2009, natural increases accounted for only 54 percent of population growth, while international immigration accounted for about 20 percent and domestic immigration for about 30 percent.[27] In the early decades of the twenty-first century, Texas was being redefined not by native-born Texans but by individuals coming to Texas to share in and contribute to the state's high-tech economic boom.

Anglos

For most of the nineteenth and twentieth centuries, the dominant ethnic group was non-Hispanic white, or Anglo. Anglos in Texas comprise a wide range of European ethnic groups, including English, Germans, Scots, Irish, Czechs, and European Jews. The first wave of Anglos came to Texas before the break with Mexico. Encouraged by impresarios such as Moses Austin and his son Stephen F. Austin, who were authorized by the Spanish and later the Mexican leaders to bring people to Texas, these Anglos sought inexpensive land. But they brought along a new set of individualistic attitudes and values about democratic government that paved the way for the Texas Revolution. Following the revolution, a new surge of Anglo immigrants came from the Deep South. Like their predecessors, they sought cheap land. But they brought with them new cultural baggage: slavery. By the time of the American Civil War, this group had come to dominate the political culture of the state. Although most Texas farmers did not own slaves themselves, the vast majority supported the institution as well as secession from the Union.

Prior to statehood, many of Texas's Anglos were European immigrants. For instance, in 1844 close to 5,000 Germans arrived and soon thereafter established the towns of New Braunfels and Fredericksburg. This painting from the 1850s shows a German American family from Fredericksburg "going visiting."

Defeat in the Civil War shattered the dominance of the traditional Anglo power structure in the state. By the end of Reconstruction, however, it had reasserted itself, establishing the three patterns that defined Texas politics for the next hundred years: the one-party Democratic state, provincialism, and business dominance. Anglos continued to dominate and define Texas's political culture throughout much of the twentieth century, but by the end of that century much had changed. As a percentage of the population, Anglo influence peaked in 1950, when 74 percent of the population was officially categorized as Anglo. This percentage began to fall, reaching 45 percent in 2010, and will likely continue to fall (see Figure 1.3).

Numbers alone do not tell the whole story. Anglos living in Texas at the end of the twentieth century were not cut from the same cloth as those who had preceded them. A new wave of Anglo immigration into Texas over the past 40 years has redefined what it means to be an Anglo in Texas. No longer can one say that an Anglo lives on a farm, holds culturally conservative values, and is firmly tied to the Democratic Party. On the contrary, he or she may be an urbanite or suburbanite who wasn't born in Texas and who votes Republican.

Latinos

Most Hispanics in Texas are people of Mexican descent.[28] Prior to independence from Spain, this included people born of Iberian (Spanish) parents as well as mestizos (people of mixed Spanish and Native American ancestry). In the early nineteenth century, approximately 5,000 people of Mexican descent were living in Texas. Although this number fluctuated considerably over the years, by 1850 it was estimated that 14,000 Texans were of Mexican origin. Texas became for many a refuge from the political and economic instability that troubled Mexico from the late 1850s to the 1920s. Despite periodic attempts to curtail the growth of the Mexican American population in Texas, it grew from an estimated 700,000 in 1930 to 1,400,000 in 1960. The 2000 census counted 5.1 million Mexican Americans living in Texas. In 2010, there were 9.5 million Hispanics residing in Texas. Texas Hispanics constituted 19 percent of all Hispanics in the United States.[29]

FIGURE 1.3
Anglo Population in Texas Counties, 2010

SOURCE: Data are drawn from the 2010 census. Texas State Data Center, www.texastribune.org/library/data/census-2010/ (accessed 5/2/12).

Anglo Population

- ▢ 0–1,000 persons (8 counties)
- ▨ 1,001–10,000 persons (91 counties)
- ▦ 10,001–100,000 persons (121 counties)
- ▪ 100,001+ persons (34 counties)

Most Latinos in Texas are Mexican American. During the first half of the twentieth century, Mexicans immigrated to Texas to work in the emerging cotton industry. This 1939 photo shows cotton pickers laboring in the sun over rows of white cotton.

Until 1900, Hispanics constituted a majority in south Texas along the border with Mexico and in certain border counties of west Texas. During the first few decades of the twentieth century, Hispanics migrated to northwest Texas and the Panhandle to work as laborers in the newly emergent cotton economy. Labor segregation limited the opportunities available to many Hispanics before World War II. After World War II, however, many Hispanics left agricultural work and took jobs in the rapidly growing urban areas of Texas. By the end of the century, Hispanics constituted majorities in the cities of San Antonio and El Paso and sizable minorities in Houston, Dallas, Austin, and Fort Worth (see Figure 1.4).

The political status of Latinos in Texas has changed considerably over the past hundred years. In the nineteenth century, numerous obstacles limited their participation in the political life of the state. Voting, particularly among the lower classes, was discouraged or tightly controlled. The white-only primary and the poll tax actively discouraged voting by Latinos. Only after World War II were Latino politicians able to escape some of the strictures that had been imposed on them by the dominant Anglo political culture of the time. A more tolerant atmosphere in the growing urban areas enabled Latino politicians to assume positions of importance in the local political community. In 1956, Henry B. Gonzalez became the first Mexican American to be elected to the Texas Senate in modern times. In the mid-1960s a political movement emerged in the Raza Unida Party, which sought to confront many of the discriminatory practices that isolated Texas Latinos from the political and economic mainstream. By the 1980s, Latino political leaders were

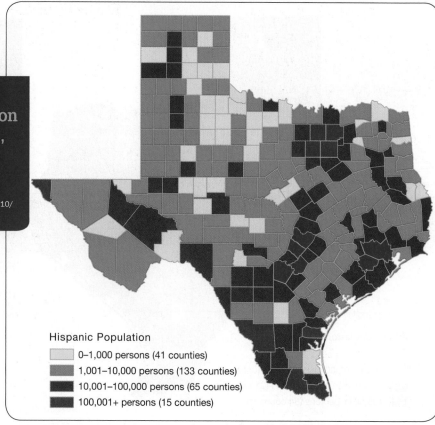

FIGURE 1.4

Hispanic Population in Texas Counties, 2010

SOURCE: Data are drawn from the 2010 census. Texas State Data Center, www.texastribune.org/library/data/census-2010/ (accessed 5/2/12).

Hispanic Population

☐ 0–1,000 persons (41 counties)

☐ 1,001–10,000 persons (133 counties)

■ 10,001–100,000 persons (65 counties)

■ 100,001+ persons (15 counties)

playing a growing role in state politics, and Latino voters were courted heavily by both political parties. The number of Latinos elected to public office rose from 1,466 in 1986 to 2,521 in 2011. After the 2010 elections, the National Association of Latino Elected and Appointed Officials Education Fund reported that 6 Latinos represented Texas in the U.S. House of Representatives, 7 Latinos were in the Texas State Senate, and 31 Latinos were elected to the Texas House of Representatives.[30] The use of the terms *Hispanic* and *Latino* can be confusing. We often use the words interchangeably to refer to people of "Spanish" descent or people from Latin America. Many statistical databases use the term *Hispanic*, as we will when presenting data from these databases.

African Americans

People of African descent were among the earliest explorers of Texas.[31] Most African Americans, however, entered Texas as slaves. Anglo Americans from the upper and lower South brought slaves with them to Texas. At first, antislavery attitudes among Spanish and Mexican authorities kept the slave population down. However, independence from Mexico lifted the restrictions on slavery, creating an incentive for southerners to expand the system of slavery westward. The number of slaves in Texas rose from 5,000 in 1830 to 11,000 in 1840 to 58,000 in 1850. By the Civil War, over 182,000 slaves lived in Texas, approximately one-third of the state's entire population.

As in most former slave states, there was initial resistance to the civil rights movement in Texas. These signs appeared in Fort Worth's Riverside section in September 1956 during a protest over a black family's moving into a previously all-white block of homes.

Emancipation for African Americans living in Texas came on June 19, 1865. Emancipation, however, did not bring anything approaching equality. Between 1865 and 1868, a series of Black Codes were passed by the state legislature and various cities that sought to restrict the rights of former slaves. Military occupation and congressional reconstruction opened up new opportunities for former slaves, who supported the radical wing of the Republican Party. Ten African American delegates helped write the Texas Constitution of 1869. Forty-three served as members of the state legislature between 1868 and 1900. The end of Reconstruction and the return to power of the Democratic Party in the mid-1870s reversed much of the progress made by former slaves in the state. In 1900, over 100,000 African Americans voted in Texas elections. By 1903, the number had fallen to under 5,000, largely because of the imposition of the poll tax in 1902 and the passage of an early version of the white-primary law in 1903. In 1923, the legislature explicitly banned blacks from voting in the Democratic primary. Segregation of the races became a guiding principle of public policy, backed by the police power of the state and reinforced by lynchings and race riots against African Americans. For all intents and purposes, African Americans had become second-class citizens, disenfranchised by the political system and marginalized by the political culture.

Federal court cases in the 1940s and 1950s offered some hope of relief to African Americans living in Texas. The white primary was outlawed in 1944 in the Supreme Court decision in *Smith v. Allwright*. In 1950, African Americans were guaranteed admission to Texas's graduate and professional schools in *Sweatt v. Painter*. Finally, the segregation of public schools was outlawed by the Supreme Court in *Brown v. Board of Education* in 1954.

Political progress was much slower. The Civil Rights Act of 1964 and the Voting Rights Act of 1965 helped to open up the political system in Texas to African Americans. In 1966, a small number of African American candidates actually began to win political office in the state. In 1972, Barbara Jordan became the first African American woman to be elected to the United States House of Representatives from Texas.

Today the African American population is concentrated in east Texas, where the southern plantation and sharecropping systems were dominant during the nineteenth century. Large numbers of African Americans had also migrated to

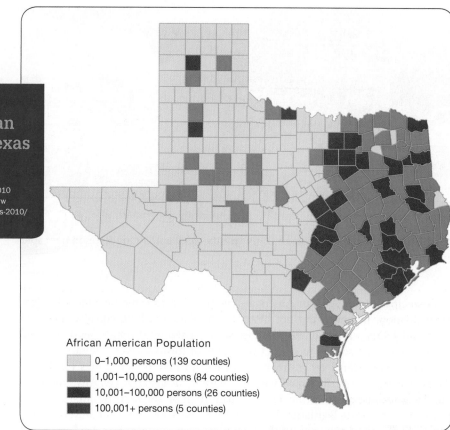

FIGURE 1.5

African American Population in Texas Counties, 2010

SOURCE: Data are drawn from the 2010 census. Texas State Data Center, www .texastribune.org/library/data/census-2010/ (accessed 5/2/12).

African American Population

- 0–1,000 persons (139 counties)
- 1,001–10,000 persons (84 counties)
- 10,001–100,000 persons (26 counties)
- 100,001+ persons (5 counties)

form sizable minorities in the urban and suburban areas of Houston and Dallas (see Figure 1.5). African American political leaders have come to play major roles in these areas as members of Congress, the state legislature, and city councils. African Americans were also elected mayors of Houston and Dallas in the late 1990s. The political influence of African Americans in Texas has not been extended to west Texas, where few African Americans live.

Age

When compared with the rest of the nation, the population of Texas is relatively young. In 2010, 27.8 percent of the population were under 18 years old, compared with 24.3 percent nationally. In addition, only 10.2 percent of the population in Texas were 65 years of age or older, compared with 12.9 percent nationally.[32] Having a relatively young population compared with those of other states presents Texas with a variety of problems and opportunities, as we shall see in later chapters.

Poverty and Wealth

Younger populations tend to be poorer, as income and poverty statistics bear out. As noted above, the 1990s were a period of rapid economic growth in Texas. Despite this growth, however, Texas continued to lag behind the nation as a whole (see Table 1.3). Per capita income in Texas, however, rose from $17,421 in 1990

forcriticalanalysis

How did the population of Texas change during the 1990s? What is its racial and ethnic composition? How do these changes complicate the idea of the "typical" Texan?

TABLE 1.3

Per Capita Income in Texas and the United States, 1990–2010 (in Nominal Nonadjusted Dollars)

	1990	1995	2006	2010
USA	$19,477	$23,076	$36,276	$40,584
Texas	$17,421	$21,033	$34,257	$39,493

SOURCE: U.S. Department of Commerce, Bureau of Economic Analysis.

to $39,493 in 2010. Texas ranked only twenty-third among the states in per capita income, up from thirty-second in 1990.

The percentage of the population in Texas living below the poverty level—a level established by the federal government—fell from 15.7 percent to 14.9 percent between 1990 and 2004, rose to 16.9 percent in 2006, and to 17.1 percent in 2009. During the same period, the national poverty rate fell from 13.5 percent to 11.7 percent, rose to 13.3 percent in 2006, and to 14.3 percent in 2009.[33]

● Urbanization

Describe the shift from a rural society to an urban one in Texas

Urbanization is the process by which people move from rural to urban areas. Suburbanization is the process by which people move out of central city areas to surrounding suburban areas. Much of Texas's history is linked to ongoing urbanization. By the end of the twentieth century, this process was largely complete, as 88 percent of the population now reside in urban areas (see Table 1.4). Suburbanization, however, continues as city populations spill over into surrounding suburban areas.

urbanization the process by which people move from rural areas to cities

Most Texas cities are the result of Anglo settlement and culture.[34] The Spanish influence on urban life in Texas grew out of efforts to extend territorial control northward out of Mexico through a series of presidios (garrisons), missions (churches), and pueblos (towns). The physical organization and planning of the towns reflected this imperial mission. For example, the largest Spanish settlement was San Antonio. It was initially established as a supply depot to missions in east Texas. Later it expanded as missions were established to convert local Native Americans to Christianity and farms were cultivated to feed the local population. By the early nineteenth century, San Antonio's population had reached 2,500. Other smaller settlements were located in east Texas, along the border with French and, later, American territory.

Anglo American influence began with the arrival of Moses Austin in 1820 in San Antonio. Soon his son Stephen F. Austin followed. The Spanish offered the Austins and other impresarios grants of land to encourage the inflow of Americans into underpopulated regions of Texas. Small towns emerged as administrative units for impresario grants. There were considerably more freedom and dynamism in

TABLE 1.4

Urbanization in Texas, 1850–2010

	1850	1900	1950	2010
Urban	4%	17%	63%	88%
Rural	96%	83%	37%	12%

SOURCES: *Statistical Abstracts of the United States: 1994* (Washington, DC: U.S. Department of Commerce, Bureau of the Census, 1994); Dallas Morning News, *Texas Almanac 2001–2002* (Dallas: Dallas Morning News, 2001); U.S. Department of Agriculture, Economic Research Service.

Anglo American urban areas than in Spanish ones. Americans brought with them a host of new interests and ideas that would transform urban life in Texas, including a new language, slavery, Protestantism, and a commitment to free enterprise and democracy. The courthouse became a central feature of many Anglo American towns, often located in the center of the town surrounded by shops.

The expansion of Anglo American urban life initially began along the Gulf Coast and gradually expanded east to west, particularly along rivers. New technologies transformed the urban landscape of Texas. Dredging technologies helped to stimulate the growth of port cities such as Houston, Galveston, Corpus Christi, and Brownsville. Railroad construction in the second half of the nineteenth century opened up new lands, which had been difficult for populations to reach, to urban development. In 1880, there were only 11 towns of 4,000 or more people in all of Texas. Following the rapid expansion of the railroads in the 1880s and 1890s, the number rose to 36. By 1910, when the railroad network of 13,110 miles was completed, Texas had 49 towns with a population of 4,000 or more. By 1920, 5 cities—Dallas, El Paso, Fort Worth, Houston, and San Antonio—had populations of more than 50,000. Later technological breakthroughs in transportation, such as cars and air travel, would reinforce the population grid laid out by the railroads.

The Urban Political Economy

political economy the complex interrelations between politics and the economy, as well as their effect on one another

Understanding the complexity of the **political economy** of Texas today demands having some sense of how Texas's three major metropolitan areas compare with each other (see Tables 1.5 and 1.6).

Houston Houston, located in Harris County, is the largest city in Texas and the fourth-largest city in the United States—with a population of 2.1 million—behind New York, Los Angeles, and Chicago. Its consolidated metropolitan area encompasses eight counties, with an estimated population of 6.1 million in 2011. Houston grew by 7.5 percent during the first decade of the twenty-first century.

The city originated in 1836 out of the entrepreneurial dreams of two brothers, Augustus Chapman Allen and John Kirby Allen, who sought to create a "great interior commercial emporium of Texas."[35] The town was named after Sam Houston, the leader of Texas's army during its war of independence from Mexico. Early settlers came from the South, bringing with them the institution of slavery. As a consequence, segregation was built into the social structure from the outset. For

How Is the Texas Population Changing?

The face of Texas is changing rapidly and will continue to change well into the future. The figures below show projections of how the Texas population will change over the next 30 years. The state's population will continue to grow quickly, especially as the number of Hispanic Texans increases. Further, most of the population growth in the state will happen in metropolitan areas—Dallas–Fort Worth, Houston, San Antonio, and Austin.

Race and Total Population

	1980			2010			2040		
= 250,000 people	White 66%	Hispanic 21%		White 47%	Hispanic 37%		White 32%	Hispanic 53%	
	Black 12%	Other 1%		Black 11%	Other 4%		Black 10%	Other 6%	

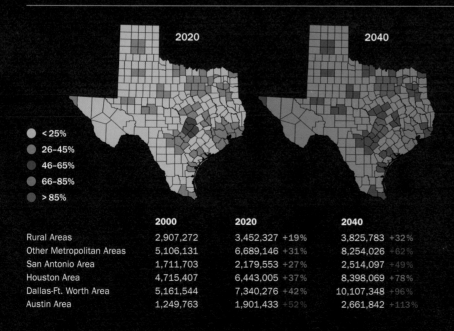

TOTAL POPULATION =	14,229,191	24,330,646	35,761,165

Geography Projected Population Growth from the year 2000, by Metropolitan Area

2020 2040

< 25%
26–45%
46–65%
66–85%
> 85%

	2000	2020	2040
Rural Areas	2,907,272	3,452,327 +19%	3,825,783 +32%
Other Metropolitan Areas	5,106,131	6,689,146 +31%	8,254,026 +62%
San Antonio Area	1,711,703	2,179,553 +27%	2,514,097 +49%
Houston Area	4,715,407	6,443,005 +37%	8,398,069 +78%
Dallas-Ft. Worth Area	5,161,544	7,340,276 +42%	10,107,348 +96%
Austin Area	1,249,763	1,901,433 +52%	2,661,842 +113%

SOURCES: Texas State Data Center; Office of State Demographer.

for critical analysis

1. How do you think the increase in the Hispanic portion will change the nature of Texas politics? Will it change the issues that the state government focuses on? Will it have an impact on what party wins elections in Texas?

2. Texas is traditionally associated with images of farming, ranching, and other elements of rural life. How do you think the growth of the urban population will change the image of Texas?

TABLE 1.5

Populations of the Largest Cities in Texas, 2010

Houston (Harris County)	2,099,451
San Antonio (Bexar County)	1,327,407
Dallas (Dallas County)	1,197,816
Austin (Travis County)	790,390
Ft. Worth (Tarrant County)	741,206
El Paso (El Paso County)	649,121

SOURCE: 2010 Census.

TABLE 1.6

Race and Ethnic Breakdown of Texas and Its Largest Counties, 2010

	WHITE	OTHER	BLACK	ASIAN	MULTIPLE RACE	HIS-PANIC*	TOTAL
Texas	70%	11%	12%	4%	3%	38%	25,145,561
Harris	57%	15%	19%	6%	3%	41%	4,092,459
Dallas	54%	16%	22%	5%	3%	38%	2,368,139
Tarrant	67%	11%	15%	5%	3%	27%	1,809,034
Bexar	73%	14%	8%	2%	4%	59%	1,714,773
Travis	69%	13%	9%	6%	4%	34%	1,024,266
El Paso	82%	11%	3%	1%	3%	82%	800,647
Collin	72%	6%	9%	11%	3%	15%	782,341

*Hispanic in this classification can be any race. Numbers are rounded.
SOURCE: 2010 U.S. Census.

the first half of the twentieth century, African Americans were either denied or given limited access to a variety of public services such as parks, schools, buses, restrooms, and restaurants. Although not enforced legally, residential segregation divided the city into a number of distinct racially divided neighborhoods for much of the twentieth century.

In the late nineteenth century, Houston's economic well-being depended on cotton and commerce. Railroads played an integral role in placing Houston at the hub of the Texas economy. The opening of the Houston Ship Channel further enhanced Houston's place in the state economy by helping to turn it into the second or third (depending on whose ranking is used) deep-water port in the United States. But it was oil that fundamentally transformed the Houston area in the twentieth century.

Oil refineries opened along the ship channel and a petrochemical industry emerged, making Houston one of the leading energy centers in the world. Today it continues to rank first in the nation in the manufacture of petroleum equipment.

By 1930, Houston had become the largest city in Texas, with a population of around 292,000 people. The population continued to expand throughout the 1940s, 1950s, and 1960s, assisted by a liberal annexation policy that enabled the city to incorporate into itself many of the outlying suburban areas. Although the oil bust in the mid-1980s slowed the city's growth, that growth continued in the 1990s, extending into suburban areas such as Clear Lake City and other urban areas such as Galveston.

Of the 2.1 million people living in Houston at the time of the 2010 census, 28.3 percent of the population were non-Hispanic white, 22.2 percent were black, and Hispanics counted for 42.4 percent of the overall population.

Dallas–Fort Worth   The Metroplex is an economic region encompassing the cities of Dallas and Fort Worth, as well as a number of other suburban cities, including Arlington (population 365,438), Mesquite (139,824), Garland (226,876), Richardson (99,223), Irving (216,290), Plano (259,841), Carrollton (119,097), Grand Prairie (175,396), Denton (113,383), and Frisco (116,989).[36] The major counties in the area are Dallas, Tarrant, and Collin. The Metroplex is joined together by a number of interlocking highways running north–south and east–west, and a major international airport that is strategically located in the national air system.

Dallas was founded as a trading post in 1841, near where two roads were to be built by the Republic.[37] By the 1850s, it had become a retail center servicing the rural areas. By 1870, the population had reached 3,000 people. The coming of the Houston and Texas Central Railroad in 1871 and the Texas and Pacific Railroad in 1873 made Dallas the first rail crossroads in Texas and transformed forever its place in the state's economy. Markets now beckoned east and north, encouraging entrepreneurs and merchants to set up shop. Cotton became a major cash crop, and the population expanded over threefold to more than 10,000 people in 1880. By the turn of the twentieth century, the city had grown to more than 42,000 people.

As with Houston, the oil economy changed the direction and scope of the city's economic life. With the discovery of oil in east Texas in 1830, Dallas became a major center for petroleum financing. By the end of World War II, the economy had diversified, making Dallas a minor manufacturing center in the nation. In the 1950s and 1960s, technology companies such as Ling-Temco-Vought (LTV) and Texas Instruments were added to the industrial mix, transforming Dallas into the third-largest technology center in the nation. The high-tech boom of the 1990s was built from the corporate infrastructure laid down in the 1950s and 1960s.

Dallas grew from 844,401 people in 1970 to 904,078 in 1980 to 1,197,816 in 2010. In 2010, 29 percent of the population were non-Hispanic white, 25 percent were black, and 42 percent were Hispanic.

Although they are locked together in important ways economically, Dallas and Fort Worth are as different as night and day. Whereas Dallas looks to the East and embodies a more corporate white-collar business culture, Fort Worth looks to the West. It is where the West begins in Texas.

In some areas of Texas, Asian immigrants are a growing force. The signs at this shopping center in Houston attest to the changing demographic landscape of Texas.

forcritical**analysis**

Based on the population growth, urbanization, and economic change of the last two decades, what do the next two decades hold for Texas? Which areas will grow in population, and will government be ready for that growth? What can or should government do to maintain and strengthen the economy of Texas?

Fort Worth originated as an army post in 1849.[38] By 1853, the post had been abandoned as new forts were located to the west. Although settlers took the fort over, population growth was slow through the early 1870s. The spark that enabled the town to begin to prosper was the rise of the cattle industry. Fort Worth was a convenient place for cowboys to rest on their cattle drives to Kansas. Cattle buyers established headquarters in the city. Gradually other businesses grew up around these key businesses. Transportation and communication links improved with the establishment of stage lines to the west and railroad lines to the north and east.

By 1900, Fort Worth was served by eight different railroad companies, many of them transporting cattle and cattle-related products to national markets. The two world wars encouraged further economic development in Fort Worth. Over 100,000 troops were trained at Camp Bowie during World War I. World War II brought an important air force base and, along with it, the aviation industry. The Consolidated Vultee Aircraft Corporation, which was later bought by General Dynamics, became the largest manufacturing concern in the city. Between 1900 and 1950, the population grew from 26,668 to 277,047. In 2010, Fort Worth's population was 741,206. The overall metropolitan area of Dallas–Fort Worth included 6.7 million people in 2011.

San Antonio   San Antonio is located in Bexar County, the fourth-largest county in Texas today. San Antonio grew out of the Spanish presidio San Antonio de Bexar, which was founded in 1718.39 In 1773, it became the capital of Spanish Texas, with a population of around 2,100 people. Because of the threats posed by Native Americans and Mexicans after the Texas Revolution, the population declined to about 800 people by 1846. On Texas's entry into the Union, however, the population took off, reaching 3,488 in 1850 and 8,235 in 1860. By the Civil War, San Antonio was the largest city in Texas.

Following the Civil War, San Antonio grew rapidly, stimulated by the building of the San Antonio Railroad in 1877. By 1880, the population had reached more than 20,000 people, mostly Anglo Americans from southern states. The population continued to grow through the first two decades of the twentieth century, reaching 161,000 by 1920. Mexican immigration increased significantly following the Mexican Revolution of 1910 and the building of a city infrastructure that provided paved roads, utilities, water, telephones, and hospitals. By midcentury, San Antonio had become a unique blend of Latino, German, and southern Anglo American cultures. Population growth slowed down in the 1930s but picked up again during World War II, reaching over 408,000 in 1950. Major military bases came to dot the landscape around San Antonio. By 1960, the population topped 587,000 people.

Today, San Antonio is Texas's second-largest city. The population of the city was 1,327,407 in 2010, and the San Antonio metropolitan area as a whole had a population of 2,150,918, making it the twenty-seventh-largest metropolitan area in the country. San Antonio's population has become increasingly Hispanic. Approximately 62 percent of the people are Hispanic, 29 percent are Anglo American, and 6 percent are African American.[40]

Unlike Houston or Dallas, San Antonio lacks high-paying manufacturing jobs, and average metropolitan income is lower than in Houston and Dallas. The economy rests on four legs: national military bases, educational institutions, tourism, and a large medical research complex.

● Thinking Critically about Texas's Political Culture

In this chapter, we have studied the political culture of Texas and seen how the state has been transformed by economic and demographic shifts over the past hundred years. Three great technological revolutions have reshaped the economic life of the state. The first—based on the production of agricultural products such as cotton and cattle and on the newly built railroad system—defined economic life in the latter decades of the nineteenth and early twentieth centuries. The second—based on the production of oil and the industries that cheap oil made possible—dominated the economy well into the second half of the twentieth century. The third—the era of high tech—has transformed the state by diversifying its economy and tying it closely to the growing international economy. Accompanying and fueling these economic revolutions have been ongoing demographic changes, which have redefined who the "typical" Texan is and where this person lives. No longer can it be said that a "typical" Texan is simply an extension of an Anglo American culture rooted in southern tradition. No longer does this person reside in a small town, living life close to the land much as his or her ancestors did. Like the economy, the people of Texas have been diversified. Increasing numbers of Hispanics from Mexico and Anglo Americans from other parts of the United States have created a new melting pot of cultures and concerns throughout the state. These cultures have come together in the big metropolitan areas across Texas.

The chapters that follow will analyze the way specific aspects of Texas politics and government work. In the process, we will explore the meaning of liberty, equality, and democracy in Texas and how these ideas are influencing Texas politics and government today.

As we have seen in this chapter, the majority of Texans today continue to view liberty through the lens of a political culture dominated by both traditionalistic and individualistic values. There is a tendency in the political culture to defer to leaders in positions of authority. But this deferential politics is checked by a healthy suspicion of giving too much power to those in authority. As a result, in Texas, government is often perceived as something that gets in the way of our individual liberty rather than something through which we accomplish collective objectives.

Two notions of equality also play important roles in Texas political life. First, there is the idea of equality of opportunity. This aspect of equality is deeply rooted in Texas's traditional individualistic political culture. The job of government is to treat individuals fairly and to ensure them a fair chance to make it on their own through their own skills and initiative. Few Texans believe that it is the task of state government to redistribute resources from the rich to the poor, ensuring some equality of result.

In addition to equality of opportunity, political equality has been an issue in Texas politics, with the growing importance of African American and Latino minorities in the state. Much of the history of Texas from 1950 to the present represents an effort to expand the political rights of these groups. Additionally, debates over the meaning of equal participation and representation at all levels of state government have reshaped the broad contours of political life in Texas and given rise to one of the bitterest and most controversial issues to face the state legislature in recent decades: congressional and legislative redistricting.

Like liberty and equality, the ideals of democratic self-government are enshrined in various constitutions under which Texas has operated since the days of the

In 2006 an estimated half million people marched in Dallas to demand fairer treatment for immigrants. As immigration has changed the demographic profile of Texas, it has also given rise to numerous political debates.

for critical analysis

In Texas political culture, governmental power is often seen as a threat to individual liberty. However, Texans also tend to value equality of opportunity and political equality for all citizens. To what extent should the Texas state government use its power to ensure equality?

Republic. The people are formally given a number of important roles to play in the political process, including choosing the members of all three branches of government and approving constitutional amendments. As we will see, however, the actual operations of state government and politics tend to work in seemingly undemocratic ways. Arcane rules in the legislative and executive branches allow power to concentrate in the hands of a few individuals. Elections of judges politicize their selection in a way unimaginable in national politics. Well-funded special-interest groups have been able to exert their influence on elections in Texas and to penetrate the legislative process. The rise to power of the Republican Party in the state may be best understood as the triumph of a new set of interests that have successfully displaced those attached to the traditional Democratic Party.

Texans in general and Texas political leaders in particular may be committed to the idea of democracy. The Texas Constitution may enshrine the values of democratic self-government. As we will see, however, the actual operations of Texas politics and government raise serious questions about what kind of democracy the state really is. The tension between the ideal and reality of democracy in Texas may come to play an important role in restructuring the political system as it responds to ongoing economic and demographic change in the state.

study guide

(S) **Practice online with:** Chapter 1 Diagnostic Quiz ▪ Chapter 1 Key Term Flashcards

Texas Political Culture

■ **Describe the defining characteristics of political culture in Texas (pp. 5–7)**

Texas political culture can best be characterized as individualistic and traditional. Texans have great pride in their state and have adopted a famous phrase "Don't mess with Texas" for those external forces wishing to change the state's way of doing things. Texas is a low tax state with distrust for large government programs. Business plays a major role in defining the political culture of the state.

Key Terms

political culture (p. 5)

moralistic political culture (p. 5)

individualistic political culture (p. 5)

traditionalistic political culture (p. 5)

elite (p. 5)

provincialism (p. 6)

Practice Quiz

1. In terms of area, how does Texas rank among the 50 states? *(p. 3)*
   a) first
   b) second
   c) third
   d) fifth
   e) seventh

2. *Provincialism* refers to *(p. 6)*
   a) a narrow view of the world.
   b) a progressive view of the value of diversity.
   c) a pro-business political culture.
   d) an urban society.
   e) a group of counties.

(S) **Practice Online**
Video exercise: *The Handbook of Texas Online*

The Land

■ **Identify the major geographic regions in Texas (pp. 7–9)**

Because of Texas's immense size, the state's topography is diverse, with East Texas's flat lands, West Texas's arid climate, and Central Texas's hill country all representing diverse ecosystems and land patterns.

Practice Quiz

3. Which of Texas's physical regions is characterized by the presence of many of the state's largest ranches? *(p. 8)*
   a) Gulf Coastal Plains
   b) Great Plains
   c) Interior Lowlands
   d) Basin and Range Province
   e) Rio Grande Valley

4. Which of Texas's physical regions is found in West Texas? *(p. 9)*
   a) Gulf Coastal Plains
   b) Great Plains
   c) Interior Lowlands
   d) Basin and Range Province
   e) Pine Belt

Economic Change in Texas

■ **Trace the evolution of Texas's economy (pp. 9–20)**

The Texas economy has undergone a series of technological transformations over the past 100 years. Once the Texas economy was grounded in cotton and ranching. Oil production came to play an important role in the twentieth century. Today, high technology and international trade play important roles in the state's economy. Texas appears to have weathered the Great Recession better than most other states.

Key Term

North American Free Trade Agreement (NAFTA) (p. 18)

Practice Quiz

5. Creative destruction *(p. 9)*
   a) destroys both old and new economies.
   b) creates new economies and destroys old ones.
   c) maintains old economies and creates new ones.
   d) creates and maintains old and new economies.
   e) does not affect economies.

6. Which industry controlled the politics and economy of Texas for most of the twentieth century? *(pp. 12–16)*
   a) cotton
   b) cattle
   c) railroad
   d) oil
   e) technology

7. Which of the following statements is true? *(p. 16)*
   a) Oil production in Texas is greater today than it was 50 years ago.
   b) Oil production longer plays an important role in the state's economy.
   c) Oil production declined in Texas in the early twenty-first century.
   d) The DFW region has become a major producer of oil in the early twenty-first century.
   e) none of the above

8. Unlike earlier eras, the Texas economy of the twenty-first century features *(p. 18)*
   a) computers, electronics, and other high-tech products.
   b) transportation, oil and natural gas, and banking.
   c) insurance, construction, and banking.
   d) ranching, oil, and tourism
   e) education, the military, and agriculture.

9. NAFTA refers to *(p. 18)*
   a) an oil company.
   b) an independent regulatory commission.
   c) an interstate road network.
   d) an interest group.
   e) an international trade agreement.

10. What is meant by the "Great Recession"? *(p. 19)*
    a) the post–Vietnam War era in the mid 1970s when housing prices rose
    b) the period of high inflation during the early 1980s
    c) a time of chronic economic problems beginning in late 2007 that drew analogies to the Great Depression of the 1930s
    d) the time when Democrats lost control of the Texas House for the first time since Reconstruction
    e) a period of high unemployment in the early 1990s

The People: Texas Demography

▇ **Explain how the population of Texas has changed over time (pp. 20–26)**

Texas demography has changed over the last century. Once dominated by Anglos, Texas now has a large Latino population that, when coupled with the African American population and other minorities, now makes Texas a majority-minority state. Despite considerable wealth on average, Texans are younger and poorer than the average American.

Practice Quiz

11. Which of the following accounts for most of Texas's population growth? *(p. 21)*
    a) immigration
    b) natural increases due to the difference between births and deaths
    c) domestic immigration
    d) NAFTA
    e) movement from rural to urban areas

12. Which of the following is not true? *(p. 23)*
    a) Hispanics are increasing as a percentage of the population in Dallas.
    b) More African Americans live in East Texas than West Texas.
    c) San Antonio has a larger Anglo population than Hispanic.
    d) Houston's largest minority population is Hispanic.
    e) The Hispanic population in Texas has grown rapidly in recent decades.

Ⓢ **Practice Online**
"Exploring Texas Politics" exercise: *Texas Demographics*

Urbanization

 Describe the shift from a rural society to an urban one in Texas (pp. 27–32)

Initially a rural state, Texas has urbanized, with Houston, San Antonio, and Dallas–Fort Worth representing the largest metropolitan areas in the state. This process of urbanization has changed the state's economy from an agricultural powerhouse to a high tech and innovative economy.

Key Terms

urbanization (p. 27)

political economy (p. 28)

Practice Quiz

13. *Urbanization* refers to a process in which *(p. 27)*
    a) people move from rural to urban areas.
    b) people from the north and west move to Texas.
    c) people move out of urban centers to the suburbs.
    d) people move out of urban centers to rural areas.
    e) minorities assume political control of a city.

14. The three major metropolitan areas in Texas are *(pp. 28–32)*
    a) Houston, Dallas–Fort Worth, and San Antonio.
    b) Houston, Dallas–Fort Worth, and El Paso.
    c) El Paso, Houston, and Austin.
    d) San Antonio, El Paso, and Brownsville-Harlingen-McAllen.
    e) San Antonio, El Paso, and Houston.

Recommended Websites

Business QuickFacts
http://quickfacts.census.gov/qfd/states/48000.html

Federal Reserve Bank of Texas
http://dallasfed.org/index.cfm

Handbook of Texas
www.tshaonline.org/handbook/online/

Office of the Governor, Economic Development and Tourism, Business and Industry Data Center
www.governor.state.tx.us/ecodev/divisions/bidc/

Texas Almanac
www.texasalmanac.com

Texas State Data Center and Office of the State Demographer
www.txsdc.utsa.edu

As a state in a federal system, Texas shares power with the national government. How much power the national government should have has long been a controversial question. These protesters want more power returned to Texas.

Texas and the Nation

WHAT GOVERNMENT DOES AND WHY IT MATTERS In 2010, Governor Rick Perry published a book that explained his thinking about the relationship between Texas and the national government. He expressed strong criticism of a powerful national government when he wrote:

> We are fed up with being overtaxed and overregulated. We are tired of being told how much salt we can put on our food, what windows we can buy for our house, what kind of cars we can drive, what kinds of guns we can own, what kind of prayers we are allowed to say and where we can say them, what political speech we are allowed to use to elect candidates, what kind of energy we can use, what kind of food we can grow, what doctor we can see, and countless other restrictions on our right to live as we see fit. We are fed up with a federal government that has the arrogance to preach to us about how to live our lives.[1]

Perry wrote that Congress was "arguably one of the most incompetent regimes with one of the worst track records of mismanagement in the history of mankind."[2] Nor did "activist judges," Democrats, President Obama, or "Washington Republicans" escape his criticisms.[3] In Perry's view, power needed to be returned to the states in order to have accountability to the people and to preserve liberty because "the very essence of America stems from a limited, decentralized government."[4]

At the heart of Perry's conservative critique is a rejection of the expansion of the national government in the twentieth century. He wrote that the early years of that century—the Progressive era or the era of Woodrow Wilson—gave rise to vast increases in the powers of the national government. In 1913 the ratification of the Sixteenth Amendment, which Perry described as "the great milestone on the road to serfdom,"[5] gave Congress the power to tax the incomes of Americans without any requirement that those taxes be returned to the states in proportion to the amounts collected. This amendment initiated the redistribution of wealth in the United States and provided the national government with huge sums of money without requiring state cooperation in federal programs.[6] The power of state governments was further eroded by the ratification of the Seventeenth Amendment, which established the direct election of U.S. senators rather than the previous system of having senators chosen by state legislatures.[7]

The New Deal of Franklin Delano Roosevelt in the 1930s only made matters worse. In Perry's view, the centralization of power in federal agencies during the New Deal "represents the second big step in the march of socialism and was the key to releasing the remaining constraints on the national government's power to do whatever it wishes."[8]

Perry's conservative critique of American government and politics in the early twenty-first century essentially boiled down to two points: first, the Wilson era and the New Deal era destroyed the rights of states by transferring power to the federal government; second, it is now necessary to "retake the reins of our government from a Washington establishment that has abused our trust."[9] This perspective is popular among some Texans today. Conservative Republicans and others who identify with the Tea Party movement, in particular, have embraced Perry's message.

Ironically, Perry's anti-Washington rhetoric likely would have surprised many of those Texas political leaders who served in key positions at the national level in both the Wilson and New Deal periods. Indeed, many of these leaders would likely have trouble understanding exactly what all the anti-Washington fuss is about today. As the national government grew in importance and power in the twentieth century, so did the role of Texas in the nation. In this chapter, we will explore the role played by leading Texans over the past hundred years in shaping our national political system and reconfiguring the role that Texas plays in it.

chaptergoals

- Understand federalism and Texas's relationship to the national government (pages 41–45)

- Trace the major changes in Texas's relationship to the national government over time (pages 46–57)

- Describe the major trends and issues related to federalism in Texas today (pages 57–63)

Texas: A State in a Federal System

Understand federalism and Texas's relationship to the national government

In the chapter opener, we discussed a particular view of federalism—as expressed by Governor Perry—in which states have a major and largely autonomous role in governance. **Federalism** is the relationship between the national government and the states, a relationship that has been the subject of intense political dispute since the American Revolution. Immediately following the United States' independence from Britain, the Articles of Confederation gave states the primary role in governance, and the national government was small and had very limited powers. The relative weakness of the national government meant that the states functioned as nearly independent entities rather than as one nation. Dissatisfaction with this system led to the U.S. Constitution.

Under the U.S. Constitution, which replaced the Articles in 1787, a federal system was created in which the national government was **sovereign**, deriving its power directly from the American people in the Preamble. Individual states were also sovereign, deriving their power from the people in their state through their state constitutions. The U.S. Constitution recognized through the Tenth Amendment that "The powers not delegated to the United States by the Constitution, nor prohibited by it to the States, are reserved to the States respectively, or to the people." The immediate effect of the Constitution was to increase national power and to delegate to the national government distinctive powers and responsibilities such as national defense and foreign policy. State governments also had separate powers and responsibilities, such as protecting public safety. Local governments were created by state governments and their powers are granted (and can be revoked) by state governments. Rather than being a part of a federal system, local governments were the creations of states, and continue to be so today.

Controversy over the exact nature of the federal system divided Americans in the late 1820s and '30s. During the Nullification Crisis in 1833, South Carolina tried to assert the right to veto (or nullify) national legislation passed by Congress. Spokesmen like John C. Calhoun argued that a strong national government was a threat to the sovereignty of states, and argued for a system along the lines of the original Articles of Confederation. Under the Articles of Confederation, the United States was a loose confederation of independent states where the Federal government derived its power from the state governments, not from the American people as a whole. President Andrew Jackson responded by threatening to use military force in support of federal law. South Carolina backed down. Although the national government had imposed its will successfully during the Nullification Crisis, the question of the exact relationship between the central government and the individual states was still open.

The Civil War was, in part, a struggle over the meaning of the federal system and the proper relationship between the national and the state governments. Southern states, including Texas, feared that a national government controlled by northern states would move to end slavery, an institution that they

federalism a system of government in which power is divided, by a constitution, between a central government and regional governments

sovereign possessing supreme political authority within a geographic area

The United States and Texas flags that fly in front of many government buildings in Texas (including Dallas's city hall, pictured here) reflect the nature of federalism. Both the national government and the state government are sovereign. The third flag is the flag of the city of Dallas.

felt was essential to their social, political, and economic way of life. They saw the creation of the Confederacy as a movement back to the older confederation system embodied in the Articles of Confederation where the central government in Richmond was weak and the individual states were strong. This vision of a confederation effectively came to a close with General Lee's surrender at the Appomattox Court House, which ended the Civil War.

Following the end of Reconstruction (the period after the Civil War when much of the South was under military occupation) and into the early twentieth century, the U.S. constitutional system operated under a system of **dual federalism**, in which the national government was relatively small in comparison to the states and in which states did most of the governing. The national government's role was more or less limited to providing for national defense and foreign policy and assisting in the development of commerce. The daily lives of citizens were chiefly affected by state governments.

This system of dual federalism was described by political scientist Morton Grodzins as **layer-cake federalism** (see Figure 2.1). Like the layers on a cake, the powers of the national government and state governments were largely separate and, one might add, the layer that was the national government's powers and responsibilities was smaller than was the layer that represented the powers and responsibilities of state governments.[10] Under layer-cake federalism, there were still clear limits to the sovereignty of states. States could not nullify national legislation, nor could they secede from the Union. But states had a major role to play in governance that was quite distinct from the role of the federal government.

Mobilization for World War I during the Woodrow Wilson era increased national power significantly, but there was a so-called return to normalcy in the 1920s, which curtailed to a degree the growing power of the national government. This "normalcy" was short-lived, as the onset of the Great Depression in 1929 brought forward new calls to change the existing federal system.

With the presidency of Franklin Roosevelt, the relationship between the national government and the states changed dramatically. Generally, federalism in the New Deal has been described as **cooperative federalism**, where national and state governments worked together to provide services—often with joint funding of programs or state administration of programs mostly funded by the national government. In fighting the Great Depression, Roosevelt pursued a variety of such

dual federalism the system of government that prevailed in the United States from 1789 to 1937, in which most fundamental governmental powers were strictly separated between the federal and state governments

layer-cake federalism a way of describing the system of dual federalism where there is no interaction between the levels of government

cooperative federalism a type of federalism existing since the New Deal era in which grants-in-aid have been used to encourage states and localities (without commanding them) to pursue nationally defined goals. Also known as "intergovernmental cooperation"

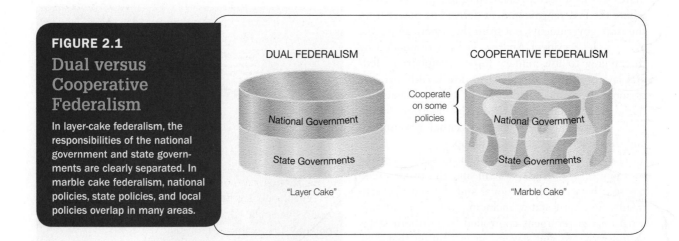

FIGURE 2.1
Dual versus Cooperative Federalism

In layer-cake federalism, the responsibilities of the national government and state governments are clearly separated. In marble cake federalism, national policies, state policies, and local policies overlap in many areas.

DUAL FEDERALISM

National Government

State Governments

"Layer Cake"

Cooperate on some policies

COOPERATIVE FEDERALISM

National Government

State Governments

"Marble Cake"

programs. The Social Security Act of 1935, for instance, changed the existing federal system in a number of fundamental ways. First, it put into place a national insurance program for the elderly (now known as the Social Security program) where individuals in all states were assessed a payroll tax on their wages. Upon retirement, "participants" were to receive a pension check. Second, the act put into place a series of state-federal programs to address particular social problems, including unemployment insurance, aid to dependent children, aid to the blind and disabled, and aid to impoverished elderly people. The basic model for these programs was that the federal government would make money available to states that established their own programs in these areas, provided they met specific administrative guidelines. Although the federal dollars came with these strings attached, the programs were state run and could differ from state to state.

In the 1960s during President Lyndon B. Johnson's Great Society, new programs were added to the Social Security Act. A Medicare program was established to provide health insurance for the elderly, paid for through a payroll tax on current workers. A Medicaid program was added to provide health care funding for individuals enrolled in the state-federal Aid to Families with Dependent Children (AFDC) program. Medicaid's funding and administration were based on the same state-federal principles as AFDC and unemployment insurance: the federal government provided funding for approved state programs. To borrow from Morton Grozdins's analogy, under these cooperative federal initiatives, layer-cake federalism became **marble-cake federalism**, characterized by significant overlaps between national and state powers.[11] Not only was the power of the national government expanding, but the sharp boundaries between the policies sponsored by the national government and those of the state governments were becoming blurred.

Federalism continued to evolve with the passage of civil rights legislation, first in 1957 and again in 1960, 1964, 1965, and 1968, when the role of the national government was expanded to protect the rights of minorities. In the process, the national government was often thrown into conflict with southern states such as Texas that persisted in trying to maintain a segregated society. President Richard M. Nixon briefly tried a somewhat different version of federalism that he called **New Federalism**. In an attempt to reduce federal control, Nixon introduced a funding mechanism called **block grants**, which allowed the states considerable leeway in spending their federal dollars. In the 1980s, President Ronald Reagan adopted Nixon's New Federalism as his own, and block grants became an important part of federal–state cooperation.

New Federalism's biggest success, however, was actually during President Bill Clinton's administration when, in 1996, major reforms were passed in welfare programs that gave the states a significant decision-making role. By the 1990s, liberals and conservatives were in agreement that welfare in America was broken. Replacing the state–federal system with a system of grants tied to federal regulations and guidelines lay at the heart of the Clinton welfare reforms, the most important since the New Deal.

In recent years some national actions have been described as **coercive federalism**, where federal regulations are used to force states to change their policies to meet national goals. Until the 2012 Supreme Court decision involving the Affordable Care Act (commonly called Obamacare) struck down the provision, states were threatened with the loss of all Medicaid funding if they did not expand their Medicaid coverage to comply with the legislation. Perhaps most disturbing for states are the federal "unfunded mandates," which are the federal requirements that the state (or local) governments pay the costs of federal policies.[12] For example,

marble-cake federalism a way of describing cooperative federalism where there is interaction between the levels of government

New Federalism attempts by Presidents Nixon and Reagan to return power to the states through block grants

block grants federal grants that allow states considerable discretion in how the funds are spent

coercive federalism federal governmental efforts to accomplish national policy goals by preempting state power, forcing states to change their policies, and forcing the expenditure of money by states without compensation by the national government

the federal Americans with Disabilities Act requires that street curbs be accessible to wheelchairs, but the federal government does not pay for the curbs. That cost is passed on to state and local governments.

A federal system of power has one distinct advantage over the centralized forms of government found in other countries: it encourages competition and creativity. Under this "competitive federalism," states are essentially 50 laboratories set up for experimentation with different approaches to policy problems to determine which approach works best. If, for example, a number of states face a problem of uninsured motorists, one state may try large criminal penalties for uninsured motorists, another may tow the cars of the uninsured, and still another may block the registration of uninsured cars. It should then be possible to examine the success of each state's policies to determine the best approach in resolving the issue.[13] It may be, of course, that differences among states are great enough that a policy solution cannot readily be transferred from one state to another, but Texas currently seems inclined to approach problems on its own without reliance on the experience of other states.

As Figure 2.2 shows, federal funds make up a large portion of the Texas state budget in recent years. If the national government's role were more limited, there would be economic repercussion for the state. The Who Are Texans? section shows how responsibility for different programs is divided between the national and state government in the 2010–11 biennium. Today, the national government is involved in so many important policy areas that a shift away from a strong national government would raise major questions about addressing a range of issues. However, as we have seen and will consider more closely in the next section, the nature of federalism has been evolving—sometimes more rapidly and sometimes more slowly—throughout history.

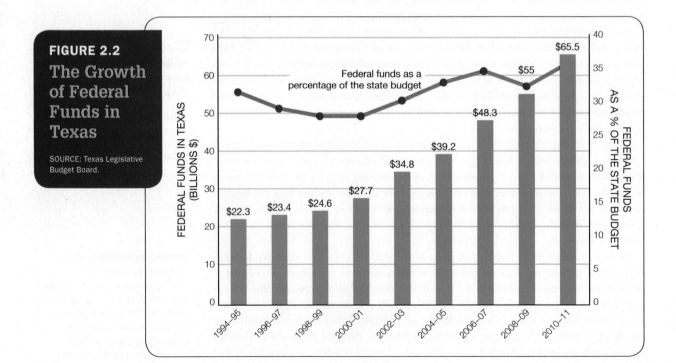

FIGURE 2.2

The Growth of Federal Funds in Texas

SOURCE: Texas Legislative Budget Board.

FEDERAL FUNDS IN TEXAS (BILLIONS $)

FEDERAL FUNDS AS A % OF THE STATE BUDGET

Federal funds as a percentage of the state budget

$22.3 | $23.4 | $24.6 | $27.7 | $34.8 | $39.2 | $48.3 | $55 | $65.5

1994–95 | 1996–97 | 1998–99 | 2000–01 | 2002–03 | 2004–05 | 2006–07 | 2008–09 | 2010–11

How Much Money from the Federal Government?

Federal grants provide states with money for programs that range from Medicaid and school lunches to tuberculosis control and immunization programs. As the chart below indicates, federal grants make up a majority of the money the state of Texas spends on health care and business and economic development, and a large share of the money spent on natural resources, education, and general government.

2010–11 Texas Budget

● = $1 billion

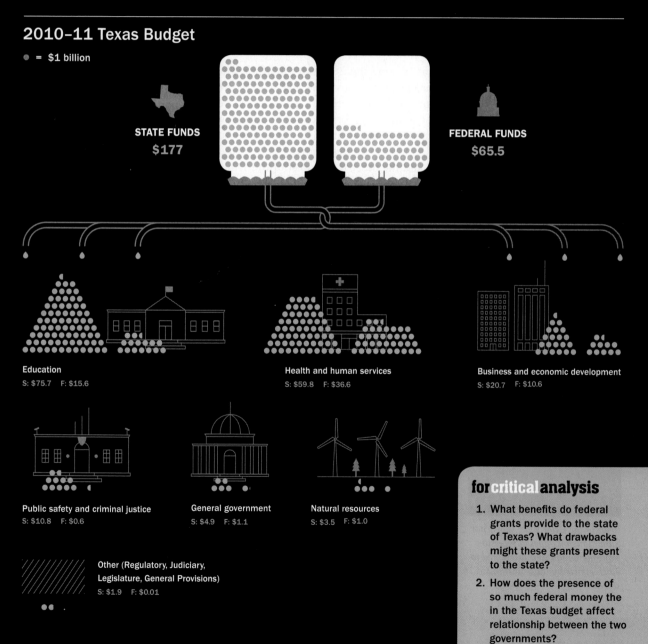

STATE FUNDS
$177

FEDERAL FUNDS
$65.5

Education
S: $75.7   F: $15.6

Health and human services
S: $59.8   F: $36.6

Business and economic development
S: $20.7   F: $10.6

Public safety and criminal justice
S: $10.8   F: $0.6

General government
S: $4.9   F: $1.1

Natural resources
S: $3.5   F: $1.0

Other (Regulatory, Judiciary, Legislature, General Provisions)
S: $1.9   F: $0.01

for critical analysis

1. What benefits do federal grants provide to the state of Texas? What drawbacks might these grants present to the state?

2. How does the presence of so much federal money the in the Texas budget affect relationship between the two governments?

SOURCE: Legislative Budget Board, "Top 100 Federal Funding Sources in the Texas State Budget," www.lbb.state.tx.us/Federal_Funds/Other_Publications/ (accessed 12/13/12).

● Texas's Evolving Role in the Nation

Trace the major changes in Texas's relationship to the national government over time

One of the eternal questions in Texas politics has been a question about federalism: What is the role of the national government relative to the states? Texas played a major role in defining federalism in the Wilson and New Deal eras. The notion of federalism offered by those Texans in these earlier periods is now being rejected by contemporary Texas leaders who seek to limit national power and increase the powers of states. In this and the following sections, we will discuss how Texas's role in the nation and its relationship to the national government have evolved over time.

Texas Joins the Union

Texas became the 28th state in 1845. The issue of Texas joining the Union was a major one that involved war with Mexico as well as the expansion of slavery. Although Texas received a good deal of political attention at the time, Texas was a backwater state for much of the nineteenth century. When the first Texans were elected to Congress in 1846, Texas had two senators and only two members in the U.S. House of Representatives. One of the two congressional districts was to the east and the other to the west of the Trinity River. Texas still had only two House members when it seceded from the Union in 1861.[14] In the early period of statehood and then secession, Sam Houston was the most important Texas political figure, serving as president of Texas, U.S. senator, and governor of Texas. His most important role in state-federal relations was his failed effort to keep Texas in the Union in 1861.

It was not until 1869 that Texas got four congressional districts, and it was not until 1897 that a Texas politician had a leadership role in Congress. Joseph Weldon Bailey, a congressman from Gainesville, Texas, was the Democratic minority leader in the House of Representatives from 1897 to 1899 and then a U.S. senator from Texas from 1901 to 1913. Bailey was an exceptionally talented orator who was described by one contemporary, Speaker of the House Champ Clark, as the "ablest member of Congress." Unfortunately, Bailey was also vain, arrogant, violent, and probably corrupt—characteristics that turned him into a political lightning rod rather than a political leader. He was, however, an important states' rights advocate in those early years, although he used states' rights to argue for the continuation of racial segregation and oppression of African Americans.[15] Texas would have to wait until the Wilson era for its real political talent to develop.

Although geographically large, Texas in 1912 had a population of only 4.1 million people out of a national population of 95.3 million. Texas had only 20 of the 531 delegates to the Electoral College who formally cast votes for the president. Texas's backwater status in national politics was further sealed by the fact that it had been, like other southern states, a single-party Democratic state since the end of Reconstruction following the Civil War. Republican domination of the presidency and Congress for much of the late nineteenth and early twentieth centuries seriously constrained the role Texas political leaders played in the affairs of national government.

Prior to the Civil War, Governor Sam Houston opposed secession from the Union and attempted to block efforts by those wishing to secede.

A Growing Role for Texas: The Progressive Era

Woodrow Wilson was elected president in 1912, only the second Democratic president since the Civil War and the first Democratic president who was part of the Progressive movement, which favored a stronger role for the national government, particularly in regulating the economy. Wilson's Progressive policies were known as the New Freedom. When Woodrow Wilson was elected president, Texas rapidly gained national political influence. Woodrow Wilson carried Texas's 20 electoral votes with almost 73 percent of the popular vote. His closest political adviser was a wealthy Texan named Edward House. The son of a Houston mayor, House was a close adviser to four Democratic governors in Texas between 1892 and 1902. House had been important to Wilson's victory in 1912 at the Democratic National Convention. He and Wilson formed a friendship that lasted until Wilson was incapacitated by a stroke at the end of his presidency. Wilson offered House any position in the cabinet except the State Department, which had been reserved for William Jennings Bryan, a major political figure of the time and a frequent Democratic presidential candidate. House declined the offer and instead served the president in an important but informal capacity. House had an especially strong role as the president's adviser in foreign matters: he was one of Wilson's peace commissioners at the end of World War I and was Wilson's second-in-command in peace negotiations. In addition to foreign policy, House was involved in the planning and implementation of tariff reform, the creation of the Federal Reserve, the income tax, trust regulation, industrial relations, and banking and currency policies.[16]

House wasn't the only Texan to cast a long shadow during the Wilson administration. Three other Texans served in important capacities in Wilson's cabinet. In 1914, Thomas Gregory, an Austin lawyer, a former regent of the University of Texas, and a close ally of House, became Attorney General of the United States. Gregory played a central role in the passage of the Espionage and Sedition Acts and the prosecution of more than 2,000 opponents to World War I. He also advised Wilson at the Versailles Peace Conference after the war.

A third influential Texan, also close to House, was Albert Burleson, who became Postmaster General of the United States. At that time, this was a very important political office with the power to award numerous patronage positions, such as town postmaster jobs and rural mail carrier jobs, to political friends and supporters of the administration. Burleson had served Texas in the U.S. House of Representatives from 1899 to 1913 before moving to the Postmaster General's position in 1913. He held that key post until 1921. Burleson and Gregory were particularly active in the area of internal security, attempting to suppress radical and socialist activity and thought.[17]

A fourth influential Texan in the Wilson administration was David Houston. On the recommendation of House, President Wilson appointed Houston as his Secretary of Agriculture. Prior to this, Houston had had a remarkable career as an academic and a college administrator. Beginning in 1902, he served for three years as president of Texas Agricultural and Mechanical College (now Texas A&M University). Then, in 1905 he was named president of the University of Texas. In 1908, Houston became president of Washington University in St. Louis. During Wilson's last year as president, Houston served as Secretary of the Treasury.[18]

It was a remarkable coup for Texas to have three of its own serving as key advisers in Wilson's cabinet. That, however, was not the full extent of the Texan influence during the Wilson presidency. Like other southern states from the former

Confederacy, Texas had great influence in Congress during the Wilson era as a result of the congressional seniority system. Under the seniority system, advancement to leadership positions of congressional committees was based on length of congressional service. Because of single-party dominance in their states, congressional members from Texas and the South could, with relative ease, build up seniority and achieve positions of power simply by being elected and re-elected in a noncompetitive political environment. In 1913, when Wilson became president, southerners chaired "twenty-two of the twenty-seven important committees of the two houses, while even two of the five remaining committees were controlled by men from the border state of Oklahoma."[19] Indeed, this was "the first time in over fifty years that the South had regained the federal domination it so often enjoyed" in the pre–Civil War era.[20] Texas's congressional delegation was the largest from the South. And although Wilson and the Progressive agenda did face strong opposition from some traditionalists like Joe Bailey, in general, the Texas

Before 1913, state legislatures selected U.S. senators for their state. State governments lost power in the national government with the ratification of the Seventeenth Amendment, which provided for direct election of senators by the people of the state. For example, the people of Texas— not the state legislature—elected Kay Bailey Hutchison to three full terms as senator before she decided not to seek reelection in 2012.

delegation to Congress firmly supported Wilson. In the Senate, Charles Culberson, also allied with Edward House, was chair of the important Judiciary Committee, and in the House of Representatives, Robert Henry chaired the Rules Committee, which set the agenda for legislation that was to be considered by the House.[21]

In spite of Culberson and Henry's formal positions, however, two other Texas members of Congress proved to have the greatest national influence in the Wilson era: Morris Sheppard and John Nance Garner. Morris Sheppard was a Texas member of the U.S. House of Representatives from 1902 until 1913 when he was elected to represent Texas in the U.S. Senate, where he served until his death in 1941. Sheppard played a key role in three issue areas: Prohibition policy, national defense, and prenatal and child health care.

In the Wilson era, one of the great political issues was the Eighteenth Amendment to the U.S. Constitution, also known as Prohibition. Progressives supported Prohibition along with other policies such as the right to vote for women, bans on child labor, and pure food and drug laws. For Progressives, Prohibition was a reform because alcohol was seen as harmful to individuals, families, and society. A ban on alcohol was a way that government could improve life in America. An ardent Prohibitionist, Sheppard became its most outspoken supporter in the Senate, and he will be forever identified as one of the leading advocates of the Prohibition Amendment to the Constitution.

Sheppard also was a strong supporter of Wilson's international policies, advocating military preparedness as well as support for the League of Nations, a keystone of Wilson's post–World War I policies.[22] Later, during the New Deal in the 1930s, Sheppard served as chairman of the Military Affairs and Census Committees. He co-sponsored the Sheppard-Towner Act of 1921, which contributed matching federal funds to states that established prenatal and child health care centers. Although considered by many to be a weak act, the Sheppard-Towner Act was an important symbolic step forward in the development of welfare and health care policies at the national level.

John Nance Garner served as a member of the U.S. House of Representatives from Texas from 1903 until 1933. From 1931 to 1933, he was Speaker of the

U.S. House of Representatives, and from 1933 to 1941, he was Vice President of the United States. Garner first gained an important role in national politics when he steered through the House of Representatives President Wilson's controversial legislation that established the Federal Reserve System. The majority leader of the House of Representatives during World War I was Claude Kitchin, who was a pacifist, and as a result, President Wilson relied on Garner to be his liaison with the House regarding World War I legislation.[23]

Assessing Progressivism The relationship between the states and the national government clearly began to change in the Wilson era. World War I led to expanded national power, as did the fear of communists, radicals, and anarchists that became especially acute in the aftermath of the Bolshevik Revolution in Russia. State governments lost power in the national government when U.S. senators were directly elected by the people of the states rather than state legislatures. With ratification of the woman's suffrage amendment to the Constitution, states no longer were the deciding force in whether women could be part of the electorate. The ratification of the income tax amendment, strongly supported by Texas political leaders, created a stronger potential income stream for the national government than the tariff—a national tax on imports—which had previously been the national government's primary source of revenue. And there was greater government regulation of the economy in the Wilson era (and even earlier in the Theodore Roosevelt administration).

At times, the Supreme Court's interpretation of the Constitution did curtail some of that economic regulation. For example, in the 1918 case of *Hammer v. Dagenhart*, the Court ruled in favor of states' rights when it held that the federal government could not ban goods produced by child labor from interstate commerce since those goods were not inherently harmful products.[24] Similarly, the Court said that the federal Sherman Anti-Trust Act could not be used to break up the sugar refining trust, which the Court deemed a form of production that was state regulated.[25] The Court limited state power over the economy as well when it interpreted "liberty of contract" to be part of the due process clause of the Fourteenth Amendment to the Constitution. This meant that states could not unreasonably interfere with the liberty of employers and employees to contract working conditions and made it difficult to regulate maximum working hours and establish minimum wage laws.[26] States were restricted in their economic regulations by the U.S. Constitution's supremacy clause, which made the Constitution supreme over laws of states.[27]

Perhaps the most important development in advancing the power of the national government over state governments in the Wilson era was the establishment of the Federal Reserve System in 1913. The Federal Reserve is a central bank for the United States and since its inception has proven to be very important in establishing monetary policy for the country. Perhaps no better example of the importance of the Federal Reserve is its role as the primary governmental agency in combating economic crises, including the current Great Recession. Prior to the Federal Reserve, the government's role in addressing national financial problems was minimal. Indeed, in the economic crisis of 1907, it was not the U.S. government that acted to contain the crisis, but a powerful American banker, J. Pierpont Morgan. With Theodore Roosevelt and his Secretary of the Treasury supporting his efforts, Morgan was able to put together financial guarantees to prevent a failure of financial markets. It was the last time that a private banker rather than government regulators would be called upon to control a financial crisis.[28]

Despite their "progressive" influence in national government, Wilson's Texas supporters remained remarkably provincial in their social attitudes. They were segregationists who supported the continuation of second-class citizenship for African Americans and Mexican Americans. The national government in their minds existed to protect national security, to create a better society through the right to vote for women and Prohibition, and to prevent economic oppression through low tariffs and through a regulated banking system. Mostly notably within Texas, Wilsonian Progressivism became evident in Prohibition and the right to vote for women. Wilson's New Freedom was a long way from the policy changes of the next period—the New Deal era—when Texans would again have a strong voice in national politics.

The New Deal and Texas

In the election of 1918, Democrats lost control of Congress, and in the election of 1920, Democrats lost the presidency. Texas, still a solidly Democratic state, lost influence in the executive and legislative branches. But even in the minority, Texas's members of Congress continued to gain seniority in both houses of Congress. After the Republican sweep in the elections of 1928, for example, John Garner became the Democratic minority leader of the House of Representatives. With the onset of the Great Depression in 1929, Texans in Congress saw their opportunity to again gain major power in the nation. In the aftermath of the 1930 election, Democrats regained control of the U.S. House of Representatives, and John Garner was the obvious choice for Speaker. Outside Texas, there was some opposition to Garner. Senator James Hamilton Lewis of Illinois urged Illinois congressman Henry Rainey to seek the Speakership. In what was an obvious attack on Garner's effort to become Speaker, Lewis wrote, "I am compelled to say to you that the memory of the day when the cry was 'Texas—everything for Texas,' under the Wilson administration, ought not now to be revived."[29] Clearly there was a perception that Texans had been too influential in the Wilson administration and that it should not be allowed to happen again.

Despite this opposition, Garner was elected Speaker in 1931 and other Texans also gained vast power in Congress. With Democratic control of the House of Representatives, numerous Texans soon gained chairs of important committees such as

During the 1930s, the Great Depression affected Texans across the state. In cities and towns, people waited in bread lines for food. Many farms went bust as crop prices plummeted. With the entire country struggling, the federal government took on a much larger role in many policy areas, through the New Deal programs.

Interstate and Foreign Commerce, Appropriations, Judiciary, Rivers and Harbors, and Agriculture. By 1931, all 18 members of the House of Representatives from Texas were Democrats.[30] With the 1932 presidential election, Speaker John Garner was the most visible member of Congress and held its most important position. He became a viable candidate for the Democratic nomination for the presidency against Franklin Roosevelt, the governor of New York. Garner was not able to defeat Roosevelt, but he did obtain the vice presidency, where he served until a breach with Roosevelt led to Garner's departure from the ticket in 1940.

In the House, Texans held numerous senior positions, and in 1937 Sam Rayburn, a Garner ally and chair of the Interstate and Foreign Commerce Committee, was elected majority leader. With the death of the Speaker in 1940, Rayburn became the new Speaker and served in that position until his death in 1961, with the exception of 1947–49 and 1953–55, when the Republicans controlled the House and Rayburn served as the Democratic minority leader. Rayburn served as Speaker longer than anyone in American history. At the time of his death, he was the longest-serving member in the history of the House, having served from 1913 to 1961. In the U.S. Senate, Morris Sheppard, the old Wilson supporter and Prohibitionist, was an advocate for military preparedness and became as strong a New Dealer as he had been an advocate of Wilson's policies. There were other strong New Dealers inside and outside Congress as well, such as Congressman Marvin Jones, who was chair of the Agriculture Committee and responsible for many of the New Deal's policies on agriculture, including the Agricultural Adjustment Act and the Farm Credit Administration Act.

With the death of James Buchanan of Texas, Chair of the Appropriations Committee, Lyndon Johnson was elected to his congressional seat in 1937 as a strong New Dealer, so strong that he campaigned and was elected on his support for Roosevelt's effort to increase the size of the Supreme Court and pack the Court with Roosevelt's political allies.

Within the administration, Jesse Jones handled finance issues for Roosevelt. A part-owner of the *Houston Chronicle*, Jones was initially appointed to be chairman of the Reconstruction Finance Corporation by President Hoover and continued in this role during the Roosevelt administration. In this position, he became a primary investor in the American economy in the 1930s for the government and President Roosevelt. From 1940 to 1945, he served as Secretary of Commerce. Jones, however, was much more conservative than Roosevelt and ultimately broke with the New Deal.[31] Different from Wilson's New Freedom, Franklin Roosevelt's New Deal emphasized a strong national regulatory role as the mechanism for ending the Great Depression, which was seen as a failure of an unregulated capitalist economy. One way that the New Deal promoted strong federal regulation was by establishing public works projects that would not otherwise be provided by the private sector or by state governments. These public works projects were also a way to build political support. National projects such as rural electrification, soil conservation, water projects, and farm-to-market roads were immensely popular with voters. Sam Rayburn, for example, was a major legislative sponsor or supporter of all these programs, and their popularity allowed him to sponsor controversial regulatory legislation such as the Securities and Exchange Commission, the Federal Communications Commission, and the breakup of giant national holding companies in the utility industry.[32] Toward the end of the 1930s, with war on the horizon, the New Deal turned toward military preparation. As in World War I, Texans were strongly supportive of national security. It was said that Senator Morris Sheppard worked himself to death in 1941 trying to get the country prepared for the forthcoming war.[33]

The New Deal and Federalism The New Deal era brought about a new relationship between the states and the national government in which the national government had broad regulatory powers over the economy and eventually, with the presidency of Lyndon Johnson, over protecting civil rights. By the 1950s and 1960s, states' rights advocates were largely confined to southern segregationists, including some Texans, who argued that the national government could not interfere with state-supported racial segregation.

Wickard v. Filburn, decided by the Supreme Court in 1942, is probably the most extreme example of how the New Deal led to a rejection of state power when it appeared to conflict with the power of the national government. Roscoe Filburn was a small farmer in Ohio who violated a national law, the Agricultural Adjustment Act of 1938, by growing an additional 239 bushels of wheat beyond the allowable limit. For this violation, he was subject to a fine of $117.11. Filburn challenged the penalty by arguing that the federal law was unconstitutional because it was based on Congress's power to regulate interstate commerce. Filburn claimed that interstate commerce was not involved in his case because he was producing the wheat within his own state for his own use, not for interstate distribution. The Court, however, held that interstate commerce was involved: if Filburn had not grown the wheat himself, he would have had to purchase it, most likely through interstate commerce. And the cumulative effect of many farmers such as Filburn growing wheat beyond their allotment for their own use would have had a substantial influence on the price and market conditions for this commodity. The decision implied that the power of Congress to regulate interstate commerce was remarkably broad.[34]

The broad interpretation of interstate commerce later became the foundation for much of the civil rights legislation passed in the Johnson administration. In 1964, Ollie McClung challenged the constitutionality of part of the 1964 Civil Rights Act as applied to his barbecue restaurant. The provision of the act prevented restaurants from refusing service to people because of their race, as restaurants were involved in interstate commerce. Ollie McClung, however, argued that his family-owned restaurant, which had been segregated since 1927, was a local business with almost no connection to interstate commerce. There was a rational justification, however, according to the Court, to find that interstate commerce was involved and that the segregation of the restaurant burdened interstate commerce. For example, the Court found that 46 percent of the meat purchased from a local supplier was actually originally procured from an out-of-state source.[35] It was also during the Johnson presidency that civil rights laws such as the 1965 Voting Rights Act were passed and provided the opportunity for Latinos and African Americans to gain political power. Pathbreaking Texas Latino leaders such as Henry B. Gonzalez and African American leaders such as Barbara Jordan began to gain power in Congress as civil rights became a reality.

In an about-face during the New Deal, the Court rejected the concept of liberty to contract, which had restricted both state and national governments from regulating employment conditions. For example, the Court's 1937 decision in *West Coast Hotel Company v. Parrish* upheld the constitutionality of Washington State's minimum wage law, noting that liberty to contract was not absolute. Subsequently, the Court overturned precedents that had banned similar minimum wage laws.[36] The elimination of liberty to contract reasoning was so great that the Court in a case decided in 1963 wrote that "it is up to legislatures, not courts, to decide on the wisdom and utility of legislation."[37]

The New Deal and Texas Politics In spite of the support of major Texas politicians for the New Deal, there was also considerable opposition. Texas now had significant oil production and, along with it, some very wealthy oilmen who generally were unsympathetic to the regulatory state that was the New Deal—unsympathetic unless the regulations benefited their pocketbooks, that is.[38] One of these benefits came in the form of tax benefits for oil production. New Deal politicians such as Sam Rayburn and Lyndon Johnson protected themselves from political retaliation from these wealthy oilmen by providing them with tax advantages.[39] Additionally, many of these oilmen and corporations benefited from the public works projects of the New Deal, and Johnson, in particular, was able to obtain large sums in campaign contributions from them.[40] The connection between that era's oil economy and the politics of the time period was never clearer than in the New Deal politicians' dependence on contributions and other support from the oil industry.

Nevertheless, there was considerable hostility to the New Deal among politicians such as Congressman Martin Dies and Governor and Senator W. Lee O'Daniel, who often condemned New Deal policies as a march toward socialism.[41] Others such as Senator Tom Connally and Congressman Hatton Summers were unwilling to accept aspects of the New Deal such as Franklin Roosevelt's effort to increase the size of the Supreme Court. They became leaders in the opposition to Roosevelt's Court Packing Plan of 1937.[42] Interestingly, Senator Connally later became one of the leading advocates for the United Nations, an international organization whose origins were with Woodrow Wilson's post–World War I proposal for a League of Nations.

John Nance Garner may have been the classic example of the ambivalence many Texans felt about the New Deal. He faithfully served as Roosevelt's vice president until 1937, when he concluded that Roosevelt was moving too far to the left with such policies as packing the Supreme Court. Even while he was vice president, Garner began to oppose the New Deal and ultimately the result was his removal from the ticket when Roosevelt ran for a third term in 1940.[43]

By 1944, a split had developed between liberals and conservatives in the Texas Democratic Party based on their opposing positions on the New Deal. A large group of Texas politicians—the liberals—were New Dealers such as Rayburn and Johnson, who continued to support the national Democratic Party and its domestic objectives. However, a substantial number of Texas political leaders constituted the conservative wing and were unwilling to accept all the aspects of the New Deal. For them, it simply meant too much national governmental power. In 1952 the conservative wing of the Democratic Party aligned with Governor Allan Shivers to vote for the popular Republican presidential candidate Dwight Eisenhower. They were dubbed "Shivercrats." Still, when it came to an issue of national security, whether it was World War II or the Cold War, liberal and conservative Texas Democrats were unified in their support of the military and of national security.

For the most part, Texas Democrats after the New Deal were united on another issue: race relations and segregation. Even the most adamant New Dealers could not accept a restructuring of Texas society. Sam Rayburn, as dedicated a New Dealer as could be found, was at least publicly a segregationist throughout his lengthy political career.[44] Lyndon Johnson was not a strong advocate of civil rights until he became president of the United States with a far different political base than he had as a Texas congressman and senator. Only with the Johnson presidency were civil rights laws passed that broke through the barriers to equal rights that had existed for minorities since the end of Reconstruction in the South after the Civil War.[45]

Texas's political strength at the national level was especially notable in much of the 1950s. Even though a Republican, Dwight Eisenhower, was president, Texan

Sam Rayburn was Speaker of the House of Representatives, and Senator Lyndon Johnson was Senate majority leader. The two men dominated the Congress and left a lasting imprint on American political life.

A Modest Break with the New Deal System: The Reagan Era in Texas

The New Deal ideology among Texas politicians did not disappear with Speaker Sam Rayburn's death in 1961 or even with President Lyndon Johnson's departure from the presidency in 1968. It continued well into the 1980s with such Texas political leaders as Speaker Jim Wright and Judiciary Committee chair Jack Brooks, both of whom were protégés of Rayburn and Johnson. The New Deal was dying in the 1980s, however, as a result of the political strength in Texas of President Ronald Reagan, who ushered in a new ideology.

Just as the New Deal promoted a national regulatory state, Ronald Reagan stressed the importance of economic deregulation and tax cuts along with traditional family values and a powerful national defense. In Texas, this perspective was represented by a new generation of Texas political leaders who were Republican. Like the Democrats before them, the Texas Republicans were strong advocates of national defense, and with the demise of the Soviet Union and the emergence of a terrorist threat, Texas Republicans showed their dedication to defense policy to be as strong as that of the Texas Wilsonians and the Texas New Dealers. To the Texas Republicans of the Reagan era, however, the New Deal ideology was flawed. It had allowed the national government to become too big and too intrusive in business, and this had stymied economic growth. As a result, the Texas Republicans focused on balancing the federal budget and reducing regulation of business in order to allow the economy to flourish. And where government programs discouraged individual work effort, Texas Republicans sought to reform those programs—and thus

Lyndon Johnson (pictured on his ranch in Texas at left) was not a strong advocate for civil rights during his years representing Texas in Congress. However, as president he had a much different political base and helped pass important civil rights legislation, including signing the 1968 Civil Rights Act into law (right).

they supported welfare reform. There were, the Texas Republicans of the Reagan era argued, private economic solutions for economic problems that did not require intervention from the national government.

President George H. W. Bush and his son, President George W. Bush, were among the Texans who supported the Reagan agenda. In Congress there was no stronger supporter of eliminating the regulatory state than Republican senator Phil Gramm. He was joined in the U.S. House of Representatives by Republican leaders such as majority leader Richard Armey and then by majority leader Tom DeLay and by the powerful Texan who chaired the House Ways and Means Committee, Bill Archer. In their view, economic growth would occur if the restrictions on that growth—high taxes and restrictive regulations on business—could be reduced.

Of this group of Reagan Republicans, Gramm was a notably transformative figure in Texas politics. He came to office as a conservative Democrat when Texas was still a part of a largely solidly Democratic South. He then switched to the Republican Party, signaling the breakup of the southern Democratic Party and an increasing ideological division between the Republicans and Democrats. As a Republican senator from Texas, he served on the Budget Committee and was a ceaseless worker for balancing the federal budget. He chaired the Senate Banking, Housing, and Urban Affairs Committee and was a leader in efforts to deregulate banking in the United States. Gramm was probably the leading spokesman for the view that market forces should drive the economy without interference from government regulation. Peter Fitzgerald, a former Senate colleague, described this strong advocate of Reagan economics as "a true dyed-in-the-wool free-market guy. He is very much a purist, an idealist, as he has a set of principles and he has never abandoned them."[46]

A Resurgence of States' Powers During the Reagan era, there was an effort to strengthen the powers of state governments versus the powers of the national government. The effort to promote a reemergence of state power is evident in Supreme Court decisions at this time. Although not dramatic reinterpretations of constitutional law, the Court's rulings did begin to place limits on Congress's ability to legislate under the interstate commerce power, and it resurrected the Tenth Amendment as a protection for the rights of states.

In *United States v. Lopez* in 1995, the Court struck down as unconstitutional the Gun Free School Zones Act of 1990 that made it a federal crime for a person to possess a firearm in a school zone. The law, passed under Congress's authority to regulate interstate commerce, was challenged when a 12th grade student in San Antonio found to be carrying a handgun at school was convicted under the statute. The Court found that Congress's power to regulate interstate commerce was not limitless. It must involve an economic activity that substantially affected interstate commerce and mere possession of a firearm in a school zone was not such activity.[47] The decision was a modification of the broad law-making powers Congress had in the post–New Deal period. Congress's power to regulate now had to have a connection to economic matters—regulation of noneconomic matters was to be left to the states. Additionally, in the wake of *Lopez* it was not enough to show some tangential connection to interstate commerce; there had to be a clear connection between Congress's regulation and interstate commerce or the powers of states were violated.

However, in *Gonzales v. Raich* (2005) the Court had the chance to narrow interstate commerce by reversing the New Deal–era decision, *Wickard v. Filburn,* and it refused the opportunity. *Gonzales* dealt with the constitutionality of a federal law

Should the federal government be able to pass national gun laws? These advocates of gun rights would certainly say no. A 1990 law passed by Congress banning guns in a school zone was struck down by the Supreme Court as an overreach of federal power, and in 2010 the Supreme Court found that the Second Amendment applies to the states as well as the national government.

that made it a crime to cultivate small amounts of marijuana for medical purposes even though the cultivation of medical marijuana was legal under California state law. The similarities of the case to *Wickard* were clear: there was no violation of state law, the product was being grown in small quantities, and the connection to interstate commerce was not at all clear—Gonzales's marijuana was going to be used for medicinal purposes in the household. Yet the Court adhered to the *Wickard* precedent and held that the national government could prohibit the production of small amounts of medical marijuana because that production could impact the illegal interstate market in marijuana.[48] Overall, the Court during and after the Reagan era was willing to place some limits on interstate commerce, but not so much that it reversed the key New Deal decision that gave the national government broad regulatory powers through the interstate commerce clause.

The Court also returned to the Tenth Amendment—the so-called states' rights amendment—some of the strength that it had lost during the New Deal era. *Printz v. United States* (1997) challenged a provision of the 1993 Brady Handgun Violence Prevention Act. The Brady Act required the attorney general to establish by the end of November 1998 a national database for instant background checks on anyone buying a handgun. Until the database could be finalized, the act required local law enforcement officials to verify that no handguns were sold to unqualified persons. Sheriffs in Montana and Arizona claimed that this provision was unconstitutional on the grounds that the federal government did not have the authority to command state and local officials to administer a federal program. The Supreme Court agreed that the law infringed on the rights of states, writing, "The Federal Government may neither issue directives requiring the States to address particular problems, nor command the States' officers, or those of their political subdivisions, to administer or enforce a federal regulatory program."[49]

The Court, however, was unwilling to place more than minimal restrictions on Congress's power to tax and spend. In *South Dakota v. Dole* (1987), the Court was faced with a question of the degree to which Congress could use its spending power to cause states to change policies. South Dakota's minimum age for purchasing alcohol was 19. In 1984, Congress enacted a law that directed the Secretary of Transportation to withhold some federal highway funds to states that did not have an age requirement of at least 21 years to purchase alcohol. While the Court did recognize that there might be circumstances where the financial inducement would be so coercive that states would be unconstitutionally compelled to change policies, South Dakota was not coerced in this case, because it would have only lost 5 percent of eligible highway funds if it had not complied with Congress's age requirement. Congress had the power, wrote the Court, to offer "relatively mild encouragement to the States to enact higher minimum drinking ages than they would otherwise choose."[50] Given that Congress has numerous grant-in-aid programs to the states, this decision continues to allow Congress broad leeway to condition its spending on state adherence to congressionally imposed requirements.

While there was some support for states' rights shown by the Court in Tenth Amendment cases such as *Printz* and some restrictions on the powers of Congress under the interstate commerce clause in cases such as *Lopez*, the Court was unwilling to restrict Congress's powers under the taxing and spending clause. States' rights was clearly a more viable constitutional argument than it had been in the 1940s, but the Supreme Court was unwilling to resurrect the Tenth Amendment to the degree that it had been used to restrict national legislation up to the early 1930s.

● Texas in the Nation Today: The Tea Party Era

> Describe the major trends and issues related to federalism in Texas today

With the Great Recession of 2008, something changed in Texas politics. The Reagan era, of course, moved Texas overwhelmingly into the Republican column. Today, Democratic domination of the state, such as in the Wilson and New Deal eras, is unimaginable. The shift to Republican dominance in Texas occurred rapidly in the 1980s and '90s. Still another change has recently arrived in the form of a powerful wing of the Texas Republican Party known as the Tea Party movement, and its champion has been Governor Rick Perry. Their perspective goes beyond the anti-regulation policies of the Reagan era to a general anti–federal government ideology that has become the most powerful force in Texas politics. Part of this thinking is libertarian—a view that government in general should not intrude in the lives of individuals. However, a major theme of this new movement in Texas politics is a sense that it was the national government that had grown too powerful, too intrusive, and too willing to spend the nation into bankruptcy.

This ideology allowed Perry to defeat front-runner Senator Kay Bailey Hutchison in the 2010 Republican primary, despite her remarkable political resume and strong conservative credentials. A successful banker and businesswoman, Hutchison had served in the Texas House of Representatives, on the National Transportation Safety Board, and was state treasurer before being elected to the U.S. Senate.[51] Perry, however, used Hutchison's national experience against her and pegged her as a Washington insider with endorsements from former vice president Dick Cheney and former president George H. W. Bush. Perry, on the other hand, had the endorsement of the ultimate outsider in politics, Sarah Palin, and he enthusiastically appealed to the pervasive anti-Washington sentiment in Texas.[52] Hutchison,

In 2012, Governor Perry ran for president, arguing that he could bring some of Texas's successes to the nation. However, his candidacy fizzled after a poor debate performance and other missteps.

said Perry, "is Washington and all things bad about Washington. I am Texas. State sovereignty. The Tenth Amendment. States' rights."[53] This strategic message helped win Perry the governorship.

Governor Perry's popularity in Texas was not enough to win him a place in national politics. In 2012 he attempted a presidential run with the widespread expectation that he would become the star of what was generally a weak field of Republican candidates. But Perry proved to be exceptionally weak as a debater. He generated little support in the Republican primaries, and finally withdrew as a candidate.

With the advent of the Great Recession and the election of President Barack Obama, two things happened. First, Texas lost enormous influence in Congress and second, Texas lost influence in the executive branch. It was a Democratic Congress and Democratic presidency and there was a scarcity of Texas Democrats. That prevented Texans from having much of a voice in national government in 2009–10. Even after Republicans gained a majority in the U.S. House in 2011, Texans were not in the highest leadership positions in Congress.

Today there are strong demands from within the state that Texas withdraw from the national political scene altogether. Unlike the previous eras in Texas politics, the current period—perhaps best described as the Tea Party era—is a time when the national government is seen as the enemy. Hallmarks of this ideology are avoidance of taxation at all costs and the assumption that government, especially the national government, is by definition undesirable. Compromise in the interest of making public policy—a belief deeply held by such past leaders as Lyndon Johnson and Sam Rayburn—is regarded as evil. When Kay Bailey Hutchison, for example, voted on a procedural matter regarding stopping a filibuster on a defense appropriations bill that was blocking consideration of the Obama health care bill in the Senate, she was criticized and picketed for voting with Democrats, even though her vote was not necessary to break the filibuster and even though it was to allow a vote on a defense bill.[54]

In the Tea Party's view, politics is no longer the effort to seek common ground among opposing interests in making policy: it is a zero-sum game in which the goal is to remain ideologically pure and to defeat Democrats rather than join with them in law-making. Senator John Cornyn (R-Tex.) came under Tea Party attack when he headed the Republican senatorial campaign committee and sent funding to Republican Senator Lisa Murkowski (R-Alaska), who was being challenged by Tea Party–backed candidate Joe Miller. Cornyn was accused of trying to re-elect a "RINO," which means a "Republican in Name Only." The Tea Party claimed Cornyn was contributing to the "mess" in Washington by backing the too-liberal Murkowski.[55] Murkowski was defeated in the primary election, but ran as an independent and won the general election.

As a result of his support for Murkowski, along with his vote for TARP, a Bush administration–initiated bailout program to deal with the economic consequences of the Great Recession, Cornyn was booed at an Austin Tea Party meeting.[56] One blog from a Tea Party supporter commented about Cornyn being booed, "The message for politicians? People are watching your votes carefully, and if you vote for big government while trying to convince us that you are for limited government, the people will not buy it. Cornyn tried to criticize Washington, but the people in Austin were well aware that Cornyn had become part of the problem."[57]

A Tea Party political action committee, Club for Growth Action, targeted Lieutenant Governor David Dewhurst in his 2012 race in the Republican primary for Hutchison's old seat in the U.S. Senate. The political action committee ran a million-dollar television ad campaign against Dewhurst in which he was labeled a "moderate"—the new derogatory label for a candidate in Texas.[58] The strength of the Tea Party proved too great for Dewhurst who was defeated by Tea Party favorite Ted Cruz in the Republican run-off primary.

Interestingly, if President Lyndon Johnson had adopted this sort of viewpoint regarding ideological purity in 1964 and had not allied with Republicans, his pathbreaking civil rights bills would have never passed. And with this ideological perspective, President Reagan could never have met regularly with Democratic Speaker Tip O'Neill and worked out compromises over drinks at the end of the day. Politics in the Tea Party era is total war as opposed to consensus building, a war to reduce government programs, reduce taxes, reduce costs, and keep power out of Washington.

The demand for ideological purity has filtered down to the state level as well. The Texas legislature was once known for its lack of partisanship but is becoming increasingly partisan. Texas House Speaker Joe Straus, a Republican, would not have won that office without support from Democrats. However, when the Speaker was chosen in the last legislative session, he was heavily criticized for his ties to Democrats.[59] In an effort to cultivate ties to Democrats, Republican state senator John Carona held a fund-raiser for a Democratic state senator, Royce West. In doing this, Carona may have jeopardized his conservative voter base; he has come under heavy criticism for supporting a Democrat.[60]

One aspect of Tea Party thought, of course, relates to how the Constitution should be interpreted. The Tea Party would like to see states' rights recognized as protected by the Tenth Amendment and the role of states in governance vastly enhanced. At the same time, the powers of the national government would be weakened, primarily through a narrowing of its power to regulate interstate commerce. According to this line of reasoning, the federal health care law commonly known as Obamacare should have been struck down as an unconstitutional, overly broad exercise of the commerce power.

A Texas law that strictly required voters to show a government-issued ID in order to cast a ballot was blocked by a federal court in 2012. The federal court found that it would discriminate against poor and minority voters.

Major Issues in Federalism Today

Texans had a major role in designing the "marble-cake federalism" that came into full bloom in the Roosevelt era. What appears to disturb Governor Perry and other advocates of states' rights is that the national government has expanded too much, intruded too much on the lives of individuals, and interfered too significantly with state government operations. These concerns are especially evident in three areas of marble-cake federalism that are vastly important issues in Texas today: health care, water policy, and immigration policy.

About one out of every four Texans does not have health insurance. The Affordable Health Care and Patient Protection Act (Obamacare) mandates health insurance for every uninsured Texan who is a legal U.S. citizen. While this legislation may be desirable public policy, it also entails an unprecedented degree of national involvement in the lives of its citizens. Never before has the national government used its powers to force an individual to buy a product from a private company. That aspect of the law, of course, is disturbing to the libertarian strain in contemporary Texas politics. In addition, the legislation could have a huge effect on state expenditures for Medicaid (health services for poor people) in future years. The effect on the state Medicaid budget disturbs those who are worried about the cost of national governmental programs.

Another policy area that is currently affected by federal-state relations is water. The growth and development of Texas will falter without adequate water supplies and this will require an expansion of the state's reservoir system. Currently, the 16-county north Texas region that includes Dallas, Collin, Denton, and Tarrant counties has a population of 6.67 million people. While that population is expected to double by 2060, the region's current water supply of 583 billion gallons of water only slightly exceeds today's demand. Yet two proposed water reservoirs for the region have been held up by regulations for years with no resolution in sight. Many of those regulations involve federal rules on issues, such as environmental impact, that serve desirable goals, but also are preventing the state from dealing with a compelling long-term problem. The effect of failing to provide adequate water for north Texas, according to the Texas Water Development Board, will cost the region $50 billion by 2060 and the loss of a half-million jobs.[61] Can Texas supply its water needs without federal support—support that has always been present in the construction of previous water projects?

Finally, the federal role in setting immigration policy has been a hotly debated issue in Texas. Within the Republican Party there are two schools of thought on immigration. One wing of the party has been adamantly opposed to new policies dealing with immigration out of fear that those policies would lead to amnesty for undocumented persons. The other wing takes a more moderate stance, as seen in the state party's 2012 platform position. This centered on a guest worker program whereby temporary immigrant workers would be permitted to work in Texas provided that they

- passed a criminal background check
- had paid all fines from possible prior immigration violations
- could secure health insurance

Tax Policy in Texas versus Other States

Our federal system allows states to enact different tax policies for the funding of state government operations. It has been said that in Texas there are two words that, when combined, are associated with political suicide: *income* and *tax*. This is not the case in many other states, such as New York or California, where residents pay state income taxes. Of course, Texans pay federal income taxes and the state receives funding for certain programs from the national government, but the state government is responsible for many of the services that are most important to residents. Texas's dominant political philosophy emphasizes low taxes and low social services.

The 2012 Texas tax structure clearly reflects the low tax mantra. Texas has no individual income tax and no corporate income tax, with the tax burden placed on a state sales tax of 6.25 percent and property tax collections. The sales tax is slightly higher in certain areas because localities can add to this burden; however, the sales tax cannot exceed 8.25 percent under state law. According to the Tax Foundation, a nonpartisan tax research group, the overall state and local tax burden in Texas is estimated at 7.9 percent, which places it sixth in the nation for lowest tax burden and below the national average of 9.8 percent. In comparison, New Jersey, New York, and Connecticut have the three highest state tax burdens in the country, with rates at or above 12 percent.

Supporters of allowing Texas and other states significant autonomy argue that variation and competition among state policies lead to better outcomes. For example, government spending is low in Texas, with many of Texas's fiscal conservatives priding themselves on keeping money in the "people's pockets." Talmadge Heflin, who served 11 terms in the Texas House and chaired the Appropriations Committee, wrote, "As of December 2011, Texas's unemployment rate has been at or below the national average for 60 consecutive months. This feat is all the more impressive given that Texas added more people than any other state between 2010 and 2011."[a] Among the 50 states, Texas has the nation's leading economy, and advocates of its tax structure give some credit to the state's fiscal policies.

On the other hand, should the poor and disadvantaged in Texas receive less help than low-income residents of other states? Low-tax, low-service states like Texas spend less money on programs to aid the poor and disadvantaged. Economist Paul Krugman argues, "While low spending may sound good in the abstract, what it amounts to in practice is low spending on children, who account directly or indirectly for a large part of government outlays at the state and local level."[b] According to the U.S. Census Bureau, Texas had a child poverty rate of 25.7 percent for 2010, the ninth highest child poverty rate in the nation.[c] Moreover, the *Houston Chronicle* reported that during a period of reduced revenue in 2011, the Texas state legislature cut school funding by $4 billion for 2012 and 2013 and reduced education grants by $1.4 billion for the same period. These budget cuts lowered Texas's annual spending to an average of $8,908 per student, while the national average is $11,463.[d]

In the abstract, voters want low taxes and high services, but if taxes are low, there isn't as much money for services. In Texas, the budget must be balanced every two years,

which in times of economic difficulties means either spending cuts or higher taxes. Texas has chosen to balance recent budgets by cutting spending, often at the expense of education and social services. Proponents of state autonomy argue that Texas is leading the nation in job creation and population growth because of its low-tax, low-services approach, but critics of this approach say that it comes at a high cost to the marginalized, the poor, and children across the state.

[a] Talmadge Heflin, "Why the Texas Economy Is Booming," *The Daily Caller*, March 5, 2012, http://dailycaller.com/2012/03/05/why-texas-economy-is-booming (accessed 12/18/12).
[b] Paul Krugman, "Leaving Children Behind," *New York Times*, February 27, 2011, www.nytimes.com/2011/02/28/opinion/28krugman.html?_r=0 (accessed 12/18/12).
[c] U.S. Census Bureau, "Table 1: Number and Percentage of Children in Poverty in the Past 12 Months by State and Puerto Rico: 2009 and 2010," November 2011, www.census.com/prod/2011pubs/acsbr10-05.pdf (accessed 12/18/12).
[d] Sommer Ingram, "Protesters in Austin Rally against Texas Education Cuts," May 21, 2011, *Houston Chronicle*, www.chron.com/news/houston-texas/article/Protesters-in-Austin-rally-against-Texas-1601524.php (accessed 12/18/12)

critical thinking questions

1. Should states or the federal government have more of a say in how taxes are collected and spent? Why?

2. If the federal government didn't collect federal income taxes from Texans and didn't provide funding for state programs, how would this affect the state budget?

Health care has been perhaps the most controversial issue in federalism in recent years. Following the passage of the Affordable Care Act in 2010, 26 states (including Texas) sued the federal government over the law.

- waived all rights to financial support from public assistance programs
- were proficient in English and completed an American civics class
- worked for employers who deducted and matched payroll taxes
- obtained an individual temporary worker biometric identification card that tracked all their address changes and any court appearances as a defendant[62]

Although its requirements are stringent, this platform position is a dramatic departure from the Texas Republican Party's previous views on immigration as well as from the very hostile views on immigration by Republicans in states such as Alabama and Arizona. However, this moderate position on immigration may simply be symbolic. When it comes to the Tea Party demand that states should be able to act to control immigration, a recent Supreme Court decision involving Arizona immigration policy establishes that much of immigration policy is preempted by the national government. While we may have marble-cake federalism with much overlap between national and state government actions, there remain some parts in the "marble cake" that are reserved for only the national government.

There has always been Texas opposition to Washington, but Texas has in the past played a major role in the Washington political scene. Since the Wilson era, Texas has produced three presidents, three vice presidents, three Speakers of the House, four majority leaders of the House, two minority leaders of the House, one majority leader of the Senate, and one minority leader of the Senate. Table 2.1 lists the Texans who held these highest political offices in the nation. These and other Texas politicians of the past also acknowledged that the federal government had a legitimate role to play in areas such as national defense, public welfare, and economic security. Even the Texan Republicans of the Reagan era, who rejected the New Deal emphasis on federal economic regulation, did not reject the national government as a whole. They did not condemn Washington or call for secession.

The Tea Party era is a new one for Texas and it is unclear how long this period will last. The new era in the relationship between Texas and the nation rejects

TABLE 2.1

Texans Holding the Highest Political Offices in the United States

POLITICAL OFFICE	OFFICEHOLDER	PARTY	TERM OF OFFICE
U.S. President*	Lyndon B. Johnson	Democrat	1963–69
	George H. W. Bush	Republican	1989–93
	George W. Bush	Republican	2001–09
U.S. Vice President	John Nance Garner	Democrat	1933–41
	Lyndon B. Johnson	Democrat	1961–63
	George H. W. Bush	Republican	1981–89
Speaker of the U.S. House of Representatives	John Nance Garner	Democrat	1931–33
	Sam Rayburn	Democrat	1940–47
			1949–53
			1955–61
	Jim Wright	Democrat	1987–89
U.S. Senate Majority Leader	Lyndon B. Johnson	Democrat	1955–61
U.S. Senate Minority Leader	Lyndon B. Johnson	Democrat	1953–55
U.S. House Majority Leader	Sam Rayburn	Democrat	1937–40
	Jim Wright	Democrat	1977–87
	Richard Armey	Republican	1995–2003
	Tom DeLay	Republican	2003–06
U.S. House Minority Leader**	John Nance Garner	Democrat	1929–31
	Sam Rayburn	Democrat	1947–49
			1953–55

* Dwight Eisenhower was born in Texas, but considered Kansas his home state.
** Joe Bailey served as Democratic Minority Leader in the U.S. House of Representatives in 1897–99, but this was prior to the Wilson era.

rather than embraces national policy and influence, and instead has promoted a philosophy that is antitax, anti-Washington, highly partisan, and pro–ideological purity. One needs to ask, however, whether it is possible for Texas to deal with such problems as health care, water, or immigration while rejecting national governmental power.

● Thinking Critically about Texas and Federalism

Texas began its role in the national government as a backwater state. Its entrance into the nation led to war with Mexico, and it was important in expanding slavery. Texas soon seceded from the Union to join the Confederacy, which was a very weak confederation of slave states. The defeat of the Confederacy led to Texas's return to the Union and Reconstruction. It was not until the late 1890s that a Texas politician—Joseph Weldon Bailey—gained a leadership role in Congress, although his personal flaws prevented him from becoming a key player on the national political scene.

Things changed for Texas during the administration of Woodrow Wilson. Texan Edward House became Wilson's key adviser, and House's political allies occupied important positions in Wilson's cabinet. During this era, Texans began to have real political clout in Congress. They played a major part in expanding the role of the national government, where they chipped away at the traditional notion of federalism and began moving the national government toward a larger and more active role in people's lives. With the coming of Franklin Roosevelt and the New Deal, Texans again rose to leadership in the executive branch and Congress, and were among the main architects of a new way of thinking about the relationship between the national and the state governments. "Dual federalism," illustrated in Figure 2.1, became a dead concept replaced by "cooperative federalism" in which the national government was even larger, more actively involved in people's lives, and much more involved in economic regulation. New Deal ideology did not die with Franklin Roosevelt, but actually continued until the era of Ronald Reagan, when some recognition of the rights of states again emerged. A large national government was not rejected in the Reagan era, but some limits were placed on national power versus the powers of states. In the modern Tea Party era, Texas power at the national level has, at least for now, declined. No Texan occupies a leadership role in the executive branch or a top leadership role in Congress, though Senator John Cornyn is advancing in the Senate Republican leadership circles and several Texans in the House hold committee chairs, including the chairmanship of the especially powerful Rules Committee. Within Texas, there is pervasive distrust of the national government, a sense that it has become too powerful and too intrusive and that its regulations are preventing or discouraging economic recovery.

Since the Wilson administration, there has always been a faction of Texas politics that has opposed the expansion of national governmental power at the expense of state power. During the Wilson era, that opposition was seen in Joseph Weldon Bailey's unsuccessful effort to become governor of Texas. Texans also opposed Franklin Roosevelt and the New Deal—for example, John Nance Garner and Jesse Jones ultimately turned against the New Deal because they saw the national government as becoming too powerful. The movement toward deregulation in the Reagan era and the corresponding expansion of state powers was strongly supported by Texans. In the Tea Party era there has been strong opposition to national power and support for state powers. The key question is whether this new dominant position on federalism will last and, most importantly, whether Texas can solve the problems it faces without strong national governmental involvement.

The Texas Constitution
amended hundreds of
In 2011, Texans voted
approved the Texas Per
School Fund Amendme
measure amended the
to make additional fun
to public school distric

study guide

 **Practice online with:** Chapter 2 Diagnostic Quiz ▪ Chapter 2 Key Term Flashcards

Texas: A State in a Federal System

■ **Understand federalism and Texas's relationship to the national government (pp. 41–45)**

The American federal system of government has evolved through a number of forms. The Constitution established a national government alongside existing state governments. Following the Civil War, various federal systems emerged including dual federalism (layer-cake federalism), cooperative federalism, marble cake federalism, New Federalism, and coercive federalism.

Key terms

federalism (p. 41)

sovereign (p. 41)

dual federalism (p. 42)

layer-cake federalism (p. 42)

cooperative federalism (p. 42)

marble-cake federalism (p. 43)

New Federalism (p. 43)

block grants (p. 43)

coercive federalism (p. 43)

Practice Quiz

1. *Federalism* refers to (p. 41)
   a) a system of government where cities are strong.
   b) a system of government where executive power is grounded in a committee of governors.
   c) a system of government where there is a national government as well as a number of regional governments.
   d) a system of government dominated by business interests.
   e) a system of government with strong parliaments.

2. The Articles of Confederation *(p. 41)*
   a) was a loose confederation of independent states that operated in the 1820s.
   b) was never accepted by a majority of the states.
   c) derived its power directly from the state governments.
   d) replaced the U.S. Constitution of 1787.
   e) outlawed effective state constitutions.

3. The relationship between the states and the national government *(pp. 41–44)*
   a) has been a matter of continuing controversy throughout the nation's history.
   b) was finally settled when the Articles of Confederation were rejected in favor of the U.S. Constitution.
   c) was resolved for all time by the Civil War.
   d) was resolved by Article 1, Section 8 of the U.S. Constitution.
   e) was not a problem in a federal system.

4. *Dual federalism (p. 42)*
   a) refers to a system of government where states do most of the governing.
   b) existed in the United States following World War II.
   c) rejected the idea that states were sovereign political entities.
   d) is the idea that there are two branches to the national legislature.
   e) drained all power from state governments.

Texas's Evolving Role in the Nation

■ **Trace the major changes in Texas's relationship to the national government over time (pp. 46–57)**

Initially, after joining the Union in 1846, Texas had little political influence at the national level. Texas lost its "backwater" status only at the beginning of the twentieth century. Texas's role in national affairs increased during the presidency of Woodrow Wilson, and Texans also played key roles in Franklin Roosevelt's New Deal Coalition. By the end of the New Deal, questions began to be raised by some leaders about the wisdom of continuing New Deal policies. But, in general, Texans remained steadfast in support of the New Deal. During the Reagan Era, Texas began moving toward the Republican Party and away from its long-standing connection with the Democratic Party.

Practice Quiz

5. Texas was a les
   ately after joinin
   a) it had a relat
   b) it was econo
   c) it had little p
   d) it was too co
   e) it was too Re

6. Texans first ass
   at the national l
   administration c
   a) Theodore Ro
   b) Lyndon B. Jo
   c) Woodrow Wil
   d) Franklin Roos
   e) Herbert Hoov

7. Which of the foll
   the Wilsonian Er
   a) Prohibition
   b) national defe
   c) child labor la
   d) pure food an
   e) rising Medica

8. Which of the foll
   a) Texas was a
      New Deal.
   b) Republicans
      ing the 1930
   c) By 1931 all
   d) John Nance
      of the House
   e) Lyndon John
      Representat

9. Roosevelt's Nev
   a) promoted a
      the economy
   b) supported na
   c) was support
   d) was oppose
   e) occured imm

10. Texans played a
    expanding the r

Texas in tl

Describe the n
federalism in T

Today Texas has con
Party. Within recent
the Tea Party, to mo
right. The policy pos
include the rejection
government social p

---

d) is concerned about federal spending
e) all of the above

15. Following the passage of "Obamacare" in 2010, opponents of the federal health care law were concerned because *(p. 60)*
    a) the law would increase the number of uninsured Texans.
    b) the state would have to spend much more on Medicaid.

---

c) it would create a new system of dual federalism.
d) it mandates health insurance for illegal immigrants.
e) the law reflects a libertarian perspective on government.

Practice Online

Video exercise: *Governor Perry and Secession*

Recommended Websites

Texas Tea Party:
texasteaparty.com

Texas Almanac:
texasalmanac.com

Dallas Tea Party:
dallas teaparty.mojo4m.com

Texas Conservative Coalition:
txcc.org

Texas State Historical Association:
tshaonline.org

The Texas Constitution

WHAT GOVERNMENT DOES AND WHY IT MATTERS Every few years, the Texas Legislature presents to the voters a list of proposed amendments to the state constitution. Voter approval is necessary for the amendments to take effect. In 2011, 10 amendments were proposed. Among these amendments was one that would allow the Texas Water Development Board to issue bonds so loans could be given for local governments for water projects and a proposed amendment that would give El Paso more borrowing authority. In 2009, 11 amendments were proposed, among them an amendment protecting private property from some property takings involving eminent domain, an amendment establishing a National Research University Fund, and an amendment allowing members of emergency services districts to serve for four years. In 2007, 16 amendments were put forward spanning a wide range of matters. Some amendments grappled with essential problems of constitutional government and public policy. Others were more technical, reflecting efforts to clean up specific language in the state constitution. Some had an air of whimsy about them that belied a serious critique: that the current state constitution is a clumsy document and is, in many respects, out of date. Such is the case with Proposition 10, an amendment proposed in 2007 to abolish the constitutional authority of the county Office of the Inspector of Hides and Animals.[1]

In 1871 the state legislature established the office for the inspection of the brands on all hides and animals that were shipped out of a county.[2] Over time, the need for inspectors declined. By 1945, only about one-third of Texas counties still had an inspector of hides and animals. Nonetheless, under constitutional amendments passed in 1954 and 1958, the office acquired constitutional status. By the 1990s, few counties still had an inspector of hides and animals, and in those that did, the office was not taken all that seriously.

In Fort Bend County, Jeff McMeans served as the inspector for 17 years, after running for the position initially as a joke in 1986. "It was the perfect office," McMeans told a *Dallas Morning News* reporter. "No pay, no office, no responsibility, no nothing." In Travis County, Glenn Maxey was elected inspector of hides and animals in 1986. Before he could file as a candidate, he had to convince the county clerk in Travis County that there really was such an office. Running unopposed, Maxey was elected, but he refused to take the oath of office, noting that his objective in running was not to win but to abolish a useless county office.

The demise of the office of inspector of hides and animals eventually took place in 2003 when the legislature changed the Agricultural Code. But the language in the constitution remained unchanged. Finally, during the 2007 session, the legislature passed a proposed amendment to the constitution (Proposition 10) that would delete any reference to the office in the constitution itself. Although there was no serious opposition to Proposition 10, some used it to draw attention to the fact that the amendment process and the state constitution itself were seriously flawed. A group of Austin Community College students rallied against Proposition 10, to show that the constitution was woefully out of date and that piecemeal amendments such as Proposition 10 only made matters worse. Not surprisingly, the proposition passed.

Efforts have been made in the past to rethink the constitutional foundations of political life in Texas. In spite of reform efforts, the Texas Constitution remains a document much disparaged and not well understood by the population as a whole. However, the Texas Constitution probably has a greater immediate impact on the lives of Texans than does the U.S. Constitution.

chaptergoals

- Identify the main functions of state constitutions (pages 71–72)
- Describe the five Texas constitutions that preceded the current constitution (pages 72–81)
- Explain the circumstances that led to the Texas Constitution that is still in use today (pages 81–83)
- Analyze the major provisions of the Texas Constitution today (pages 83–89)
- Describe modern efforts to change the Texas Constitution (pages 89–98)

The Role of a State Constitution

Identify the main functions of state constitutions

State **constitutions** perform a number of important functions. They legitimate state political institutions by clearly explaining the source of their power and authority. State constitutions also delegate power, explaining which powers are granted to particular institutions and individuals and how those powers are to be used. They prevent the concentration of political power by providing political mechanisms that check and balance the powers of one political institution or individual officeholder against another. Finally, they define the limits of political power. Through declarations of rights, state constitutions explicitly forbid the intrusion of certain kinds of governmental activities into the lives of individuals.

The idea of constitutional government in Texas since its first constitution has been heavily indebted to the larger American experience. Five ideas unite the U.S. and Texas constitutional experiences. First, political power in both the United States and Texas is ultimately derived from the people. Political power is something that is artificially created through the constitution by a conscious act of the people. Second, political power is divided into three separate parts and placed in separate branches of government. The legislative, executive, and judicial branches of government have their own unique powers and corresponding duties and obligations. Third, the U.S. and Texas constitutions structure political power in such a way that the power of one branch is checked and balanced by the power of the other two branches. The idea of checks and balances reflects a common concern among the framers of the U.S. Constitution and the authors of Texas's various constitutions that the intent of writing a constitution was not just to establish effective governing institutions. Its purpose was also to create political institutions that would not tyrannize the very people who established them. The concern for preventing the emergence of tyranny is also found in a fourth idea that underlies the U.S. and Texas constitutions: the idea of individual rights. Government is explicitly forbidden to violate a number of particular rights that the people possess.

The final idea embodied in both the U.S. and Texas constitutions is that of **federalism**. Federalism is the division of government into a central government and a series of regional governments (see Chapter 2). Both kinds of government exercise direct authority over individual citizens of the United States and of each particular state. Article IV, Section 4, of the U.S. Constitution guarantees that every state in the Union will have a "Republican Form of Government." Curiously, no attempt is made to explain what exactly a "Republican Form of Government" entails. The Tenth Amendment to the U.S. Constitution also recognizes the importance of the idea of federalism to the American political system. It reads: "The powers not delegated to the United States by the Constitution, nor prohibited by it to the States, are reserved to the States respectively, or to the people." According to the U.S. Constitution, enormous reservoirs of political power are thus derived from the people who reside in the states themselves.

However, some important differences distinguish the constitutional experience of Texas from that of the United States. Most important is the subordinate role that Texas has in the federal system. Article VI of the U.S. Constitution contains the **supremacy clause**, declaring the Constitution and the laws of the United States to be "the supreme Law of the Land." The supremacy clause requires all judges in every state to be bound by the U.S. Constitution, notwithstanding the

constitution the legal structure of a government, which establishes its power and authority as well as the limits on that power

federalism a system of government in which power is divided, by a constitution, between a central government and regional governments

supremacy clause Article VI of the U.S. Constitution, which states that the Constitution and laws passed by the national government and all treaties are the supreme law of the land and superior to all laws adopted by any state or any subdivision

laws or constitution of their particular state. In matters of disagreement, the U.S. Constitution thus takes precedence over the Texas Constitution.

One of the major issues of the Civil War was how the federal system was to be understood. Was the United States a confederation of autonomous sovereign states that were ultimately independent political entities capable of secession (much like the current European Union)? Was the United States a perpetual union of states that were ultimately in a subordinate relationship to the central government? The results of the war and the ratification of the Fourteenth Amendment in 1868 ultimately resolved this question in terms of the latter. The idea that the United States was a perpetual union composed of subordinate states would have profound implications for constitutional government in Texas throughout the late nineteenth and twentieth centuries. The incorporation of the Bill of Rights through the Fourteenth Amendment, which made much of the Bill of Rights apply to the states, became a dominant theme of constitutional law in the twentieth century. The Fourteenth Amendment effectively placed restrictions on Texas government and public policy that went far beyond those laid out in Texas's own constitution.

Another major difference between the U.S. and Texas constitutions lies in the **necessary and proper clause** of Article I, Section 8. Section 8 begins by listing in detail the specific powers granted to Congress by the Constitution. The Founders apparently wanted to limit the scope of national government activities. But Section 8 concludes by granting Congress the power necessary to accomplish its constitutional tasks. The net effect of this clause was to provide a constitutional basis for an enormous expansion of central government activities over the next 200 plus years.

Drafters of Texas's various constitutions generally have been unwilling to grant such an enormous loophole in the exercise of governmental power. Although granting state government the power to accomplish certain tasks, Texas constitutions have generally denied officeholders broad grants of discretionary power to accomplish their goals.

necessary and proper clause
Article I, Section 8, of the U.S. Constitution; it provides Congress with the authority to make all laws "necessary and proper" to carry out its powers

● The First Texas Constitutions

> Describe the five Texas constitutions that preceded the current constitution

Since declaring independence from Mexico, Texas has had six constitutions. Each was shaped by historical developments of its time and, following the first constitution, attempted to address the shortcomings of each previous constitution. In this section, we look at the five Texas constitutions that preceded the current constitution. First, though, we consider the constitution that governed Texas when it was part of Mexico.

The Constitution of Coahuila y Tejas, 1827 Despite the growing fears of American expansionism following the Louisiana Purchase, in 1803 Spanish Texas was still sparsely populated. In 1804, the population of Spanish Texas was estimated to be 3,605. In 1811, Juan Bautista de las Casas launched the first revolt against Spanish rule in San Antonio. The so-called Casas Revolt was successfully put down by the summer of 1811. The next year, a second challenge to Spanish rule took place along the border between Texas and the United States. After capturing Nacogdoches, La Bahia, and San Antonio, rebel forces under José Bernardo Gutiérrez de Lara issued a declaration of independence from New Spain and drafted a constitution.

This 1844 cartoon satirized congressional opposition to the annexation of Texas. Personified as a beautiful young woman, Texas is holding a cornucopia filled with flowers. Though James K. Polk, elected to the presidency in 1844, welcomes Texas, the Whig Party leader Senator Henry Clay, with arms folded, warns, "Stand back, Madam Texas! For we are more holy than thou! Do you think we will have anything to do with gamblers, horse-racers, and licentious profligates?"

By 1813, however, this revolt had also been put down, and bloody reprisals had depopulated the state. Texas remained part of New Spain until the Mexican War of Independence.[3]

The Mexican War of Independence grew out of a series of revolts against Spanish rule during the Napoleonic Wars. Burdened by debts brought on by a crippling war with France, Spain sought to extract more wealth from its colonies. The forced abdication of Ferdinand VII in favor of Napoleon's brother Joseph in 1808 and an intensifying economic crisis in New Spain in 1809 and 1810 undermined the legitimacy of Spanish rule. Revolts broke out in Guanajuato and spread throughout Mexico and its Texas province. Although these rebellions were initially put down by royalist forces loyal to Spain, by 1820 local revolts and guerrilla actions had helped to weaken continued royal rule from Spain. On August 24, 1821, Mexico was formally granted independence by Spain.

Because Texas was part of Mexico, the first federal constitution that it operated under was the Mexican Constitution. At the national level, there were two houses of Congress. The lower house was composed of deputies serving two-year terms. In the upper house, senators served four-year terms and were selected by state legislatures. The president and vice president were elected for four-year terms by the legislative bodies of the states. There was a supreme court, composed of 11 judges, and an attorney general. Although the Mexican Constitution mandated separate legislative, executive, and judicial branches, no attempt was made to define the scope of states rights in the Mexican confederation. Local affairs remained independent of the central government. Although the Mexican Constitution embodied many of the ideas found in the U.S. Constitution, there was one important difference: Catholicism was established as the state religion and was supported financially by the state.[4]

Under the Mexican Constitution, the state of Coahuila and the sparsely populated province of Texas were combined together into the state of Coahuila and Texas. Saltillo, Mexico, was the capital. More than two years were spent drafting a constitution for the new state. It was finally published on March 11, 1827.

The state was formally divided into three separate districts, with Texas composing the District of Bexar. Legislative power for the state was placed in a **unicameral** legislature composed of 12 deputies elected by the people. The people of the District of Bexar (Texas) elected 2 of these. Along with wide-ranging legislative powers, the legislature was also empowered to elect state officials when no majority emerged from the popular vote, to serve as a grand jury in political and military matters, and to regulate the army and militia. Executive power was vested in a governor and a vice governor, each elected by the people for a four-year term. Judicial power was placed in state courts. The Constitution of 1827 formally guaranteed citizens the right to liberty, security, property, and equality. Language in the Constitution of 1827 also supported efforts to curtail the spread of slavery, an institution of vital importance to planters who were immigrating from the American South. The legislature was ordered to promote education and freedom of the press. As in the Mexican federal constitution, Catholicism was the established state religion.[5]

unicameral comprising one body or house, as in a one-house legislature

The Constitution of the Republic of Texas, 1836

Texas's break with Mexico was in large part a constitutional crisis that culminated in separation. Political conventions held in San Felipe de Austin in 1832 and 1833 reflected a growing discontent among Texans over their place in the Mexican federal system. Along with demands for a more liberal immigration policy for people from the United States and for the establishment of English- and Spanish-speaking primary schools, calls for separate statehood for Texas emerged from the conventions. The 1833 convention actually drafted a constitution for this newly proposed state modeled on the Massachusetts Constitution of 1780. Stephen F. Austin's attempt to bring the proposed constitution to the attention of the central government in Mexico City led to his imprisonment, which, in turn, pushed Texas closer to open rebellion against the central Mexican government.

On November 7, 1835, a declaration was adopted by a meeting of state political leaders at San Felipe, which stated the reasons Texans were beginning to take up arms against the Mexican government. The declaration proclaimed that Texas was rising up in defense of its rights and liberties as well as the republican principles articulated in the Mexican Constitution of 1824. This declaration was but a prelude to the formal Texas Declaration of Independence that emerged out of the convention of 1836 held at Washington-on-the-Brazos.

Of the 59 delegates attending the Convention of 1836, only 10 had lived in Texas prior to 1830. Two had arrived as late as 1836. Thirty-nine of the delegates were from southern slave states, 6 were from the border state of Kentucky, 7 were from northern states, 3 were from Mexico (including 2 born in Texas), and 4 were from other English-speaking lands.[6] The final products of the convention—the Texas Declaration of Independence and the Constitution of 1836—reflected the interests and values of these participants.

In their own Declaration of Independence, delegates to the convention proclaimed that the federal constitutional regime they had been invited to live under by the rulers of Mexico had been replaced by a military tyranny that combined a "despotism of

UNANIMOUS

DECLARATION OF INDEPENDENCE,

BY THE

DELEGATES OF THE PEOPLE OF TEXAS,

IN GENERAL CONVENTION,

AT THE TOWN OF WASHINGTON,

ON THE SECOND DAY OF MARCH, 1836.

RICHARD ELLIS, *President.*

The Texas Declaration of Independence was written by George C. Childress and adopted at the Convention of 1836. Childress modeled the document on the American Declaration of Independence.

the sword and the priesthood." Echoing the American Declaration of Independence, they presented a long list of grievances against the central government, including the failure to provide freedom of religion, a system of public education, and trial by jury.

The Texas Declaration of Independence Like the Founders during the American Revolution, leaders of the Texas Revolution felt they needed to justify their actions in print. Written by George C. Childress and adopted by the general convention at Washington-on-the-Brazos on March 2, 1836, the Texas Declaration of Independence stated why it was necessary to separate from Mexico and create an independent republic. Not surprisingly, the document draws heavily on the ideas of John Locke and Thomas Jefferson for inspiration. The description of the role of the government, "to protect the lives, liberty, and property of the people," repeated verbatim Locke's litany of the primary reasons for establishing government. Like Jefferson's Declaration, Texas's declaration catalogues a list of grievances against the Mexican regime. According to Texas's declaration, the existing government had abdicated its duties to protect the governed and had broken the trustee relationship that binds a people to those in authority. By dissolving civil society into its original elements, the government had forced the people to assert their inalienable right of self-preservation and to take political affairs into their own hands again. The "melancholy conclusion" of Texas's declaration echoed ideas that Locke and Jefferson would have understood well: any government that stripped a people of their liberty was unacceptable to those raised on principles of self-government. Self-preservation demanded "eternal political separation" from the very state (Mexico) that had invited them to settle in Texas.

After declaring Texas a separate republic independent from Mexico, the convention proceeded to draft and pass a new constitution reflecting these republican sentiments. Resembling the U.S. Constitution in being brief and flexible (fewer than 6,500 words), the 1836 Constitution established an elected chief executive with considerable powers, a **bicameral** legislature, and a four-tiered judicial system composed of justice, county, district, and supreme courts.[7] Power was divided among these three branches, and a system of checks and balances was put into place. Complicated procedures were included for amending the constitution, and a bill of rights was elaborated.

bicameral having a legislative assembly composed of two chambers or houses

A number of important provisions from Spanish-Mexican law were adapted for the Texas Republic in the constitution, including the idea of community property, homestead exemptions and protections, and debtor relief. The values of American democracy percolated through the document. White male suffrage was guaranteed. Ministers and priests were ineligible for public office. But one of the most important aspects of the Constitution of 1836, at least from the perspective of newly immigrated Americans from the South, may have been the defense of slavery as an institution.

The Constitution of Coahuila y Tejas of 1827 had challenged, albeit unsuccessfully, the existence of slavery as an institution. Although the 1836 Constitution of the Republic of Texas outlawed the importation of slaves from Africa, it guaranteed that slaveholders could keep their property and that new slaveholding immigrants could bring their slaves into Texas with them. The results of this constitutional protection were monumental. In 1836, Texas had a population of 38,470, including 5,000 slaves. By 1850, the slave population had grown to 58,161, over one-quarter of the state's population. By 1860, there were more than 182,566 slaves, accounting for more than 30 percent of the state's population.[8] To all intents and purposes, the Constitution of 1836 not only saved slavery as an institution in Texas but also provided the protections needed for it to flourish.

It was one thing to declare independence from Mexico, but quite another to win independence. Only after the Battle of San Jacinto, where on April 21 Sam Houston's force of 900 men overran the 1,300-man force of Santa Anna and captured Santa Anna himself, did Texas become an independent state.[9]

The Texas State Constitution of 1845

Although the 1836 Constitution called for annexation by the United States, Texas remained an independent republic for nine years. There were concerns in the United States that if Texas were admitted to the Union, it would be as a slave state. Texas's admission to the Union could alter the delicate balance between slave and free states and further divide the nation over the sensitive subject of slavery. Additionally, it was feared that annexation by the United States would lead to war with Mexico. The defeated Mexican general and dictator Santa Anna had repudiated the Treaty of Velasco, which had ended the war between Texas and Mexico. Still

The lowering of the Republic flag marked Texas's annexation to the Union on March 1, 1845. A state constitution was drafted shortly thereafter to reflect Texas's new role.

claiming Texas as part of its own territory, Mexico undoubtedly would have gone to war to protect what it felt to be rightfully its own.

Hesitation over admitting Texas to the Union was overcome by the mid-1840s. On March 1, 1845, the U.S. Congress approved a resolution that brought Texas into the Union as a state. The annexation resolution had a number of interesting provisions. First, the Republic of Texas ceded to the United States all military armaments, bases, and facilities pertaining to public defense. Second, Texas retained a right to all "its vacant and unappropriated lands" as well as to its public debts. This was no small matter, because Texas claimed an enormous amount of land that extended far beyond its present state boundaries. The boundary issues were not resolved until Congress passed the Compromise of 1850 which, among other things, established Texas's boundaries in exchange for a payment from the federal government where some of the funds were used to pay Texas's debts. Finally, Texas was given permission to break up into four additional states when population proved adequate.

On July 4, 1845, Anson Jones, fourth and final president of the Republic of Texas, called a convention in Austin to draft a state constitution. Drafters of the constitution relied heavily on the Constitution of 1836, although the final document ended up being almost twice as long. The familiar doctrines of separation of powers, checks and balances, and individual rights defined the basic design of government.

Under the Constitution of 1845, the legislature would be composed of two houses. The House of Representatives would have between 45 and 90 members, elected for two-year terms. Members were required to be at least 21 years of age. The Senate would be composed of between 19 and 33 members, elected for four-year terms. Half of the Senate would be elected every two years. As in the U.S. Constitution, revenue bills would originate in the House. Executive vetoes could be overturned by a two-thirds vote of each house. In a separate article on education, the legislature was ordered to establish a public school system and to set aside lands to support a Permanent School Fund. Another interesting power granted to the legislature was the power to select the treasurer and comptroller in a joint session.

This constitution provided for an elected governor and lieutenant governor. The governor's term was set at two years. He could serve only four years as governor in any six-year period. Among the executive powers granted to the governor were the powers to convene and adjourn the legislature, to veto legislation, to grant pardons and reprieves, and to command the state militia. The governor also had the power to appoint the attorney general, secretary of state, and district and supreme court judges, subject to the approval of the Senate.

The Constitution of 1845 established a judicial branch consisting of a supreme court composed of three judges, district courts, and lower courts deemed necessary by the legislature. Judges on the higher courts were to be appointed to six-year terms and could be removed from office subject to a two-thirds vote of both houses of the legislature.

Amending the Constitution of 1845 was difficult. After being proposed by a two-thirds vote of each house, amendments had to be approved by a majority of the voters. In the next legislature, another two-thirds vote of each house was necessary for ratification. Only one amendment was ever made to the Constitution of 1845. In 1850, an amendment was added to provide for the election of state officials who were originally appointed by the governor or by the legislature.[10]

This constitution retained some of the unusual provisions from the annexation resolution. Texas could divide itself into as many as five states and was responsible for paying its own foreign debt. It would retain title to its public lands, which could be sold to pay its debt. There was even a provision allowing Texas to fly its flag at the same height as the U.S. flag.

The Constitution of 1861: Texas Joins the Confederacy

The issue of slavery had delayed Texas's admission into the United States for nine years, until 1845. It drove Texas from the Union in 1861. By 1860, slavery had become a vital institution to the Texas economy. Concentrated in east Texas and along the Gulf Coast, slaves had come to constitute 30 percent of the population. However, in large sections of the state, particularly in the north and west, the economy was based on ranching or corn and wheat production rather than cotton. There slavery was virtually nonexistent. The question of whether Texas should secede was a controversial one that divided the state along regional and ethnic as well as party lines.

This image shows what the Texas State House looked like in the 1850s. Texas's first constitution after joining the Union as a state was ratified in 1845. It lasted until 1861 when Texas seceded from the Union along with other southern states.

Pressure to secede mounted following the presidential election of Abraham Lincoln in November 1860. A staunch Unionist, Governor Sam Houston refused to convene a special session of the legislature to discuss secession. Seeking to bypass Houston, a number of influential political leaders in the state, including the chief justice of the Texas Supreme Court, called for a special convention in January 1861 to consider secession. Giving in to the pressure, Houston called a special session of the legislature in the hopes of undercutting the upcoming secession convention. The legislature, however, had other ideas, validating the call for the convention and turning its chambers over to the convention.

Lawyers and slaveholders dominated the secession convention. Lawyers composed 40 percent of the delegates; slaveholders composed 70 percent. The Texas Ordinance of Secession, produced by the convention on February 2, 1861, reflected this proslavery membership. In striking language, it proclaimed that the northern states had broken faith with Texas, particularly regarding the institution of slavery. Northerners had violated the very laws and constitution of the federal Union by appealing to a "higher law" that trampled on the rights of Texans. In language that people living in the twenty-first century find hard to understand, the Ordinance of Secession proclaimed,

> We hold as undeniable truths that the governments of the various States, and of the confederacy itself, were established exclusively by the white race, for themselves and their posterity; that the African race had no agency in their establishment; that they were rightfully held and regarded as an inferior and dependent race, and in that condition only could their existence in this country be rendered beneficial and tolerable.[11]

Texas voters approved secession from the Union on February 23, 1861. The secession convention reconvened to enact a new constitution to guide the state as it entered the **Confederacy**. There were surprisingly few changes in the final document. This constitution was similar to the Constitution of 1845 except that references to the United States of America were replaced with references to the Confederate States of America. Public officials had to declare allegiance to the Confederacy, and slavery and states' rights were defended. A clause in the 1845 Constitution that provided for the emancipation of slaves was eliminated, and freeing slaves was declared illegal. But for the most part, the document accepted the existing constitutional framework. Controversial proposals, such as resuming the African slave trade, were rejected. The move out of the Union into the Confederacy may have been a radical one, but the new constitution was conservative insofar as it reaffirmed the existing constitutional order in the state.[12]

Confederacy the Confederate States of America, those southern states that seceded from the United States in late 1860 and 1861 and argued that the power of the states was more important than the power of the central government

The Constitution of 1866: Texas Rejoins the Union

Defeat in the Civil War led to the institution of another state constitution in 1866. The provisional governor, Andrew Jackson Hamilton, called a constitutional convention on November 15, 1865, a little over six months after the surrender of Lee's army in Virginia. Delegates were elected on January 8, 1866, and the convention was held February 7. Few former secessionists were excluded from voting, with the result that there were strong Unionist and secessionist factions at the convention.

A number of actions were taken to bring the state into compliance with President Andrew Johnson's policy of Reconstruction, including the rejection of the right to secession, a repudiation of the war debt incurred by the state, and an acceptance of the abolition of slavery. The convention granted freedmen fundamental rights to their persons and property and gave them the right to sue and be sued as well as the right to contract with others. However, there was little support for extending suffrage to blacks, and they were banned from holding public office. The convention also made a few changes to the existing constitutional system in Texas. These changes came to be known as the Constitution of 1866.

As in the two previous constitutions, the size of the House was set between 45 and 90, and that of the Senate between 19 and 33. Terms of office remained the same as under the 1845 and 1861 constitutions, although salaries were increased. Reapportionment was to be based on the number of white male citizens, who would be counted in a census every 10 years.

The governor's salary was also increased, and the term was extended to 4 years, with a limit of 8 years in any 12-year period. The governor was also granted, for the first time, a line-item veto on appropriations. The comptroller and the treasurer were to be elected by the voters for 4-year terms.

Under the new constitution, the state supreme court was expanded from three to five judges and terms were increased to 10 years. Their salaries also were increased. The chief justice was to be selected from the five judges on the supreme court. District court judges were to be elected for 8-year terms, and the attorney general for a 4-year term.

Voters ratified the Constitution of 1866 in June in a relatively close referendum, 28,119 to 23,400. The close vote was attributed to a widespread unhappiness with the increase in salaries of the various state officers.[13]

The Reconstruction Constitution of 1869

In 1869, Texas wrote still another constitution to meet the requirements of the Congressional Reconstruction Acts of 1867. A vote calling for a constitutional convention was ordered by General Winfield Scott Hancock, the commander of the Texas and Louisiana military district, in early 1868. Against Democratic opposition, **Radical Republicans** easily won the vote for a convention by 44,689 to 11,440. Of the 90 delegates to the convention, only 6 had served in the previous constitutional convention. Ten were blacks. The vast majority represented the interests of various wings in the Republican Party. The convention was a rancorous affair as delegates argued over a wide range of issues, including railroad charters, lawlessness in the state, and whether laws passed during the war years were legal. In the final days of the convention, delegates finally got down to the constitutional matters and the problems of accepting the Thirteenth and Fourteenth Amendments. Although delegates never completed their task of reworking the Constitution of 1866, their efforts were published under orders by military officials and became the Constitution of 1869.

A number of features of the Constitution of 1869 stand out.[14] The U.S. Constitution was declared to be the supreme law of the land. Slavery was forbidden, and blacks were given the right to vote. Fourteenth Amendment guarantees of equality before the law were recognized. Additionally, the constitution altered the relationship among the three branches of government.

The House of Representatives was set at 90 and the Senate at 30 members. Senatorial terms were extended to six years, with one-third of the seats to be elected every biennium. Legislative sessions were to be held annually.

The most critical changes were in the executive branch and the courts. The powers of the governor were vastly expanded. Among other things, the governor was given wide-ranging appointment powers that included the power to appoint judges. The state supreme court was reduced from five to three judges. The term

Radical Republicans a bloc of Republicans in the U.S. Congress who pushed through the adoption of black suffrage as well as an extended period of military occupation of the South following the Civil War

of supreme court judges was also lowered to nine years, with one new judge to be appointed every three years. Salaries for state officials were increased.

A Republican affiliated with the Radical faction of the party and a former Union general, Edmund Davis, governed under this constitution. Davis had vast authority, since the constitution had centralized power in the executive while reducing local governmental control. Varying interpretations exist of the government provided by Davis, though the popular perception at the time was that Davis presided over a corrupt, extravagant administration that eventually turned to the state police and the militia to attempt to maintain its regime.

In 1872 the Democrats regained control of the state government, and in 1873 the Democrat Richard Coke was elected governor. Davis attempted to maintain control over the governor's office by having his handpicked supreme court invalidate Coke's election. Davis refused to give up his office and surrounded himself with state police in the capitol building. However, when Democrats slipped past guards and gathered upstairs in the capitol building to organize a government, Davis was unable to obtain federal troops to retain him in office. Democrats were able to form a government, and Davis left office.

● The Constitution of 1876

> **Explain the circumstances that led to the Texas Constitution that is still in use today**

To prevent another government such as Davis's, efforts were made to write a new constitution. In 1874 a constitution was proposed and later rejected by a sitting legislature.[15] Finally, in 1875 a constitutional convention was called. Three delegates were selected by popular vote from each of the 30 senatorial districts. The final composition of the convention included 75 white Democrats and 15 Republicans, 6 of whom were black. Not one of the elected delegates had participated in the constitutional convention of 1868–69. Forty of the delegates were farmers, and 40 were members of the **Grange**, a militant farming organization that had emerged to improve the plight of farmers.

The document that emerged from this convention, the Constitution of 1876, is still the basis for Texas government today. In an era of agriculture when prices and incomes were low and when little was demanded or expected from government, much in the 1876 Constitution made sense. However, one might question whether a constitution designed primarily by white males for whites in a rural agrarian society—and for the purpose of keeping the likes of Edmund Davis from ever controlling the state again—is the best foundation for government in the modern era.

The framers were committed to a constitution with four major themes. First, they wanted strong popular control of state government. Second, they believed that a constitution should seriously limit the power of state government. Third, they sought economy in government. Fourth, the framers sought to promote agrarian interests, particularly those of small farmers, who formed the basis of support for the Grange movement.

Popular control of state government meant that the governor's vast appointment powers were limited by making judges and other public officials subject to election. But popular control of the government did not mean that all the electorate voted. When the framers of the 1876 Constitution thought of popular control of state government, they thought of control by white males.

Grange a militant farmers' movement of the late nineteenth century that fought for improved conditions for farmers

The example of Davis's reign motivated the revision of executive branch power in the Constitution of 1876. The framers of that constitution sought popular control of state government in order to limit the appointment powers of the governor as provided by the Constitution of 1869.

for critical analysis

Consider the characteristics of the constitutions adopted prior to 1876. What were the major provisions of each? Which were incorporated into the present Texas Constitution? Why does the state constitution place so many limits on state government? What changes could be made to the constitution to increase its effectiveness?

In the effort to limit the powers of state government, the constitution placed great restrictions on the actions of government, restrictions that could be modified only through a complex constitutional amendment process. Executive authority was diffused among numerous officeholders, rather than concentrated in the hands of the governor. Although subsequently changed by constitutional amendment, an initial provision further limited gubernatorial power by setting a two-year term limit for the office. The legislature was part-time, ordinarily sitting for a proscribed time period every other year. This was in contrast to the 1869 Constitution, which provided that the legislature meet in annual sessions.

Economy in government was accomplished in several ways. The constitution restricted the extent of government debt and of government's power to tax. In addition, there were limits on the salaries of state officials, especially those of legislators. A major economic depression had begun in 1873, and many Texans were experiencing economic hardship. One way money was saved was by decentralizing public education. Schools were segregated, and compulsory education laws were eliminated. By having local control over education, white landowners could avoid paying taxes for the education of black students.

Texas at that time was an agricultural state. Wishing to protect agrarian interests, the framers wrote provisions protecting homesteads and restricting institutions that at that time were perceived to be harmful to farmers, such as banks and railroads. Greater responsibility was placed on local instead of state officials. There were also detailed regulations on railroad competition, freight and passenger rates, and railroad construction incentives.

Even in its earliest stages, the Texas Constitution of 1876 was a lengthy, rigid, and detailed document, and purposely so. Regulations curtailing government power were placed not in statutes where they could easily be reversed, but in the body of the constitution. The goal of this design was to ensure that the Radical Republicans and Edmund Davis would never again be able to reign and spend in Texas. They, of course, never did, although over the years the constitution became an increasingly unwieldy document.

● The Constitution of Texas Today

Analyze the major provisions of the Texas Constitution today

The U.S. Constitution has two great virtues: brevity and flexibility. Neither of these virtues can be said to characterize the Texas Constitution. The U.S. Constitution is limited to 7 short articles and 27 amendments, and takes up only 8 pages of the *World Almanac*. Much in the federal document is left unsaid, allowing lawmaking to be accomplished by statute. In contrast, in 2012 the Texas Constitution contained 16 articles (Table 3.1; another article that concerned Spanish and Mexican land titles has been deleted from the constitution) and had been amended 474 times (Table 3.2). Many

---

TABLE 3.1

The Texas Constitution: An Overview

Article I: The Bill of Rights

Article II: Separation of Powers in State Government

Article III: The State Legislature

Article IV: The Plural Executive

Article V: The Judicial Department

Article VI: Suffrage in Texas

Article VII: Public Education in Texas

Article VIII: Taxation and State Revenues

Articles IX and XI: Concerning Local Government, including Counties and Municipal Corporations

Article X: Empowering the State to Regulate Railroads and to Create the Texas Railroad Commission

Article XII: Empowering the State to Create General Laws for Corporations

Article XIII: Concerning Spanish and Mexican Land Titles, Now Deleted from the Constitution

Article XIV: Creates the General Land Office to Deal with Registering Land Titles

Article XV: Impeachment Provisions

Article XVI: General Provisions Covering a Wide Range of Topics

Article XVII: Amendment Procedures

of the articles are lengthy, complex affairs, taking up over 67 pages of text in one edition of the *Texas Almanac*. But it is not just the length that differentiates the two constitutions. There is a difference in tone. The Texas Constitution reflects the writers' fears of what government could do if the principle of **limited government** was not clearly established.

In addition to its severe limits on executive power, the Texas Constitution also addresses a number of specific policy problems directly in the text, turning what might appear to be matters of public policy into issues of constitutional authority. By granting a variety of boards and districts a special place in the constitution, the framers set out additional checks and balances that make it difficult for governors to exercise power effectively. Quite unintentionally, the Texas Constitution became a place where special interests could seek to promote and protect their own agendas, even in the face of considerable political opposition.

The contrasts in character between the federal and Texas constitutions are a direct reflection of the differences in their framers' underlying goals. The U.S. Constitution was written to overcome the liabilities of the Articles of Confederation and create a government that could act effectively in the public welfare in a variety of policy areas. The Texas Constitution was written to prevent the expansion of governmental authority and the return of a system of political power that was perceived as acting against the interests of the people.

The Preamble

The preamble to the Texas Constitution is surprisingly short: "Humbly invoking the blessings of Almighty God, the people of the State of Texas do ordain and establish this Constitution." This brevity is more than made up for in what follows.

Article I: Bill of Rights

Article I of the U.S. Constitution establishes and delegates power to the legislative branch of government. One of the overriding concerns of the Founders was to create a legislature that could act effectively in public affairs. What came to be known as the Bill of Rights—the first 10 amendments to the Constitution—was added after the original Constitution was drafted and approved.

In contrast, the Texas Constitution puts its Bill of Rights up front as Article I, well before any discussion of the legislature, the executive, or the courts. From the beginning, the purpose of the Texas Constitution was not simply to create a set of institutions that could wield political power. It was to limit the way political power is used and to prevent it from being abused.

The Texas Bill of Rights embodies certain ideas captured in the U.S. Bill of Rights. All "free men" are declared to have free and equal rights that cannot be denied or abridged because of sex, race, color, creed, or national origin. Freedom of religious worship is guaranteed, and there will be no religious test for office. Liberty of speech and press are guaranteed. Individuals are protected from unreasonable search and seizure, from excessive bail, from bills of attainder or ex post facto laws, and from double jeopardy. Article I also guarantees an individual a right to trial by jury and the right to bear arms "in the lawful defense of himself or the State; but the Legislature shall have the power, by law, to regulate the wearing of arms, with a view to prevent crime" (Article I, Section 23).

Article I also contains some ideas that move beyond those guaranteed by the first 10 amendments to the U.S. Constitution. The right to **republican government**,

limited government a principle of constitutional government; a government whose powers are defined and limited by a constitution

republican government a representative democracy, a system of government in which power is derived from the people

something clearly stated in the main body of the U.S. Constitution but not in the U.S. Bill of Rights, is powerfully articulated in the first two sections of Article I. According to Article I of the Texas Constitution, all political power is inherent in the people, and the people of Texas have at all times the "inalienable right to alter, reform or abolish their government in such manner as they may think expedient" (Article I, Section 2).

The differences between the Texas Bill of Rights and the U.S. Bill of Rights are not simply matters of where best to articulate a philosophy of republican government. They also involve very concrete matters of public policy. Section 26, for example, forbids monopolies that are contrary to the public interest, and states that the law of primogeniture and entail (a law designed to keep large landed properties together by restricting inheritance to the firstborn) will never be in effect in the state. Although monopolies remain a public concern today, primogeniture and entail do not. Section 11 grapples with the complicated issue of bail and under what specific circumstances an individual can be denied bail. Significantly, Section 11 has been the subject of three major constitutional revisions: in 1955, 1977, and 1993. Section 30, adopted in 1989, provides a long list of the "rights of crime victims," including the right to be treated fairly and with dignity, the right to be protected from the accused, and the right to restitution. Although these are important matters of public policy for Texas today, they could hardly be considered proper material for the U.S. Constitution.

Article II: The Powers of Government

Like the U.S. Constitution, Article II divides the power of government in Texas into three distinct branches: the legislative, the executive, and the judicial (see Figure 3.1). It also stipulates that no one in any one branch shall be attached to either of the other branches, except where explicitly permitted (as in the case of the lieutenant governor's role in the Senate). The article—one short paragraph of text—assures that a version of the **separation of powers** doctrine found in the U.S. Constitution will be embodied in Texas institutions.

separation of powers the division of governmental power among several institutions that must cooperate in decision making

Article III: Legislative Department

Article II is one of the shortest articles in the Texas Constitution. Article III is the longest, comprising almost one-third of the text. Like Article I of the U.S. Constitution, Article III of the Texas Constitution vests legislative power in two houses: a Senate of 31 members and a House of Representatives of no more than 150 members. It stipulates the terms of office and qualifications. House members serve two-year terms, whereas senators serve four-year terms, half being elected every two years. House members must be citizens of the United States, must be at least 21 years of age, and must have resided in the state for two years and in their district for one year. Senators must be citizens of the United States, must be at least 26 years old, and must have resided in the state for five years and in their districts for one year. In addition, Article III provides for the selection of officers in both houses of the legislature, states when and for how long the legislature shall meet (Section 5), and explains how the legislative proceedings will be conducted (Sections 29–41) and how representative districts will be apportioned (Sections 25, 26, and 28).

Like Article I, Texas's Bill of Rights, Article III moves well beyond the U.S. Constitution, putting limits on what the legislature can do. For example, it puts limits on legislators' salaries and makes it difficult to increase those salaries. Article III

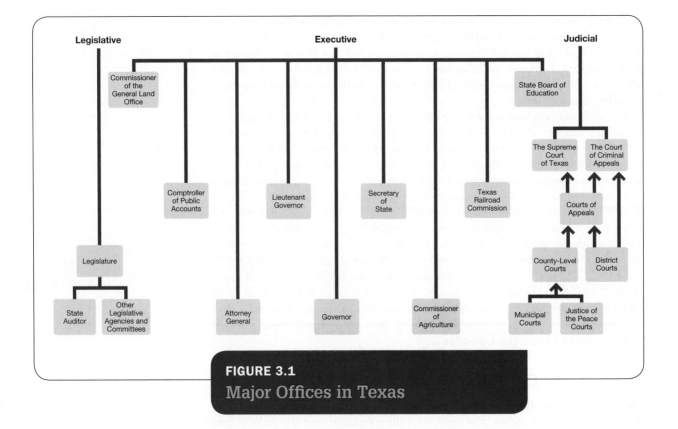

FIGURE 3.1

Major Offices in Texas

also creates a bipartisan Texas Ethics Commission whose job, among other things, is to recommend salary increases for members of the legislature and to set per diem rates for legislators and the lieutenant governor. Article III, Section 49(a), also subjects the legislature to the actions of the comptroller of public accounts, whose duty is to prepare a report prior to the legislative session on the financial condition of the state treasury and to provide estimates of future expenditures by the state. This provision of the Texas Constitution effectively limits the state legislature to the financial calculations and endorsements of the comptroller, a check on the legislature all but unimaginable to the writers of the U.S. Constitution.

Putting constraints on certain legislative actions is only part of the story. The largest portion of Article III (Sections 47–64) is dedicated to addressing a variety of policy problems, including lotteries, emergency service districts, the problem of debt creation, problems surrounding the Veterans' Land Board and the Texas Water Development Board, Texas park development, the creation of a state medical education board, and even the establishment of an economic development fund in support of the now defunct superconducting supercollider.

Article IV: Executive Department

Article II of the U.S. Constitution concentrates executive power in the presidency. The desire was to create a more effective and more responsible executive than had been possible under the Articles of Confederation. In contrast, Article IV of the Texas Constitution states that the executive shall consist of six distinct offices: the governor, who serves as the chief executive; the lieutenant governor, who serves as the president of the Senate; the secretary of state, who keeps the official seals of the state; the comptroller of public accounts; the commissioner of the General Land Office; and the attorney general, who acts as the state's chief legal officer. With the exception of the secretary of state, who is appointed by the governor and approved by the Senate, all other offices are elected by qualified voters every four years. Besides creating a **plural executive**, Article IV guarantees its members will have independent political bases in the electorate. This provides an additional check against any concentration of powers in the hands of any one person.

plural executive an executive branch in which power is fragmented because the election of statewide officeholders is independent of the election of the governor

Article V: Judicial Department

Article III of the U.S. Constitution succinctly provides for a Supreme Court and empowers Congress to create any necessary lower courts. Nothing could be further from the detailed discussion of the state courts found in Article V of the Texas Constitution. Besides creating one supreme court to hear civil cases and one court of criminal appeals to hear criminal cases, Article V provides for such lesser courts as courts of appeal, district courts, commissioner's courts, and justice of the peace courts, and empowers the legislature to establish other courts as deemed necessary. It also goes into such details as the retirement and compensation of judges, the jurisdictions of the various courts, and the duties of judges; it states what to do in the case of court vacancies, and includes a series of discussions on particular issues involving the lower courts.

An even greater difference between the federal Constitution and the Texas Constitution is the crucial role the latter gives to elections. Federal judges are appointed by the executive and approved by the Senate. In Texas, the people elect state judges. Nine supreme court and nine court of criminal appeals judges are elected at large in the state. Lower court positions are elected by voters in their relevant geographic locations. Much like the U.S. Constitution, the Texas Constitution seeks to create an independent judiciary that can check and balance the other two branches of government. But it seeks an additional check as well. It wants the people to watch over the courts.

Article VI: Suffrage

Article VI contains a short but detailed discussion about who may vote in Texas. It also empowers the legislature to enact laws regulating voter registration and the selection of electors for president and vice president.

Article VII: Education

The concerns found in the Texas Declaration of Independence over the need for public schools to promote a republican form of government are directly addressed in Article VII. Section 1 makes it a duty of the state legislature to support and maintain "an efficient system of public free schools." The Texas Supreme Court's interpretation of this provision as applying to school funding in the state has led to the current political battles over school finance. Sections 2–8 provide for their funding and the creation of a State Board of Education to oversee the operations of elementary and secondary education in the state. State universities are the subject of over half of Article VII, where detailed discussions of the funding and operations of particular state institutions are put directly into the text.

Article VIII: Taxation and Revenue

The complex issue of taxation is the subject of Article VIII. Once again we find a highly detailed account of several important policy issues built directly into the text of the constitution. One of the most controversial sections of the Texas Constitution centers on the issue of the income tax. Section 1 enables the legislature to tax the income of individuals and businesses. This power, however, is subject to Section 24, which was passed by the 73rd legislature in 1993. Section 24 requires that the registered voters in the state approve a personal income tax and that the proceeds from this tax be dedicated to education and tax relief. As with other portions of the constitution, the net effect of these provisions is to curtail severely what the state legislature can do and how it is to do it. If Section 24 of Article VIII is any indication, the public fear of unresponsive and potentially tyrannical government was as alive during the 1990s as it was in 1876.

Articles IX and XI: Local Government

These articles provide highly detailed discussions of the creation, organization, and operation of counties and municipal corporations.

Articles X, XII, XIII, and XIV

These heavily revised articles deal with a series of specific topics: the railroads (X), private corporations (XII), Spanish and Mexican land titles (XIII), and public lands (XIV). Article X empowers the state to regulate railroads and to establish the Railroad Commission. Article XII empowers the state to create general laws creating private corporations and protecting the public and individual stockholders. Article XIII, now entirely deleted from the constitution, dealt with the nineteenth-century issue of Spanish and Mexican land titles. Article XIV created a General Land Office to deal with the registration of land titles.

Article XV: Impeachment

impeachment under the Texas Constitution, the formal charge by the House of Representatives that leads to trial in the Senate and possible removal of a state official

Impeachment is, in the U.S. Constitution, one of the major checks Congress holds against both the executive and judicial branches of government. The House of Representatives holds the power to impeach an individual; the Senate is responsible for conducting trials. A two-thirds vote in the Senate following impeachment by the House leads to the removal of an individual from office.

A similar process is provided for in Article XV of the Texas Constitution. The House has the power to impeach. The Senate has the power to try the governor, lieutenant governor, attorney general, land-office commissioner, and comptroller, as well as judges of the supreme court, the courts of appeal, and district courts. Conviction requires a two-thirds vote of the senators present. In contrast to the U.S. Constitution, the Texas Constitution rules that all officers against whom articles of impeachment are proffered are suspended from their office. The governor is empowered to appoint a person to fill the vacancy until the decision on impeachment is reached.

Despite these similarities to the impeachment procedures in the U.S. Constitution, the Texas Constitution has its own caveats. Most notably, the Texas Constitution does not explicitly define impeachable offenses in terms of "Treason, Bribery, or other high Crimes and Misdemeanors," as the U.S. Constitution does. The House and Senate (and the courts) decide what constitutes an impeachable offense.[16] In addition, the supreme court has original jurisdiction to hear and determine whether district court judges are competent to discharge their judicial duties. The governor may also remove judges of the supreme court, courts of appeal, and district courts when requested by the two-thirds vote of each legislature. Significantly, the reasons for removing a judge in this case need not rise to the level of an impeachable offense, but need only involve a "willful neglect of duty, incompetence, habitual drunkenness, oppression in office, or other reasonable cause" (Article XV, Section 8). The barriers to removing a judge by political means are thus, at least on paper, much lower in Texas than in national government.

In 1980, Section 9 was added to Article XV, providing a new way to remove officials appointed by the governor. With the advice and consent of two-thirds of the members of the senate present, a governor may remove an appointed public official. If the legislature is not in session, the governor is empowered to call a special two-day session to consider the proposed removal.

Article XVI: General Provisions

Article XVI is one of the lengthiest in the Texas Constitution and has no parallel in the U.S. Constitution. It is literally a catchall article tackling a variety of issues ranging from official oaths of office to community property to banking corporations and stock laws to the election of the Texas Railroad Commission to the state retirement systems. Here, perhaps more than anywhere else, we see the complexity and confusion of the philosophy reflected in Texas's Constitution.

Article XVII: Amending the Constitution

Like the U.S. Constitution, the Texas Constitution explicitly delineates how it can be amended. Essentially, amendments undergo a four-stage process: First, the legislature must meet in either regular or special session and propose amendments. Second, these amendments must be approved by a two-thirds vote of all the members elected to each house. Third, a brief statement explaining the amendments must be published twice in each recognized newspaper in the state that meets the publication requirements for official state notices. Finally, the amendments must be approved by a majority of the state voters.

● Recent Attempts to Rewrite the Texas Constitution

Describe modern efforts to change the Texas Constitution

Given the difficulty of amending the state constitution, a surprising number of amendments have been proposed since 1876. A considerable number of these have been turned down in the popular vote. As Table 3.2 shows, demands for amending the Constitution have intensified in recent years, as legislators have dealt with the problem of making changes in public policy while being constrained by an unwieldy constitutional document.

Sharpstown and the Failed Constitutional Reforms of 1974

A drive to rewrite the Texas Constitution grew out of a major stock fraud that broke in the early 1970s, involving the Sharpstown State Bank and the National

TABLE 3.2

Amending the Texas Constitution

(The Constitution of Texas has been amended 474 times since its inception in 1876)

YEARS	NUMBER PROPOSED	NUMBER ADOPTED
1876–1900	31	17
1901–20	56	21
1921–40	71	47
1941–60	78	59
1961–80	151	98
1981–2000	180	148
2001–10	79	77
2011	10	7
Totals	656	474

SOURCE: Texas Legislative Council and Texas Secretary of State.

Bankers Life Insurance Corporation. Following the 1970 elections, which had been dominated, as generally was the case, by the conservative wing of the Democratic Party, a suit was filed in Dallas federal court. Attorneys for the Securities and Exchange Commission alleged that a number of influential Democrats, including Governor Preston Smith, the state Democratic chairman and state banking board member Elmer Baum, Speaker of the House Gus Mutscher, and others, had been bribed. By the fall of 1971, Mutscher and two of his associates had been indicted. On March 15, 1972, they were convicted and sentenced to five years' probation.

The convictions fueled a firestorm in the state to "throw the rascals out." During the 1972 elections, "reform" candidates dominated the Democratic primary and the general election. The conservative rancher-banker Dolph Briscoe became governor, but only by a plurality, making him the first governor in the history of the state not to receive a majority of the popular vote. Other reform-minded candidates such as William P. Hobby Jr. and John Hill were successful. Hobby won the lieutenant governor's race, while Hill became attorney general, defeating the three-term Democratic incumbent Crawford C. Martin. When the smoke cleared, half of the House seats were occupied by new members, and the Senate had witnessed a higher-than-normal rate of turnover. The elections had one other outcome: an amendment was passed empowering the legislature to sit as a constitutional convention whose task would be to rewrite the Constitution.[17]

The constitutional convention met on January 8, 1974, in Austin. The idea was for the convention to draft a new constitution that would then be presented to state voters for ratification. Originally scheduled to last 90 days, the convention was extended to 150 days. Even so, it did not have enough time. Bitter politics, coupled with the intense demands of highly mobilized special interests, made it impossible to reach the necessary agreement. In the end, proponents of a new constitution failed to achieve a two-thirds majority by three votes (118 to 62, with 1 abstention).

Why Is the Texas Constitution So Long?

State Constitution Length (estimated)

- < 19,999 words
- 20,000–39,999 words
- 40,000–59,999 words
- 60,000–79,999 words
- > 79,999 words

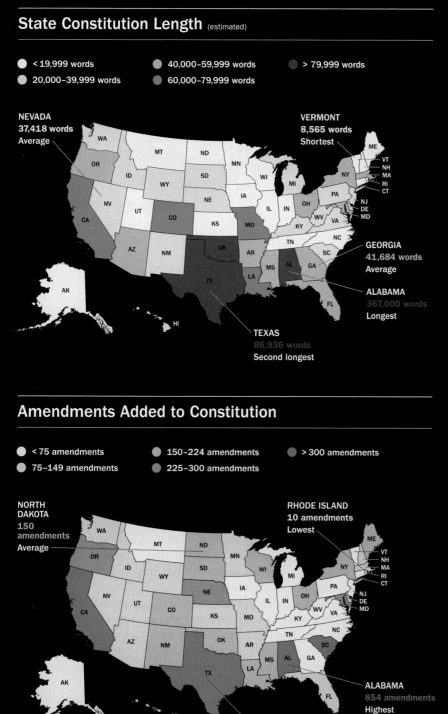

NEVADA
37,418 words
Average

VERMONT
8,565 words
Shortest

GEORGIA
41,684 words
Average

ALABAMA
367,000 words
Longest

TEXAS
86,936 words
Second longest

The Texas Constitution is the second longest state constitution in the United States. The framers of the Texas Constitution gave the state government very specific powers so that the government could not use ambiguity to expand its powers. As a result, the Texas Constitution requires frequent amendments to address situations not covered specifically in the original constitution. The Texas Constitution has been amended 467 times as of 2010, fourth most of any state.

Amendments Added to Constitution

- < 75 amendments
- 75–149 amendments
- 150–224 amendments
- 225–300 amendments
- > 300 amendments

NORTH DAKOTA
150 amendments
Average

RHODE ISLAND
10 amendments
Lowest

ALABAMA
854 amendments
Highest

TEXAS
467 amendments
Fourth highest

for critical analysis

1. How would such a long and detailed state constitution achieve the framers' goal of limiting the scope and power of government in Texas?

2. The U.S. Constitution is a much shorter document than the Texas Constitution and has only 27 amendments. Why would a shorter constitution lead to fewer amendments?

—By BOB TAYLOR, Times Herald Staff Cartoonist

"This baby has a wart...off with his head!"

The Sharpstown State Bank scandal led to a demand for a new constitution to replace the outmoded 1876 document. This cartoon, which shows Governor Dolph Briscoe regally proclaiming, "This baby has a wart . . . off with his head!" satirizes Briscoe's stance against the new constitution.

forcriticalanalysis

What was the rationale for attempting to rewrite the constitution in 1974 and 1999? What changes were proposed? Why did these attempts fail?

The movement to rewrite the constitution did not die at the convention. During the next session of the legislature, eight constitutional amendments were passed that effectively would have rewritten the constitution through the normal amendment process. Each proposal, however, was turned down by the electorate in a special election on November 4, 1975. The Constitution of 1876 remained alive, if not well.

The 1999 Ratliff-Junell Proposal

For the first time since the unsuccessful effort to revise the constitution in the mid-1970s, state senator Bill Ratliff and state representative Rob Junell, both powerhouses in the state legislature, proposed a new constitution for Texas in 1999. Ratliff argued, "It's time for Texas to have a constitution that's appropriate for the twenty-first century." They were concerned that the 1876 Constitution was too restrictive and cumbersome for modern government. It is lengthy, cluttered, and disorganized. The document had become so chaotic that in both 1999 and 2001, amendments were approved "to eliminate duplicative, executed, obsolete, archaic, and ineffective provisions" in the constitution.

Among the major Ratliff-Junell proposals was that the governor would be given the authority to appoint several state officeholders who are now elected. Additionally, the executive branch would be reorganized so that the governor would have an appointed cabinet of department heads, subject to senate confirmation, much as the U.S. president does. With that proposal, only the lieutenant governor, the attorney general, and the state comptroller would be elected.

The governor would also be given the power to appoint all appellate and district judges. Afterward, the judges would be subject to voter approval in retention elections—where they have no opponent on the ballot but where voters are asked if they wish to retain the appointed judge in office for a specified time period. Ratliff argued that the changes would make the governor more accountable for how state government works.

The legislature would remain part-time and would continue to meet in regular session every other year. It would also convene in a special 15-day "veto session," in order to consider overriding any gubernatorial vetoes from previous sessions. State senators now serve four-year terms and state representatives two-year terms. Under the proposed constitution, these terms would be increased to six years for state senators and four years for state representatives. For the first time, there would also be term limits so that representatives' service would be limited to eight regular sessions in the House or 16 years in office, and senators' service could not exceed nine regular sessions in the Senate or 18 years in office.

Although county government would remain as it is today, local voters would be given the authority to abolish their own county's obsolete offices without state-wide approval through constitutional amendments.

Even as it was proposed, its sponsors realized that the revamped constitution would be tough to pass. And they were right—it did not pass, but suffered the fate of earlier efforts to change the 1876 Constitution.

Recent Amendments

In the 2011 constitutional amendment elections, voters were asked to consider 10 proposed amendments. Seven of the amendments passed, although only approximately 5.2 percent of registered voters bothered to vote. One thing that is clear about elections that deal with constitutional amendments is that voting participation is invariably low. Table 3.3 compares the percentage turnout of registered voters in November special elections on constitutional amendments with the percentage turnout in presidential elections (which tend to produce the highest turnout). There are two likely reasons for the low voter turnout in constitutional amendment elections: (1) Constitutional amendment elections are held in "off" years when there are no elections with candidates on the ballot. Because of this, the political parties take a less active role in getting out the vote, and there are no candidates to generate voter turnout. As a result, advertising campaigns to get out the vote are frequently limited only to the activities of interest groups that support or oppose the issues on the ballot. (2) Many of the amendments are relatively insignificant to most voters.

Most of the 2011 proposed constitutional amendments listed in Table 3.4 were uncontroversial. The controversial ones were those that the Tea Party and other antitax groups saw as increasing the financial burden upon Texans. For example, Proposition 4 was defeated because it would have expanded the ability of counties to issue bonds to finance the development of unproductive areas where those bonds were to be repaid with property tax revenues. Critics of the proposal argued that it would clear the way for new toll roads. Proposition 7 was defeated because it would have given El Paso new borrowing authority. Proposition 8 passed the legislature with bipartisan support. It would have given property owners the opportunity to opt out of agricultural or wildlife conservation property tax exemptions in favor of water conservation property tax exemptions. The Tea Party successfully opposed the proposition on the grounds that it would shift the tax burden to others.[18]

In 2005 social conservatives urged Texans to vote in favor of Proposition 2, which defined marriage in Texas as the union of one man and one woman. This appeal to traditional values contributed to relatively high turnout, and Proposition 2 passed by more than a 3-to-1 margin.

TABLE 3.3

Voter Turnout in Texas Constitutional Amendment Elections Compared with Texas Turnout for Presidential Elections

ELECTION	% TURNOUT OF REGISTERED VOTERS
2011 constitutional amendment	5.2
2009 constitutional amendment	8.2
2008 presidential	59.5
2007 constitutional amendment (November)	8.4
2007 constitutional amendment (May)	7.1
2005 constitutional amendment	17.97
2004 presidential	56.6
2003 constitutional amendment	12.2
2001 constitutional amendment	6.9
2000 presidential	51.8
1999 constitutional amendment	8.38
1997 constitutional amendment (August)	6.94
1997 constitutional amendment (November)	10.6
1996 presidential	52.24
1995 constitutional amendment	7.86
1993 constitutional amendment	12.59
1992 presidential	72.92
1991 constitutional amendment	26.25

SOURCE: Texas Secretary of State.

While the Tea Party and other antitax groups could not defeat all of the propositions they opposed, low voter turnout enabled them to exert a significant influence. Indeed, their defeat of three proposals broke the modern pattern in which amendments are routinely approved. For example, between 2001 and 2010, 77 of 79 proposed amendments were approved.

Highly visible, controversial propositions can lead to higher turnout. For example, in 2003, voter participation rose to 12.2 percent, well over twice the turnout in 2011. That was because in 2003, Proposition 12 authorized the legislature to limit noneconomic damages assessed against a provider of medical or health care. After January 1, 2005, the legislature could place limits on awards in other types of cases as well. A major change in the state's tort law, Proposition 12 prompted a voter turnout in the 2003 constitutional amendment election that was the highest for such an election since 1993.[19]

Approved with only about 51 percent support of the voters, Proposition 12 inspired the costliest battle ever waged in Texas over a proposed state constitutional amendment. Donations to support the amendment came largely from doc-

TABLE 3.4

Passed Constitutional Amendments, November 8, 2011

Proposition 1 (S.J.R. 14).The constitutional amendment authorizing the legislature to provide for an exemption from ad valorem taxation of all or part of the market value of the residence homestead of the surviving spouse of a 100 percent or totally disabled veteran.

Proposition 2 (S.J.R. 4). The constitutional amendment providing for the issuance of additional general obligation bonds by the Texas Water Development Board in an amount not to exceed $6 billion at any time outstanding.

Proposition 3 (S.J.R. 50). The constitutional amendment providing for the issuance of general obligation bonds of the State of Texas to finance educational loans to students.

Proposition 5 (S.J.R. 26). The constitutional amendment authorizing the legislature to allow cities or counties to enter into interlocal contracts with other cities or counties without the imposition of a tax or the provision of a sinking fund.

Proposition 6 (H.J.R. 109). The constitutional amendment clarifying references to the permanent school fund, allowing the General Land Office to distribute revenue from permanent school fund land or other properties to the available school fund to provide additional funding for public education and providing for an increase in the market value of the permanent school fund for the purpose of allowing increased distributions from the available school fund.

Proposition 9 (S.J.R. 9). The constitutional amendment authorizing the governor to grant a pardon to a person who successfully completes a term of deferred adjudication community supervision.

Proposition 10 (S.J.R. 37). The constitutional amendment to change the length of the unexpired term that causes the automatic resignation of certain elected county or district officeholders if they become candidates for another office.

SOURCE: Texas Legislative Council.

tors, hospitals, medical groups, insurance companies, and businesses. Amendment supporters spent $7.8 million in the campaign to get the amendment approved. Opponents of the amendment spent $9.3 million, with most of the money coming from lawyers and law firms.[20] Much of the campaign focused on the caps of noneconomic damages for medical malpractice awards. Supporters argued that huge medical malpractice awards were driving doctors from medical practice and reducing the availability of medical care for Texans. Opponents, on the other hand, claimed that the proposal reduced access to the courts for Texans and provided no control over the underlying problem of medical malpractice. And although the immediate consequence of the battle was a reduction in the amount of noneconomic damages that could be awarded in medical malpractice cases, the language of the amendment allows for reduction of damage awards in other types of cases in the future. It was a close vote, but a victory for the new Republican-controlled Texas government, which was sympathetic to tort reform efforts. At the same time, it was a defeat for Democrats who had been unsympathetic toward tort reform, and it was a real blow for trial lawyers—once a mighty interest group in Texas politics but now left with only a fraction of their former political influence.[21]

Most of the 2005 proposed constitutional amendments were, like the previously discussed propositions, of significance only to a narrow group of people.

Proposition 2 and Same-Sex Marriage

In November 2005, Texans went to the polls to vote on Proposition 2 to amend the Texas Constitution, a measure aimed at prohibiting same-sex marriages in the state. While the state legislature was not likely to pass a law allowing same-sex marriages at that time, supporters of Proposition 2 wanted the ban on such marriages enshrined in the state constitution in order to prevent any future legislative attempts. The measure passed with nearly 76 percent of Texans voting in support of the proposition.

However, Proposition 2's language was criticized during the campaign because of its ambiguity. The exact wording of the amendment was as follows:

> (a) Marriage in this state shall consist only of the union of one man and one woman. (b) This state or a political subdivision of this state may not create or recognize any legal status identical or similar to marriage.

Opponents argued that section b of the amendment would, if interpreted literally, actually ban traditional marriage, as marriage is "identical to marriage."

In 2009, a same-sex couple living in Texas who were married in 2006 in Massachusetts, where such marriages are legal, filed for divorce in Texas. Their filing for divorce was problematic, as their marriage had not been recognized in Texas because of Proposition 2. The couple sued the state, claiming that Proposition 2 violated the full faith and credit clause of the U.S. Constitution, which stipulates that licenses issued by one state must be recognized in other states. They also claimed that it violated the equal protection clause, which gives all citizens the right to equal protection under the law. A federal district court judge in Dallas agreed with the plaintiffs, although the State of Texas appealed the ruling, argu-

ing that the equal protection clause was not violated as a result of Proposition 2. In 2010, the Fifth Circuit Court of Appeals overruled the district court, claiming that Texas had the right to pass Proposition 2 and that the equal protection clause was not violated. Texas remains one of many states where same-sex marriages are not recognized.

This case illustrates the trade-offs between minority rights and majority rule in a democracy. The majority of Texans had approved Proposition 2, denying

marriage rights to same-sex couples. In democracies, majorities rule, but minorities retain certain rights under the Constitution. The equal protection clause was written in order to ensure that no class of citizens would be treated differently or in a second-class manner. The U.S. Supreme Court has developed suspect classifications such as race and ethnicity so that when laws single out a group of people, they must have a rational basis and advance a legitimate governmental interest. Does Proposition 2 have a rational basis and advance a legitimate governmental interest?

Proponents argue that Proposition 2 does have a rational basis—the defense of the one flesh union between one man and one woman, a complementarity that cannot exist between two men or two women. They also believe that society is better off when marriages between one man and one woman unite to create families with children. Families, they argue, are the cornerstone of civilization and must be protected against the spread of alternative lifestyles.

Opponents argue that gay men and lesbians wishing to enter into marriage arrangements should be allowed to do so. They argue that they should be entitled to the same tax benefits, visitation rights, and societal respect for their mutual commitment. Society, they say, should encourage monogamy and the establishment and continuance of life-long commitments. They claim that such laws as Proposition 2 are not rational and only reflect anti-gay sentiment.

critical thinking questions

1. Is Proposition 2 a violation of the equal protection clause?
2. How do we balance the rights of minority groups, such as gays and lesbians, with the will of the majority?

Amendments to the state constitution affect many areas of Texans' lives. The amendments passed in 2011 included one intended to help address drought in Texas by making additional funds available to local governments for water projects.

For example, one of the nine proposed amendments provided for clearing land titles in Upshur and Smith Counties. Another authorized the legislature to provide for a six-year term for a board member of a regional mobility authority. Yet the turnout in this election was much higher than is typically seen in constitutional amendment elections. The reason was Proposition 2, which defined marriage in Texas as the union of one man and one woman. The proposition also prohibited the state or any political subdivision of the state from creating or recognizing any legal status identical to or similar to marriage. The proposition generated a strongly favorable vote—1,723,782 in favor versus 536,913 against. Unlike Proposition 12 in 2003, this was not an economic battle involving interests concerned with tort law; rather, this was an issue pitting social conservatives against those more sympathetic to gay rights. The strength of the social conservative vote in the state was, of course, remarkable, since the amendment carried by more than a 3-to-1 margin. Many churches and religious organizations strongly supported the proposed amendment. Their activities probably generated the relatively high voter turnout. The proposition was unusual in that people felt it was important to their lives because it affected their value systems. Although it is doubtful the amendment was necessary to support the traditional concept of marriage and although the ambiguity of the provision rejecting any legal status similar to marriage is disturbing, a significant part of the voting population apparently believed that it was important to vote their moral values, even if the proposal was largely symbolic.

Although most constitutional amendments are not of great importance, there are some notable exceptions. Table 3.5 identifies some of those amendments that, like Proposition 12 in 2003 or Proposition 2 in 2005, have had great significance in the public policy of the state.

TABLE 3.5

Some Important Constitutional Amendments

In 1894, Texans strongly supported an amendment providing for the election of railroad commissioners. In later years, when Texas became a major oil producer, the railroad commission gained the authority to regulate oil production and became the most powerful elected regulatory agency in the country.

In 1902, Texans by a huge majority backed an amendment "requiring all persons subject to a poll tax to have paid a poll tax and to hold a receipt for same before they offer to vote at any election in this state, and fixing the time of payment of said tax." The poll tax required a payment of money prior to voting. The effect was to reduce the size of the electorate, limiting the opportunity of those with lower incomes to vote.

In 1919, the same year the national prohibition amendment was ratified, Texas ratified a state prohibition amendment.

In 1935, Texans repealed statewide prohibition. In its place was a local option whereby local communities chose whether alcohol would be sold in those communities. This was two years after repeal of national prohibition.

In 1954, Texans passed an amendment requiring women to serve on juries. Previous to that, women were exempt on the grounds that they were needed at home as the center of home life.

In 1966, Texans repealed the poll tax as a voting requirement in the face of pressures from the U.S. Supreme Court and from a national constitutional amendment that eliminated the poll tax in national elections.

In 1972, Texans overwhelmingly passed a constitutional amendment "to provide that equality under the law shall not be denied or abridged because of sex, race, color, creed or national origin." This amendment was primarily seen as an equal rights amendment banning sex discrimination, since federal civil rights statutes largely dealt with discrimination on other grounds. It was the state version of a proposed sexual equal rights amendment that was never ratified and made part of the U.S. Constitution.

In 2003, a constitutional amendment promoting the tort reform agenda passed that placed limitations on lawsuits. In "civil lawsuits against doctors and health care providers, and other actions," the legislature was authorized "to determine limitations on non-economic damages."

In 2005 a constitutional amendment was passed "providing that marriage in this state consists only of the union of one man and one woman and prohibiting this state or a political subdivision of this state from creating or recognizing any legal status identical or similar to marriage." The amendment was passed in response to the movement toward the recognition of civil unions and same-sex marriage in some states.

In 2009, Texans supported an amendment establishing "the national research university fund to enable emerging research universities in this state to achieve national prominence as major research universities." The amendment was a recognition that the Texas economy would benefit by the development of nationally recognized research universities in the state.

In 2009, in reaction to a U.S. Supreme Court decision involving eminent domain—the taking of private property for public use—that was seen as unsympathetic to property rights, Texans passed an amendment "to prohibit the taking, damaging, or destroying of private property for public use unless the action is for the ownership, use, and enjoyment of the property by the State, a political subdivision of the State, the public at large, or entities granted the power of eminent domain under law or for the elimination of urban blight on a particular parcel of property, but not for certain economic development or enhancements of tax revenue purpose."

● Thinking Critically about the Texas Constitution

In this chapter, we explored the history of constitutional government in Texas. We analyzed the seven constitutions under which Texas has been governed and explained the similarities and differences between the U.S. Constitution and Texas's current constitution (the Constitution of 1876). We also discussed attempts over the past 30 years to replace this constitution with a new one. The ideas of liberty and equality are enshrined in the Texas Constitution as they are in the U.S. Constitution. In some ways, the Texas Constitution does a better job of protecting liberty and providing for equality than does the U.S. Constitution. Where the Texas Constitution most fundamentally differs from the U.S. Constitution is in its view of democracy. Although championing democratic forms of government, the writers of the Texas Constitution were even more suspicious of centralized institutions of power than were the Founders of the United States. The Texas Constitution places serious constraints on the Texas Legislature's ability to act as an independent body. It creates a weak plural executive, in which executive power is limited and decentralized. Finally, the Texas Constitution subjects the courts to periodic elections. In Texas, the institutions of democracy were never meant to be too far removed from the guiding hand of the people.

A number of additional themes were emphasized in this chapter. First, Texas's current constitution is far more complex than its predecessors or the U.S. Constitution. Matters that are considered public policy in most other states often must be addressed as constitutional issues in Texas. Second, the Texas Constitution is based on a general distrust of politicians and political power. It was originally written to prevent the expansion of political power that had taken place during Reconstruction and to make sure that political power could not be centralized in a way that might hurt the liberties and civil rights of the people. By limiting and decentralizing power, the Texas Constitution makes it hard to implement and successfully administer public policies. Third, the Texas Constitution has been a difficult document to replace. Although amended 474 times, it has not been replaced by a new constitution to date and will probably not be replaced in the future. One reason for this is that mobilizing support for a wholesale reworking of the constitution has proven to be difficult. Another is that the general distrust of government and political power that gave birth to the Constitution of 1876 continues to hold sway among the citizenry.

Many people see some desirable features in the Texas Constitution. Like many state constitutions, the Texas Constitution has a Bill of Rights. Nor are all the rights in the Texas Bill of Rights merely a duplication of those in the U.S. Constitution. To some extent, the Texas Bill of Rights provides more constitutional protections than does the U.S. Constitution. State constitutions may do this under the doctrine of independent state grounds. That is, although a state constitution may provide more rights than the U.S. Constitution, it may not take away rights granted by the U.S. Constitution. One may think of the U.S. Constitution as a baseline to which states can add but not subtract protections. One of the most interesting Texas rights is an amendment adopted in 1972. It states, "Equality under the law shall not be denied or abridged because of sex, race, color, creed, or national origin. This amendment is self-operative." Although the amendment is not the subject of much litigation, note that it provides explicit protection from sex discrimination, something that is not mentioned in the U.S. Constitution. It is, in fact, a state version of the federal Equal

for critical analysis

How does the supremacy clause of the U.S. Constitution affect Texas government?

Rights Amendment, which was almost ratified in the 1970s but which never quite received sufficient support from the states to become a part of the U.S. Constitution.

Still, in spite of its positive aspects, the Texas Constitution is a lengthy, confusing, and highly restrictive document. Yet efforts to drastically change the document seem doomed to failure. There is little public outcry over the large numbers of amendments on which voters regularly must cast ballots. Additionally, the Texas Constitution provides protections for the interests of key groups in Texas society, groups that are reluctant to give up those protections in exchange for a more flexible document.

study guide

(S) **Practice online with:** Chapter 3 Diagnostic Quiz ■ Chapter 3 Key Term Flashcards

The Role of a State Constitution

■ **Identify the main functions of state constitutions (pages 71–72)**

The state constitution is the governing document of the state much in the same way the U.S. Constitution sets up the framework for the nation as a whole. Many of the ideas found in the U.S. Constitution are also found in Texas's constitutions, including republican government, separation of powers, checks and balances, and individual rights.

Key Terms

constitution (p. 71)

federalism (p. 71)

supremacy clause (p. 71)

necessary and proper clause (p. 72)

Practice Quiz

1. Which idea is contained in both the U.S. and Texas constitutions? *(p. 71)*
   a) separation of powers
   b) Keynesianism
   c) laissez-faire economics
   d) *Rebus sic stantibus*
   e) none of the above

2. Which of the following is *not* an important function of a state constitution? *(p. 71)*
   a) prevents the concentration of political power
   b) delegates power to individuals and institutions
   c) allows government to intrude in the lives of businesses and individuals
   d) legitimizes political institutions
   e) limits application of U.S. Constitution

3. Which part of the U.S. Constitution reserves power to the states? *(p. 71)*
   a) Article I
   b) Article VI
   c) First Amendment
   d) Tenth Amendment
   e) Nineteenth Amendment

4. Under the U.S. Constitution, the government of Texas is most limited by *(p. 72)*
   a) Article IV of the U.S. Constitution.
   b) the implied powers clause and the Tenth Amendment of the U.S. Constitution.
   c) the Fourteenth Amendment of the U.S. Constitution.
   d) All matter equally.
   e) None matter.

 Practice Online
Video exercise: *Governor Mark White on the Separation of Powers*

The First Texas Constitutions

■ **Describe the five Texas constitutions that preceded the current constitution (pages 72–81)**

Texas has had six constitutions reflecting the concerns of the historical periods in which they were written. The Civil War and Reconstruction played a major role in shaping Texans' attitudes toward the dangers of strong state government.

Key Terms

unicameral (p. 74)

bicameral (p. 76)

Confederacy (p. 79)

Radical Republicans (p. 80)

Practice Quiz

5. The Constitution of 1861 *(p. 79)*
   a) generally accepted the existing constitutional framework.
   b) guided Texas's entry into the Confederate States of America.
   c) supported slavery.
   d) defended states' rights.
   e) all of the above

6. A unique feature of the Constitution of 1869 was that *(p. 80)*
   a) explicitly rejected the power of the federal government in Texas.
   b) fewer than 1 percent of voters opposed it.
   c) it was less than four pages long.
   d) it was never submitted to the voters.
   e) it is considered the best of Texas's constitutions.

The Constitution of 1876

 Explain the circumstances that led to the Texas Constitution that is still in use today (pages 81–83)

The Constitution of 1876 sought to limit the powers that had been wielded under the previous constitution by Republican governor Edmund Davis. It remains, though much amended, the existing state constitution of Texas.

Key Term

Grange (p. 81)

Practice Quiz

7. A new Texas Constitution was written *(pp. 80–83)*
   a) when Reconstruction ended.
   b) when the Compromise of 1850 was adopted.
   c) at the start of World War I.
   d) in 1999.
   e) none of the above

8. The present Texas Constitution *(pp. 81–82)*
   a) is well organized and well written.
   b) is considered to be one of the best of the 50 state constitutions.
   c) delegates a great deal of power to the governor.

   d) severely limits the power of the governor and other state officials.
   e) all of the above

9. The Constitution of 1876 was a reaction to the Reconstruction Constitution of 1869 because *(pp. 81–83)*
   a) the 1869 Constitution was too short.
   b) the 1869 Constitution forbade slavery.
   c) the 1869 Constitution increased state officials' salaries.
   d) the 1869 Constitution was seen as giving the governor too much power.
   e) none of the above

10. Those who wrote the Constitution of 1876 wanted to return control of government to the people. By "the people" they meant *(p. 81)*
    a) all adult citizens of Texas.
    b) all adult male citizens of Texas.
    c) all adult white male citizens of Texas.
    d) all citizens except carpetbaggers and scalawags.
    e) none of the above

 Practice Online
"Exploring Texas Politics" exercise: *The Texas Constitution*

The Constitution of Texas Today

Analyze the major provisions of the Texas Constitution today (pages 83–89)

Today's Texas constitution is lengthy and includes over 400 amendments. It limits the power of state government and tries to prevent the concentration of power in the hands of one person.

Key Terms

limited government (p. 84)

republican government (p. 84)

separation of powers (p. 85)

plural executive (p. 87)

impeachment (p. 88)

Practice Quiz

11. Article I of the Texas Constitution *(p. 84)*
    a) contains the Texas Bill of Rights.
    b) renounces the use of the death penalty.
    c) rejects the U.S. Constitution's Bill of Rights.
    d) recognizes the supremacy of the national government.
    e) accepts the principle of rapprochement.

12. The Texas Bill of Rights *(pp. 84–85)*
    a) guarantees some rights not found in the U.S. Bill of Rights.
    b) duplicates the U.S. Bill of Rights.
    c) is unusual, since state constitutions generally do not have Bills of Rights.
    d) guarantees gay marriage.
    e) outlaws abortion

13. The Texas Constitution requires that Texas judges *(p. 87)*
    a) be appointed by the governor.
    b) be a member of the Republican Party.
    c) be senior lawyers.
    d) be elected by the people.
    e) cannot receive campaign contributions.

Practice Online
"Who Are Texans?" interactive exercise: *Why Is the Texas Constitution So Long?*

Recent Attempts to Rewrite the Texas Constitution

 Describe modern efforts to change the Texas Constitution (pages 89–98)

Recent attempts to rewrite the Texas constitution have been unsuccessful. Amendments continue to be the easiest way to modify the document.

Practice Quiz

14. A new constitution for Texas *(pp. 89–98)*
    a) is unlikely to be ratified before 2015.
    b) is scheduled for a vote in 2014.
    c) has a 50–50 chance of being ratified.
    d) has a very small chance of being written and ratified.
    e) none of the above

15. Voter turnout for constitutional amendment elections could be improved if *(p. 93)*
    a) they were held at the same time as presidential elections.
    b) there were more voter awareness of the proposed amendments.
    c) the amendments involved significant issues for voters.
    d) all of the above
    e) none of the above

Recommended Websites

Handbook of the State of Texas
www.tshaonline.org/handbook/online/

Texas Constitution
www.constitution.legis.state.tx.us/

Texas Constitutions 1824–76
http://tarlton.law.utexas.edu/constitutions/

In 2012 the Democratic Party of Texas held their state convention in Houston. Democrats dominated Texas politics for nearly a century, but today the Republican Party is dominant. Why did this shift occur, and how do party politics affect Texans?

Political Parties in Texas

WHAT GOVERNMENT DOES AND WHY IT MATTERS In 2011, state representative J. M. Lozano of Kingsville declared that he would switch from the Democratic Party to the Republican Party. Lozano became the second Latino in the 150-member state legislature to switch to the majority party that year. Why was this switch important, and what does it tell us about the significance of political parties in Texas?

Thanks to Lozano's switch and those of two other former Democrats following the 2010 elections, Republicans for the first time exceeded 100 members in the Texas House of Representatives. This was important because it meant that Republicans now had a "supermajority" enabling them to pass legislation with little interference from the minority party.

Lozano's switch also serves as a window into two parallel developments in Texas politics: the rise of the Republican Party and the growing importance of Latinos in the state. In this chapter we will explore how Lozano's switch was emblematic of a larger shift among Texans from the Democratic Party to the Republican Party in recent decades. Not long ago, Democrats were the majority party in Texas and held virtually all important statewide posts and won most elections. However, Republicans have gradually come to dominate state politics.

We will also see that while most Latinos still identify with the Democratic Party, some Latino elected officials and a substantial minority of the Latino population identify as Republican. Several Latinos have won statewide office in recent years, including Victor Carrillo to the Railroad Commission and Dan Morales as attorney general. In contrast with African Americans, who have remained solidly Democratic as a group, Latinos are more willing to cross party lines and vote for Republicans. For example, Latino votes were a factor in Republican George W. Bush's victory in the governor's races of 1994 and 1998. Bush received nearly 40 percent of the Latino vote in 1998, and his success signaled the possibility that Latinos might be gradually shifting to the Republican Party. Although a large-scale shift of Latinos toward the Republicans has not yet come to pass, and some observers doubt that it is likely, the underlying reality remains that Republicans cannot ignore a group that makes up nearly 40 percent of the state's population if they expect to continue winning elections in twenty-first-century Texas.

Lozano's story also highlights the important role parties play in democracy. Voters rely on parties as brand labels or cues to determine where a candidate stands on the important issues of the day. This has not always been the case, however. In Texas, as we will explore in this chapter, conservatives and liberals alike belonged to the Democratic Party for most of the post–Civil War period until the mid-1990s. Competition between candidates took place in the Democratic primary, which was in essence the real election. Because there were so many more Democrats than Republicans in Texas, the winner of the Democratic primary could be confident of getting more votes than the Republican opponent in the general election. A major problem with this system, however, was the exclusion of African Americans and Latinos from the Democratic primary through barriers such as the poll tax and white primary, which the U.S. Supreme Court declared unconstitutional in 1966 (for Texas state elections) and 1944, respectively.

It is important to understand political parties and their structure because knowledge of the rules in government is essential to advancing public policy. Because parties play such a large role in government processes, we must know how parties are organized, how candidates are selected, and how partisanship influences public policy. This chapter will address the history of political parties in Texas, the current party system, and what the future holds for the party system in the state.

chaptergoals

- Describe the main functions of state party organizations (pages 107–17)

- Trace the evolution of the party system in Texas (pages 117–23)

- Analyze how ideological divisions and demographic change affect Texas political parties (pages 124–28)

The Role of Political Parties in Texas Politics

Describe the main functions of state party organizations

Political parties help candidates win elections and assist voters in making their electoral choices. Perhaps the most important function of parties in Texas is that they provide a label under which candidates can run and with which voters can identify. Because Texas elects large numbers of officeholders, it is unlikely that voters will be familiar with the views or the qualifications of every candidate. However, Texas voters overwhelmingly identify with or lean toward either the Republican Party or the Democratic Party.[1] Those voters use the party affiliation of the candidates as a way to decide for whom to vote. Thus, for many voters, without other information, the party label becomes the standard they apply in casting a ballot for a candidate. Voters often use the party label as a cue to the ideology of candidates. A voter may assume that, for example, a Republican candidate is a "conservative" and may vote for or against that candidate because of the ideology that a party affiliation implies.[2]

Parties to some extent help in raising money for candidates' campaigns and in assisting candidates with legal requirements and training for a campaign. They sometimes recruit candidates for political races, although in Texas any candidate may run in a party primary, and, if victorious in the primary, will become the party nominee. Parties also assist in "getting out the vote" for candidates through phone banks, door-to-door contacts, and other efforts.

Once a candidate is elected to office, party affiliation helps in organizing the government. Governors will usually appoint people who are members of their own party. Increasingly, the Texas Legislature is divided by party. Public officials may also feel a greater sense of loyalty and cooperation toward other public officials of their party. After all, they often campaign together and make appearances at the same

One of the most important functions of political parties is to select candidates to run for office under the party label. The Republican Party of Texas officially announced their candidates for office at their 2012 convention in Fort Worth.

political events, and their fortunes often rise and fall together based on the popularity of the party. In that sense, the banding together of officeholders with the same party affiliation provides voters an opportunity to hold the party accountable for its policies or its failures.

Texas Parties in the National Context

States differ in terms of the strength of the political parties, and parties also tend to have less power at the state level than they do in the national government. For example, in neighboring Louisiana, the parties are relatively weak. In the Louisiana legislature, even though the majority party controls committee assignments, chairs of committees sometimes include a mix of Democrats and Republicans. This has historically also been true in Texas. The current speaker of the Texas House, Joe Straus from San Antonio, is considered a moderate Republican and owes his election to the speakership to many Democrats in the legislature who voted to elect him speaker. In recognition of their support, Straus made some Democrats committee chairs. This would never happen in the U.S. Congress, as parties are much more important in national politics. In Congress, the majority party gives leadership positions like committee chairs only to its own loyal party members.

Why might parties at the state level have less power? Tip O'Neill, the former Speaker of the U.S. House, used to say that "all politics is local," and this certainly rings true in Texas. Local issues are usually not ideological in nature. They often deal with who is most effective at creating jobs and keeping districts safe for residents. Voters in local races are therefore likely to be influenced by these concerns in addition to hot-button issues such as abortion and gay marriage. This means that partisanship has been less important in running the everyday business of the state. To be sure, ideological issues might matter in certain state-level elections during some election years. **Partisan polarization**, which is the degree to which Republicans have become more conservative and Democrats have become more liberal, is beginning to become more pronounced in the Texas Legislature. Partisan polarization in politics means that it is increasingly difficult for politicians to compromise on important policy issues. Compromise is often considered a sign of weakness and caving in to the other side.

Party politics in Texas is similar to party politics in some other southern states, but there are important differences. Other southern states have had historically larger African American populations than Texas. As we will discuss later, African Americans are generally loyal Democrats. They constitute nearly 30 percent of the population in Mississippi and Louisiana, for example. In Texas, African Americans are concentrated in east Texas and in the major urban areas, and represent only 11 or 12 percent of the state's population. Another major difference between Texas and some other southern states is Texas's large Hispanic population, which currently is estimated at 38 percent of the state's population. Like African Americans, Hispanics tend to be Democrats, but not to the same degree.

To a certain extent, Texas is similar to New Mexico, Arizona, and Colorado in terms of its large Hispanic population. In contrast with the Hispanic population in Arizona, however, Tejanos (Texans of Mexican descent) are more likely to have resided in the state

partisan polarization the degree to which Republicans have become more conservative and Democrats have become more liberal

As compared with the U.S. Congress, the Texas Legislature is less partisan. Here, Republican Speaker Joe Straus meets with members of the Texas House Democratic Caucus.

for generations. In Arizona, the Sonora Desert region is the largest gateway for Mexican immigration, and new immigrants in Arizona exhibit political behavior that differs from that of their Tejano counterparts in many ways. For example, new immigrants are even more likely than Tejanos to identify as Democrats and to see the Democratic Party as more supportive of immigrant rights.

Public Attitudes about Parties

Texans, like many Americans, are increasingly identifying as independent. However, in practice many self-identified independents lean toward either Democratic or Republican affiliation. What is the source of these political leanings? The process of **political socialization** occurs throughout our early years, when our parents, religious leaders, teachers, and others influence our partisan identifications. While this can change over time for many people, we often retain the same political beliefs as those of our parents. How does partisan affiliation affect Texas voters? According to a May 2012 *Texas Tribune* poll, 56 percent of respondents cited party affiliation as either very or somewhat important when deciding for whom to vote. Party identification acts as an important cue that signals what candidates stand for. For the most part, when we see an "R" or a "D" next to a candidate's name, we make certain assumptions about the positions the candidate takes. Of course, other candidates characteristics matter too; in the same poll, voters also cited the candidate's record, issue positions, and character as important considerations in their voting choices.[3]

political socialization the introduction of individuals into the political culture; learning the underlying beliefs and values on which the political system is based

In Texas, the Republican Party has complete control of state government, and voters continue to re-elect Republicans to all levels of government. This does not mean that there is no competition within the Republican Party, however. Republican primaries often pit conservatives against moderates. An example of this was the Republican gubernatorial primary between Governor Rick Perry and Senator Kay Bailey Hutchison in 2009. Perry positioned himself to the right of Hutchison, even though she had compiled a conservative voting record in the U.S. Senate since her election in 1994.

At the conservative end of the spectrum, the Tea Party movement is particularly strong in Texas. In the *Texas Tribune* poll, nearly 18 percent of respondents said that they would vote for a Tea Party candidate if the movement organized as a third party. When asked about the Tea Party's influence on the state Republican Party, respondents were split: 29 percent felt that the Tea Party had too much influence, 23 percent thought their degree of influence was about right, and 23 percent thought that they had too little influence. According to this poll, roughly 34 percent of voters in Texas would support a generic Democratic candidate, while 45 percent would support a generic Republican candidate.[4] This leaves a substantial remainder of "swing" voters who ultimately decide elections. Since their control of state government gives Republicans a built-in advantage, it is increasingly difficult for Democrats to win statewide.

The Contemporary Republican Party in Texas

Texas Republicans are currently in what Paul Burka of the *Texas Monthly* considers a "divided moment." Established pro-business Republicans have dominated state politics in recent years, but the nascent Tea Party movement has begun to influence state legislative races as well as major statewide races.

Consider the U.S. Senate race in 2012. The Republican candidate, Lieutenant Governor David Dewhurst, had the endorsement of Governor Rick Perry and many of the state's political leaders. However, former solicitor general Ted Cruz, a darling of the Tea Party movement, posed a significant challenge to Dewhurst especially in terms of grassroots support. In May 2012, Senator Rand Paul (R-Ky.) and Representative Ron Paul (R-Lake Jackson) endorsed Cruz at the Texas capitol, signaling an important divide within the state Republican Party. Former Alaska governor and 2008 vice presidential candidate Sarah Palin and former senator Rick Santorum of Pennsylvania would also later endorse Cruz. Dewhurst responded by running advertisements with former Arkansas governor Mike Huckabee endorsing his campaign.

This left Texas Republicans in a difficult situation. Who was the real conservative in the Senate race? Third-party groups supporting Cruz also ran ads criticizing Dewhurst for being too moderate, a charge that is not particularly helpful in a Republican primary. Dallas mayor Tom Leppert ran political ads criticizing both Cruz and Dewhurst for being "empty suits." He touted his credentials as a business leader who would create jobs, while criticizing Dewhurst for being an insider and state government official with endorsements from the state's political establishment. Dewhurst criticized Cruz for his involvement in representing a company that outsourced jobs to China. Ultimately, Cruz won the primary as well as the general election.

Texas Republicans currently hold all of the major statewide elected offices. The governor, lieutenant governor, comptroller, attorney general, members of the state supreme court, and the railroad commissioners are all Republicans. Texas Democrats have attempted to recruit challengers for these offices, but have come up short. As the Senate race in 2012 demonstrates, the major competition for important statewide offices occurs during the Republican primary, much in the same way the Democratic primary used to fulfill this role when Texas was a Democratic state.

The Republican Party in Texas has not always been so powerful. Prior to 1994, Democrats held many statewide offices in Texas. Ann Richards, the state's last Democratic governor, was a proud liberal, as was former U.S. senator Ralph Yarborough, who championed the Bilingual Education Act in 1968. However, few pundits seriously thought that the Democratic candidates for the U.S. Senate seat in 2012 had a realistic chance of winning the general election in November. This is a remarkable change from only 10 years prior, when Democrat Ron Kirk was seen as a more formidable candidate for statewide office, even though on election day he lost to Senator John Cornyn by double-digits.

The Contemporary Democratic Party in Texas

Texas Democrats have been relegated to minority status in the state since 1994. By that year, the shift of conservative white Democrats in Texas to the Republican Party was complete. To be sure, Democrats controlled the Texas House until 2002, but Republicans held every statewide office. Other southern states, such as Arkansas, still have Democratic legislatures and statewide elected officials; however, these officeholders are more conservative than the national Democratic Party. In West Virginia, for example, Democrats dominate state government, but in presidential elections, the state often votes Republican. Before 1994, Texas exhibited similar voting patterns, but now Republicans are elected to all statewide offices at the state and federal levels.

Most Texas Democrats today would be classified as liberal. The party's base is made up of African Americans, Latinos, and white liberals in urban areas. Most white liberals are located in Austin, Houston, Dallas, and San Antonio, and have often moved to Texas from other parts of the country. This coalition, however, is currently not large enough to win many elections in statewide races. Most whites in the state have settled into the Republican Party, and because whites turn out to vote at much higher rates than Latinos, who are the fastest growing minority group in the state, Republicans have won recent elections. Democrats hope to mobilize Latinos, who constitute nearly 40 percent of the state's population, to encourage them to vote. Sixty-nine percent of Texas Latinos are American citizens by birth, but voter turnout rates among Texas Latinos are lower than their Anglo counterparts. It will require extensive efforts to register and bring Latino voters to the polls in force to change this.

No Democrat has won Texas in a presidential race since Jimmy Carter in 1976. In 2012, Republican presidential candidate Mitt Romney won 57 percent of the vote in Texas, while Barack Obama won just 41 percent. Democrats also fared poorly in the U.S. Senate race to replace retiring senator Kay Bailey Hutchison; Ted Cruz, the Republican nominee, won the office easily.

This does not mean that Texas Democrats do not have influence in certain localities. In Travis County, the home of Austin, Democrats dominate city government. Other major cities, including Houston and San Antonio, have Democratic mayors and city councils. However, this influence does not extend to statewide elections. When Democrat Bill White, the former mayor of Houston, ran for governor in 2010, he lost to Rick Perry.

Most of the nine Democrats representing Texas in the U.S. Congress are either Latino or African American. Lloyd Doggett of Austin and Gene Green of Houston are the only two white Democrats representing Texas in Congress. This suggests that the majority of Texas Democrats are minorities, and with the growth of the minority population in the state, the party makeup will become more minority and less white. This demographic change in Texas makes the state more similar to its southern neighbors. In the Deep South, the Democratic Party is mostly an African American party. This is not true in the Northeast, where more whites identify as Democrats than in the South.

Democratic and Republican Party Organization

Although many Texans proclaim that they are "registered Republicans" or "registered Democrats," Texas does not have a system of party registration. Registered voters may vote in either the Democratic or Republican primary. When they do vote in a primary, their voter registration card will be stamped "Democrat" or "Republican" to prevent them from voting in the other primary as well.

One of the most important functions of political parties is to select candidates to run for office under the party label. Today that is done through primary elections. If several candidates are running for the party nomination in a primary election, it may be that none receives a majority vote. In that case, the party will hold a runoff election to determine who will be nominated. Primaries were not always used to select the party nominee. During the nineteenth century, candidates were nominated at party conventions, but early in the twentieth century the state moved to the primary as a way to select candidates.

To understand how the parties are organized, think first in terms of the permanent organization of the party and then in terms of the temporary (campaign) organization (see Figure 4.1). In each election **precinct**, a **precinct chair** will be elected in the party primary. The precinct chair will head the precinct convention and will also serve on the party's **county executive committee.** In the primary, the **county chair** will also be elected. The county chair will head the county executive committee,

precinct the most basic level of political organization at the local level

precinct chair the local party official, elected in the party's primary election, who heads the precinct convention and serves on the party's county executive committee

county executive committee the party group, made up of a party's county chair and precinct chairs, that is responsible for running a county's primary elections and planning county conventions

county chair the county party official who heads the county executive committee

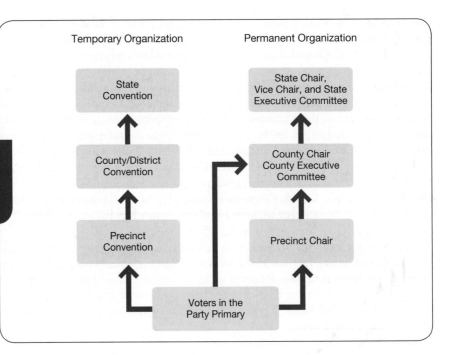

FIGURE 4.1
Party Organization in Texas

Temporary Organization

State Convention

↑

County/District Convention

↑

Precinct Convention

↑

Permanent Organization

State Chair, Vice Chair, and State Executive Committee

↑

County Chair County Executive Committee

↑

Precinct Chair

↑

Voters in the Party Primary

state executive committee
the committee responsible for governing a party's activities throughout the state

state chair and **vice chair** the top two state-level leaders in the party

precinct convention a meeting held by a political party to select delegates for the county convention and to submit resolutions to the party's state platform; precinct conventions are held on the day of the party's primary election and are open to anyone who voted in that election

county convention a meeting held by a political party following its precinct conventions, for the purpose of electing delegates to its state convention

state convention a party meeting held every two years for the purpose of nominating candidates for statewide office, adopting a platform, electing the party's leadership, and in presidential election years selecting delegates for the national convention and choosing presidential electors

which is composed of the chair and the precinct chairs. The main responsibility of the county executive committee is to run the county primary and plan the county conventions. There may be other district committees as well for political divisions that do not correspond to the county lines.

At the state level, there is a **state executive committee,** which includes a **state chair** and **vice chair.** These officers are selected every two years at the state party conventions. The state executive committee accepts filings by candidates for statewide office. It helps raise funds for the party, and it helps establish party policy. Both the Democratic and Republican parties also employ professional staff to run day-to-day operations and to assist with special problems that affect the party.

The temporary organization of the party includes the **precinct conventions.** The main role of the precinct conventions is to select delegates to the **county convention** and possibly to submit resolutions that may eventually become part of the party platform.

Delegates chosen by the precinct convention then go to the county conventions (or in urban areas, to district conventions). These conventions will elect delegates to the **state convention.** Both the Democratic and Republican parties hold state conventions every other year. These conventions certify the nominees of the party for statewide office; adopt a platform; and elect a chair, a vice chair, and a state executive committee. In presidential election years, the state conventions select delegates for the national party conventions; elect delegates for the national party committee; and choose presidential electors, who, if the party's choice for president carries the state in the election, will formally cast the state's electoral votes for the president in the electoral college.

Conflict occurs not only between political parties but also within the parties. Battles for control of a state party have often been fought in Texas politics, where rival ideological and other interest groups have struggled to control precinct, county, and state conventions and to elect their candidates for precinct chair,

Political parties in Texas are organized at the precinct level, the county level, and the state level. This photo shows the Fayette County Republican Headquarters in La Grange.

county chair, and state executive committee. In the 1950s, struggles for control of the Democratic Party between liberals and conservatives were fierce. There have also been calmer times in Texas politics, when involvement in the parties has been minimal and battles have been few. Sometimes, apathy has been so great that precinct conventions have been sparsely attended and offices such as precinct chair have gone unfilled.

Third Parties in Texas

In Texas, as in many other states, the two parties in power have made it difficult for third parties to gain access to the ballot. In essence, both parties agree that a third competitor is not a net positive for either party. Third-party candidates rarely win elections in Texas.

In Texas, third parties have emerged at certain points in history, mainly because of a particular issue. For example, racial integration was the issue in 1948 when the States' Rights Democratic Party, or **Dixiecrats,** rallied behind segregationist Strom Thurmond for president instead of Democratic Party candidate Harry Truman. The Dixiecrat movement, however, did not last very long, mainly because Dwight Eisenhower became an acceptable Republican for many southern Democrats in the 1950s. In 1960 most southern Democrats voted against Democrat John F. Kennedy, despite the presence of Lyndon Johnson on the ticket as Kennedy's running mate, making the election much closer than expected in terms of the popular vote. Segregation continued to be the issue for southern Democrats in the 1968 presidential election when they supported Alabama governor George Wallace, who ran as a third-party candidate, instead of the liberal Democratic candidate, Minnesota senator Hubert Humphrey.

The civil rights movement in the 1960s planted the seeds for an independent Latino movement named **La Raza Unida,** meaning "united race." Jose Angel Gutierrez led the party at its inception, which was concentrated in Zavala County. La Raza Unida developed into a third party in Texas and was able to win races in Crystal City and other small towns in south Texas. The party was able to do this

Dixiecrats conservative Democrats who abandoned the national Democratic Party in the 1948 presidential election

La Raza Unida Party political party formed in Texas in order to bring attention to the concerns of Mexican Americans

Third-Party Ballot Access in Texas

In Texas, as in most other states, nearly all state legislators and members of the executive branch are members of one of the two major political parties: the Democratic Party or the Republican Party. As discussed in this chapter, the state parties hold primary elections in order to determine who their candidates will be for the general election. Are voters limited to choosing between the two major parties? Not necessarily. Third parties can get their candidates on the ballot. For example, Libertarian Party presidential candidate Gary Johnson (pictured here) appeared on the ballot in all 50 states in 2012. However, ballot access is difficult in Texas because of laws passed by the legislature. This results in many general elections between the candidates of the two major political parties only.[a]

Texas requires parties that did not get 5 percent of the vote in a previous statewide race to collect a minimum number of signatures for their petition to get on the ballot. The number must equal at least 1 percent of the total number who voted in the most recent gubernatorial election. Other states have similar requirements for ballot access. However, in Texas, parties that hope to qualify for inclusion on the ballot by petition are also required to notify the state that they intend to do so. This law is unique to Texas.

The intention form is usually due in January of election years.[b] Many third parties point out that this requirement discriminates against parties that are formed in the spring of election years, because by then it is too late to complete the form. The law was passed in 1993 but if Texas had a law like this in 1912, Theodore Roosevelt could not have put his new Progressive Party on the ballot, because even the idea for the party did not occur to Roosevelt until after he failed to get the Republican presidential nomination in June 1912.

The last new party formed in the United States in *an election year* that

proved to have a fairly strong ability to get on ballots was the Natural Law Party. It was formed in April 1992. Of course, the Texas law didn't exist that year. Since the formation of the Natural Law Party in 1992, all the new parties formed in the United States that have had any heft have been formed in the odd years before the election. The January deadline does not seem necessary for purposes of administering elections because a party cannot begin to petition until after the primary anyway. For example, in 2012 a party could not have begun to petition until April. If a new party were formed in the spring that had not existed as of January 2, 2012, it would have been too late to file the intention form necessary to get on the ballot in Texas. The law requiring the intention form is currently being challenged in federal court.

Should Texas make it easier or more difficult for third parties to gain access to the ballot? Proponents of the law argue that adding more uncertainty to the political process by allowing more names on the ballot only muddies the waters, as historical election returns indicate that one of the two major party candidates will most likely win. Adding third parties to ballots might thwart the will of the people by allowing a candi-

date to win without majority support. Some point to the presidential election of 2000, when Vice President Al Gore lost Florida's electoral votes and thus the election because of the presence of Green Party candidate Ralph Nader on the Florida ballot.

Opponents of the law argue that the two major political parties have joined forces to eliminate competition.[c] This leads to strict ballot access laws, requiring stringent deadlines and, in some cases, unrealistic numbers of signatures of registered voters in a given area. Opponents also argue that in a democracy, access to the ballot should be open so that voters have a true say on Election Day. Limiting the ballot to only two parties severely restricts the will of the people.

[a] Ross Ramsey, "Smaller Parties Refuse to Be Counted Out," *New York Times*, April 6, 2012, p. A19.
[b] Texas Secretary of State, www.sos.state.tx.us/elections/forms/181004.pdf (accessed 10/29/12).
[c] The Coalition for Free and Open Elections, http://cofoe.org; Ballot Access News, www.ballot-access.org (accessed 11/28/12).

critical thinking questions

1. Should every party be allowed a spot on the ballot, regardless of their chances of winning votes? Why or why not?

2. What would be the ideal way to regulate ballot access? How should access to the ballot be determined?

Independent candidates face considerable challenges in elections. Although the musician and writer Kinky Friedman's 2006 candidacy for governor attracted major media attention, Friedman received only 12.4 percent of the vote.

by taking advantage of nonpartisan elections in many cities and towns. Even today, many cities, such as Austin, conduct nonpartisan elections. This does not mean that the candidates running for office do not belong to political parties. It just means that their party affiliation is not listed on the ballot. Reformers in many cities pushed for this so that voters would vote on the basis of candidate qualifications rather than by political party. La Raza Unida won many of these races in Zavala County and other surrounding counties, so that at one point, the party was able to take control of some city councils, school boards, and even the top city job of mayor. By 1972, the party nearly cost Democrat Dolph Briscoe the governorship because of the candidacy of Ramsey Muñiz. While this movement ultimately faded away, as most third-party movements do, it marked the growing influence of Latinos in the state.

An enduring third party which has been able to gain access to the Texas ballot box has been the Libertarian Party. Libertarians believe in limited government and can be considered fiscal conservatives and social liberals. U.S. Representative Ron Paul of Lake Jackson, nominally a Republican, ran for president in 1988 as a Libertarian, and his isolationist views on foreign policy, in particular, are quite distinct from those of other Republicans. Libertarians are particularly active in some of the major cities, including Austin. While they do not win very many elections, they can influence politics in other ways. For example, the major parties may adopt some of the positions promoted by Libertarians (or members of other minor parties) in order to win their support in runoff elections.

The most recent case involving a significant threat to the major-party candidates was the 2006 election for governor. Rick Perry was seen as a vulnerable incumbent, especially during a year that was not particularly favorable for Republicans. Democrat Chris Bell, a former Houston member of Congress, won the Democratic nomination, but two major independent candidates also ran for governor. They were former comptroller Carole Keeton Strayhorn from Austin and musician and humorist Kinky Friedman, whose catchy slogan was "Why the hell not?" When all the ballots were counted, Perry was re-elected governor with 39 percent of the vote. While it is not clear that a two-way race between Bell and Perry would have ensured a Bell victory, the candidacies of Strayhorn and Friedman damaged whatever mandate Perry could claim from a victory without a majority.

Why don't people vote for third parties? The United States employs what is known as a "first past the post," **single-member district** electoral system. Under a first past the post system, only the candidate who wins the plurality of votes, that is, the most votes, is elected. According to **Duverger's Law**, this type of voting system tends to favor a two-party system because a vote for a third-party candidate generally does not result in a win. Consider the 2006 governor's race in which Perry won with less than an outright majority. Although Friedman and Strayhorn made a good showing for third-party candidates, they still only received 12.4 percent and 18.1 percent of the vote, respectively. Even if a runoff election had occurred, it would have been between the top two vote getters, Perry and Bell. This is not to say that a vote for a third-party candidate is "wasted," because major-party candidates as well as the parties themselves can often be responsive to voters who might have voted for a third-party candidate. Winning candidates often run in future elections and would like to appeal to constituents who might not have supported them in the past.

In contrast, some other countries use a system of **proportional representation** that encourages third-party voting because even if a party wins only 10 percent of the vote in an election, it will still win 10 percent of the seats in the legislature or other representative body. Voters in these countries are therefore more likely to vote for third and minor parties, because they will almost certainly be able to elect at least one of these candidates.

Many American voters believe that their votes would be wasted if they voted for a third-party candidate. This expectation is rational, as the history of elections shows that a Republican or Democrat will almost always win. Most voters logically decide that it makes more sense to vote for the major party candidate whose ideology is closest to their own.

The Occupy and Tea Party Movements in Texas

The recent **Occupy** and **Tea Party movements** have become prominent nationwide and in Texas. Occupy has held demonstrations in Austin and other major Texas cities, protesting the influence of big banks and Wall Street on American politics. Tea Party advocates, however, have had greater influence in Texas mainly because of their libertarian anti-tax message, which resonates with many Texans. The implications of these anti-tax policies in Texas means less funding for K–12 and higher education and fewer social services, such as children's health care programs.

Tea Party organizers have not yet sought to run a third-party candidate in elections, however. Instead, they have tried to influence Republican primary elections (see Figure 4.2). They believe that they can have more influence in state politics if they become a force to be reckoned with within the Republican Party. Undoubtedly, this is a wise strategy given the history of defeat for third parties, not only in the state but nationwide. Tea Party groups have focused their efforts on key statewide races. They have campaigned against incumbents, such as Speaker Straus of San Antonio, whom they deem to be too moderate. While the Tea Party has had some success in terms of defeating incumbents and nominating

single-member district an electorate that is allowed to elect only one representative for each district

Duverger's Law the observation that in a single-member district system of electing representatives, a two-party system will emerge

proportional representation a multi-member district system that allows each political party representation in proportion to its percentage of the total vote

Occupy movement political movement aimed at limiting the influence of Wall Street and big corporations in American politics. Created following government bailouts in 2008

Tea Party movement created after Barack Obama's election, a political movement that advocates lower government spending, lower taxes, and limited government

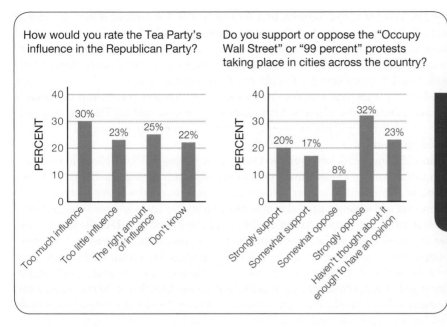

How would you rate the Tea Party's influence in the Republican Party?

Too much influence: 30%
Too little influence: 23%
The right amount of influence: 25%
Don't know: 22%

Do you support or oppose the "Occupy Wall Street" or "99 percent" protests taking place in cities across the country?

Strongly support: 20%
Somewhat support: 17%
Somewhat oppose: 8%
Strongly oppose: 32%
Haven't thought about it enough to have an opinion: 23%

FIGURE 4.2

Tea Party and Occupy Wall Street Support in Texas

SOURCE: Texas Politics Project at the University of Texas at Austin.

preferred candidates, it remains to be seen whether the movement will fade and be co-opted by the Republican Party or continue to be an independent influence. Ted Cruz's victory in the U.S. Senate runoff in July 2012 seemed to suggest that the Tea Party movement has been co-opted by the Republican Party.

● Texas's History as a One-Party State

Trace the evolution of the party system in Texas

In order to understand the present partisan environment in Texas, let us look at the history of partisanship in Texas since the end of the Civil War. With the defeat of the Republican governor Edmund J. Davis in 1873, Texas entered a period of Democratic dominance that would last for over a century. Often the Republican Party would not contest major state offices, and other parties, such as the Populist or People's Party, though having some influence for brief periods, did not have staying power. In general elections, it was a foregone conclusion that the Democratic nominee would win. If there was a meaningful election contest, it was in the Democratic Party primary.

Republicans tended to have a limited role in Texas politics. Most commonly, people remained Republicans in the hope of gaining political patronage (usually local postmaster or rural mail carrier positions) when Republican presidents were in office. Some Republicans were businesspeople unhappy with the liberal policies of Democratic presidents such as Franklin Delano Roosevelt or Harry Truman. However, the Republican Party was not a threat to Democratic dominance in the state. Indeed, Republicans interested in patronage from the national government may have had an incentive to keep the Republican Party small, as the fewer the Republicans, the less the competition for patronage positions. When the father of the late senator Lloyd Bentsen first moved to the Rio Grande Valley, he visited with R. B. Creager, who was then state chairman of the Republican Party. Lloyd Bentsen, Sr., told Creager that he wanted to get involved in the Republican Party because his father had been a devoted Republican in South Dakota. Rather than welcoming Bentsen into the Republican Party, Creager told Bentsen, "You go back to Mission [Texas] and join the Democratic Party, because what's best for Texas is for every state in the union to have a two-party system and for Texas to be a one-party state. When you have a one-party state, your men stay in Congress longer and build up seniority."[5]

In 1952 and 1956, however, the Democratic governor Allan Shivers led a movement often known as the **Shivercrat movement**, which presaged a dramatic change in party alignments a quarter century later. Governor Shivers was a conservative Democrat and widely regarded as one of the most able Texas governors of the twentieth century. He supported the candidacy of the Republican Dwight Eisenhower for the presidency against the Democratic nominee, Adlai Stevenson. Stevenson opposed the Texas position on the Tidelands, offshore lands claimed by both Texas and the national government, which were believed to contain oil. Additionally, Stevenson was much more liberal than Shivers, and Eisenhower was a famous and popular hero of World War II. Governor Shivers not only supported Eisenhower for the presidency, he and all statewide officeholders except the agriculture commissioner, John White, ran on the ballot as Democrats *and* Republicans. It was an act of party disloyalty condemned by loyal Democrats such as Speaker of the U.S. House of Representatives Sam Rayburn, and it led to much tension in the Democratic Party between liberal and conservative Democrats as well as between party loyalists and the Shivercrats.

The Shivercrat movement sent a strong message that many conservative Democrats were philosophically opposed to the national Democratic Party and, although they were unwilling to embrace the Republican Party fully, they found the Republican Party more compatible with their views. A pattern in voting known as **presidential Republicanism** was strengthening, whereby conservative Texas voters would vote Democratic for state offices but vote Republican for presidential candidates. With the Shivercrat movement, those conservatives were more numerous and more closely aligned with the Republican Party. Presidential Republicanism would persist in Texas and other southern states until Republicans began to get elected in state and local races in the 1990s and beyond.

Still, in state elections, the Democratic Party was overwhelmingly the dominant party. There might be pockets of the state where Republicans showed strength. Traditionally, in the post–Civil War era, the "German counties" in the Texas Hill Country, which were settled by German immigrants, showed Republican leanings. Dallas County, whose voters were influenced by a powerful group of conservative businesspeople and a conservative newspaper, the *Dallas News*, showed early Republican strength, electing a very conservative Republican congressman in the 1950s. However, for the most part, the Democratic Party was so dominant in state elections that the Republican Party did not field opponents to the Democratic nominees.

During this era, the Democratic Party was an umbrella party that held a variety of groups and interests. Liberals and conservatives belonged to the party, as did members of labor unions, businesspeople, farmers, and city dwellers. Often liberals and conservatives within the party battled for control of the party and its offices. But when liberals and conservatives were not engaged in periodic intraparty bat-

Shivercrat movement a movement led by the Texas governor Allan Shivers during the 1950s in which conservative Democrats in Texas supported Republican candidate Dwight Eisenhower for the presidency because many of those conservative Democrats believed that the national Democratic Party had become too liberal

presidential Republicanism a voting pattern in which conservatives vote Democratic for state offices but Republican for presidential candidates

Although the Democratic Party dominated state politics for much of the twentieth century, by the 1950s it faced internal divisions between liberal and conservative Democrats. Governor Allan Shivers (third from left) was a conservative Democrat who encouraged supporters to vote for Republican Dwight Eisenhower in the 1952 and 1956 presidential races.

tles, battles that occurred with considerable regularity, what political organization existed tended to be based on personal ties and personal popularity of individual candidates.

Until about the 1940s, Texas politics was often chaotic and confused. By about the mid-1940s, however, a split between liberals and conservatives developed in the Democratic Party that focused on New Deal economic policies and civil rights measures. This liberal-conservative split became a characteristic division within the Democratic Party, and liberals and conservatives battled in the party primaries. Between the mid-1940s and the mid-1970s, the victor in these primary squabbles would then go on to win the general election. However, by the late 1970s, the winner of the Democratic primary had to face a significant conservative challenge from Republicans in the general election.[6]

The Era of Conservative Democrats

After Reconstruction and through the mid-twentieth century, conservative Democrats were in control of state government. These Democratic officeholders were conservative on fiscal and racial issues and exerted a powerful influence in the region as well as in Congress. This may seem somewhat hard to fathom in today's political environment, where Democrats are seen as liberal and Republicans as conservative, but recall that the Republican Party was initially started in Illinois as an anti-slavery party. Conservative Democrats in the early to mid-twentieth century were not particularly favorable to policies that would make it easier for African Americans to vote or participate in civic life in an equal manner. Many southern Democrats were elected to Congress and gained seniority in the Democratic-controlled U.S. Congress. Northern Democrats, however, had always been more liberal than their southern counterparts and did not like the growing influence of the South on policy matters in Washington.

In the many contests between conservative Democrats and liberal Democrats within Texas when that party was the only game in town, the conservatives usually won because of the sheer fact that there were more conservatives than liberals in the state. However, some liberals did emerge, such as U.S. Senator Ralph Yarborough, and to some extent, President Lyndon B. Johnson. Even though the two men were political adversaries, they both held progressive views, unlike many of their white Texas counterparts. U.S. Senator Lloyd Bentsen, who served the state during the 1980s, became the vice presidential candidate for Michael Dukakis in 1988 but was unable to win the state for his running mate. Instead, Republican George H. W. Bush, who had moved to Texas from Connecticut, carried the state and the general election. The Reagan Revolution had reached Texas and from that point on, the Democratic Party in the state shrank to become the minority party.

The Growth of the Republican Party

for critical analysis

Consider how electoral decisions could be made if candidates were not identified by party membership. Would it be more or less difficult for individuals to discover the candidates' views on the issues? Would fund-raising be more or less difficult?

One of the most important developments in Texas politics has been the growth of the Republican Party (see Figure 4.3). In the 1950s, more than 60 percent of Texans identified with the Democratic Party and fewer than 10 percent identified themselves as Republicans. The remainder considered themselves independents. In the 1960s, Republican identification in Texas rose above 10 percent; Democratic identification remained above 60 percent; and identification with independents dropped slightly. The 1970s saw a decline in Democratic affiliation and an increase in Republican affiliation. That pattern of increase of Texans who identified themselves as Republicans and decline among those who identified themselves as Democrats accelerated during the 1980s.[7] In 2008, Texans who identified themselves as Republicans saw a drop from 37 percent in 2004 to 33 percent, whereas Democratic Party affiliation remained steady at 30 percent.[8] A 2009

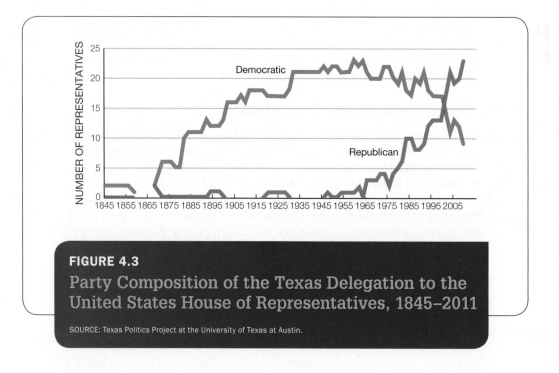

FIGURE 4.3

Party Composition of the Texas Delegation to the United States House of Representatives, 1845–2011

SOURCE: Texas Politics Project at the University of Texas at Austin.

When Did Texas Become Republican?

The Republican Party is the dominant party in Texas. However, this is a fairly recent development. Before the 1970s, Texans were less likely than the rest of the nation to support Republican presidential candidates. And it was only in the 1990s and the early 2000s that Republicans came to hold a majority of seats in the Texas delegation to the U.S. House and in the Texas legislature.

Republican Share of the Presidential Vote

■ Texas ■ National

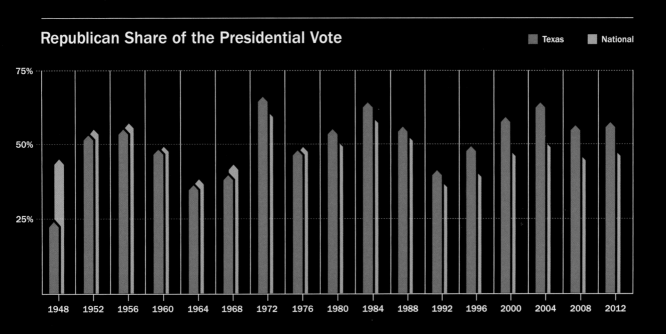

Republican Share of Offices Held

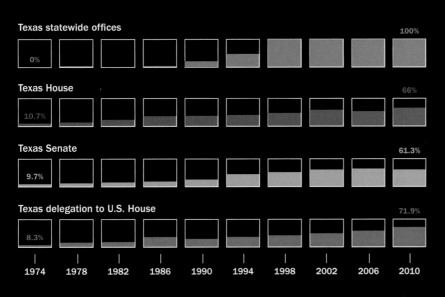

Texas statewide offices — 0% ... 100%

Texas House — 10.7% ... 66%

Texas Senate — 9.7% ... 61.3%

Texas delegation to U.S. House — 8.3% ... 71.9%

1974 1978 1982 1986 1990 1994 1998 2002 2006 2010

SOURCES: First figure: 1948–2004 data from the CQ Elections and Voting Collection. 2008 data from the Associated Press. Second figure: 1974–2002 data from Republican Party of Texas. 2004–10 data calculated by author from election results archived at the Texas Secretary of State.

for critical analysis

1. Consider the timing of the shift toward the Republican Party in Texas. What factors contributed to this shift?

2. The figures show that in the last few elections, the growth of the Texas Republican Party has leveled out somewhat. Do you think the growth of the Texas Republican Party has stalled, or will the party's strength continue to grow in Texas?

Gallup poll study identified Texas as being a competitive state with Republican leanings.[9] However, there is a difference between potential voters who respond to surveys and actual voters. Among actual voters, Texas is strongly Republican in statewide elections.

In the first quarter of the twentieth century, the Republican Party was only a token party. In the state legislature, for example, Republicans never held more than one seat in the Texas Senate and never more than two seats in the Texas House from 1903 to 1927. From 1927 to 1951, there were no Republicans in the Texas Legislature, and then a lone Republican was elected from Dallas to serve only one term in the Texas House. It was another decade before Republicans were again elected to the legislature, when two served in the Texas House. Then in 1962, six Republicans were elected to the House from Dallas County and one from Midland County. By 1963, there were 10 Republicans in the Texas House and none in the Texas Senate.[10]

As Table 4.1 shows, as late as 1974, there were not many more than 75 Republican officeholders in the entire state of Texas. One of those officeholders was U.S. Senator John Tower, and there were two Texas Republicans in the U.S. House of Representatives. No Republicans were elected to state office in statewide elections. There were only 3 Republicans in the Texas Senate and only 16 Republicans in the Texas House of Representatives. Ronald Reagan's election as president in 1980 marked a significant change in how Texans began to vote not only in presidential elections but also in state elections. The Reagan era ushered in a period when conservative Democrats began to switch to the Republican Party in record numbers. This switch became more evident at the end of the Reagan and Bush years when Texas became a Republican state not only in presidential races but also state races. By contrast, in 2012 both U.S. senators from Texas were Republican and 24 Texas members of the U.S. House of Representatives were Republican. A majority of the Texas Senate, 19 of the 31 members, and the Texas House of Representatives, 95 of the 150 members, was Republican.

It was a record of remarkable Republican growth and Democratic decline. By 1998, every statewide elected official was Republican. (This remained true in 2012 as well.) That included the governor, lieutenant governor, attorney general, comptroller, land commissioner, agriculture commissioner, all three mem-

TABLE 4.1

Growth of the Republican Party in Texas

YEAR	U.S. SENATE	OTHER STATEWIDE	U.S. HOUSE	TEXAS SENATE	TEXAS HOUSE	COUNTY OFFICE	DISTRICT OFFICE	SCHOOL BOARD	TOTAL
1974	1	0	2	3	16	53	NA	NA	75+
1980	1	1	5	7	35	166	NA	NA	215+
1990	1	6	8	8	57	547	170	5	802
2000	2	27	13	16	72	1,233	336	10	1,709
2010	2	27	23	19	101	1,500	386	11	2,069
2012	2	27	24	19	95	NA	NA	NA	NA

SOURCE: Republican Party of Texas.

bers of the Texas Railroad Commission, and all nine members of both the Texas Supreme Court and the Texas Court of Criminal Appeals. Only 20 years earlier, William Clements was the first statewide official elected as a Republican since Reconstruction.

The Disappearance of Conservative Democrats

Conservative Democrats, also known as **Blue Dog Democrats**, are becoming an endangered species in Texas and in the rest of the South. Such Democrats never left the party they grew up in, and they have become marginalized in the national party because of their social conservatism. Many of these Democrats are opposed to abortion and gay marriage while supportive of gun rights. These positions put them at odds with the prevailing consensus in the Democratic Party. Some of the few conservative Democrats elected to Congress in recent years even refused to support Nancy Pelosi of San Francisco as their party leader because of their divergence from her more liberal views.

By 2012, all of the conservative Democrats elected to represent Texas in the U.S. Congress had retired, switched parties, or lost their elections. For example, former congressman Chet Edwards was a conservative Democrat who represented Crawford, the home of former president George W. Bush. In the 2010 elections, Edwards lost his bid for re-election to Republican Bill Flores, a businessman. Congressman Ralph Hall of Rockwall switched to the Republican Party in 2004 after spending many years as a conservative Democrat. He switched parties in order to have more influence in Congress's governing party, although just two years later, the Democrats retook control of the U.S. House.

The biggest losses for conservative Democrats came following the 2003 redistricting cycle, spearheaded by Tom DeLay. As House majority leader, DeLay wanted to take advantage of the new Republican majority in the state legislature in order to redraw congressional districts, which he thought were too favorable to Democrats. Although controversial, DeLay was able to succeed in organizing a dramatic redistricting session, which put many conservative Democrats from Texas at risk of losing their seats.

After this episode, two Texas Democrats, Representatives Charles Stenholm and Max Sandlin, lost their seats to Republicans. Another Democrat, Jim Turner, decided not to seek re-election in his newly configured district in east Texas. This left liberal Lloyd Doggett of Austin as the only white Democrat representing a majority white congressional district in Texas. Gene Green of Houston represents a majority-minority district.

The pattern we observe in Congress is also present at the state legislative level. Twelve of the 74 Democrats in the Texas House of Representatives are considered conservative in research conducted by Mark Jones of Rice University. Note, that this is relative to other Democrats, not Republicans. The most conservative Democrat in the Texas House is still more liberal than the most liberal Republican. In the most recent legislative session, however, Allan Ritter of Nederland, who was one of the 12 mentioned earlier, switched to the Republican Party.

In today's political environment, the influence of conservative Democrats and liberal Republicans is very limited. At the national level and in Texas, conservatives are disproportionately members of the Republican Party and liberals are members of the Democratic Party. In many races, there are a shrinking number of truly independent voters who can swing elections. Often, both parties attempt to mobilize their own bases instead of trying to reach these swing voters.

Blue Dog Democrats another name for conservative Democrats, mostly from the South

● Issues in Texas Party Politics

Analyze how ideological divisions and demographic change affect Texas political parties

Both the Democrats and the Republicans have factions within the party, and these factions emphasize different issues. For example, the Democratic Party in Texas has a large Latino base, which is very interested in the issue of immigration. The Republican Party has a strong and growing Tea Party contingent, which is making the party more antitax and fiscally conservative. In this section, we will examine some of these conflicts both between and within the major parties.

Party Unity and Disunity

All groups have opposing factions within them, and political parties are no exception. When a party becomes dominant in a state, these factional battles become particularly important because the stakes are higher for the factions of the dominant party.

When the Democratic Party was the dominant party in Texas, factional battles were common between liberals and conservatives in the party. These conflicts in the Democratic Party were especially notable during the 1950s in the struggles between the pro-Eisenhower conservative Democrats, led by Allan Shivers, and the pro-Stevenson liberal and loyalist Democrats, led by Sam Rayburn, Lyndon Johnson, and Ralph Yarborough. Now that the Republican Party is the dominant party in Texas, major factional battles have occurred for control of that party. One faction is the religious right. This group includes religious conservatives who are especially concerned with social issues such as abortion, prayer in public schools and at school events, the teaching of evolution in public schools, and the perceived decline in family values. The other major segment of the party is composed of economic conservatives. This group is primarily concerned with reduced government spending, lower taxes, and greater emphasis on free enterprise. At the end of the day, however, these factions often end up supporting their party candidate in the general election.

In the 2006 primary, some Republicans, including two of the party's largest contributors in Texas, believed that some Republicans in the Texas House were too moderate and spent money to try to defeat them.[11] At least six Republican incumbents were aided by last-minute contributions from a political action committee that poured about $300,000 into their campaigns to help protect them from Republican challengers. Nevertheless, two of the six incumbents were defeated and one was thrown into a runoff.[12] The 2010 primary battle between Kay Bailey Hutchison and Rick Perry suggests that the ideological tensions in the Republican Party continue between what is essentially a conservative faction and an even more conservative faction. The latter faction has been identified with the Tea Party movement.

To maintain their political strength, the Republican Party has to keep these factional disputes within the party. For years, the Democratic Party battles between its liberal and conservative wings were kept inside the party because there was no rival party where one of the factions could go. Eventually the Republican Party emerged as a home where many conservative Democrats felt comfortable. Conceivably, the factional disputes in the Republican Party could lead one of the factions—most likely the more moderate Republicans—to move to the Democratic Party.

Urban, Rural, and Suburban Influences on Partisanship

As in the rest of the country, one of the major divides in political party affiliation is rural versus urban. Today's large suburban populations must be added to this equation. The growth of suburban enclaves around major cities such as the Dallas–Fort Worth metroplex, Houston, and San Antonio has profoundly changed politics. Prior to the growth of suburbia, people lived either in cities or in rural areas. Rural residents were often cattle ranchers or farmers. As cattle raising and farming became more mechanized and large companies displaced local farmers, it became less profitable to run family farms. Many rural residents relocated to urban areas to work in banks, oil companies, or other industries.

During the 1950s, the federal government embarked on a major project to connect cities through an interstate highway system. One consequence of this system was that it made it easier for workers to travel to and from urban areas. For those who wanted to escape urban congestion, it became easier to move to the outskirts of the city and travel by car to their jobs. While mass transit facilitated suburban commuting in other parts of the country, in Texas, taxpayers were unwilling to fund these infrastructure investments.

Texas's interstate highway system encouraged the process of "white flight," the mass exodus of more affluent whites from urban areas to suburban areas. This left urban areas with eroding tax bases and remaining poor minority populations, who did not have the luxury of purchasing automobiles to commute between city and suburb.

The political result of this changing demographic is that cities have become more Democratic, even in Texas, where the urban strongholds of Austin, Dallas, and Houston deliver the most Democratic votes in the state. Rural areas have remained solidly conservative and have become Republican in Texas, and suburban areas can best be described as hybrid areas with pockets of Republicans and Democrats depending on the specific area and local issues.

Another consequence is that voters tend to settle in places with like-minded people so that cities tend to attract more Democrats, and suburban and rural areas tend to attract more Republicans. This reinforces the political proclivities already established in such communities. A recent book, *Our Patchwork Nation*, by Dante Chinni and James Gimpel explores this phenomenon nationwide, arguing that different communities have distinct political characteristics.[13]

The tensions introduced by suburbanization are clearly seen in Dallas County over the last decade. As Dallas County has urbanized and the suburbs have extended to adjoining counties, Dallas County has been transformed into an urban, Democratic county. In the media coverage of the 2000 presidential election, one small judicial race in Dallas County was almost overlooked. Only one puzzled article on the race's results appeared in the *Dallas Morning News*.[14] A three-time Republican judge, Bill Rhea, won re-election against a first-time Democratic candidate, Mary Ann Huey. That should have been no surprise. By the late 1980s, the only Democrat who could win a judicial race in Dallas County was Ron Chapman, a Democratic judge who happened to share the name of the most popular disk jockey in the county.[15] In the early 1980s, there had been a wholesale rush of incumbent Democratic judges to the Republican Party. Although varying explanations were given by the party switchers, perhaps the most honest and straightforward was by Judge Richard Mays: "My political philosophy about general things has nothing to do with me [*sic*] being a judge. . . . That's not the reason I'm switching parties. The reason I'm switching is that to be a judge in Dallas County you need to be a

State Senator Leticia Van de Putte, of San Antonio, is one of a growing number of influential Hispanics in the Democratic Party in Texas. Here, she makes an announcement about helping indentured servants, who are brought over the border and then forced to work, often under harsh conditions, to pay off their "debt" to the traffickers who transported them.

Republican." With Mays's switch in August 1985, 32 of the 36 district judges in Dallas County were Republicans, though none were Republicans before 1978.[16] It would, of course, not take long until all judges in Dallas County were Republican.[17]

So what was remarkable about that one district court race between a Democratic challenger and a longtime Republican incumbent, other than the fact that a Democrat had the temerity to challenge an incumbent in a Republican bastion such as Dallas County? Out of 560,558 votes cast, only 4,150 votes separated the two candidates. In other words, a three-term Republican judge with no scandal or other controversy surrounding his name won with only 50.3 percent of the vote. It is no wonder that the judge commented, "I'm thrilled to be serving again and duly humbled by the vote count."[18] Even more astounding, Judge Rhea's Democratic opponent, Mary Ann Huey, had run with no money, no political experience, and no support from the legal community. She ran in the same year that George W. Bush was the presidential nominee, with no other Democratic judicial candidates on the ballot at the county level, and with little more than audacity on her side.

Judge Rhea's humbling experience, of course, was not caused by his judicial performance but rather by demographic changes. The Republican base in Dallas County has moved to places such as Collin, Denton, and Rockwall counties. That suburban growth has changed those traditionally Democratic counties into Republican counties, but has left the old Republican base—Dallas—with a larger African American and an even larger Latino population and has returned to the Democratic column that it left a little more than 20 years ago.

In the 2004 elections, George W. Bush carried Dallas County by fewer than 10,000 votes (50.72 percent), and Dallas County elected Democrats as sheriff and four countywide elected judges. The 2006 elections in Dallas County were truly a watershed in the county's politics. A Democrat was elected county judge, a Democrat was elected district attorney, and all 42 Democrats who ran for Dallas County judgeships were elected. Democrats continued their sweep of countywide elections in 2008, 2010, and 2012.

In 2008, Harris County also dramatically shifted to the Democratic column, electing a large number of Democrats to county office. It seemed to be following in Dallas County's footsteps. However, the 2010 elections moved Harris County back into the Republican column, and in 2012, Harris County was a virtual tie between Obama and Romney.

African Americans in Texas Political Parties

In Texas, African Americans are a smaller percentage of the population than in neighboring Louisiana. Approximately 12 percent of the state population is African American, and most of that population is concentrated in east Texas as well as in the major cities of Houston, Dallas, San Antonio, and Austin. Depending on the election, the vast majority of African Americans cast their votes for Democrats. This is not unusual, as African Americans in other parts of the country are similarly loyal to the Democratic Party.

This is not to say that all African Americans are Democrats. Former railroad commissioner Michael Williams became the first black Republican to be elected to the statewide post. Texas Supreme Court Chief Justice Wallace Jefferson is also an African American Republican, and was elected by voters to his position. Other than Williams and Jefferson, only two other African Americans have been elected to statewide office in recent years.

African Americans have been elected mayors of important cities in Texas. Democrat Lee Brown became Houston's first African American mayor in 1997, and Democrat Ron Kirk became Dallas's first African American mayor in 1995. In 2002, Kirk ran for the U.S. Senate but lost to white Republican John Cornyn. Kirk is now the U.S. trade representative, appointed by President Obama in 2009.

Latinos and the Future of Party Politics in Texas

The 2002 elections raised serious questions about how soon the Latino vote would transform politics in Texas. In an attempt to break the lock that the Republicans had on statewide offices, the Democratic Party put forward a "Dream Team" with Tony Sanchez, a wealthy Latino businessman from Laredo, running for governor alongside Ron Kirk running for the U.S. Senate and John Sharp (a former state comptroller and white conservative Democrat) running for lieutenant governor. The idea was to mobilize minority voters to vote for the Democratic ticket while holding traditional white voters. The strategy failed dismally as Sanchez lost to the Republican candidate Perry (40 percent to 58 percent), Kirk lost to the Republican Cornyn (43 percent to 55 percent), and Sharp lost to the Republican Dewhurst (46 percent to 52 percent). Especially disappointing because Sanchez was the first Latino major party nominee for governor, Latino voter turnout was only 32.8 percent. The Democratic "Dream Team" became a nightmare. Sanchez had money and spent it with abandon, but he was a poor campaigner who could not even mobilize the Latino vote.

Additionally, Democrats didn't anticipate the grassroots get-out-the-vote effort put forth by the Republicans. Republican straight-ticket voting in key urban and suburban counties across the state appeared to have outdistanced Democratic straight-ticket voting. Further, it appeared that the negative campaigning, particularly that directed at Tony Sanchez, may have undercut support for the Democratic ticket among traditional white conservative voters. Bob Stein, a political science

for critical analysis

What is the significance of Latino population growth to parties in Texas?

TABLE 4.2

Racial/Ethnic Groups' Share of Texas's Population and the State's 2008 Vote

GROUP	% SHARE OF POPULATION	% SHARE OF ELIGIBLE VOTERS
White	50.5	61.5
Hispanic	37.4	25.5
African American	12	13

SOURCE: Pew Hispanic Center, "Hispanics in the 2008 Election: Texas," February 20, 2008.

professor at Rice University, estimates that 15 percent of Democrats abandoned Sanchez because of questions raised by his involvement in a failed savings and loan bank that was accused of laundering money for Mexican drug kingpins.

The 2010 election has been described as a Republican tsunami running throughout the nation. Texas experienced this wave in three important ways. First, four Democratic incumbent U.S. Congressmen were defeated. Second, Republicans maintained their monopoly over statewide elected offices. Third, Republicans gained 22 seats in the Texas House. A conservative majority reasserted itself in Texas politics. Since the 2010 elections, two Latino members of the state house have switched parties. Aaron Peña of Edinburg and J. C. Lozano of Kingsville became Republicans.

Despite the final results of the 2008 and 2010 elections, few commentators were willing to dismiss the growing importance of the Latino vote in the state. One indication of that importance is that in 2010, it was estimated that Hispanics made up about 20 percent of the registered voters in Texas.[19]

However, Hispanics have not fully realized their potential voting strength. Table 4.2 shows Hispanic voting in comparison to that of other racial and ethnic groups, comparing the group's share of the population with its share of voters in the 2008 election. It does seem likely that Hispanics will at some point significantly increase their share of the vote in Texas, although one obstacle may be that some are not citizens and are ineligible to vote.[20] When Hispanic voting does increase, the key question will be whether Republicans can make inroads into the Hispanic vote to the extent necessary to keep the Democratic Party from emerging as a dominant party in Texas once again. As of 2012, according to the Pew Hispanic Center, Latinos constitute about 38 percent of the Texas population and 25 percent of the eligible voters, yet they are only 24 percent of registered voters and only 20 percent of actual voters.

● Thinking Critically about Parties in Texas

We often think of conflict in politics between the Democratic and Republican parties, especially in government. While this is certainly true, conflict can also occur within political parties among different factions. These factions usually compromise to support their candidates during the general election. Political parties therefore provide a structure through which candidates strive to win office. The two major parties in Texas are the Democratic and the Republican parties, although most of the elected officials in the state are Republican (see Figure 4.4). In south

Texas, however, Democrats control many cities, towns, and school boards because of the large Latino population, which is overwhelmingly Democratic.

One of the most striking developments in Texas politics over the past 20 to 25 years is that one-party Democratic dominance is gone from the Texas political scene. That decline in Democratic dominance corresponds to the rise of the Republican Party in Texas. In 2012 every statewide elected officeholder in Texas was a Republican.

Currently, the most dangerous conflict within the Republican Party is the split between religious social conservatives and economic conservatives who have a low-taxing, low-spending agenda. This split was strikingly revealed in the primary battle between Governor Rick Perry and Senator Kay Bailey Hutchison. Perry's victory in the primary may signal the triumph of the social conservatives and their increasingly powerful role in the state's politics. However, Republicans are not necessarily secure as the dominant party. It is important that the Republican Party grow and expand its base of support. One of the Republican Party's great weaknesses is its lack of support among Latinos, the fastest-growing ethnic group in Texas. If the Republicans are to continue their remarkable successes in Texas politics, they will have to make greater inroads with Latino voters.

Democrats still have a significant base of support in urban counties with large minority populations and with older Texans and with liberals. For Texas to be a competitive two-party state, the Democrats need to win some statewide elections. The party needs to regroup and redirect its appeal to Texans. Most important, if the Democratic Party is to do more than lose elections, it must do what parties have traditionally done in states that have political machines. That is, it must get out the vote. In part, the key to success in future Texas elections is a party's ability to mobilize the Latino vote in the state.

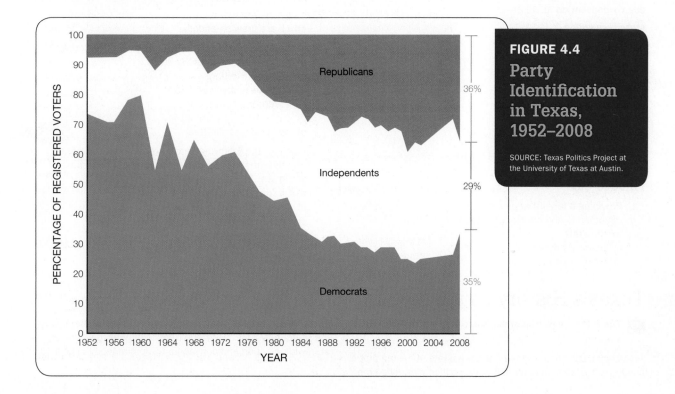

FIGURE 4.4

Party Identification in Texas, 1952–2008

SOURCE: Texas Politics Project at the University of Texas at Austin.

study guide

The Role of Political Parties in Texas Politics

■ **Describe the main functions of state party organizations (pp. 107–17)**

In Texas, political parties serve as brand labels for voters to determine whom to vote for in elections that have little or no publicity. Texas political parties also have conventions and committees that help their members organize and mobilize in elections.

Key Terms

partisan polarization (p. 108)

political socialization (p. 109)

precinct (p. 111)

precinct chair (p. 111)

county executive committee (p. 111)

county chair (p. 111)

state executive committee (p. 112)

state chair and **vice chair** (p. 112)

precinct convention (p. 112)

county convention (p. 112)

state convention (p. 112)

Dixiecrats (p. 113)

La Raza Unida Party (p. 113)

single-member district (p. 116)

Duverger's Law (p. 116)

proportional representation (p. 116)

Occupy movement (p. 116)

Tea Party movement (p. 116)

Practice Quiz

1. Providing a label that helps voters identify those seeking office is an important function of *(p. 107)*
   a) the state.
   b) political parties.
   c) interest groups.
   d) regional and subregional governments.
   e) the president.

2. The process by which political parties become more distant from each other in terms of ideology is *(p. 108)*
   a) partisan convergence.
   b) partisan polarization.
   c) partisan conventions.
   d) partisan equilibrium.
   e) partisan deliverance.

3. All of the following groups constitute the Democratic Party base in Texas *except (p. 110)*
   a) business leaders.
   b) Latinos.
   c) African Americans.
   d) white liberals.
   e) urban residents.

4. Which minority group is the fastest growing in Texas? *(p. 111)*
   a) African Americans
   b) Latinos
   c) Asian Americans
   d) Native Americans
   e) All are growing equally.

5. In the state of Texas, the highest level of temporary party organization is the *(p. 112)*
   a) state convention.
   b) state executive committee.
   c) governor's convention.
   d) civil executive committee.
   e) speaker's committee.

6. Which of the following third parties and movements had the most success in winning elections in post–World War II Texas? *(pp. 114–15)*
   a) La Raza Unida Party
   b) The Occupy movement
   c) The Green Party
   d) The Kinky Friedman movement
   e) The Constitution Party

Texas's History as a One-Party State

■ **Trace the evolution of the party system in Texas (pp. 117–23)**

Texas has traditionally been a one-party state, meaning that one party has been in control of state politics for a long time.

In the post–Civil War period, the Democrats held power in the state, but since 1994, the Republicans have won every statewide election and consequently dominate state politics.

Key Terms

Shivercrat movement (p. 118)

presidential Republicanism (p. 118)

Blue Dog Democrats (p. 123)

Practice Quiz

7. The Shivercrat movement was *(p. 118)*
   a) a group of conservative Democrats in Texas who supported Eisenhower for president.
   b) a group of liberal Democrats who supported equal rights for all Americans.
   c) a group of conservative Republicans who rejected the Obama administration.
   d) a group of liberal Republicans who rejected the Bush administration.
   e) a group of Libertarians.

8. In Texas, the Republican Party became the dominant party in *(p. 122)*
   a) the 1950s.
   b) the 1960s.
   c) the 1970s.
   d) the 1980s.
   e) the 1990s.

9. Blue Dog Democrats were *(p. 123)*
   a) northeastern Democrats with conservative views.
   b) southern Democrats with liberal views.
   c) southern Democrats with conservative views.
   d) northern Democrats with liberal views.
   e) western Democrats with liberal views.

10. Presidential Republicanism refers to which of the following? *(p. 118)*
   a) Texans voting for Republican local candidates
   b) Texans voting for Republican presidents and Democrats for state offices
   c) Texans voting for Republican presidents and Republicans for state offices
   d) Texans voting for Democratic local candidates
   e) Texans voting for third-party candidates at all levels

Issues in Texas Party Politics

■ **Analyze how ideological divisions and demographic change affect Texas political parties (pp. 124–28)**

Texas is a diverse state with divisions between north and south and east and west. Latinos currently constitute nearly 40 percent of the state's population and currently favor the Democratic Party, although their registration and turnout rates are lower than those of the other major demographic groups.

Practice Quiz

11. Which of the following is *not* true? *(p. 125)*
   a) Cities in Texas have become more Democratic.
   b) Cities in Texas are dominated by third parties.
   c) Rural areas of Texas are solidly Republican.
   d) Texas suburbs contain pockets of both Democrats and Republicans.
   e) Democrats dominate elections in Dallas County.

12. African Americans in Texas *(p. 127)*
   a) tend to cast their votes for Democrats.
   b) are a large part of the Republican base.
   c) vote mainly for independent candidates.
   d) make up less than 10 percent of the population.
   e) split their votes evenly between the Democratic and Republican parties.

Ⓢ **Practice Online**
"Exploring Texas Politics" exercise: *The Latino Vote in Texas*

Recommended Websites

Libertarian Party of Texas
www.tx.lp.org

Republican Party of Texas
www.texasgop.org

Texas Democrats
www.txdemocrats.org

Texas Tribune
www.texastribune.org

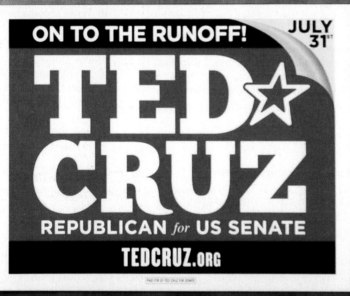

In 2012, Ted Cruz won the U.S. Senate race in Texas after defeating Lieutenant Governor David Dewhurst in the Republican primary. During the primary race, Cruz argued that Dewhurst was not a true conservative.

Elections in Texas

WHAT GOVERNMENT DOES AND WHY IT MATTERS In 2011, U.S. Senator Kay Bailey Hutchison announced that she would not run for re-election in the 2012 election. The last time Texas had an open Senate seat was when Phil Gramm retired in 2002. He was replaced by John Cornyn, who had been the attorney general of the state. At the time, Ron Kirk, the former mayor of Dallas, was a formidable Democratic candidate but ended up losing to Cornyn in the general election.

Hutchison's retirement threw open a bitter race in the Republican primary. Lieutenant Governor David Dewhurst became the party's candidate endorsed by Governor Perry and the rest of the state's leadership. Not only did Dewhurst have most of the major endorsements, but as a self-made millionaire, he also had the most money.

Club for Growth, a national conservative organization, endorsed former solicitor general Ted Cruz, a son of a Cuban immigrant who attended Princeton University and Harvard Law School. Cruz became the favorite of Tea Party activists who appreciated his message of low taxes and limited government. *National Review* magazine also endorsed Cruz, and many observers saw him as a telegenic candidate who could appeal to the large Latino constituency.

Dallas mayor Tom Leppert, a millionaire like Dewhurst, also entered the race and blanketed the airwaves with ads deriding his principal opponents as empty suits. Leppert ran as a "conservative businessman" in the mold of Mitt Romney, the 2012 Republican nominee for president. ESPN commentator Craig James also entered the race but was never able to gain traction, as the other three candidates and their larger set of endorsements and money drowned him out.

The political ads in this Senate race became nastier by the day. Dewhurst accused Cruz of representing a business that closed its American operations and moved to China. Cruz accused Dewhurst of being a moderate and a tax raiser, a toxic accusation in Texas. In a controversial radio advertisement, Dewhurst then accused Cruz of supporting amnesty for illegal immigrants. This led Cruz to accuse Dewhurst of trying to remind voters of Cruz's ethnicity, a possible liability in a Republican primary.

Preelection polls showed Dewhurst with a lead in the race, but just short of the 50 percent he needed to avoid a runoff with the second-place finisher. Cruz was second in the polls, with Dallas mayor Tom Leppert rounding out the field. On May 29, the primary election results confirmed the polls: Dewhurst finished first with 45 percent of the vote against Cruz, who finished second with 34 percent of the vote. In the July 31 runoff, Ted Cruz surprised many pundits by receiving 57 percent of the vote against Dewhurst's 43 percent, thus making him the Republican nominee for the U.S. Senate from Texas.

On the Democratic side, former state representative Paul Sadler ran against several other candidates, but the race received virtually no attention, mainly because the Democrat was not expected to beat the winner of the Republican primary. And, indeed, Cruz easily defeated Sadler in the general election.

Why should it matter who is elected to represent Texas in the Senate? The U.S. Senate is composed of only 100 members, 2 from each state. Each senator has enormous political power compared to a member of the House of Representatives. Senators can help set the policy agenda in Washington and help bring jobs and businesses to the state. Senators fight to ensure that the interests of their states are adequately represented at the national level.

While this high-profile Senate election received more attention than usual from voters, the reality is that all elections matter for public policy in Texas. Elections to the city council, school board, and state legislature make a huge difference in our lives. Education funding, health care policy, tax policy, and environmental policy are all affected by whom we elect to represent us, whether at the national or local level.

chaptergoals

- **Describe the types of elections held in Texas and how they work** (pages 135–38)

- **Explain how the rules for voting affect turnout among different groups of Texans** (pages 138–53)

- **Present the main features of election campaigns in Texas** (pages 153–57)

Features of Elections in Texas

Describe the types of elections held in Texas and how they work

Elections are the most important vehicles by which the people express themselves in the democratic process in Texas. At the national level, elections are limited to the selection of the president and vice president (via the Electoral College) and members of Congress. In Texas, however, voters select candidates for various offices in all three statewide branches of government (the legislature, executive, and judiciary), as well as in numerous local elections. Texans also vote for changes to the state Constitution, which can alter public policy in the state. In theory, such elections are meant to enable the people to exercise some direct control over each branch. In practice, however, one-party dominance and low levels of voter participation have often told a different story, leaving the government exposed to special interests and big money.

Elections are the mechanisms people use to select leaders, authorize actions by government, and borrow money on behalf of government. In Texas, there are a multitude of elections: primary elections, general elections, city elections, school board elections, special elections, elections for community college boards of regents and the boards of directors for many special districts, and bond elections for city, county, and state governments.

Primary Elections

Primary elections are the first elections held in an electoral cycle. In Texas, they are generally held on the second Tuesday in March of even-numbered years. Primary elections determine the party's nominees for the general election. They are conducted by the political party and funded jointly by the party and the state. Essentially, parties collect filing fees from those seeking nomination and use these funds to pay for their share of holding the primary election.

Both parties conduct primaries in all of Texas's 254 counties. Within each county, voters cast ballots in precincts. The number of voting precincts varies depending on the population of the county. Less-populated counties such as Loving and Kennedy have as few as 6 precincts, whereas Harris County contains more than 1,000 voting precincts.[1]

Republicans seeking their party's nomination file papers and pay a filing fee to the Republican Party. Likewise, Democrats file papers and pay a filing fee to the Democratic Party. If several Republicans (or Democrats) seek the office of governor, they will campaign against each other and one will be chosen to run in the general election. Winning the primary election requires an absolute majority. The party's nominees must have more votes than all opponents combined. If no candidate receives an absolute majority, there is a **runoff primary** generally held the second Tuesday in April between the two candidates receiving the most votes. Voters who participate in the Republican Party primary cannot vote in a Democratic runoff; likewise, anyone who voted in the Democratic Party primary cannot vote in a Republican runoff. However, those who voted in neither the Democratic nor Republican primary can vote in either the Republican or Democratic runoff primary.

An **open primary** allows any registered voter to cast a ballot in either, but not both, primaries. There are no party restrictions. One can consider oneself a Republican and vote in the Democratic primary or can leave home intending to vote in the Democratic primary, change one's mind, and vote in the Republican primary.

primary election a ballot vote in which citizens select a party's nominee for the general election

runoff primary a second primary election held between the two candidates who received the most votes in the first primary election if no candidate in the first primary election had received a majority

open primary a primary election in which any registered voter can participate in the contest, regardless of party affiliation

closed primary a primary election in which only registered members of a particular political party can vote

The Texas Constitution and election laws call the Texas system a **closed primary**, because one must declare one's party affiliation before voting, but in practice it is an open primary. Before receiving a primary ballot, the voter signs a roll sheet indicating eligibility to vote and pledging to support the party's candidates. By signing the roll sheet, the voter makes a declaration of party affiliation prior to voting. However, because the voter declares a party affiliation only a few moments prior to voting in the primary, the primary is closed only in the narrowest sense of the term. These declarations in no way bind a voter to support the party's candidates in future elections. Many other states have true closed primaries in that only registered party members can vote in these elections. Each state decides how it will run primary elections.

General Election

general election the election in which voters cast ballots to select public officials

The **general election** is held the first Tuesday following the first Monday in November of even-numbered years. The Democratic Party's nominee runs against the nominee of the Republican Party. It is possible that independent and minor-party candidates will also appear on the general election ballot.

Major state officials (governor, lieutenant governor, comptroller of public accounts, attorney general, and so on) are elected in nonpresidential election years. This arrangement seeks to prevent popular presidential candidates from influencing the outcomes of Texas races. For example, it is possible that a popular Republican presidential candidate might draw more than the usual number of Republican votes, and an unusually large Republican presidential vote might swing the election for statewide candidates running under the Republican banner. Likewise, it prevents an uncommonly popular statewide candidate from influencing the presidential election. If statewide elections were held in presidential election years, a Democratic candidate for governor, for example, might influence Texas's presidential voting by increasing the number of votes for Democratic candidates in general.

General elections are held in November to select national and state officeholders. Members of city councils, school boards, and other local government entities are also selected by general elections; however, these elections usually take place outside the traditional early November time period. In many cases, this means very low voter turnout. For example, in the Austin municipal elections in May 2012, there was a record low turnout of only 10 percent of the city's registered voters. City leaders have proposed moving the election to November in the future to encourage a larger proportion of voters to participate.

Special Elections

special election an election that is not held on a regularly scheduled basis; in Texas, a special election is called to fill a vacancy in office, to give approval for the state government to borrow money, or to ratify amendments to the Texas Constitution

In Texas, **special elections** are used to fill vacancies in office, to give approval to borrow money, or to ratify or reject amendments to the Texas Constitution. The dates for special elections are specified by the Texas Legislature. If a Texas senator resigns, for example, the governor will call a special election to fill the vacancy.

Texas laws require voter approval before any governmental agency in Texas can borrow money and undertake long-term debt. If the local school district wants to borrow money to build a new high school and repair three elementary schools, a special election must be held. During the election, voters decide whether they will allow the school board to borrow the money.

The legislature proposes amendments to the Texas Constitution, and the voters in a special election ratify them.

Some blame the relatively low voter turnout for Texas elections on the frequency of elections and the large number of candidates. Also, state officials are not elected in presidential election years, when voter participation tends to be highest.

Running as an Independent

It is unusual for a candidate to run for office in Texas as an independent. One reason is that there are substantial requirements for getting one's name on the ballot. Additionally, an independent candidate lacks the political support of party organizations and the advantage of having a party label on the ballot. As we saw in Chapter 4, however, in 2006 Texas had two independent candidates for governor: Kinky Friedman and former Austin mayor Carole Keeton Strayhorn, the state comptroller, who had been elected to that office as a Republican.

Both candidates were obviously hoping that an independent candidacy would attract the votes of Democrats who believed that a Democratic candidate for governor could not win in Texas. They also were hoping to get substantial votes from Republicans disaffected with the policies and performance of the Republican governor, Rick Perry. Strayhorn, in particular, seemed to have strong appeal to Democrats who usually contributed large sums to Democratic nominees. One study of Strayhorn's contributions from July through December of 2005, for example, found that 52 percent of her campaign funds were from people who had given exclusively or almost exclusively to Democrats over the previous five years.[2]

In general, however, independents have a hard time getting on the ballot in Texas. Texas decides its own requirements for getting on the ballot, and these vary by state. Some states make it easier for independents to get on the ballot, but the process in Texas is relatively difficult. For Friedman and Strayhorn to get on the ballot, for example, they had to meet the following requirements:

1. The candidates must obtain signatures on a petition from registered voters. The signatures must equal 1 percent of the total votes in the last governor's race. This meant that Friedman and Strayhorn each had to obtain 45,540 signatures.

2. The signatures must come from registered voters who did not participate in any political party primary election.

3. Signature collection cannot begin until the day after the last primary election. In 2006 this was March 8.

4. Voters may sign only one candidate's petition. If they sign both, only the first signature provided will count.[3]

The two major political parties don't agree on much, but they do agree on keeping competitors out. Making it difficult for independents to get their names on the ballot helps ensure that the two major political parties will continue to dominate politics in the state well into the future. Elections may be open in Texas, but they work through the dominant political parties, helping to solidify their control over the political process and the major political offices in the state. The electoral performances of Friedman and Strayhorn also point to the difficulties of independent candidacy in that both of these candidates received only a small fraction of the overall vote.

● Participation in Texas Elections

> **Explain how the rules for voting affect turnout among different groups of Texans**

When we think of political participation, we often think of voting. This is the most basic and fundamental duty citizens have in democracy. Other forms of political participation include signing petitions, protesting, and writing letters to the newspaper and elected officials, some of which we will discuss later in this chapter and others we will discuss in future chapters. Here, we begin by examining the history of voting in the state and the regulations and procedures surrounding voting rights. Issues include who can vote, how easy it is to register to vote, and why so few Texans vote.

Earlier Restrictions on the Franchise

For much of the period of one-party Democratic control that began in the late nineteenth century, there were restrictions on the franchise.

Nineteenth Amendment ratified in 1919, amendment guaranteeing women the right to vote

suffrage term referring to the right to vote

Women Women were allowed to vote in primaries and party conventions in Texas in 1918 and obtained the right to vote in all elections as a result of the **Nineteenth Amendment** to the U.S. Constitution in 1920. However, some of the most influential politicians in the state were opposed to the franchise for women. Joseph Weldon Bailey, for example, who had been Democratic leader in the U.S. House of Representatives and later the informal Democratic leader in the U.S. Senate, was an eloquent opponent of women's **suffrage**, arguing that women could not vote because they could not perform the three basic duties of citizenship: jury service, *posse comitatus* service (citizens who are deputized to deal with an emergency), and military service. He believed that women's morals dictated their beliefs and that women would force their beliefs on men. The result, he felt, would be prohibition of alcohol.[4] Tinie Wells, the wife of Jim Wells, perhaps the most influential south Texas political leader of his day, was also an important and influential spokesperson for the anti–women's suffrage movement.[5] Governor "Farmer Jim" Ferguson was another opponent of women's suffrage, but when he was impeached, his successor, William P. Hobby, proved a key supporter of women's right to vote. It was Governor Hobby who called the legislature into special session in 1919 to consider the Nineteenth Amendment. Thus Texas became the ninth state and the first state in the South to ratify the women's suffrage amendment.[6]

The Poll Tax Minorities had an even tougher time gaining access to the ballot in Texas. In the early part of the twentieth century, powerful political bosses had economic power and personal influence over Latino voters. They used this power to support national politicians such as John Nance Garner. Garner represented a huge part of south Texas, which stretched from Laredo to Corpus Christi and then north almost to San Antonio. A lifelong Democrat, he began his service in the House of Representatives in 1903 and served until 1933. From 1931 to 1933, he was Speaker of the U.S. House of Representatives, and from 1933 to 1941, he was vice president of the United States. He is most famous for his quip that the vice presidency was not worth more than a bucket of warm spit. Garner was the first Speaker from Texas and the first vice president from Texas. His south Texas political base was secured by votes that were controlled by the south Texas political bosses.[7]

One restriction on voting that affected poor people in general during this era was the **poll tax**. Enacted in 1902, it required voters to pay a tax, presumably to cover the costs of elections. That tax was usually between $1.50 and $1.75. It was a small sum, but it had to be paid in advance of the election and, in the first third of the century, the tax could be one, two, or even more days' wages for a farm worker. Thus, it tended to disenfranchise poorer people.

The south Texas political bosses used the poll tax to great advantage. They would purchase large numbers of poll tax receipts and provide those receipts to their supporters, who often depended on the bosses for jobs and other economic, legal, and political assistance, and who therefore would vote as the bosses wanted.

poll tax a state-imposed tax on voters as a prerequisite for voting. Poll taxes were rendered unconstitutional in national elections by the Twenty-Fourth Amendment, and in state elections by the Supreme Court in 1966

Participation in elections in Texas is low relative to that in other states. In the past, there were restrictions on the franchise. One such restriction that discouraged poor people from voting was the poll tax, which remained legal in Texas until 1966. Here, voters are asked to pay the poll tax and then vote against Pappy O'Daniel.

early registration the requirement that a voter register long before the general election; in effect in Texas until 1971

white primary primary election in which only white voters are eligible to participate

Jaybird Party after the white primary was ruled unconstitutional, this offshoot Democratic party pre-selected candidates for the Democratic primary and prohibited African Americans from participating

Although the poll tax was made illegal in federal elections in 1964 by the passage of the Twenty-Fourth Amendment to the U.S. Constitution, it remained legal in state elections in Texas until 1966, when it was held unconstitutional.[8] After the elimination of the poll tax, Texas continued to require **early registration** for voting—registration more than nine months before the general election. Early registration was required on a yearly basis. This requirement effectively prevented migrant workers from voting. These provisions lasted until 1971, when they were voided by the federal courts.[9] Texas even prohibited anyone who was not a property owner from voting in revenue bond and tax elections until the practice was stopped by federal courts in 1975.[10] Texas also required an unusually long period of residency. Until 1970, voters had to have lived in the state for at least one year and to have lived in the county for at least six months prior to voting. This was another restriction on the franchise that was struck down by the federal courts.[11]

The White Primary The most oppressive restriction on the franchise, however, was designed to minimize the political strength of African American voters. It was the **white primary**. This practice came under scrutiny by federal courts numerous times in the 21 years between 1923 and 1944; yet each time, the Texas Legislature and state parties found a way to maintain the white primary and exclude black voters. In 1923 the Texas Legislature flatly prohibited African Americans from voting in the Democratic primary. Since Texas was a one-party state at this time the effect, of course, was to prevent African Americans from participating in the only "real" election contests. Texas was able to do this because of a 1921 U.S. Supreme Court decision, *Newberry v. United States*, which dealt with a federal campaign-expenditures law. In interpreting the law, the Court stated that the primary election was "in no real sense part of the manner of holding the election."[12] This cleared the way for southern states, including Texas, to discriminate against African Americans in the primaries.

In 1927, however, the Supreme Court struck down the Texas white primary law, claiming that the legal ban on black participation was a violation of the equal protection clause of the Constitution.[13] In response, the Texas Legislature passed another law that authorized the political parties, through their state executive committees, to determine the qualifications for voting in the primaries. That law, of course, allowed the parties to create white primaries. The theory was that what a state could not do directly because of the Fourteenth Amendment, it could authorize political parties to do. However, in *Nixon v. Condon* (1932), the U.S. Supreme Court held that the state executive committees were acting as agents of the state and were discriminating in violation of the Fourteenth Amendment.[14] As a result, the Texas Democratic Party convention, acting on its own authority and without any state law, passed a resolution that confined party membership to white citizens. That case was also appealed to the U.S. Supreme Court and, in *Grovey v. Townsend* (1935), the Court held there was no violation of the Fourteenth Amendment. The Fourteenth Amendment requires "equal protection under the law" for individuals of all races. However, the Court said that this requirement applied only to "state action," not action by private groups. Since there was no state law authorizing the white primary, the Court believed there was no "state action," only discrimination by a private organization, the Democratic Party, which is not banned by the Fourteenth Amendment.[15] Thus, the Court upheld the white primary until 1944, when, in *Smith v. Allwright*, it decided that the operation of primary elections involved so much state action and so much public responsibility that the white primary did involve unconstitutional state action.[16]

Even with the *Smith* decision, at least one Texas county held unofficial primaries by the **Jaybird Party**. This was a Democratic political organization that excluded

African Americans. The winners in the Jaybird primary then entered the regular Democratic Party primary, in which they were never defeated for county office and where they seldom had opposition. In *Terry v. Adams*, the U.S. Supreme Court finally ruled that the Jaybird primary was an integral, and the only effective, part of the elective process in the county. Thus, the Fifteenth Amendment (which deals with the right to vote) was applicable, and the white "preprimary" primary of the Jaybird Party was ruled unconstitutional.[17]

What made the white primary restriction work for Democrats during this era was the fact that Texas was a one-party state, where elections were decided in the Democratic Party primary. If Texas had had a competitive two-party system during this era, the state might have had a more difficult time imposing and maintaining these restrictions on the franchise. In a competitive two-party system, to obtain and retain power, both parties would have to search for ways to build and increase their base of support in order to be the victorious party. In a one-party system, there is a greater incentive to restrict participation in the party in order to retain control over it. Losers in a battle for control of a one-party system essentially have no place to go. If they cannot maintain a place in the dominant party's councils, then they have no other avenue for expressing their political views.

Expanding the Franchise

At least since the 1940s, there has been a gradual expansion of the franchise in Texas. Much of that expansion was brought about by litigation in the federal courts, often by African American and Latino civil rights organizations. For example, the National Association for the Advancement of Colored People (NAACP) filed lawsuits throughout the 1960s and 1970s challenging laws that restricted or otherwise stunted African American political advancement. The Mexican American Legal Defense and Education Fund (MALDEF) has also been active in monitoring any changes in electoral laws and challenging them if they prevented Latino political advancement.

Federal laws also played an important role in the expansion of the franchise. The most important of these laws was the **Voting Rights Act of 1965**, which applied to Texas as a result of congressional amendments after 1975. The Voting Rights Act was a piece of legislation initially aimed at ensuring that African Americans were not discriminated against at the polls. The year prior to the passage of this bill, Congress had passed the Civil Rights Act, which dealt with ensuring the equality of African Americans in terms of access to businesses, hotels, and other public facilities. President Lyndon B. Johnson signed both laws even though he knew it would damage his political popularity in the South.

Voting Rights Act of 1965 important legislation passed in order to ensure that African Americans would be guaranteed the right to vote. Renewed several times since 1965, the act also prevents the dilution of minority voting strength

The Voting Rights Act has without question had an important influence on elections in Texas. One provision of the law was to send federal examiners to southern states to register voters. In many southern states, blacks were systematically excluded from the ability to register to vote, much less attempt to vote. In Mississippi, only about 7 percent of blacks were registered to vote prior to 1965, but by 1967, more than 67 percent had been registered to vote. This demonstrates the success of the Voting Rights Act in its efforts to ensure equal access to the ballot.

Section 2 of the Voting Rights Act involves a nationwide prohibition against the abridgement of voting rights on the basis of race or ethnicity. Because this affects all states, some localities outside of the South have been sued in federal court alleging violations of voting rights on the basis of race or ethnicity.

The Voting Rights Act has been renewed several times since 1965, and new provisions have been added since then. For example, bilingual ballots are now required in certain areas where more than 5 percent of voters speak another language. This ensures that voters who cannot speak English are not disenfranchised. Texas has complied with the renewals of the Voting Rights Act.

Contracting the Franchise?

Highly partisan legislation passed in 2011 may make it more difficult for some people to vote. Over Democratic opposition, the Republican majority in the Texas Legislature passed a voter identification law that requires a photo identification in order to vote. Republicans claimed that the photo identification requirement is necessary in order to prevent voter fraud. Democrats, in contrast, have argued that evidence of voter fraud is minimal and that the law will make it harder for low-income persons, students, and the elderly (all of whom typically support Democrats) to vote.[18] Forms of photo identification that are acceptable are a driver's license, an election identification certificate, a Department of Public Safety personal ID card, a U.S. military ID, a U.S. citizenship certificate, a U.S. passport, and a Department of Public Safety–issued concealed handgun license.[19] Photo ID cards issued by colleges and universities are not acceptable. It remains to be seen if the Texas voter ID law will ultimately be upheld by the Appellate courts. State political leaders, such as Governor Perry and Attorney General Abbott, have argued that Texas should not be singled out along with other southern states and subjected to the special scrutiny, and should be allowed to have a voter ID law without any approval process. The You Decide section takes a closer look at this issue.

Qualifications to Vote

Today, meeting the qualifications to register to vote in Texas is relatively easy. A voter must be

1. eighteen years of age
2. a U.S. citizen
3. a resident of Texas for 30 days
4. a resident of the county for 30 days

To be eligible to vote, one must be a registered voter for 30 days preceding the election and a resident of the voting precinct on the day of the election. Two groups of citizens cannot vote even if they meet all the preceding qualifications: felons who have not completed their sentences and those judged by a court to be mentally incompetent.

About 70.3 percent of the state's voting-age population is registered to vote.[20] The **motor voter law**,[21] which allows individuals to register to vote when applying for or renewing driver's licenses, is one factor in increased registration. Public schools distribute voter registration cards as students turn 18. Cooperative efforts between the secretary of state's office and corporations such as Diamond Shamrock, Stop 'n' Go, and the Southland Corporation (which operates 7-Eleven stores) also increase the number of registered voters. Most colleges and universities also have registration drives to encourage young people to register to vote. In 2011, Texas had about 13 million registered voters out of a voting-age population of just under 18.3 million.[22]

motor voter law a national act, passed in 1993, that requires states to allow people to register to vote when applying for a driver's license

Voter Identification Laws

In 2011 the Texas Legislature passed a law that would require all voters to present photo identification when they presented themselves to vote in an election. Prior to the law, Texans could present a voter registration certificate, which does not carry a photograph. Not all photo identifications are allowed under the new law. Student identification cards are not considered valid, but state-issued concealed weapons permits are. If a voter shows up to the polls without valid photo identification, they may cast a provisional ballot. They are then required to return to the registrar's office with photo identification within six days.

Supporters of the law argue that it is necessary to reduce fraud. They claim that fraud is often undetected and difficult to prosecute, so the absence of high rates of prosecutions of voter fraud does not mean that it is not a problem that should be addressed. They suggest that it is important to ensure the integrity of the election system and point out that one needs to show photo identification to board airplanes and conduct official business and transactions with banks and other organizations. They also argue that requiring photo identification will provide an assurance to the citizens of the state that elections are free from fraud. Supporters believe that having the potential of penalties for breaking the law will deter any attempts to commit fraud. They also point to public opinion polls showing that the majority of Texans support the simple proposition that one must show a photo identification to prove who you are in order to vote.

Opponents of the law argue that requiring photo identification to vote would have a disparate impact on elderly, disabled, and minority voters,

especially Hispanics who are less likely to possess photo identification. Opponents claim that the measure is not really about preserving the integrity of the electoral system, but it is meant to minimize Democratic turnout in order to help the state Republican Party keep its hold on power. In addition, they point to studies that show there is no real problem concerning voter fraud in Texas. In essence, the law is a solution in search of a problem. Those who oppose the law claim that it is expensive and puts an undue burden on the poor and disadvantaged by making them go through additional steps to vote. The law does provide for free photo identification, but in some rural areas, opponents argue, the nearest Department of Public Safety office is far away and not easily accessible.

Because Texas is subject to the Voting Rights Act of 1965, any changes to Texas elections must be approved by the Department of Justice or the District of Columbia federal district court. In 2012 the Department of Justice refused to approve the voter identification law because it would disproportionately affect Hispanic voters, who are less likely to hold photo identification. Under the Voting Rights Act, new legislation that has the effect of harming the minority community's ability to vote or elect candidates of choice is illegal. Texas Attorney General Greg Abbott, a Republican, has appealed the ruling claiming that the federal government should not intervene with the state's right to pass legislation, and that the Obama Administration has "waged a war on Texas."

However the dispute is decided, the question remains whether voter identification laws are on balance positive or negative. There are legitimate arguments for and against the legislation, but one thing is clear: Republicans strongly support the measure and Democrats have attempted to stop the measure. This fact alone suggests that Republicans believe they will electorally benefit from the law, while Democrats believe they will be harmed. Should this be an important consideration when deciding the trade-offs?

critical thinking question

1. Do the arguments for the legislation outweigh the arguments against it? Is there a way to compromise on this issue? If so, what would a compromise look like?

Low Voter Turnout

In most elections, fewer than 50 percent of U.S. citizens vote.[23] Even fewer Texans exercise their right to vote, especially young people. Historically, Texans rank in the bottom third in terms of voter participation. Table 5.1 provides data on the abysmal turnout of registered voters in the various types of recent Texas elections.

TABLE 5.1

Turnout by Registered Voters in Texas Elections

ELECTION	PERCENTAGE OF VOTING TURNOUT TO REGISTERED VOTERS
2000 Democratic Primary (Presidential)	6.8
2000 Republican Primary (Presidential)	9.7
2000 Democratic Runoff Primary	2.1
2000 Republican Runoff Primary	1.9
2000 General Election (Presidential)	51.8
2001 Special Election (Constitutional Amendments)	6.9
2002 Democratic Primary (Gubernatorial)	8.4
2002 Republican Primary (Gubernatorial)	5.1
2002 General Election (Gubernatorial)	36.2
2003 Special Election (Constitutional)	12.2
2004 Democratic Primary (Presidential)	6.8
2004 Republican Primary (Presidential)	5.6
2004 General Election (Presidential)	56.6
2005 Special Election (Constitutional Amendments)	18.0
2006 Democratic Primary (Gubernatorial)	4.0
2006 Republican Primary (Gubernatorial)	5.2
2006 General Election (Gubernatorial)	33.6
2007 November Special Election (Constitutional Amendments)	8.7
2008 General Election (Presidential)	59.5
2009 November Special Election (Constitutional Amendments)	8.2
2010 Democratic Primary (Gubernatorial)	5.2
2010 Republican Primary (Gubernatorial)	11.4
2010 General Election (Gubernatorial)	38.0
2011 November Special Election	5.0
2012 Republican Primary (Presidential)	11.3
2012 Democratic Primary (Presidential)	5.0

SOURCES: Texas Secretary of State; Christy Hoppe, "Primary Draws Lowest Turnout in Decades," *Dallas Morning News*, March 10, 2006, p. 3A.

Considering the ease of registration and the ability to vote early, voter participation should be higher. Why do so few Texans vote?

A more detailed analysis reveals several factors that may contribute to low participation rates:

1. low levels of educational attainment
2. low per capita income
3. high rate of poverty
4. location in the South
5. young population
6. traditionalistic and individualistic political culture
7. candidate-centered elections and little party competition
8. Lack of media attention to substantive political issues
9. large numbers of undocumented residents and felons

Education and income appear to be the two most important factors in determining whether someone votes, and this is often referred to as socioeconomic status (SES). In Texas, low levels of education and high levels of poverty are both the strongest predictors of low voter participation. While college students and other young adults were mobilized by President Obama's election in 2008, the fact remains that voter turnout among this demographic is low.

In the southern states that composed the Confederacy, individuals participate in smaller numbers than in other parts of the United States. Texas was part of the Confederacy, and its level of participation is consistent with lower levels of voting in the South. The average age of Texans is less than the national average, and young people vote in smaller numbers; this may also contribute to Texas's low turnout rate.

In 2010 only 38 percent of registered voters cast ballots in the Texas gubernatorial election. Turnout is higher in presidential elections in Texas but still below the national average.

According to the political scientist Daniel Elazar, Texas's political culture is traditionalistic and individualistic (see Chapter 1).[24] Low levels of voting characterize these cultures. In a traditionalistic political culture, the political and economic elite discourage voting. People choose not to vote in individualistic cultures because of real or perceived corruption in government.

Interestingly, there are still other possible explanations for low voter participation in Texas. In keeping with the Texas tradition of decentralized government, there are so many elections in Texas and so many candidates for office that voters are simply overloaded with elections and candidates. Note that as shown in Table 5.1, voter participation was much higher in the general election than in the special constitutional election. If there were fewer elections, the ballot might be longer, but voter turnout would likely be higher, because more voters would be attracted to at least some races or issues on the ballot. Additionally, the practice of having elections in nonpresidential election years decreases voter turnout because the highest voter participation tends to occur for presidential elections. A third problem is that most elections in Texas involve very low-visibility offices. Voters likely know little about the candidates for these positions or the offices themselves, and such a lack of knowledge would naturally discourage voter participation. Efforts have been made in a number of states, most notably Washington, to increase voter knowledge by having the state provide biographical information about the candidates to voters, but Texas makes little effort to enhance voter knowledge of candidates. Independent groups such as the League of Women Voters often provide voter guides, but only readers of newspapers or those who actively seek these voter guides out benefit from this information. Finally, some suggest that the new voter identification law will reduce voter turnout even more.

Early Voting

Early voting is a procedure that increases the polling period from 12 hours on Election Day to an additional two weeks prior to the election. The legislature has allowed early voting in an effort to increase participation. It is designed for those who have trouble getting to the polls between 7 A.M. and 7 P.M. on Election Day. For most elections, early voting commences on the 17th day before the elections and ends four days prior to Election Day.

Voting early is basically the same as voting on Election Day. An individual appears at one of the designated polling places, sometimes the local supermarket, presents appropriate identification, and receives and casts a ballot. Each general election has seen an increase in early voting, but overall turnout has increased only modestly. Those who normally vote on the official Election Day simply cast their ballots early.

Predictions that Democrats would benefit from early voting did not hold true after Texas moved strongly into the Republican column. Republican candidates for the highest office on the ballot get a much larger proportion of early votes than do the Democratic candidates. In 2004, for example, 63 percent of the early votes for president in Texas were cast for George W. Bush, compared with 37 percent of the early votes for John Kerry. In seven of the nine elections examined, however, Republicans got a slightly smaller proportion of overall votes (votes cast in early voting plus Election Day voting) than early votes. And in five of the nine elections, Democrats got a slightly larger proportion of overall votes than early votes. This suggests that early voting has been a bit more beneficial to Republicans than to Democrats, although the advantage has been very slight (Table 5.2).

forcriticalanalysis
Voter participation in Texas is among the lowest in the nation. What accounts for the state's low levels of participation? What can be done to increase voter participation in the short term? In the long term?

early voting a procedure that allows voters to cast ballots during the two-week period before the regularly scheduled election date

How Did Texans Vote in 2012?

	Race	Pop.%	🫏 = Obama	🐘 = Romney		

National

Race	Pop.%		Obama	Romney
White	72%		39%	59%
Black	13%		93%	6%
Hispanic	10%		71%	27%
Asian	3%		73%	26%
Other	2%		58%	38%

Texas

Race	Pop.%		Obama	Romney
White	67%		25%	70%
Black	12%		88%	9%
Hispanic	21%		53%	42%
Asian				
Other				

Note: Data on Asian American voters and other groups were not available from Texas exit polls.

California

Race	Pop.%		Obama	Romney
White	55%		44%	54%
Black	8%		96%	4%
Hispanic	23%		70%	29%
Asian	12%		77%	22%
Other	3%		52%	38%

Voters in Texas are known for their conservatism and their support of the Republican Party. In 2012, while the country voted for Barack Obama over Mitt Romney by a 51–48 margin, Texas went for Romney 57–41.

In Texas, these exit polls show that Romney won in large part because he won an overwhelming share of white voters. Obama won among African American and Hispanic voters in Texas by similar numbers to what he won nationally. Romney won 70 percent of white votes in Texas, 11 points better than the 59 percent of white voters he won nationally. Compare this to California, a state with similar demographics to Texas: Romney won only 54 percent of California's white voters.

for critical analysis

1. Why do you think Romney appealed to white Texans more than he appealed to white voters in the rest of the country? How distinct does this make Texans?

2. As we've seen in earlier chapters, the Hispanic population of Texas is growing over time. How might this growth change the outcomes of future elections in Texas?

SOURCE: Texas data from the YouGov Texas poll, Oct. 31–Nov. 3, 2012. National and California data from the EMR Exit Polls, 2012. Downloaded from CNN.com (accessed 11/12/12).

TABLE 5.2

Early Voting and Overall Voting by Party in Texas

YEAR	OFFICE	EARLY/OVERALL VOTES FOR REPUBLICANS (% OF TOTAL)	EARLY/OVERALL VOTES FOR DEMOCRATS (% OF TOTAL)
1994	Senate	62/61	37/38
1996	President	52/49	45/44
1998	Governor	68/69	32/31
2000	President	63/59	35/38
2002	Senator	57/55	42/43
2004	President	63/61	37/38
2006	Senator	56/56	44/44
2008	President	54/55	45/44
2010	Governor	56/55	41/42

SOURCE: Texas Secretary of State.

Racial and Ethnic Variations in Voting and Participation

While Texas is a state with a larger percentage of minorities than non-Hispanic whites, this does not mean that the majority of the state's voters are minorities. As a result of a variety of factors, including the large undocumented population consisting of mostly Latinos from Mexico and Latin America and the lower rate of voter turnout for Latino citizens, non-Hispanic whites wield considerable influence in the state electorate.

Because most African Americans and Latinos tend to vote for Democrats and non-Hispanic whites tend to vote for Republicans, the balance of power in most state elections currently tilts toward Republicans. Democrats hope that as more Latinos become citizens, they will register and turn out to vote, but these hopes have yet to fully materialize.

Public Opinion Differences on Issues Public opinion on issues varies according to race and ethnicity. In a book entitled *Divided by Color*, Donald Kinder and Lynn Sanders show that the views of African Americans and whites are remarkably different on issues ranging from the death penalty to affirmative action.[25] For example, according to a February 2010 *Texas Tribune* survey, 83 percent of whites supported the death penalty, while 57 percent of African Americans and 76 percent of Latinos supported the death penalty. Significantly more African Americans, however, expressed doubts that the death penalty is implemented in a fair, non-biased manner. In the same survey, only 22 percent of African Americans felt the death penalty was implemented fairly compared with 66 percent of whites.[26] In most cases, African Americans are more liberal than whites on political issues.

One issue with remarkable convergence on public opinion between blacks and whites is gay marriage. In Texas, according to a June 2009 *Texas Tribune* survey, only 22 percent of African Americans, 28 percent of whites, and 32 percent of Latinos supported gay marriage.[27] This is why Texas is one of several states that were able to pass a state constitutional amendment defining marriage in the state as between one man and one woman. While the gulf in public opinion is more pronounced between African Americans and whites compared to Latinos and whites, even the latter two groups differ on attitudes about public policy, especially the role of government.

Consider the issue of immigration policy. Most Latinos surveyed in Texas support the DREAM Act, a policy that would allow undocumented students who serve in the military or graduate from college to become citizens. According to a May 2010 *Texas Tribune* poll, 78 percent of whites in Texas strongly oppose this policy, especially the version that allows college graduates to become citizens.[28] For conservatives, this amounts to an unacceptable form of amnesty for illegal immigrants. In contrast, a minority of Latinos (43 percent) strongly oppose the DREAM Act. Whites are also more likely than Latinos to support restrictive immigration policies, although African Americans are just as likely to support such immigration policies.

Regarding education policy, Latinos in Texas are more likely to support a greater role for government in public education. In general, Latinos view education as a more important policy issue than their Anglo counterparts. This could be for several reasons. First, Latinos are generally poorer and less educated than the majority white population and correctly see educational attainment as a key to success. Second, many Latinos are immigrants who view education as the ticket to the American Dream. Finally, Latinos have the highest high school dropout rates, and this reality has important ramifications for social, political, and economic advancement.

One related issue area with a significant divide in opinion between Anglos and Latinos is bilingual education. Most Latinos in Texas support the use of bilingual education—instruction in English and Spanish until students can transition to full English instruction. On the other hand, most Anglos oppose this policy, and support total immersion in English. A May 2010 *Texas Tribune* poll shows that 55 percent of white Texans strongly supported ending bilingual education, while only 22 percent of Latinos supported this position. Forty-four percent of Latinos strongly opposed ending bilingual education, while only 15 percent of whites strongly opposed ending bilingual education.[29] This policy, along with attitudes about an English Only law for Texas, is one of the most polarized by ethnicity in the state.

Redistricting in Texas

Every 10 years, the U.S. Census is charged with counting how many people live in the United States. The process of **reapportionment** involves re-calculating how many congressional districts each state will receive based on the state's population. For example, Texas gained four new congressional seats following the 2010 Census because of the explosive population growth of the state. Since the House of Representatives is capped at 435 members, other states had to lose some of their congressional seats. States such as New York lost congressional seats because their populations had decreased during the previous 10 years. The state legislature is tasked with drawing new congressional districts every 10 years to comply with the new overall number of seats allowed.

In 2011 the Texas Legislature drew new congressional districts (Figure 5.1A), a process called **redistricting**. This is a blatantly political procedure because the majority party uses it to retain power by creating as many friendly districts as it can. The Republicans in charge of the legislature attempted to draw as many Republican-voting districts as possible. If Democrats had been in control, they would have tried to maximize their number of seats as well. Because more than 67 percent of the population growth in Texas was a result of Latino immigration and birth rates among native-born Latinos and foreign-born Latinos, Latino leaders in the state

reapportionment process that takes place every 10 years to determine how many congressional seats each state will receive, depending on population shifts

redistricting the process of redrawing election districts and redistributing legislative representatives in the Texas House, Texas Senate, and U.S. House. This usually happens every 10 years to reflect shifts in population or in response to legal challenges in existing districts

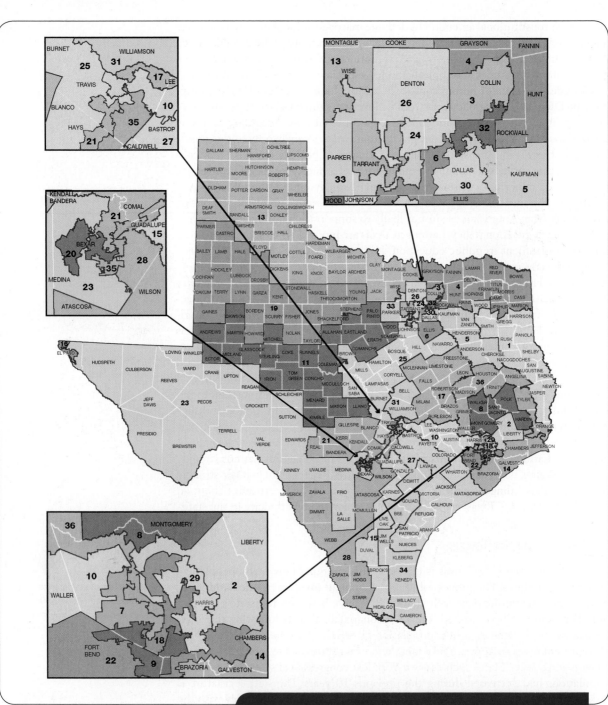

FIGURE 5.1A

Texas U.S. Congressional District Maps: Legislature Plan

The district map drawn by the Republican majority in the Texas Legislature in 2011 was designed to help Republicans win as many U.S. House seats as possible. However, Latino leaders complained that the plan didn't create more Latino-majority districts.

SOURCE: The Texas Legislative Council.

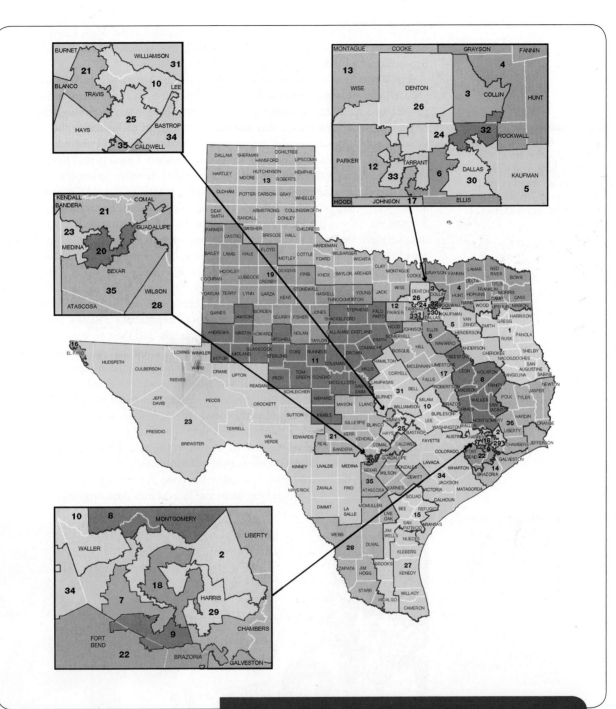

FIGURE 5.1B

Texas U.S. Congressional District Maps: Court Plan

By comparing the court-approved plan above with the Republican legislature's plan at left, we can see district lines were changed to comply with the Voting Rights Act and to create one new Latino-majority district (District 35, stretching from Bexar County to Travis County).

SOURCE: The Texas Legislative Council.

wanted at least two of the new seats to be majority Latino. Most Latino-majority districts in the state tend not to elect Republicans, which put the Republican-led legislature in a bind.

The terms by which Texas must comply with the Voting Rights Act further complicated the situation. Section 5 of the act requires that any changes to election procedures, including the drawing of new district lines, must go through the process of **preclearance**. This means that the U.S. Department of Justice or the District of Columbia Federal Court must approve the new district lines in order to make sure that the voting rights of minorities are not diminished. Districts that have been created to help minorities win cannot be dismantled in order to benefit a particular political party. For the most part, it is the southern states of the old Confederacy that are subject to this provision. Attorney General Greg Abbott has argued that Section 5 of the act violates the Tenth Amendment to the U.S. Constitution because it singles out particular states for preclearance. The preclearance requirement is but on example of the conflict between Texas and the federal government on a number of issues (see Chapter 2). Governor Perry has frequently criticized the federal government for its regulations and mandates. Nevertheless, Section 5 is still the law of the land.

In the 2011 redistricting round, several lawsuits were filed by different parties challenging the districts created by the Texas Legislature, and the federal court stepped in (Figure 5.1B). Ultimately, the legislature and the court created one new congressional district with a majority Latino population that stretched from Bexar County to Travis County along Interstate 35. The three other new districts were designed to elect Republicans. This was accomplished by splitting Travis County, the seat of Austin, into five congressional districts in order to dilute the Democratic vote. Since most Travis County voters are white Democrats, there are no protections under the law for diluting their vote. The U.S. representative for Austin, Democrat Lloyd Doggett, was forced to run in the new Latino majority district, since the other four districts were majority Republican.

Because of the federal court's lengthy process, the Texas primary was pushed back to May 29, 2012, much later than the late March date originally scheduled.

preclearance provision under Section 5 of the Voting Rights Act of 1965 requiring any changes to election procedures or district lines to be approved by the U.S. Department of Justice or the U.S. district court for the District of Columbia

In recent elections, immigration policy has been an issue as candidates try to balance concerns about illegal immigration with calls for immigrants' rights. In 2006 supporters of immigrants' rights participated in massive demonstrations in Texas.

This meant that Texas voters were not afforded a real choice in the Republican presidential primary, because Mitt Romney effectively clinched the nomination prior to May 29. While Texas voters could still vote in the primary, Romney was virtually assured of the nomination by that point.

One possible solution to reforming redistricting is to take the process away from the legislature. In Texas, the state legislature decides how the district lines will be drawn, and critics often say that this is the only time when politicians choose their voters and not the other way around. Some states, such as Arizona, however, have taken the responsibility away from the legislature and created an independent redistricting commission. Such a commission, supporters argue, would create fairer districts in Texas without the influence of politicians who have a vested interest in protecting their seats and political parties. According to a May 2011 *Texas Tribune* poll, 40 percent of respondents voiced support in principle for such a system, while 30 percent were opposed, and 30 percent were unsure of the plan.[30] Changing the system of redistricting will be challenging because legislators of both parties greatly benefit from the ability to influence how district lines are drawn.

Contemporary Barriers to Voting

While the days of poll taxes are over, there are still barriers to voting in contemporary Texas. For example, in many cities, council members are elected at-large, meaning that there are no individual districts for the city. Consider a city that has 10 city council seats and is 20 percent African American, 25 percent Latino, and 55 percent white. In at-large races, the white majority could theoretically capture all of the city's 10 council seats. If the city had a single-member district system, there would be a distinct possibility that at least four of the seats would be held by minorities. Austin has an at-large system of electing city council members, but is currently considering changing the system in order to provide for better geographic and racial representation.

Other tactics for preventing certain groups from voting include reducing the number of polling places in certain areas, the presence of broken voting machines, misleading information provided to voters, and voter intimidation. While such practices are becoming less frequent, there are still reports of them in every contested election.

● Campaigns

> **Present the main features of election campaigns in Texas**

Political campaigns are efforts of candidates to win support of the voters. The goal of the campaign is to attain sufficient support to win the primary election in March and the general election in November. Some campaigns last a year or more; however, the more accepted practice is to limit the campaign to a few weeks before the election. In Texas, campaigns to win the party primary begin in January and continue to the second Tuesday in March. Labor Day is the traditional start of the general election campaign, which lasts from early September to the first Tuesday following the first Monday in November. However, in recent elections, statewide campaigns began even earlier than September.

In 2010 and 2012 interestingly, the distinguishing feature of the campaigns was the lack of emphasis on state issues, including the pressing issue of the state budget.

Instead, Republicans ran against the national Democratic administration, whereas Democrats tried to distance themselves from President Obama and his policies.

Campaigns involve attempts to reach the voters through print and electronic media, the mail, door-to-door campaigning, speeches to large and small groups, coffee hours, and telephone solicitation. Costs are enormous. During the 1980s and 1990s, candidates for statewide races spent as much as $30 million. A new record up to that point for campaign spending was set in the 2002 gubernatorial race, when the Democrat Tony Sanchez and the Republican Rick Perry spent a total of $88 million. In 2006 the amount raised in the gubernatorial race fell to $53.4 million, 28.7 percent of which went to the two independent candidates, Carole Keeton Strayhorn and Kinky Friedman. In 2010 total campaign contributions by Democrats seeking the governorship came to nearly $37 million and total contributions by Republicans came to nearly $55 million—an amount far larger than the $30 million raised by Republicans in 2006 because of the primary challenge to Rick Perry by Kay Bailey Hutchison. For all statewide offices, Republican campaign contributions overwhelmed Democratic campaign contributions. Total contributions in state House and state Senate races were also far greater for Republicans than for Democrats. There is no question, then, that money is important for candidate success in Texas. Candidates must continually raise money by hosting fundraisers with donors, making phone calls to potential donors, and setting up websites that make it easy for ordinary citizens to contribute.(Table 5.3 and Table 5.4).

Candidates who run in Texas for federal office, such as the U.S. Congress, are subject to federal campaign finance laws, which are stricter than state laws and which impose limits for campaign contributions. Candidates for state offices, however, are subject to state laws enacted in 1991 when the Texas Ethics Commission (TEC) was established. State candidates and lobbyists must file quarterly reports with the TEC, although there are no limits to campaign contributions for state races. The state imposes a moratorium on contributions to state legislators just prior to the beginning of a legislative session.

In some places in the United States, the parties have a major role in the running of political campaigns. That is not the case in Texas. Here the candidates have the major responsibility for campaign strategy, for running their campaigns, and for raising money. At times, party leaders will try to recruit individuals to run for office, especially if no candidates volunteer to seek an office or if the candidates appear to be weak ones. For the most part, the benefit of the party to a candidate in Texas is that the party provides the party label under which the candidate runs. That "Democratic" or "Republican" label is, of course, important to candidates because many voters use the party label in casting their votes, especially for low-visibility races. The party also contains numerous activists whom the candidate can tap for campaign tasks such as manning phone banks, preparing mailings, and posting campaign ads. Additionally, the party does provide some support for the candidate, most commonly through campaigns to get out the vote for the party's candidates. Campaigning in Texas, however, is generally left up to the candidate, and in that effort, the parties take a secondary role.

Name recognition is essential for candidates. Incumbents hold a distinct advantage in this regard. Officeholders have many ways to achieve name visibility. They can mail out news releases, send newsletters to their constituents, appear on radio talk shows, and give speeches to civic clubs. Newspaper coverage and local television news coverage of the politician can increase name recognition. Challengers have a more difficult time getting this crucial name visibility, although new media sources such as Facebook and Twitter accounts can help both incumbents and challengers gain name recognition, especially among young people.

TABLE 5.3

Amount Raised by All Candidates in Texas, 2010, Listed by Political Party*

OFFICE	DEMOCRAT	REPUBLICAN	THIRD-PARTY
Governor	$36,994,646	$54,682,462	0
Judicial	$401,025	$2,592,108	$110
Other Statewide	$3,150,119	$21,387,407	$1,547
House	$28,780,507	$48,634,984	$26,552
Senate	$3,979,924	$6,991,616	$23,007

*Excludes contributions to candidates not up for election in 2010 and one candidate for state senate who withdrew.
SOURCE: Calculated from Institute on Money in State Politics.

TABLE 5.4

Campaign Contributions in Statewide Executive Offices: Texas General Elections 2010

OFFICE	CANDIDATE	$ CONTRIBUTED	% VOTE*
Governor	R. Perry (R)	$39,328,540	54.97
	B. White (D)	$26,291,535	42.29
Lt. Governor	D. Dewhurst (R)	$9,240,480	61.78
	L. Chavez-Thompson	$958,040	34.83
Agriculture Commissioner	Todd Staples (R)	$1,742,941	60.82
	Hank Gilbert (D)	$336,363	35.79
Attorney General	Greg Abbott (R)	$5,828,370	64.05
	Barbara Radnafsky (D)	$1,135,031	33.66
Comptroller	Susan Combs (R)	$2,744,001	83.16
	None		
Land Commissioner	Jerry Patterson (R)	$864,688	61.66
	Hector Uribe (D)	$102,487	35.28
Railroad Commissioner	David Porter (R)	$564,488	59.40
	Jeff Weems (D)	$287,248	36.23

*Numbers do not add to 100 percent because of the presence of third-party candidates.
SOURCES: Institute on Money in State Politics and Texas Secretary of State.

The case of William R. Clements illustrates the importance of name recognition. In 1978, William R. Clements was a political unknown. He spent thousands of dollars of his own fortune to gain name recognition. He leased hundreds of billboards throughout the state. Each had a blue background with white letters proclaiming "CLEMENTS." In the print media, early ads bore the simple message, "ELECT CLEMENTS." The unprecedented scale of this advertising effort made Clements's name better known among the voters in Texas. This, in turn, stimulated interest in his campaign's message. Clements won the race for governor, becoming the first Republican to hold that office in Texas since the end of Reconstruction.

Payments for media ads account for the greatest expense in most campaigns. In metropolitan areas, television, radio, and print advertising are very costly. Full-page ads in metropolitan newspapers can cost as much as $40,000. Candidates for metropolitan districts in the Texas House of Representatives and Texas Senate need to reach only a small portion of the population, but they are forced to purchase ads in media sources that go to hundreds of thousands of people not represented. In rural areas, any individual ad is relatively inexpensive. However, candidates must advertise in dozens of small newspapers and radio stations, and the costs add up.

Even more important, the campaigns must be well designed. A slipup in a well-funded campaign can do great harm, as David Dewhurst discovered in the early stages of his 2002 campaign for lieutenant governor. Dewhurst's personal wealth and his willingness to spend it had already pushed Bill Ratliff, the state senator elected by his colleagues to succeed Rick Perry as lieutenant governor, out of the race for the office. And Dewhurst was not remiss in spending money. He purchased a very expensive four-page ad in *Texas Monthly* that was intended to advertise his appointment by Governor Perry as the state's new chairman of the Governor's Task Force on Homeland Security. In the wake of the September 11, 2001, terrorist attacks, such an appointment might be turned into an important political asset. Indeed, Dewhurst listed "protecting the physical safety of all Texans" as the top issue in his campaign. In the ad, however, a military officer appears in dress uniform against a background of the American flag. Unfortunately for Dewhurst, the officer is not wearing an American military uniform, but the uniform of the German Luftwaffe with German military insignia and a name tag bearing a German flag. Alongside the picture is a plea from Dewhurst to support "the brave men and women of our armed forces." Such an ad can be a candidate's worst nightmare. Dewhurst had spent a substantial sum to show in a widely circulated, full-color magazine on glossy paper that the person in charge of homeland security for the state did not know the difference between an American officer and a German officer![31]

Some impressive but limited evidence indicates that television can be a very valuable tool for a Texas political candidate. On four occasions in the 1990s, Republican Supreme Court candidates were challenged in the primary by candidates with little, if any, organized support and minimal funding. Yet the insurgent candidates all showed great strength in areas where the established candidates did not run television ads. Of course, there may be additional explanations for the strength of established candidates in areas where ads were shown. Perhaps the candidates worked harder in those areas or were better organized. And in some areas, candidates may have had stronger name recognition than their opponents.[32]

None of the insurgent candidates had the resources to run television ads; only the established candidates did, and only in some media markets. It was the support the established candidates received in the areas where they ran television ads that led to their victories. It is important to note that since the data all relate to the Republican primary, the effect of the political party label is controlled. If we compare the percentage difference in votes for established candidates in areas where television ads were run with votes in areas where no ads were run, the difference is remarkable: established candidates received between 12 percent and 18.5 percent more votes in media markets where they bought television time.[33]

In one of the closest races of 2012, Democrat Pete Gallego (pictured here) defeated U.S. Congressman Francisco Canseco in District 23 (R.-San Antonio). The campaigns and outside groups spent millions on advertising, much of which was negative.

Given the myriad factors that may explain electoral success, we should beware of imputing victory in these judicial races solely to television ads. On the other hand, the general pattern of high margins of victory in areas where television was used is so powerful that it cannot be ignored.

● Thinking Critically about Elections in Texas

Elections in Texas are essential to the state's functioning democracy. It is important to think critically about how elections are structured and who benefits from the types of districts that are created by the state legislature. Because of the single-member district system, third parties are disadvantaged in state politics, and this has important implications for how policy is made.

The state has a formal process for candidates who want to serve their fellow citizens in elective office. The candidate must first run in a party primary; then, if the candidate does not receive a majority of the votes, he or she must run in a runoff primary. Ideally, the battles of primaries and runoff primaries will be forgotten and the party will come together in support of the nominee in order to win the election. However, what often happens is that the primaries and runoffs create enormous conflicts and divisions within the party that are not healed. The opposition then exploits those party divisions so that their candidate can win the election.

Redistricting in Texas has been very controversial since the passage of the Voting Rights Act in 1965. Texas is subject to additional constraints when it draws new district lines, and the federal courts have stepped in to make sure that the voting rights of African Americans and Latinos have not diminished. Election results are greatly influenced by the kind of districts that are drawn, which is why it is so important to pay close attention to this process, which occurs by law every ten years. Districts do not just arise out of thin air—politicians create them to advance their own interests as well as their party's goals.

While Republicans have won every statewide election since 1994, the growing Latino population and increased diversification of the state may change this in years to come. While not as strongly Democratic as African Americans, Latinos in Texas are more likely to identify as Democrats. As more Latinos register to vote and participate in state elections, Texas may once again become a competitive two-party state.

Politics is everywhere in Texas. Campaigns—especially statewide campaigns—are therefore very expensive. For the most part, the candidates themselves must raise the money necessary to win an election. Gubernatorial campaigns can cost $40 million or more. One effect of the high cost of campaigns in Texas is that candidates are often very wealthy individuals willing to use their own money in their campaigns.

Although Texas once tried to narrow the franchise, primarily by limiting the right to vote through poll taxes and white primaries, in recent years it has tried to expand the franchise through the motor voter law and through early voting. Yet voter participation in Texas is quite low. That is probably because of the demographics of Texas voters, but it may also be a result of the scheduling of elections in Texas, the vast number of elections, and the large number of low-visibility candidates for office. Participation in elections is important because public policies are determined by who is elected to office. For example, policies related to funding for higher education that affect all college students in Texas are dependent on elected officials and the people they appoint. It also remains to be seen whether the state's new voter identification law will have an impact on voter turnout in the state.

Ⓢ **Practice online with:** Chapter 5 Diagnostic Quiz ▪ Chapter 5 Key Term Flashcards

Features of Elections in Texas

■ **Describe the types of elections held in Texas and how they work (pp. 135–38)**

Texas allows all registered voters the choice to vote in one party primary during an election season. Should a candidate not receive a majority of votes in a primary, a runoff is held to determine who the party nominee will be. The general election ultimately decides who is elected to office.

Key Terms

primary election (p. 135)

runoff primary (p. 135)

open primary (p. 135)

closed primary (p. 136)

general election (p. 136)

special election (p. 136)

Practice Quiz

1. In a primary election, *(p. 135)*
   a) voters choose all local officials who will hold office in the following year.
   b) voters select federal officials for office.
   c) voters select their party's candidate for a general election.
   d) voters choose third-party candidates.
   e) voters cast ballots on proposed constitutional amendments.

2. Which of the following is *not* a type of election found in Texas? *(pp. 135–36)*
   a) general
   b) primary
   c) distinguished
   d) special
   e) runoff primary

3. Officially, Texas has a *(p. 136)*
   a) joint primary.
   b) extended primary.
   c) open primary.
   d) closed primary.
   e) jumbled primary.

4. The first Tuesday following the first Monday in November of even-numbered years is the day for which election? *(p. 136)*
   a) primary election
   b) runoff primary
   c) runoff for the general election
   d) secondary election
   e) general election

5. When are gubernatorial elections held? *(p. 136)*
   a) during presidential election years
   b) during odd-numbered years
   c) during even-numbered years that are not presidential election years.
   d) every year
   e) every six months

Participation in Texas Elections

■ **Explain how the rules for voting affect turnout among different groups of Texans (pp. 138–53)**

Participation in Texas elections varies by election. Turnout is lowest in party primaries, followed by elections when a presidential candidate is not on the ballot. Latinos and those of lower socioeconomic status are also less likely to vote in state elections.

Key Terms

Nineteenth Amendment (p. 138)

suffrage (p. 138)

poll tax (p. 139)

early registration (p. 140)

white primary (p. 140)

Jaybird Party (p. 140)

Voting Rights Act of 1965 (p. 141)

motor voter law (p. 142)

early voting (p. 146)

reapportionment (p. 149)

redistricting (p. 149)

preclearance (p. 152)

Practice Quiz

6. Which of the following is true? *(p. 139)*
   a) Poll taxes are legal.
   b) Women acquired the right to vote in the original 1876 Texas Constitution.
   c) The poll tax restricted the participation of poor people in the general election.
   d) You do not have to be a resident of Texas to vote in Texas.
   e) Latinos vote at higher rates than African Americans.

7. In which of the following elections is voter turnout the highest? *(p. 144)*
   a) presidential elections
   b) gubernatorial general elections
   c) city elections
   d) runoff elections
   e) off-year congressional elections

8. The two most important factors in determining whether someone will vote are *(p. 145)*
   a) income and education.
   b) education and family history of voting.
   c) income and gender.
   d) party membership and gender.
   e) ethnicity and race.

9. Who has benefited the most from early voting? *(p. 146)*
   a) Republicans
   b) Democrats
   c) All parties have benefited equally
   d) Independents
   e) Greens

10. The procedure by which certain states, such as Texas, are required to obtain approval every time they make changes to districts is called *(p. 152)*
    a) redistricting.
    b) reapportionment.
    c) preclearance.
    d) external validation.
    e) judicial review.

 Practice Online
Video exercise: *Voter ID Laws*

Campaigns

■ **Present the main features of election campaigns in Texas (pp. 153–57)**

Because of Texas's size, statewide campaigns can be expensive. There are several major media markets, which makes television advertising very expensive. Grassroots efforts to mobilize voters is also costly because of the large territory. This means wealthy candidates are often on the ballot.

Practice Quiz

11. The distinguishing feature of the 2010 and 2012 campaigns in Texas was *(p. 153)*
    a) the increased presence of third party candidates.
    b) the lack of emphasis on state issues.
    c) the candidates' focus on the state budget.
    d) the unusually low levels of money spent on media ads.
    e) the candidates' focus on welfare reforms.

12. The traditional start of the campaign season is *(p. 153)*
    a) Memorial Day.
    b) Labor Day.
    c) Christmas.
    d) Thanksgiving.
    e) Veterans Day.

13. Who is the first Republican to become Texas governor since Reconstruction? *(p. 155)*
    a) William Clements
    b) Rick Perry
    c) George W. Bush
    d) Ann Richards
    e) Kinky Friedman

14. The most costly item for most political campaigns is *(p. 156)*
    a) travel.
    b) security.
    c) fund-raising.
    d) media.
    e) food.

15. In 2002, David Dewhurst's ad in the *Texas Monthly* featuring German veterans hurt in his campaign for which office? *(p. 156)*
    a) state Senate
    b) U.S. Senate
    c) lieutenant governor
    d) governor
    e) attorney general

Practice Online
Video exercise: *Party Values*

Recommended Websites

Texas Secretary of State
www.sos.state.tx.us/

Texas Tribune
www.texastribune.org

The highway construction industry had a strong interest in the Trans-Texas Corridor project and attempted to forward that interest through lobbying and campaign contributions. Here, construction company executives appear with Governor Perry and transportation officials after signing a contract related to the proposed project.

Interest Groups and Lobbying

WHAT GOVERNMENT DOES AND WHY IT MATTERS In 2002, Governor Rick Perry proposed the Trans-Texas Corridor. It was to be the largest privatized tollway in the United States, consisting of 4,000 miles of state roads at a cost of $175 billion. The idea of privatized roads was nothing new. Indiana, for example, has a 157-mile toll road that has been leased to a private entity since 2006, and Chicago has leased its 8-mile Skyway since 2004. It was the massive size of the Trans-Texas Corridor, however, that made Governor Perry's proposal so extraordinary.

In June 2003, Governor Perry signed legislation that authorized the Trans-Texas Corridor and expanded the powers of the Texas Department of Transportation to include road privatization. The creation of such a vast new highway system would be an enormous boon to the highway construction industry. Accordingly, the industry tried to promote its interests in the highway system through campaign contributions to key politicians. Prior to Governor Perry's announcement of his highway plan, three major construction industry companies (Zachry Construction, Pate Engineers, and Othon) had made political contributions totaling $113,280 from 1999 to 2000. In the 2002 election cycle after Governor Perry announced his construction plans, these three companies tripled their contributions. The same occurred with the construction companies Williams Brothers, Ballenger Construction, Parsons Corporation, and Klotz Associates. Contractors were particularly interested in contributing to Lt. Governor David Dewhurst, who possesses significant power in the Texas Senate. Governor Perry also received large contributions, as did state senators who sit on the Senate Transportation Committee. The Trans-Texas Corridor contractors also spent somewhere between $2,770,000 and $6,130,000 (exact amounts are unknown because Texas reporting laws provide for huge ranges in lobbying contracts) on 163 different contracts with lobbyists.

As the size of the project sank into the public consciousness, opposition emerged, most notably from the landowners who became aware of the massive acreage that would be condemned for the Corridor. In 2005 property owners were angered by the U.S. Supreme Court decision in *Kelo v. City of New London*,[1] which upheld the condemnation of private property in order to enhance city revenues. That led to public outcry in Texas (and to a considerable degree nationwide) favoring private property rights over the taking of property for questionable public uses. The public outcry increased when estimates were made that these privatized roads could still cost Texans billions of dollars. Interest group discontent soon spread to the political arena. During the 2006 primary and election seasons, all Governor Perry's opponents came out against the Trans-Texas Corridor, as did both political parties in their official platforms.

Responding to this overwhelming opposition, the Department of Transportation in 2009 decided to abandon the idea of a Trans-Texas Corridor, replacing it with a series of more traditional right-of-way improvements in the state's transportation and utility infrastructure. In 2010 the Federal Highway Administration formally ended the project by issuing a "no action" ruling on the proposal. This had the effect of canceling the agreement between the Texas Department of Transportation and the private construction companies. The final nail in the coffin came at the end of the 2011 legislative session when a bill ending the proposal passed both houses and was signed by the governor. The controversy over the Trans-Texas Corridor continued to haunt Perry throughout the 2012 Republican presidential primary debates.

The case of the Trans-Texas Corridor is a classic example of interest-group politics where powerful economic and political interests are mobilized both for and against controversial pieces of legislation. We will explore interest group politics in Texas in more detail in this chapter.

chaptergoals

- **Define interest groups and describe the major ways they try to influence Texas government** (pages 163–72)

- **Describe the role of PACs in Texas elections** (pages 172–75)

- **Explain how ordinary individuals can influence Texas government** (pages 175–76)

Interest Groups in the Political Process

Define interest groups and describe the major ways they try to influence Texas government

It is probably true that all of us have political interests, goals, or objectives that can be achieved with governmental intervention. Many of us, however, will never act to achieve those goals. A few of us may speak privately to a legislator or other official. However, some of us will join with others to try to convince the government to help us achieve our interests. When we do that, we have formed an **interest group**.

It has often been claimed that business-oriented interest groups dominate the Texas Legislature. Using campaign contributions, political pressure, and sometimes corruption, "The Lobby," as pro-business groups were called, was once purported to run Texas government. Some of the most influential business leaders of the state belonged to the "8F Crowd." 8F was the number on a suite of rooms at the Lamar Hotel in Houston, where George R. Brown held court. Brown was a founder of Brown & Root, one of the world's largest construction firms and until April 2007 part of the even larger Halliburton Company. He met regularly with other fabulously wealthy Texans such as Jesse Jones of Texas Commerce Bank and Tenneco, Gus Wortham of American General Insurance, and James Elkins of the Vinson & Elkins law firm. These men socialized together and worked together to promote their political interests. For 40 years they were considered the kingmakers in Texas politics who determined much of the important policy of state government.[2]

interest group an organization established to influence the government's programs and policies

Lobbying, derided by some as "Austin's oldest profession," is big business in Texas. When the legislature is in session, many lobbyists can be spotted around the capitol waiting to meet with legislators. When the legislature is not in session, lobbyists are often busy with campaign activities.

The "8F Crowd" was, of course, an interest group—an elite, wealthy, powerful, pro-business interest group. Although the "8F Crowd" is long gone from the Texas political scene, much of what they did is still done in Texas politics by other interest groups, though no modern-day group is ascribed the influence that was allegedly held by the "8F Crowd."

Nevertheless, Texas is known as a state that has long had powerful interest groups. During the Texas Constitutional Convention of 1875, an interest group played an important role. That was the Grange, a powerful farmers' organization, of which many of the framers were members. As Chapter 3 indicated, the Constitution of 1876 reflected many of the values of Grange members. It was a document for rural Texas that was pro–small farmer and opposed to a powerful state government.

With the development of a strong oil and gas industry in Texas in the first half of the twentieth century, the oil industry began playing an important role in state politics. In one-party states, interest groups often become powerful political actors, perhaps because one-party states tend to have a small number of important sectors in their economies and limited economic development. However, Texas has in the past 20 years moved from a Democratic one-party system to a competitive two-party system to a Republican-dominated system. And with an expanding Hispanic vote, it may soon become a more competitive two-party system again. It also now has a strong and diversified economy. Yet interest groups maintain great influence.[3]

Interest Groups and Policy Makers

Interest groups want something from policy makers: they want policy that is beneficial for their groups. On the other hand, policy makers benefit from developing relationships with interest groups. From those groups, the policy maker gains information, since the interest groups can provide substantial expertise in areas that are their special concern. Additionally, interest groups can provide campaign funds to the policy maker. In a state as large as Texas, with numerous media markets and with some party competition, considerable campaign funds are necessary to run and win elections. An interest group can help raise money from its membership for a candidate sympathetic to the interest group's goals. Also, interest groups can supply votes to the policy maker. They can assist in mobilizing their own groups, and they can supply campaign workers to distribute campaign leaflets and to operate phone banks to get out the vote. Interest groups can also publicize issues through press conferences, press releases, publications, conferences, and hearings and even by filing lawsuits. Finally, interest groups can engage in research and education programs. It has become increasingly common for interest groups to engage in public education programs by running advertisements in the Texas media explaining why their particular approaches to a public policy problem would be more beneficial to Texans in general.

Unlike a private citizen interested in and involved in politics, larger or better-funded interest groups have several advantages: (1) time; (2) money; (3) expertise; and (4) continuity.

Although concerned citizens do have an impact on public policy in Texas, organized and well-funded interest groups have an advantage in affecting the policy process. It is difficult for a concerned citizen from Houston to spend time in Austin developing relationships with policy makers and trying to convince those policy makers to support public policies that are compatible with the individual's goals. On the other hand, if that individual joins with like-minded people to create an organized interest group, the group may have a greater likelihood of achieving policy goals. It might be possible to fund an office in Austin with a staff that could monitor events in state government on a daily basis and develop relationships with key policy makers. Additionally, although some individuals in Texas do have the money to provide substantial campaign support to policy makers, even those individuals can get more "bang for the buck" if they join with others in **bundling** their funds into a larger contribution from the interest group. The creation of an organized interest group also allows for the development of a staff. The staff can gain in-depth knowledge of an area of policy far greater than could be gained by most individuals working alone. Also, an individual may be intensely concerned with an issue in one legislative session, but may find it difficult to sustain that interest over a period of many legislative sessions. The larger, better-funded, more successful organized interest groups have continuity. They are in Austin, developing relationships with policy makers and presenting the views of the organization day in and day out, year in and year out. The result is that legislators and other policy makers can develop long-standing relationships with the interest groups and the groups' representatives in Austin.

On September 15, 2010, Governor Perry received a briefing on tort reform at the Austin airport. He then flew to Houston and was taken to the Petroleum Club, where he dined with the tort reform political action committee (PAC) of an interest group, Texans for Lawsuit Reform. He was then driven to Mach Industrial Group in Houston, where he held a press conference about his endorsement by the PAC.[4] It was an important day for Perry—though not surprising—he had gotten the official support of a group described as "arguably the most powerful interest group in Texas politics, in large part because of the massive amounts of money it raises from the state's business community."[5] Texans for Lawsuit Reform helped reshape the Texas Supreme Court into a more pro-business court, and it has reshaped the legislature into a more pro-business body. With Texans for Lawsuit Reform on Perry's side, he had an incredibly powerful and wealthy interest group backing him in the 2010 election. And Texans for Lawsuit Reform knew it could help re-elect a pro-business candidate to the governorship.

Types of Interest Groups and Lobbyists

Interest groups strive to influence public opinion, to make their views known to policy makers, and to elect and support policy makers who are friendly to their points of view. To accomplish these goals, interest groups usually maintain **lobbyists** in Austin who try to gain access to policy makers and communicate their objectives to them. There are several different types of lobbyists. Some interest groups have full-time staffs in Austin whose members work as lobbyists. One form of interest group is, of course, a corporation, and companies often have government relations departments that lobby for the companies' interests. Lobbyists may be employed by an interest group to deal with one issue, or they may be employed by an interest group on a regular basis. Some lobbyists represent only one client; others will represent large numbers of clients. All lobbyists, however, must be able to reach and communicate with policy makers. Corporate interest groups tend to use either government relations departments or law firms to represent their interests in Austin. Often industries have broad interests that need representation. For example, an insurance company may have one specific interest it wishes to have represented. However, the insurance industry as a whole also has a wide range of issues that need representation, and thus it will form an industry-wide interest group.

bundling the interest-group practice of combining campaign contributions from several sources into one larger contribution from the group, so as to increase the group's impact on the candidate

lobbyist an individual employed by an interest group who tries to influence governmental decisions on behalf of that group

Some interest groups focus on a single issue, such as abortion. When Texas passed a law requiring women to undergo a sonogram 24 hours before having an abortion, anti-abortion groups applauded the measure, but some women's groups protested against it.

Interest groups may also represent professional groups. One of the most influential professional groups in Austin is the Texas Medical Association, which represents the interests of doctors in state government. Other professional groups represent accountants, chiropractors, opticians, dentists, and teachers.

That teachers are an important interest group suggests still another type of interest group—public-employee interest groups. Public school teachers may be the largest and most effective of these groups, but firefighters, police officers, and even justices of the peace and constables all are represented in Austin.

Some interest groups are formed with a single issue in mind. For example, an interest group may be concerned about the regulation of abortion or school vouchers or tort reform or the environment. Other interest groups are concerned with multiple issues that affect the groups. Public school teachers, for example, are concerned about job security, qualifications of teachers, health insurance, pensions, salaries, and other matters that affect the lives of their members.

Civil rights groups such as the National Association for the Advancement of Colored People, the League of United Latin American Citizens, or the Mexican American Legal Defense Fund are concerned about civil rights issues affecting the lives primarily of African Americans and Latinos. Interestingly, not only do these groups often try to influence public opinion and the legislature, but they have had notable success in representing their groups' interests through litigation, especially in the federal courts.

Other public interest groups try to promote consumer, environmental, and general public issues. Examples of these groups are Public Citizen, the Sierra Club, and Common Cause. Groups such as the Sierra Club work to promote environmental interests, whereas groups such as Public Citizen and Common Cause tend to have broader interests and work to promote more open government. These groups rarely have much funding, but they often can provide policy makers with information and expertise. In addition, they can mobilize their membership to support or oppose bills, and they can publicize matters that are important to their goals.

Getting Access to Policy Makers

In order to communicate the goals of their interest groups to policy makers, lobbyists must first gain access to those policy makers. Gaining access to policy makers, of course, imposes on the time of legislators, so lobbyists will often spend significant sums entertaining them. That entertainment is one of the most criticized aspects of lobbying. But from the lobbyists' perspective, entertainment is an important tool for reaching policy makers and putting them in a congenial frame of mind. Entertainment by lobbyists can involve expensive dinners, golfing, and other activities. For example, lobbyists for Texas Utilities (TXU) bought a $300 saddle for one state representative and a $200 bench for another. TXU lobbyists also treated a state senator to a trip to the Masters golf tournament and picked up the dinner tab, as well. One House member received a gun as a gift, another received a jacket, and several got "deer-processing" costs paid for by these lobbyists.[6]

When Representative Lon Burnam proposed legislation to regulate consumer versions of "stun guns," the lobbyist for TASER International as a joke gave Burnam a gift of a pink "stun gun" valued at more than $150. The "stun gun" was, of course, a minor expenditure.[7] Others are much more lavish. When Governor Perry wanted to go to the Rose Bowl game, the trucking lobby picked up the costs of a private jet for $14,580. The former Texas Motor Transportation Association president who arranged the trip said, "Let's face it, if you have a way to help the sitting governor get somewhere he wants to be and to help our industry get where it needs to be, to me it becomes a no-brainer."[8] In the first two months of 2011, lobbyists spent more than $1.2 million, with much of that money going toward events, goods, and gifts for lawmakers and others in state government.[9]

Texas lawmakers receive only $600 per month plus $150 a day when on legislative business, but lawmakers are permitted to use campaign contributions for expenses associated with holding office. This allows interest groups to fund significant lavish benefits for lawmakers. Indeed, about one-third of the spending of North Texas lawmakers—about $3.4 million of roughly $10 million in 2007–09—has gone to fund things other than campaign expenditures. Senator Florence Shapiro, for example, has used her contributions to fund a car lease for a Mercedes Benz and to pay for conference stays at the Ritz-Carlton in Palm Beach, the Venetian in Las Vegas, and the Hay-Adams in Washington, D.C. Thirty-six North Texas lawmakers spent nearly $560,000 on travel and entertainment, $470,000 on Austin living expenses, and $290,000 on food.[10]

Sometimes lobbyists have long-standing personal ties to policy makers, and those bonds can be invaluable to the lobbyists' clients. Access to policy makers may also be gained by building support for an issue among their constituents. Constituents may be encouraged, for example, to write or call legislators about a bill and offer their opinions. Essentially, the interest group tries to mobilize interested voters to get involved in the political process on behalf of the groups' goals.

One important way of gaining access to those in government is to employ former officials as lobbyists. A lobbyist who is a former legislator often has friends in the legislature and can use that friendship to gain access. Additionally, a former legislator often is in an exceptionally good position to understand the personal relationships and informal power centers that must be contacted to accomplish a legislative objective. As a result, some of the best-paid lobbyists in Austin are former Texas state officials and often are former legislators.

In 2010, 65 registered lobbyists were former legislators. What they have in common is knowledge of "how to pass bills, to kill them, whom to talk to, which clerks are friendly, whose birthdays are coming up—all inside stuff that makes the government machine whir."[11] Other especially valuable lobbyists have been former committee clerks for major committees and chiefs of staff of members who were on major committees.[12] Ten recently retired lawmakers were lobbyists in the 2009 legislative session. The 10 had a total of 68 lobbying contracts allowing them to generate between $2,025,000 and $3,890,000 in fees. One gets a sense of the value of these ex-legislators-turned-lobbyists from the explanation Representative Jim Pitts gave for sponsoring an amendment that was pushed by an AT&T lobbyist and former legislator, Pat Heggerty. The amendment would have forced the state to pay for rerouting phone lines for road projects. Said Representative Pitts of the amendment, "I was just trying to help Pat out."[13] The amendment later failed to pass.

It is not only former legislators who can move on to successful lobbying careers. Forty Perry aides either have left the administration to become lobbyists or have joined the administration after having been lobbyists. Some have moved back and forth from administration to lobbying in a revolving door fashion. Five of Perry's closest campaign aides have been lobbyists. Two of his ex-aides are now lobbyists who are also heading pro-Perry PACs.[14]

One former-legislator-turned-lobbyist who reversed course and went back into the legislature is Todd Hunter. Hunter had served in the legislature from 1989

Is He a Lobbyist?

Lobbyists are individuals hired by interest groups to advocate on their behalf to state lawmakers. Organizations ranging from business groups to environmental groups to teachers' groups all employ lobbyists to advance their agendas. Not all groups technically lobby legislators. They might occasionally interact with a legislator, but their goal is to advocate on behalf of their agenda in general terms. But sometimes the line can be blurred between lobbying and general advocacy. This distinction is crucial because in Texas, as in many other states, there are laws requiring lobbyists to register and report their activities in a spirit of full disclosure so that the public can see precisely how much money is being spent to influence legislators.

Consider the case of the interest group Empower Texans and its subsidiary known as Texans for Fiscal Responsibility. The organization is committed to increasing the number of conservative legislators in Texas and promoting conservative ideals. It has aligned with the Tea Party wing of the Republican Party in calling for reduced taxes and budget cuts to balance the state budget. Notably, Empower Texans and Texans for Fiscal Responsibility have refused to endorse some Republican incumbents in the state legislature, instead supporting opponents who are more conservative.

In 2012, two Republicans who were not endorsed by Empower Texans and Texans for Fiscal Responsibility filed a complaint with the Texas Ethics Commission (TEC) claiming that the head of these groups, Michael Quinn Sullivan, had lobbied during the most recent legislative session despite the fact that he was not registered. In Texas, lobbyists must register with the TEC in order to conduct their activities. They must also reveal their clients and how much they are compensated for their services.

The two state representatives, Jim Keffer and Vicki Truitt, allege that Sullivan communicated with state rep-

Michael Quinn Sullivan
President, Texans for Fiscal Responsibility

resentatives and their staff about their priorities for the legislative session. In particular, they claim that the group opposed the re-election of Speaker Straus within the Texas House in favor of a more conservative legislator. In addition, the group lobbied the legislature to oppose the use of the state's $9.6 billion Rainy Day Fund to balance the state budget. The complaint alleges that the group actively lobbied legislators and did not merely take public positions on these issues.

Keffer and Truitt also allege that Texans for Fiscal Responsibility failed to file campaign finance disclosure forms for the last quarter of 2011, as required by state law. They insist that it is hard to believe that the organization did not make contributions to politicians during this period. Because Sullivan did not register, he did not reveal who was funding his organization. In addition, the law requires that any expenditures over $100 by an

organization must be documented and reported. The complaint suggests that the group did not reveal expenditures.

Sullivan claims that the two legislators are upset that they were not endorsed by Texans for Fiscal Responsibility and did not receive campaign contributions. In particular, Truitt's Republican opponent in the 2012 primary was endorsed by the organization, and Sullivan actively campaigned against her in the past. He argues that the timing of the complaint is suspect coming soon before an election and that discussions with legislators are not the primary purpose of the organization.

The TEC was expected to investigate the allegations and decide whether to pursue any additional measures against the group. If the commission finds that the group indeed lobbied and failed to register, then it would be fined. The same is true if the commission finds that campaign contributions were made in violation of Texas law.

critical thinking questions

1. What exactly is a lobbyist? How is a lobbying different from general advocacy? Why do you think Texas disclosure laws are different for lobbyists than for general advocacy groups?

2. Based on the limited information above, is Michael Quinn Sullivan a lobbyist? Should he have registered with the state? Why or why not?

to 1997. An active lobbyist as late as 2007, he was elected to the Texas House in 2008.[15] Jerry Patterson, now Texas land commissioner, was a state senator, became a lobbyist, and was able to move to his current statewide office with little criticism of his role as a lobbyist. However, David Sibley, a state senator who became a lobbyist and then tried to regain his old position, caught tremendous political flak for this decision and, to a considerable degree, lost the Republican primary because of that career choice.[16] The issue of lobbying by former officials and their staffs is a significant one, as there is concern that policy decisions may be made with an eye toward future lucrative lobbying jobs.

Texas has only weak laws dealing with lobbying by former government officials. A former member of the governing body or a former executive head of a regulatory agency cannot lobby the agency for two years after leaving office. Senior employees or former officers of Texas regulatory agencies cannot ever lobby a government entity on matters they were involved in when employed by the government. However, there are no legal restrictions on lobbying by a former governor, former lieutenant governor, former legislator, or any former aides to these officials.[17]

In March 2012 there were 1,377 registered lobbyists in Texas.[18] This is a decrease from the 1,836 registered lobbyists in 2011, probably because more lobbying was needed in 2011 when the legislature was in session compared to 2012 when it was not in session. An analysis that was done of the lobbying reports in 2011 found these lobbyists had 2,908 clients.[19] Because of the loose nature of the Texas reporting laws, it is unclear what these lobbyists were paid, but it was as much as $345 million in 2011.[20] Over the past 10 years, lobbyists in Texas have been paid as much as $2.8 billion. Some Texas lobbyists make enormous sums. Thirty of them reported maximum lobbying incomes of at least $1.5 million.[21]

Once lobbyists obtain access to policy makers, they provide information that may be useful. For example, they may explain how a bill benefits a legislator's district, or how it benefits the state, or how it is perceived as being unfair. Since the staffs of Texas legislators are small, lobbyists perform useful functions by explaining what numerous bills are intended to do. They may even write bills to be introduced by friendly legislators or write amendments to bills. Almost certainly, if a bill affects the interests of a lobbyist's client and reaches a point in the process where hearings are held on the bill, the lobbyist will arrange for testimony to be given at the hearing explaining the interest group's viewpoint on the proposed legislation.

Lobbyists do not limit their activities to the legislative process, of course. Rules proposed by the bureaucracy or the courts can affect the interests of lobbyists' clients. Lobbyists will testify at hearings on rules and try to provide information to administrators in face-to-face meetings as well.

There is always a concern that lobbyists may corrupt policy makers by bribing them in order to accomplish the interest groups' policy objectives. Early in the twentieth century, Sam Rayburn, later a famed U.S. congressman and Speaker of the House, served in the Texas House of Representatives for six years. At that time, he was especially concerned with corruption and refused to accept free meals and entertainment from lobbyists. He called some of his fellow legislators "steak men." By that he meant that the legislators would sell their votes on a bill for a steak dinner at the Driskill Hotel in Austin. "Steak men" (and women) may still exist in Texas politics, but, for the most part, lobbyists provide information, campaign contributions, and political support (or opposition) rather than bribes.

Still, from time to time lobbying does stoop to very low levels. In 1989, "Bo" Pilgrim, a large poultry producer, distributed $10,000 checks to state senators in the capitol while he was lobbying them on workers' compensation reform. Perhaps even more troubling, some senators accepted the checks until media attention forced them to reconsider. Yet this practice of offering $10,000 while asking for a senator to vote on a specific bill was not illegal. A year later, the Speaker of the Texas House of Representatives, "Gib" Lewis, got in trouble for his close relationship with a law firm that specialized in collecting delinquent taxes for local governments. In 1991, Speaker Lewis was indicted for receipt of an illegal gift from the law firm. Ultimately, Lewis plea-bargained and received a minor penalty. The result of these scandals, however, was legislation that created a state ethics commission. The legislation imposed additional lobbying reporting requirements and restrictions on speaking fees that interest groups paid legislators and pleasure trips that lobbyists provided. By no means was the law a major regulation of or restriction on lobbying practices, but it did put some limits on lobbying behavior.

Who Represents Ordinary Texans?

Another problem with lobbying was well described by the director of a public-interest lobby, Craig McDonald: "Legislators are rubbing shoulders with . . . lobbyists, almost all of whom hustle for business interests. While corporate interests dominate our legislative process, there is virtually no counterbalancing lobby to represent ordinary Texans. Nowhere on the list of Texas's biggest lobby spenders will you find a single group dedicated to the interests of consumers, the environment or human services. No wonder these citizen interests repeatedly get steamrolled in Austin."[22]

Figure 6.1 classifies the interests represented by the registered lobbyists and estimates the value of those lobbying expenditures. The Who Are Texans? box on p. 171 looks at campaign contributions to Texas legislators in 2010. Although the categories in both are very broad, it is clear that business interests dominate in

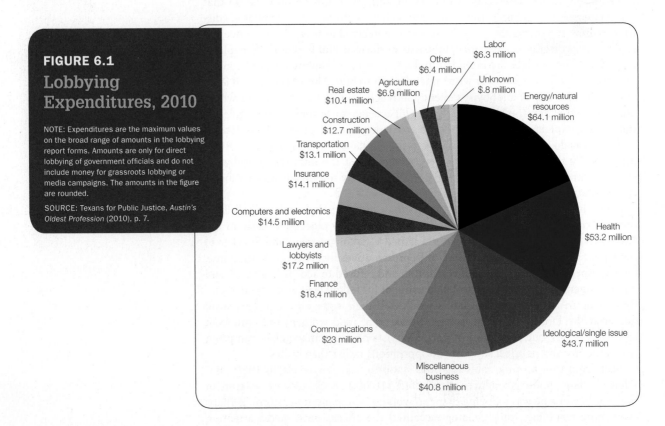

FIGURE 6.1
Lobbying Expenditures, 2010

NOTE: Expenditures are the maximum values on the broad range of amounts in the lobbying report forms. Amounts are only for direct lobbying of government officials and do not include money for grassroots lobbying or media campaigns. The amounts in the figure are rounded.

SOURCE: Texans for Public Justice, *Austin's Oldest Profession* (2010), p. 7.

Labor $6.3 million
Other $6.4 million
Agriculture $6.9 million
Unknown $.8 million
Real estate $10.4 million
Energy/natural resources $64.1 million
Construction $12.7 million
Transportation $13.1 million
Insurance $14.1 million
Computers and electronics $14.5 million
Health $53.2 million
Lawyers and lobbyists $17.2 million
Finance $18.4 million
Communications $23 million
Ideological/single issue $43.7 million
Miscellaneous business $40.8 million

Who Represents Me?

nterest groups try to achieve favorable policies not only by lobbying members of the Texas legislature directly but also by influencing who becomes members of the legislature in the first place by donating to the election campaigns of favored candidates. The chart below breaks down contributions from employees of different industries by party in 2010.

Contributions to Texas Legislature Candidates in 2010

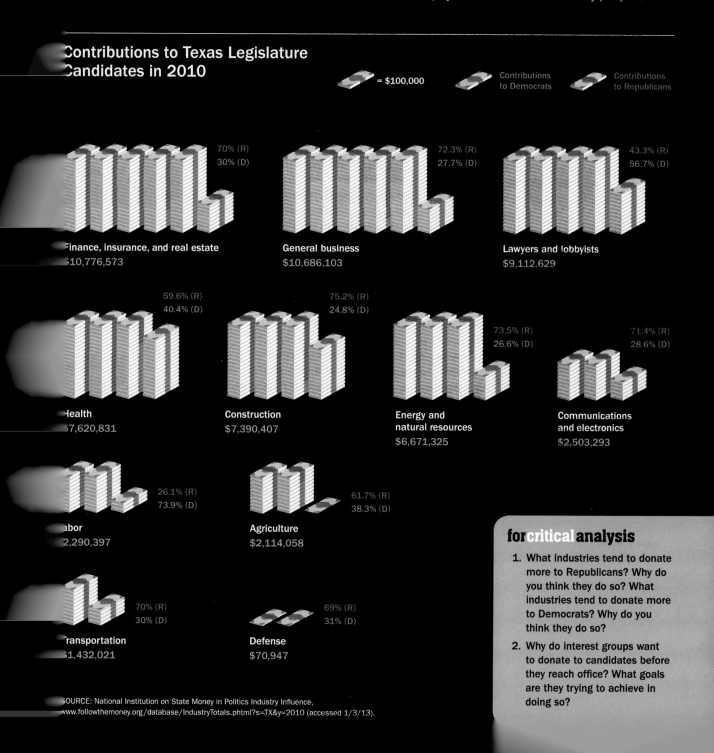

= $100,000   Contributions to Democrats   Contributions to Republicans

Finance, insurance, and real estate
$10,776,573
70% (R)
30% (D)

General business
$10,686,103
72.3% (R)
27.7% (D)

Lawyers and lobbyists
$9,112,629
43.3% (R)
56.7% (D)

Health
$7,620,831
59.6% (R)
40.4% (D)

Construction
$7,390,407
75.2% (R)
24.8% (D)

Energy and natural resources
$6,671,325
73.5% (R)
26.6% (D)

Communications and electronics
$2,503,293
71.4% (R)
28.6% (D)

Labor
$2,290,397
26.1% (R)
73.9% (D)

Agriculture
$2,114,058
61.7% (R)
38.3% (D)

Transportation
$1,432,021
70% (R)
30% (D)

Defense
$70,947
69% (R)
31% (D)

SOURCE: National Institution on State Money in Politics Industry Influence, www.followthemoney.org/database/IndustryTotals.phtml?s=TX&y=2010 (accessed 1/3/13).

for critical analysis

1. What industries tend to donate more to Republicans? Why do you think they do so? What industries tend to donate more to Democrats? Why do you think they do so?

2. Why do interest groups want to donate to candidates before they reach office? What goals are they trying to achieve in doing so?

Texas government. Of course, many issues considered by Texas government may pit one business interest against another, and sometimes a business or professional organization may find itself aligned with consumer interests. For example, the Texas Trial Lawyers Association, an organization of plaintiffs' lawyers in Texas, frequently allies with consumer interests. Many of the clients of these lawyers are consumers who sue large businesses. The interests of these lawyers and their clients are especially close, since the lawyers are paid on a contingent fee basis, which means they don't receive payment unless their clients receive payment. It is also the case that lobbying is not all there is to the representation of interests in Austin. Interest groups without money may still mobilize their members in order to accomplish their objectives, or they may influence public opinion.

Still, there is no question that money does help in politics. Figure 6.1 and the data in the Who Are Texans box provide support for concern that in this battle of mostly business interests, there may not be an objective voice, or at least a voice for the public interest, that reaches the ears of legislators.

● Another Side to Lobbying

Describe the role of PACs in Texas elections

Lobbyists in Texas represent mostly business interests, and they are active in trying to gain access to government officials and inform them of the legislative desires of their clients. But interest groups are not simply information channels between business and government. They also promote the political interests of elected officials who support their viewpoints and oppose the interests of those who do not. One major way that interest groups engage in this activity is by making campaign contributions. Interest groups may encourage individual members to make contributions to candidates, or they may collect funds from their members, bundling those funds as a donation from the interest group. When this is done, the interest group creates a **political action committee (PAC)** to make the contribution.

political action committee (PAC) a private group that raises and distributes funds for use in election campaigns

There are numerous reasons for forming a political action committee. A candidate is more likely to notice a substantial contribution from a PAC than many small contributions from individual members of an interest group. Additionally, the lobbyist who delivers a substantial PAC check to a candidate can more likely gain political access than can a lobbyist who simply asks interest group members to mail individual checks. The PAC becomes a way for the interest group to send a message to the candidate that its members care strongly enough about their agenda that they are prepared to back those goals with money. In some cases, a PAC can even serve as an intermediary to provide money to candidates that the PAC's members might not want to support publicly.

issue advocacy independent spending by individuals or interest groups on a campaign issue but not directly tied to a particular candidate

PACs may give money directly to the candidate, or they may engage in **issue advocacy** that supports the candidate but is independent of the candidate's control. The candidate does not report these independent expenditures on contribution disclosure statements. PACs may also spend money to support an issue rather than a specific candidate or to support such activities as "get-out-the-vote" campaigns. In 2008, about 55 percent of the money given to Democratic and Republican legislative candidates was given by PACs. About 45 percent of the money was given by individuals.[23]

Campaign contributions can be, to a considerable degree, divided in terms of the economic interests represented by the contributors. The Who Are Texans box in this chapter shows that the largest contributor was the finance, insurance, and real estate sector. This sector is a major part of the Texas economy and is subject to significant state regulation. That is also true of general business, energy and natural resources, construction, and health. In contrast to business, political parties, agriculture, and even candidates providing funds to their own campaigns, labor represents a small amount of campaign spending.

Getting Out the Vote

The Texas Medical Association constructed a grassroots campaign in 1988 to elect its slate of candidates to the Texas Supreme Court. Physicians were encouraged to give to TEXPAC, the medical association PAC. They were also encouraged to make individual contributions to certain candidates. Additionally, physicians were given slate cards with recommended candidates, literature endorsing candidates, and even expensively produced videotapes. They were asked not only to encourage families and friends to vote for the candidates endorsed by the medical association but also to encourage their patients to vote for them. The effort by the medical association was remarkable for its fund-raising success and for its reaching and mobilizing the grass roots.[24] It was probably the most successful get-out-the-vote campaign ever run by an interest group in Texas.

Most efforts by interest groups, however, are far less sophisticated. Generally, interest groups' PACs simply provide resources for the candidates to get out the vote. Unfortunately for the interest groups, sometimes they misjudge the political viability of the candidates they support. Backing an unsuccessful candidate results in a waste of the interest group's funds and the likely alienation of the winning candidate. In the 2010 primary campaign, Texans for Lawsuit Reform, the pro-business and pro–tort reform interest group that has had spectacular successes in forwarding its agenda over the past 15 years, suffered a remarkable failure. Although it had contributed $602,290 to 28 candidates, 53 percent of this money was spent on 4 incumbent candidates who lost their primaries, and another 28 percent of their money was spent on 3 candidates—2 of them incumbents— who were forced into a runoff election. Obviously, Texans for Lawsuit Reform thought these candidates were important for achieving its agenda, but it is questionable how desirable it is for an interest group to pump huge amounts of money into the campaigns of incumbent candidates who do not have the political strength even to win in their own party primary elections. And the high degree of financial support for candidates can be hurtful to the candidate. In one of these races, the winning candidate's main issue was that the defeated incumbent had received money from an organization known for giving huge sums to Republican candidates. This, contended the winner, was proof that the incumbent Democrat was not a real Democrat but a Republican with a Democratic label.[25]

Nevertheless, Texans for Lawsuit Reform scored impressive victories in the 2010 general election. It gave more than $550,000 to Republican Marva Beck to defeat Democratic representative Jim Dunnam and $300,000 to Republican Larry Gonzales to defeat Democrat Diana Maldonado.[26]

Defeating Opponents

Generally, incumbents have a huge advantage over challengers in an election. Since they are officeholders, they usually have greater name recognition than challengers, and it is easy for incumbents to get publicity by holding town hall meetings, by

TABLE 6.1

Average Dollars Raised by Incumbents and Challengers for the Texas Legislature, 2010

OFFICE	INCUMBENTS	CHALLENGERS
House	$349,233	$139,862
Senate	$656,908	$43,687

SOURCE: National Institute on Money in State Politics.

announcing the relocation of new businesses to the district, or simply by attending community events. Additionally, they usually have an established network of supporters who helped them get into office at least once previously. There are two great exceptions to incumbency advantage: (1) scandal can destroy incumbency advantage, and (2) redistricting can ruin the political base of incumbents.

Except in cases of scandal or redistricting, however, it is far safer for interest groups to try to work with incumbents. Campaign money, for example, overwhelmingly goes to incumbents. In the 2010 campaign for the Texas House of Representatives, as Table 6.1 shows, incumbents raised two and one half times the amount raised by challengers, and in the Texas Senate incumbents raised 15 times the amount raised by challengers. Incumbents win elections to an overwhelming degree.[27]

Of course, sometimes an interest group does not want to help a candidate or even pressure a candidate; it wants to defeat that candidate. This can be a risky strategy because if the candidate wins, then the interest group will be faced with not only an unfriendly public official but also one displeased with the interest group for its opposition. When that happens, the interest group will often "get well" or "get on the late train." This means that the interest group will make a substantial political contribution to the winning candidate whom it formerly opposed. Often, winning candidates have significant campaign debts after a grueling election battle, and they appreciate the late contributions of former enemies, which are offered as a way of making amends.

Although "late-train" contributions may improve the relationship between officials and interest groups, usually candidates reserve a special loyalty for those supporters who backed them early. Without support at the very beginning of a campaign, it is hard for a candidate to build an organization and get the support necessary to make a decent campaign start. That is why early supporters are so valuable. The best lobbyists start early in trying to develop relationships with candidates and with new legislators. One national PAC, EMILY's List (EMILY stands for Early Money Is Like Yeast), is funded by women and provides early campaign contributions to female candidates. Legislators remember who was with them at the beginning of their political careers—and this can be immensely beneficial to the lobby that cultivated that early relationship.[28]

Sometimes PACs give to both candidates as a way to avoid alienating either one, though the possibility remains that such dual giving will wind up alienating both. At other times, interest groups simply don't care if they alienate a candidate. The 2010 Democratic primary election between State Representatives Tara Rios Ybarra and Jose Manuel Lozano highlighted the lines that can clearly separate interest groups during a campaign. Texans for Lawsuit Reform contributed $256,610 to Ybarra, which was 56 percent of her campaign funds. Ybarra lost to Lozano, who was backed by trial lawyers who were not the least bit sympathetic to the goals of Texans for Lawsuit Reform.[29]

An extraordinary battle occurred in the 2012 Republican primary where Texans for Lawsuit Reform backed Railroad Commissioner Elizabeth Ames Jones in her challenge to Republican state senator Jeff Wentworth. Wentworth served nearly five years in the Texas House before being elected to the state senate in 1992. He

Former governor Ann Richards received support from the PAC EMILY's List early in her career. EMILY's List is a national organization that provides campaign funding to female candidates.

appeared to be well established and unbeatable. An early poll showed him with a large lead. But although Wentworth supported 21 of 23 bills considered by Texans for Lawsuit Reform to be "major" legislation, he angered the interest group by criticizing a 2003 constitutional amendment that limited the amounts patients could receive in medical malpractice suits. He also voted against a bill that reduced the amount of money coastal homeowners could receive after hurricanes. While Wentworth was defeated, it was not by Jones, but by Donna Campbell who had Tea Party backing. Nevertheless, Wentworth blamed his defeat on the "mammoth $2 million-plus negative campaign launched against me by Texans for Lawsuit Reform."[30] The defeat no doubt sent a message to Republican lawmakers that they had better not cross Texans for Lawsuit Reform.

When an interest group is convinced that it cannot work with a public official, the interest group may undertake an all-out effort to defeat that official. But spending money by no means guarantees success. Dr. James Leininger is one of the biggest contributors to Republican candidates. In the 2006 election cycle, he gave over $5 million to Republican candidates in Texas, either through individual contributions or by giving to PACs that then made contributions. Leininger and some of the PACs he supports are strong supporters of school vouchers. Much of this money backed challengers to Republican incumbents who were unfavorable to vouchers. The effort was unsuccessful and the result, according to Texans for Public Justice, was a legislature "even less receptive to vouchers than its predecessor."[31]

● Individuals as Lobbyists

> **Explain how ordinary individuals can influence Texas government**

Sometimes ordinary individuals can have a remarkable impact on public policy, although interest groups clearly have an advantage in influencing the legislative process. Nevertheless, a persistent individual with a well-reasoned argument can make a difference. For example, Tyrus Burks lost his wife and two children in a late-night electrical fire in West Dallas. Burks did not awaken in time to save them because he is deaf and did not hear the audible smoke alarm. Texas's state property code required the installation of audible smoke alarms but not visual alarms. In 2009, Burks became an advocate for a bill that would require property managers to buy and install visual smoke alarms if hearing-impaired tenants requested them and to put the alarms in visible locations such as bedrooms. Supported by state senator Royce West, the Sephra Burks Law, named for Tyrus's wife, who was also deaf, went into effect at the start of 2010. Tyrus Burks was an active lobbyist for the bill and gave legislative testimony in support of it with the aid of a sign language interpreter.

Burks's efforts benefited from the support of the Texas Apartment Association, a major interest group representing apartment property interests, who backed the bill. Burks's story was tragic and his argument was compelling. It would have been difficult for opposition to emerge against such a proposal. Still, his efforts resulted in a major victory for the deaf, who are protected by such a law requiring visual smoke alarms in only three other states and the District of Columbia.[32] Burks's achievement demonstrates that individuals can, at least sometimes, be successful lobbyists.

Occasionally, ordinary individuals can have a direct influence on policy. Barbara Brown, of Plano, lobbied local government and the state legislature to get better bicycle safety laws and programs passed. Brown's son was killed in an accident while riding his bicycle.

● Thinking Critically about Interest Groups

Interest groups play an important role in Texas politics even though Texas is no longer a one-party state with limited economic development. Even with two major political parties and a diverse economy, Texas politics cannot be understood without also examining the role of interest groups. Interest groups in Texas have a notable pro-business flavor. Labor is weak in Texas, and its role in the political process is quite limited. Trial lawyers are an especially wealthy and important interest group that promotes liberal policies in Texas, but with the growth of the Republican Party and tort reform interest groups, the influence of the trial lawyers has waned.

Though no single interest group or coalition of interest groups dominates Texas politics, by far most lobbyists represent business interests, and the bulk of PAC money comes from business interests. Often, of course, businesses are pitted against one another in the political process. Also, public interest, civil rights, consumer, and environmental groups may still be successful by mobilizing public opinion and influencing the media. However, there are only a few interest groups that offer alternatives to business perspectives on policy issues. Less frequently, ordinary individuals are able to influence public policy. Although they tend to be at a disadvantage in terms of money and other resources, dedicated individuals with a compelling argument sometimes succeed in lobbying for specific legislation. This is especially true when they are pursuing goals that do not put them in conflict with well-organized and well-funded interest groups.

Interest Groups in the Political Process

■ **Define interest groups and describe the major ways they try to influence Texas government (pp. 163–72)**

Interest groups in Texas are organizations of interested citizens who band together to influence public policy. Lobbyists are hired to cultivate relationships with legislators and convince them of their clients' interests. The goal of lobbyists is to gain access to policy makers to persuade them to support the positions of the interest group.

Key Terms

interest group (p. 163)

bundling (p. 165)

lobbyist (p. 165)

Practice Quiz

1. The "8F Crowd" *(p. 163)*
   a) was a group of legislators who failed the eighth grade.
   b) was a group of extremely wealthy Texans who met in Suite 8F of the Lamar Hotel in Houston and controlled Texas politics for 40 years.
   c) were 25 legislators who boycotted the eighth session of the legislature in order to prevent the legislators from taking any action because it lacked a quorum.
   d) was made up of eight lobbyists who were close friends of the governor.
   e) were the eight most powerful officials in the state who met in Suite F of the Austin State Office Building.

2. Interest groups provide public officials with all the following *except (p. 164)*
   a) information.
   b) money.
   c) media coverage.
   d) votes.
   e) committee assignments.

3. The goals of interest groups include all *except (pp. 164–65)*
   a) electing people to office in order who support the groups' goals.
   b) influencing those who control government.
   c) educating the public and members about issues of importance to the group.
   d) providing campaign funds for favored candidates.
   e) maintaining a heterogeneous membership.

4. Interest groups have an advantage over individuals in influencing policy because interest groups usually have *(pp. 164–65)*
   a) more time to influence officials.
   b) greater expertise than individuals.
   c) more money to influence elections.
   d) more staff.
   e) all of the above.

5. When PACs combine small contributions from many sources to form one large contribution, it is called *(p. 165)*
   a) bundling.
   b) compacting.
   c) cracking.
   d) polling.
   e) packing.

6. The most important thing interest groups need to be effective is *(p. 166)*
   a) the support of a majority of Texans.
   b) office space in Austin.
   c) a variety of issues on which to lobby.
   d) a large, paid staff.
   e) access to politicians.

7. Trial lawyers are which type of interest group? *(p. 166)*
   a) professional group.
   b) public employee group.
   c) single-issue group.
   d) consumer group.
   e) business group.

8. Interest groups often hire former legislators as lobbyists to *(p. 167)*
   a) gain greater access to current legislators.
   b) benefit from the policy expertise of former legislators.
   c) benefit from the personal "insider" knowledge of the former legislator.
   d) all of the above.
   e) none of the above.

9. Lobbying takes place in the *(p. 169)*
   a) legislative branch only.
   b) legislative and executive branches only.
   c) executive and judicial branches.
   d) time immediately before an election.
   e) legislative, executive, and judicial branches.

(S) **Practice Online**
Interactive simulation: *Interest Groups and Lobbying*

Another Side to Lobbying

 Describe the role of PACs in Texas elections (pp. 172–75)

Political action committees are private groups that raise and distribute funds for election campaigns. Interest groups play a major role in getting out the vote. Interest group money can play a major role in defeating as well as electing candidates.

Key Terms

political action committee (PAC) (p. 172)

issue advocacy (p. 172)

Practice Quiz

10. Lobbyists are *(p. 172)*
    a) all corrupt.
    b) all unethical.
    c) important sources of information for legislators.
    d) harmful to the democratic process.
    e) never retired legislators.

11. In Texas, the most powerful interest groups represent which interests? *(p. 172)*
    a) consumer
    b) civil rights
    c) business
    d) owners of oil wells
    e) public employee

12. PACs are used to *(pp. 172–73)*
    a) stir the public's interest in politics.
    b) raise money from individuals, which is then bundled and given to candidates.
    c) create media campaigns to influence the course of government.
    d) create grass-roots campaigns.
    e) all of the above.

13. One of the most important grassroots tactics of interest groups is *(p. 173)*
    a) gain support from all the mayors of town in a district.
    b) to get out the vote.
    c) to form political alliances with executive and legislative leaders.
    d) to lobby the judicial branch of national and state government.
    e) to interpret the needs of their members.

14. Interest groups have a hard time defeating incumbent legislators unless *(p. 174)*
    a) the legislator is involved in scandal.
    b) the legislator has been redistricted.
    c) the legislator's positions have generated overwhelming opposition in the district.
    d) all of the above.
    e) none of the above.

 Practice Online
Video exercise: *PACs and Lobbying Expenditures*

Individuals as Lobbyists

 Explain how ordinary individuals can influence Texas government (pp. 175–76)

Citizens can lobby their legislators by calling, writing, or visiting their offices. Industries and well-financed interests can afford professional lobbyists to try to influence legislation, but legislators will listen to individual citizens, especially if they join together in large numbers.

Practice Quiz

15. Individuals have the best chance to influence public policy when they *(p. 175)*
    a) are not opposed by organized interest groups.
    b) are polite.
    c) entertain legislators.
    d) vote.
    e) live in Austin.

Recommended Websites

Texans for Public Justice
www.tpj.org

Texas Ethics Commission
www.ethics.state.tx.us/

Texas Medical Association
www.texmed.org

Texas Trial Lawyers Association
www.ttla.com/TX/

TEXPAC
www.texpac.org

Texans for Lawsuit Reform
www.tortreform.com/

Like the U.S. Congress, the Texas Legislature is bicameral, with two chambers: a house of representatives and a senate. Here, members of the Texas House of Representatives take a break during the 2011 session.

The Texas Legislature

7

WHAT GOVERNMENT DOES AND WHY IT MATTERS The Speaker is the most powerful member of the Texas House of Representatives. One might expect that the Speaker would be selected by a simple vote of the majority party in caucus as in the U.S. House of Representatives. In recent years, however, a different dynamic has led to the election of the Speaker, one that reflects the tensions that have broken out between moderates and conservatives in the majority Republican Party. The story of the speakership is also the story of the shifting sands of political life in Texas.

Following the 2002 election, Republicans seized control of the House for the first time in over 100 years with an 88-to-62 majority. They elected Tom Craddick, a conservative businessman from Midland, to lead them. A Republican stalwart since 1968 when he was first elected to the Texas House, Craddick had long promoted a partisan agenda. Assuming power in the midst of a fiscal crisis that gripped the state, Craddick began pushing a conservative Republican agenda that included lawsuit limitations, private school vouchers, pro-business legislation, and congressional redistricting. By the end of the term, bad blood had spilled across party lines as 50 Democratic members of the House fled the state for Oklahoma, seeking to deny the Speaker a quorum.

In 2008 the bad blood in the House spilled over into the Republican Party as a bitter fight broke out between the conservative Speaker and disgruntled moderate Republicans. Failing to defeat Craddick's re-election to a third term as Speaker at the beginning of the session, opponents tried to remove him from office at the end of the session by a motion on the House floor. Although this effort failed, a group of 11 moderate Republicans let it be known after the 2008 elections that they would not support the conservative Craddick for another term as Speaker. By January 2009, a makeshift coalition of 72 Democrats and disgruntled Republicans had come out in support of Representative Joe Straus, a moderate Republican from San Antonio, to replace Craddick as Speaker. Socially conservative Republicans tried to mobilize against Straus's candidacy, but their efforts failed as the coalition of Democrats and insurgent Republicans held fast, ushering in a new period of moderate Republican leadership in the House. The price that Democrats in the House extracted from Straus was steep: 16 chairmanships went to Democrats and 18 to Republicans, many of a moderate ideological stamp.

This alignment of political forces was only temporary as the 2010 election pushed the legislature back toward the right. The Republican majority increased as the party took control of 99 of the 150 seats in the House. Soon after the election, two Democratic members switched to the Republican Party, creating a supermajority for the Republicans. Another member switched in early 2012, bringing the Republican supermajority to 102. That Republican majority, however, dropped to 95 after the 2012 election. The 2011 session was dominated by conservative policies on issues such as spending cuts, immigration, abortion, and gay marriage. Speaker Joe Straus, facing conservative opposition in the aftermath of the 2010 election, had the votes necessary for re-election as Speaker. But throughout the session he was forced to move in a more conservative direction, abandoning many issues that concerned Democrats who supported him in his rise to the speakership. One problem that he faced in the 2013 legislative session was the loss of major leaders from both parties with whom he worked. This included the retirement of such experienced and respected legislators as State Representatives Jerry Madden, Scott Hochberg, Pete Gallego, Will Harnett, and Burt Solomon. Straus hoped to remain Speaker after the 2012 election cycle. But the political interests he will serve in the future will likely be much more conservative than the moderate interests that initially put him into office.[1]

chaptergoals

- Describe the bicameral organization of the legislature and the rules for membership (pages 183–87)

- Explain when the legislature meets (pages 187–89)

- Outline the legislative and nonlegislative powers of the legislature (pages 189–91)

- Trace the process through which law is made in Texas (pages 191–98)

- Describe the roles of other state officials in shaping legislation (pages 198–99)

- Analyze how party leadership and redistricting affect power in the legislature (pages 200–207)

● Structure of the Texas Legislature

Describe the bicameral organization of the legislature and the rules for membership

The Texas state legislature is the most important representative institution in the state. Members share many of the duties and responsibilities that are taken up at the national level by members of the U.S. Congress. Like members of the U.S. Congress, the members of the Texas House and Senate are responsible for bringing the interests and concerns of their constituencies directly into the democratic political processes. But the important constitutional and institutional differences between the U.S. Congress and the Texas state legislature must be taken into account if we are to understand the role that the state legislature plays in democracy in Texas.

bicameral having a legislative assembly composed of two chambers or houses

Bicameralism

Like the U.S. Congress and all the states except Nebraska, Texas has a **bicameral** legislature, with two chambers: the Texas House of Representatives and the Texas Senate. Its 150 House members and 31 senators meet in regular session for 140 days every odd-numbered year. Senators serve four-year terms, and House members serve for two years. Each represents a single-member district. Members of the Texas House represent approximately 168,000 people. Senators represent over 811,000 constituents. A state senator now represents more people than does a member of the U.S. House of Representatives. Elections are held in November of even-numbered years, and senators and House members take office in January of odd-numbered years.

Bicameralism creates interesting dynamics in a legislature. For one thing, it means that before a law is passed, it will be voted on by two deliberative bodies representing different constituencies. In 2009, for example, the Texas Senate passed legislation to allow college students and faculty with concealed handgun licenses to carry their firearms on campus. That legislation, however, was killed in the Texas House of Representatives.[2] In 2011, the Texas Senate again passed a bill with an amendment allowing guns on campus, and in the Texas House, the bill had support from a majority of members. However, the bill failed in the House because of a successful parliamentary objection that the gun amendment was not germane to the bill it amended, which dealt with scholarships.[3] If a bill cannot be killed in one house, it can be killed or modified in the other body.

One effect of bicameralism in Texas is that the author of a bill in one house whose bill has been amended in the other body has the option of accepting or rejecting the amendment. If the author accepts the amendment, the bill moves forward; if the author rejects the amendment, the bill is killed.

Before becoming law in Texas, a bill must pass in both houses of the legislature. In 2009 and 2011, the Texas Senate passed bills to allow concealed firearms on college campuses, but the bill did not pass in the Texas House and thus failed to become law.

FIREARMS
PROHIBITED ON PREMISES
—
PROHIBIDAS
LAS ARMAS DE FUEGO
EN ESTA AREA

Bicameralism allows a member of one legislative body to retaliate against a member of either body for not cooperating on desired legislation. A "local and consent" calendar in the House is usually reserved for uncontroversial bills or bills limited to a localized problem. In order for a bill to be passed from that calendar, it has to pass without the objection of any member of the House. That requirement provides a perfect opportunity for members to retaliate against other members for perceived slights.[4]

Membership

The constitutional requirements for becoming a member of the Texas Legislature are minimal. A senator must be a U.S. citizen, a qualified voter, and a resident of the state for at least five years and of the district for at least one year. Additionally, the senator must be at least 26 years of age. Members of the House must be at least 21, U.S. citizens, qualified voters, and residents of the state for two years and of the district for one year. These requirements are in keeping with the political philosophy of those who wrote the Constitution of 1876. They believed holding public office required little or no formal training and should be open to most citizens.

In Texas, the typical legislator is white, male, Protestant, college educated, and affluent, and has a professional or business occupation. These characteristics do not mean that a poor high school dropout who is a day laborer cannot be elected to the state legislature, but they do indicate that individuals with most of these informal characteristics have a distinct advantage. Members of the legislature must have jobs that allow them the flexibility to campaign for office and to work in the legislature for 140 days every other year, as well as in special legislative sessions and meetings of committees when the legislature is not in session. Thus, about one-third of the members of the legislature are attorneys. The legal profession is one of the few careers that pays well and offers the necessary degree of time flexibility a legislator needs. Lawyers who serve in the legislature may even gain increased legal business either from interests with legislative concerns or because of the enhanced visibility of a lawyer-legislator.[5]

Although the "typical" member of the Texas state legislature is white and male, women and minority groups have increased their representation in recent years. For example, state Senator Leticia Van de Putte has become a prominent figure in Texas politics.

Who Are the Members of the Texas Legislature?

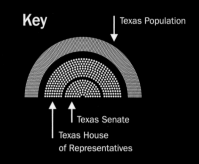

Key

Texas Population

Texas Senate

Texas House
of Representatives

Gender

	Texas Pop.	Texas House	Texas Senate
Female	50%	21%	19%
Male	50%	79%	81%

Race

	Texas Pop.	Texas House	Texas Senate
White	45%	68%	71%
Black	12%	11%	7%
Hispanic	38%	20%	23%
Asian	4%	1%	0

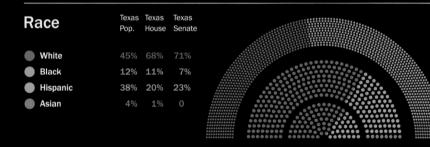

Education

	Texas Pop.	Texas House	Texas Senate
< HS diploma	20%	0	0
High school grad.	48%	9%	7%
Associate's degree	6%	2%	0
Bachelor's degree	17%	41%	39%
Graduate degree	9%	51%	55%

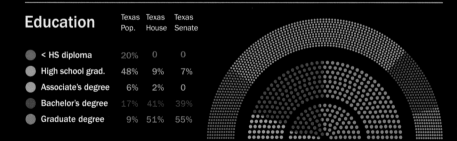

Occupation

- Business
- Attorney
- Community service
- Health care
- Education
- Other

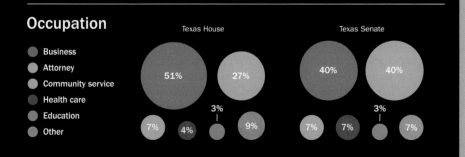

Texas House — 51% 27% 3% 7% 4% 9%

Texas Senate — 40% 40% 3% 7% 7% 7%

The Texas legislature is designed to be a representative body, which looks and sounds like the state as a whole. How well does the legislature represent Texas? In many ways, the legislature does not look like Texas. The data to the left are for the Texas legislature in 2011–12. The state is evenly split between men and women, while the legislature is four-fifths male. While the state has no ethnic majority in its population, more than two-thirds of Texas legislators are white. Perhaps the biggest differences, though, relate to socioeconomic status. Over half of the members of the legislature hold graduate degrees, while only 9 percent of the population does.

for critical analysis

1. How much do you think the racial, gender, and socio-economic makeup of the Texas legislature matter to the type of laws that the legislature passes? If the legislature had more people of color, more women, or more middle class members, would it pass different policies?

2. Why do you think that members of the Texas legislature come from the more educated, higher socioeconomic groups? Does the structure of the Texas legislature encourage or discourage people from particular occupations to run?

SOURCES: For Texas House, numbers calculated by author based on data from the Directory of Elected Officials of the Texas Tribune: www.texastribune.org/directory/. State demographic data calculated from the US Census Bureau American Community Survey, www.census.gov.

TABLE 7.1

Gender and Minority Membership in the Texas Legislature

	% OF TEXAS POPULATION	% OF 2011 TEXAS HOUSE MEMBERSHIP	% OF 2011 TEXAS SENATE MEMBERSHIP
Men	50%	78%	81%
Women	50	21	19
African American	12	11	6
Anglo	47	61	71
Hispanic	38	27	23
Asian	4	1	0

SOURCES: *Texas State Directory*; Texas House Legislative Black Caucus; National Association of Latino Elected and Appointed Officials. State demographic data calculated from the 2010 Census.

per diem daily payment to a public official engaged in state business

Legislators in Texas cannot expect to live on their legislative salaries. In keeping with the Texas constitutional tradition of a low-cost, part-time legislature, Texas representatives receive a salary of only $7,200 a year. Legislators also receive a payment of $150 a day when the legislature is in session. When the legislature is not in session, legislators may claim up to 12 days per month of **per diem** pay if they are in Austin on official business, or 16 days if they are committee chairs. The legislators themselves determine what qualifies as official business. It is common to pay expenses from officeholder expense accounts and to pocket the per diem so that it becomes a salary supplement. Legislative retirement pensions are very generous. The pension is tied to district judges' salaries, which are $125,000 a year. That salary is multiplied by the years of service of the legislator times 2.3 percent That amount would be the lawmaker's pension as long as the lawmaker served at least eight years. With 8 years of service, the lawmaker can start collecting a pension at age 60. With 10 years of service, a lawmaker can start collecting at age 50.[6]

Originally, per diem rates were set by the Texas Constitution, and a constitutional amendment was necessary to change this. In 1991, Texans adopted an amendment allowing the Texas Ethics Commission to propose changes in legislative salaries, which then require voter approval. To date, the commission has not recommended a salary increase. At the start of each regular session, the Ethics Commission sets the legislative per diem. In the 2011 session, with major belt-tightening throughout state government, the legislature asked the Texas Ethics Commission to reduce their scheduled per diem of $168 a day to $150.[7] One Texas legislator found a way to increase his income by billing both the state and his campaign funds for his travel expenses. Representative Joe Driver of Garland pled guilty to a third-degree felony for double billing thousands of dollars in expenses. His conviction raises questions about how closely legislators' expenses are monitored.[8]

Table 7.1 shows the proportions of minorities and women serving in the legislature. Although those numbers have increased over the years, they are not in proportion to their strength in the population of Texas. Civil rights laws have increased voting by minorities, and those laws provide protection for minority political districts. Thus, more minority officeholders have been elected and, as the Hispanic population in Texas increases, additional Latino legislators will be elected. Women have also had an increased role in politics, especially since the 1970s, and as a result, it is likely that additional women will be elected to legislative office.

Sessions of the Legislature

Explain when the legislature meets

Not all state legislatures meet for the same time periods. Some state legislatures meet every year like the U.S. Congress. Texas's legislature generally meets every other year unless they are called by the governor to meet between regular meetings.

regular session the 140-day period during which the Texas Legislature meets to consider and pass bills; occurs only in odd-numbered years

biennial occurring every two years

Regular Sessions

The Texas Constitution specifies that **regular sessions** of the Texas Legislature be held for 140 days in odd-numbered years. The **biennial** legislative sessions have their origin in the nineteenth-century idea that legislative service is a part-time job and a belief that short, biennial sessions would limit the power of the legislature. For a few years, legislators were encouraged to end their work early by being paid for only 120 days of service.

Thousands of bills and resolutions are introduced into the legislature during a regular session, and the 140-day limitation places a considerable restriction on the legislature's ability to deal with this workload. Hundreds of bills pass in the last hours of a legislative session, most with little or no debate. More die in the end-of-session crush of business because there isn't time to consider them.

Special Sessions

If the legislature does not complete its agenda before the end of the legislative session or if problems arise between regular sessions, the governor may call a **special session**. Special sessions last no more than 30 days, but there is no limit to the number of special sessions a governor can call and the governor sets their agenda. Texas has averaged one special session a year since 1876, although years may go by with no special session, whereas in some years there may be three or four sessions.

The ability to call and set the agenda of a special session provides the governor with control over which issues are discussed and what bills are passed. In many instances, the governor, the Speaker of the Texas House, the lieutenant governor, and various committee chairs will meet to decide what will be done to solve the problem at hand. Once the leaders address the issue and develop solutions, the governor calls the special session.

Once the session begins, the governor can open it to different issues. At times, the governor bargains for a legislator's vote in return for adding to the special session agenda an issue of importance to that legislator. In 2003, Governor Perry called three special sessions of the legislature to address congressional redistricting. In 2004, a fourth special session was called to address school finance. In 2005, in addition to the regular session, two special sessions addressed school finance. There was also a special session in 2006, 2009, and 2011.

Between legislative sessions, members serve on interim committees that may require a few days of their time each month. Legislators are also frequently called on to present programs to schools, colleges, and civic clubs. They supervise the staff

for critical analysis

Texas is the second-largest state and the second most populous state. Can a legislature that meets only 140 days every other year meet the needs of this modern, urban state? Will changes in the economy make a full-time legislature necessary?

special session a legislative session called by the governor that addresses an agenda set by him or her and that lasts no longer than 30 days

A Full-Time or Part-Time Legislature?

The Texas Legislature is a part-time, citizen legislature. It meets only once every two years for 140 days. Members of the Texas House are elected for two-year terms and are paid $7,200 per year. They receive a per diem allowance for expenses while they are in session. Members of the Texas Senate are elected for four-year terms and receive the same pay. If special issues arise outside of the regular session, then the governor can call a special session to deal with a specific issue.

It is interesting to contrast the Texas Legislature with a professional, full-time legislature, such as New York's. The New York Legislature meets year-round, and members are paid $79,500 per year. The New York legislature is considered professional because legislators are committed to being full-time representatives. Texas's legislators generally have other forms of employment, as not many people can live on $7,200 per year. The U.S. Congress is more similar to the New York Legislature and can be considered a professional legislature because members of Congress serve year-round.

As a candidate for president in 2011 and 2012, Governor Rick Perry campaigned on adapting the Texas model to the U.S. Congress. He proposed that members of Congress should have their pay cut to similar levels. Currently, members of Congress are paid $174,000 per year and are required to meet year-round, with the exception of August and some holidays. Perry argued that the Texas model works much better because it requires legislators to have jobs in the private sector and it reduces the propensity to corruption. Perry argued that the Founders intended a "citizen" Congress with members only serving for a few terms and retaining their regular employment. This vision also fits with the principle of limited government—the principle that Congress or the legislature really should have a small role and the more they are in session, the more temptations they have to pass laws restricting liberties.

Opponents argue that the Texas model is not one that should be adopted for the U.S. Congress or other legislatures. Legislators are not any less prone to corruption under the Texas model. Under either model, lobbyists attempt to influence policy makers, and the fact that legislators have private-sector jobs does not minimize this possibility. Meeting once every two years reduces the time to deliberate and make sensible policies. In Texas, critics argue that the legislative session is rushed, and legislators rely too heavily on staff who work year-round and are more familiar with the ins and outs of policy making. The rush of completing the legislation necessary to govern the state often leaves important issues unresolved, leading to the need for more special sessions. Members who are not independently wealthy are unable to legislate effectively because they cannot just leave their jobs for 140 days at a time every two years. All of these factors result in a less productive and less professional legislature.

Your vision of the proper role of government will likely affect where you come down on this issue. Liberals, who prefer an active government, would probably prefer a full-time legislature which actively addresses social problems. Conservatives, who are not supporters of government activity in the economy, are more likely to support a minimal role for legislators so that citizens are free to make their own choices without governmental interference.

Why should citizens care about this issue? The political process matters, and how legislative institutions are designed makes a difference in terms of policy outcomes.

critical thinking questions

1. Are you more convinced by the arguments for a part-time legislature or a full-time legislature? What are the advantages and disadvantages of each approach?

2. Is a compromise possible between Texas's 140-day session and a full-time approach?

of their district offices and address the needs of their constituents. Special sessions, interim committee meetings, speeches, and constituent services require long hours, with little remuneration. Many members devote more than 40 hours a week to legislative business in addition to maintaining their full-time jobs.

When Texas was a rural, predominantly agricultural state, biennial sessions worked well; however, Texas has moved beyond this description. In the twenty-first century, Texas is a modern state with more than 80 percent of its population living in metropolitan areas. Population growth continues at a rapid rate. Texas is home to many high-tech and biotech corporations. It is a center for medical research, and hosts the headquarters for NASA and the Lyndon Johnson Space Center. The state's gross domestic product exceeds that of many nations. Part-time legislators serving biennial 140-day sessions may not work well anymore in allowing the state to respond quickly and effectively to problems that arise.

Powers of the Legislature

> **Outline the legislative and nonlegislative powers of the legislature**

The Texas Legislature sets public policy by passing bills and resolutions, but it also supervises the state bureaucracy through the budgetary process and the Sunset Act, an act that provides for the review and, when deemed appropriate, the termination of state agencies. This supervision is achieved using legislative and nonlegislative powers. Legislative powers consist of passing bills and resolutions. Nonlegislative powers are those functions falling outside the lawmaking function.

Legislative Powers

Bills   Revenue bills must begin in the House of Representatives. All other bills may start in either the House or the Senate. For decades, a **bill** would be introduced in either the House or the Senate and work its way through the legislative process in that chamber. A bill introduced in the Senate would be passed by the Senate prior to going to the House. Today, it is customary for a bill to be introduced into the House and the same bill, a companion bill, to be introduced into the Senate at the same time. This simultaneous consideration of bills saves time in the legislature.

There are three classifications of bills in the Texas Legislature: (1) local bills, (2) special bills, and (3) general bills. **Local bills** affect only units of local government such as a city, a county, special districts, or more than one city in a county. A local bill, for example, might allow a county to create a sports authority or to establish a community college. **Special bills** give individuals or corporations an exemption from state law. A special bill could grant compensation to an individual wrongly convicted and sentenced to prison. **General bills** apply to all people and/or property in the state. General bills define criminal behavior; establish standards for divorce, child custody, or bankruptcy; and address other matters affecting people and property throughout the state.

Resolutions   There are three types of **resolutions** in the Texas Legislature: (1) concurrent resolutions, (2) joint resolutions, and (3) simple resolutions. **Concurrent resolutions** must pass both the House and Senate, and except for resolutions setting the time of adjournment, they require the governor's signature. These resolutions

bill a proposed law that has been sponsored by a member of the legislature and submitted to the clerk of the House or Senate

local bill a bill affecting only units of local government, such as a city, county, or special district

special bill a bill that gives an individual or corporation a special exemption from state law

general bill a bill that applies to all people and/or property in the state

resolution an expression of opinion on an issue by a legislative body

concurrent resolution a resolution of interest to both chambers of the legislature and which must pass both the House and Senate and generally be signed by the governor involve issues of interest to both chambers. They may request information from a state agency or call on Congress for some action. Senate Concurrent Resolution 6 might, for example, call on Congress to propose an amendment requiring a balanced federal budget.

joint resolution a resolution, commonly a proposed amendment to the Texas Constitution or ratification of an amendment to the U.S. Constitution, that must pass both the House and Senate but which does not require the governor's signature

Joint resolutions require passage in both the House and Senate but do not require the governor's signature. The most common use of joint resolutions is to propose amendments to the Texas Constitution or to ratify amendments to the U.S. Constitution. Resolutions that propose amendments to the Texas Constitution require a two-thirds vote of the membership of both houses of the state legislature. Ratification of amendments to the U.S. Constitution requires a majority vote in both the Texas House and Senate.

simple resolution a resolution that concerns only the Texas House or Senate, such as the adoption of a rule or the appointment of an employee, and which does not require the governor's signature

Simple resolutions concern only the Texas House or the Senate, and they do not require the governor's signature. They are used to adopt rules, to request opinions from the attorney general, to appoint employees to office in the House or Senate, or to honor outstanding achievements by Texas residents. For example, SR 27 could recognize the achievements of a Nobel Prize winner or the San Jacinto College baseball program for accomplishments in the National Junior College Athletic Association.

Resolutions of honor or recognition are acted on without debate and without requiring members to read the resolution. Resolutions are mostly symbolic acts that are designed to promote goodwill with voters. However, at times these simple symbolic acts can go terribly wrong. A Fort Worth doctor was twice honored by the Texas House of Representatives as the "doctor of the day." It was then, to the embarrassment of the House and the legislators who introduced him to the House, reported that the doctor was a registered sex offender who had been convicted of having a sexual relationship with a seventeen-year-old female patient.[9]

Nonlegislative Powers

Nonlegislative powers include the power to serve constituents, electoral powers, investigative powers, directive and supervisory powers, and judicial powers. The functions of these powers fall outside the scope of passing bills and resolutions; however, the passage of legislation may be necessary to exercise these powers.

constituent a person living in the district from which an official is elected

Legislators have the power to get things done for or in the name of **constituents**. Efforts on behalf of constituents may involve legislative activity, such as introducing a bill or voting on a resolution. Often, however, working on behalf of constituents involves nonlegislative activity, such as arranging an appointment for a constituent with a government agency that regulates some aspect of the constituent's life, writing a letter of recommendation for a constituent, or giving a speech to a civic group in the legislator's district.

electoral power the legislature's mandated role in counting returns in the elections for governor and lieutenant governor

Electoral powers of the legislature consist of formally counting returns in the elections for governor and lieutenant governor. This is accomplished during a joint session of the legislature when it is organized for the regular session.

investigative power the power, exercised by the House, the Senate, or both chambers jointly, to investigate problems facing the state

Investigative powers can be exercised by the House of Representatives, by the Senate, or jointly by both bodies. The legislature can undertake to investigate problems facing the state, the integrity of a state agency, or almost anything else it wishes. A special investigative committee is established by a simple resolution creating the committee, establishing the jurisdiction of the committee, and explaining the need for the investigation. If the special committee is formed in the House, the Speaker appoints the members of the committee. The lieutenant governor appoints members for special committees in the Senate. The Speaker and the lieutenant governor share appointments if it is a joint investigation.

Directive and supervisory powers enable the legislature to have considerable control over the executive branch of government. The legislature determines the size of the appropriation each agency has to spend for the next two years. The amount of money an agency has determines how well it can carry out its goals and objectives. A review of each agency of state government takes place every 12 years.

Judicial powers include the ability of the House to impeach members of the executive and judicial branches of state government. On **impeachment**, a trial takes place in the Senate. A majority vote of the House is required to bring charges, and a two-thirds vote of senators attending is necessary to convict an individual of the impeachment charges. Unlike the U.S. Constitution, the Texas Constitution does not explicitly define what constitutes an impeachable offense. This will be determined by the House and Senate in the impeachment process itself.[10]

Each body can compel attendance at regular and special sessions. More than once, Texas Rangers have handcuffed absent members and brought them to the legislature. On rare occasions, a chamber will punish nonmembers who disrupt proceedings by imprisoning them for up to 48 hours. The House and Senate judge the qualifications of members and can expel a member for cause.

How a Bill Becomes a Law in Texas

> Trace the process through which law is made in Texas

Anyone can write a bill, but only members of the legislature can introduce a bill. Bills may be written by members of the executive branch, by lobbyists, by constituents, or by local governmental entities. Legislators may also write bills, often with the help of a legislative staff expert in drafting legislation. There are, of course, innumerable reasons for drafting and introducing a bill.

Revenue bills must start in the House of Representatives. Other bills can start in either the House or Senate. During the 82nd Legislature regular session that met in 2011, a total of 5,796 bills were introduced in the legislature. Of those bills, 1,379 passed the legislature, and the governor vetoed 25 of them.[11]

Figure 7.1 shows the flow of a bill from the time it is introduced in the Texas House of Representatives to final passage and submission to the governor. A bill introduced in the Senate would follow the same procedure in reverse. Examining this figure suggests that the process of how a bill becomes law is long, detailed, and cumbersome. However, when the process is distilled to its basic parts, there are only six steps in how a bill becomes law. For a bill that starts in the House these steps are (1) **introduction**, (2) **referral**, (3) **consideration by standing committee**, and (4) **floor action**. Steps (1) through (4) are repeated in the Senate. Step (5) is action by a **conference committee** and approval by both houses, and finally, (6) is **action by the governor**.

Introduction in the House

A legislator introduces a bill by placing copies of the bill with the clerk of the House. In the Senate, the secretary of the Senate receives the bill. The clerk or secretary numbers the bill and enrolls it by recording its number, title, caption, and sponsor in a ledger. Similar information is entered into a computer.

---

directive and supervisory power the legislature's power over the executive branch; for example, the legislature determines the size of appropriations for state agencies

judicial power the power of the House to impeach and of the Senate to convict members of the executive and judicial branches of state government

impeachment according to the Texas Constitution, the formal charge by the House of Representatives that leads to a trial in the Senate and possibly to the removal of a state official

introduction the first step in the legislative process, during which a member of the legislature gets an idea for a bill and files a copy of it with the clerk of the House or secretary of the Senate

referral the second step in the legislative process, during which a bill is assigned to the appropriate standing committee by the Speaker (for House bills) or the lieutenant governor (for Senate bills)

consideration by standing committee the third step in the legislative process, during which a bill is killed, amended, or heard by a standing committee

floor action the fourth step in the legislative process, during which a bill referred by a standing committee is scheduled for floor debate by the Calendars Committee

conference committee a joint committee created to work out a compromise on House and Senate versions of a piece of legislation

action by the governor the final step in the legislative process, during which the governor signs, vetoes, or refuses to sign a bill

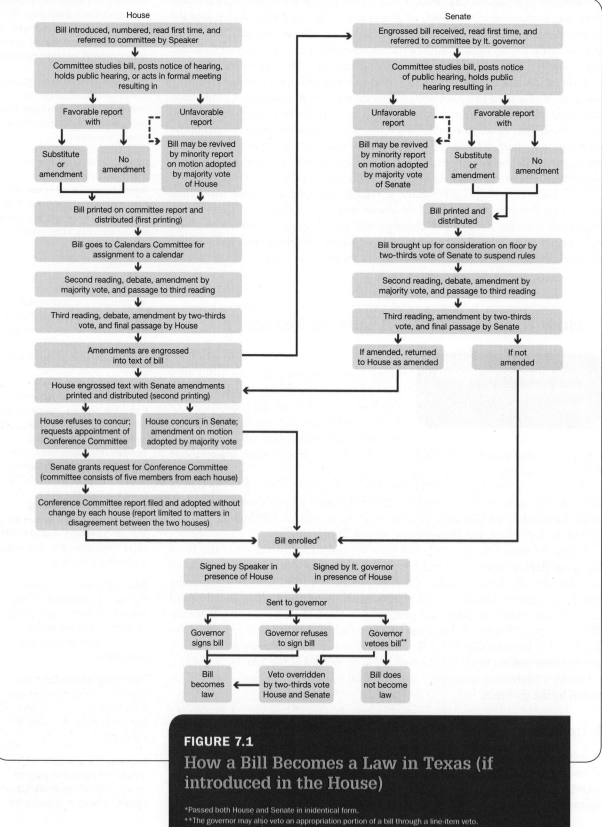

House

Bill introduced, numbered, read first time, and referred to committee by Speaker

Committee studies bill, posts notice of hearing, holds public hearing, or acts in formal meeting resulting in

Favorable report with

Unfavorable report

Substitute or amendment

No amendment

Bill may be revived by minority report on motion adopted by majority vote of House

Bill printed on committee report and distributed (first printing)

Bill goes to Calendars Committee for assignment to a calendar

Second reading, debate, amendment by majority vote, and passage to third reading

Third reading, debate, amendment by two-thirds vote, and final passage by House

Amendments are engrossed into text of bill

House engrossed text with Senate amendments printed and distributed (second printing)

House refuses to concur; requests appointment of Conference Committee

House concurs in Senate; amendment on motion adopted by majority vote

Senate grants request for Conference Committee (committee consists of five members from each house)

Conference Committee report filed and adopted without change by each house (report limited to matters in disagreement between the two houses)

Senate

Engrossed bill received, read first time, and referred to committee by lt. governor

Committee studies bill, posts notice of public hearing, holds public hearing resulting in

Unfavorable report

Favorable report with

Bill may be revived by minority report on motion adopted by majority vote of Senate

Substitute or amendment

No amendment

Bill printed and distributed

Bill brought up for consideration on floor by two-thirds vote of Senate to suspend rules

Second reading, debate, amendment by majority vote, and passage to third reading

Third reading, amendment by two-thirds vote, and final passage by Senate

If amended, returned to House as amended

If not amended

Bill enrolled*

Signed by Speaker in presence of House

Signed by lt. governor in presence of House

Sent to governor

Governor signs bill

Governor refuses to sign bill

Governor vetoes bill**

Bill becomes law

Veto overridden by two-thirds vote House and Senate

Bill does not become law

FIGURE 7.1

How a Bill Becomes a Law in Texas (if introduced in the House)

*Passed both House and Senate in inidentical form.
**The governor may also veto an appropriation portion of a bill through a line-item veto.
SOURCE: Texas State Senate, *Citizen Handbook*.

Rules of the legislature require that the bill be read on three separate occasions. After enrollment, the bill is read for the first time by its number, title, and caption. There is great variation in the number of bills introduced by various members of the legislature. Senator John Whitmire of Houston, for example, introduced 5 bills in one legislative session; Senator Eliot Shapleigh of El Paso filed nearly 100 bills. The variation is related, in part, to the political philosophy of the legislators. Whitmire, for example, believes his constituents think there are already too many laws and that his job is to look at legislation that ought to be killed or opposed. Others believe that constituents judge them on the number of bills they introduce. Still others think it is important to represent the views of their constituents by introducing the bills their district wants. Still others file bills they know will be defeated, simply to make a point.[12]

Referral

After undergoing first reading, the bill is assigned to a standing committee by the Speaker. In the Senate, the lieutenant governor assigns it to a committee. Since committees in the Texas Legislature have overlapping jurisdictions, the Speaker and lieutenant governor can assign a bill to a friendly committee or an unfriendly one. The committee to which a bill is assigned can determine whether the bill survives or dies in committee.

Committee Action

Every bill introduced in the Texas Legislature is assigned to a **standing committee**, and the vast majority of bills die in committee. The chair of the committee kills most by pigeonholing. **Pigeonholing** means that the committee chair sets the bill aside and never brings it before the committee.

Standing committees are considered the "workhorses" of the legislature (see Table 7.2). If the bill does not die, it most likely is amended. Few bills leave the committee in the same form as they arrived. Parts of several bills can also be combined to form a single bill. Changes are made to make the bill more acceptable to the entire legislature or to meet the political desires of the leadership or members of the committee. Hearings can take place to allow experts and the public to educate committee members on the good and bad points of the bill. In the Senate, all bills reported by the committee must have a public hearing.

standing committee a permanent committee with the power to propose and write legislation that covers a particular subject, such as finance or agriculture

pigeonholing a step in the legislative process during which a bill is killed by the chair of the standing committee to which it was referred, as a result of his or her setting the bill aside and not bringing it before the committee

Floor Action

In the House, bills referred by a standing committee go next to the Calendars Committee, which, after consulting the Speaker, schedules bills for debate. In the Senate, the lieutenant governor controls the agenda and decides when a bill will be considered.

The Speaker determines the length of debate in the House. Customarily, each member is allowed 10 minutes of debate. Early in the session when the agenda is not crowded, debate may last longer. Later in the session when there is a crush of legislative business, debate will be more limited. Some bills will be voted on without debate; however, important or controversial bills are usually allocated adequate time. Debate in the Senate is unlimited, which means it is possible for a senator to **filibuster**. A filibuster occurs when a senator talks for a lengthy period of time in an effort to kill a bill or to obtain amendments or other compromises. There are

filibuster a tactic used by members of the Senate to prevent action on legislation they oppose by continuously holding the floor and speaking until the majority backs down. Once given the floor, senators have unlimited time to speak, and it requires a vote of three-fifths of the Senate to end a filibuster

TABLE 7.2

Standing Committees of the Texas Senate and House (82nd Legislature)

SENATE COMMITTEES

Administration	Finance	Jurisprudence
Agriculture & Rural Affairs	Government Organization	Natural Resources
Business & Commerce	Health & Human Services	Nominations
Criminal Justice	Higher Education	State Affairs
Economic Development	Intergovernmental Relations	Transportation & Homeland Security
Education	International Relations & Trade	Veterans Affairs & Military Installations

HOUSE COMMITTEES

Agriculture & Livestock	Environmental Regulation	Pensions, Investments & Financial Services
Appropriations	General Investigating & Ethics	Public Education
Border & Intergovernmental Affairs	Government Efficiency and Reform	Public Health
Business & Industry	Higher Education	Redistricting
Calendars	Homeland Security & Public Safety	Rules & Resolutions
Corrections	House Administration	State Affairs
County Affairs	Human Services	Technology
Criminal Jurisprudence	Insurance	Transportation
Culture, Recreation & Tourism	Judiciary & Civil Jurisprudence	Urban Affairs
Defense & Veterans' Affairs	Land & Resource Management	Ways & Means
Economic & Small Business Development	Licensing & Administrative Procedures	
Elections	Local & Consent Calendars	
Energy Resources	Natural Resources	

certain rules that apply to the filibuster in the Texas Senate that are quite different from those in the U.S. Senate. There is no eating or drinking during a filibuster. Senators must stand at their desks and may not lean, sit, or use their desk or chair in any way. Remarks must be confined to the issue under consideration. Finally, one must speak in an audible voice.

In the past 72 years, there have been more than 100 filibusters. The longest filibuster was in 1977 by Senator Bill Meier, who spoke for 43 hours. Given the time constraints under which the Texas Legislature operates, even the threat of a filibuster may be sufficient to kill or force changes in a bill.

Another tactic used in both the House and the Senate to prevent or delay passage of a bill is called "chubbing." Here, one or more members debate bills at length to slow down the legislative process. Like the filibuster, this is a particularly effective tactic as the legislative session draws to a close.

Sponsors of a bill are expected to gather sufficient votes to pass the bill. In fact, before the Calendars Committee schedules the bill for floor debate, sponsors often assure the committee that they have enough votes to pass the bill.

The Texas Senate has a rule that bills shall be considered according to the "regular order of business." This means that bills and resolutions are considered on second reading and listed in the order in which the committee report was received by the Secretary of the Senate. Bills and resolutions are considered on the third reading in the order in which they were passed on the second reading. In order to conduct business, especially when dealing with legislation that is controversial, this "regular order" blocks consideration of legislation because it can be considered only if the Senate suspends this rule requiring consideration in order. A two-thirds vote is required to suspend the rules. Thus, for all practical purposes, legislation in the Senate must have two-thirds support to pass rather than a simple majority. In the 2011 legislative session, the highly partisan issue of requiring an identification document to vote was excluded from the two-thirds rule, which made it possible for Senate Republicans to pass the legislation.

When a bill passes both the House and Senate, it is examined. If there are differences between the bill passed by the House and that passed by the Senate, the two bills are sent to a conference committee.

Before a law is passed in Texas, it is voted on by the two chambers of the legislature—the House and the Senate. Here, former state senator Jeff Wentworth casts a vote; raising one finger means "yes" and two fingers mean "no."

Conference Committee

Bills must pass the House and Senate in exactly the same form. If the bill is different in any way, it is sent to a conference committee. Conference committees have 10 members: 5 members from the House appointed by the Speaker, and 5 members from the Senate appointed by the lieutenant governor.

Under legislative rules, the conference committee consists of 5 members from the House and Senate. Senate rules require that 2 members of the standing committee that considered the bill must be appointed. Unless specifically instructed, the conference committee cannot change parts of the bill that are the same. Changes are made and compromises reached only on parts of the bill that differ.

Once a compromise is reached, the report of the conference committee goes to the House and Senate. It can be debated in each chamber, but the report cannot be changed. It must be either accepted or rejected as is. If either chamber fails to approve the report of the conference committee, the bill is dead. Although it is possible for the conference committee to try a second time to reach a compromise, it is unusual for conference committees to do so.

If the report is agreed to in both chambers of the legislature, a final copy of the bill is prepared. The Speaker of the House, the clerk of the House, the president of the Senate (lieutenant governor), and the secretary of the Senate sign the bill. The next stop is the governor's desk.

The Governor

veto according to the Texas Constitution, the governor's power to turn down legislation; can be overridden by a two-thirds vote of both the House and Senate

post-adjournment veto a veto of a bill that occurs after the legislature adjourns, thus preventing the legislature from overriding it

The governor can influence legislation through the veto or the line-item veto. The threat of a veto can be powerful, as legislators often try to take the governor's preferences into account and avoid a veto.

It is the governor's responsibility to sign or **veto** legislation. During the first 130 days of a regular session, the governor has 10 days from the time a bill arrives on his desk to sign or veto the legislation. If he neither signs nor vetoes the bill in the 10 days, it becomes law without his signature. In the last 10 days of a session, he has 20 days from the time the bill arrives on his desk to sign or veto the legislation. Again, if he does neither, it becomes law without his signature. Unlike the U.S. president, who may sometimes kill a bill without signing it through what is called a "pocket veto," the Texas governor does not have this power.

The governor's veto can be overridden by a two-thirds vote of both the House and Senate. Anytime the governor vetoes a bill, he attaches a message explaining why it was vetoed. It is then returned to the chamber that originated the bill. If the presiding officer elects to allow a vote to override the veto, a vote is scheduled. Only two vetoes have been overridden in more than 70 years.

Many bills arrive on the governor's desk in the last few days of a session. Almost all important or controversial bills reach the governor in the waning moments of a session. If the governor wants to veto a bill that comes to him from day 131 to day 140, he simply waits until the legislature adjourns to exercise the veto. His veto cannot be overridden because the legislature has adjourned. Vetoing legislation after legislative adjournment is called a **post-adjournment veto**, or a strong veto, since the legislature has no opportunity to overturn the veto. The post-adjournment veto

TABLE 7.3

Total Number of Vetoes by Texas Governors

YEAR	GOVERNOR	TOTAL VETOES
2011	Perry	25
2009	Perry	38
2007	Perry	54
2005	Perry	19
2003	Perry	48
2001	Perry	82*
1999	Bush	33
1997	Bush	37
1995	Bush	25
1993	Richards	26
1991	Richards	36

*Record number of vetoes by a Texas governor.
SOURCE: Texas Legislature, "Legislative Statistics," April 20, 2010; Legislative Reference Library of Texas, "Bill Statistics."

provides the governor with an excellent bargaining tool, since he can threaten a veto unless changes are made in a bill.

The governor also has a **line-item veto** that allows him or her to sign a bill and draw lines through specific items, deleting them from the bill. Except for the items that the governor has deleted, the bill becomes law. In Texas, the line-item veto applies only to the state's omnibus appropriations bill. Governor Perry used the line-item veto in 2009 to reduce the state budget by $97.2 million in general revenue and $288.9 from all funding sources.[13] In 2011, it was expected that Governor Perry would veto the funding for the Texas Historical Commission, as he had earlier proposed the abolition of the commission. Surprisingly, he did not do so.[14] Table 7.3 provides the total number of vetoes by Texas governors since 1991.

line-item veto the power of the executive to veto specific provisions (lines) of an appropriations bill passed by the legislature

Other Ways in Which the Governor Influences Legislation   Message power is the governor's ability to communicate with the legislature. Early in each session, the governor delivers a State of the State message that is similar to the president's State of the Union message. In this address, the governor puts forth a vision for Texas and what legislation will accomplish that vision. If the governor chooses to submit an executive budget, a letter stating why this budget should be adopted accompanies it.

Periodically, the governor will visit with legislators to gain their vote on a bill. A personal visit can be persuasive, but increasingly, it is members of the governor's paid staff who are sent on these legislative visits. Like lobbyists for corporations and interest groups, the governor's representatives use their skills to encourage passage of bills the governor favors and to kill bills the governor opposes. However, there is a problem with this practice. The Texas Constitution forbids use of tax dollars to influence the legislature, and the governor's staff is, of course, paid through tax dollars. The governor's representatives avoid this ban by claiming they are simply providing needed information to the legislators. One should not underestimate the informal power that the governor has to influence legislation.

Additional Players in the Legislative Process

Describe the roles of other state officials in shaping legislation

In addition to the legislators and the governor, there are others involved in the lawmaking process during both regular and special sessions. One official, the comptroller, has direct involvement in the legislative process, while other players are involved indirectly.

The Comptroller of Public Accounts

The comptroller of public accounts issues revenue estimates to inform the legislature of the amount of money it can spend in the next two years. Texas's operating budgets must balance. The Texas Constitution forbids borrowing money to conduct the daily operations of government. The estimate provided by the comptroller sets the limit on state spending. If the legislature wants to spend more than the comptroller estimates, it must enhance revenue—that is, increase taxes and fees.

The comptroller's estimates can be political in nature. The comptroller can provide a low revenue estimate and tell the legislature that the estimate will remain low until it passes bills the comptroller wants. On passage of those bills, the comptroller can revise the estimate to increase the spending limit and allow the legislature to complete its business.

The media can influence the legislative agenda through the stories that they cover. Accordingly, legislators try to attract media attention that will support their positions. Here, House Speaker Joe Straus speaks at a press conference.

The Media

Media can determine issues of importance by the selection of stories they cover. If the media cover more stories on crime, crime and criminal justice issues will move toward the top of the legislature's agenda. A media focus on corporate fraud, rising homeowners insurance rates, alcohol-related traffic deaths, or poor performance by Texas public school students will increase legislative attention to these issues.

The media inform the public about the issues the legislature is considering and about the job the legislature is doing during the session. Media coverage of the legislature provides the public with needed information on what is going on in Austin. Stories portraying the legislature as modern, efficient, and hardworking provide the public with a positive image of the legislature, whereas stories about legislators sleeping at their desks or killing legislation on technicalities provide a negative image.

The Courts

Federal and state courts influence the legislative agenda. In recent years, the courts' scrutiny has included the prison system, the state's treatment of patients in state mental hospitals, the funding of public education, and equality of funding for colleges and universities in South Texas. The ability to rule acts of the legislature and actions of state agencies unconstitutional gives courts significant power over issues the legislature addresses. To a remarkable degree, state and federal courts have issued decisions that have forced the Texas Legislature to act in areas that the legislature would have preferred to avoid—largely because action required a significant expenditure of money. For example, many recent legislative actions directed toward criminal justice and public education are responses to court rulings.

Lobbyists

During a regular session, roughly 1,800 individuals register as lobbyists and attempt to influence the legislature. A lobbyist's responsibility is to convince legislators to support the interest the lobbyist represents. Lobbyists want legislators' votes on bills. At the least, they desire access to legislators.

The Public

Individuals can influence legislators. Legislators are evaluated at each election. If the people believe their elected officials are representing them well, legislators are re-elected. A legislator who fails to live up to expectations might not be re-elected.

The public can serve as lobbyists. Letters, e-mail, or telephone calls urging representatives or senators to vote a certain way constitute a lobbying effort. Members of the public can also write legislation, but must convince at least one legislator to sponsor it and introduce it for consideration by the legislature.

The public and interest groups may also influence the legislature. During a special session in which the legislature dealt with tax reduction, these Houston-area realtors and others demonstrated in favor of property tax relief.

Power in the Legislature

Analyze how party leadership and redistricting affect power in the legislature

Among the most powerful political figures in Texas are the leaders of the House and Senate. They play a key role in structuring the committees of the legislature, setting the state's political agenda, and passing (or defeating) bills.

Leadership

Speaker the chief presiding officer of the House of Representatives. The Speaker is the most important party and House leader, and can influence the legislative agenda, the fate of individual pieces of legislation, and members' positions within the House

The **Speaker** of the Texas House of Representatives and the lieutenant governor are two of the most powerful political figures in the state. Republican representative Joe Straus of San Antonio is currently the Speaker of the House. Republican David Dewhurst is the current lieutenant governor. The Texas House and Senate endow both officials with considerable control over the legislative process. It is fair to say that either of them can usually kill legislation they oppose, and often they have the power to pass legislation they support.

Members of the House elect the Speaker at the beginning of the regular session. Additionally, at the start of each regular session, members of the House adopt rules that give the Speaker institutional powers sufficient to control the work of the House. Speakers usually are the dominant figures in the Texas House and wield vast power.

One of the most interesting developments in modern times in the Texas Legislature was the turmoil surrounding the 2002–08 speakership of Republican Tom Craddick. Craddick first challenged the Democratic Speaker "Pete" Laney and ultimately displaced Laney when the Republicans gained control of the House. Craddick worked to redistrict Texas congressional districts so as to increase substantially the number of Republicans in the Texas congressional delegation. As Speaker, Craddick was accused of micromanaging the House, of taking discretion away from committee chairs, and of insisting that members support his views on key issues even when contrary to the desires of their constituents. Republicans also lost seats in the Texas House between 2004 and 2006—a loss blamed in part on Craddick's leadership. The result was an open rebellion against Craddick, who was able to retain his position in the 2007 session only by resorting to a questionable parliamentary maneuver: he refused to recognize a motion to "vacate the chair," which would have caused a vote on his fate as Speaker.[15] It is doubtful that such dissension over a Speaker has occurred since Ira Evans was removed as Speaker in 1871.[16] In 2009, Craddick lost his speakership to Joe Straus, a Republican from San Antonio, who was elected Speaker by a coalition of anti-Craddick Republicans and Democrats. Straus faced opposition in 2011 from conservatives who saw him as too moderate and as too favorable to Democrats, but Straus was able to retain his position as Speaker.

The lieutenant governor is elected statewide to a four-year term. His or her major responsibility is to serve as president of the Senate and to preside over the Senate. Unlike the Speaker, the lieutenant governor is not a member of the Senate, simply its presiding officer, who may vote only to break a tie.

The Speaker of the House is one of the most powerful people in Texas politics. In 2009, Tom Craddick (left) was replaced as Speaker by Joe Straus (right).

At the start of each regular session, senators adopt rules that the Senate will follow for the next two years. These rules give the lieutenant governor enormous control of the work of the Senate.

Centralizing Power: Sources of the Leadership's Power

The operation of the Texas Legislature is significantly different from that of the U.S. Congress. In the U.S. Congress, the leader of the president's party in the House and the Senate is the president's spokesperson in that house of Congress. Additionally, the level of partisanship is high. Committee appointments are made in such a way that the majority party controls every important committee, and chairs of those committees are always members of the majority party. Each house of Congress has majority party leadership and minority party leadership. Such divisions do not exist in the Texas Legislature. No member of the Texas Legislature is formally known as the governor's spokesperson.

Although there is partisanship in the Texas Legislature, it is not at the level found in the U.S. Congress. There is no majority and minority party leadership, for example. Committee assignments and committee chairmanship appointments cross party lines so that in the Texas House, for example, where the majority party is now Republican, a Democrat may chair an important committee and successfully sponsor important legislation.[17] This somewhat nonpartisan structure of the Texas Legislature is important from the perspective of leadership. If the governor has no leader in the legislature, and if the membership does not owe allegiance to party leaders in the legislature, then leadership and power are further centralized in the Speaker and lieutenant governor. The Speaker and lieutenant governor can make appointments with limited regard for party affiliation, thus ensuring that members will be loyal to them rather than to the party.

Nevertheless, the redistricting controversy in 2003 did result in a more partisan legislature in 2005. It is clear that since that time, the Texas Legislature has moved into a more partisan era. Other factors may also undermine the tradition of nonpartisan politics in the state legislature. Most of the powers of the Speaker and of the lieutenant governor are granted by the rules that each chamber's membership votes on at the beginning of the legislative session. The powers of the Speaker and of the lieutenant governor could potentially be greatly reduced if the members of the legislature so chose. One could, for example, imagine a future Republican Senate that would reduce the powers of the lieutenant governor over the Texas Senate if a Democrat were elected lieutenant governor. Of course, one of the first rules that would have to change is the requirement of a two-thirds vote for a bill in the Senate to be voted on out of order. Indeed, the two-thirds rule in the state Senate encourages some degree of bipartisanship, because Republicans do not quite control two-thirds of the Senate and so need Democratic votes.

The two-thirds rule came under attack in the 2009 special session of the legislature and it continued to be criticized in 2011, mainly because the requirement of such a large supermajority makes it difficult to pass bills that arouse partisan tensions. Democrats support the rule because with it, Democratic support is needed to pass any bill in the Senate. Some Republicans wanted to abandon the rule in order to allow their majority to pass legislation without Democratic support. Others want to weaken the requirement of a supermajority by having a three-fifths rule instead of a two-thirds rule. Still other Republicans are inclined to support the long precedent of a two-thirds requirement. At least for the time being, the two-thirds rule remains. However, it can be easily changed at some point, as the rules of the Senate are passed by majority vote.[18]

for critical analysis

Who are the most important leaders in the Texas Legislature? What are their powers? How does the battle over redistricting illustrate the party politics within the legislature?

In 2011, Representative J. M. Lozano announced that he was leaving the Democrats and joining the House Republicans. This switch gave the Republicans a supermajority of 100 members in the House, enabling them to pass legislation without fear of Democratic interference.

recognition The power to control floor debate by recognizing who can speak before the House and Senate

The Republican congressional redistricting bill in 2003 led to abandonment of the two-thirds rule for that bill so that redistricting that was beneficial to Republicans could be passed. That bill would have been impossible to pass without changes in the rules that allowed passage by majority vote. In the 2009 special session of the legislature, the Texas Senate passed a highly partisan bill that required voters to show identification solely because the two-thirds rule was abandoned for that bill.[19] It was not until 2011, when the Texas Senate again abandoned the two-thirds rule, that the voter identification bill became law.

As the Texas Senate becomes more partisan, it seems likely that there will be increased use of special rule changes to allow for the passage of controversial bills, a lowering of the two-thirds supermajority requirement for passing a bill, or a complete abandonment of the two-thirds rule in favor of majority rule.

The structure of the Texas Legislature and the lack of formal lines of gubernatorial authority in the legislature are very important in centralizing power in the hands of the Speaker and the lieutenant governor. However, these officials have other important sources of power as well. One of those powers—a power especially important in the Texas House—is the power of **recognition**. The Senate rule allowing unlimited debate decreases the lieutenant governor's power in this area. In the House, the Speaker controls legislative debate, including who speaks and how long debate will last. On occasion, the Speaker ignores or skips a member seeking recognition to speak. This is a signal to other members of the House that this individual has fallen from the Speaker's good graces. That ability to pick and choose among those desiring to speak on the House floor, however, allows the Speaker to structure the debate and to affect the outcome of legislation.

As mentioned earlier, the Senate has a rule that for bills to be voted on, they must be taken in order and, for a bill to be taken out of order, there must be a two-thirds vote. Given the vast powers of the lieutenant governor, on issues that are important to him, he can usually control the votes of at least one-third of the membership. Thus, if a bill is opposed by the lieutenant governor, he can frequently prevent it from being taken out of order for consideration.

One of the most important sources of power for the Speaker and the lieutenant governor is the committee assignment power. The committees on which legislators serve are important to individual members and to the presiding officer. For members, assignments to powerful committees increase their prestige in the legislature. Committee assignment also affects how well constituents are represented. Assigning members to standing committees is one of the most important duties of the lieutenant governor and the Speaker.

The Speaker and the lieutenant governor have major roles in appointing the membership of committees, appointing chairs of committees, and setting the legislative agenda. Party affiliation and seniority are of only moderate importance in committee assignments. The most important factor in committee assignments is the members' relationships with the presiding officer. In order to maintain control over the legislature, the Speaker and lieutenant governor use their committee assignment powers to appoint members who are loyal to them and who support their legislative agendas. When chairs and vice chairs of important committees are appointed, usually only the most loyal friends and allies of the Speaker and lieutenant governor are chosen. In 2011, 6 of the 18 standing committee chairs in the Senate were Democrats. Eleven of the 36 standing committee chairs in the House were Democrats.

Not only do the Speaker and the lieutenant governor have vast committee assignment powers, but committees in the Texas Legislature also have overlapping jurisdiction. Although each bill must be assigned to a committee, it can be assigned to more than one committee. Since the Speaker and the lieutenant governor assign bills to committees in their respective chambers, they use the bill assignment power to influence the fate of the bill. They can, for example, assign bills they oppose to committees they believe hostile to the bill and those they support to committees they believe will favor the bill.

Since bills must pass the House and Senate in exactly the same form, the Speaker and the lieutenant governor can exercise still another important influence on policy through their power to appoint conference committees. As we have seen, if any differences exist in a bill passed by both the House and the Senate, the bill goes to a conference committee that works out the differences in the House and Senate versions. By appointing the conference committee members, the Speaker and lieutenant governor can affect the language and even the fate of the bill.

Redistricting

One of the most controversial and partisan issues is **redistricting**—the redrawing of district lines for the Texas House, the Texas Senate, and the U.S. House of Representatives, which must be done at least every 10 years, after the federal census.

There are 150 Texas House districts and 31 Texas Senate districts. One senator or one member of the House represents each district. This is called representation by **single-member districts**.

After each census, the legislature draws new boundaries for each Texas House and Senate district. Newly drawn districts for the Texas House and Senate must contain an almost equal number of people in order to ensure equal representation. That requirement guarantees that each person's vote counts the same whether the vote is cast in Houston, Big Lake, El Paso, Presidio, Brownsville, or Commerce.

For much of the first half of the twentieth century, Texas and other states failed to draw new boundaries, and even after U.S. Supreme Court decisions, Texas did not do so willingly. Not until the U.S. Supreme Court's decisions in *Baker v. Carr* (1962) and *Reynolds v. Sims* (1964), compelling the legislature to draw new districts,

redistricting the process of redrawing election districts and redistributing legislative representatives in the Texas House, Texas Senate, and U.S. House. This usually happens every 10 years to reflect shifts in population or in response to legal challenges in existing districts

single-member district a district in which one official is elected rather than multiple officials

one-person, one-vote principle
the principle that all districts should have roughly equal populations

were boundaries drawn that represented the population fairly.[20] These and subsequent decisions meant that Texas had to draw legislative districts of roughly equal populations—a concept known as the **one-person, one-vote principle**.

Congressional redistricting is also a responsibility of the legislature. Once the U.S. Congress apportions itself, the Texas Legislature divides Texas into the appropriate number of congressional districts. According to the 1964 Supreme Court case *Wesberry v. Sanders*, each state's U.S. House districts must be equal in population.[21] Depending on how the districts are drawn, the representation of the two political parties in the U.S. House of Representatives can be significantly changed. Indeed, reapportionment can so change the division of the parties that control of the U.S. House of Representatives can be affected. Thus, maneuvering over redistricting is highly partisan.

If the legislature fails to redistrict at the first regular session after the census, the task falls to the Legislative Redistricting Board (LRB). The LRB has five ex officio members: the lieutenant governor, the Speaker of the House, the attorney general, the commissioner of the General Land Office, and the comptroller of public accounts.

When the legislature adjourns without redistricting, the LRB convenes. The LRB must meet within 90 days of legislative adjournment and complete its responsibilities within another 60 days. Even here, the influence of the Speaker and the lieutenant governor is clearly visible.

Texas redistricting plans must comply with the federal Voting Rights Act which, among other things, protects minorities from being disadvantaged by a redistricting plan. A federal court can temporarily redraw district lines if a redistricting violates this law.

Partisan differences in the state legislature resulted in the failure to pass a redistricting plan in 2001 during its regular session, transferring the responsibility to the Republican-dominated LRB. On a split vote, the board developed redistricting plans that appeared to favor the Republican Party. The board's decision, in turn, was appealed to the federal courts. A three-judge panel, composed of two Democrats and one Republican, approved the lines drawn for the state Senate, noting that the U.S. Justice Department had determined that the plan did not violate the Voting Rights Act. However, the court modified the board's plan for the House,

In 2006 the U.S. Supreme Court upheld most of the new boundaries drawn in the Republicans' controversial redistricting but found that some of the redrawn districts failed to protect minority voting rights. Here, Governor Perry displays the new redistricting map. The new map drawn by Republicans after the 2010 census again went to federal courts.

arguing that the Department of Justice had rejected the plan because it was seen as diluting Hispanic voting strength in three areas of the state. The court felt that its role in the entire redistricting process was constrained. In their decision, the judges commented that "federal courts have a limited role in considering challenges to pre-cleared, legislatively adopted redistricting plans."[22]

The final plan approved by the court appeared to be a great victory for the Republican Party. Twenty-seven incumbent Democrats found themselves placed in districts with other Democratic incumbents. Four Democrats who chaired key committees announced that they would not seek re-election. Many observers felt that redistricting would make the Republicans the majority party in the House and would maintain their majority status in the Senate. And many doubted that the Speaker of the House, Democrat Pete Laney, would be able to mobilize the votes needed for re-election to the speakership in the next session. After the 2002 elections, these observers were proven correct.[23]

Power and Partisanship in the Redistricting Battle

Republican control of the Texas House and Senate in 2002 heralded more than simply a shift in party control of the legislature. With Republican control came a significant decline in the harmonious, bipartisan spirit that had largely governed the Texas Legislature. The Republican leadership, especially House Speaker Tom Craddick, chose to govern in a more partisan fashion. Additionally, a number of Democrats in the House who saw their power slipping away chose a rebellious course. They worked to make Craddick's speakership a difficult one, obstructing Republican legislative efforts as much as possible.

This new partisan tension in the Texas Legislature rose to a fever pitch in 2003 when Republicans, with the support of the Republican majority leader Tom DeLay, sought to alter the Texas congressional districts for partisan advantage. The Republican goal was to increase Republican representation in the Texas congressional delegation and, in so doing, help ensure a continuing Republican majority in the U.S. House of Representatives. The Republican effort was unconventional in that it occurred in mid-cycle—that is, it was the second redistricting after the 2000 census. As a rule, redistricting occurs only once after each decennial census, although there is no legal requirement that this be the case.

After the 2000 census, the Texas Legislature could not agree on redistricting, and a federal court devised a plan. The 2000 congressional redistricting gave the Democrats an advantage. With control of the state legislature, however, Republicans argued that the existing redistricting plan was unsatisfactory because it reflected a Democratic majority that no longer existed. Republicans wanted a plan that more clearly reflected Republican voting in Texas.[24] In 2000, Democrats won 17 congressional seats and Republicans won 13, even though Republicans won 59 percent of votes in the state and Democrats received only 40 percent. In 2002, Democrats got only 41 percent of the statewide vote, but they won 17 seats to 15 for the Republicans. In fact, since 1996, Republicans had never received less than 55 percent of the statewide vote, and Democrats never won more than 44 percent, yet Republicans were a minority in the Texas congressional delegation. With the new redistricting plan in 2004, Republicans got 58 percent of the statewide vote and elected 21 members of Congress from Texas. Democrats got 41 percent of the statewide vote and elected 11 members of Congress from Texas.[25]

Although the Texas Legislature is not as susceptible to partisan squabbling as the U.S. Congress, flare-ups between the Democrats and Republicans do occur. For example, in this photo, Texas House Democrats celebrate their return to Texas in May 2003, after spending four days in Ardmore, Oklahoma, to kill a GOP-produced congressional redistricting plan.

The Republican congressional redistricting plan was not enacted without political turmoil, however. At the end of 2003, 51 Democrats from the state legislature walked out and gathered in Ardmore, Oklahoma, where the Texas state police did not have jurisdiction to bring them back to the state capitol. The result was that a quorum could not be reached to pass the plan. The Democratic legislators did not return to Austin until redistricting was taken off the agenda. A special legislative session was called to deal with redistricting, but the two-thirds rule in the state Senate prevented the bill from being passed. In a second special session that was called to deal with redistricting, 11 of the 12 Democratic members of the Senate fled to Albuquerque in order to prevent a Senate vote. Finally, a third special session produced a plan that passed both houses of the legislature.[26]

Most notable about the 2004 redistricting was that seven incumbent congressional Democrats were targeted for defeat. A lawsuit that challenged the redistricting on the grounds that it diluted minority votes stressed that the Democrats had been elected with minority support. The lawsuit also pointed out that these seven Democrats had either been paired so that they had to run against another incumbent or had been given a more Republican district.[27] A case before the U.S. Supreme Court challenged the extremely partisan gerrymandering of the Texas redistricting, its reduction of the strength of minority voters, and its use of the now outdated 2000 census. The Court did find that there had been a reduction in the strength of minority voters. However, the extremely partisan gerrymander and the mid-decennial redistricting using the 2000 census were upheld. For the most part, Republicans were successful in reshaping the partisan composition of the Texas delegation to the U.S. House of Representatives. However, the 2006 election led to Democratic control of the U.S. House and to a Texas congressional delegation with vastly weakened power due to the loss of key Democrats in the redistricting.[28]

The 2010 census led to another round of redistricting for the Texas Legislature and the U.S. House of Representatives. The overwhelmingly Republican legislature designed a redistricting plan strongly favorable to Republicans, but the plan ran afoul of a federal court which held that minority voting rights were violated. The court ordered a redistricting plan that was more favorable to Democrats.

● Thinking Critically about the Texas Legislature

The Texas Legislature has undergone great changes and continues to do so. Perhaps the most significant change has been the increasing partisanship. The Texas Legislature is less partisan than the U.S. Congress, but the Texas party divide was especially notable under Speaker Tom Craddick, during the redistricting battles, and during the battles over a voter identification law in 2009 and 2011.

The two-thirds rule in the Texas Senate is under attack. That rule requires considerable consensus to pass legislation from that body. If the two-thirds rule is reduced to a three-fifths rule or even majority rule, there will be renewed partisanship and rancor in the Texas Senate.

The Texas Legislature seems in some ways like an archaic institution. Unless there are special sessions, it meets once every two years and is a part-time body with very limited compensation for its members. The structure of the legislature, however, has survived since the 1876 Constitution, and there seems little likelihood that the structure will soon change.

Especially notable regarding the legislature is the vast power held by the Speaker and the lieutenant governor. The 1876 Constitution showed its distrust of a powerful governor, and the result is that in Texas the governor must share political influence with two other major powers in Texas government—the Speaker and the lieutenant governor, over whom the governor exerts no formal control. Still, the revolt against Speaker Craddick does remind us that it is perilous for the Speaker to try to exert so much power that he becomes subject to rebuke from a constituency whose views he ultimately must reflect—the views of a majority of the members of the Texas House.

study guide

(S) **Practice online with:** Chapter 7 Diagnostic Quiz ■ Chapter 7 Key Term Flashcards

Structure of the Texas Legislature

■ **Describe the bicameral organization of the legislature and the rules for membership (pp. 183–87)**

The Texas Legislature is bicameral. The leader of the House is the Speaker, and the Lieutenant Governor presides over the Texas Senate. Although the typical member of the legislature is white and male, women and minorities have increased their representation in recent years.

Key Terms

bicameral (p. 183)

per diem (p. 186)

Practice Quiz

1. There are _____ members of the Texas Senate, and state senators serve a _____ year term. *(p. 183)*
   a) 31/4
   b) 100/6
   c) 150/2
   d) 300/6
   e) 435/2

2. Texas House members differ from Texas Senate members because *(p. 183)*
   a) House members represent smaller districts and are subject to more frequent elections.
   b) House members represent people and senators represent counties.
   c) House members are elected from single-member districts and senators from multimember districts.
   d) House members have term limits and senators do not have term limits.
   e) House members must live in the state for 10 years before standing for election.

(S) **Practice Online**
"Who Are Texans?" interactive exercise: *Who Are the Members of the Texas Legislature?*

Sessions of the Legislature

■ **Explain when the legislature meets (pp. 187–89)**

The Texas Legislature meets once every two years for 140 days and additionally as required in special sessions called by the governor. Special sessions must have a specific purpose, such as redistricting or school finance.

Key Terms

regular session (p. 187)

biennial (p. 187)

special session (p. 187)

Practice Quiz

3. The Texas Legislature meets in regular session *(p. 187)*
   a) 90 days every year.
   b) 180 days every year.
   c) 140 days each odd-numbered year and 60 days each even-numbered year.
   d) 140 days each odd-numbered year.
   e) 180 days each even-numbered year.

4. The agenda for a special session of the Texas Legislature is set by the *(p. 187)*
   a) lieutenant governor and the Speaker of the House.
   b) governor.
   c) Texas Supreme Court.
   d) chair of the Joint committee on Special Sessions.
   e) agenda-setting committee.

Powers of the Legislature

■ **Outline the legislative and nonlegislative powers of the legislature (pp. 189–91)**

The Texas Legislature passes bills and resolutions and supervises the state bureaucracy through the budgetary process and sunset legislation.

Key Terms

bill (p. 189)

local bill (p. 189)

special bill (p. 189)

general bill (p. 189)

resolution (p. 189)

concurrent resolution (p. 189)

joint resolution (p. 190)

simple resolution (p. 190)

constituent (p. 190)

electoral power (p. 190)

investigative power (p. 190)

directive and supervisory power (p. 191)

judicial power (p. 191)

impeachment (p. 191)

> **⑤ Practice Online**
> Video exercise: *Senator Eliot Shapleigh—A Day in the Life of a Texas Legislator*

How a Bill Becomes a Law in Texas

■ **Trace the process through which law is made in Texas (pp. 191–98)**

The Process of a how a bill becomes a law is similar to the federal level. A key difference is the governor's use of the line item veto by which he can eliminate individual appropriations or line itemsin the state budget. Additionally, the lieutenant governor and the Speaker of the Texas House have exceptionally strong powers. The committee system plays a major role in shaping the legislative process.

Key Terms

introduction (p. 191)

referral (p. 191)

consideration by standing committee (p. 191)

floor action (p. 191)

conference committee (p. 191)

action by the governor (p. 191)

standing committee (p. 193)

pigeonholing (p. 193)

filibuster (p. 193)

veto (p. 196)

post-adjournment veto (p. 196)

line-item veto (p. 197)

Practice Quiz

5. If a bill fails to pass the Texas House and Texas Senate in exactly the same form, the bill *(p. 195)*
   a) dies.
   b) is returned to the standing committee in the House or Senate that originally considered the bill.
   c) is sent to a conference committee.
   d) is sent to the governor, who decides which version of the bill will be signed.
   e) becomes a law.

6. The _____ provides the governor with a powerful tool with which to bargain with the legislature. *(pp. 196–97)*
   a) ability to introduce five bills in a regular session
   b) post-adjournment veto
   c) pocket veto
   d) message power
   e) initiative

Additional Players in the Legislative Process

■ **Describe the roles of other state officials in shaping legislation (pp. 198–99)**

Other than the two leaders in the House and the Senate, committee chairs have enormous influence in crafting legislation in Texas. The Comptroller plays an important role in legislation by issuing revenue estimates to inform the legislation about the money available for the legislature to spend.

Practice Quiz

7. Which state official, in large part, determines the total amount of money the legislature may appropriate? *(p. 198)*
   a) governor
   b) lieutenant governor
   c) treasury
   d) comptroller of public accounts
   e) attorney general

Power in the Legislature

■ **Analyze how party leadership and redistricting affect power in the legislature (pp. 200–207)**

The Speaker of the House and the lieutenant governor are the most important actors in the legislature. Together they help to centralize power in the legislature, and they facilitate or prevent the passage of legislation. The legislature has become increasingly partisan with one of the most partisan issues involving redistricting.

Key Terms

Speaker (p. 200)

recognition (p. 202)

redistricting (p. 203)

single-member districts (p. 203)

one-person, one-vote principle (p. 204)

Practice Quiz

8. The two most powerful political figures in the Texas Legislature are the *(p. 200)*
   a) governor and the lieutenant governor.
   b) governor and the attorney general.
   c) Speaker of the House and the governor.
   d) Speaker of the House and the lieutenant governor.
   e) Chairs of the finance committee in each house.

9. The Speaker of the Texas House is chosen *(p. 200)*
   a) in a statewide election.
   b) in a party-line vote by members of the Texas House.
   c) by a majority of the members of the House whether Democrat or Republican.
   d) by seniority in the House.
   e) by lot.

10. The lieutenant governor is the presiding officer of *(p. 200)*
    a) the Texas Senate.
    b) the governor's cabinet.
    c) the Texas Legislature.
    d) the Legislative Conference committees.
    e) the Treasury.

11. The chairs of the Texas House committees are *(p. 201)*
    a) of the same party as the Speaker.
    b) selected on the basis of seniority.
    c) chosen because of their experience.
    d) both Democrats and Republicans.
    e) independents.

12. The ability of the lieutenant governor and the Speaker of the House to control the final outcome of legislation comes from their power to *(p. 203)*
    a) appoint members of conference committees.
    b) refuse to approve the work of standing committees.
    c) exercise the legislative line-item veto.
    d) change up to three lines in any bill.
    e) control floor debate.

13. An important issue for the legislature at least every 10 years is *(p. 203)*
    a) adopting a budget.
    b) deciding the order of succession to the office of governor.
    c) impeaching the lieutenant governor.
    d) redistricting.
    e) electing the president.

14. In recent years, the Texas Legislature has *(p. 205)*
    a) become more partisan.
    b) become less partisan.
    c) become more experienced in lawmaking.
    d) been more inclined to let the governor make policy.
    e) been more respectful of county officials.

 Practice Online
Interactive simulation: *A Member of the Speaker's Team*

Recommended Websites

Chron.com—*Houston Chronicle*
www.chron.com/new/politics/

Speaker of the Texas House of Representatives
www.house.state.tx.us/speaker/welcome.htm

Texas Legislative Council
www.tlc.state.tx.us

Texas Legislature Online
www.capitol.state.tx.us

Texas Lieutenant Governor
www.senate.state.tx.us/75r/LtGov/Ltgov.htm

Window on State Government (Comptroller of Public Accounts) www.window.state.tx.us

Although the governor is the most visible leader in Texas politics, Texas governors have fewer powers than governors in other states. This is in keeping with Texans' mistrust of excessive governmental power. Like other Texas governors before him, Governor Rick Perry has frequently been checked by the legislature.

The Texas Executive Branch

WHAT GOVERNMENT DOES AND WHY IT MATTERS Candidates for the governorship in Texas can pursue several electoral strategies when seeking office. For example, they can try to direct attention to state issues, emphasizing their special abilities to address the concerns and problems facing Texans today. Alternatively, an unpopular presidential administration can drive state and local candidates to focus on their differences with national leaders and why the state and local candidates are better able to address the needs of the state. Or candidates can embrace a popular presidential administration and try to identify themselves with its larger vision of where the state and nation must go. By nationalizing the election, candidates seek to move the electorate's attention away from state politics to national politics.

The Texas Constitution limits the intrusion of national politics into state elections by scheduling the election of its governor and other executive officers every four years in "off-presidential years." Holding elections in off-presidential years, however, is no guarantee that national politics does not intrude into statewide elections. Indeed, the 2010 election was a classic example of how gubernatorial elections can be nationalized.

Governor Rick Perry rode anti-Washington sentiment to victory in the 2010 Republican primary and carried these anti-Washington themes into the general election campaign. Perry portrayed himself as a leader who would protect Texas from the excesses of the Obama administration. Although Perry's legislative accomplishments in two and a half terms as governor were modest at best, his popularity rose as his anti-Washington, anti-Democrat, anti-Obama message intensified.

Perry refused to debate his Democratic opponent Bill White on television, citing his opponent's failure to release certain tax returns as a reason. Commentators from the press were highly critical of this decision, bemoaning the fact that the key issues facing the state would never be discussed in an open forum. Conversation about the issues that ensued was largely one-sided, either between the press and one candidate or across campaign ads. One of the most important consequences of this limited debate over the issues was that Perry was able to sidestep discussing the most difficult issue that was facing the state—a burgeoning budget deficit.

Perry's strategy of nationalizing the 2010 gubernatorial race was highly successful. The week following the election, he published his first book: *Fed Up! Our Fight to Save America from Washington*. The book reads less like a conclusion to a race for the governorship than it does a preface to a future campaign for national office. Its anti-Washington theme is typical of Perry's 2010 campaign, which focused not on state issues—even as pressing as a gargantuan budget deficit—but on the evils of Washington and national power.

After the 2011 legislative session, Perry launched a national campaign for the Republican presidential nomination. Following an initial surge in the polls, the Perry campaign sputtered along after a series of gaffes by the candidate and his supporters. Unlike his predecessor in the governorship, George W. Bush, Perry had considerable difficulty translating his popularity in Texas into a national political presence.

chaptergoals

- Describe the powers of the Texas governor and the limits of the governor's power (pages 215–26)

- Identify the other elected officials who make up the plural executive (pages 226–34)

- Explain the roles played by boards, commissions, and regulatory agencies (pages 235–40)

● The Governor

Describe the powers of the Texas governor and the limits of the governor's power

At the national level, the president represents and is responsible to the people as a whole. The president is the spokesperson for the government and the people in national and international affairs. Throughout the twentieth century, various presidents parlayed the powers granted them by the U.S. Constitution into what some commentators call the "imperial presidency." The governorship in Texas is not an analogous imperial one. Compared with the president, the governor of Texas is weak. Executive power in Texas is divided among a number of separately elected officials, all of whom are elected by and responsible to the people as a whole. This plural executive has important implications for democratic life in the Lone Star State.

Although the governor of Texas is the most visible state official, Texas's governor has far less formal power than most governors. In 1983, a study of the appointment, budget, removal, and organizational powers of governors ranked Texas's governor forty-ninth in the nation, ahead only of the governor of South Carolina.[1] In 1990, a study of gubernatorial authority in the nation also ranked Texas's governor forty-ninth, ahead of the governor of Rhode Island.[2]

To understand the restrictions placed on the office, it is necessary to remember that the Constitution of 1876 was a reaction to the Reconstruction government that existed in Texas following the Civil War. During Reconstruction, the governor was very powerful, and many regarded state government as oppressive and corrupt. When a new constitution was drafted at the end of the Reconstruction era, Texans did their best to ensure that no state official had extensive power. The Texas Constitution of 1876 placed strict limits on the governor's ability to control the people appointed to office and almost eliminated the possibility that appointees to office could be removed. Power was further fragmented among other officeholders, who are collectively known as the plural executive. Each of these officeholders is elected and has separate and distinct responsibilities. Members of major state boards, such as the Railroad Commission and the State Board of Education, are also elected and are largely outside the control of the governor.

Governors who are successful in pushing their programs through the legislature and seeing them implemented by the bureaucracy are able to use the limited formal powers available to them, exercise their personal political power, exploit the prestige of the office of governor, and marshal various special interests to their cause. One political writer likens the office of governor to a bronco that breaks most who attempt to ride it and will be successfully handled by very few. In short, successful governors are successful politicians.[3]

Former state representative Brian McCall has written about the modern Texas governorship, arguing that Texas governors can be quite powerful in spite of the weaknesses of the office that are inherent in the Texas Constitution. He points out that governors who develop a collaborative relationship with the legislature can realize many of their goals if they are flexible, have a vision, are willing to motivate others to achieve that vision, and will work cooperatively with the legislature. McCall notes that when former governor Allan Shivers was asked about the weak governorship of Texas, he responded, "I never thought it was weak. I had all the

for critical analysis

What can governors do to overcome the inherent weakness of the position? What are the implications for democratic government of a weak chief executive?

power I needed." McCall, in stressing that the Texas governorship can be parlayed into a position of power by capable individuals, noted that the governor has the only power to call special sessions of the legislature. The governor can pardon criminals and can permit fugitives to be extradited to other states. The governor appoints people to state governing boards and commissions. Only the governor can declare martial law. Only the governor can veto acts of the legislature. Through the traditional State of the State address delivered at the beginning of every legislative session, the governor can outline state priorities and convince others of the importance of those priorities. The governor can be a major persuasive force in mobilizing interest groups, editorial boards of newspapers, and opinion leaders to support his or her agenda.

Not all governors have the personal skills to turn the office into a powerful one. Some have been unable to develop a collaborative relationship with the legislature. Others have not had the interest or the ability to develop their own vision and political agenda. Still others have been unable to accomplish their goals because of economic downturns that have limited their resources. However, McCall argues that modern governors such as John Connally, Ann Richards, and George Bush have had the persuasive skills that have enabled them to achieve major political objectives in spite of the constitutional limitations on the powers of the office.[4]

Still, even many successful governors have not acted as if the job is a demanding one. George W. Bush, according to McCall, would typically arrive at the office by eight in the morning, leave for a run and a workout at 11:40 A.M., return at 1:30 P.M., and play video golf or computer solitaire until 3 P.M.[5] Governor Perry was so detached from the operation of state government that he did not receive a full briefing on the raid on a polygamist cult that put 400 children in protective custody and involved a half-dozen state agencies and 1,000 state personnel until five days after the event. One review of Governor Perry's schedule during the first four months of the 2011 legislative session showed that he averaged only 21 hours per week on state business and took six three-day weekends.[6]

George W. Bush was governor of Texas from 1995 until he was elected president of the United States in 2000. Here, Bush is seen campaigning for re-election as governor in 1998. Like Rick Perry, Bush was able to achieve a number of his political goals as governor, despite the limited powers of the office.

Qualifications

Only three formal constitutional qualifications are required to become governor of Texas. Article IV of the Texas Constitution requires the governor to (1) be at least 30 years of age; (2) be a U.S. citizen; and (3) live in Texas five years immediately before election. Texas governors have tended to be male, white, conservative, either personally wealthy or with access to wealth, Protestant, and middle-aged, and they have had considerable prior political experience.

Women compose more than 50 percent of the population of the United States and Texas, but only two women—Miriam Ferguson (1925–27, 1933–35) and Ann Richards (1991–95)—have served as governor of Texas.

William Clements's victory over John Hill in the gubernatorial campaign of 1978 was the first time since Reconstruction that a Republican had won the office. George W. Bush was the second Republican elected governor and the first individual elected for two consecutive four-year terms.

Access to money is important because running for governor is inordinately expensive. A campaign for the governorship can cost tens of millions of dollars, and few Texans have that kind of money. The 2010 gubernatorial campaign set a record, costing about $91 million when all primary and general election candidates are considered. Tony Sanchez, the Democratic nominee for governor in 2002, spent over $66 million in that campaign, a record for an individual candidate. About $60 million of those funds came from his family's fortune in a losing effort for the governor's mansion.

Sam Kinch, a former editor of *Texas Weekly*, suggests that prior political experience is an important consideration in selecting a governor. Kinch maintains that although experience may not mean that someone will be a better governor, it does mean he or she is more likely to know how to handle the pressures of the office.[7]

Election and Term of Office

Before 1974, Texas governors served two-year terms, with most being elected to a maximum of two consecutive two-year terms. As Table 8.1 shows, there have been exceptions, such as Coke Stevenson, Price Daniel, and John Connally, who each served for six years, or Allan Shivers, who served for eight years. In 1972, Texas voters adopted a constitutional amendment changing the governor's term to four years. In 1974, Dolph Briscoe was the first governor elected to a four-year term of office. Rick Perry, who has served as governor since 2000, has been the longest serving Texas governor.

Gubernatorial elections are held in off-years (years in which a president is not elected) to minimize the effect of presidential elections on the selection of the Texas governor. The Texas legislature, controlled at the time by Democrats, designed the off-year system to eliminate the possibility that a popular Republican presidential candidate would bring votes to a Republican candidate for governor. Likewise, party leaders wanted to negate the chances of an unpopular Democratic presidential candidate costing a Democratic gubernatorial candidate votes in the general election. Unfortunately, because of this timing, voter turnout in gubernatorial contests is relatively low.

Campaigns

Campaigns for governor of Texas last at least 10 months. Candidates hit the campaign trail in January of an election year to win their party's primary election in March; then they continue campaigning until the November general election.

TABLE 8.1

Governors of Texas and Their Terms of Office since 1874

Richard Coke	1874–76	Miriam Ferguson	1933–35
Richard B. Hubbard	1876–79	James V. Allred	1935–39
Oran M. Roberts	1879–83	W. Lee O'Daniel	1939–41
John Ireland	1883–87	Coke Stevenson	1941–47
Lawrence S. Ross	1887–91	Beauford H. Jester	1947–49
James S. Hogg	1891–95	Allan Shivers	1949–57
Charles A. Culberson	1895–99	Price Daniel	1957–63
Joseph D. Sayers	1899–1903	John Connally	1963–69
S. W. T. Lanham	1903–07	Preston Smith	1969–73
Thomas M. Campbell	1907–11	Dolph Briscoe	1973–79*
Oscar B. Colquitt	1911–15	William Clements	1979–83
James E. Ferguson	1915–17	Mark White	1983–87
William P. Hobby	1917–21	William Clements	1987–91
Pat M. Neff	1921–25	Ann Richards	1991–95
Miriam Ferguson	1925–27	George W. Bush	1995–2000**
Dan Moody	1927–31	Rick Perry	2000–
Ross Sterling	1931–33		

*Term changed to four years with the 1974 general election.
**Resigned to become president of the United States.
SOURCE: Dallas Morning News, *Texas Almanac and State Industrial Guide 1998–99* (Dallas: A. H. Belo, 1999).

Successful candidates spend thousands of hours and millions of dollars campaigning. The money goes to pay staff salaries and for travel, opinion polls, telephone banks, direct mailings, and advertisements in print and broadcast media. Texas is so large that statewide candidates must purchase print and electronic advertisements in 19 media markets to reach every corner of the state.

In the 2010 Republican primary, Kay Bailey Hutchison spent over $14 million in her losing battle against Rick Perry. Perry spent nearly $13 million in the primary. Overall, Perry spent about $39 million and Bill White spent about $26 million in their campaigns. That is $14.37 for every vote Perry received and $12.48 for every vote White received. High-priced campaigns illustrate that successful candidates need personal wealth or access to wealth.

Removal of a Governor

In Texas, the only constitutional method of removing a governor from office is by **impeachment** and conviction. "To impeach" means to accuse or to indict, and impeachment is similar to a true bill (indictment) by a grand jury. The Texas Constitution notes that the governor may be impeached but does not give any grounds for impeachment. Possible justifications for impeachment are failure to perform the duties of governor, gross incompetence, or official misconduct.

impeachment the formal charge by the House of Representatives that leads to a trial in the Senate and the possible removal of a state official

Impeachment begins in the Texas House of Representatives. A majority vote of the Texas House is required to impeach, or to bring charges. If the House votes for impeachment, the trial takes place in the Texas Senate. One or more members of the Texas House prosecute the case, and the chief justice of the Supreme Court of Texas presides over the impeachment proceedings. A two-thirds vote of the senators present and voting is necessary to convict. If convicted, the governor is removed from office and disqualified from holding any other state office.

Any member of the executive or judicial branch may be impeached. Once the House votes for impeachment charges against an official, that individual is suspended from office and cannot exercise any of his duties. Governor James Ferguson was the only Texas governor to be impeached and convicted.

Succession

The Texas Constitution provides for the lieutenant governor to become governor if the office becomes vacant through impeachment and conviction, death, resignation, or the governor's absence from the state.

In December 2000, a succession occurred when Governor George W. Bush became president-elect of the United States and resigned as governor. Lieutenant Governor Rick Perry immediately took the oath to become governor of Texas. The *Houston Chronicle* has characterized Rick Perry as "a politician who so looks the part that it's been joked that he was ordered straight from central casting."[8] Perry, a former state legislator from Haskell, was a conservative Democrat who switched to the Republican Party in 1990 and ran successfully for commissioner of agriculture. His six years in the Texas House, eight years as head of a major state agency, and two years as lieutenant governor and president of the Texas Senate provided him with a great deal more experience than any other governor of the last three decades.[9]

Governor Rick Perry spent millions of dollars on his 2010 campaign for re-election, as he first fended off a serious challenge from Kay Bailey Hutchison in the Republican primary election and then campaigned in the general election.

Should the governor leave the bounds of the state, the lieutenant governor becomes acting governor. If the governor is impeached, the lieutenant governor serves as acting governor before and during the trial. While serving as acting governor, the lieutenant governor earns the governor's daily salary, which is far better than the $20 earned as lieutenant governor. (However, a governor who is absent from the state still earns the same daily salary.)

When out of the state, the governor is legally entitled to Department of Public Safety protection. George W. Bush spent part of 1999 and 2000 campaigning to be president of the United States. During fiscal year 1999, it cost Texans an additional $2,365,000 to provide protection for the governor while he was on the presidential campaign trail.[10] In 1992, Governor Ann Richards was often out of the state campaigning for Bill Clinton, and the Texas taxpayers picked up the cost of her security detail. Governor Perry was also out of the state a great deal during his campaign for the 2012 Republican presidential nomination.

Constitutionally, the governor's office is weak. Former lieutenant governor Bill Hobby noted that about the only way he knew when he was acting governor was by a note his secretary left on his daily calendar.[11] In the first three months of 2000, Rick Perry, then lieutenant governor, served as acting governor more days than George W. Bush was in the state to serve as governor. Perry's press secretary commented that the added duties of being acting governor were not very noticeable and that those duties made little difference in Perry's schedule.[12] State government takes little notice of the governor's absences. Former Speaker of the Texas House Pete Laney has said that the governor's office is "holding court and cutting ribbons" and in 2000 commented on Governor Bush's out-of-state campaigning by saying, "I guess we've been doing pretty well without [a governor]."[13]

Legislation further defines succession from the governor to the lieutenant governor, to the president pro tempore of the Texas Senate, Speaker of the House, attorney general, and the chief judges of the Texas courts of appeal in descending order.

Compensation

The governor's salary is set by the legislature. Texas pays its governor $150,000 annually. In addition to this salary, the governor receives use of an official mansion near the capitol grounds, although fire damage prevented its use as an official residence from June 2008 to the summer of 2011. Governors and the legislature often squabble about the amount of money needed for upkeep of the mansion and its grounds. The governor also receives use of a limousine, a state-owned aircraft, and a personal staff.

Staff

The governor's staff consists of nearly 250 individuals. This includes a chief of staff, a deputy chief of staff, a general counsel, and a press secretary. A scheduler coordinates the governor's appointments, personal appearances, and work schedule. Governor Perry has 35 staff members who focus solely on policy issues.[14]

The staff keeps the governor informed about issues and problems facing the state, and it may suggest courses of action. In addition, during a four-year term, a governor makes several thousand appointments to various state posts. It is impossible for a governor to be acquainted personally with each appointee. Some of the staff find qualified individuals for each post and recommend them to the governor. Other staff members track legislation. They talk with legislators, especially key people such as committee chairpersons. The staff lets the governor know when his or her personal touch might make a difference in the outcome of legislation. For each bill that passes the legislature, a staff member prepares a summary of the bill with a recommendation that the governor sign or veto the bill.

Recent governors have used their staffs to be more accessible to the public. Governor Perry, like his immediate predecessors, wants his staff to be no more than a phone call away from those who need assistance. In theory, individuals need only call a member of the governor's staff to receive help or find out where to go for help. The Office of the Governor has a Citizen's Assistance Hotline that handles thousands of calls each year from Texans needing assistance with their problems with state government.

Executive Powers of the Governor

Texas has a board or agency form of government. Approximately 200 state boards, commissions, and agencies make up the executive branch of Texas government. Agencies may be as obscure as the Texas Funeral Commission or the State Preservation Board or as well-known as the Public Utilities Commission of Texas or the

Who Re-Elected Governor Perry in 2010?

Rick Perry is from Paint Creek, Texas, a rural community in Haskell County. Bill White served as mayor of Houston, Texas's largest city. The results of the 2010 governor's election reflect this urban/rural divide between the two candidates. Perry did best in rural counties, especially in his native West Texas. Outside of the Rio Grande Valley, White did best in the urban counties.

2010 Election Results, by County

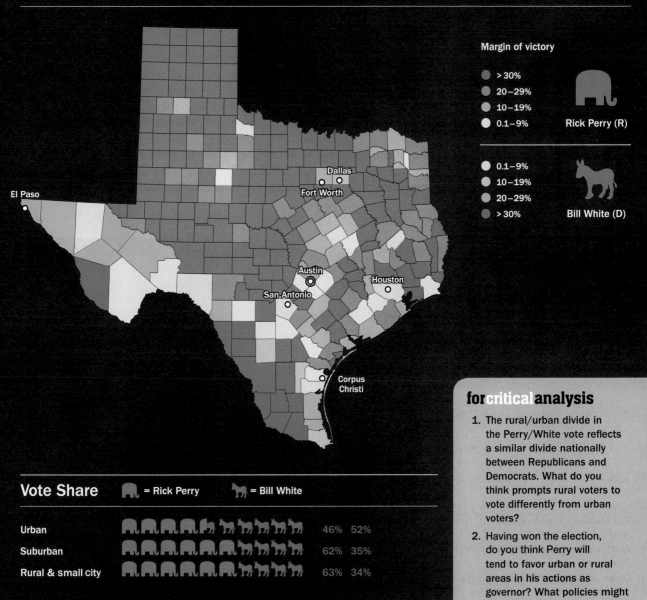

Margin of victory

- > 30%
- 20–29%
- 10–19%
- 0.1–9%   **Rick Perry (R)**

- 0.1–9%
- 10–19%
- 20–29%
- > 30%   **Bill White (D)**

Vote Share   = Rick Perry   = Bill White

		Perry	White
Urban		46%	52%
Suburban		62%	35%
Rural & small city		63%	34%

SOURCE: Texas Secretary of State

for critical analysis

1. The rural/urban divide in the Perry/White vote reflects a similar divide nationally between Republicans and Democrats. What do you think prompts rural voters to vote differently from urban voters?

2. Having won the election, do you think Perry will tend to favor urban or rural areas in his actions as governor? What policies might he support that will be more favorable to rural areas?

Texas Department of Human Services, but each is important to its constituents. These multimember boards are the policy-making bodies for their agencies. They employ and oversee the people who operate the agencies on a daily basis.

appointment the power of the chief executive, whether the president of the United States or the governor of a state, to appoint persons to office

Appointment Power The governor's power of **appointment** is the most significant executive power. It allows a degree of control over about 200 state agencies. Governor Perry's long tenure has allowed him to appoint more than 4,000 people to these boards, and through these appointments he has been able to exert control throughout state government. One lobbyist described Perry's appointees as much different from Governor Bush's in that they "appear to be much more concerned with the larger political context and what sort of direction, either signaled or voiced, is coming from the governor's office."[15]

The power of appointment enables the governor to exercise the power of **patronage**. It permits the governor to reward supporters by appointing them to office. Most of the offices pay very little, but they do offer supporters some prestige. The governor can also use the appointment power to repay political favors by appointing friends and associates of legislators to office as well as to garner political IOUs from politicians. Most important, a governor can use the appointment power to influence agency policy. To a great degree, the effectiveness of a governor's use of the appointment power will determine the governor's success in office.

patronage the resources available to higher officials, usually opportunities to make partisan appointments to offices and to confer grants, licenses, or special favors to supporters

A governor, however, must exert some care in appointments. In 2007 there was a scandal within the Texas Youth Commission, which has authority over institutionalized juveniles. It became clear that not only was there a widespread pattern of physical and sexual abuse of juveniles in the facilities, but authorities tried to cover up the abuse. As a result, Governor Perry's appointees had to resign from the commission, and it was necessary to reorganize the agency.

The authority to appoint many state officials is an important executive power. In 2008, Rick Perry appointed Esperanza "Hope" Andrade as Texas secretary of state.

The governor appoints people to office, but the Texas Senate must also confirm them. However, because the Senate may not meet for almost two years, the appointee takes office immediately and does not wait for Senate confirmation. An important limitation on the power of the governor to appoint persons to office is the requirement that the individual's state senator must approve the appointment. This is known as **senatorial courtesy** and applies regardless of the party affiliation of the governor, senator, or appointee. Usually, if the appointee's senator concurs in the appointment, the remainder of the Senate will agree. However, if the appointee's senator opposes the appointment, the remainder of the Senate will also oppose the appointment.

The process for removing an appointee is also complicated. A governor cannot remove an appointee who refuses to resign unless the governor can show cause and get two-thirds of the Texas Senate to approve.[16] This complex procedure for the termination of members of boards and commissions, along with the practice of senatorial courtesy, can be a significant limitation on the governor's power to influence the policies of state agencies. Chairs of boards, however, serve at the pleasure of the governor and so can easily be removed if they do something that displeases the governor.

Budgetary Power Officially, the Texas governor is the state's chief budget officer. As such, governors submit an **executive budget** to the legislature. This budget suggests a plan for revenue and expenditure for Texas, but more important, it indicates the governor's priorities for the state in the next biennium.

In 1949, in an effort to gain more control over the state's budget, the legislature established the Legislative Budget Board (LBB), which is responsible for preparing a **legislative budget**. Thus, two budgets are prepared and submitted to the legislature: an executive budget by the governor and a legislative budget by the LBB. As a creation of the legislature, the LBB's budget proposal receives more consideration by the House and Senate than the governor's recommendations, and in recent years the governor's budget has fallen into disuse. Legend has it that the governor's budget has been used as a doorstop and a paperweight, and one diminutive legislator used two copies as a booster in his office chair. In 1989, Governor Clements recognized the futility of submitting an executive budget and simply endorsed the recommendations of the LBB. Ann Richards followed Clements's precedent, but Governor George Bush took a more active role in budget preparation and Governor Perry was very involved in dealing with the state's 2011 budgetary shortfall.

The governor has some control over the final appropriations bill through the use of the line-item veto; however, the governor cannot impound funds or transfer funds from one agency to another, even if circumstances change from the time the money was appropriated. Overall, the budgetary process does not provide the governor with an effective means of controlling state agencies.

Military Power The governor is commander in chief of the state's National Guard units when they are not under presidential orders. These units are headed by the adjutant general, who is appointed by the governor. The governor can declare martial law, which suspends most civil authority and imposes military rule over an area. Martial law can be declared in the event of a riot, flood, hurricane, tornado, or other disaster to protect lives and property.

Police Power In Texas, law enforcement and police power are primarily a local responsibility, and the governor has few responsibilities in this area. The governor

senatorial courtesy the practice whereby the president, before formally nominating a person for a federal judgeship, seeks the indication that senators from the candidate's own state support the nomination; in Texas, the practice whereby the governor seeks the indication that the senator from the candidate's home supports the nomination

executive budget the state budget prepared and submitted by the governor to the legislature, which indicates the governor's spending priorities. The executive budget is overshadowed in terms of importance by the legislative budget

legislative budget the state budget that is prepared and submitted by the Legislative Budget Board (LBB) and that is fully considered by the House and Senate

for critical analysis
What are the governor's formal powers? How does the governor exercise these powers?

Deployment of the state's national guard in times of emergency is one aspect of the governor's military power. Here, Texas National Guard troops deliver relief supplies after Hurricane Ike in 2009.

appoints, with Senate approval, the three-member Public Safety Commission that directs the work of the Department of Public Safety (DPS). The DPS is responsible for highway traffic enforcement (highway patrol), drivers' licensing, motor vehicle inspection, truck weighing stations, and the Texas Rangers. When circumstances warrant, the governor can assume command of the Rangers, an elite, highly trained force of about 100 officers. If there is evidence of ongoing violence or corruption, the governor can use informal powers, the prestige of the governor's office, and appeals to the media to compel appropriate action from local law enforcement officials.

Legislative Powers of the Governor

As we saw earlier, the governor's legislative powers include message power, power of the veto, and the authority to call special sessions and set their agendas. If a governor uses these powers effectively, he or she can have considerable control over the state's legislative business, but they do not enhance his or her ability to control the executive branch of state government.

Message Power Any communication between the governor and the legislature is part of the message power. Early in each regular session, the governor delivers a State of the State message. In this speech to a joint session of the legislature, the governor explains his or her plan for the state in the coming two years. The governor may propose specific programs or simply set general goals for the state. The speech is covered by most news media, and it is often broadcast on public television and radio stations.

If the governor submits an executive budget, he or she may address the legislature on the important items in the proposed plan of spending and revenue. At the very least, the budget proposal is forwarded to the legislature with a letter briefly explaining the budget.

Lobbying by governors is part of the message power. Governors try to pass or defeat bills important to them. For example, early in 1991, Governor Ann Richards successfully lobbied for legislation that would expand higher educational opportunities in the Rio Grande Valley and that resulted in the creation of the University of Texas at Brownsville.

Although Governor Bill Clements personally lobbied the legislature, he preferred to use his five full-time paid lobbyists to influence the legislature. Although not exactly part of the governor's message power, the use of lobbyists is an effective way for a governor to communicate with and influence the legislature.

Veto Power Governors of Texas can sign or **veto** legislation—but in most cases they sign legislation. In the 82nd Legislature (2011), Governor Perry vetoed 25 bills. Since becoming governor in 2000, Perry has vetoed 273 bills.[17]

When the governor vetoes a bill after the legislature adjourns, it is called a **post-adjournment** or strong veto. This veto is absolute, because the legislature that passed the vetoed bills no longer exists. As a result, if the governor decides to veto a bill, it stays vetoed.

Texas governors possess the **line-item veto**, which is the ability to veto individual parts of an appropriations bill. The governor signs the bill but strikes out particular lines in the bill. Items struck from the bill do not become law, but the remainder of the appropriations bill does.

In 2007, Governor Perry used the line-item veto to cut $646.5 million from the total state budget. One of his most controversial vetoes was for group insurance contributions for community and junior colleges that came to $153 million. He cut another $36 million in special-item funding for higher education, such as $2 million for obesity research at the Texas Cooperative Extension and $5 million for public health programs at the University of Texas Health Science Center at Houston.[18]

This line-item veto allows Texas governors considerable control over appropriations to state agencies, and this power can be used by the governor to reduce state expenditures or to punish agencies or programs disfavored by the governor.[19] It is one important power of the governor that is greater than that of the president of the United States, who does not have the power to issue a line-item veto because the U.S. Supreme Court has held that such a power violates separation of powers in the U.S. Constitution.

Special Sessions Special sessions of the Texas legislature are called by the governor, last for no more than 30 days, and may consider only those items placed on the agenda by the governor. **Special sessions** are called to address critical problems that have arisen since the last regular session. The nature of special sessions allows the legislature to focus attention on specific issues.

From 1989 through 2011, the legislature met in 19 special sessions. These sessions considered the complicated and divisive issues of reform of workers' compensation laws, public school finance, reapportionment, and voter identification. The sessions ranged from 30 days to 2 days, with six of the sessions occurring in 1989–90 and five occurring from 2005 through 2011.[20]

Judicial Powers of the Governor

Texas elects each of its appellate and district court judges, but when vacancies occur because of the death, resignation, or retirement of the incumbent or as a result of creation of new courts, the governor is responsible for appointing individuals to fill these vacancies.

Once appointed to office, judges tend to remain in office. More than 95 percent of incumbents win re-election. Through this power to appoint judges, the governor has considerable influence over the Texas judicial system.

veto the governor's power to turn down legislation; can be overridden by a two-thirds vote of both the House and Senate

post-adjournment veto a veto of a bill that occurs after the legislature adjourns, thus preventing the legislature from overriding it

line-item veto the power of the executive to veto specific provisions (lines) of an appropriations bill passed by the legislature

special session a legislative session called by the governor that addresses an agenda set by him or her and that lasts no longer than 30 days

Clemency normally includes the power to issue pardons, grant paroles, and issue reprieves. The governor's power in this area is severely limited because of abuses of previous governors. Pardons can be granted only on the recommendation of the Board of Pardons and Paroles. Texas governors can neither grant nor deny paroles. Governors have the ability to grant each person condemned to death one 30-day reprieve. Additional reprieves and any other act of clemency must be recommended by the Board of Pardons and Paroles.

The Office and Its Occupants

People often expect governors to be able to do things they are not equipped to do. They are expected to be chief executives in more than name only despite being granted little in the way of formal power. Constitutionally and statutorily, the governor is ill-equipped to exert control and direction over the Texas bureaucracy.

John Connally was regarded as a strong governor, whereas Dolph Briscoe was regarded as weak. In part, the difference was that Connally actively sought to lead. As governor, he had a dynamic personality, whereas Briscoe was more retiring in his personal style and did not seek to have the impact Connally had. Allan Shivers was an imperial governor, as Richard Nixon was called an imperial president. Preston Smith was described as one of the most ordinary people ever to serve as governor. Smith is seldom given credit for doing anything as governor, yet he established the first actual planning organization in Texas government. Rick Perry has used his lengthy service and his appointment powers over state boards and commissions to exert unusually strong control over the operation of government.

In large part, the office of governor is what the person holding the position makes it. Whether the governor is viewed as strong or weak depends on how the governor conducts him- or herself in office, uses the position's formal power, and exercises political influence.

● The Plural Executive

> **Identify the other elected officials who make up the plural executive**

plural executive an executive branch in which power is fragmented because the election of statewide officeholders is independent of the election of the governor

When Texans drafted a constitution in 1876, they chose to limit executive power and disperse it through several elected officials called the **plural executive**. Texans elect six of the seven people who make up the plural executive: the governor, lieutenant governor, attorney general, comptroller of public accounts, commissioner of the General Land Office, and commissioner of agriculture (see Table 8.2 and Table 8.3). The governor appoints the seventh person, the secretary of state. Except for the lieutenant governor, who receives the same salary as a legislator, salaries of members of the plural executive are set by the legislature. Additionally, two major regulatory agencies, the Railroad Commission of Texas and the State Board of Education, are run by officials who are independently elected. The result is vast fragmentation of responsibility for public policy in the state.

Elections are partisan, and each member of the plural executive may choose to operate independently of the others. At times, members of the plural executive may be in competition with each other, often because of conflicting personal ambitions. That occurred when John Hill was attorney general and sought to take the governorship from Dolph Briscoe, and when Mark White was attorney general and sought the governorship from Bill Clements. Because of the difficulty of defeating incumbents, however, it is far more likely that members of the plural executive will wait for a vacancy in a more prestigious office before seeking that higher office. Champions of the plural executive believe that it limits the power of executive officials and makes these officers more accountable to the public. Opponents assert the plural executive is inefficient and does not promote good government. The governor is a member of the plural executive, but this multipart executive limits the governor's control of the executive branch because he or she has little authority over this group.

One can get a sense of the importance of the various positions in the plural executive simply by looking at the campaign contributions received by winning candidates for these offices in the 2010 elections. Table 8.4 shows the contributions

TABLE 8.2

Elected Officials in Texas with Executive Responsibilities

SINGLE-ELECTED EXECUTIVES	MULTI-ELECTED EXECUTIVES
Governor	Railroad Commission (3 members)
Lieutenant Governor	
Attorney General	
Land Commissioner	State Board of Education (15 members)
Agriculture Commissioner	
Comptroller	

TABLE 8.3

State Executive Officeholders, 2013

Governor	Rick Perry (Republican)
Lieutenant Governor	David Dewhurst (Republican)
Attorney General	Greg Abbott (Republican)
Comptroller of Public Accounts	Susan Combs (Republican)
Commissioner of the General Land Office	Jerry Patterson (Republican)
Commissioner of Agriculture	Todd Staples (Republican)
Railroad Commissioners	Barry Smitherman (Republican)
	David Porter (Republican)
	Christi Craddick (Republican)
Secretary of State (appointed)	John Steen (Republican)

TABLE 8.4

Campaign Contributions in 2010 and the Plural Executive

OFFICE	LOSING CANDIDATE	CONTRIBUTIONS TO LOSER	WINNING CANDIDATE	CONTRIBUTIONS TO WINNER
Governor	B. White (Dem.)	$26,291,535	R. Perry (Rep.)	$39,328,540
Lieutenant Governor	L. Chavez-Thompson (Dem.)	958,040	D. Dewhurst (Rep.)	9,240,480
Attorney General	B. Radnotsky (Dem.)	1,135,031	G. Abbott (Rep.)	5,828,370
Comptroller	(No Dem. candidate)	0	S. Combs (Rep.)	2,744,001
Agriculture Commissioner	P. Gilbert (Dem.)	336,363	T. Staples (Rep.)	1,742,941
Land Commissioner	H. Uribe (Dem.)	102,487	J. Patterson (Rep.)	864,688

SOURCE: National Institute on Money in State Politics.

received by both the Democratic and the Republican nominees in 2010. Governor Rick Perry, the incumbent Republican, received over $39 million in contributions. In contrast, his Democratic opponent, Bill White, received much less. The incumbent Republican lieutenant governor David Dewhurst had over $9 million in contributions, compared with only about $958,000 in contributions for his opponent. The winning candidate for attorney general had nearly $6 million in contributions, the winning candidate for comptroller more than $2.7 million in contributions even though she had no Democratic opponent. The agriculture commissioner had more than $1.7 million, and the land commissioner had more than $864,000. Two things are especially notable about these figures. One is the enormous amounts of money that are contributed to candidates for the plural executive offices. The other is how lopsided the contributions are in favor of the Republican candidates. It is a sign of the strength of the Republican Party and the weakness of the Democratic Party in Texas elections that Republican candidates raise so much more money for their campaigns than do Democratic candidates.

Secretary of State

secretary of state state official, appointed by the governor, whose primary responsibility is administering elections

Strangely, given Texas's fragmentation of power, the governor does appoint the Texas **secretary of state**, even though this office is an elective one in 37 other states.[21] Though once considered a "glorified keeper of certain state records," the secretary of state is now an important officer.[22] The secretary of state has myriad responsibilities, and the appointment of a secretary of state is one of the governor's most important tasks.

As Texas's chief election official, the secretary of state conducts voter registration drives. His or her office works with organizations such as the League of Women Voters to increase the number of registered voters. The secretary of state's office also collects election-night returns from county judges and county clerks and makes the results available to the media. This service provides media and voters with a convenient method of receiving the latest official election returns in Texas.

All debt and Uniform Commercial Code filings are placed with the secretary of state's office. When any individual borrows money from a financial institution, a copy of the loan agreement is placed in the secretary of state's office.

Lieutenant Governor

The **lieutenant governor** has executive responsibilities, such as serving as acting governor when the governor is out of state and succeeding a governor who resigns, is incapacitated, or is impeached. The real power of the office of lieutenant governor, however, is derived from its place in the legislative process.

lieutenant governor the second-highest elected official in the state and president of the state Senate

According to the Texas Constitution, the lieutenant governor is the "Constitutional President of the Senate" and has the right to debate and vote on all issues when the Senate sits as a "Committee of the Whole." The Texas Constitution also grants the lieutenant governor the power to cast a deciding vote in the Senate when there is a tie. Like the Speaker of the House, the lieutenant governor signs all bills and resolutions. The constitution names the lieutenant governor to the Legislative Redistricting Board, a five-member committee that apportions the state into senatorial and House districts if the legislature fails to do so following a census. Other powers of the lieutenant governor are derived from various statutes passed by the legislature. For example, the lieutenant governor is chair of the LBB and is a member of a number of other boards and committees, including the Legislative Audit Committee, the Legislative Education Board, the Cash Management Committee, and the Bond Review Board.

The Texas Constitution grants the Senate the power to make its own rules, and lieutenant governors traditionally have been granted significant legislative power by the Senate itself. The Senate rules empower the lieutenant governor to decide all parliamentary questions and to use discretion in following Senate procedural rules. The lieutenant governor is also empowered to set up standing and special committees and to appoint committee members and chairs of the committees. The Senate rules, and not just the Texas Constitution, make the lieutenant governor one of the most powerful political leaders in the state. New Senate rules passed by a future Senate could, of course, substantially alter the power possessed by the lieutenant governor.

Republican David Dewhurst was re-elected as lieutenant governor of Texas in 2010. The lieutenant governor's most important powers derive from his or her role in the legislature.

Political Style of Lieutenant Governors Bob Bullock served as lieutenant governor of Texas from 1991 to 1999. A force in Texas politics for over 40 years, he was one of the strongest and most effective lieutenant governors Texas politics had ever seen. He took a bluff, rough, tough, head-knocking approach to leadership. He was feared and respected by friends and foes alike.

His successor, Rick Perry, brought a very different style to the office. The first Republican elected lieutenant governor in over 100 years, Perry had served two terms as the Texas commissioner of agriculture from 1985 to 1991. Prior to that, he served in the Texas House of Representatives, representing a rural west Texas district as a Democrat. His switch to the Republican Party reflected the broader movement of rural conservatives in the 1980s and 1990s. Expectations for Perry were low when he assumed office. In contrast to Bullock, Perry had a low-key style. But his style was appreciated by senators long under the demanding eye of Bob Bullock. Perry compared himself with a football player following in the footsteps of the Heisman Trophy winner Ricky Williams from the University of Texas. Like a running back imagining himself scoring a touchdown, Perry actually practiced banging a gavel in the empty Senate chamber. Perry's situation was also made more difficult by the fact that then–incumbent governor George W. Bush was actively pursuing the presidency, leaving additional jobs and uncertainties on Perry's shoulders.

Democratic senator John Whitmire, whom Perry had removed as chairman of the Senate Criminal Justice Committee, may have offered the best evaluation of Perry's leadership ability when commenting on a newspaper article that claimed Perry had lost control of the Senate during a debate over hate-crime legislation. Whitmire said, "I don't know how in the hell you say he lost control of the Senate. Was it a major difference in the way Bullock would have done it? Yeah. Serious difference. But I think members kind of appreciated the fact he didn't use his position as lieutenant governor to strong-arm members into positions that were contrary to their districts. Do I agree with all his decisions or operations, philosophy? Of course not. Essentially he was a freshman. . . . I'm sure he would be the first to tell you he learned by doing. No one's ever tried to govern us while the governor's been running for president. He had a good session."[23]

When George W. Bush became president and Lieutenant Governor Rick Perry became governor, the Senate elected one of its members to serve as lieutenant governor. That person was Bill Ratliff, a Republican from Mount Pleasant who was chairman of the powerful Senate Finance Committee. Ratliff had been in the Senate since 1989. A civil engineer, Ratliff was a strong believer in bipartisanship and was fascinated by the policy-making process. Known for his candor and moderation, he quickly alienated conservatives in his party when he named the Democratic senator Rodney Ellis of Houston as his replacement as chairman of the Finance Committee. As the presiding officer of the Senate, Ratliff oversaw a legislative session that had considerable accomplishments, such as passage of a statewide teacher health plan and the extension of Medicaid coverage to hundreds of thousands of poor children.

One poll showed Ratliff the leader in a Republican primary for lieutenant governor, and so he announced he would seek the office in the next election. However, one of his opponents was Land Commissioner David Dewhurst, who claimed he would spend tens of millions of dollars of his own money in the race. Ratliff soon ran into trouble with Republican contributors whom he needed in order to compete with Dewhurst's money. Ratliff quickly discovered that his political moderation was not favored by many contributors and, with love for policy but distaste for politics, Ratliff concluded he should withdraw and not be a candidate for the office. One of his advisers suggested that Ratliff claim he was dropping out of the race because of a fatal disease. The fatal disease, noted Ratliff, was "independence and moderation."[24]

Dewhurst successfully ran for lieutenant governor in 2002 and was re-elected in 2006 and in 2010. As lieutenant governor, Dewhurst is in very different political circumstances from his two Republican predecessors, Perry and Ratliff. Republicans held a majority in the Senate throughout the Dewhurst years. Though Dewhurst pledged to work with state Democrats and appointed some as committee chairmen, partisanship became an increasingly divisive force in the state Senate under Dewhurst. Far more low-key than Bob Bullock and much less dominant a personality, Dewhurst has proven an effective lieutenant governor who unsuccessfully sought to replace Kay Bailey Hutchison as U.S. senator from Texas.

for critical analysis

How does the power of the lieutenant governor differ from that of the governor?

Attorney General

The **attorney general** (AG) is elected to a four-year term and acts as the chief lawyer for the state of Texas. The AG is, in effect, head of Texas's civil law firm. Currently the Texas AG oversees the work of over 700 lawyers.

The AG's office is concerned primarily with civil matters. When a lawsuit is filed against the state or by the state, the AG manages the legal activities surrounding that lawsuit. Any time a state agency needs legal representation, the AG's office represents the agency. In any lawsuit to which Texas is a party, the AG's office has full responsibility to resolve the case and can litigate, compromise, settle, or choose not to pursue the suit.

One of the more important powers of the AG's office comes from the opinion process. Any agency of state or local government can ask the AG's office for an advisory opinion on the legality of an action. The AG's office will rule on the question, and the ruling has the force of law unless overturned by a court or the legislature.

Probably the most controversial and criticized aspect of the work of the AG's office is child support collection. Almost one-half of the AG's 4,000 employees are involved in collecting child support, and they have collected more than $21 billion since Greg Abbott became attorney general. However, this program is the subject of intense criticism because much child support remains uncollected.

The AG's office has little responsibility in criminal law but may appoint a special prosecutor if a local district attorney asks the AG for assistance. This can happen when there is a potential conflict of interest, as, for example, if the district attorney is a friend of or works with a local official who is under criminal investigation. In one recent case, lawyers from the AG's office prosecuted a state district judge in Collin County on bribery charges.

Generally, criminal cases in Texas are prosecuted by district or county attorneys elected in each county. The county is usually responsible for the costs of the trial and for all appeals in state court. If a criminal case is appealed to the federal courts, the AG's office assumes responsibility.[25]

attorney general elected state official who serves as the state's chief civil lawyer

land commissioner elected state official who is the manager of most publicly owned lands

The General Land Office is influential in large part because it awards oil and gas exploration rights for publicly owned lands. Land Commissioner Jerry Patterson was re-elected in 2010.

Commissioner of the General Land Office

The General Land Office (GLO) is the oldest state agency in Texas. Historically the **land commissioner** gave away land. Today, the GLO is the land manager for most publicly owned lands in Texas. Texas owns or has mineral interest in 13 million acres of land in the state, plus all submerged lands up to 10.35 miles into the Gulf of Mexico. All but 28 of Texas's 254 counties have some of these public lands.

The GLO also awards grazing and oil and gas exploration rights on this land. Thousands of producing oil and gas wells are found on state-owned land and are managed by the GLO. These responsibilities make the office of land commissioner quite influential. A significant portion of royalties on oil and natural gas produced by these wells goes to the Permanent School Fund and the Permanent University Fund.

The commissioner also manages the Veterans' Land Program, through which the state makes low-cost loans to Texas veterans. The program includes loans for land, housing, and home improvements. Recently, the GLO was given authority over some environmental matters. The land commissioner is responsible for environmental quality on public lands and waters, especially along the Texas coast. All of Texas's Gulf Coast beaches are publicly owned and under the jurisdiction of the GLO.

The commissioner of
agriculture, the land
commissioner, the state
comptroller, and the
attorney general each
head agencies that have
significant responsibility
for the operation of state
government. To what extent
is the public aware of these
agencies and the major role
they play in government?

In recent years, the commissioner of the GLO, Jerry Patterson, was involved in considerable controversy over the disposition of 9,269 acres of state land in the Christmas Mountains just north of Big Bend National Park. The Christmas Mountains land was under the control of the GLO and Patterson offered to sell the land to either public or private entities. After a public outcry over the proposed sale, the National Park Service expressed interest in accepting a donation of the land. However, Patterson, who is staunchly pro-hunting and pro-handgun, rejected the proposed donation because at the time the National Park Service banned hunting and the carrying of handguns in national parks. Finally, in 2011, the land was transferred to the Texas State University System, where it will serve as an "outdoor classroom." To satisfy Patterson's concerns, it was agreed that the land will be open to those who are licensed to carry handguns and to hunting.[26]

Commissioner of Agriculture

agricultural commissioner
elected state official who is
primarily responsible for enforcing
agricultural laws

The **agricultural commissioner** is primarily responsible for enforcing agricultural laws. These include administration of animal quarantine laws, inspection of food, and enforcement of disease- and pest-control programs. Enforcement of the state's laws helps to ensure that Texas's farm products are of high quality and are disease free.

The Department of Agriculture checks weights and measures. Each year a representative of the department checks each motor fuel pump to make sure that it dispenses the correct amount of fuel. Scales used by grocery stores and markets are checked to guarantee that they weigh products correctly.

Farming and ranching are big business in Texas. Although a large number of small family farms exist in the state, large corporate farms increasingly dominate Texas agriculture. These large agribusinesses are greatly affected by the decisions of the commissioner. Such decisions can increase or decrease the cost of production. Changes in production costs affect the profit margins of these agribusinesses and ultimately the price consumers pay for food products.

Comptroller of Public Accounts

comptroller elected state official
who directs the collection of taxes
and other revenues

The **comptroller** is a powerful state official because he or she directs the collection of tax and nontax revenues and issues an evaluation and estimate of anticipated state revenues before each legislative session. Tax collection is the most visible function of the comptroller. The taxes collected by the comptroller include the general sales tax, severance tax on natural resources, motor fuel tax, inheritance tax, most occupational taxes, and many minor taxes.

Although collecting billions in revenue is important, estimating revenues provides the comptroller with more power. These estimates, issued monthly during legislative sessions, are vital to the appropriations process because the legislature is prohibited from spending more than the comptroller estimates will be available. Final passage of any appropriations bill is contingent on the comptroller's certifying that revenues will be available to cover the monies spent in the appropriation. Because most bills require the expenditure of monies, this certification function provides the comptroller with significant power over the legislative process. If the comptroller is unable to certify that monies are available to pay for the appropriation, the legislature must reduce the appropriation or increase revenues. More than just an auditor, accountant, and tax collector, the comptroller is a key figure in the appropriations process.

A Plural or Single Executive?

In many ways, the Texas executive branch is similar to the federal executive branch. The governor, like the president, has the power to veto legislation and is the leader of the state. One important difference is the "cabinet" of the governor. The president appoints his or her cabinet, including the secretaries of the Treasury, Agriculture, and State, to name a few. Presidential candidates run on the same ticket with a vice presidential candidate, whom they choose and who will serve with them if elected. In Texas, only the secretary of state is appointed by the governor. The comptroller of public accounts, the attorney general, the land commissioner, and even the lieutenant governor are elected separately. We call this system a plural executive because executive power is balanced among different officeholders.

Many other states follow the federal model so that when the governor and lieutenant governor are elected to office together, they can appoint all of the relevant officeholders to run the executive branch. In this instance, the attorney general, the secretary of state, the agriculture commissioner, and all other "cabinet" officials are appointed by the governor and serve at his or her pleasure. This is similar to the federal model or single executive model.

Advocates of the plural executive model, such as that used in Texas, argue that a system of checks and balances within the executive branch helps guard against abuse of power. The Texas Constitution intentionally provides for a weak governorship, and the plural executive is one way to guarantee this. If the attorney general and other statewide officials are not beholden to the governor, they will not necessarily support the governor's agenda. This is an important way to keep the governor in check and prevent abuses of executive power. It is also a more democratic form of governance. Voters might decide that the Democratic candidate for attorney general is more qualified while the Republican candidate for governor is more qualified. In this case, the voters select candidates for each individual office, rather than taking the risk that the governor will appoint someone whom they do not support.

Opponents of the plural executive model argue that there are already enough checks and balances built into the three branches of state government. The plural executive only makes it more difficult for the governor to govern effectively and creates a counterproductive tug of war among all of the separately elected officials for more influence. In the federal model, the president can decide who is best suited for a particular role and delegate power accordingly. The Texas governor, on the other hand, cannot give orders to the lieutenant governor or the attorney general, thus making it more difficult to run the state.

As of 2012, in Texas all of the state-wide elected officials are Republicans, but this does not guarantee policy unity. While Attorney General Greg Abbott and Governor Rick Perry (both pictured above) have agreed on some of the major issues, such as the state of Texas suing the federal government over the Affordable Care Act because of the individual mandate to purchase

health insurance, this cooperation is not necessarily the norm. In states with a mix of Democrats and Republicans in the plural executive, disagreement is even more common.

In Texas's recent past, Republican governor George W. Bush had to work alongside Democratic lieutenant governor Bob Bullock in order to pass his legislative agenda. Some observers saw this as a positive effect of the plural executive, because it required compromise for the good of the state. Opponents of the plural executive might have seen this as a negative effect, because it undermined the power of the governor to implement his agenda. Each form of governance has its benefits and its costs for democracy.

critical thinking questions

1. The plural executive is more democratic because it gives more power to the people to elect individuals to serve in different executive capacities, but is this necessarily good for effective governance if it leads to more stalemate and gridlock?

2. If you were to design a state executive branch, how would you decide whether to have a plural executive or a single executive? What are the pros and cons of each model?

In 1996, the office of state treasurer was eliminated, and the comptroller of public accounts assumed the duties of that office. Since then, the comptroller of public accounts has been the official custodian of state funds and is responsible for the safety of the state's money and for investing that money.

To ensure the safety of Texas's money, funds are deposited only in financial institutions designated by the State Depository Board as eligible to receive state monies. Deposits are required to earn as much money as possible. The more money earned as interest on deposits, the fewer tax dollars are needed.

An interesting responsibility of the comptroller is returning abandoned money and property to their rightful owners. In October of each year, the comptroller publishes a list of individuals with unclaimed property. One list included $117,000 in a forgotten savings account, a certificate of deposit for $104,000, gold coins, diamond rings, family photos, and rare baseball trading cards. Money or property that remains unclaimed goes to the state.

Accountability of the Plural Executive

Except for the secretary of state, each member of the plural executive is directly accountable to the people of Texas through elections. The plural executive is accountable to the legislature in three ways: the budgetary process, Sunset Review and the impeachment process.

The legislature can demonstrate its satisfaction, or lack thereof, with an agency of the plural executive by the amount of money it appropriates to that agency. A significant increase in appropriations indicates an agency in good standing with the legislature, whereas little or no increase in funds indicates legislative displeasure. Sunset Review can lead to reforms of an agency and even its elimination.

The Texas Constitution, not the legislature, creates most of the plural executive. Impeachment and conviction are the ultimate check on an elected official. The Texas House of Representatives can impeach an official for such things as criminal activity or gross malfeasance in office. The Texas Senate then tries the official. If convicted by the Senate, the official is removed from office.

for critical analysis

What are the effects of a plural executive on accountability in state government?

The Plural Executive and the Governor

The plural executive dilutes the ability of the governor to control state government. The governor appoints the secretary of state but has no control over other members of the plural executive. Officials are elected independently, and they do not run as a slate. They do not answer to the governor, and they do not serve as a cabinet. They tend to operate their offices as independent fiefdoms, and they jealously guard their turf. The plural executive can make state government appear as if it is going in several different directions at once. This is especially true when members of the plural executive are political rivals. For example, widely publicized tensions between Governor Rick Perry and Comptroller Carole Strayhorn led to Strayhorn's unsuccessful campaign as an independent against Perry in 2006.

With each member of the plural executive having separate and distinct responsibilities, state government and statewide planning lack cohesiveness. However, the plural executive is a product of Texas's history and environment. Like much of Texas government, it was a result of the public's negative reaction to Governor Edmund J. Davis at the close of Reconstruction.

Boards, Commissions, and Regulatory Agencies

Explain the roles played by boards, commissions, and regulatory agencies

The state **bureaucracy** in Texas has approximately 200 state boards and commissions as well as major agencies within the plural executive. In addition to the agencies under the direct control of the single executives who are part of the elected plural executive, there are also (1) agencies run by multimember boards appointed by the governor and confirmed by the Senate; (2) agencies with single executives appointed by the governor and confirmed by the Senate; and (3) agencies run by multimember boards elected by the people.

Governor Perry's lengthy service has given him enormous influence throughout state government, as he is the only Texas governor in modern history to have made every appointment in state government that a governor can make—and he has also made numerous appointments to vacancies in office such as the Texas appellate courts and scores of district judgeships. State law usually sets the terms of persons on state boards at four or six years. As a result, each new governor spends a great deal of time replacing holdover appointments from previous governors. With Perry's lengthy tenure as governor, however, those holdover appointments are long gone. The result, according to former state representative and author Brian McCall, is that "in this regard, [Perry] is by far the most powerful governor in Texas history. No governor has been able to do what he has done."

Perry has placed many of his closest advisers in key positions, which has spread not only his personal influence but also his personal political philosophy of a pro-business state government. To compare Perry's influence with previous governors, McCall noted that Governor Preston Smith in 1969 was able to appoint the entire board of regents at Texas Tech by getting an amendment inserted into a Minor bill that changed the name of Texas Technological to Texas Tech University. When the name change took effect, the entire board of regents lost their positions and Smith was able to appoint the board. Perry has appointed the entire boards of 17 public colleges and universities and has had a voice in selecting the chancellors of those universities.[27]

Perry has also been willing to discipline board members who have displeased him. For example, in 2009, he refused to reappoint three members of the Texas Forensic Science Board two days before they were to examine a flawed arson investigation. Perry also appointed a new chair of the Forensic Science Board, who abruptly canceled its meeting, and the review of the arson case never took place.[28] In that same year, a Texas Tech regent who was a Perry appointee claimed that a former Perry staff member had told him to resign from the Board of Regents because the regent had endorsed Kay Bailey Hutchison in the Republican primary for governor.[29]

Not all of Perry's nominees have been approved by the overwhelmingly Republican state senate. His nominee for the Board of Pardons and Paroles, best known for her political activism and opposition to sex-toy parties in the Burleson, Texas area, was turned down by the Senate with an overwhelming 27-to-4 vote against her confirmation. State senator John Whitmire, a Democrat and the chair of the Senate Criminal Justice Committee, argued that she was turned down not because the issue was a partisan one, but simply because she was not qualified for a position that considers "life and death matters."[30]

bureaucracy the complex structure of offices, tasks, rules, and principles of organization that are employed by all large-scale institutions to coordinate the work of their personnel

Multimember Appointed Boards

Most boards and commissions in Texas are headed by members appointed by the governor and confirmed by the Senate. Multimember commissions with heads appointed by the governor include innocuous agencies, such as the Bandera County River Authority, the State Seed and Plant Board, the Caddo Lake Compact Commission, and the Texas Funeral Commission. There are also better-known agencies, such as the Texas Alcoholic Beverage Commission, the Department of Parks and Wildlife, the Texas Youth Commission, and the Texas Department of Corrections. Except in the case of a major controversy, such as the sexual abuse scandal that embroiled the Texas Youth Commission in 2007, these agencies work in anonymity, although several of them have a direct effect on the lives of Texans. One such example is the Public Utilities Commission.

Public Utilities Commission (PUC) More than any other agency, the Public Utilities Commission (PUC) has a direct effect on consumers' pocketbooks. Before 1975, cities in Texas set utility rates. The PUC was established in 1975, in part to protect consumers and to curb the rate at which utility costs were increasing. The commission is responsible for setting all local telephone and some electric rates.

Local telephone rates vary from one part of Texas to another, but all rates in a service area are the same. The commission also determines the maximum charge for pay telephones and approves additional services such as caller ID, call waiting, and call forwarding. A rule that took effect in September 1999 prohibits an individual's local service from being disconnected for nonpayment of long-distance bills. Another regulation by the PUC establishes a "no call" list for phone numbers of Texas residents who do not wish to receive telemarketing calls from companies that do not have a business relationship with the phone customer.

With the introduction of retail competition to the electric industry, the PUC has had a major role in providing information to consumers and in setting requirements

The Department of Parks and Wildlife is an agency in the Texas executive branch and is led by a board appointed by the governor. The department manages natural resources and fishing, hunting, and outdoor recreation in the state. Here, an employee measures fish caught near Corpus Christi.

for providers of electric services. The PUC maintains a website that allows electric customers to compare the costs of electricity from the various electric service providers.

Appointed Single Executives

The Texas Department of Insurance Whereas the PUC is run by a multimember body appointed by the governor and confirmed by the Texas Senate, the Texas Department of Insurance is run by one commissioner appointed by the governor for a two-year term and confirmed by the Senate. This single-member appointive system has been in effect since 1993, when governance of the agency by a three-member appointed board was abandoned in favor of single-member governance. The purpose of the Department of Insurance is to regulate the insurance market in Texas, a complicated task that affects most Texans.[31]

In the early 2000s Texas was faced with huge increases in the cost of homeowners' insurance brought on at least in part by major increases in insurance claims, most notably for mold damage. From the first quarter of 2000 to the fourth quarter of 2001, the number of mold claims increased from 1,050 to 14,706. Additionally, the costs of these claims increased significantly to the point that insurance payments became greater than insurance premiums. And with a declining economy during this period, insurance companies were no longer making substantial profits on their investment of insurance premiums. Homeowner premiums increased rapidly. Between 2001 and 2002, homeowners' premiums rose 21.8 percent. Some companies chose not to write any new homeowners' policies; other companies simply pulled out of the Texas market. In 1997, 166 companies were writing homeowners' policies in Texas; by 2003, only 101 companies were writing such policies.

In response, the Texas Department of Insurance began to deregulate insurance coverage so that, for example, policies could be written that charged more for complete mold coverage, less for reduced mold coverage, and significantly less for no mold coverage.

The legislature also stepped into the homeowners' insurance cost issue, which by 2002–03 was reaching crisis proportions. One effect of the legislature's involvement was a "file and use" regulatory system that was implemented at the end of 2004. This system allowed insurers to institute new rates immediately after filing them with the Texas Department of Insurance. The commissioner of insurance can then disapprove of the new rates and may force the company to issue rebates to policyholders.[32] Thus, the commissioner of insurance appears to wield great power over insurance rates but only after those rates have gone into effect.

In 2007, Insurance Commissioner Mike Geeslin canceled Allstate's 5.9 percent rate hike, but Allstate got a court order allowing it to keep charging higher rates, at least temporarily. State Farm has been battling the Department of Insurance for years after ignoring an order from the commissioner to cut its rates by 12 percent.

State Farm's battle with the Texas Insurance Department has taken on the characteristics of a marathon. The company has shown no sign of compromising with the state in its legal battle over the state's claim that it overcharged homeowners. Additionally, in 2009–10 it twice filed to increase its insurance rates and ignored the insurance commissioner's claim that customers deserved a break from increases. The result was a 35 percent boost in insurance rates for many customers in Dallas and nearby counties. It has also successfully sued the Texas Department of Insurance to keep the agency from publicizing documents related to its rate increases.

State Farm's obstinacy in dealing with the Insurance Commission means that for a 10-year-old brick home in north Dallas with an insured value of $150,000, the premium would average about $1,679 per year compared with the average premium charged by other companies of $1,298 per year.[33] While the department's battles with Allstate and State Farm continue, insurance companies have been reducing coverage of homes on the Texas coast out of fear that a hurricane could cause the companies major losses.[34]

Although insurance companies advocate less regulation, consumer groups argue that the insurance commissioner has inadequate powers to deal with insurance companies. Indeed, it is doubtful that the commissioner has sufficient power to force an uncooperative insurer to comply with his or her decisions. The commissioner is also faced with the seemingly intractable problem of keeping rates low and coverage available in hurricane-prone areas to which more and more people are moving.

Multimember Elected Boards

Members of two state agencies are elected by the voters: the Railroad Commission of Texas and the State Board of Education. The Railroad Commission has 3 members elected statewide to six-year terms of office. One of the 3 members is elected every two years. The Board of Education is a 15-member board elected to four-year terms from single-member districts.

Railroad Commission of Texas (RRC) At one time, the Railroad Commission of Texas (RRC) was one of the most powerful state agencies in the nation. It regulated intrastate railroads, trucks, and bus transportation and supervised the oil and natural gas industry in Texas. For most of the RRC's existence, regulation of the oil and gas industry was the RRC's primary focus.

Today, the RRC is a shadow of its former self. Court decisions, deregulation of the transportation industry, other state and federal legislation, and the decline in the nation's dependence on Texas's crude oil production have diminished the commission's power. In 2005 the RRC's limited authority over railroads was transferred to the Texas Department of Transportation, so the RRC now has no authority over what was once its major reason for existence. During the RRC's heyday when Texas was a major oil producer, the commission limited production to conserve oil and to maintain prices. Because it restricted oil production, the RRC was one of the most economically significant governmental bodies on the national and international stage. As oil production shifted to the Middle East, the RRC became the model for OPEC, the Organization of Petroleum Exporting Countries, which also seeks to limit oil production to maintain prices. At one time, members of the Texas RRC wielded such vast economic power that they were among the state's most influential politicians. As the power of the office has been weakened through declining oil production in the state and decreasing dependence on Texas oil, it has become increasingly difficult for railroad commissioners to move into higher offices, and their political visibility has waned.

State Board of Education (SBOE) The State Board of Education (SBOE) sets policy for public education (pre-kindergarten to twelfth-grade programs supported by the state government) in Texas. The education bureaucracy that enforces the SBOE's rules and regulations is called the Texas Education Agency (TEA). Together these two bodies control public education in Texas by determining

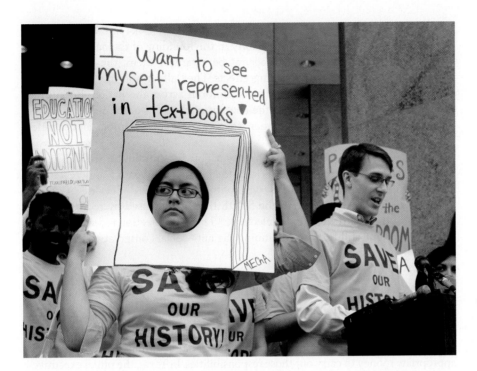

The State Board of Education sets policy for public education, from pre-kindergarten through 12th grade. In recent years, some of the board's decisions concerning curriculums and textbooks have generated controversy.

licensing requirements for public school teachers, setting minimum high school graduation criteria for recommended or advanced curriculums, establishing standards for accreditation of public schools, and selecting public school textbooks.

Texas spends millions of dollars each year purchasing textbooks, and the state furnishes these books without charge to students. Books must meet stringent criteria, and because the state buys so many textbooks, publishers print books especially for students in Texas. Often states that spend less money on textbooks than Texas must purchase those originally printed for Texas.

The commissioner of education is appointed by the governor from a list of candidates submitted by the SBOE. He or she is administrative head of the TEA and serves as adviser to the SBOE. The commissioner of education is at the apex of the public education bureaucracy in Texas.

In recent years, the Texas SBOE has become an ideological battleground. In 2009, that conflict led the board to review how evolution was taught. In what was a partial defeat for the social conservatives, no longer would teachers be required to teach "strengths and weaknesses" of evolution, although they would be encouraged to teach "all sides." Other battles have broken out over other aspects of educational policy. For example, one policy goal was that high school students were to learn how the cultural contributions of "people from various racial, ethnic, gender, and religious groups shape American culture." One of the leading social conservatives on the board proposed an unsuccessful amendment that would delete the words "from various racial, ethnic, gender, and religious groups." That suggested, of course, that teaching would not focus on the role of those specific groups in shaping American culture. Another amendment proposed that students be required to evaluate the contributions of significant Americans—Thurgood Marshall, Billy Graham, Newt Gingrich, William F. Buckley Jr., Hillary Rodham Clinton, and Edward Kennedy. All passed the board except for Edward Kennedy. Other issues involve whether César

Chávez was significant enough to be in social studies textbooks and whether greater emphasis should be placed on Christianity in the founding of the nation.

Although many Texas voters may not be aware of them, the battles fought within the SBOE have wide-reaching effects. They affect not only the education of Texas schoolchildren, but also that of children across the nation. Because the state's textbook market is so large, the content of the textbooks used in Texas sets the tone for textbook content in other states that are less populous and therefore have smaller markets for texts.[35]

As a result of the 2010 elections, there was a power shift on the SBOE when the leader of the social conservatives who was the chair of the board was defeated. The 2012 elections created a new battle for control of the board. Because of changes in the single-member districts of the SBOE that were caused by redistricting, all members of the board were up for election.[36] The 2012 election reduced the social conservative blue still further, continuing the anti–social conservative trend begun in the 2010 elections.

Making Agencies Accountable

In a democracy, elected officials are ultimately responsible to the voters. Appointed officials are indirectly accountable to the people through the elected officials who appoint them. Both are responsible to legislatures that determine responsibilities and appropriate money to carry out those responsibilities. In Texas, the plural executive is responsible to the legislature for its biennial funding and to the voters for re-election. The myriad state agencies look to the legislature for funding, and once every 12 years they must justify their existence to the **Sunset Advisory Commission (SAC)**.

Sunset Advisory Commission (SAC) a commission created in 1975 for the purpose of reviewing the effectiveness of state agencies

The 12-member SAC has 5 members from the Texas Senate and 1 public member appointed by the lieutenant governor. Five members from the Texas House and 1 public member are appointed by the Speaker of the Texas House.

The Sunset Review Act created the SAC in 1977. The act established specific criteria to be considered in evaluating the continuing need for an agency. One of several laws enacted in the mid-1970s to bring more openness and accountability to Texas government, the Sunset process establishes a date on which an agency is abolished unless the legislature passes a bill for the agency to continue in operation.

During its Sunset review, an agency must, among other things, document its efficiency, the extent to which it meets legislative mandates, and its promptness and effectiveness in handling complaints, and it must establish the continuing need for its services. The review process is lengthy, lasting almost two years.

After a thorough study of an agency, the SAC recommends one of three actions to the legislature: (1) the agency continues as is, with no change in its organization or functions; (2) the agency continues but with changes (reorganization, a new focus for the agency, or merger with other agencies); or (3) the agency is abolished.

If option 1 or 2 is recommended, specific action by the legislature is required before the date of the agency's abolition. Option 1 requires specific legislation to re-create the agency in its existing form. Option 2 requires the legislature to re-create the agency with some or all of the changes recommended by the SAC. If the legislature agrees the agency should be abolished, no action is necessary. It will expire at the Sunset deadline; the sun sets and the agency is no more.

Each state agency has been through the Sunset process. The legislature has allowed the sun to set on more than 58 agencies; 12 agencies have been merged with existing bodies. Since 1978, the legislature has accepted the majority of recommendations of the SAC.

for critical analysis

What is the source of power of Texas bureaucratic agencies? How are these agencies held accountable to other elected public officials or the public?

Thinking Critically about the Executive in Texas

At the national level, the president is elected, through the Electoral College, by the people as a whole. The president is the spokesperson for the nation in the world and is the commander in chief of the armed forces. When there is a national crisis, the people look to the president for leadership. Throughout the twentieth century, the power and authority of the presidency increased significantly, often at the expense of Congress. American democracy has become an executive-led system, with a weak Congress and a partially demobilized electorate.

Such is not the case in Texas. The fear of a strong executive who could ignore the wishes of either the legislature or the people, as was the case during Reconstruction in Texas, led in 1876 to a constitution that created a plural executive. The governor is the chief executive officer in the state, elected directly by the popular vote of all the people of Texas. People turn to the governor for leadership and direction during times of crisis. But compared with that of the president, the power of the Texas governor is more limited. Many key executive officials, including the lieutenant governor, the attorney general, the comptroller, and the land commissioner, are elected—like the governor—directly by the people. These members of the plural executive, along with other popularly elected statewide boards and commissions, possess power and authority that under other constitutional arrangements the governor might possess. As has been noted throughout this chapter, Governor Perry's ability to accumulate power in the governor's office is unprecedented in recent history. That his successors will be able to wield the limited powers of the governor as efficiently is by no means certain.

The existence of an institutionally weak office of the governor and a plural executive has a number of important implications for democracy in Texas. First, because power and authority are divided among a number of distinct officers, no individual is fully responsible for executive initiatives in the state. Indeed, executive officials can struggle with each other for power as they seek to move the state government in different directions. Partisanship can exacerbate the natural conflict built into the executive branch in Texas. A Democratic lieutenant governor may or may not be willing to work closely with a Republican governor. But the worst clashes may be among executive officials of the same party. The fight between Governor Rick Perry and Comptroller Caroline Strayhorn, both Republicans, culminating in Strayhorn's running against the incumbent governor as an independent in 2006, was a recent example of a fundamental truth in Texas politics: the executive does not have to speak with one voice or in harmony with itself.

A second consequence of the plural executive for democracy in Texas is that it has given rise to a powerful executive officer in the state legislature, outside the office of the governor. The lieutenant governor has become, along with the Speaker of the House, one of the two most important officials in the state legislature. The lieutenant governor, not the governor, runs the Senate. The lieutenant governor, not the governor, is the executive branch's chief legislative official.

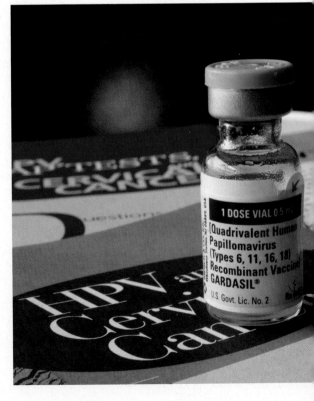

Governor Perry experienced a significant check from the legislature in 2007 after he issued an executive order for girls in Texas to be vaccinated against HPV, a sexually transmitted disease linked to cervical cancer. The legislature passed a bill overturning the order.

The dispersal of power and authority among a number of different executive offices in the state has a third consequence for democracy in the state. Additional points of access are created for interest groups seeking to influence government and public policy, making it easier for special interests to impose their will on the policy-making process. The 2012 elections have continued the Republican Party's firm hold over the plural executive and will have major consequences for policy and politics in Texas.

study guide

(S) **Practice online with:** Chapter 8 Diagnostic Quiz ■ Chapter 8 Key Term Flashcards

The Governor

■ **Describe the powers of the Texas governor and the limits of the governor's power (pp. 215–26)**

Although the Texas governor is considered weak compared to other states, the power of appointing members to boards has made Governor Rick Perry the most powerful governor in state history largely because of his long tenure. Among the executive powers the governor possesses are appointment, budgetary, military, and police powers. Among his legislative powers are message and veto powers and the ability to call special sessions of the legislature.

Key Terms

impeachment (p. 218)

appointment (p. 222)

patronage (p. 222)

senatorial courtesy (p. 223)

executive budget (p. 223)

legislative budget (p. 223)

veto (p. 225)

post-adjournment veto (p. 225)

line-item veto (p. 225)

special session (p. 225)

Practice Quiz

1. Which of the following is *not* necessary to become governor of Texas? *(p. 217)*
   a) A governor must be at least 30 years of age.
   b) A governor must have lived in Texas for at least five years.
   c) A governor must be a U.S. citizen.
   d) A governor must be a lawyer.
   e) A governor must have substantial campaign funding.

2. The election for governor of Texas is held in an off-year in order to *(p. 217)*
   a) increase voter participation in elections in odd-numbered years.

b) influence the presidential vote in Texas.
   c) decrease the likelihood of voter fraud.
   d) give governors an opportunity to campaign for presidential candidates.
   e) prevent the presidential vote in Texas from influencing the election of state officials.

3. The only constitutional method of removing the governor is *(p. 218)*
   a) *quo warranto* proceedings.
   b) *ex post facto* removal.
   c) a vote of no confidence.
   d) impeachment.
   e) impeachment and conviction.

4. The governor's most effective power in controlling the executive branch of state government is the power *(p. 222)*
   a) of the veto.
   b) of appointment.
   c) of removal.
   d) of judicial review.
   e) to create a state budget.

5. The governor's veto is absolute when it is a *(p. 225)*
   a) line-item veto.
   b) special veto.
   c) budgetary veto.
   d) post-adjournment veto.
   e) select veto.

6. The governor can grant *(p. 226)*
   a) pardons.
   b) suspended sentences.
   c) probation.
   d) retrials.
   e) parole.

(S) **Practice Online**
"Exploring Texas Politics" exercise: *The Power of the Veto*

The Plural Executive

■ **Identify the other elected officials who make up the plural executive (pp. 226–34)**

Unlike the national level, the governor does not appoint a "cabinet." Voters in Texas elect the lieutenant governor and other major statewide offices in separate elections. This disperses power within the executive branch, which means that executive officers must compromise not only with the legislature, but within the executive branch.

Key Terms

plural executive (p. 226)

secretary of state (p. 228)

lieutenant governor (p. 229)

attorney general (p. 231)

land commissioner (p. 231)

agricultural commissioner (p. 232)

comptroller (p. 232)

Practice Quiz

7. Which member of the plural executive is appointed? *(p. 228)*
   a) secretary of state
   b) land commissioner
   c) lieutenant governor
   d) comptroller of public accounts
   e) attorney general

8. The attorney general is *(p. 231)*
   a) part of the governor's Cabinet.
   b) elected independently of the governor.

c) appointed by the Texas Supreme Court.
d) the governor's lawyer.
e) chosen by the State Bar of Texas.

9. The land commissioner *(p. 231)*
   a) records all property deeds.
   b) administers state land.
   c) surveys property in Texas.
   d) is appointed by the state Senate.
   e) administers Big Bend National Park.

10. Members of the plural executive are accountable to the *(p. 234)*
    a) voters and the governor.
    b) legislature and voters.
    c) constitution.
    d) state supreme court.
    e) legislature.

 Practice Online
"Exploring Texas Politics" exercise: *The Lieutenant Governor in Texas*

Boards, Commissions, and Regulatory Agencies

■ **Explain the roles played by boards, commissions, and regulatory agencies (pp. 235–40)**

The governor's most important power is the ability to appoint people to boards, commissions, and regulatory agencies. Such institutions have important powers to interpret state regulations and make a difference in the lives of everyday Texans.

Key Terms

bureaucracy (p. 235)

Sunset Advisory Commission (SAC) (p. 240)

Practice Quiz

11. The Public Utilities Commission *(p. 236–37)*
    a) regulates some electric rates.
    b) regulates local phone rates.
    C) maintains a website so consumers can compare electric rates.
    d) maintains a "do not call" registry.
    e) All of the above are features of the Public Utilities Commission.

12. The Texas Department of Insurance *(p. 237)*
    a) has limited power to regulate insurance rates.
    b) collects the penalties for not buying health insurance under Obamacare.
    C) sells insurance for mold coverage.

d) is run by a five-member elected board.
e) All of the above are features of the Texas Department of Insurance.

13. The Railroad Commission of Texas *(p. 238)*
    a) is responsible for the safety of the state's railroads.
    b) issues bonds to support the state's transportation needs.
    c) regulates oil and gas production in Texas.
    d) approves mergers of railroads.
    e) is the most powerful agency in the state.

14. The State Board of Education *(pp. 238–39)*
    a) has a major role in determining the books used in Texas public schools.
    b) is appointed by the legislature.
    c) reviews applications to state colleges and universities.
    d) is responsible for school property tax rates.
    e) governs local boards of education.

15. Which agency investigates the performance of state agencies and recommends whether an agency should be abolished, continued as is, or continued with changes? *(p. 240)*
    a) Legislative Budget Board
    b) Legislative Research Bureau
    c) Texas Research League
    d) Public Utilities Commission
    e) Sunset Advisory Commission

Recommended Websites

Attorney General of Texas
www.oag.state.tx.us/

Lieutenant Governor of Texas
www.ltgov.state.tx.us/

Office of the Governor
www.governor.state.tx.us/

Railroad Commission of Texas
www.rrc.state.tx.us/

Sunset Advisory Commission
www.sunset.state.tx.us/

Texas Department of Agriculture
www.agr.state.tx.us/

Texas General Land Office
www.glo.state.tx.us/

Texas Secretary of State
www.sos.state.tx.us/

Window on State Government (Comptroller's Office)
www.window.state.tx.us/

Texas courts are responsible for securing liberty and equality under the law. The judges who preside over Texas courts are elected, and this method of selection may influence judges' behavior, as they try to win favor with voters.

The Texas Judiciary

WHAT GOVERNMENT DOES AND WHY IT MATTERS The presiding judge of the Texas Court of Criminal Appeals, Sharon Keller, has cultivated a "tough on crime" image. Her campaign literature, for example, has shown a figure behind bars with the headline, "He won't be voting for Judge Sharon Keller."

However, Keller may have crossed the line in terms of her harshness toward criminal defendants on September 25, 2007. That evening, Michael Richard was scheduled to die by lethal injection. Earlier that day, the Supreme Court of the United States had agreed to hear a challenge to the constitutionality of death by lethal injection. Ordinarily, that would lead to a petition to the Court of Criminal Appeals for a stay of execution, in order to wait for the decision of the U.S. Supreme Court.

Things went terribly wrong. The lawyers for Michael Richard were working against a tight deadline for their petition, and they claimed they experienced computer problems that created a delay in preparing their documents. They called the Court of Criminal Appeals and asked that the court stay open an extra 20 minutes so that the stay of execution request could be filed. Judge Keller refused to keep the court open. In making this decision, she did not consult with other judges on the court, some of whom were working in the same building. Other judges on the court have stated that they would have stayed late to hear the appeal if they had known about it. Michael Richard was executed that evening.

Complaints were filed against Judge Keller with the State Commission on Judicial Conduct. The hearing officer, known as a special master, found plenty of blame to go around in this case. He found that the Texas Defender Service, which provided legal representation for Michael Richard, was unable to show that it actually had computer problems that made it unable to file the claim on time. In fact, the Texas Defender Service did not even contemplate filing a lethal injection claim until over two hours after the Supreme Court had agreed to hear a lethal injection case, and then it assigned a junior attorney to prepare documents, the first of which was not ready until 4:45 P.M. and all of which were not completed until 5:56 P.M. that day. Nor did the Court of Criminal Appeals escape criticism. And though Judge Keller's behavior did not, according to the special master, justify removal from office or reprimand, it "was not exemplary of a public servant." He stated, "Although [Judge Keller] says that if she could do it all over again she would not change any of her actions, this cannot be true. Any reasonable person, having gone through this ordeal, surely would realize that open communication, particularly during the hectic few hours before an execution, would benefit the interests of justice. Further, her judgment in not keeping the clerk's office open past 5:00 to allow the TDS to file was highly questionable. In sum, there is a valid reason why many in the legal community are not proud of Judge Keller's actions."[1] Interestingly, in the fall of 2010, a special court of review dismissed the public warning against Keller on the grounds that a warning cannot be a penalty following a formal proceeding against a judge.

This episode is noteworthy for two reasons: (1) Texas judges are elected, which encourages judges and judicial candidates to behave in ways that may cultivate the favor of voters even as the judges seem to sidestep notions of justice; and (2) one reason that Texas is the death penalty capital of the nation may be that it has a partisan election system for selecting not only judges but also the district attorneys, who prosecute crimes.

chaptergoals

- Describe how the Texas court system is organized (pages 249–53)

- Explain the legal process and the differences between criminal and civil law (pages 254–56)

- Evaluate the process for selecting judges in Texas (pages 256–68)

- Assess the impact of recent changes related to tort reform, litigation, and disciplining judges (pages 268–72)

Court Structure

Describe how the Texas court system is organized

Like the federal courts, the state and local courts in Texas are responsible for securing liberty and equality under the law. However, the democratic mechanisms put into place in Texas to select judges and to hold them accountable for their actions are quite different from those at the national level. Federal judges are appointed by the president and confirmed by the Senate. They have lifetime appointments. This means that federal judges, subject to good behavior in office, are free from the ebb and flow of democratic politics. They do not have to cater to public opinion and are empowered to interpret the law as they see fit, without fear of reprisal at the polls. In Texas, however, judges are elected to office. Although they may initially be appointed to their offices, sooner or later they are responsible to the people for their decisions in office. Election of judges brings not only the people but also interest groups into the selection and retention of judges. The influence of special interest money in judicial campaigns raises important questions about the relationship between the rule of law and the nature of democratic politics.

Texas has a large and complex court structure consisting of a hodgepodge of courts with overlapping jurisdiction (see Figure 9.1). Additionally, some courts have specialized jurisdiction, whereas others have broad authority to handle a variety of cases. At the highest level for civil cases is the **Texas Supreme Court**, which consists of nine justices, including a chief justice. This court hears civil and juvenile cases only and, at the state level, it has final appellate jurisdiction. The only requirements for being a Texas Supreme Court justice are that one must be a citizen of the United States and a resident of Texas, be at least 35 years of age, and

Texas Supreme Court the highest civil court in Texas; consists of nine justices and has final state appellate authority over civil cases

The Texas Supreme Court is the highest civil court in Texas. The court consists of nine justices (pictured here as of 2012).

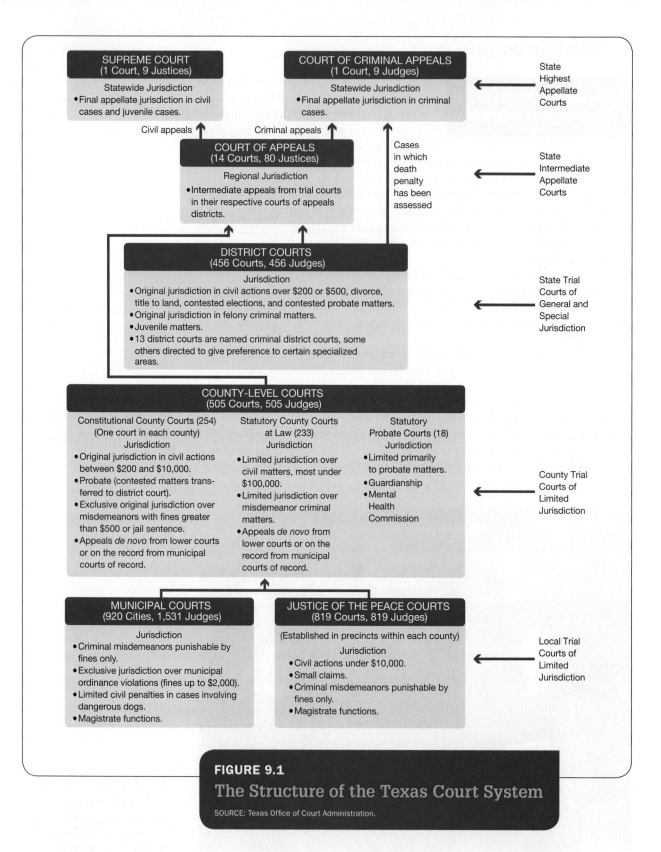

FIGURE 9.1

The Structure of the Texas Court System

SOURCE: Texas Office of Court Administration.

have been either a practicing lawyer or judge for at least 10 years. The term of a justice is six years, with at least three justices being elected every two years.

The **Texas Court of Criminal Appeals** is the highest appeals court in the state for criminal cases. This court also has nine judges, including a presiding judge. The pay, terms, and qualifications of Court of Criminal Appeals judges are the same as for the Texas Supreme Court. Perhaps the most important task of the Court of Criminal Appeals is its jurisdiction over automatic appeals in death penalty cases.

Both the Supreme Court and the Court of Criminal Appeals have appellate jurisdiction. This means that they have the authority to review the decisions of lower courts to determine whether legal principles and court procedures were followed correctly. This authority also provides the power to order that a case be retried if mistakes were made. Texas has 14 other appellate courts, located in various parts of the state, which have both criminal and civil jurisdiction. These courts are intermediate appellate courts and hear appeals from the trial courts. Usually, before the Supreme Court or the Court of Criminal Appeals hears a case, the initial appeal has been heard by one of the **courts of appeals**. These courts have intermediate appellate jurisdiction in various regions of the state for both civil, juvenile, and criminal cases. Presently, there are 80 judges who serve on the 14 courts of appeals, which range in size from 3 to 13 judges. Although there are occasions when every judge on a court of appeal will hear a case, mostly appeals at this level are heard by panels of three judges. The requirements for a court of appeals justice are the same as those for justices of the higher courts. Each of the 14 courts has one chief justice.

The major trial courts in Texas are the **district courts**. Each county has at least one district court, although rural parts of Texas may have several counties that are served by one district court. Urban counties have many district courts. Harris County (Houston), for example, has 59 district courts and Dallas County has 48. District courts usually have general jurisdiction, meaning that they hear a broad range of civil and criminal cases. However, in urban counties, some district courts

Texas Court of Criminal Appeals the highest criminal court in Texas; consists of nine justices and has final state appellate authority over criminal cases

courts of appeals the 14 intermediate-level appellate courts that hear appeals from district and county courts to determine whether the decisions of these lower courts followed legal principles and court procedures

district courts the major trial courts in Texas, which usually have general jurisdiction over a broad range of civil and criminal cases

The Texas Court of Criminal Appeals is the highest court in the state for criminal cases. Like the Texas Supreme Court, it has nine justice (pictured here as of 2012).

with specialized jurisdiction hear only civil, criminal, juvenile, or family law matters. Those district courts having general jurisdiction would hear felony criminal cases, divorces, land disputes, election contests, and civil lawsuits. Currently, there are 456 district judges, 9 State Supreme Court judges, 9 court of criminal appeals judges, and 80 court of appeals judges.

Texas is unusual in having the office of **county judge** in each of its 254 counties. Not only does the county judge preside over the county commissioners court and thus have responsibilities for administration of county government, but the county judge also presides over the county court. Often these **county courts** have jurisdiction over uncontested probate cases and over the more serious misdemeanor criminal offenses involving fines greater than $500 or a jail sentence as well as over civil cases where the amounts in dispute are relatively small, generally in the $200 to $10,000 range. The county court may also hear appeals from municipal courts or from justice of the peace courts. Thus, the county judge combines political-administrative functions with some judicial functions. However, in the more populated counties, there are county courts at law and sometimes probate courts. As a result, in the larger counties most, and sometimes all, of the county judges' judicial duties are now performed by other courts.

In larger counties, there are **statutory county courts at law**. Since the county courts at law were created by statute, often at widely different times, the jurisdiction of these courts varies significantly. Usually, the county courts at law hear appeals from justices of the peace and from municipal courts. In civil cases, they usually hear cases involving sums greater than would be heard by a justice of the peace court, but less than would be heard by district courts. Typically, county courts at law hear civil cases involving less than $100,000. In comparison to the district courts, the county courts at law would hear less serious criminal offenses.

Some of the county courts at law have specialized jurisdiction; most commonly these are in the most urban counties, where some of the courts will have only civil jurisdiction and others only criminal jurisdiction. Currently there are 233 county court at law judges.

In the most urban areas of the state, the legislature has created courts known as **statutory probate courts**. These courts are highly specialized, as their primary activity involves probate matters that relate to the disposition of property of deceased persons. They may also deal with matters relating to guardianship of people unable to handle their own affairs, and they may handle mental-health commitments. In other parts of the state, depending on the statute, probate matters may be heard by the county court, the county court at law, or the district court. Currently, there are 18 statutory probate court judges.

Each county in Texas has between one and eight justice of the peace precincts, depending on population, although large urban counties have more than one judge in each precinct. Harris County, for example, has two in each of eight precincts. Within each precinct are **justice of the peace courts**. There are 819 justice of the peace courts in Texas. These courts hear class C misdemeanors, which are less serious crimes. They also have jurisdiction over minor civil matters, and they function as small claims courts. Suits in small claims court must be for less than $10,000, but the suits can be handled more informally in small claims court than in a higher level court and they can be handled without a lawyer. Judges may issue search and arrest warrants. In counties without medical examiners, judges may fulfill the administrative functions of coroners.

Justices of the peace mostly handle traffic misdemeanors. Of the more than 2.45 million criminal cases disposed of by justice of the peace courts in the year ending August 31, 2010, more than 1.9 million were traffic misdemeanors. In contrast, justice of the peace courts heard only about 546,000 civil cases.[2]

county judge the person in each of Texas's 254 counties who presides over the county court and the county commissioners court, with responsibility for the administration of county government; some county judges carry out judicial responsibilities

county courts the courts that exist in some counties that are presided over by county judges

statutory county courts at law courts that tend to hear less serious cases than those heard by district courts

statutory probate courts specialized courts whose jurisdiction is limited to probate and guardianship matters

justice of the peace courts local trial courts with limited jurisdiction over small claims and very minor criminal misdemeanors

Justices of the peace have faced considerable criticism in recent years. In Dallas County, an auditor discovered 22,000 unprocessed traffic cases. The justice of the peace had failed to collect as much as $2 million in fines. Unlike any other judge in Texas except for the county judge (who is often an administrator rather than a judge), 92 percent of the 819 justices of the peace in Texas are non-lawyers, and the lack of justices' legal credentials has led to considerable debate in the state.[3] The office has its origins in medieval England and has existed in Texas since 1837, even before statehood. In the days of the frontier, justices of the peace provided legal authority where no other existed. Indeed, the famed Judge Roy Bean was a justice of the peace. The initial idea was that a justice of the peace would be a respected person in the community who was chosen for ability, judgment, and integrity. Today, as the former State Bar president Frank Newton has pointed out, "In almost every large metropolitan area, there are some JPs who do virtually nothing and sort of get lost in the shuffle. People don't tend to get all excited about JP elections. Most people don't know what a JP does. JP is not a very prestigious job."[4]

Municipal courts have been created by the legislature in each of the incorporated cities of the state. There are 920 cities and towns in Texas that have these courts; larger cities have multiple courts. There are 1,531 municipal court judges in the state. Municipal courts have jurisdiction over violations of city **ordinances** and, concurrent with justice of the peace courts, have jurisdiction over class C misdemeanors, for which the punishment for conviction is a fine. Municipal judges may issue search and arrest warrants, but they have only limited civil jurisdiction.[5] Municipal courts, like justice of the peace courts, function primarily as traffic courts. In the year ending August 31, 2010, municipal courts disposed of almost 7 million cases. About 5.1 million of these cases were non-parking traffic misdemeanors; another 663,091 were parking cases.[6]

Great controversy has erupted in the city of Dallas where the city council has demanded that municipal judges—there are 11 full-time and 18 part-time municipal judges in Dallas—get tougher with offenders or lose their judicial appointments. In particular, city officials have claimed that the judges give too many trial postponements, set fines too low, and don't hold accused violators accountable for ignoring citations.[7]

municipal courts local trial courts with limited jurisdiction over violations of city ordinances and very minor criminal misdemeanors; municipal courts are located in each of Texas's incorporated cities and towns

ordinance a regulation enacted by a city government

The boxes of evidence that the State of Texas prepared for the trial against tobacco companies in 1997 occupied an entire gym in Texarkana. In a civil case, the plaintiff bears the burden of proof and must demonstrate that the defendant is more than not likely responsible for the harm suffered by the plaintiff.

The Legal Process

Explain the legal process and the differences between criminal and civil law

Just as the Texas Supreme Court hears civil cases and the Texas Court of Criminal Appeals hears criminal cases, it is useful to think of the law as divided into these parts. **Civil law** involves a dispute, usually between private individuals over relationships, obligations, and responsibility. Though there are exceptions with a violation of the civil law, the remedy is often for the offending party to pay compensation to the injured party.

In contrast, **criminal law** involves the violation of concepts of right and wrong as defined by criminal statutes. In criminal law, the state accuses individuals of violations and, if found guilty, the violator is subject to punishment. In some cases, that punishment may involve loss of liberty or even loss of life.

In civil law, an aggrieved person will usually obtain a lawyer and file a petition that details the **complaint** against the person accused of causing the harm. The petition is filed with the clerk of court, who issues a citation against the defendant. The defendant will usually file an **answer** explaining why the allegations are not valid. Depending on the issue, the amounts of money that may be awarded as damages, and the probability of success, the aggrieved person may be able to obtain the services of a lawyer on a **contingent fee** basis. This means that the lawyer will not charge the individual if the case is lost but will obtain a portion of the damages awarded if the case is won. It is not unusual for such contingent fee arrangements to involve one-third or more of the damages award plus expenses. Lawyers who handle cases on contingent fee agreements often handle personal-injury cases and are known as trial lawyers. Traditionally, these lawyers will contribute money to judicial candidates who are sympathetic to plaintiffs. They make money only if they win, so they have a strong economic interest in supporting judicial candidates who are sympathetic to plaintiffs and to the awarding of large damages.

The person being sued either will have to hire an attorney on his or her own or, if insured, will be represented by an attorney paid for by the insurance company. Fee arrangements vary for civil defense lawyers, but often they are paid by the hour, in which case they get paid whether they win or lose. Their economic incentives to contribute money to judicial campaigns may be different from the incentives trial lawyers have, but civil defense lawyers do contribute large sums to judicial campaigns in order to elect judges who support their views on tort law.

The court to which a civil case is taken depends on the type of case and the amount of money involved. Most commonly, a civil case will be settled, meaning the dispute is resolved without going to court. Settlements may, however, occur during trial, sometimes immediately before a jury renders its decision. If a case is not settled and goes to trial, it may be heard either by a judge or, if requested by either side, by a jury. Although civil jury cases do not have to be unanimous in Texas, the burden of proof is on the plaintiff. The standard of proof that the plaintiff must meet is **preponderance of the evidence**. That means that the plaintiff must show that it is more likely than not that the defendant is the cause of the harm suffered by the plaintiff.

Civil cases may involve tiny amounts of damages or they may involve billions of dollars, which have the potential of breaking huge corporations, such as happened in the 1980s when Pennzoil successfully sued Texaco in a dispute over the takeover of the Getty Oil Company.[8]

civil law a branch of law that deals with disputes, usually between private individuals over relationships, obligation, and responsibility

criminal law the branch of law that regulates the conduct of individuals, defines crimes, and specifies punishment for criminal acts

complaint the presentation of a grievance by the plaintiff in a civil case

answer the presentation of a defendant's defense against an allegation in a civil case

contingent fee a fee paid to the lawyer in a civil case and which is contingent on winning the case

preponderance of the evidence the standard of proof in a civil jury case, by which the plaintiff must show that the defendant is more likely than not the cause of the harm suffered by the plaintiff

Civil case verdicts may, of course, be appealed. Appeals are usually from the trial court to the intermediate court of appeal and perhaps further to the state supreme court. Given the cost of appeals and the delay that is involved, it is not unusual for some settlement to be reached after the verdict, but before the case goes through the appellate process. For example, a plaintiff might agree to settle for much less than the verdict in the case to avoid the expense and delay of further appeals.

In criminal cases, the state alleges a violation of a criminal law and is usually represented in court by a prosecutor. Some prosecutors are career prosecutors with vast trial experience. These people will often prosecute the most difficult and complex cases, such as felonies and **capital cases**. However, because the pay of prosecutors is often much lower than that of private lawyers who do litigation in the private sector, it is common for most prosecutors to be quite young and inexperienced. Once they gain trial experience, prosecutors commonly move into the private sector.

capital case a criminal case in which the death penalty is a possible punishment

Defendants may hire criminal defense attorneys, who usually charge a flat fee to handle the case. Criminal defense lawyers, of course, do not work on a contingent fee basis. Since most criminal defendants are found guilty, criminal defense lawyers often prefer to obtain as much of their fee as possible in advance of the verdict.

Some parts of Texas have public defender offices where salaried lawyers provide at least some adult indigent criminal defense services in a county. Bexar County has established the first public defender office for indigent criminal appeals. Travis County has a public defender office representing only indigents with mental impairments.[9] A public defender office represents indigents in capital cases in west Texas.[10]

In Texas, indigent criminal defendants are more commonly represented by court-appointed lawyers. These are lawyers appointed by the judge to represent a defendant. Usually, these government-paid fees are less than would be charged to nonindigent defendants. Thus, some lawyers are reluctant to fulfill court appointments; others may not put the time and energy into a court-appointed case that they would if they were privately paid; others take court appointments because they have a limited number of paying clients; and still others take court appointments to gain experience. Concern over the poor quality of legal representation provided indigent criminal defendants, especially in capital cases, led to legislation in 2001 to increase the pay and qualifications of court-appointed lawyers.

Serious crimes are **felonies**. In those cases, as well as many lesser offenses known as **misdemeanors**, prior to the trial there will be an indictment by a grand jury. In Texas, a **grand jury** consists of 12 persons who sit for two to six months. Depending on the county, a grand jury may meet only once or twice, or it may meet several times a week. Although sometimes grand juries are selected randomly from a pool of qualified citizens, mostly Texas grand jurors are chosen by a commissioner system. A district judge will appoint several grand jury commissioners, who will then select 15 to 20 citizens of the county. The first 12 who are qualified become the grand jury.[11]

felony a serious criminal offense, punishable by a prison sentence or a fine. A capital felony is possibly punishable by death.

misdemeanor a minor criminal offense, usually punishable by a small fine or a short jail sentence

Grand juries can inquire into any criminal matter but usually spend most of their time on felony crimes. They work in secret and rely heavily on the information provided by the prosecutor, though in some cases grand juries will work quite independently of the prosecutor. These grand juries are called runaway grand juries because the prosecutor has lost control of them, but such cases are very rare. If nine of the grand jurors decide a trial is warranted, they will indict a suspect. An **indictment** is also known as a "true bill." On the other hand, sometimes a grand jury does not believe a trial is warranted. In those cases, the grand jury issues a "no bill" decision.

grand jury jury that determines whether sufficient evidence is available to justify a trial; grand juries do not rule on the accused's guilt or innocence

indictment a written statement issued by a grand jury that charges a suspect with a crime and states that a trial is warranted

Although a suspect has the right to trial by jury, he or she may waive that right and undergo a **bench trial** before the judge only. Most commonly, the suspect

bench trial a trial held without a jury and before only a judge

In 2008 members of the Fundamentalist Church of Jesus Christ of Latter Day Saints appealed to the Texas courts after Child Protective Services took more than 400 children from the polygamist compound into custody. The Texas Supreme Court affirmed a lower-court ruling that state officials had acted improperly.

plea bargain negotiated agreement in a criminal case in which a defendant agrees to plead guilty in return for the state's agreement to reduce the severity of the criminal charge or prison sentence the defendant is facing

beyond a reasonable doubt the legal standard in criminal cases, which requires the prosecution to prove that a reasonable doubt of innocence does not exist

will engage in a **plea bargain**. With plea bargaining, a suspect agrees to plead guilty in exchange for a lighter sentence than might be imposed if the suspect were found guilty at trial. Approximately 97 percent of criminal convictions in Texas are the result of plea bargains.[12] If the suspect does choose trial by jury, felony juries will have 12 members; misdemeanor juries will have six members. There must be a unanimous verdict of guilty or not guilty. If the jurors are not unanimous, the result is a hung jury and a mistrial is declared. The prosecutor may then choose to retry the suspect. In addition to the requirement of unanimity in jury decisions, another important difference between civil and criminal cases is the standard of proof. In criminal cases, rather than the standard of preponderance of the evidence, the standard is **beyond a reasonable doubt**. This means that the prosecutor must prove the charges against the defendant, and they must be proven to a very high standard so that a reasonable doubt of innocence does not exist.

If a guilty verdict is returned, there will be a separate hearing on the sentence, which in Texas is sometimes also determined by the jury. At the sentencing hearing, factors such as prior record and background will be considered, even though these factors could not be considered at the trial portion of the proceeding.

Of course a defendant may also appeal a verdict. Usually, the appeals are by a convicted defendant who alleges that an error in the trial may have affected the case's outcome. In rare cases, a prosecutor may also appeal. For the most part, however, criminal defendants will appeal their convictions to an intermediate appeals court and perhaps further to the Texas Court of Criminal Appeals. In capital cases, however, the appeal will be directly to the Texas Court of Criminal Appeals.

● Judicial Politics

Evaluate the process for selecting judges in Texas

Although there are still generalist lawyers who handle all sorts of cases, much of the practice of law is very specialized. Thus, in the civil process, trial lawyers and civil defense lawyers tend to back opposing candidates for judgeships. It is not unusual for trial lawyers to support one candidate, often the Democrat, who is more likely to be the more liberal, or pro-plaintiff, candidate, and for the civil defense lawyers to support the Republican, who is more likely to be the conservative, or pro-defendant, candidate. The civil defense lawyers will often align themselves with business groups and with professional groups, such as medical doctors, to support judges inclined to favor the civil defense side.

In the criminal process, it is sometimes possible to see criminal defense lawyers backing one candidate and prosecutors backing the other. Some prosecutors' offices are quite political, and the prosecutors will publicly support pro-prosecution judicial candidates. They will often be aligned with victims' rights groups. Criminal defense lawyers, on the other hand, will often back one of their own in contested criminal court races.

One big difference in the campaigns of civil court judges versus criminal court judges is the amount of money involved. Enormous amounts can be involved in civil cases, and so it is worth lots of money to trial lawyers and civil defense interests to elect candidates favorable to their point of view. On the other hand, with the exception of a relatively few highly paid criminal defense lawyers, the practice of criminal law is not very lucrative. Prosecutors are on salary, and usually the salaries are not large. Criminal defense lawyers often represent clients with little money. And most criminal cases are plea-bargained. The economic incentives to contribute large sums to criminal court races don't exist. The result is that a strong candidate for the Texas Supreme Court may raise in the neighborhood of $1,000,000 for a campaign, whereas a strong candidate for the Texas Court of Criminal Appeals may raise $100,000. However, as Texas has become predominantly Republican at the statewide level, hard-fought contests between Democrats and Republicans for the Texas Supreme Court and the Texas Court of Criminal Appeals have become rare.

Initial Appointment of Judges by the Governor

A notable aspect of the Texas judiciary is that with the exception of municipal judges, who tend to be appointed by local governments, all judges are elected in partisan elections. Still, because the governor appoints district and appellate judges to the bench to fill vacancies prior to an election or to fill judgeships on new courts, large percentages of judges initially get on the bench through appointment. Although there has been some controversy over the relatively small number of appointments of minorities made by some governors, gubernatorial appointment

for critical analysis

What is the most important feature of how judges are selected in Texas? What does this feature reveal about Texas politics more broadly?

Is justice for sale in Texas? Because statewide judicial races have been increasingly expensive, candidates for judgeships have been forced to raise more money. This, in turn, has led to criticism that judicial decisions are, in effect, being bought.

Elected or Appointed Judges?

Federal judges are appointed for life by the president, with the advice and consent of the U.S. Senate. To be sure, federal judges can't just rest on their laurels and not do their jobs once they are appointed. The same impeachment process that can remove the president is also applicable to federal judges. Indeed, several federal judges have been impeached and removed from office, usually because of illegal activities. Many states follow the federal model so that the governor appoints state judges with the advice and consent of the state senate.

In Texas, however, state judges are not appointed by the governor with the advice and consent of the state senate. Members of the Texas Supreme Court and the Court of Criminal Appeals, as well as all lower state courts, are elected to their posts by the voters. What if a Texas judge is not doing his or her job properly or engages in illegal activity? In this case, a judge can be reprimanded by a state commission. A judge can also be removed by the governor, provided the legislature agrees with two-third majorities in both houses. A judge can be impeached in a process similar to the one at the federal level. Finally, the Texas Supreme Court can remove a lower court judge due to malfeasance or just cause.

Is there an alternative to appointing or electing judges? Many "good government" advocates support merit selection. Merit selection involves a commission which vets potential judges based on their character and temperament. A group of approved judicial nominees is then presented to the governor who appoints one as judge. After a period of time, that judge runs in a retention election. The judge does not face an opponent, but the ballot question asks voters whether the judge should be retained in office.

REBECA MARTINEZ

for **4th Court of Appeals**
EXPERIENCE · FAIRNESS · JUSTICE

Supporters of the Texas model argue that judges should be accountable to the electorate. If judges are insulated from the public, then they can render decisions without accountability. Elections hold judges accountable to the voters. This leads criminal court judges to run campaigns touting their tough sentencing practices and "zero tolerance" for criminals. Texas model supporters maintain that the alternative is undemocratic because elites would choose judges who would become entrenched in their positions and make rulings without any fear of public backlash.

Opponents argue that the Texas model inevitably leads to corruption because lawyers and other interests can make campaign contributions to judges, which might influence their rulings. Especially in civil cases, Texas judges could sell out to the highest bidder. According to critics of judicial elections, in criminal cases, the rights of the accused might not be taken as seri-

ously, as the public consistently favors tough rulings and sentences on criminals. Strong partisanship also prevents Texans from choosing the best-qualified judges, as voters tend to vote based on party affiliations rather than merit.

Some Texas state legislators have proposed changing the judicial selection system. However, doing so would generally require a constitutional amendment, which is not easy to implement. The larger debate revolves around whether it is possible to keep politics out of judicial selection. Gubernatorial appointments also involve political considerations. Some observers have suggested that Texas Supreme Court and appellate court judges should be appointed, while lower court judges should be elected. This hybrid system might be an effective compromise to ensure responsiveness at a certain level. As in most political debates, there are clear tradeoffs involved in deciding which approach is best.

critical thinking questions

1. **What do you think? Should judges be elected or appointed? Is merit selection an effective compromise?**

2. **Should the selection system vary according to type of judge?**

TABLE 9.1

Percentage of Judges Obtaining Their Position Initially through Appointment

YEAR	TRIAL COURTS* (%)	APPELLATE COURTS** (%)
1962	57	50
1984	67	51
1998	46	40
2001	34	38
2003	43	43
2006	43	50
2009	36	51
2011	37	52

*Trial courts are the district and criminal district courts.
**Appellate courts are the supreme court, the court of criminal appeals, and the courts of appeal.
SOURCES: Anthony Champagne, "The Selection and Retention of Judges in Texas," *Southwestern Law Journal* 40 (May 1986): 66; Texas Office of Court Administration, "Profile of Appellate and Trial Judges" as of September 1, 1998, 2001, 2003, 2006, and 2009 and March 1, 2011.

has generated little additional controversy.[13] Table 9.1 shows the percentage of district and appellate judges who have initially gained their seats through appointment by the governor. Currently, about 52 percent of appellate judges and 37 percent of the trial judges initially got on the bench through appointment.[14] Still, the controversial issue in Texas judicial politics deals with how the remaining judges obtained their seats and how all judges retain their seats if they wish to remain in office. That controversy involves the partisan election of judges in Texas.

The Elections Become Highly Partisan

Until 1978, the selection of judges in partisan elections did not create much concern. Texas was overwhelmingly a Democratic state, and judges were elected as Democrats. The only real competition occurred in the Democratic primary, and with the political advantage of incumbency, judges were rarely defeated even in the primary. Competition in judicial races occurred in those relatively rare cases where there was an open seat in which no incumbent sought office. Beginning in 1978, however, changes began to occur in Texas judicial politics. William Clements, the first Republican governor since Reconstruction, was elected. The governor has the power to appoint judges to the district and higher courts when new courts have been created or when a judicial vacancy occurs as a result of death, resignation, or retirement. Unlike the previous Democratic governors, who appointed members of the Democratic Party, Clements began appointing Republicans. With that advantage of incumbency and with the increasing popularity of the Republican party label, some of the Republican judges began to win re-election.

Helped by the popularity of Ronald Reagan in Texas, other Republicans began seeking judicial offices and winning. Thus, by the early 1980s, in statewide elections and in several counties in Texas, competition began to appear in judicial races. With that competition, incumbent judges began to be defeated. Sensing the growth of Republican strength, a number of Democratic judges changed to a Republican Party affiliation. From 1980 through July 24, 1985, 13 district and appellate judges changed from the Democratic to the Republican Party; 11 county court judges switched; and 5 justices of the peace changed parties. Judge Don Koons switched parties in early 1985 and explained his move to the Republican Party by saying: "I ran as a Democrat in 1982. It was a long, tough year, but we won. On the other hand, it cost a lot more money and time away from the bench to run as a Democrat. The work suffers some, and you've got to be always hustling money."[15] Koons apparently believed that with the emerging strength of the Republican Party, a switch in party affiliation would make his job more secure.

Judicial elections became more expensive because judicial candidates needed money to run meaningful campaigns. In particular, campaigns that used television advertising became very expensive because of high media costs.

Judicial candidates needed money because judicial races tend to have low-visibility campaigns in which voters are unaware of the candidates. The races tend to be overshadowed by higher-visibility races, such as the race for governor or U.S. senator. Money was needed to give judicial candidates some degree of name visibility by voters. However, in general, Texas voters do not give much money to judicial campaigns. Instead, it is lawyers, interest groups, and potential litigants who tend to be donors in judicial races.[16] That has raised concerns about the neutrality of Texas judges who are deciding cases that involve the financial interests of persons who have given them campaign funds. A Texas poll found that 83 percent of the public thought that judges were strongly or somewhat influenced by contributions in their decisions. Ninety-nine percent of lawyers believed that campaign contributions have at least some influence on judges. Perhaps even more striking, 86 percent of judges reported that they believed campaign contributions had at least some influence on judicial decisions.[17]

Contributions for judicial races in Texas can sometimes amount to several hundred thousand dollars, especially for hotly contested district court races or appellate races. In general, however, the most expensive races are for the Texas Supreme

In 2012, Democrat Keith Hampton ran against Sharon Keller for presiding judge of the Court of Criminal Appeals. Although he ran a fairly strong campaign, Hampton faced a major difficulty because Texas has more Republicans than Democrats, and voters tend to follow party labels in judicial races. Keller defeated Hampton 55.5 percent to 41.2 percent in the general election.

Court. When races are contested between Democratic and Republican candidates, a candidate can raise well over $1 million, though these hard-fought races are increasingly rare as statewide elections have moved into the Republican column. That is because these are statewide races and because this court sets the tone of tort law throughout the state, so a great deal of money is needed and a great deal can be raised. Table 9.2 shows the average contribution to Texas Supreme Court candidates for each election period from 1982 through 2010. The contribution data are reported for those races that were contested by both a Republican and a Democratic candidate. In the 2000 Supreme Court elections, the Republicans were so strong that no Democrat even bothered to run for any position on the Texas Supreme Court.

In spite of judicial campaigns, however, voters often know little about judicial candidates. As a result, they vote not for the best-qualified person to be a judge,

TABLE 9.2

Average Contributions to Texas Supreme Court Candidates*

YEAR	AVERAGE FOR ALL CANDIDATES	AVERAGE FOR WINNING CANDIDATES
1980	$155,033	$298,167
1982**	173,174	332,998
1984**	967,405	1,922,183
1986	519,309	1,024,817
1988	859,413	842,148
1990	970,154	1,544,939
1992	1,096,001	1,096,687
1994	1,499,577	1,627,285
1996	656,190	1,277,127
1998	521,519	829,794
2000	NA[†]	584,719[††]
2002[‡]	425,474	568,430
2004**	394,906	548,685
2006**	995,218	1,792,523
2008	654,819	910,973
2010	438,854	744,033

* Averages are reported for candidates from contested races featuring both a Republican and Democratic candidate.
** The 1982, 1984, 2004, and 2006 elections each featured only one contested race with both a Democratic and Republican candidate.
[†] No Democrats ran in the three Supreme Court elections in 2000.
[††] Average campaign contributions for the three victorious Republicans; none had a Democratic opponent.
[‡] Chief Justice Tom Phillips ran for re-election and refused to accept any campaign contributions beyond his cash on hand, which amounted to $19,433. His Democratic opponent, however, raised almost no funds—$12,815. Phillips was the victor in this race, which lowers the average contributions for this year.
SOURCES: Kyle Cheek and Anthony Champagne, Judicial Politics in Texas (New York: Peter Lang, 2005), p. 38; Institute on Money in State Politics.

but for the party label. As the Republican Party has become increasingly dominant in statewide races, it is the Republican label, rather than the qualifications or experience of judicial candidates, that has determined the outcome of judicial races. Related to the importance of party label in judicial races is the effect of top-of-the-ticket voting. In 1984 the popularity of Ronald Reagan seemed to help Texas judicial candidacies as many voters cast straight or almost straight Republican ballots. In that year, Reagan received nearly 64 percent of the presidential vote in Texas. All four Republican incumbent district judges who were challenged by Democrats won. Sixteen Democratic incumbent district judges were challenged by Republicans. Only three of those Democrats won. In contrast, in 1982, U.S. Senator Lloyd Bentsen ran for re-election. Bentsen was a very popular senator and a Democrat. His candidacy on the Democratic ballot seems to have encouraged voters to cast ballots for Democrats further down on the ticket. Bentsen received slightly more than 59 percent of the vote in Texas. In that year, 26 Republican incumbent district judges faced Democratic opposition; only 14 won. Yet 16 Democratic district judges faced opposition, and 14 won.[18]

Even voters who try to make a serious effort to learn about judicial candidates can have a hard time. In Houston, for example, voters are faced with ballots loaded with so many judicial candidates that it becomes nearly impossible to be an informed voter. In 1994 one of the most extreme examples of a long judicial ballot occurred in Harris County, where voters were faced with 45 judicial elections that were primary elections and then 8 runoff primary elections. In the general election, there were 59 contested judicial elections and 16 more elections where the judicial candidate was unopposed. In 2010, Harris County voters cast ballots in 10 contested appellate court races and 36 contested district court races.

The Name Game

In 1994, Cathy Herasimchuk ran for the Texas Court of Criminal Appeals. In a three-way Republican primary, she won only 26 percent of the statewide vote. The candidates in the Democratic and Republican primaries who did make the runoff for that seat all had simple, easy-to-spell and easy-to-pronounce names. Herasimchuk was appointed to the Court of Criminal Appeals in 2001, but in running for election to the court in 2002, she realized she had a problem with her name. As she said, "Everybody told me you couldn't win city dog catcher with the name Herasimchuk, and they all turned out to be accurate." Herasimchuk's problems getting elected certainly had nothing to do with her credentials. She has been a Harris County prosecutor, a criminal defense lawyer, an adviser to then-governor Bush, and a law school lecturer. When she successfully ran in 2002, she did so under her maiden name—Cathy Cochran.[19]

for critical analysis

How does the selection process influence who becomes a judge in Texas?

The name game continued in the 2008 elections for judges in Harris County. Most Republican judges in that county were swept out of office, but four Republicans survived. They had all been challenged by Democrats with unusual names. As a result, the incumbent Republican judge Sharon McCally was able to defeat the Democratic challenger Ashish Mahendru; Republican judge Mark Kent Ellis defeated Democrat Mekisha Murray; Judge Patricia Kerrigan, a Republican, defeated the Democrat Andres Pereira; and Judge Joseph Halback defeated his Democratic challenger, Goodwille Pierre.[20]

Some have claimed that a Latino name will hurt candidates in Republican primaries. In reference to judicial races, for example, Justice David Medina was defeated by John Devine in the 2012 Republican run-off primary for the Texas Supreme Court, and in 2002, Justice Xavier Rodriguez was defeated in the Republican primary for the Texas Supreme Court by Steve Smith. There have been other

How Do Texans Choose Their Judges?

Texans elect many, many judges. Most voters know little about the individual judicial candidates, and use the party affiliations of the candidates to fill in the gaps about who the candidate is and what type of judge he or she will be. As a result, voters often vote "straight party," punching one place on the ballot to vote for all the nominees of their party.

The results of the 2010 election show how closely the results of district judge elections track straight ticket voting. The graphs below compare the percentage of the vote won by the average district court judicial candidate to the percentage of gubernatorial votes won in Texas's five largest counties.

Vote Share of Gubernatorial Candidates and District Judges, 2010

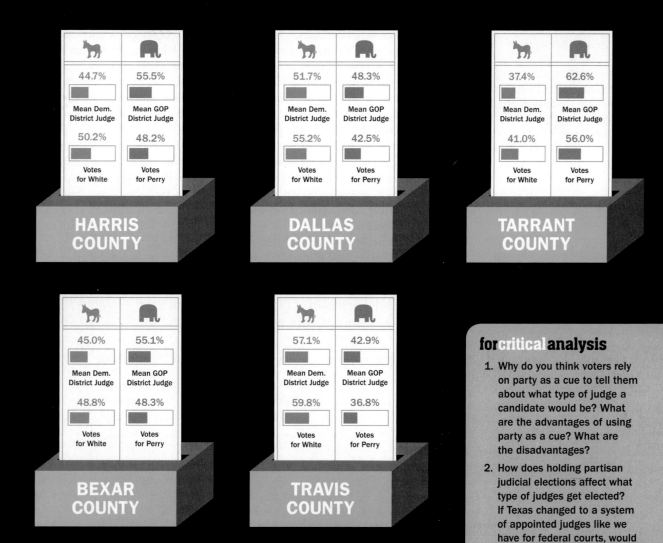

HARRIS COUNTY
44.7% Mean Dem. District Judge
55.5% Mean GOP District Judge
50.2% Votes for White
48.2% Votes for Perry

DALLAS COUNTY
51.7% Mean Dem. District Judge
48.3% Mean GOP District Judge
55.2% Votes for White
42.5% Votes for Perry

TARRANT COUNTY
37.4% Mean Dem. District Judge
62.6% Mean GOP District Judge
41.0% Votes for White
56.0% Votes for Perry

BEXAR COUNTY
45.0% Mean Dem. District Judge
55.1% Mean GOP District Judge
48.8% Votes for White
48.3% Votes for Perry

TRAVIS COUNTY
57.1% Mean Dem. District Judge
42.9% Mean GOP District Judge
59.8% Votes for White
36.8% Votes for Perry

for critical analysis

1. Why do you think voters rely on party as a cue to tell them about what type of judge a candidate would be? What are the advantages of using party as a cue? What are the disadvantages?

2. How does holding partisan judicial elections affect what type of judges get elected? If Texas changed to a system of appointed judges like we have for federal courts, would a different type of judge be selected? If so, why?

SOURCE: Data are from the appropriate County Clerk office.

Note: Percentages are all two-party vote share. "Mean GOP (or Dem.) District Judge" is the mean vote share for all Republican (or Democrat) district judge candidates in that county.

non-judicial Republican primary elections where persons with Latino names have been defeated by persons with Anglo names. However, the victory of Ted Cruz over David Dewhurst in the 2012 Republican run-off primary for U.S. senator from Texas suggests that the assertion that there is ethnic bias in Republican primary voting may be overblown.[21]

Minority Representation in the Texas Judiciary

Minority groups have been concerned that countywide and larger partisan judicial races make it difficult for minorities to get elected to judgeships—and that Texas judges do not reflect the diversity of the state. Table 9.3 lists the ethnicity of Texas judges as of March 1, 2011.

Although women do not make up 50 percent of the judiciary as they do of the population, there is a higher proportion of women in the Texas judiciary than of minorities. Women were at one time a great rarity on the bench. In 1970 only 1 percent of the nation's judiciary was female. As late as 1979 only 4 percent of the nation's judges were women.[22] In Texas, the first woman to serve as a state judge was Sarah Hughes, who was appointed in 1935 and who served as a district judge until 1961, when she was appointed to the federal bench. Famous for a number of her decisions, including one that forced Dallas County to build a new jail, she is probably best known as the judge who swore in Lyndon Johnson as president after the assassination of John F. Kennedy. In March 2011, however, 41 percent of appellate judges in Texas were women, and 28 percent of district judges were women. Thirty-five percent of county court-at-law judges were female, as were 33 percent of the probate judges. Sixteen percent of county judges, 35 percent of municipal judges, and 35 percent of justices of the peace were women.[23]

Different interpretations have been offered for the low numbers of minorities on the bench. The lack of racial and ethnic diversity on the bench is a nationwide problem. Ninety-two percent of the state judges in the nation are white.[24] Civil rights groups in several states with elective judiciaries, including Texas, have argued that white voters dominate countywide and larger districts and will vote against minority judicial candidates. Civil rights organizations representing Latinos and African Americans have argued that for minorities to get elected to office, there must be smaller judicial districts where minority voters make up the majority.

for critical analysis

Few minorities hold judicial office in Texas. Although African Americans and Hispanics make up 50 percent of the Texas population, relatively few Texas judges belong to these groups. Offer at least three suggestions, including alternative election methods, to increase the number of minorities holding judicial office in Texas.

TABLE 9.3

Race and Ethnicity of Texas Judges, 2011

RACE AND ETHNIC STATUS	APPEALS COURTS	DISTRICT COURTS	COUNTY COURTS AT LAW	PROBATE COURTS	COUNTY COURTS	MUNICIPAL COURTS	JP COURTS
% White	85%	77%	72%	78%	91%	78%	77%
% Black	3%	5%	4%	0%	1%	5%	3%
% Hispanic	11%	16%	23%	22%	8%	15%	20%
% Other	1%	2%	1%	0%	0%	3%	0%
Total number of responding judges	93	373	164	9	176	1,069	555

SOURCE: Texas Office of Court Administration, "Profile of Appellate and Trial Judges," March 1, 2011.

An alternative argument is that minority candidates in Texas, like minority voters, tend to be Democrats at a time when Republicans increasingly are winning judicial races. Thus, minorities do not get elected to judicial office because they run as Democrats.[25] Still another argument is that there are few minority judges because there are few minority lawyers and, with the exception of county judges and justices of the peace, judges in Texas must be lawyers.

The issue of minority representation on the bench has been the subject of major concern by minority and civil rights leaders in Texas. It was also the subject of prolonged federal litigation. In 1989 a case was tried in federal court in Midland. The case, *League of United Latin American Citizens v. Mattox*, was a suit against countywide election of judges in 10 of the larger counties in Texas.[26] The suit, filed by minority plaintiffs, argued that countywide election of judges diluted the strength of minority voters and violated the Voting Rights Act. The trial judge agreed with the plaintiffs and, after a political solution failed, ordered that judges be elected in nonpartisan elections from smaller judicial districts. The trial court order, however, was blocked by the Fifth Circuit, which is the federal court of appeals for the region that includes Texas.[27] The case was then appealed to the U.S. Supreme Court, along with a Louisiana case; the Supreme Court held that the Voting Rights Act did apply to judicial elections.[28] The case was then returned to the Fifth Circuit to examine whether minority voting strength was diluted and to determine the state's interest in maintaining countywide elections. Ordinarily, the federal courts of appeal do not preside as an entire group to hear cases; instead, they hear cases in panels of three judges. Such a panel decided in favor of the minority plaintiffs, and a settlement seemed to be reached with the state to have elections of judges from smaller districts in the larger counties. However, in important cases, it is sometimes possible to appeal a decision of a panel of three judges to the entire court of appeal. When this happens, the court is said to sit *en banc*. That happened when some of the defendants in the suit were unhappy with the settlement, and the entire Fifth Circuit ruled in 1993 that party affiliation of minority candidates explained the failure of minority judicial candidates to win election rather than the candidates' minority status. Thus, countywide election of judges was not illegal, and there was no legal need to reduce the size of districts from which judges were elected.[29]

Since that decision, minority leaders and minority groups have continued to express concerns about the small numbers of minority judges, but any solution that would involve smaller districts would have to result from an act of the legislature rather than the actions of a federal court. Judicial reform bills in the legislature since this decision have included provisions for smaller judicial districts, but those bills have not passed. Perhaps the strongest judicial reform bill was one backed by then-Democratic lieutenant governor, Bob Bullock, who created a task force to try to develop an acceptable compromise on the judicial selection issue. The proposed constitutional amendment designed by the task force passed the Texas Senate in 1995 but failed to pass the Texas House. Under the plan, all appellate judges would be appointed by the governor. District judges, on the other hand, would be chosen from county commissioner precincts in nonpartisan elections. After serving for a time, they would run countywide in **retention elections**, in which there would be a "yes" or "no" vote on their retention in office and where they would face no opponent on the ballot.

On the surface, the compromise seemed to offer something for almost everyone. Because the governor appointed appellate judges, judges would have greater career security and no worries about campaign funding. The business community,

en banc referring to an appellate hearing with all judges participating

retention election an election in which voters decide whether to keep an incumbent in office by voting "yes" or "no" to retain the incumbent and where there is no opposing candidate

recognizing that Texas tended to elect conservative governors and was increasingly likely to elect conservative Republican governors, got appointed appellate judges. Nonpartisan elections would protect trial judges from party sweeps in which judges are voted out of office solely because of their party affiliation. Minorities would get smaller judicial districts for the major trial courts. But what looked like a great compromise fell through. Although African Americans supported the compromise, Latinos did not. The two largest counties in Texas—Harris and Dallas—elected a total of 96 of the 386 district judges then chosen in Texas. Under the compromise, one-fourth of Harris and Dallas county judges would be elected from each of the county commissioners' precincts in that county. Both Dallas and Harris counties had three white county commissioners and one African American. Latinos, on the other hand, elected no county commissioner and believed that the compromise would not promote the election of more Latino judges. They believed that to elect Latino judges, considerably smaller districts were needed. As a result, much Latino support was not forthcoming. Further, the political parties opposed the compromise. Nonpartisan elections might protect the interests of judges, but they weakened the political parties. Additionally, an appointive system for appellate judges reduced the number of elective offices, thereby reducing the role of the political parties. Although his powers would have increased with an appointed appellate judiciary, Governor George W. Bush opposed the compromise, probably because he did not want to oppose the Republican Party. Because the plan had the support of Lieutenant Governor Bob Bullock and because he gave the legislation priority on his legislative agenda that year, it passed the Texas Senate. However, the proposal died in the Texas House. The Bullock proposal was probably the best hope for judicial change for a long time to come.[30]

One of the business community's underlying concerns about smaller districts seemed to be a fear that small districts might create a narrower electorate for judges. That narrow electorate might in some areas prove unduly sympathetic to plaintiffs who file suit against businesses. Whatever the cause of the low number of minority judges, the lack of diversity on the bench, the role of money in judicial races, the defeat of incumbents, the importance of party label, top-of-the-ticket voting, and the "name game" have all created support for alternative judicial selection systems.

Alternative Means of Selection

Judges are selected in the United States by a variety of ways. One way is through appointment by the governor and approval by the state Senate. This method is used in Texas to select judges to new courts or courts where there has been a death, resignation, or retirement during a judicial term. It is also similar to the system for selecting federal judges, who are appointed by the president and confirmed by vote of the U.S. Senate. However, this method of judicial selection is contrary to Texas's traditional distrust of a powerful chief executive. At a time when Texas governors are Republicans, it also is not a system that Democrats tend to favor.

Another system for selecting judges is nonpartisan election. Such a system for selecting judges in Texas would eliminate much of the partisan politics, but, at the same time, it would make it more difficult for candidates to reach voters. This is because in a truly nonpartisan election, judicial candidates would have to run for office without the benefit of political parties. In some states that have ostensibly nonpartisan elections, such as Ohio, the parties continue to take an active role to the point that it is difficult to distinguish that type of nonpartisan system from a partisan election system. If Texas instituted a truly nonpartisan system, however, candidates would require even more campaign money to reach voters they could no longer reach through the mechanisms of the political parties.

Most commonly, however, judicial reformers argue for a system of judicial selection that is commonly called **merit selection** of judges. In this system, a blue-ribbon committee consisting of lawyers and lay people supplies to the governor the names of a small number of candidates for a judgeship. The governor makes the judicial appointment from this list, and after the judge serves for a brief time, he or she runs in a retention election. In a retention election, the incumbent does not have an opponent. Instead voters are asked whether the incumbent should be retained for another term of office. The voters then vote "yes" or "no" on the judge's retention. As might be expected in an election where one does not have an opponent, the incumbent usually wins. One study of retention elections found that only 1.6 percent of incumbent judges were defeated in retention elections.[31] Yet from time to time, interest groups will organize against a judge in a retention election and spend a great deal of money trying to defeat him or her; sometimes those efforts have been successful. One of the great concerns about merit selection is the nature of the merit selection commission, because those commissioners filter out all but a handful of prospective judges. Some are quite fearful of this centralized method of determining who should be judges, and although there is much support for merit selection in Texas, there is also much opposition.[32]

In recent years, one of the most popular reform proposals has been a system known as "appoint-elect-retain." Under this system, the governor would appoint a judge with confirmation by two-thirds of the state Senate. The governor-appointed nominee would not assume office until confirmed by the Senate, which would meet year-round for the purpose of dealing with judicial confirmations. In the first election thereafter, the judge would run in a contested nonpartisan election and subsequently in retention elections. This is, of course, a hybrid plan that encompasses aspects of gubernatorial appointment, nonpartisan election, and merit selection.

Another reform plan would have appellate vacancies filled by gubernatorial appointment with senatorial confirmation. The appellate judges would then run in nonpartisan elections followed by retention elections. In Dallas, Tarrant, and Bexar counties, district court judges would be elected from county commissioner precincts rather than from one district encompassing the entire county. Additionally, in Harris County, district judges would be elected from smaller geographic regions than county commissioner precincts. Supporters of this plan tend to believe that it would increase the number of minority judges, especially trial court judges in urban areas. Of course, this is also a hybrid plan designed to combine various reform proposals in order to gain sufficient support to become the new way Texas selects its judges.

At least for the time being, however, it seems likely that not much will change in the way Texas selects its judges. Restructuring the system would be a major change, and these are always difficult to initiate. Changing might upset many voters, who like being able to vote for judges, and it would surely upset the political parties, which like having large numbers of judicial candidates running under their party label. It might also upset lawyers accustomed to the traditional ways of selecting judges and even judges who have benefited from the present system. That has led some to argue that judicial reform needs to be less drastic and more incremental. These reformers have suggested lengthening judicial terms of office on the grounds that longer terms mean fewer election contests and therefore less need for campaign money, less of a chance for defeat of incumbents, and less involvement of

In 2009, Rick Perry appointed Eva Guzman—the first Latina woman to serve on the Texas Supreme Court—to fill a vacancy on the court. Guzman was elected to a full term in the 2010 election.

merit selection a judicial reform under which judges would be nominated by a blue-ribbon committee, appointed by the governor, and, after a brief period in office, would run in a retention election

judges in politics. Another proposed incremental reform is to remove judges from the straight party vote. This means that a voter would actually have to cast a ballot for the judicial candidate rather than simply voting for everyone on the Republican or Democratic column by casting a straight party vote. Such a reform would remove judicial candidates from the effects of top-of-the-ticket voting. It would, of course, also reduce the votes that judges receive and lessen their dependence and reliance on the political parties. Still another suggested reform is to increase the levels of experience needed to serve on the bench. The idea is that even if judicial races are subject to the whims of voters, high qualifications for judges would mean that there would be experienced judges on the bench rather than highly inexperienced judges who won simply because they were good campaigners or because they had the right party affiliation in that election year.

Judicial Campaign Fairness Act a judicial reform under which campaign contributions are limited by the amount that a judicial candidate can receive from donors

Perhaps the most significant judicial reform in Texas is the **Judicial Campaign Fairness Act**. Texas is the only state with a campaign finance regulation of this type. Among the most important aspects of compliance with the act are campaign contribution limitations. For example, statewide judicial candidates limit themselves to contributions of no more than $5,000 from any individual in any election. Additionally, statewide candidates can receive no more than $30,000 per election from any law firm. Although the amounts of money that can be donated are still quite high, there has been a significant reduction from contribution amounts in the 1980s when, prior to the act, some donors would give candidates $25,000, $50,000, and even more in campaign contributions. A recent strengthening of campaign contribution limits requires that if a judge receives campaign contributions from a party to a lawsuit, or if the party's lawyer had made contributions in excess of the limits in the Judicial Campaign Fairness Act, the judge would recuse him- or herself from the case.[33]

For many, the role of money in judicial campaigns is the most troubling issue in Texas judicial politics. As long as judges are elected, however, money will be necessary to run judicial campaigns, and where elections are competitive, a great deal of campaign money will be necessary.

● Issues in the Texas Court System

> **Assess the impact of recent changes related to tort reform, litigation, and disciplining judges**

One of the most important issues in Texas has been tort reform, which is the effort to change the system for awarding damages in lawsuits where harm is claimed. Tort reform has had important effects on the Texas judiciary.

Civil Cases and Tort Reform

Figure 9.2 shows the numbers of civil cases disposed of by the courts of appeal and the trial courts in 1990, 1998, 2000, 2003, 2006, and 2010. The Texas court system is overloaded and would not be able to function adequately without the aid of visiting judges, retired or defeated judges who continue hearing cases in order to assist with the growing caseloads.

The Texas Supreme Court sets the tone for civil cases throughout the state. Most important of those types of cases, because of the large amounts of money involved,

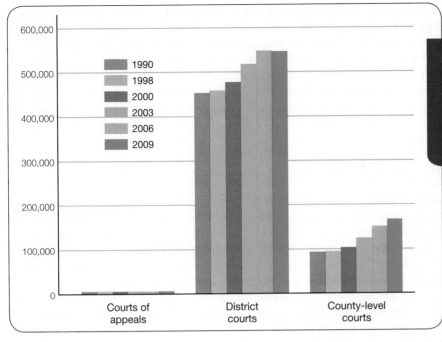

FIGURE 9.2

Civil Cases
Disposed Of by
Texas Courts

SOURCE: Texas Office of Court Administration.

is tort law. Tort law refers to civil cases in which one person has been harmed by the actions of another. For example, medical malpractice cases are a common type of tort case. In the early to mid-1980s, the court tended to be sympathetic to the plaintiffs' positions in tort cases. That is, the court tended to support the side in a case that was suing businesses, professionals, and insurance companies. However, in 1988, more justices began to be elected who favored the defendants in civil lawsuits. One reason for this change was that in 1988, Republican justices began to be elected, and they were more conservative than many of the previous justices, who were Democrats. Another explanation is that interest groups that were harmed by the pro-plaintiff tendencies of the court began to organize, raise and spend money, and elect justices more sympathetic to their perspective.

In the 1980s, plaintiffs' lawyers—lawyers who sue businesses, professionals, and insurance companies—worked to elect pro-plaintiff justices. The tide turned, and business, professional, and insurance interests were now electing pro-defense justices. In 1996–97 civil defendants won three-fourths of the time, and insurance companies won almost all their substantive cases. Physicians, hospitals, and pharmaceutical companies won all seven of their cases before the Texas Supreme Court. In 1997–98 civil defendants won 69 percent of the time.[34] However, by 1998–99, the court was not as strongly pro-defendant, perhaps because of several new justices on the court who were regarded as somewhat moderate in their judicial philosophy. In insurance cases, defendants won only 40 percent of the time; plaintiffs won 40 percent of the time; and the decision of the court was a split decision 20 percent of the time. Defendants in medical cases (typically hospitals or doctors), however, still won 100 percent of the time.[35] Most recently, the court seems to have shifted strongly in favor of civil defendants. A study of the decisions of the Texas Supreme Court in tort cases found that defendants won 87 percent of the time.[36] Still another study of the Texas courts of appeal also found a strongly pro-defendant pattern in civil matters. When plaintiffs in tort cases won at the trial court level and the defendants appealed, the appellate course reversed the decision 49 percent of the time. When defendants in civil cases prevailed and the plaintiffs appealed, the trial court decision was reversed only 25 percent of the time. The authors of this study add, "Tort reform measures enacted by the legislature, as well as Texas Supreme Court decisions favoring tort defendants, have discouraged some . . . plaintiffs from filing suit at all."[37] It is this power of the Texas Supreme Court to set the tone in civil cases that makes that court a political battleground, since millions—even billions—of dollars can be at stake as a result of the court's decisions.

The Role of Lawyers

Lawyers occupy a crucial role in the legal process. In order to practice law, one must be a licensed lawyer and in order to be licensed in Texas, it is generally necessary to complete a Juris Doctor (JD) degree at a law school accredited by the American Bar Association. Usually this degree takes three years beyond the bachelor's degree if the law student attends full-time. After completing law school, it is necessary for a prospective lawyer to take the state bar exam.

After passing the Texas state bar, one may be sworn as a lawyer in Texas. Texas has an integrated bar, which means that all licensed lawyers in the state must join and pay dues to the State Bar of Texas. That agency offers a variety of services to lawyers such as insurance plans, a journal, and professional meetings. Since lawyers must undergo continuing education, the State Bar authorizes continuing education credit for a number of educational programs. That body is unusual in that it is not only a professional organization of lawyers, but also an agency of government that is charged with enforcing ethical standards for the profession. Lawyers can be disciplined for a variety of infractions ranging from discipline for serious criminal behavior, to failing to keep a client informed of the status of a legal matter, to promptly paying out funds from a legal settlement. The State Bar may also enforce rules against illegal efforts to generate litigation. In 2012, for example, a Houston lawyer was disciplined for permitting a non-lawyer to make a number of telephone calls from the lawyer's office to patient rooms at a large Houston hospital for the purpose of soliciting legal business for the lawyer.[38]

Illegal generation of litigation is commonly known as barratry, and the state legislature has become so concerned about lawyers inappropriately generating legal business that in 2011 it passed new legislation that allows for a penalty of up to $10,000 and the recovery of attorney's fees. The goal of the new legislation was to prevent what is commonly known as "ambulance chasing," something that appears to continue to be a problem in spite of long-standing State Bar rules against it. Some of the horror stories of barratry include people being solicited to sign contracts with lawyers for lawsuits at home, in hospitals, and even during funerals. At times the relatives of accident victims have been offered large payments to sign a contract with a particular lawyer to file a lawsuit.[39]

It is too early to assess the value of the new law in discouraging barratry, though three months after the law was passed, the first barratry lawsuit was filed against two south Texas lawyers who were accused of firing their office manager when she refused to sign a contract with them where the office manager would receive a bonus payment for illegally soliciting and referring cases to the lawyers.[40] In 2012 state representative Ronald Reynolds was arrested for the crime of barratry. Reynolds, who was a supporter of the new barratry law in 2011, was charged with illegally soliciting clients on his own and through the office of a chiropractor. The alleged scheme to solicit clients was discovered when a "runner"—a person used by an attorney to solicit clients for the attorney—approached an attorney who was involved in a car accident. The "runner" tried to get the attorney in the accident to hire Representative Reynolds to represent her, but the accident victim instead reported that solicitation to authorities.[41]

In 2010 there were slightly more than 77,000 active lawyers in Texas and more than 1.2 million active lawyers in the United States. In Texas, 30.56 active lawyers exist for every 10,000 people and in the United States as a whole, 38.42 active lawyers exist for every 10,000 people.[42] With the decline in the number of legal jobs during the Great Recession, both in Texas and nationally, there is much discussion about whether there are too many lawyers, although it seems likely that the demand for lawyers will increase with an improvement in the economy. Of course, lawyers trained in out-of-state law schools may take the bar exam and be licensed in Texas, but the state has a substantial number of law schools: the University of Texas, Texas Tech, Texas Southern, St. Mary's, South Texas, SMU, Baylor, and Texas Wesleyan. There are plans for still another law school in Dallas, the University of North Texas School of Law, which may open in 2014. In spite of the weakened job market for lawyers, Texas has law schools aplenty and there remains high demand among students for a legal education.

The legal process in Texas relies on lawyers. Constitutional county court judges are not required to be lawyers, and justices of the peace do not have to be lawyers, but all other judges must be "learned in the law," a term found in the Texas Constitution whose meaning has come to require a law degree. Even justice of the peace courts, which in theory are informal courts where people can easily resolve their minor criminal and civil issues, often have rules of operation that would be confusing to non-lawyers—the Texas Rules of Civil Procedure and Evidence, for example, apply to civil cases in justice of the peace courts, although not when justices of the peace sit as judges in small claims courts, a distinction which itself is confusing to nonlawyers—and much of the litigation in justice of the peace courts involves lawyers who, for example, are representing businesses trying to collect debts or apartment complexes trying to evict a tenant. Of course, in civil and criminal litigation, it is possible for a layperson to pursue a case without a lawyer, but it is generally recognized that non-lawyers are at a significant disadvantage if they are without legal help in either a civil or a criminal proceeding.

Discipline of Judges

The State Commission on Judicial Conduct was created by a constitutional amendment in 1965. It is charged with investigating allegations of judicial misconduct and disability and is charged with discipline of judges. There are 13 members on the commission and they serve six-year terms. Members of the commission are unpaid. The commission also has a staff of 14. In 2011 the commission spent nearly $997,000, mostly on staff salaries. The commission is an unusual hybrid agency in that two attorney members are appointed by the state bar, the six judicial members are appointed by the Supreme Court of Texas with one of the judicial members being an appellate judge, one a county court at law judge, one a constitutional county judge, one a district judge, one a justice of the peace, and one a municipal judge. There are five citizen members who can neither be lawyers nor be judges who are appointed by the governor. The state Senate confirms the commission members.

In dealing with disciplinary issues involving Texas judges, the commission relies on complaints from the public, from attorneys, and from members of the judiciary.

In 2011 there were 1,119 complaints filed with the commission, but 607 were immediately dismissed for failure of the complaint to allege misconduct. A common complaint is that the person disagrees with the judge's decision, but, of course, this is not a violation of the Code of Judicial Conduct, which is the ethical code promulgated by the Supreme Court of Texas that is enforced by the commission along with certain legislative requirements on judges. Indeed, one of the problems of the commission is that it is responsible for forcing requirements that the Supreme Court of Texas places on judges and laws passed by the legislature that affect judges. Potentially, there could be a conflict between the Texas Supreme Court rules and the legislatively imposed requirements, in which case it would be unclear what the commission should do. Still another problem with the commission is that because it deals with ethical issues of judges, its decision making is done behind closed doors and thus the commission lacks openness and transparency in decision making. Still, other than impeachment by the legislature or criminal prosecution of judges, both rare and extreme measures, the commission is the only mechanism for regulating ethical and legal conduct of Texas judges.

In 2011 the commission imposed 34 sanctions on judges and three suspensions of judges. In addition, the commission accepted five resignations of judges who chose to resign rather than to be sanctioned. The commission can recommend public censure or removal of a judge or the judge's involuntary retirement to a seven-judge review tribunal that is composed of the chief justice of Texas and six appellate judges. The review tribunal's decision can be appealed by the affected judge to the Supreme Court of Texas. No such case occurred in 2011. Other decisions of the commission can be appealed by the affected judge to a court of review consisting of three appellate judges. No such case occurred in 2011.

Most of the disciplinary actions of the commission involve private sanctions of the judge. In 2011, 27 of the 34 sanctions were of a private nature and consisted of the commission providing a private admonition, warning, or reprimand to the judge (admonitions are less severe sanctions than are warnings, which are less severe than are reprimands). In one case, a judge was ordered to obtain additional training and in 12 cases, judges were privately sanctioned and ordered to obtain additional training. In only seven cases were sanctions made public. Three were public admonitions, two were warnings, one was a reprimand, and one was a public sanction with an order for continuing education of the judge. Public reprimands do have especially serious consequences for judges, as often when judges retire, they become visiting judges where they are paid to hear cases when sitting judges are on vacation or where dockets are overloaded and they also continue to be paid retirement income. Judges who receive a public reprimand are not allowed to serve as visiting judges.[43]

● Thinking Critically about the Judiciary in Texas

Texas elects its judges in partisan judicial elections. For many years, when the Democratic Party was dominant, Texas judicial elections were staid, low-budget, noncompetitive events. However, with the growth of the Republican Party, judicial elections became highly political, and large amounts of money have been raised for judicial candidates, especially in Texas Supreme Court races. Often these judicial races pitted business interests against candidates backed by the plaintiffs' bar because the Texas Supreme Court sets the tone of tort law in the state. These elections have calmed down in recent years as the Democratic Party has weakened and, at least in statewide races, judicial elections have become less competitive.

There have been problems in Texas judicial races, in large part because voters often don't know much about judicial candidates. As a result, voters often decide on the basis of the candidate's party affiliation or the candidate's name appeal. The result has been the election of several judicial candidates who lacked significant qualifications for the job.

Numerous efforts have been proposed to change the way judges are selected in Texas. There have been efforts to change the system of selection to "merit selection" and to nonpartisan election. Minority groups have pushed to reduce the size of judicial districts in order to increase the election of minority judges. However, no change so far has been successful. No majority coalition can agree on appropriate changes in the judicial selection system, and significant opposition to change comes from groups such as the political parties and business interests. Additionally, Texans seem satisfied with the current system of selection and seem to prefer to elect their judges. Recent injustices in the Texas criminal system do raise questions about how the system can be improved. One might speculate that a criminal justice system in which both judges and prosecutors are elected creates political pressures to gain convictions at all costs.

Texas courts handle large caseloads of both civil and criminal cases. The highest civil court in the state is the Texas Supreme Court, currently an all-Republican court elected with strong support from business interests. The court has been severely criticized for being too sympathetic to those interests. The highest criminal court in the state is the Texas Court of Criminal Appeals. That court is also an all-Republican court, which was elected with strong support from prosecutors and victims' rights groups. Perhaps its most important function is as the appellate court for the death penalty in the state.

Because the Texas court system affects the liberty and especially the pocketbooks of Texans, it will continue to be an area of concern and controversy. And the most controversial area of Texas justice will continue to be the process by which judges are selected.

study guide

Court Structure

■ **Describe how the Texas court system is organized (pp. 249–53)**

The appellate court system in Texas is divided into civil and criminal tracks with the Texas Supreme Court being the highest state level court for civil cases and the Texas Criminal Court of Appeals being the highest for criminal cases. Texas has an intermediate appellate court system and trial courts that range from district courts for the most important criminal and civil cases, to county courts for less important criminal and civil cases, to justice of the peace and municipal courts for settling the lowest level of conflicts.

Key Terms

Texas Supreme Court (p. 249)

Texas Court of Criminal Appeals (p. 251)

courts of appeals (p. 251)

district courts (p. 251)

county judge (p. 252)

county courts (p. 252)

statutory county courts at law (p. 252)

statutory probate courts (p. 252)

justice of the peace courts (p. 252)

municipal courts (p. 253)

ordinance (p. 253)

Practice Quiz

1. The highest criminal court in the state of Texas is the *(p. 251)*
   a) Texas Supreme Court.
   b) Texas Court of Appeals.
   c) Texas Court of Criminal Appeals.
   d) county court.
   e) district court.

2. The major trial courts in Texas are the *(p.251)*
   a) courts of appeals.
   b) justice of the peace courts.
   c) district courts.
   d) municipal courts.
   e) county courts.

3. Which of the following judges do not have to be lawyers? *(p. 253)*
   a) Texas Supreme Court justices
   b) district judges
   c) justices of the peace
   d) Texas Criminal Court of Appeals justices
   e) probate judges

> (S) **Practice Online**
> Interactive simulation: *Monday Morning in Travis County*

The Legal Process

■ **Explain the legal process and the differences between criminal and civil law (pp. 254–56)**

Civil and criminal law is dramatically different with the burden of proof relying on different standards. Plaintiffs are the initiators of legal actions in civil cases. Defendants in civil cases respond to accusations made against them. Civil cases may lead to trial or dismissal by a judge. They may also be resolved by a settlement between the parties. The state is a prosecutor in a criminal case, and the accused individual is the defendant. Criminal cases can result in a trial, a dismissal, or a plea bargain.

Key Terms

civil law (p. 254)

criminal law (p. 254)

complaint (p. 254)

answer (p. 254)

contingent fee (p. 254)

preponderance of the evidence (p. 254)

capital case (p. 255)

felony (p. 255)

misdemeanor (p. 255)

grand jury (p. 255)

indictment (p. 255)

bench trial (p. 255)

plea bargain (p. 256)

beyond a reasonable doubt (p. 256)

Practice Quiz

4. Grand juries *(p. 255)*
   a) determine the guilt of defendants.
   b) decide whether a trial of an accused is warranted.
   c) agree to plea bargains.
   d) recommend that defendants undergo bench trials.
   e) hear appeals of convictions.

5. On conviction, the criminal's punishment is determined *(p. 256)*
   a) by the Grand Jury.
   b) in a separate hearing by the jury or judge that determined the person's guilt.
   c) by the prosecuting attorney.
   d) by the prosecuting and defense attorneys.
   e) by the Texas Court of Criminal Appeals

Practice Online
"Exploring Texas Politics" exercise: *The Texas Judiciary*

Judicial Politics

■ **Evaluate the process for selecting judges in Texas (pp. 256–68)**

Unlike federal judges, Texas judges are elected in partisan elections. Partisan elections make judges accountable to voters, but critics claim that unqualified judges are elected solely because of their party labels. These critics advocate alternatives for choosing judges such as merit selection. Minorities are not proportionately represented, possibly in part because most judges are elected from large Anglo-dominated districts.

Key Terms

en banc (p. 265)

retention election (p. 265)

merit selection (p. 267)

Judicial Campaign Fairness Act (p. 268)

Practice Quiz

6. In civil cases, defense lawyers often align themselves with *(p. 256)*
   a) business and industry.
   b) the grand jury.
   c) groups that support workers.
   d) judges supported by the Democratic Party.
   e) labor groups.

7. Texas's movement from being a Democratic to a Republican state led to *(pp. 259–60)*
   a) defeats of large numbers of incumbent judges.
   b) party switching by incumbent judges.
   c) large campaign contributions to judges.
   d) election of more Republican judges.
   e) all of the above.

8. In Texas, which event marked the rise of the Republican Party and partisan judicial elections? *(p. 259)*
   a) the election of President Ronald Reagan
   b) the impeachment of William Jefferson Clinton
   c) the appointment of Tom Phillips as Chief Justice of the United States
   d) the election of Bill Clements as governor of Texas
   e) the Shivercrat movement

9. Which of the following groups has the largest number of judges? *(p. 264)*
   a) African Americans
   b) American Indians
   c) Asian Americans
   d) Hispanics
   e) women

10. Elections lost due to party membership rather than race or ethnicity do not violate *(p. 265)*
    a) the Fifth Amendment to the U.S. Constitution.
    b) Fair Elections Act.
    c) Article I of the Texas Constitution.
    d) *Clements v. Maddox.*
    e) the Voting Rights Act.

Practice Online
Video exercise: *Judicial Campaigns*

Issues in the Texas Court System

 Assess the impact of recent changes related to tort reform, litigation, and disciplining judges (pp. 268–72)

Texas courts make decisions affecting Texans on a variety of issues, including the ultimate penalty of death and tort cases such as medical malpractice.

Practice Quiz

11. How likely is Texas to change its method of selecting judicial candidates? *(p. 267)*
    a) Texas is scheduled to change to the Missouri Plan in January 2015.
    b) extremely likely in the next two decades
    c) likely in the next decade
    d) likely in 2013
    e) unlikely

12. Which of the following sets campaign contribution limits for judicial candidates in Texas? *(p. 268)*
    a) Judicial Campaign Fairness Act
    b) Judicial Campaign Law
    c) Equal Justice Act
    d) Code of Judicial Conduct
    e) Federal Rules of Civil Procedure

13. Philosophically, in the past few years, Texas courts became *(p. 269)*
    a) more pro-defendant in civil cases.
    b) more liberal.
    c) more pro-defendant in criminal cases.
    d) more conservative.
    e) hostile to tort reform.

14. All lawyers who regularly practice in Texas *(p. 270)*
    a) must be members of the State bar of Texas.
    b) must have graduated from a Texas law school.
    c) must appear in court at least twice a year.
    d) must volunteer to sit on grand juries.
    e) do not need any additional training once they have a law license.

15. The State Commission on Judicial Conduct *(p. 271)*
    a) screens judicial candidates to determine if they are qualified to be judges.
    b) offers continuing education courses for judges.
    c) investigates complaints of ethical violations by judges.
    d) recommends trial judges for promotion to appellate courts.
    e) makes rules governing the conduct of judges.

Recommended Websites

The Supreme Court of Texas
www.supreme.courts.state.tx.us/

Texans for Public Justice
www.tpj.org

Texas Court of Criminal Appeals
www.cca.courts.state.tx.us/

Texas Courts Online: Texas Court Structure
www.courts.state.tx.us/

In 2011, Michael Morton was released from prison based on new DNA testing in his case. He served over 20 years in prison before another man was arrested for the crime. DNA evidence has revealed a series of wrongful convictions, raising questions about criminal justice in Texas.

Crime and Corrections Policy

WHAT GOVERNMENT DOES AND WHY IT MATTERS On August 13, 1986, Christine Morton was beaten to death at her home in Austin. Her husband, Michael Morton, was charged with the murder and was prosecuted by Williamson County district attorney Ken Anderson. Michael received a life sentence for the murder, though he persisted in claiming his innocence and argued that some unknown intruder must have killed his wife after he had gone to work. The day after the murder, Christine's brother had found a bloodstained blue bandana near the crime scene and he had turned it over to detectives. In 2005, Michael asked for DNA testing on several items including the blue bandana.

District Attorney Ken Anderson had by this time been appointed to a state district judgeship by Governor Rick Perry, who then appointed John Bradley, an assistant district attorney under Anderson, as the new district attorney. Bradley was known as a tough prosecutor, and he opposed the requests for DNA testing, claiming there was no way the testing would lead to some "mystery killer." Michael Morton's lawyers were, argued District Attorney Bradley, "grasping at straws." Morton's lawyers suspected that key evidence had been withheld in the case and so they sought investigative materials in Morton's case. Bradley opposed those requests as well. In 2008, Bradley was forced to turn over the investigative materials and Morton's defense lawyers discovered that Eric Morton, who was three years old at the time of his mother's murder, had seen the murder and described the killer as a "monster" who had red gloves and a big mustache. He also had said that the killer was not his father.

Defense lawyers discovered other information as well from the newly released files of the case. Police reports noted that there was a check to Christine that was cashed with a forged signature after her death, and there were also reports of fraudulent use of her credit card after her death. There were also neighbors' statements to police that a man was seen parked in a green van near the Morton home on several occasions before the murder. Contrary to a legal requirement that prosecutors share exculpatory materials, this information had not been provided to the defense lawyers.

Then, in 2010, DNA testing on the blue bandana was allowed. DNA was found on the bandana to belong to the victim, Christine, and to a man whose DNA was in a national database as a result of an arrest in California. That man was Mark Alan Norwood. On October 4, 2011, Michael Morton was released from prison—he had been convicted in 1987. Mark Alan Norwood was arrested on November 9, 2011, for the murder of Christine Morton. He is also a suspect in another murder of a woman in 1988.

District Attorney Bradley now says that when defense lawyers bring him a case to review, his perspective will be different. He was defeated for re-election in 2012. Judge Ken Anderson is currently facing a court of inquiry that is examining his conduct in withholding evidence during Michael Morton's trial. And Morton is free and will receive financial restitution from the state for the quarter century that he spent in prison for a murder he did not commit. This case highlights several aspects of the criminal justice system in Texas and raises questions about how it works. In this chapter we will look both at the basics of the criminal justice system and at recent issues related to criminal justice in Texas.[1]

chaptergoals

- Identify the major classifications of crime under Texas law and the types of punishments that may be imposed (pages 281–83)

- Outline the procedural steps that occur after a person is arrested (pages 283–88)

- Describe prisons and corrections policy in Texas (pages 289–99)

- Explain why Texas's criminal justice system is often controversial (pages 299–304)

- Consider recent proposals to improve Texas's criminal justice system (pages 304–5)

Categorizing Crime in Texas

Identify the major classifications of crime under Texas law and the types of punishments that may be imposed

Crimes, of course, have different levels of seriousness, and punishments vary according to the legislature's classification of the seriousness of the crime. As is shown in Table 10.1, in the Texas criminal justice system, crimes are classified as felonies or misdemeanors.

Felonies

A **felony** is a serious criminal offense that subjects a person to state prison punishment. Fines can be up to $10,000, and prison punishment can range from six months to the death penalty. The right to vote, to have a gun, or to have certain occupational licenses can also be taken away, although in Texas voting rights for felons are restored after the sentence has been fully discharged. The most serious felony is capital murder, for which the penalty can be death or life imprisonment without parole. The next most serious felony is a first degree felony, for which the punishment can be 5 to 99 years in a state prison and a possible fine of up to $10,000. First degree felonies include such crimes as aggravated assault on a public servant, aggravated kidnapping, aggravated sexual assault, and arson of a habitation. A crime defined as "aggravated" involves the use of some sort of weapon. A second degree felony is punished with a sentence of 2 to 20 years in state prison and a possible fine of up to $10,000. Second degree felonies include such crimes as arson, bigamy, bribery, robbery, sexual assault, manslaughter, and possession of

felony a serious criminal offense, punishable by a prison sentence or a fine. A capital felony is punishable by death.

TABLE 10.1

Classification of Crimes

FELONY CRIMES	PENALTIES*
Capital murder	Death or life without parole
First degree	5 to 99 years in state prison; fine up to $10,000
Second degree	2 to 20 years in state prison; fine up to $10,000
Third degree	2 to 10 years in state prison; fine up to $10,000
State jail	180 days to 2 years in a state jail; fine up to $10,000

MISDEMEANOR CRIMES	PENALTIES*
Class A	No more than 1 year in county jail; fine up to $4,000
Class B	No more than 180 days in county jail; fine up to $2,000
Class C	Fine up to $500

*In many cases, probation is a possible substitute for serving jail or prison time. If jail or prison time is imposed, it is possible to obtain parole or early release.

SOURCES: "Texas Criminal Laws & Penalties," Texas Criminal Defense Lawyer, www.mytexasdefenselawyer.com; Fred Dahr, "Crimes and Punishment in Texas State Court," www.texasdefenselaw.com.

While possession of a small amount of marijuana is a misdemeanor, possession of larger amounts and selling drugs are felonies. Here, a Fort Worth police captain holds a press conference on an investigation into a drug-dealing ring.

misdemeanor a minor criminal offense usually punishable by a small fine or short jail sentence

probation punishment where an offender is not imprisoned but remains in the community under specified rules and under the supervision of a probation officer

parole the conditional release of an offender who has served some prison time, under specified rules and under the supervision of a parole officer

50 to 2,000 pounds of marijuana. A third degree felony is punished with a sentence of 2 to 10 years in state prison and a possible fine of up to $10,000. Examples of third degree felonies include a stalking conviction, a third driving while intoxicated (DWI) charge, or a third offense of violation of a protective order. The last category of felonies, state jail felonies, result in 180 days to two years in a state jail and a possible fine of up to $10,000. Examples of a state jail felony include burglary of a building, DWI with a child as a passenger, forgery of a check, and possession of less than one gram of a controlled substance.

Misdemeanors

Misdemeanors are less serious crimes, for which the fine is $4,000 or less and the sentence is up to one year in the county jail. No rights such as the right to vote, right to possess a weapon, or rights to have some occupational licenses are lost as a result of a misdemeanor conviction. There are three classes of misdemeanors. The most serious is a class A misdemeanor, for which the fine is not more than $4,000 and the sentence would not be more than one year in the county jail. Examples of class A misdemeanors include burglary of a vehicle, a second DWI offense, public lewdness, and possession of two to four ounces of marijuana. Class B misdemeanors are punishable with a sentence of up to 180 days in the county jail and a fine not to exceed $2,000. Examples of class B misdemeanors are prostitution, terroristic threats, a first DWI charge, criminal trespass, and possession of two ounces or less of marijuana. Finally, class C misdemeanors are punished with fines not to exceed $500 and involve such crimes as public intoxication, disorderly conduct, and a minor in possession of alcohol.

Punishing Crime

In some cases, the judge may allow **probation**, or community supervision, rather than a jail or prison sentence, especially if it is the defendant's first conviction. Probation is a suspension of the jail or prison sentence with the understanding that the defendant will meet certain requirements that are imposed by the court. These requirements usually include reporting to a probation officer on a regular basis, holding a steady job, paying fines or restitution, and abstaining from alcohol or drug use. Generally, community supervision can run up to 2 years for misdemeanors and up to 10 years for felonies, although if a probationer is compliant with the rules of community supervision, it is possible to obtain early release from probation after serving one-third of the term.[2]

Violation of probation requirements can result in being sent to jail or prison to serve out the remainder of the sentence behind bars. Often prosecutors know that people with lengthy probation sentences will find it difficult to comply with all of the requirements. So, in cases where they believe it will be difficult to get a conviction, they might agree to a plea bargain allowing community supervision for a long period. They expect that the defendant will violate probation and spend time in jail or prison.

People who are sentenced to prison may be released on **parole** after a period of time behind bars. This decision to grant parole is made by the Texas Board of

Pardons and Paroles. The agency is composed of a chair and six board members. Members of the board serve six-year staggered terms. The board makes recommendations about state prisoners' sentences, clemency, parole, and supervision. In order for the governor to alter a prisoner's sentence, a majority of the board must support the change. The board also determines which prisoners are to be released on parole, determines conditions of parole, determines revocation of parole, and recommends clemency matters to the governor.

People serving time for capital crimes are not eligible for parole, and generally those convicted of other violent crimes must serve at least half their sentence before being considered for parole. People convicted of nonviolent crimes must serve at least one-fourth of their sentences or 15 years, whichever is less, before being considered for parole. A complex formula is used by the Board of Pardons and Paroles that considers the crime, when it was committed, the time served, and the behavior of the inmate, so that no simple rule generally applies to offenders. If a prisoner is granted parole, he or she must comply with the requirements imposed on the parole or, like probation violators, he or she can be sent to prison for the remainder of the sentence.[3]

There are also sentencing enhancements where sentences are increased or the classification of the crime is increased in certain circumstances. Previous convictions can be used to enhance the punishment for a crime. For example, a DWI offense is a class B misdemeanor, but a second DWI is a class A misdemeanor, and a third DWI is a third degree felony. That means, of course, that a second or third DWI conviction will result in more serious penalties than will the first DWI offense.

Texas enhances sentences for repeat felony offenders as well. If a person who commits a third degree felony has a prior felony conviction, that person is sentenced for a second degree felony. Similarly, a second degree felony is punished as a first degree felony if the person had a prior felony conviction. A person convicted of a third felony can be sentenced to life imprisonment based on a **"three strikes" provision** in the penal code, and in some cases, such as sexual assault cases, two felony convictions are sufficient for life imprisonment.

"three strikes" provision a law that allows persons convicted of three felonies (or in some cases two felonies) to be sentenced to life imprisonment

● The Criminal Justice Process

Outline the procedural steps that occur after a person is arrested

There are several procedural steps that occur after a person is arrested and prior to the determination of guilt or innocence. In Texas, as in most other states, this process may take months or even years. The major procedural steps are listed below.

Arraignment and Posting Bail

Generally, when a person is arrested for a felony or misdemeanor and jailed rather than ticketed, he or she will be arraigned before a judge. At the arraignment, the charges will be explained to the accused, and he or she will be reminded of the due process rights—such as the right to remain silent and the right to an attorney. Generally, bail will be set at this point. In some cases, a date will be determined for the judge to review the charges against the defendant.

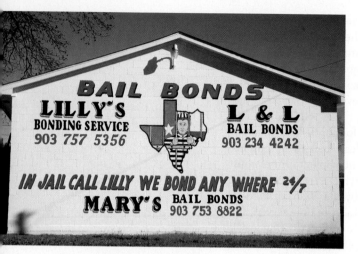

After being charged, a defendant may be released on bail until the trial. **Bail** is money that is provided by the defendant to assure his or her appearance in court. Usually, if a defendant does not show up for trial, the bail is forfeited. If the defendant appears as required, the bail money is returned. An individual may put up the entire sum for bail in order to be released from prison pending trial. Often, however, bail is more than the accused can pay, and so he or she will arrange with a bail bondsman to pay the bail in exchange for a nonrefundable payment that is often 10 percent of the amount but can be higher. A recent scandal involving bail bondsmen in Dallas County is leading to a reconsideration of how bail bonds are administered in that county. In Dallas, many bail bondsmen have had accused persons flee, but they have not forfeited the bail money for those persons. Additionally, many bail bondsmen can use property as security for their bonds and have gotten unusually high valuations on their property to support the bail bonds that they underwrite. This means that the property guaranteeing the bail does not actually equal the value of the bail, which means people are being released from jail for less than the amount of money that should be provided to guarantee their appearance at trial.

After being charged, a defendant may be released on bail. If the individual does not have enough money to post bail, he or she may make arrangements with a bail bondsman, who posts bail in exchange for a nonrefundable payment.

bail payment of money to the state as an assurance that an accused person who is released from jail pending trial will appear for trial; if the accused does not appear, the bail is forfeited

If a person cannot provide bail on the person's own or cannot pay a bondsman, the accused possibly can be released on personal recognizance, which is the accused's promise to appear. This process is most likely if the accused has ties in the community such as a family or employment and does not have a criminal record. If an accused person cannot provide bail, he or she usually will be held in jail pending the trial.

Grand Jury Indictment

grand jury jury that determines whether sufficient evidence is available to justify a trial; grand juries do not rule on the accused's guilt or innocence

Although the procedure can vary, generally after arraignment, a felony case will be presented to a **grand jury** which consists of 12 persons who will hear the case to determine if there is sufficient evidence to hold the accused for trial. Grand juries do not find people guilty of a crime, but instead will vote a "true bill," meaning that they find probable cause that an accused person has committed the crime, or they will return a "no bill," meaning that they did not find probable cause. A person would, of course, be held for trial only if a grand jury voted a "true bill." A grand jury indictment is far from conviction, as all a grand jury determines is the existence of probable cause and usually the grand jury's decision is based only on a presentation made by the prosecutor. In a trial, to find a person guilty, there must be a finding of guilt "beyond a reasonable doubt," which is a demanding standard of proof for a prosecutor, and at a trial the defense is also heard and has the opportunity to cross-examine witnesses and present the defense's version of events. The major criticism of the grand jury is that it usually hears only what the prosecutor chooses to let it hear and that it serves as a "rubber stamp" for the prosecutor's decision.

Pretrial Hearings

After indictment for a felony, there will likely be a number of pretrial hearings in which the accused will formally plead guilty or not guilty, the trial is scheduled, and various motions may be presented such as motions to move the trial or motions to exclude certain evidence. These hearings vary in length but in most cases are quite brief. In a criminal trial, a common motion is one to exclude certain evidence on the grounds that the evidence was seized in violation of the 4th Amendment, meaning that it was illegally seized. In these instances, the judge examines the facts of the seizure and determines whether the evidence was legally seized and therefore can be used at trial.

Although plea bargaining can occur even during a trial and even after a finding of guilt but before sentencing, the prosecution and the defense will often discuss a punishment in exchange for a guilty plea and reach an agreement before the trial.

Trial and Sentencing

If the case does go to trial, a defendant may waive the right to a jury trial and have the determination of guilt made by a judge. A jury trial may be waived in cases where a judge is perceived as more inclined to be favorable because of past decisions by the judge or because the crime is believed to be one that would inflame the emotions of jurors, resulting in less favorable treatment. A defendant may also have a jury trial but waive the right to sentencing by a jury so that the judge determines the sentence if there is a guilty verdict. In Texas, felony juries are composed of 12 people and misdemeanor juries are composed of 6. Decisions by criminal juries must be unanimous, and for both felonies and misdemeanors the standard of proof is "beyond a reasonable doubt." If the jury's decision in a felony case is not unanimous, the case results in a mistrial, and the prosecutor must decide whether to retry the defendant.

If the defendant is acquitted (found not guilty), the defendant is, of course, set free. If the defendant is found guilty, there will be a jail or prison sentence or probation and/or a fine. A defendant may appeal a determination of guilt, meaning that the defendant asks a higher court to reconsider the lower court's decision. Very minor criminal cases that are heard by municipal courts or by justice of the peace courts can be appealed to the county courts. More serious misdemeanors and felonies, however, are heard by county or district courts, and appeals from county courts or district courts will be to one of the 14 courts of appeal in Texas. An appeal beyond the Texas courts of appeal will be to the highest criminal court in Texas, the Texas Court of Criminal Appeals. In rare events where a question of U.S. constitutional or statutory law is raised, it may also be possible to appeal to the federal courts.

Does the Criminal Justice System Create Criminals?

In some cases, the requirements of the Texas criminal justice system can be quite burdensome on individuals. For some people, complying with the rules of the process can be difficult and even financially impossible. One common crime in Texas, especially among younger offenders, is possession of less than two ounces of marijuana. Although Travis County treats this crime as the equivalent of a typical traffic offense where the police officer tickets the offender, in other Texas counties offenders will be taken to a local jail to be held until the bond hearing and until they can make bail. Commonly, the bail on such a charge would be $500, which means that the full $500 will have to be posted with the county, or a bail bondsman

Before the trial, hearings may be held to hear motions from either side, such as a motion to exclude certain evidence or to move the trial. Here, lawyers in the Andrea Yates case speak to the judge in a pretrial hearing.

will have to be retained for roughly a $50 nonrefundable fee. After bail is posted, the defendant will eventually have to go to trial in a county-court-at-law. Some defendants hire an attorney, which may cost $1,000 to $3,000 for the entire process in this type of case; others may appear in court without an attorney. It would not be unusual for a first offense to result in at least a $500 fine plus court costs, a sentence of 30 hours of community service, a sentence of 15 hours in an approved drug education course, and nine months' probation where the defendant would pay a fee for each visit to the probation officer and any drug testing required by the probation officer. After court costs, probation costs, and the fine, the offender will probably have spent about $1,000 to $1,200, excluding legal fees.

While on probation, the offender will not be allowed to use drugs or alcohol and will be subject to testing. There will be a required visit with a drug counselor and regular trips to a probation officer. Travel will be restricted. If the offender is in compliance, he or she will probably get early release from probation. If not, probation could be full length and jail time is possible. Additionally, because this is a drug case, the driver's license of the offender will be suspended for six months. If driving is necessary for the offender, in order to be in compliance, the offender must go to court and obtain an occupational driver's license in order to drive to and from work or care for family matters. Filing this paperwork can easily cost nearly $300 not counting possible attorney's fees. Additionally, the offender will have to purchase an SR-22 automobile insurance policy for two years in order to drive legally. This is a high-risk insurance policy where the insurance company reports directly to the state that the offender has automobile insurance coverage. This type of insurance can cost twice as much as a regular insurance policy. Thus, an arrest for possession of a marijuana cigarette can easily cost more than $5,000 to $7,000 overall in fines, court costs, insurance charges, probation fees, and attorney costs, not to mention time in jail after arrest and, if the marijuana was found in the offender's vehicle, towing and impoundment charges. Failure to comply with all probation requirements can lead to violation of probation and other criminal charges such as driving with a suspended license or driving without proper insurance.

The structure of the criminal justice process even for minor crimes such as a class B misdemeanor may deter future crimes because of the severity of punishment, but the cost and penalty structure also seems to encourage failure and further criminality by the offender.

Crime and Texas District Attorneys

Ordinarily when we think of the criminal justice system, we think of the police who make arrests and the Texas criminal courts that adjudicate those criminal cases. The most important actors in the Texas criminal justice system, however, are probably the prosecuting attorneys. Some counties have an elected county attorney whose office represents the state in misdemeanor criminal cases. The county attorney usually provides legal advice to the county commissioners as well, although generally the **county attorney** does not represent the county in civil cases. Counties with elected county attorneys also have elected **district attorneys**. They represent the state in felony cases. There are counties that have merged the offices of county and district attorney into a combined office that represents the state in both misdemeanor and felony cases. Often, when the office of county and district attorney is merged, it is called the office of the criminal district attorney.[4]

In the urban counties in Texas, the office of the district attorney is huge, encompassing several hundred lawyers, investigators, and support staff. In the most rural counties, the district attorney's office may be composed of only one or two lawyers.

county attorney an elected official in some counties who prosecutes misdemeanor cases

district attorney public official who prosecutes the more serious criminal cases in the district court

The head of every district attorney's office in Texas is an elected officer who runs under a party label. The term of office is four years. And, as the chief prosecuting officer of the county or district, the district attorney has the responsibility for criminal prosecutions within the district attorney's jurisdiction. This means that the district attorneys generally campaign as officials who are "tough on crime," and they brag about high conviction rates. If they appear too lenient or their conviction rates are too low, political opponents will emerge who will accuse them of not doing their job appropriately. Because prosecutors often deal with people who have committed terrible crimes, they often see the worst aspects of humanity, and this also may lead to a "tough on crime" approach. A Parker County prosecutor wrote in a periodical widely read by other prosecutors of the mindset that prosecutors develop in the course of their work, "Like many of you, I've become jaded. The past nine years as a felony prosecutor has convinced me that an unending supply of humanity is willing to lie, cheat, steal, maim, or kill for the smallest reasons or for no reason at all. I had begun to think that my conscience could no longer be shocked, regardless of the facts and circumstances of any case I prosecuted."[5] Thus, the political pressures of the job coupled with the experiences one has in the job do not incline prosecutors to be sympathetic in their dealings with defendants.

District attorneys and other prosecutors try to maintain high conviction rates in order to keep their positions. However, after a series of wrongful convictions by overzealous prosecutors, some have called for reform. A 2012 campaign ad for Travis County DA Rosemary Lehmberg stressed reform.

Prosecutors must maintain high conviction rates in order to keep their positions. One way that high conviction rates are maintained is through plea bargaining. In a **plea bargain**, a prosecutor will meet with the accused or his lawyer and offer a sentence in exchange for a plea of guilty. The prosecutor's offer might involve reducing the charge, dropping some of the charges, or recommending a lighter sentence than the defendant might get at trial if found guilty. Plea bargaining is not only necessary politically for an elected district attorney to maintain high conviction rates, but also crucial in managing the limited resources of the prosecutor's office and the courts. Prosecuting a case that goes to trial after a defendant pleads not guilty can cost thousands and even millions of dollars and uses up the time of employees. If plea bargaining were suddenly abandoned in Texas, the criminal justice system would quickly come to a halt as a result of a massive overflow of trials. There is often an incentive for defense lawyers to plea bargain as well. In many cases, defense lawyers can generate more income by representing numerous defendants (who often have limited resources) in plea negations than they can in a few time-consuming trials. And, of course, plea bargains can benefit defendants, even innocent defendants, in that they get an assured sentence that may be less than they would receive if they went to trial and were found guilty and sentenced by either a judge or a jury.

In almost all cases that involve plea bargaining, the judge with jurisdiction over the case will agree with the bargain made by the district attorney's office. For one thing, plea bargains reduce the crowded dockets of judges. Without a trial, the judge cannot be aware of the strengths and weaknesses of the state's case and so will generally recognize that the district attorney is in a far better position to determine the appropriate sentence.

The district attorney has prosecutorial discretion, which includes the power to charge or not charge a person with a crime. Even when a case is presented before a grand jury to determine if a criminal indictment should be issued, the grand jury is dependent on the prosecutor to present the evidence that may lead to an

plea bargain a negotiated agreement in a criminal case in which a defendant agrees to plead guilty in return for the state's agreement to reduce the severity of the criminal charge or prison sentence the defendant is facing

indictment, and a prosecutor has great discretion in choosing to go before a grand jury and in deciding to accept or not accept the decision of a particular grand jury. There have been several recent examples of the vast power of the district attorney in the state's criminal justice process. Prosecutors are powerful enough to even go after judges. In Collin County in late 2011, District Judge Suzanne Wooten was convicted of six counts of bribery, one count of money laundering, tampering with a government record, and engaging in an organized criminal activity. In order to get the indictment of Judge Wooten that led to her conviction, the district attorney had to go before at least six different grand juries. The first five grand juries did not decide to indict. It was an extraordinary example of prosecutors shopping for a grand jury that would finally indict someone they had targeted. After Wooten was convicted at trial, she faced the possibility of a 20-year sentence. Prosecutors then offered her a sentencing deal. She would get 10 years' probation, get a $10,000 fine, and have to do 1,000 hours community service. She took the deal even though it meant that she also had to agree not to appeal the conviction, which protected the prosecution from an appeal and from further controversy over whether the case was tainted by local politics.[6]

In another case, a Dallas County judge held a prosecutor in contempt for not following a court order. The judge had ordered the prosecutor to hand over the criminal histories of police officers, and the assistant district attorney had objected, claiming the district attorney's office was not required to do so and that federal law prohibited that information from being provided to defense lawyers. The assistant district attorney who refused was confined by being ordered to remain in the courtroom. Later the judge suspended her decision to hold the assistant district attorney in contempt and agreed to hold a hearing about the matter. However, prior to the hearing, the district attorney's office began a grand jury investigation of the judge for official oppression. Ultimately, cooler heads prevailed and, at least as of fall 2012, the district attorney dropped a grand jury subpoena against the judge.[7] Nevertheless, a clear message seems to be that even judges, who are commonly perceived as all-powerful within the legal process, should be cautious when dealing with the power of a district attorney.

In Harris County, a grand jury investigated the district attorney's office over allegations that assistant district attorneys who prosecute DWI cases knew about possible problems with the Houston Police Department's breath alcohol vehicles and violated the law by not telling defendants about those concerns. There had been charges that the breath alcohol tests conducted by the vehicles were not accurate because of overheating and electrical spikes. It was highly unusual for a grand jury to take on an investigation of a district attorney's office, but again, the power of the district attorney was evident in a report issued by the grand jury in 2012. The report claimed that the district attorney's office had investigated the grand jurors, two judges, and a political opponent of the district attorney. It also criticized a prosecutor for refusing to testify and the district attorney's office for "unexpected resistance." When the grand jury issued its one-page report criticizing the Harris County district attorney's office, the district attorney called a press conference and attacked the grand jury, claiming, "This politically motivated investigation, I would submit to you, is an outrage. It's an abuse of power and a corruption of the criminal justice system. For months our office has been hounded, and there have been a torrent of grand jury leaks."[8] When district attorneys can mobilize the power of the state to prosecute and attempt to intimidate judges and grand juries, it emphasizes their power in the criminal justice system and power over ordinary citizens they charge with wrongdoing.

● Crime, Corrections, and the Texas Prison System

Describe prisons and corrections policy in Texas

It has long been claimed that Texas does things in a big way. That is certainly true of its levels of crime and the way it deals with criminals. As of August 31, 2010, there were 154,795 offenders incarcerated in the state's prisons, state jails, and substance abuse facilities.[9] These numbers exclude those incarcerated in municipal and county facilities. In 2010 the average cost per day for each bed in the state's correctional facilities was $50.79.[10]

History of the Prison System

Shortly after Texas joined the Union, construction was authorized for a state penitentiary in Huntsville. The 225-cell facility opened in 1849. It confined prisoners in single cells at night and congregated inmates during the day to work in silence. From 1870 to 1883, the entire prison system was leased to private contractors who used the labor of inmates in exchange for providing maintenance and security for prisoners. After 1883, convicts in the Texas prison system were leased to railroads, planters, and others who provided the prisoners with food and clothing and paid a stipend to the state. These leasing arrangements were abandoned in 1910 as a result of scandals and abuses of the system.[11]

Although Texas moved to a state-run system, abuses continued. In 1924 an investigation of the system found cruel and brutal treatment of prisoners, inefficient management, and inadequate care of inmates. That investigation led to the creation of a state prison board, which supervised the work of a general prison manager. Still, however, the abuses continued. By the mid-1940s, the Texas prison system was considered one of the worst in the United States. In 1974 the Joint Committee on Prison Reform submitted findings to the legislature that were very critical of the Texas prison system. It found fault with numerous aspects of the prison system's operation—from living and working conditions for inmates to classification of inmates to medical care to staff training. Still, nothing much happened.[12]

The event that had the most dramatic effect on the operation of the Texas prison system in modern times was a federal court case, *Ruiz v. Estelle*.[13] Lawsuits filed by prisoners are nothing new. During the tenure of W. J. Estelle Jr., the prison director from 1973 to 1983 and the defendant in the *Ruiz* case, prisoners filed 19,696 cases in the federal courts in Texas, a caseload amounting to about 20 percent of the federal court docket in Texas during that period.[14] However, the *Ruiz* case was exceptional. It was a class-action suit on behalf of inmates that began in 1972, and it focused on issues of crowding in the system, security and supervision, health care, discipline, and access to the courts. In 1980 the federal court concluded that inmates' constitutionally guaranteed rights had been violated. Texas joined several other states in having its prison system declared unconstitutional.

David Ruiz (right) and other Texas prison inmates filed a class-action lawsuit demanding stronger rights for prisoners. The case resulted in changes in how Texas prisons operated.

The result was the appointment by the court of a special master, a court officer, to oversee the Texas prison system to eliminate the constitutional problems such as overcrowding, improper supervision of inmates, and improper care of inmates. There was a massive reform of the system, one that had to be imposed by the federal courts, because the state seemed unwilling or unable to reform its own prison system. Federal court supervision of the prison system ended in 2002.

For a long time, many in Texas government were resistant to federal court supervision of the prison system, arguing, for example, that the *Ruiz* decision involved federal court judicial activism and interfered with the rights of the state. In order to reduce the overcrowding in state prisons to comply with *Ruiz*, the state also encouraged the early release of prisoners, some of whom reentered society and committed further crimes. *Ruiz* did, however, help turn the criminal justice system into a major public policy issue in Texas.

The Prison System Today

The Texas prison system is operated by the Texas Department of Criminal Justice. This agency is run by a nine-member board that is appointed by the governor, and board members serve staggered six-year terms. The board hires an executive director to lead the sprawling agency, and it is responsible for developing the rules and regulations that govern the entire state prison system.[15] Figure 10.1 shows the locations of the Texas Department of Criminal Justice facilities.

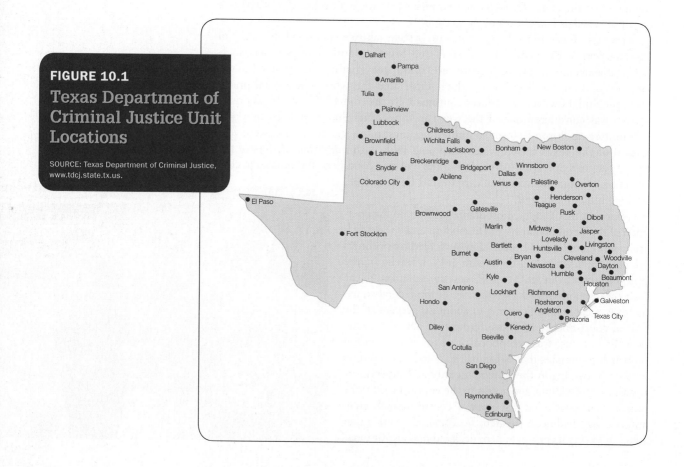

FIGURE 10.1

Texas Department of Criminal Justice Unit Locations

SOURCE: Texas Department of Criminal Justice, www.tdcj.state.tx.us.

How Does Criminal Justice in Texas Compare to Other States?

Incarceration Rate, 2010 per 100,000 residents

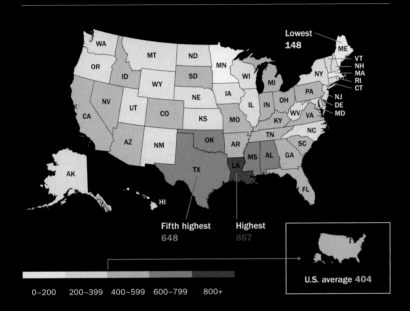

Lowest
148

Fifth highest
648

Highest
867

U.S. average 404

0–200   200–399   400–599   600–799   800+

The Texas criminal justice system is known for high incarceration rates. In 2010, 648 out of every 100,000 Texans were sentenced to one year or more in the state prison system, and rates in other recent years are similar. Texas is also known for its harsh punishments of criminals, especially the use of the death penalty. Since the U.S. Supreme Court reinstated the death penalty in 1978, Texas has executed 482 people: four times more than any other state.

Total Executions, 1976–2012

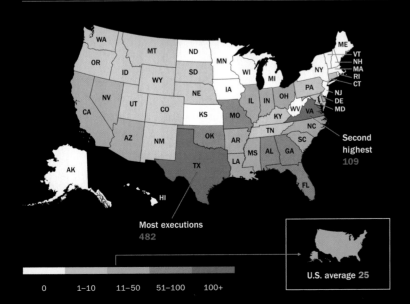

Second highest
109

Most executions
482

U.S. average 25

0   1–10   11–50   51–100   100+

SOURCES: Incarceration rate: U.S. Department of Justice, Bureau of Justice Statistics. Executions: Death Penalty Information Center www.deathpenaltyinfo.org/number-executions-state-and-region-1976 (accessed 6/7/12).

for critical analysis

1. What elements of Texas political culture or public opinion may contribute to the willingness to use the death penalty and to have high incarceration rates?

2. Examine the regional patterns on the two maps. Do certain regions of the country have high incarceration rates and death penalty usage? What do you think explains these regional patterns?

There have been dramatic increases in the costs of prison construction and prison maintenance in Texas over time. Operating costs of Texas prisons rose from $147 million in 1982 to $609 million in 1990 to nearly $1.5 billion in 1996 and over $2.8 billion in 2008. In 2011 the total operating budget for the Texas Department of Criminal Justice was $3.06 billion. Despite a steady increase in prison operating costs, prison construction costs have varied from year to year. In 1982, $126 million was spent on prison construction, but in 1990 only $24 million was spent. The greatest period of prison construction was from 1991 through 1995. During those years, nearly $1.4 billion was spent on prison construction. In 2011 prison construction costs were $62.4 million.[16] In the wake of estimates in 2007 that Texas would need 17,000 new prison beds costing $1 billion by 2012, the Texas Legislature increased the capacity of prison alternatives such as drug treatment and halfway homes, much cheaper alternatives to prison.[17]

Until 2007, when the Texas Legislature began to seriously address alternatives to imprisonment, the state government had significantly increased the incarceration of offenders by building more prisons. In 2011, however, for the first time in Texas history, the state actually closed a prison—the century-old Central Unit in Sugarland. State leaders also announced plans to close three juvenile detention centers with its move toward rehabilitation, crime prevention, and cost-cutting.

From 1976 to 1990, the rate of property crime in Texas rose 38 percent, and the violent crime rate rose 113 percent. During the same time period, prison expansion did not keep up with the increase in the crime rate. Instead, generous early-release policies were used to move prisoners out of jail to allow room for newly convicted

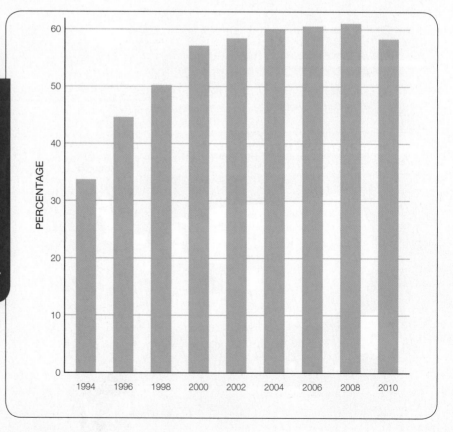

FIGURE 10.2

Percentage of Prison Sentence Served by Texas Inmates

SOURCES: Criminal Justice Policy Council, "Percentage of Prison Sentence Served for All Release Types, Fiscal Years 1994–2004"; Texas Department of Criminal Justice, Fiscal Year 2006 Statistical Report; Texas Department of Criminal Justice, Fiscal Year 2008 Statistical Report; Texas Department of Criminal Justice, "Fiscal Year 2011 Operating Budget and Fiscal Years 2012–2013 Legislative Appropriations Request," August 16, 2010.

inmates. With prison expansion, however, early-release policies were reduced. In 1990, for example, 38,000 prisoners were given early release from prison; however, even with a much larger prison population in 1997, only slightly more than 28,000 prisoners were given early release.[18] The steady lengthening of sentences is shown in Figure 10.2. In 1994 prisoners on average were released after serving one-third of their sentences. In 2010 prisoners were serving about 58 percent of their sentences before being released.[19]

As shown in Figure 10.3, the Texas prison population has soared, especially since about 1992. In 1980, at the time of the *Ruiz* case, the Texas prison population consisted of fewer than 30,000 inmates. A decade later, in 1990, there were slightly more than 49,000 inmates in Texas prisons. Only seven years later in 1997, there were almost 130,000 inmates in state prisons. In 2000 the number of inmates in state prisons had jumped to over 150,000, dropping back to about 145,000 in 2002 and to 139,316 in 2010. Put another way, there were more than 4.5 inmates in state prisons in 2010 for every inmate in state correctional facilities in 1980.[20]

For much of the 1980s, the rates of violent and property crime in Texas were especially high. By the mid-1990s, however, those rates had dropped. Some observers argued that the reduction in the crime rate is caused by the increased incarceration of offenders.[21] There may also be other causes, however. Other analysts have suggested demographic change determines the size of the prison population. The most prison-prone group in society is males between the ages of 20 and 29. If that demographic group is large, then we would expect the prison population to also be large.[22] Indeed, 92 percent of Texas prisoners are male, and the average age of prisoners is only 37 years.[23] Of course, changes in laws and treatment practices also affect the crime rate and the incarceration rate. Long sentences for habitual criminals, for example, are relatively new, as are long sentences for the use of a firearm in the commission of a crime.[24] The number of prison inmates per 100,000 population in Texas at the end of 2009 was 648. The national average was 502.

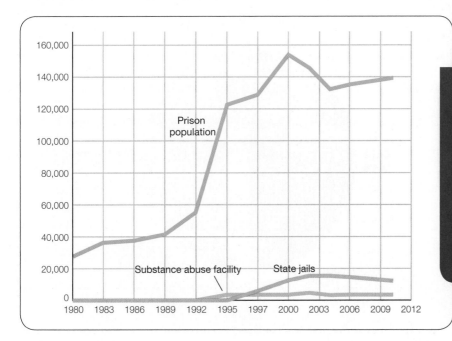

FIGURE 10.3

Texas Inmate Population, 1980–2010

SOURCES: Associated Texans Against Crime Annual Report, 1998; Texas Department of Criminal Justice, "Fiscal Year 2004 Statistics"; Criminal Justice Policy Council, "Texas Department of Criminal Justice State Incarcerated Population, Fiscal Years 1988–2002"; and Texas Department of Criminal Justice, 2006, 2008, and 2010 Statistical Report.

California and New York, the closest states in population to Texas, incarcerate 458 per 100,000 population and 298 per 100,000, respectively. Only Louisiana, Mississippi, and Oklahoma have a higher rate of incarceration than Texas. Texas had 12.2 percent of the nation's total state prison population in January 1, 2010. Only the federal system had more prisoners under its jurisdiction.[25] In spite of its high rate of incarceration, Texas ranked high in crime. A study of crime rates nationwide found Texas ranked 37 in the United States in crime where a ranking of 1 is the least crime and 50 is the greatest crime ranking.[26]

As Figure 10.4 shows, Texas imprisons mostly violent offenders. In 2010, 51 percent of Texas inmates had been convicted of violent offenses and 17 percent had been convicted of property offenses. Nearly 18 percent of the inmate population was convicted of drug offenses.[27] Whether imprisonment for drug offenses is an appropriate remedy for the drug problem has been debated, but it is interesting to note that about one in five people in Texas prisons are there because of drugs.

It is especially difficult for felons to gain legitimate employment after their release—so much so that the federal government offers a large tax credit to employers who will give jobs to people who have been convicted of a felony and have served their sentence. This difficulty in finding legal employment makes it more likely that former prisoners will commit further crimes. Another problem that inmates face once they leave prison is that the average sentence in a Texas prison is 19.2 years. After serving substantial time in prison, it is hard to readjust to life in the free world, and support structures such as family members have often died or removed the inmate from their lives. Still another difficulty is that 44.3 percent of inmates in Texas prisons do not have a high school diploma or GED and their average educational achievement is slightly less than 8 years.[28] That lack of education makes adjustment to life and legitimate employment outside of prison an extremely difficult experience.

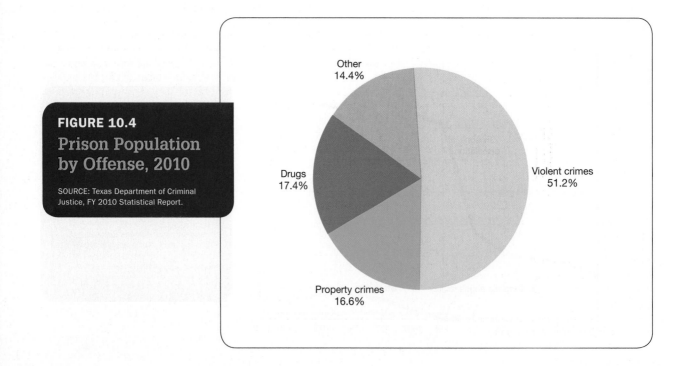

FIGURE 10.4
Prison Population by Offense, 2010

SOURCE: Texas Department of Criminal Justice, FY 2010 Statistical Report.

Other
14.4%

Drugs
17.4%

Violent crimes
51.2%

Property crimes
16.6%

Concealed Weapons on Campus

Most Texas inmates were convicted of violent crimes. Can gun laws help prevent violent crime? In May 2011, the Texas Senate approved legislation sponsored by Senator Jeff Wentworth (R–San Antonio) to allow the carrying of concealed handguns on public college campuses. Officials at the University of Texas and Texas A&M argued that they did not want the law to be implemented on their campuses. Some student groups organized on both sides of the issue. While the legislation was eventually defeated, proponents have not given up and continue to push for similar legislation.

Are college campuses with "gun-free zones" some of the safest places in Texas, or do they represent a prime place for criminal predators seeking easy unarmed prey in "victim zones"? Do more guns lead to more crime or enhance collective security? Would you feel more or less secure with the prospect that your fellow student may be legally concealing a handgun as an exercise of liberty? The first two questions can be answered with data, and the latter question is an opinion-based question, but they all involve trade-offs between liberty, public safety, public law, and collective security.

The politics of gun control has been and continues to be a polarizing topic in the United States, and many people already have their minds made up and are unwilling to seriously consider alternative viewpoints on firearms-related legislation. As the topic changes from laws regulating the constitutional "right to keep and bear arms" to laws expanding access to firearms and the "right to carry" firearms, the issue becomes even more controversial. These divergent viewpoints are evident in the reactions to tragic events such as shooting massacres.

On April 16, 2007, Seung-Hui Cho shot 49 people—killing 32—on the campus of Virginia Tech. In the wake of the shooting, law enforcement determined that Cho had illegally bought the firearms after having been declared mentally ill and "an imminent danger to self or others" over one year prior to the shootings. As a result, a "mental health loophole" was identified in the firearms background check process, and federal and state governments passed legislation seeking to close the loophole.

Since the April 2007 Virginia Tech shooting exposed potential risks on university campuses, concealed carry advocates have expressed concerns about student safety offering that students, faculty, and staff should have the right to carry weapons on college campuses. In 2004, the Utah legislature passed a law expressly allowing concealed weapons on college campuses in the state, including the possession of firearms in student housing. Proponents of carrying concealed handguns on college campuses have argued that firearms have not and will not have a negative impact on the learning environment, with some pointing to Utah's concealed carry law as a model. However, while most people might agree that an individual has a right to self-defense in his or her home, many dispute whether student housing on college campuses should be included.

NO WEAPONS ALLOWED
Except licensed concealed handgun.
Handgun license holders MUST show permit upon request.

NINGUNAS ARMAS PERMITIDAS

Opponents of carrying concealed handguns on college campuses have argued that the presence of concealed weapons in a classroom would be disruptive to the learning environment and represent a safety hazard. They claim that the risk of an accidental or an intentional discharge on campus increases if more firearms are present. Moreover, opponents often contend that institutions of intellectual activity are not the place for weapons. They argue that concealed handgun carriers may lack the necessary training to defend themselves, let alone others, while proponents argue that with law enforcement several minutes away, concealed handgun carriers can potentially defend themselves and others.

critical thinking questions

1. If opponents and proponents of concealed weapons on campus cannot agree, how should lawmakers determine what policy to pass? Can you think of a compromise that might be proposed?

2. Do you think allowing concealed weapons would make your campus safer or less safe? Can you find any data online that support your view?

During the administration of Governor Ann Richards, there was recognition that very large proportions of prisoners were involved with alcoholism, drug addiction, and drug-related crimes. An effort was made to create alcohol- and drug-abuse treatment programs within the prison system to help alleviate these problems, although the problems remain severe. In 2007 the Texas Legislature again spent resources on prison alternatives, which have helped reduce the need for new prison construction.

The Death Penalty

The most serious aspect of the criminal justice system in Texas, and one of the most controversial, is the death penalty. One study of the death penalty found that, nationwide, 68 percent of death penalty appeals were successful between 1973 and 1995, but Texas appeals were successful only 52 percent of the time. Another study found that after Texas created a new and faster system for handling death penalty appeals in 1995, only 8 of 278 cases were overturned by the Texas Court of Criminal Appeals.[29] Another reason for the lack of success of defendants in death penalty cases has to do with the quality of legal representation defendants receive if they have a court-appointed lawyer. One study found that more than 100 death-row inmates in Texas have been represented by court-appointed attorneys with troubled histories whose performance became an issue on appeal. In one case, for example, a lawyer with no permanent license to practice law and no background in capital murder cases was appointed to handle a death penalty appeal even though he had practiced law less than two years. And the Texas Court of Criminal Appeals let him stay on the case even when he asked the court to delay the appeal so that he could take an introductory course in death penalty defense. While that lawyer did get an extension to take his class, he still missed a filing deadline and filed his brief only after the court threatened him with jail for contempt. When it came time for him to argue the case before the court, he did not show. The court left him on the case and denied the appeal, noting that 6 of his 11 arguments were inadequately briefed and presented nothing for review. That lawyer was paid $8,647 by Smith County for his work on the case and subsequently lost his probationary law license when he bounced checks for state bar dues and occupational taxes and failed to appear at a board hearing to defend himself. The board expressed concern that if he continued to practice law, there was a "likelihood that he would harm a client, obstruct the administration of justice, or violate [state bar rules]."[30]

Texas has led the nation in the number of executions since the death penalty was reinstated in 1976. Of the top 15 counties in the United States that have issued death sentences since 1976, 9 of the counties have been in Texas. Harris County, where Houston is located, is the number one county in the United States to impose death sentences since 1976. One hundred fifteen death sentences have come from Harris County alone. Dallas County, where Dallas is located, is the number two county in the United States for death sentences, and it has imposed 46 death sentences. The number three county is Tarrant County, where Fort Worth is located. It has imposed 36 death sentences. The number five county in the United States for death sentences is Bexar County, where San Antonio is located. It has imposed 31 death sentences. Montgomery County, Texas, is number seven in the country, with 14 death sentences; Jefferson County is the number eight county, with 12 death sentences; Brazos, Nueces, and Potter Counties are the number nine, ten, and eleven counties in the United States with 11 death sentences each.[31] Since

1977, lethal injection has been the means for execution in Texas. The first execution by lethal injection was on December 7, 1982. Beginning in 1923, the state ordered that executions be carried out in Huntsville by electrocution. Prior to that time, each county was responsible for carrying out executions.[32] In March 2011, Texas replaced sodium thiopental with pentobarbital in the three-drug execution cocktail that is used for lethal injection. That was because the maker of sodium thiopental quit producing the drug after there were international protests over its use as an execution drug in the United States. Texas is now facing a similar problem with its use of pentobarbital. Its manufacturer has said that it will seek to block its use for executions, and the price of the drug has already dramatically increased. In order to stop a future shortage of execution drugs in Texas, Texas prison officials are trying to obtain a ruling from the Texas attorney general that would allow them to keep secret information about where execution drugs come from or how much they cost. There are already reports that Texas may switch to propofol (the drug involved in the death of entertainer Michael Jackson) as the supply of pentobarbital dries up.[33]

Texas executed 472 people from December 7, 1982, through July 21, 2011. As of July 2011, there were 311 people on death row.[34]

In Texas, one is subject to the death penalty for the murder of a public safety officer, fireman, or correctional employee; murder during commission of a kidnapping, burglary, robbery, aggravated rape, or arson; murder for hire; multiple murders; murder during a prison escape; murder by a prison inmate serving a life sentence; or murder of a child under the age of six.

A stay on death row can be a lengthy one, even in Texas. The average time spent on death row prior to execution is 10.6 years, although the time varies considerably. One inmate under a death sentence waived his appeals and spent only a little more than eight months on death row prior to execution. On the other hand, David Lee

Texas has made greater use of the death penalty than other states, but opponents argue that the legal system does not do enough to protect defendants in death penalty cases. In 2007, Johnny Ray Conner became the 400th person to be executed in Texas since 1982. In this photo, his family and death penalty opponents demonstrate against his execution.

Powell spent 31 years on death row prior to being executed in 2010.[35] A death sentence carried out in February 1998, however, initiated the greatest controversy over the death penalty. The case of Karla Faye Tucker, a convicted ax murderer, generated national demands for clemency. Tucker was widely believed to have undergone a religious conversion after her 1983 conviction. She was also attractive and articulate and was the first woman in modern times condemned to be executed in Texas. Supporters of her execution argued that her gender, appearance, articulateness, and possible religious conversion were irrelevant to the fact that she was a convicted murderer who should be treated like others in similar situations.

One of the issues involving the death penalty is whether all offenders are treated in the same way. There is a racial and ethnic disparity such that minorities, especially African Americans, are disproportionately represented on death row. On July 28, 2011, there were 122 African Americans on death row, 92 Hispanics, 93 whites, and 4 of "other" racial and ethnic classifications. Since 1982, 218 whites have been executed, 173 African Americans, 79 Hispanics, and 2 of "other" racial and ethnic groups. It may be that there is a bias in the criminal justice system such that minorities are disproportionately subject to the death penalty, although a counterargument is that the murder rate is higher among minorities. When the issue of whether there was racial bias in the imposition of the death penalty was presented to the Supreme Court, the Court refused to strike down the death penalty on the basis of statistical generalizations—essentially saying that there had to be evidence of racial bias in the imposition of the death penalty in the specific case presented to the Court.[36]

The Texas Board of Pardons and Paroles votes on clemency for death-row inmates. Both a federal and a state judge have been highly critical of this process.[37] The board was originally considered to be a remedy for possible corruption in clemency granted by the governor. Prior to 1936, the governor essentially had unlimited power to grant clemency. This power was often abused, especially by Governor Miriam Ferguson, who granted 4,000 requests for commutations of sentences in 1922 alone. It was widely believed that payments were made for many of these acts of executive clemency. In reaction, a constitutional amendment was passed in 1936 that charged the board with giving the governor recommendations on clemency. Without such a recommendation, the governor can only grant a single 30-day reprieve. No other state so limits the powers of the governor.

In August 2007, the board recommended commutation of Kenneth Foster's sentence to be executed—only seven hours before Foster was scheduled to die. Governor Perry commuted Foster's sentence to life imprisonment about one hour later.[38] Foster's much-publicized case seemed to challenge two aspects of the death penalty in Texas: (1) Foster had been tried simultaneously with the other capital defendants rather than getting a separate trial; and (2) he was the getaway driver in the crime and not the actual shooter in the robbery and murder.

Though Texas has been called the nation's "Death Penalty Capital," in recent years the number of death penalties imposed in the state has dropped. One study of the Texas death penalty compared its imposition from 1992 to 1996 with its imposition from 2005 to 2009 and noted there was a 70 percent drop in death sentences. One explanation was a decline in capital murder convictions over this time period, and another was that beginning in 2005, Texas juries could impose a sentence of life without parole. Additionally, U.S. Supreme Court decisions now prevent execution of juveniles or the mentally retarded. The cost of death penalty prosecutions has greatly reduced death penalty prosecutions in all but the 12 largest counties. Finally, Harris County was the major county for imposing the death penalty in Texas. Because of changes in district attorneys there, scandal in the Houston crime lab, and improvements in the quality of capital defense work in Houston, there has been a huge drop in the imposition of the death penalty in Harris County.[39]

● The Integrity of the Texas Criminal Justice System

> **Explain why Texas's criminal justice system is often controversial**

In recent years, numerous controversial issues and cases have raised questions about how criminal justice works in Texas. Earlier in the chapter we discussed concerns with prosecutorial abuses of power and with the difficulty some people may have in complying with the rules of the criminal justice process. Here, we consider whether aggressive use of the death penalty, wrongful convictions, and flawed evidence procedures are compromising the integrity of the criminal justice system. At the end of this section, we consider some of the reforms that have been attempted and proposed as ways to address concerns about criminal justice in Texas.

The Death Penalty and Wrongful Convictions. Texas has been more aggressive than any other state in imposing the death penalty. Yet as Texas continues to execute people, in 2000 Illinois suspended the death penalty after revelations of a number of wrongful convictions. New Jersey, North Carolina, and California are all considering moratoriums on the death penalty. Since 1989, 280 people wrongfully convicted of crimes in 34 states have been cleared as a result of DNA testing, including 17 people who served time on death row. The average prison time served by an exoneree was 13 years.[40] In the summer of 2005, Supreme Court Justice John Paul Stevens publicly noted that DNA evidence had shown that a number of death sentences had been erroneously imposed.[41]

This concern about the death penalty has even affected the internal dynamics of the Texas Court of Criminal Appeals, which is the state's court of last resort for death penalty appeals. Judge Tom Price challenged Presiding Judge Sharon Keller in the Republican primary in 2006 in part because he thought Judge Keller was too strict in her support of the decisions of trial courts in death penalty and other criminal cases. The Price-Keller primary battle reflected an emerging concern in Texas that the state has been too free in its imposition of the death penalty and too unquestioning of the evidence that leads to the imposition of criminal punishments.

Texas is the home of more verified wrongful convictions than any other state. Forty-four exonerations have occurred in Texas as a result of DNA testing.[42] Dallas County has emerged as the national leader in DNA exonerations of wrongfully convicted men. By late 2011, 22 men in Dallas County were exonerated by DNA evidence.[43]

Problems with Police Procedures and Evidence Concerns about wrongful convictions are often related to the methods police and prosecutors use to convict suspects. One reason for the large number of DNA exonerations in Dallas County is simply that Dallas County has a policy of preserving physical evidence for lengthy

DNA evidence has been at the center of numerous recent legal controversies in Texas. In Dallas, new DNA technology led to the exonerations of 20 men who had been wrongfully convicted. Larry Fuller (right) served 25 years in prison before he was proven innocent by DNA testing and exonerated in 2006.

periods of time, but others point to a pattern of convictions based on eyewitness identification with little or questionable forensic evidence. Many of the wrongfully convicted were prosecuted during the administration of District Attorney Henry Wade, whose office was known for high conviction rates. Critics claimed his office prized those high conviction rates above all else.[44]

Immediately after he became Dallas County district attorney in 2007, Craig Watkins did something no other Texas district attorney had ever done; he created a Conviction Integrity Unit in his office to investigate post-conviction claims of actual innocence, to identify valid claims, and to then take appropriate action. Interestingly, with the exception of one case, every exoneration case that was investigated by the Conviction Integrity Union involved mistaken eyewitness identification. At some point before their trial testimony, each eyewitness became certain that the innocent man was the criminal. In most cases, the innocent man was in the photo spread or the police lineup even though there was no specific reason to believe that he was the criminal. Being wrongly chosen in the lineup or photo spread by the eyewitness became the evidence against the innocent man. In many cases that was the only evidence against the innocent man, and in every case it was the most compelling evidence against him. That has led to a suggestion that there needs to be some minimum threshold of probability that those displayed in the photo spread or the lineup actually committed the crime. Additionally, it has been suggested that pretrial identification procedures be done in a way recognized by scientific best practices rather than in a haphazard, potentially unreliable way.[45] For example, with photo spreads, eyewitnesses are provided six photographs and asked if they recognize anyone in the photographs. However, sometimes those in the photographs are wearing distinguishing clothing or they are smiling or posed differently. One case examined by the Innocence Project of Texas, an organization that works on claims of innocence of those who have been imprisoned, involved a photo spread of six persons. A rape victim had told the police that the rapist was wearing a blue windbreaker. Only one person in the photo spread was wearing a blue windbreaker.

There have also been problems with the handling of evidence sent to state and local crime labs. In 2002 the Houston Police Department Crime Laboratory was closed. An independent audit of the lab's DNA section had identified enormous problems. Analysts did not know how to do their jobs, and supervisors were also incompetent. There was no quality control system and few standardized procedures. Other sections of the lab had problems as well, but the most serious were in the DNA section. Harris County sends more people to death row than any other county in America, and it had done thousands of other tests in non-death-penalty cases. All these tests were now placed in doubt. One of the first retests of the lab's work showed that a man who had been convicted of rape in 1998 at the age of 16 and had been given a 25-year sentence largely on the basis of DNA evidence was actually innocent. The problem with the lab was that as DNA technology changed, the analysts got no training in new methods, were overworked, and were following procedures inconsistently. Additionally, the lab was never inspected by an outside agency and did not seek accreditation. Nor were judges, prosecutors, and defense attorneys able to spot the lab's sloppy work—they had not kept up with DNA technology either. The lab's facilities were not conducive to good forensic science. The roof leaked over the DNA section of the crime lab, and the leaks were never patched. In 2001, when Tropical Storm Allison hit Houston, water poured through the roof, and DNA evidence in three dozen murder and rape cases was soaked. Bloody water was seen seeping out of evidence boxes.[46] DNA is often seen as the definitive proof of guilt or innocence in many serious crimes, but it is hardly definitive when the facilities are defective and the analysts are incompetent.

Another area of concern is the use of dog scent evidence to convict persons accused of crimes. Some prosecutors have claimed this evidence is as powerful as DNA evidence in supporting a conviction. This technique does not involve following a scent or picking out a package of drugs by trained dogs. Instead, it involves distinguishing different odors among people, identifying one odor, and then matching that odor to evidence obtained from a crime scene. A dog will be introduced to a scent sample collected at a crime scene. It will then be presented with a series of containers with similar scents—one taken from a suspect and others taken from other people matching the general description of the suspect. The dog will communicate to its handler if the first scent matches one of the scents in the containers. The handler will then testify that the dog accurately picked out the scent of a particular person or suspect. It is called a "scent lineup" and it has become a prosecution tool in Texas. The problem is that scent lineups are not reliable scientific evidence. Though some prosecutors in Texas have used them since the mid-1990s, defense lawyers have only recently successfully challenged them. The result is that the Innocence Project of Texas is now trying to identify persons in Texas who were convicted on the basis of scent lineups in the belief that this evidence is invalid and that those prisoners can be exonerated.[47]

The Willingham Case The case of Cameron Todd Willingham raises serious questions about whether questionable evidence led to the execution of an innocent man for the arson murders of his three children. In 1991, Willingham's three girls were killed in a fire at their home shortly before Christmas. Willingham was convicted of starting the fire that killed them. Even though he was offered a plea bargain of a life sentence, he refused the plea, claiming that he was innocent. Willingham was executed in 2004. His conviction was largely based on expert testimony that the fire was arson. To a great extent, that testimony was based on the opinion that the fire had burned so hot that a fire accelerant must have been used to start the fire.

Additionally, forensic tests had found evidence of an accelerant on the front porch of the house. However, before Willingham was executed, a noted arson expert examined the case and prepared a report that showed that the fire patterns that were relied upon by the forensic experts who testified for the prosecution could have occurred without the presence of an accelerant and that the prosecution experts were relying on outdated information about the behavior of fire to reach their conclusions. That report was submitted to the Board of Pardons and Paroles, but the board rejected the plea for clemency.

After Willingham's execution, reporters for the *Chicago Tribune* investigated the case and asked three fire experts to examine the evidence. They concluded that the fire was not arson. Later, the Innocence Project of Texas asked four fire experts to review the Willingham case. They all agreed that the fire was not arson.

In 2005, Texas created a commission, the Texas Forensic Science Commission, to investigate claims of error or misconduct by forensic scientists. A fire scientist was hired by the commission to investigate the Willingham case and he too concluded there was no evidence that the fire was arson.[48] In September 2009, 48 hours prior to the review of the report by the Texas Forensic Science Commission, Governor Perry replaced the head of the commission and two of its members. The meeting of the commission was canceled as a result. Earlier, Governor Perry had expressed confidence in Willingham's guilt, called the critics of the original arson investigation "supposed experts," and said that he had not "seen anything that would cause me to think that the decision [to execute Willingham] was not correct."[49] The commission, however, did not drop the Willingham case, which remained under their review.

In July 2011, Attorney General Greg Abbott issued a ruling that restricted the further investigation of the Willingham case after a new commission chair showed greater interest in investigating the case. Nevertheless, cases of persons now in prison on arson charges are being reviewed by the Innocence Project to determine if their imprisonment was due to bad arson science.[50]

The Tulia Drug Arrests Other widely publicized matters have also contributed to the questions raised about the adequacy of the Texas criminal justice system in protecting the innocent. One of those matters in particular became a national scandal—drug arrests in 1999 in Tulia, Texas. An undercover narcotics officer was responsible for the arrests of 47 persons in Tulia; 38 of them were black and made up about 20 percent of the black adults in the town. The defendants were zealously prosecuted. Though they were charged with possessing only small amounts of cocaine, the defendants, including those with no prior records, received long sentences—including one as long as 361 years. The undercover officer was supported by local authorities even as questions about his veracity mounted, and he was even named Officer of the Year in Texas. Doubts about the arrests and convictions, however, did not die. The officer never wore a wire, never videotaped his alleged drug buys, and was never observed by another officer. Indeed, most of his alleged drug buys had no corroboration at all.

Two and a half years after the last trials of the Tulia defendants, the undercover officer had been fired from two later narcotics assignments. It became clear that he had no undercover narcotics experience prior to coming to Tulia and that he had left jobs as a deputy sheriff in two other towns, leaving behind significant unpaid debts. One of the sheriffs who had employed him had filed criminal charges against him, which meant that he was indicted while working undercover in Tulia. Accusations were also made against him that he had racist attitudes as well as difficulties with telling the truth.

It eventually became clear that the Tulia drug busts were a massive miscarriage of justice. Thirty-five of the 47 defendants were pardoned by the governor; 9 had their charges dismissed prior to trial or were placed on deferred adjudication. One was a juvenile at the time of his alleged crime and so will not have an adult criminal record. The remaining two were sent to prison on probation violations. The disturbing factor is that without the efforts of a small number of concerned citizens, lawyers, and the press, this gross abuse of the criminal justice process would have remained undetected and unresolved.[51]

Nor was the Tulia affair the only major problem with drug arrests. In 2001 the Dallas Police Department agreed to pay an informant $1,000 per kilogram of confiscated drugs. Although the informant did know actual drug dealers, he realized they were dangerous, so he found harmless persons—Mexican immigrants and legal residents—on whom he could plant drugs. Apparently the informant also realized he could make more money with less risk if he passed off gypsum as cocaine. (Gypsum is a substance found in billiard-cue chalk.) Convictions on dozens of drug cases were obtained without even testing to see if the seized material contained real drugs. The informant was the Dallas Police Department's highest paid in 2001, earning more than $210,000 for the seizure of nearly 1,000 pounds of cocaine and amphetamines that turned out to be fake drugs. Twenty fake drug cases were multi-kilo seizures, and two were the largest busts in the history of the Dallas police. Yet nothing seemed to arouse the suspicions of the police about the arrests. This scandal reached deep into the police department, where there was a lack of supervision of undercover officers and an extreme push for numbers in terms of amounts of drugs seized and number of arrests. The implausibility of some of the arrests is amazing: a lone mechanic working under his car, with no guns or cash seized; a drug buy on credit, according to the uncorroborated word of a confidential informant; and a seizure of 25 kilos of fake cocaine, for example. Nor did the district attorney's office escape blame: its policy was not to test seized drugs unless plea bargains failed and a case went to trial. When more than 80 of the drug cases were dismissed, Dallas district attorney Bill Hill went on television and insisted that many of those who were released were guilty. Were it not for the efforts of some criminal defense attorneys who were suspicious of the drug seizures, the Dallas Police Department might well still be seizing huge quantities of gypsum and paying its informant and Texas might be sending innocent men and women to prison.[52]

The Graves Case The case of Anthony Graves is one of the most disturbing incidents in the Texas criminal justice system. Graves was imprisoned in 1992 for a horrific murder of a family in Somerville, Texas. Texas Rangers quickly identified a suspect, Robert Carter, who implicated Anthony Graves. However, Carter's statement was badly flawed; the Rangers did not seek to determine the veracity of the statement. Graves was arrested based solely on the word of Robert Carter. Graves had witnesses who placed him elsewhere and Carter recanted his statement. Snitches at the jail then claimed Graves confessed, though their claims were flimsy.

The Burleson County district attorney withheld evidence from the defense that Carter had claimed to have committed the murders himself. The district attorney also made a deal with Carter that Carter would not be questioned about his wife's involvement if he testified. Carter implicated Graves at trial, though he later recanted. Graves got the death penalty.

In 2000 the district attorney appeared on a television show about capital punishment and admitted that before Carter had taken the stand, Carter had recanted.

Does Texas's criminal justice system need to be reformed? Some observers feel that, beyond problems with wrongful convictions, the emphasis on imprisonment and the large number of inmates in Texas is a concern.

It is a gross violation for a prosecutor to withhold such evidence from the defense. Graves was granted a new trial. This time the prosecution was handled by a special prosecutor from Harris County who was known as one of that county's most aggressive prosecutors. That prosecutor found no credible evidence that implicated Graves. The special prosecutor squarely placed the blame on the former Burleson County district attorney, saying Graves's trial had been a "travesty." Graves was finally released in 2010.[53]

Reforms

Consider recent proposals to improve Texas's criminal justice system

Improvements in the Texas criminal justice system have occurred. Texas is no longer handling its crime problem solely by incarceration. The number of drug treatment programs has increased and there is greater emphasis on imprisonment as a last response to criminal behavior and more emphasis on community supervision such as requiring increased reporting to probation officers, community service, electronic monitoring of offenders, or mandatory treatment for alcohol or drug addiction as a first response. Parole supervision costs $4 a day for a prisoner as opposed to about $50 a day for incarceration. Probation costs are about 10 percent the cost of prison.[54] The result has been a decline in prison construction and even the beginning of prison closings. Efforts are being made to compensate those who are wrongfully convicted. Texas has one of the most generous compensation systems in the nation for the wrongfully convicted. If a wrongfully convicted person waives his or her right to sue the state and is not convicted of further felonies after exoneration, he or she will receive a lump sum payment of $80,000 for each year wrongfully served in prison as well as an additional yearly payment during his or her lifetime that can amount to as much as $80,000 per year. Some police departments are modifying their procedures for obtaining eyewitness evidence. For example, the Dallas Police Department has changed the way lineups are conducted so that the police officer administering the photographic lineup does not know who the actual suspect is, thus avoiding the police officer providing cues to the witness as to which photo to pick. Additionally, photos are now shown by the Dallas police sequentially rather than as a group. Research has shown that this helps prevent witnesses from comparing the photos and choosing the photo that most closely resembles the suspect rather than picking the suspect's picture. Finally, some Texas district attorneys, most notably the district attorneys in Dallas and Harris Counties, have recognized the problem of wrongful conviction and have appointed prosecutors who review claims of wrongful convictions and who take a cooperative approach toward lawyers working with various innocence projects that exist to provide legal representation to people who claim they have been wrongfully convicted.

● Thinking Critically about Criminal Justice in Texas

Perhaps the criminal justice system in Texas works well. Overall, the previous examples may be exceptions to the rule. However, the documented problems with evidence, the Willingham case, the Tulia drug arrests, the Anthony Graves case, and the Michael Morton case discussed in the introduction to this chapter do raise questions about whether the criminal justice system in Texas is working as well as it should.

One of the issues facing Texas is the fairness of the process toward those accused of crime. Will Texas, for example, decide that there needs to be greater quality in the representation of people accused of crime so that the problems in the system can be identified and resolved before a person is convicted and imprisoned for a lengthy period? Dallas County district attorney Craig Watkins has received national acclaim by offering a new perspective on the role of a district attorney. Watkins sees the role of a prosecutor as not only convicting the guilty, but also as protecting the innocent charged with crime.

Texas is recognizing that the cost of imprisoning offenders is enormous and that there are alternatives to prison, especially for nonviolent offenders. The issue of the future will be whether Texas will continue pursuing alternatives to prison for offenders. On a related note, the death penalty has declined in its imposition in Texas. Will that pattern continue with urban counties reducing the imposition of the death penalty and with life without parole being increasingly seen as a reasonable alternative punishment? Finally, many states are reducing the penalties for some crimes such as possession of small amounts of marijuana. Will Texas join the national movement toward decriminalization? Crime and corrections have always been a major issue in Texas politics, and we may be on the cusp of major changes in this area.

study guide

(S) **Practice online with:** Chapter 10 Diagnostic Quiz ▪ Chapter 10 Key Term Flashcards

Categorizing Crime in Texas

■ **Identify the major classifications of crime under Texas law and the types of punishments that may be imposed (pp. 281–83)**

Crimes are categorized along a number of dimensions. The most serious crimes are felonies. The less serious crimes are misdemeanors. Within each classification are various degrees of crime based upon the severity of the offenses. The more serious the crime, the greater are the penalties.

Key Terms

felony (p. 281)

misdemeanor (p. 282)

probation (p. 282)

parole (p. 282)

"three strikes" provision (p. 283)

Practice Quiz

1. The most serious crimes are classified as *(p. 281)*
   a) felonies.
   b) misdemeanors.
   c) trial-eligible crimes.
   d) grand jury felonies.
   e) county court-at-law crimes.

2. Probation refers to *(p. 282)*
   a) a judge's initial term in office.
   b) a suspension of the jail or prison sentence.
   c) a court in the local state court system.
   d) release into the community after time in prison.
   e) failure to pay bail.

3. Which of the following is true? *(p. 283)*
   a) Parole is granted by the governor.
   b) Members of the Texas Board of Pardons and Paroles are elected by the legislature every two years.
   c) People convicted of capital crimes are not eligible for parole.
   d) The death penalty is required in all serious felonies.
   e) Texas does not enhance the sentence of repeat felony offenders.

The Criminal Justice Process

■ **Outline the procedural steps that occur after a person is arrested (pp. 283–88)**

There are a number of stages in the criminal justice process, including arrest, arraignment, possible posting of bail, possible grand jury indictment, pre-trial hearings, and either plea bargaining or trial. If a person is found guilty, he or she will be sentenced, after which there may be appeals. Within this process, the most important actor is probably the district attorney who is the key decision maker with regard to charging a suspect, presenting evidence to a grand jury, plea bargaining or recommending a sentence to a jury or judge.

Key Terms

bail (p. 284)

grand jury (p. 284)

county attorney (p. 286)

district attorney (p. 286)

plea bargain (p. 287)

Practice Quiz

4. Grand juries *(p. 284)*
   a) review all decisions made by a trial judge.
   b) determine if witnesses are telling the truth by voting "True bills" or "False bills."
   c) determine if there is probable cause to prosecute an individual for a crime.
   d) hear trials involving the death penalty.
   e) hear trials in district court.

5. District attorneys may have the most important roles in the criminal justice process because *(pp. 287–88)*
   a) they have the power to charge people with crimes.
   b) they have the power to plea-bargain with defendants.
   c) they usually make the only presentation before grand juries.
   d) all of the above.
   e) none of the above.

6. Which of the following statements about plea bargaining is true? *(p. 287)*
   a) Plea bargaining threatens to overwhelm the limited resources of a prosecutor's office.
   b) Plea bargaining does not benefit defendants.
   c) Plea bargains are made by defendants with district attorneys and agreed to by a judge.
   d) All are true.
   e) None are true.

Crime, Corrections and the Texas Prison System

■ **Describe prisons and corrections policy in Texas (pp. 289–99)**

The Texas prison system is one of the largest in the nation. A major federal court decision (*Ruiz v. Estelle*) found serious overcrowding in the prison system. A series of reforms have been implemented to address the concerns raised by the decision. There has been an effort to lessen the number of people in prison through community supervision. While Texas remains the death penalty capital of the United States, fewer death penalties have been imposed recently than in earlier years.

Practice Quiz

7. The Texas prison system *(pp. 289–94)*
   a) was vastly affected by a federal court decision, *Ruiz v. Estelle*, that declared that the overcrowded system was unconstitutional.
   b) holds mostly persons convicted of violent crimes.
   c) is a very costly way of dealing with crime as opposed to community supervision such as drug and alcohol programs and probation and parole.
   d) is beginning to contract in size after a long period of expansion.
   e) All of the above are true of the Texas prison system.

8. The Texas Department of Criminal Justice in Texas *(p. 290)*
   a) is run by a nine-member board appointed by the governor.
   b) is run by an elected body.
   c) runs the court system for felony murder.
   d) establishes sentencing guidelines for crimes.
   e) grants probation to those convicted of crimes.

9. The death penalty *(p. 298)*
   a) is imposed in Texas for all murders.
   b) has been imposed less frequently since Texas allowed juries to sentence a defendant to life without parole.
   c) is carried out in county where the crime occurred.
   d) is carried out with an electric chair.
   e) cannot be carried out without approval by the Texas Board of Pardons and Parole.

 Practice Online
"Exploring Texas Politics" exercise: *Crime and Corrections Policy*

The Integrity of the Texas Criminal Justice System

 Explain why Texas's criminal justice system is often controversial (pp. 299–304)

Texas has had a significant number of people who have been wrongfully convicted. Numerous recent cases in which convictions were overturned have raised questions about the criminal justice system in Texas.

Practice Quiz

10. People have been wrongfully convicted in Texas because of *(pp. 299–304)*
    a) police misconduct.
    b) bad or outdated forensic science.
    c) mistaken identifications.
    d) prosecutorial misconduct.
    e) all of the above reasons.

11. An advance in which technology has conclusively proved the innocence of a large number of convicted people is *(p. 299)*
    a) drug testing.
    b) ballistics testing.
    c) DNA analysis.
    d) fire science.
    e) fingerprinting.

Reforms

 Consider recent proposals to improve Texas's criminal justice system (pp. 304–5)

Recent reforms that have been enacted may help reduce the number of wrongful convictions in Texas and improve the fairness of the criminal justice system. Reforms also may rely more on rehabilitation programs and less on incarceration as a solution to crime.

Practice Quiz

12. Reforms in the criminal justice process include *(pp. 304–5)*
    a) financial compensation for people wrongfully convicted.
    b) changes to suspect line-ups so that the police officer in charge of the line-up does not know who the actual suspect is.
    c) expanding drug treatment programs.
    d) showing photos in photo identifications to witnesses sequentially rather than at the same time to reduce the danger of witnesses comparing photos and choosing the one that best fits their memory of the assailant.
    e) All of the above are reforms to the criminal justice process.

13. Probation costs are *(p. 304)*
    a) about 10 percent the cost of prison.
    b) 10 percent higher than the cost of prison.
    c) the same as the cost of prison.
    d) half the cost of prison.
    e) double the cost of prison.

Recommended Websites

Texas Criminal Justice Coalition
criminaljusticecoalition.org

Texas Department of Criminal Justice
tdcj.state.tx.us

Texas Coalition to Abolish the Death Penalty
tcadp.org

The Stand Down Texas Project
standdown.typepad.com/weblog/

Innocence Project
innocenceproject.org

In 2010 students at UT Austin protested against cuts in education spending and increases in tuition costs. As lawmakers work to balance the state budget, the decisions they make about taxes and spending affect all Texans.

Public Finance in Texas

WHAT GOVERNMENT DOES AND WHY IT MATTERS For college students, the state budget might appear to be pretty far removed from everyday life. Decisions made in Austin every two years may seem to have little to do with attending class, preparing for an exam, or getting everything in order for a timely graduation. But like it or not, the budgetary decisions made by legislators every two years affect students where it matters most: in the pocketbook.

In 2003, state political leaders found themselves staring at a $10 billion shortfall in the upcoming budget period. Mandated by the state constitution to maintain a balanced budget, they needed to find new and creative ways to close the budget gap without raising taxes. One method was to cut higher education funding.

Prior to 2003, tuition and fee rates for state universities had been set by the state legislature, and in Texas they tended to be low, particularly when compared to those in other states. Costs ranged from $2,870 per year at Texas A&M at Texarkana to $4,912 per year at the University of Texas at Austin. The average statewide cost was $4,064 per year. General revenues funded a large portion of the state university's education budget. In 2003, as a trade-off for a 2 percent cut in the higher education budget, the legislature gave the regents of the various state schools the authority to raise tuition to make up the difference.[1]

Tuition costs skyrocketed across the country in the first decade of the twenty-first century. Labor-intensive instruction and other high fixed expenditures fueled these increases. Texas higher education was not spared these inflationary pressures. Granted the discretion to increase tuition and fees by the legislature, universities across the state lined up to solve their own budget problems by raising tuition and fees on their students. Tuition and fees for Texas A&M at Texarkana rose 71 percent between 2003 and 2011 to $5,204 per year. At the University of Texas (UT) at Austin, they rose 80 percent to $9,796 per year, and at the University of Texas at Dallas, they rose 110 percent from $5,244 per year to $11,014 per year. Overall, the average cost of attending a four-year institution in Texas for a year rose 90 percent from $3,864 to $7,342. Although this was below the national average of $8,244 per year for an in-state public institution, higher education had become an expensive commodity in Texas.[2]

In response to the budget crisis of 2011, cuts in higher education were again made and pressures to increase tuition at most state institutions continued unabated.[3] The president of UT Austin had been locked in a struggle with the UT System Board of Regents over micromanaging higher education on a variety of issues in 2011. This conflict spilled over in the debate over how much students should pay to attend the university. While accepting the proposals from most member schools for increases in tuition and fees between 2 and 4 percent for the next budgetary period, the Board of Regents, all of whom were appointed by Governor Perry, turned down a UT Austin proposal to increase tuition for in-state undergraduates by 2.6 percent. To offset some of the lost revenues, the board allocated $6.6 million to UT Austin for the next two years out of the state's Permanent University Fund. But a clear message was being sent to the universities: the board was not in the business of rubber-stamping universities' requests for higher tuition and fees. Like the decisions about the state budget facing legislators in Austin, tuition and fees decisions faced by university boards of regents were becoming deeply political.[4]

chaptergoals

- Explain the purpose of the state budget and what is typically included (pages 313–14)

- Describe the general pattern of state spending in Texas and where state revenue comes from (pages 314–24)

- Describe how the money in the budget is organized into specific funds (pages 324–27)

- Outline the constitutional provisions that affect how the state budget is made (pages 327–30)

- Identify the major steps and players in making the state budget (pages 330–33)

- Analyze major budget crises in Texas (pages 333–37)

What Is the Budget?

One of the most distinguishing characteristics about public finance in Texas is that the state constitution mandates that the legislature operate within a "balanced budget." On its face, the idea of a balanced budget is straightforward. A budget, according to *Webster's Dictionary*, is an "estimate of future financial income and outgo." A balanced budget would exist whenever the projected income from tax revenues is equal to or exceeds the projected expenditure. But public finance is a complicated business and the devil is in the details. There are actually a number of different ways to talk about the funds that constitute the "budget." One way to look at them is to divide them into the following five broad budgetary categories.

- The **General Revenues Fund budget** is a nondedicated revenue account and is the state's primary operating fund. It is the place where most state taxes and fees flow. It also includes three educational funds (the Available School Fund, the State Textbook Fund, and the Foundation School Fund). Expenditures may be made directly from the nondedicated funds and may be transferred to special funds or accounts for allocation.

- The **General Revenue–Dedicated Funds budget** includes funds dedicated to specific purposes. In 1991, 200 special funds were brought into the General Revenue–Dedicated Funds Account as part of a budget reform and consolidation package. These include such funds as the State Parks Account and the college operating accounts (which hold tuition funds). Generally speaking, the legislature can appropriate money from these accounts only for their dedicated purposes.

- The **Federal Funds budget** includes all grants, payments, or reimbursements received from the federal government by state agencies and institutions.

- The **Other Funds budget** consists of all other funds flowing into the state treasury not included in the other methods of financing. These include, among other funds, the State Highway Fund, trust funds, and revenue held in certain local higher education accounts.

- The **All Funds budget** is the aggregate of all of the above budgets, referring to all spending that goes through agencies, including federal and state programs.

Appropriations from these funds for the period 2012–13 are shown in Table 11.1.

Some important things must be noted about this complicated system of public financing through these various budgets. First, the state budget involves huge amounts of money. For the 2012–13 biennium, more than $55.4 billion was appropriated for Health and Human Services activities (encompassing the Medicaid and Temporary Assistance for Needy Families programs). There were $72.9 billion appropriated for education, including $50.8 billion for public education and $22.1 billion for higher education, and $23.7 billion appropriated for business and economic development. Second, much of this money lies outside the direct control of the legislature. Trust funds and other dedicated funds exist for particular purposes and are hard to manipulate for other budgetary purposes. Legislators seeking to balance the budget are often left with relatively few places to cut expenditures. Given its large proportion of the General Revenues Fund budget, education is often at the top of the list. Third, federal expenditures have a very important

General Revenues Fund budget a budget for a nondedicated revenue account that functions as the state's primary operating fund

General Revenue–Dedicated Funds budget a budget composed of funds for dedicated revenues that target money for specific purposes

Federal Funds budget a state budget that includes all grants, payments, or reimbursements received from the federal government by state agencies and institutions

Other Funds budget a budget consisting of all other funds flowing into the state treasury that are not included in other state budgets. This includes the Texas Highway Fund, various trust funds operated by the state, and certain revenues held for local higher education accounts.

All Funds budget the budget that aggregates all monies flowing into the state treasury and all state spending

TABLE 11.1

Texas Budgetary Funds Appropriated, 2012–13 (in billions of dollars)

General Revenue Fund budget:	$81.290
General Revenue-Dedicated Funds budget:	$6.380
Federal Funds budget:	$54.661
Other Funds budget:	$31.153
All Funds budget:	$173.484

SOURCES: Legislative Budget Board, *Fiscal Size-Up: 2012–13 Biennium*, January 2012.

role in shaping the overall direction of the state budget. The bulk of federal funds expenditures is in two areas: health and human services, and education. Strings are often attached to these monies. If legislators want federal dollars, they must spend state dollars first. Figure 11.1 highlights the increasingly important role that federal dollars have played in spending patterns in Texas. Unadjusted expenditures from General Revenue Funds (state funds) have increased modestly between 1992–93 and 2012–13. But expenditures from the All Funds budget (which takes into account federal spending) have exploded during the same period. The pressure to maximize federal dollars flowing into Texas is often in opposition to legislators' desires to minimize state spending and not raise taxes.

Spending and Revenue in Texas

> **Describe the general pattern of state spending in Texas and where state revenue comes from**

Texas has a reputation of being a "low service, low tax" state that seeks to maintain a favorable environment for business. In this section, we will look at the general pattern of state spending in Texas, as well as taxes and other sources of revenue in the state.

Trends in State Spending

For the most part, Texas's reputation as a low-spending state is well earned.[5] On a variety of measures, Texas spends less than other states. Among the 50 states, Texas ranked 47th on per capita state government expenditures. Texas spending of $4,468 per person was far below the U.S. average of $5,950. On a per capita basis, Texas ranks 33rd in educational spending, 44th in highway spending, 25th in hospital spending, and 44th in public welfare spending.[6] Texas also ranked low when compared to other states on the per capita federal dollars flowing into the state. In 2009, Texas took in $9,164 per capita from the federal government, ranking it 42nd among the states, well below the national state average of $10,396.[7]

The trend in overall spending reveals a similar story, particularly in recent years. As Figure 11.1 shows, in unadjusted dollars (that is, dollars spent not tak-

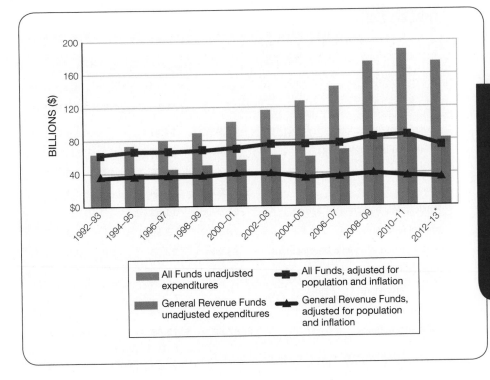

FIGURE 11.1

Trends in State Government Expenditures, 1992–93 to 2012–13 Biennia

*Appropriated

SOURCE: Legislative Budget Board, Comptroller of Public Accounts.

ing into account inflation or population increases), spending in Texas rose from $34.855 billion in the 1992–93 biennium to $81.290 billion in the 2012–13 biennium. However, in real per capita dollars (that is, dollars spent controlling for inflation and population increases), state spending actually fell from $34.855 billion to $33.944 billion.

When considering state and federal spending in Texas together (see the All Funds State Budget in Figure 11.1), the story is a little bit different. Unadjusted spending for all funds (state and federal) in Texas rose from $62.784 billion in 1992–93 to $173.484 billion in 2012–13. But in real per capita dollars, spending in the same periods rose from $62.784 billion to $72.440 billion. In other words, between the 1992–93 budget and the 2012–13 budget, federal real per capita spending increased in Texas by 15.4 percent while state real per capita spending declined by 2.6 percent.

The number of workers employed by Texas was smaller than that of many other states. In 2009, there were 126 state employees for every 10,000 people living in Texas. This figure was far below the U.S. state average of 142 state employees for every 10,000 state residents, ranking Texas 44th among the 50 states. Interestingly, though, Texas ranked only a little behind New York at 41st with 130 state employees per 10,000 people, and ahead of California at 46th with 110 state employees per 10,000 people.[8]

Revenue in Texas

Spending and size of government are only part of Texas's "low service, low tax" reputation. The taxes that fund government are the other dimension. And once again, Texas's reputation is well earned. Texas is one of nine states that still do not have a personal income tax. There is a high sales tax in Texas of 6.25 percent,

TABLE 11.2

Summary of All Funds State Budget Allocation by Biennium (in billions of dollars)

	2011–12	2012–13	PERCENT CHANGE
Governmental functions	$5.03	$4.47	−11.1%
Health and human services	65.46	55.43	−15.3
Education	76.42	72.87	−4.6
Judiciary	0.67	0.64	−4.4
Public safety and criminal Justice	12.07	11.51	−4.7
Natural resources	3.56	3.89	9.2
Business and economic Development	23.20	23.66	2.0
Regulatory	0.74	0.68	−7.9
General provisions	0	0	0
Legislature	.37	.34	−7.9
Total all functions	**$187.52**	**$173.48**	**−7.5%**

SOURCES: Legislative Budget Board, *Fiscal Size-Up 2012–13*, p. 6.

the tenth highest in the nation. Combined state and local sales taxes in the state can reach 8.25 percent.[9] State sales taxes per capita in 2007 were $1,704, ranking Texas 48th among the 50 states.

Although Texas state taxes are low compared with other states' taxes, local taxes are a different story. In 2008, Texas ranked 17th among the states in terms

After the legislature passes the biennial state budget, the state comptroller certifies the budget, confirming that it is within current revenue estimates for the period. Here, State Comptroller Susan Combs discusses the 2012–13 budget.

of property taxes paid per capita, at $1,393. When state and local taxes are taken together, however, Texas remains a low-tax state. Combined state and local taxes were $3,197 per capita in 2009, ranking Texas 45th in the nation. A 2011 study conducted by the Tax Foundation concluded that Texas had the 13th most business-friendly tax system.[10]

Government and public policy in Texas are funded from a variety of sources, including sales tax, severance taxes on oil and natural gas produced in the state, licensing income, interest and dividends, and federal aid (Table 11.3). In 2012–13, 44.1 percent of state revenues are expected to come from taxes of one sort or another. Many of these taxes are based on complex formulas. People often are unaware that they are paying them. But they are important sources of state revenue.

Sales and Use Tax The most important single tax financing Texas government is the sales tax. Today, the sales tax in Texas is 6.25 percent of the retail sales price of tangible personal property and selected services. Together county, city, and metropolitan transit authorities are allowed to impose an additional 2 percent sales and use tax. For the 2012–13 biennium, the sales and use tax is expected to account for 56.3 percent of the total tax collections in the state.[11]

Oil Production and Regulation Taxes The oil severance tax is 4.6 percent of the market value of oil produced in the state. The tax income from oil production fluctuates with the price of oil and the volume of oil produced in Texas. For 2010, the average price of oil per barrel was $72.75, and Texas produced 324.8 million barrels. In 2011, the average price was $87.85 per barrel, and Texas produced 377.7 million barrels. Revenues produced by the oil severance tax increased to $2.48 billion in the 2010–11 biennium and are projected to be about $2.9 billion for 2012–13. In the past 30 years, the percent that oil production taxes have contributed to total state revenue has varied considerably, from less than 1 percent to over 5 percent.

TABLE 11.3

State Revenue Biennial Comparison, by Source, 2010–11 and 2012–13 Biennia (in billions of dollars)

REVENUE	2010–11	2012–13	PERCENT CHANGE
Tax collections	$74.2251	$80.5761	8.6%
Federal receipts	75.2871	71.2478	−5.4
Fees, fines, licenses, and penalties	14.7395	14.9873	1.7
Interest and investment income	2.0932	1.7990	−14.1
Lottery	3.3094	3.3908	2.5
Land income	2.2224	1.4087	−36.6
Other revenue sources	9.7514	9.6821	−0.7
Total net revenue	**$181.6281**	**$183.0917**	**0.8**

SOURCES: Texas legislative Budget Board, Fiscal Size-Up 2012–13 biennium.

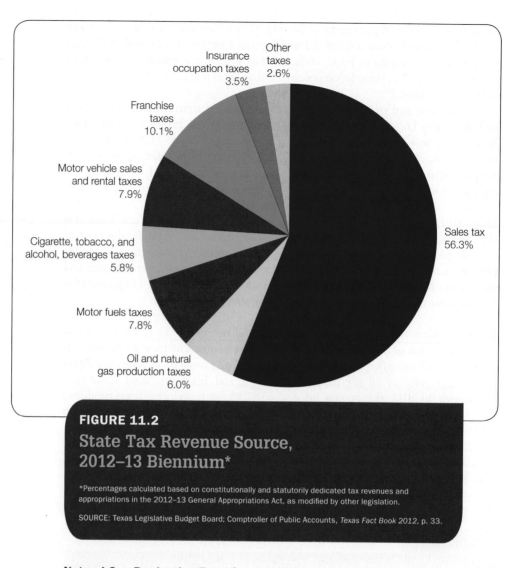

FIGURE 11.2

State Tax Revenue Source, 2012–13 Biennium*

*Percentages calculated based on constitutionally and statutorily dedicated tax revenues and appropriations in the 2012–13 General Appropriations Act, as modified by other legislation.

SOURCE: Texas Legislative Budget Board; Comptroller of Public Accounts, *Texas Fact Book 2012*, p. 33.

Natural Gas Production Tax There is a 7.5 percent tax on the market value of all natural gas produced in the state. As with the oil tax, the tax raised from natural gas depends on the price and the amount produced. Revenues from natural gas fell significantly from $734 million, or 6.9 percent of state revenues in 1980 to $489 million, or a little more than 1 percent of state revenues in 1997. Prices rose to $3.96 per thousand cubic feet in 2010 and $4.13 per thousand cubic feet in 2011. For the 2010–11 biennium, $1.84 billion flowed into the state treasury from the natural gas tax, and that amount is projected to increase to $2.29 billion in the 2012–13 biennium.

Motor Fuels Tax The motor fuels tax in Texas is 20 cents per gallon of gasoline and diesel fuel. There is a 15 cents per gallon tax on liquefied gas. In 2012–13, the motor fuels tax is projected to generate approximately $6.3 billion, or 7.8 percent of all state revenues.

Motor Vehicle Sales and Rentals and Manufactured Home Sales Tax There is a 6.25 percent tax on the sales price of all motor vehicles in the state. There is also a 10 percent tax on all rental vehicles up to 35 days and 6.25 percent thereafter.

The state of Texas collects a tax of 20 cents per gallon on motor fuels. The federal government collects an additional 18.4 cents per gallon, but Texans still pay less tax on gasoline than residents of some other states.

Newly manufactured homes are also taxed at 5 percent of 65 percent of the sales price. Because of the effects of the economic slowdown brought on by the Great Recession , motor vehicle sales and rental taxes declined by 5.6 percent in the 2010–11 biennium to $5.6 billion. More favorable projections for 2012–13 anticipate a 13 percent increase, which would result in $6.4 billion in tax revenues.

Corporate Franchise Tax The so-called franchise tax is imposed on all corporations in Texas. Prior to 2008, the tax was imposed on taxable capital and on earned surplus. Under changes put into place in 2006, the franchise tax became a "margins tax" based on the "taxable margin." The "taxable margin" is the lesser value derived from one of three methods of calculation: (1) 70 percent of total revenue, (2) total revenue minus cost of goods sold, or (3) total revenue minus total compensation and benefits. The goals of the legislature in reworking the franchise tax were to make it more difficult for corporations to escape the tax and to offset some of the costs of property tax reform. There were some serious miscalculations, however, as we will discuss later, and the taxes generated were far less than expected. The $4.4 billion generated in 2009 was almost 30 percent less than originally forecast. For the 2012–13 biennium, tax receipts from the franchise tax are anticipated to rise to $8.1 billion.

Tobacco Taxes Texas imposes a variety of taxes on cigarettes and tobacco products. For example, every pack of 20 cigarettes has a $1.41 tax per pack and every pack of 25 cigarettes has a $1.76 tax per pack included in the purchase price. The tax on tobacco products like cigars, snuff, chewing tobacco, and smoking tobacco is based on the manufacturer's listed net weight. This tax rose from $1.00 per ounce in 2012 to $1.22 in 2013. Approximately 88 percent of tobacco taxes are derived from cigarette sales, the remainder from other tobacco products. Revenues from these taxes are expected to total $2.8 billion for the 2012–13 biennium, a decrease of 3.7 percent from 2011–12.

Like the franchise tax reforms, increases in the tobacco taxes passed in 2006 were linked to property tax relief (see the following discussion). Tax revenues generated by the tax rate in place before 2007 go directly into the General Revenues

Fund. The excess above this amount goes into the Property Tax Relief Fund. A portion of the other tax increase on tobacco products put into effect in 2007 goes to a Physician Education Loan Repayment program. The remainder of the excess goes into the Property Tax Relief Fund.[12]

Alcoholic Beverage Taxes As with tobacco, a variety of taxes are imposed on alcoholic beverages. For example, beer is taxed at the rate of $6.00 per 31-gallon barrel. Liquor is taxed at the rate of $2.40 per gallon. Mixed drinks are taxed at 14 percent of gross receipts. This tax took in $1.7 billion in the 2011–12 biennium and is expected to generate over $1.8 billion in 2012–13.

Insurance Occupation Taxes A complex schedule of tax rates is applied to insurance premiums. For example, life, health, and accident insurance is taxed at the rate of 1.75 percent on gross premium receipts. In 2012–13, insurance premium taxes are expected to be $2.9 billion, up from $2.7 billion in 2010–12.

Utility Taxes There is a tax of one-sixth of 1 percent on the gross receipts of public utilities. For gas, electric, and water utilities there is a tax on gross receipts ranging from .581 percent in towns of fewer than 2,500 people to 1.07 percent in cities of between 2,500 and 9,999 people to 1.997 percent in cities of 10,000 or more. There is also a tax on gas utility administration of one-half of 1 percent of the gross income of gas utilities. In 2012–13, $972.8 billion is expected to be raised by utility taxes, up from $936.5 million in 2010–11.

Hotel and Motel Tax This state tax is 6 percent of the hotel and motel occupancy bill paid by the occupant. It is expected to generate $748 million in the 2012–13 biennium.

Inheritance Tax Federal tax reforms in 2001 effectively eliminated the Texas inheritance tax by 2005. However, that law is scheduled to sunset (that is, it will expire) in 2012 along with other portions of the Bush tax cuts. No one in Washington or Austin knows what will happen to these tax cuts as of this writing. For the purposes of budgetary planning, the Legislative Budgeting Board (LBB) assumed that new income from inheritance taxes will be zero. Taxpayers with tax liabilities from previous bienniums, however, are expected to generate approximately $1.9 billion in revenue from the state inheritance tax.

Other Taxes. There are a small number of other taxes on such items as attorney services, cement, sulfur, coin-operated machines, and bingo rental receipts that are expected to generate $375.1 million for the 2012–13 biennium.

The Question of the Income Tax in Texas

regressive tax a type of tax where the tax burden falls more heavily on lower-income individuals

Many commentators have complained that the tax system in Texas is too **regressive**.[13] By this they mean that the tax burden in the state falls more heavily on lower-income individuals. Sales and use taxes such as those found in Texas are generally considered to be regressive. Property taxes on individuals and businesses are generally considered to be somewhat regressive. Poor homeowners and renters generally pay more of their income in property taxes than do the wealthy.

There have been occasional calls for the institution of a state income tax in Texas. Supporters argue that not only is the income tax a more reliable source

Who Pays the Highest State Taxes?

Texas has one of the lowest tax rates in the country. One reason taxes are so low in the state is that Texas is one of only nine states with no income tax on wages, as shown on the map. This keeps the overall tax rates down, but also means that the state's tax revenues come primarily from sales and property taxes. As the second chart below shows, these taxes are regressive—those with less income pay a higher share of their income in taxes; those with higher incomes pay a lower share of their income in taxes.

Top State Income Tax Rates

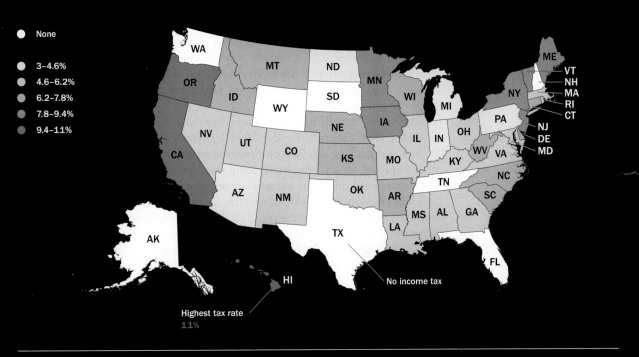

- None
- 3–4.6%
- 4.6–6.2%
- 6.2–7.8%
- 7.8–9.4%
- 9.4–11%

No income tax

Highest tax rate
11%

Taxes as a Percentage of Income in Texas

Annual Income

● Sales tax ● Property tax

< $29,233	$29,233–$52,960	$52,960–$80,882	$80,882–$126,460	> $126,460
6% $1,473	3.4% $2,177	2.9% $2,989	2.5% $4,089	1.3% $6,507
5.3% $1,273	2.9% $1,809	2.4% $2,462	2.2% $3,652	1.6% $7,555

for critical analysis

1. What are the advantages of not having an income tax in the state of Texas?

2. How would an income tax provide a method for the well-off to pay more in taxes than the poor? Where do you stand on this issue? Why?

SOURCES: The Tax Foundation, "Top Marginal State Income Tax Rates, Tax Year 2011," http://taxfoundation.org/article/map-top-marginal-state-income-tax-rates-tax-year-2011 (accessed 11/30/12).

progressive tax a type of tax where the tax burden falls more heavily on upper-income individuals

of revenue for the state, it can also be made fairer. Unlike sales and use taxes, which are applied equally to everyone whatever their income, income taxes can be made **progressive**. With a progressive income tax, people with lower income pay a lower tax rate than people with higher income. Progressive income taxes thus place a higher tax burden on the rich than on the poor. A 2009 study conducted by the Institute on Taxation and Economic Policy found that among the states Texas had the fifth most regressive tax system in the nation, behind Washington, Florida, South Dakota, and Tennessee. The study estimated that in Texas people with incomes at the bottom 20 percent paid 20 percent of their income in state and local taxes, while those with incomes in the upper 1 percent paid only 3.3 percent of their income in taxes.[14]

Few politicians have ever been willing to support an income tax. One of the attractive features of Texas to business has always been the absence of an income tax. It was not until the late 1980s and early 1990s that the first serious attempt to put a state income tax in place was undertaken. Responding to mounting budgetary pressures, the retiring lieutenant governor, Bill Hobby, came out in favor of an income tax in late 1989. Bob Bullock, Hobby's successor, announced in early 1991 that he would actively campaign for an income tax. A blue-ribbon panel chaired by former governor John Connally was charged with looking into new revenue sources for the state. The committee ended up recommending to the legislature both a corporate and a personal income tax, but not without generating an enormous amount of controversy.[15]

matching funds federal monies going to a state based on state spending for a program

Chairman Connally himself opposed the income-tax recommendations, as did Governor Ann Richards. By the 1993 legislative session, Lieutenant Governor Bullock was backing off. Bullock proposed a constitutional amendment requiring voter approval of any personal income tax. Moreover, the amendment specified that funds raised under the personal income tax be used to support public education. The amendment quickly passed the 73rd legislature and was overwhelmingly approved by voters on November 2, 1993. As this amendment effectively gave the electorate a veto over any proposal for an income tax, it is unlikely that Texans will have a personal income tax in the foreseeable future.

TABLE 11.4

Estimated State Revenue Collections, 2012–13 Biennium

Federal funds	38.9%
Sales tax	24.8%
Other receipts	16.1%
Motor vehicle sales and rental tax	3.5%
Other taxes	5.3%
Franchise tax	4.5%
Motor fuels tax	3.4%
Severance tax	2.6%
Investment income	1.0%

SOURCES: Legislative Budget Board, *Fiscal Size-Up. 2012–13 Biennium*. January 2012.

Other State Revenue

Next to taxes, the second-largest source of revenue for Texas is the federal government (see Table 11.4). Historically, Texas spends relatively little, compared with other states, for state-federal programs. As a result, the federal grants and **matching funds** (federal monies going to a state based on state spending for a program) also have been relatively low. Nevertheless, federal aid to Texas skyrocketed in the 1980s because of the expansion of transportation and human-services programs. For the 2012–13 biennium, federal funds accounted for $71.2 billion, about 38.9 percent of the total appropriations. This was down from $75.3 billion in the previous biennium. Of this amount, $31.1 billion was for Medicaid.[16]

In addition to federal monies, there are a number of other revenue sources, including interest income, licenses and fees, the sales of goods and services provided by the state, and land income. Two other sources in recent years have had a major impact on monies flowing into the state budget. A state lottery was passed by the state legislature in July 1991 and approved by the voters that November. Although the lottery was passed by voters overwhelmingly, attitudes about the appropriateness of using gambling as a source of state revenues are mixed. Some argue that the lottery unfairly takes money from people who can least afford it by fooling them into thinking that they, too, can strike it rich if only they have a little luck. Large numbers of people from all social classes continue to play the lottery. In 2009, 42 percent of Texans claimed that they had played a lottery game in the previous year. The average monthly dollar amount spent on any lottery game was $45.21. Despite the lottery's popularity, revenues generated by it are still projected to be about $3.3 billion for the 2012–13 biennium, only 1.8 percent of total state revenue.[17]

A second major source of nontax revenue is a result of the settlement the state reached with tobacco companies in January 1998. Under the settlement, Texas would receive over $17.3 billion over the next 25 years, and an additional

TABLE 11.5

Tax Collections Biennial Comparison, by Source, 2010–11 and 2012–13 Biennia (in billions of dollars)

	2010–11	2012–13	PERCENT CHANGE
Sales tax	$41.109	$45.325	10.3%
Oil production taxes	2.482	2.520	1.5
Natural gas production tax	1.835	2.290	24.8
Motor fuel taxes	6.146	6.304	2.6
Motor vehicle sales and rental taxes	5.608	6.353	13.3
Franchise tax	7.788	8.171	4.9
Cigarette and tobacco taxes	2.948	2.839	-3.7
Alcoholic beverage taxes	1.671	1.825	9.2
Insurance occupation taxes	2.674	2.854	6.7
Utility taxes	9.365	.973	3.9
Inheritance tax	.002	0.0	−100.0
Hotel occupancy tax	6.796	.748	10.0
Other taxes	3.442	.375	9.0
Total tax collections	**$74.225**	**$80.576**	**8.6%**

NOTE: Biennial change and percentage change have been calculated on actual amounts before rounding in all tables and graphics in this chapter. Totals may not sum due to rounding.
SOURCE: Comptroller of Public Accounts 2012–13 Certification Revenue Estimate, December 2011, *Texas Fact Book 2012*, p. 32.

The lottery, approved by Texas voters in 1991, generates over $1.6 billion in state revenue every year.

$580 million every year thereafter, from the tobacco industry. The largest payment—$3.3 billion—came up front, while the remainder was to be spread out over the remaining 25 years. Nationwide, states received a total of $246 billion in the final settlement reached with the tobacco industry. The Texas Comptroller's Office projects that Texas tobacco settlement receipts will total $945.1 million in 2012–13, down from the $964.6 million received in 2010–11.[18]

● State Funds

Describe how the money in the budget is organized into specific funds

Money comes into state coffers from a variety of sources and is dispersed in a wide range of activities. But money spent by the state doesn't just flow into and out of one pot. There are, in fact, 400 funds in the state treasury whose monies are directed to a wide variety of functions. Understanding how money flows into and out of these funds lies at the heart of mastering the state budget. Among the most important funds are the following.

As previously mentioned, the **General Revenues Fund** consists of two parts: nondedicated general revenue and general revenue-dedicated accounts. The nondedicated revenue is the state's primary operating fund and is the place where most state taxes and fees flow. In 1991, 200 special funds were brought into the General Revenue-Dedicated-Funds account as part of a budget reform and consolidation package. Expenditures may be made directly from the nondedicated funds and may be transferred to special funds or accounts for allocation.

General Revenues Fund the state's primary operating fund

The **Permanent School Fund (PSF)** was created in 1854 with a $2 million appropriation by the legislature to fund primary and secondary schools. The Constitution of 1876, along with subsequent acts, stipulated that certain lands and sales from these lands would constitute the PSF. The second-largest educational endowment in the country, the PSF is managed by the state board of education. The fund distributes money to school districts across the state based upon attendance and guarantees bonds issued by local school boards, enabling them to get lower interest rates in the bond markets. Over $2 billion was distributed to school districts in the 2012–13 biennium. At the end of fiscal year 2011, the fund balance was $26.9 billion.[19]

The **State Highway Fund** comes from a variety of sources, including motor vehicle registration fees, the federal highway fund, and the sales tax on motor lubricants. A significant portion of the motor fuel tax initially is deposited in the General Revenue Fund and then allocated to the State Highway Fund. The purposes of the State Highway Fund are constructing, maintaining, and policing roadways in Texas; and acquiring rights of way. Over $9.4 billion were allocated from this fund in the 2012–13 biennium, with more than 77 percent of the monies going to the Texas Department of Transportation.[20]

The **Economic Stabilization Fund (ESF)**, commonly known as the *Rainy Day Fund*, was established through constitutional amendment in 1988 to provide relief during times of financial distress. The fund is generated by a formula involving the base year of 1987. If collections from oil and gas taxes exceed the 1987 base year amount, 75 percent is transferred to the fund. Transfers are made in February by the comptroller. Half of any "unencumbered" general revenue, that is, revenue not already targeted for a specific purpose, also goes into the fund. The legislature has the authority to contribute additional funds but never has.

Few thought that large sums would accumulate in the fund. The first transfer of funds from oil and gas tax revenues of $18.5 million took place in 1990. The ESF account balance was kept below $100 million until 2001, when deposits transferred into the account exceeded $700 million. In 2003, the ESF was depleted to help solve the impending $10 billion budget shortfall. In 2003 and 2005, the legislature appropriated ESF monies to a variety of agencies, including the Teachers' Retirement System, various health and human service agencies, the governor's office, and the Texas Education Agency. Rising tax revenues from oil and gas production in the first decade of the twenty-first century flooded the ESF with funds. By the end of fiscal year 2011, the Texas Rainy Day Fund had grown to over $8.1 billion and contained more cash than similar funds in any other state. Only Alaska, also awash in oil and gas revenues, had a fund that approached that of Texas. The debate over whether or how to use the Rainy Day Fund to close the budget shortfall was a major issue during the 2011 legislative session on the 2012–13 budget.[21]

To appreciate the importance of the operations of Texas's 400 funds and the complexity that they introduce into the budgetary process, one need only look at a few funds lying at the heart of higher education. Legislative goals are met through the creation of these funds and the allocation and reallocation of funds to and from them. Some funds, such as the Permanent University Trust Fund or the Higher Education Fund, were established to channel money directly to certain institutions of higher education. Others, like the National Research University Fund, operate in order to encourage universities to behave in certain ways and to achieve a specific set of legislative objectives.

The **Permanent University Trust Fund (PUF)** contributes to the support of most institutions in the University of Texas and Texas A&M University systems. Originally established in 1876 by a land grant of 1 million acres, the fund contains approximately 2.1 million acres in 24 west Texas counties. Under provisions in the state constitution, all surface lease income goes into the Available University

Permanent School Fund (PSF) fund created in 1854, which provides monies for primary and secondary schools

State Highway Fund fund that supports the construction, maintenance, policing of roadways, and acquires rights of way; funded through a variety of taxes such as motor vehicle registration fees, the federal highway fund, and the sales tax on motor lubricants

Economic Stabilization Fund (ESF) established by constitutional amendment in 1988 to provide funds for the state during times of financial stress, commonly known as the *Rainy Day Fund*

Permanent University Trust Fund (PUF) established in 1876 and funded from the proceeds from land owned by the state; monies go to various universities in the UT and Texas A&M systems

Tapping the Rainy Day Fund

Many states, including Texas, have savings accounts or "rainy day funds." Texas's rainy day fund is more formally known as the Economic Stabilization Fund (ESF), and Texas voters passed a constitutional amendment mandating the fund in November 1988. Discussion of this fund reached a fevered pitch during the 2010 legislative session, when Texas faced a budget shortfall. Some Texans thought it was a "rainy day" and urged the state government to tap the fund for education and health services. Others believed that the fund should be preserved for the future and should be used only in extreme circumstances. Unlike the federal government, Texas state government cannot approve a budget deficit and must pass a balanced budget every two years.

The ESF's interest-bearing savings provide a financial cushion for economically challenging times. As of early 2012, this cushion contained nearly $9.4 billion representing the fund's highest balance since its establishment. According to Texas Comptroller of Public Accounts Susan Combs, "If the state's annual oil and/or gas production tax collections exceed those collected in fiscal 1987, 75 percent of the amount above that level is transferred into the fund."[a] The Texas ESF receives a yearly distribution and is primarily funded through taxes on the state's gas and oil production, though the state legislature can make other sources of funding available for it.

When Is the State Allowed to Access the Money?
The Texas Constitution provides that the ESF can be spent to "prevent or eliminate a temporary cash deficiency in general revenue" and/or for general appropriations. But these two general categories of appropriation, which are used to determine how the state legislature can access the ESF's funds, require differing degrees of legislative approval. When the state's budget revenues decline, appropriations from the fund can be used to offset a budget deficit

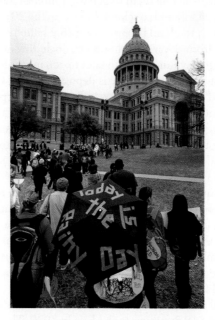

(even in the middle of a biennial budget period), but such appropriations require a three-fifths majority vote of approval by the Texas Legislature. In all other circumstances, such as using the ESF to balance a budget, appropriations from the ESF require a larger two-thirds majority vote. This is a difficult threshold to meet.

Before 2011, ESF funds had been used only twice—in fiscal years 2003 and 2005. In 2003, with the ESF containing over $900 million and Texas facing a nearly $10 billion budget gap, the Texas Legislature appropriated most of the ESF's funds. Over these two fiscal years, funds were directly appropriated to the Teacher Retirement System,

Texas Health and Human Services, the Governor's Office, and the Texas Education Agency. In 2011, Governor Perry also authorized the use of the funds, but in a limited way, to plug a budget gap from the previous two years.

What Are the Trade-Offs of Accessing the Money?
Political will is the primary motivating factor legislators face when deciding whether to access the Rainy Day Fund. Opponents of tapping the ESF have claimed it is best not to tap the fund, as economic problems can persist and economic conditions might become worse, especially if the economy does not recover as predicted. Also, while Texas's ESF funding formula has been quite successful in recent years with the growth in oil and gas prices, this formula does not guarantee success, as the tax revenue from the energy sector has fluctuated quite significantly. Finally, opponents claim that tapping the ESF could potentially damage Texas's bond rating, especially if the reserves are not replenished quickly.

Proponents of accessing the ESF have claimed that Texas should not shortchange its commitments in areas like public education, which took a large hit during the 2011 legislative session. In addition, proponents argue that we should use the money to uphold our commitments to the elderly and the poor who rely on state assistance.

[a]http://www.window.state.tx.us/comptrol/fnotes/ fn1102/

critical thinking questions

1. Is there room for compromise on the use of the ESF? Should a percentage be used, and if so, how much? Which types of programs should the ESF be used for if there is a budget shortfall?

2. Why is political will the biggest factor for legislators in deciding whether to use the fund or not? Should they base their decision purely on what they think a majority of constituents want, or should they consider other factors as well?

Fund (AUF), a fund set up to distribute PUF monies. Mineral income and the proceeds from the sale of PUF lands go into PUF and are invested. In 1999, an amendment to the constitution authorized the UT Board of Regents to channel investment income into the AUF. Two-thirds of the monies going to AUF go to the UT system; one-third to the Texas A&M system. The first obligation of any income earned by PUF is to pay the debt service on outstanding PUF bonds. The estimated value of the PUF in October 2011 was approximately $12.5 billion.[22]

The **Higher Education Fund (HEF)** was established by a constitutional amendment for universities that did not have access to PUF monies. It is funded through the General Revenue Fund. Appropriations for the HEF are projected to be $525 million for the 2012–13 biennium. An advisory committee made up of member institutions provides input to the Texas Higher Education Coordinating Board, which in turn makes recommendations to the legislature for budgetary allocation to each school out of the HEF.

The **National Research University Fund (NRUF)** was established through a 2009 constitutional amendment to provide a source of funding for universities seeking to achieve national prominence as research institutions. Under the amendment, money was transferred from the HEF to the NRUF. UT Austin and Texas A&M are already considered to be national research institutions and therefore do not qualify for this fund. Eligibility criteria as well as distribution rules were established in 2011 by the legislature. An institution must be identified as an emerging research university by the Higher Education Coordinating Board and must expend at least $45 million in specifically defined types of research. In addition, universities must meet at least four of the following criteria to qualify: (1) maintain an endowment of at least $400 million in the two preceding academic years; (2) produce 200 Ph.D. degrees during the previous two years; (3) have a freshman class of high academic achievement; (4) be designated as a member of the Association of Research Libraries, have a Phi Beta Kappa Chapter, or be a member of Phi Kappa Phi; (5) have a certain number of tenured faculty who have demonstrated excellence by winning a Nobel Prize or other prestigious fellowships, or have been elected to one of the National Academies; and (6) have a demonstrable excellence in graduate education. In early 2012, the value of the fund was approximately $550 million.

In 2011, seven universities were designated as emerging research universities, each of which could have access to these funds if certain criteria were met. They were Texas Tech University, the University of Texas at Arlington, the University of Texas at Dallas, the University of Texas at El Paso, the University of Texas at San Antonio, the University of Houston, and the University of North Texas. In January 2012, Texas Tech and the University of Houston were identified by the Coordinating Board as being eligible to receive some of these NRUF monies subject to meeting a state audit.[23]

Higher Education Fund (HEF) a state higher education fund for universities not having access to PUF monies

National Research University Fund (NRUF) established in 2009 to provide funding to universities seeking to achieve national prominence as research institutions

● The Texas Constitution and the Budget

Outline the constitutional provisions that affect how the state budget is made

A number of constitutional factors affect the way the budget is made in Texas. Probably the biggest constraint on the budgetary process has to do with time limits. The legislature is compelled to write a two-year, or biennial, budget because of the constitutional provision that the legislature may meet in regular session only once every two years. One of the effects of this restricted time frame is to force government agencies to project their budgetary needs well in advance of any clear understanding of the particular problems they may be facing during the biennium. In addition, the legislature can meet for only 140 days in regular session. This seriously limits the amount of time that the legislature can spend analyzing the budget or developing innovative responses to pressing matters of public importance.

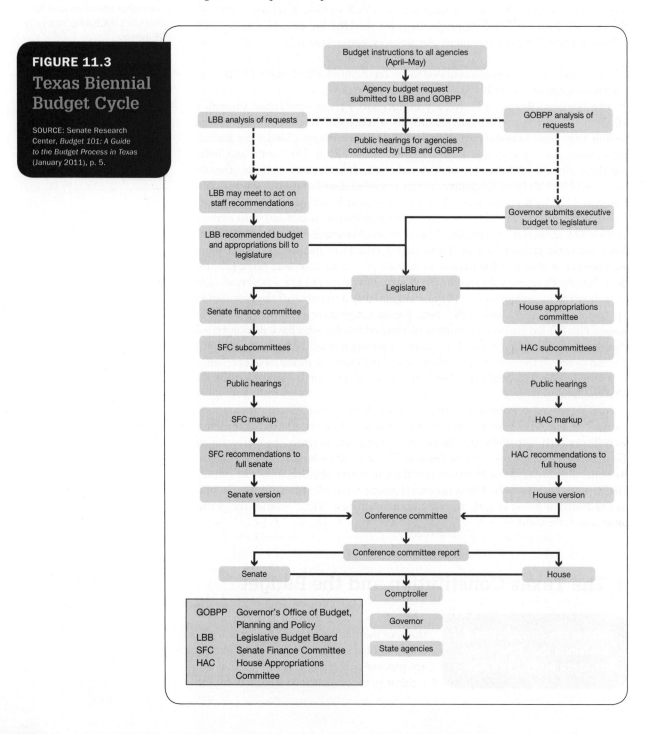

FIGURE 11.3

Texas Biennial Budget Cycle

SOURCE: Senate Research Center, *Budget 101: A Guide to the Budget Process in Texas* (January 2011), p. 5.

Another important factor is that a large portion of the biennial budget is dedicated for special purposes by federal law or by the Texas Constitution or state statute. These dedicated funds include federal monies earmarked for financing health care for the poor (Medicaid), as well as state funds for highways, education, teachers' retirement, and numerous other purposes. The purpose of dedicated funds is not difficult to understand. Supporters of particular programs want to create a stable revenue source for priority programs. But in protecting their own programs, supporters encourage other interests to do likewise, with the result that the legislature loses control of a large portion of the budget.

Finally, a number of specific constitutional provisions constrain the legislature's control of the budget.[24]

The Pay-as-You-Go Limit **Article III, Section 49a**, of the Texas Constitution, requires the state to maintain a balanced budget. All bills that get as far as **appropriations** in the legislative process must be sent to the comptroller of public accounts so the comptroller can certify that they are within available budget limit projections. One of the most important consequences of the pay-as-you-go limit is to put the comptroller at the heart of the budget process. In 2011, the comptroller certified that the 2012–13 General Appropriations Act and other appropriations acts passed during the 2011 session met the pay-as-you-go requirements.

Article III, Section 49a portion of the Texas Constitution that requires the state to maintain a balanced budget

appropriations authorization by the legislature to a government agency or body to spend up to a particular amount of money

The Welfare Spending Limit Article III, Section 51a, provides that the amount of money the state pays for assistance to or on behalf of needy dependent children and their caretakers shall not exceed 1 percent of the state budget in any biennium. This article sets a constitutional limit on the amount of money that the state may pay out to welfare beneficiaries under the Temporary Assistance for Needy Families program (TANF). The total state budget appropriated by the 82nd legislature was $173.5 billion, instituting a welfare spending limit of over $1.7 billion. State funds appropriated for TANF, however, were only $134.6 million, far below the 1 percent limit. Note that state expenditures on Medicaid are not included in this spending limit.

The Limit on the Growth of Certain Appropriations Article VIII, Section 22, which was passed in 1978, specifies that the growth in appropriations cannot be more than the growth of the state's economy, not counting dedicated spending as specified in the state constitution. This means that when the state's economy shrinks, appropriations also have to shrink. The LBB is responsible for determining what the proper financial figures are to meet this mandate. Under Texas law, the LBB determines this by dividing the estimated total state personal income for the next biennium by the estimated total state personal income for the current biennium. The LBB may adopt "a more comprehensive definition of the rate of growth" if the alternative definition is approved by a special committee composed of the governor, the Speaker of the House, and the comptroller.[25]

One might think that there might be times that the LBB would be reluctant to perform its constitutional duties. Adopting particularly dismal projections derived from the growth formula hardly makes one popular politically. But there are checks in place to make sure that the projections are made and the limit on growth is delivered in a timely fashion to the legislature. Under law, the LBB is prohibited from distributing the budget or the appropriation bill to either the legislature or the governor until this limit on the rate of growth of appropriations has been adopted. If the LBB fails to adopt a growth (and a spending limit), the rate of growth in the state's economy is treated as if it were zero. State revenues not dedicated by the

Texas Constitution to particular functions must remain at the same level as in the previous biennium.

Budget-Execution Authority Under a constitutional amendment passed in 1985 (now Article XVI, Section 69), the legislature was empowered to establish rules for the expenditure of funds by state agencies. Today this means that between legislative sessions, the governor or the LBB may propose (1) that an agency stop spending money appropriated to it in the budget; (2) that money be transferred from one agency to another; or (3) that the purpose for an appropriation to a particular agency be changed. If the governor proposes the changes, the LBB must approve or amend the proposal. If the LBB proposes the changes, the governor must approve or amend the proposal.

Limitation on Debt Payable from the General Revenue Fund The state constitution also limits the amount of debt the state can incur. Under a 1997 amendment to Article III, Section 49(j), the legislature cannot authorize additional debt if the resulting **debt service** is greater than 5 percent of the average General Revenue Fund revenue for the three preceding fiscal years (this excludes dedicated spending). Basically, Texas state debt cannot be more than five percent of state revenue.

One of the consequences of this constitutional debt limit is that compared to other states (as well as to the federal government), the Texas debt burden is relatively low. A 2010 U.S. Census study calculated that Texas's per capita debt burden was $1,228. This contrasted with per capita debts of $6,277 in New York, $4,412 in Illinois, and $3,641 in California. Among the largest 10 states, Texas's per capita state tax burden was the smallest.[26]

debt service money spent by the state to pay off debt; includes interest and principal payments

● The Budgetary Process

> **Identify the major steps and players in setting the state budget**

In theory, Texas has a "dual-budget" system. This means that responsibility for preparing an initial draft of the budget is shared by the governor through the Governor's Office of Budget, Planning, and Policy (GOBPP) and the legislature through the LBB. In practice, the budget is primarily the responsibility of the legislature.

In 1967, the legislature designated the governor the chief planning officer of the state. The GOBPP was created in 1976, through the consolidation of an older agency, the Division of Planning Coordination, with the GOBPP. The GOBPP is responsible for advising the governor regarding fiscal matters. It prepares the governor's budget recommendations for the legislature and monitors state appropriations and operations. It also serves the governor in a variety of other capacities, including providing analysis on fiscal and economic matters and coordinating federal programs in the state as well as assisting in the operations of various regional and state planning councils.

Before 1949, there was little coordination in public budgeting. Financial procedures varied, and state agencies were funded by individual appropriations. In 1949, a law was enacted to establish the 10-member LBB, whose primary job would be to recommend appropriations for all agencies of state government. The board is chaired by the lieutenant governor. The vice chair is the Speaker of the House. Other members include the chairs of the House Appropriations Committee, the House Committee on Ways and Means, the Senate Finance Committee, and the Senate State Affairs Committee. Two additional members from the Senate and the House are chosen by the lieutenant governor and the Speaker, respectively.

The LBB appoints a budget director, who brings together budgeting requests from the various state agencies and prepares appropriations bills for them. Since 1973, the LBB has also been responsible for evaluating agency programs and developing estimates of the probable costs of implementing legislation introduced in a legislative session. The LBB's draft budget, not the governor's, is the basis for final legislation. Table 11.6 summarizes the duties of key players in the budgetary process.

Preparing and implementing a budget are complex matters. The budgetary process involves two stages. In the first stage, the LBB develops a draft budget based on requests supplied by state agencies. This draft budget follows a series of steps. First, strategic plans are developed by each agency. A strategic plan includes (1) a mission statement, (2) a statement about the goals of the agency, (3) a discussion of the population served by the agency, (4) an explanation of the means that will be used

TABLE 11.6

Key Players in the Budgetary Process

The Legislative Budget Board (LBB)

1. Adopts a constitutional spending limit
2. Prepares a general appropriations bill
3. Prepares agency performance reports
4. Guides, reviews, and finalizes agency strategic plans
5. Prepares fiscal notes regarding costs and impacts of proposed legislation
6. Engages in "budget execution actions" in conjunction with the governor by transferring money from one assigned purpose to another purpose or to another agency

The Governor and the Governor's Office of Budget of Planning and Policy

1. Develop a strategic plan for the state
2. Help to develop agency Legislative Appropriation Requests (LAR)
3. Hold LAR hearings, often in conjunction with the legislature
4. Deliver a governor's appropriations budget and a general appropriations bill at the beginning of the legislative session
5. Exercise a line-item veto after an appropriations bill is passed by the legislature
6. Engage in "budget execution actions" in conjunction with the LBB by transferring money from one assigned purpose to another purpose or to another agency

The Comptroller of Public Accounts

1. Submits a statement regarding the estimated anticipated revenues for the coming biennium
2. Certifies that an appropriations bill is in balance with projected state revenues
3. Collects state taxes
4. Tracks 600 separate revenue and spending funds and making sure that agencies stay within their budgets.

The State Auditor's Office develops independent audits of state agencies, including institutions of higher education. These audits are used to evaluate agencies.

to achieve these goals, and (5) an identification of the measures to be used to assess the agency's success in meeting these goals. This information provides the basis for LBB funding recommendations for each agency. In the spring or early summer prior to the legislative session, the LBB sends out detailed Legislative Appropriation Request (LAR) instructions to the agencies. Hearings are then held by the LBB and by the GOBPP with each agency where the agency's strategic plan and LAR are discussed. LARs become the starting point for the appropriations bill that is prepared by the LBB. *Legislative Budget Estimates* is a publication of the LBB that contains information on the proposed appropriations bill, including expenditures for previous bienniums and proposed expenditures for the next biennium.[27]

While the draft budgets are being prepared, the comptroller's office prepares the Biennial Revenue Estimate (BRE). The BRE is a detailed forecast of the total revenue that the state is expected to take in over the next biennium. The Texas Constitution requires that the BRE contain "an itemized estimate of the anticipated revenue . . . to be credited during the succeeding biennium."[28] The BRE includes other information to assist legislators in the budget process, including (1) statements about the anticipated revenue from different sources; (2) an analysis of the economic outlook facing Texas and the nation; and (3) a detailed accounting of the funds in the state treasury. The comptroller effectively sets a ceiling on what the state legislature may spend. Although the legislature can override the comptroller's estimates with a four-fifths vote of each house, this has never happened. The BRE is updated by the comptroller when economic conditions change significantly and for special sessions of the legislature.[29]

The second stage of the budget process involves the legislative process. By the seventh day of each regular session, appropriations bills are submitted by the LBB to the House Appropriations Committee and the Senate Finance Committee. Traditionally, the bills are introduced to these committees by their respective chairs, although any member may do so. The bills then work their way through the committee system of each house separately and are subject to hearings, debates, and revisions. This process of drafting the bill is referred to as a "markup." Final versions of the budget are prepared by the House Appropriations Committee and the Senate Finance Committee. Each house then votes on the bill. Differences between the two versions of the bill are reconciled in a conference committee.

The conference committee is composed of representatives from the Senate and the House. Senate members are selected by the lieutenant governor or the president pro tempore of the Senate. The senator sponsoring the bill, traditionally the chairman of the Senate Finance Committee, appoints the chair of the Senate conferees. At least two members from the Senate Finance Committee must sit on the conference committee. The Speaker of the House appoints all conferees from the House as well as the chair of the House conferees. Traditionally, Senate and House representatives alternate each session in chairing the conference committee.

Specific rules govern how disagreements between the Senate and House versions of the appropriations bills are to be handled.[30]

- Items that appear in both versions of the bill must be included in the final conference committee report.
- Items that appear in both versions of the bill with identical amounts allocated to them may not be changed by the committee.
- Items that appear in both versions of the bill with differing amounts allocated to them cannot be eliminated. The committee has the discretion to fund these items at a level not larger than the larger allocation or smaller than the smaller allocation.

- Items that appear in one version of the bill but not the other can be included or eliminated from the final bill subject to the discretion of the committee. However, no more money may be allocated to that item than is found in the original version of the bill.

- Items found in neither version of the bill may not be included in the final conference report. However, the conference committee has the discretion to propose the appropriation of money for bills that already have been passed by the legislature.

While constraining the discretionary authority of the committee to a degree, these rules still leave considerable room for political maneuvering on the part of the committee. Membership on this important committee is a highly prized commodity. Once the bill passes the conference committee, it is returned to both houses for final passage.

Under Article III, Section 49a of the Texas Constitution, the comptroller has the formal authority to "certify" the budget. This means that the comptroller confirms that the comptroller's office has analyzed the budget and concluded that it is within the current revenue estimates. For all intents and purposes, the budget is being declared balanced. If the general appropriations bill is not certified by the comptroller, it is returned to the house in which it originated. The legislature must then either decrease expenditures or raise revenues to make up the difference. According to provisions set out in Article III, Section 49a, under conditions of "imperative public necessity" the legislature may with a four-fifths vote in each house decide to spend in excess of anticipated revenue.

After certification, the budget moves on to the governor, who can sign, not sign, or veto the entire bill or exercise the line-item veto. With the line-item veto, in particular, the governor has the power to unravel some of the compromises that legislators may have forged to get the bill through the committee system. The line-item veto also potentially gives the governor enormous power to limit expenditures in targeted certain areas. Of course, line-item vetoes exercised too vigorously in one session can come back to haunt the governor's legislative agenda in the next session.

The appropriations bill takes effect on September 1 in odd-numbered years. All agencies are bound by it. Monitoring agency compliance with the budget is the job of the LBB and the state auditor's office. The governor and LBB have the authority to execute the budget. This includes the power to shift funds between agency programs or between agencies if necessary when the legislature is not in session. This power to execute the budget is an important one. It has been a tool used by the governor and LBB to cope with the unanticipated shortfalls in the state budget by ordering state agencies to cut their expenditures in the middle of a biennium.

Budget Crises in Twenty-First-Century Texas

Analyze major budget crises in Texas

The 1970s and early 1980s were boom years for the Texas economy. Rising inflation coupled with high oil prices and rapid economic growth drove the economy forward.[31] Tax increases were unnecessary as tax revenues soared. The problem facing the legislature was not how to balance the budget, but how to spend revenue windfalls. There were no tax increases in Texas during this time.

The collapse of oil prices and a sputtering state economy in the mid-1980s, particularly severe in real estate and construction, brought on a serious budget crisis. As projected deficits mounted, tax increases became commonplace. Between 1985 and 1986, state tax collections fell. Income from the oil severance tax alone dropped 28 percent. Tax rates were increased, and the tax base was broadened in almost every year between 1984 and 1991.

As the state's economy turned around in the early 1990s, the budgetary situation brightened considerably. However, renewed budget surpluses did not bring a return to the spending patterns of the pre–oil crash years. Business and political leaders from both parties expressed an ongoing concern that taxes were becoming burdensome, perhaps placing Texas at a disadvantage with other states in trying to create a favorable environment for business. Additionally, a growing concern that state government was expanding too fast sparked demands for making government more efficient. With the recession beginning in 2008, all this changed. Over the next four years, political leaders in the state faced a series of budget crises that proliferated as the Great Recession worked its way through the economy and into the federal and state budgets.

The 2011 legislative session was a particularly difficult one.[32] From the outset, legislators knew that difficult budgetary choices would have to be faced. For two years, Texas had dodged the worst effects of the Great Recession. But in 2011, hard decisions were going to have to be made to balance the budget.

Two factors had delayed the full impact of the recession upon the Texas budget. First, LBB projections in January 2009 for tax revenues for the 2010–11 biennium grossly underestimated the impact that the recession would have upon tax revenues. The projection had anticipated a surplus of $2.1 billion in General Revenues and $3 billion set aside for property tax relief from the previous budget, making the 2010–11 financial outlook appear to be quite secure. But in reality the surpluses had evaporated, revealing the budget to be far too optimistic and exposing policy makers to some difficult decisions. Second, Texas had been initially protected from the worst of the recession by an infusion of federal funding. In an effort to fight the recession at the national level, the federal government instituted a surge of deficit spending under the American Recovery and Reinvestment Act passed in February 2009. This enabled the 2009 Texas Legislature to appropriate $6.4 billion in federal funds to cover a projected General Revenues Fund gap and maintain educational and health and human services programs sponsored with the federal government. By the end of the 2010–11 biennium, the federal dollars coming into the state rose to $8.0 billion, largely as a result of higher-than-expected caseloads for Medicaid, as well as an expansion of that program through federal legislation.

The pressures on the budget continued unabated through 2009 and 2010. One of the chief effects of the Great Recession across the country was the sharp contraction in real estate prices.[33] Low interest rates supported by Federal Reserve policy along with loose credit standards had led to a "bubble" in real estate that had pushed up property values through the early years of the twenty-first century. The real estate bubble popped in 2008, bringing many banks to their knees as the value of their portfolios plunged with collapsing real estate prices. Banks turned to Washington for assistance and were ultimately bailed out by a massive intrusion of the federal government into the banking system.

Although Texas escaped the worst of the real estate collapse, largely because the real estate bubble had been more muted in Texas than elsewhere, credit tightened and property values declined across the state through 2007, 2008, and 2009. As property values declined, so did property tax revenues. What had been a banking crisis at the national level became a funding crisis at the state and local levels, particularly for schools, community colleges, and health districts where funding was based largely on property taxes. In addition, sales tax receipts in Texas fell for the first time in 2009 since 2003. Sales tax receipts fell each month from February 2009 to April 2010 in Texas.

By January 2011, the comptroller projected a $4.3 billion shortfall in general tax revenues against projected expenses for fiscal year 2011, the second year of the previous biennium. The deficit projections for the 2012–13 biennium were even worse, putting the shortfall in general tax revenue at around $17 billion. Taking into account increasing demands for Medicaid and school district funding put the general revenue shortfall for the coming biennium somewhere between $24 and $27 billion.

The Great Recession was not the only cause of the financial shortfall. There were also long-term structural problems facing the budget brought on by property tax reform. In 2006, the legislature required schools to reduce their school property tax rates by one-third. The reasons were complicated. The Texas Supreme Court had ruled in *West Orange Cove ISD v. Neeley* that school districts needed to have some "meaningful discretion" in the setting of property tax rates.[34] If all property tax rates were set at the maximum allowed under law, a situation found in many districts, the court concluded that a statewide property tax essentially would have been put into place, and this was a violation of the state constitution prohibiting such a statewide property tax. Lowering property tax rates was thus one way to bring the existing property tax into compliance with the court's ruling.

Lowering property tax rates, however, would have serious funding implications for public schools. In an effort to replace lost property tax revenues and maintain funding levels at the schools, the legislature also increased the state corporate franchise tax and the cigarette tax. The LBB calculated that lost revenue from the property tax cut would be $14.2 billion for the next 2014–15 biennium. Tax increases would bring in $8.3 billion. From the outset, there was thus a projected shortfall of $5.9 billion for the next 2013–14 biennium. Proponents argued that this shortfall would evaporate as new tax collections grew. Unfortunately, these optimistic predictions were wrong. The new taxes actually brought in $3.78 billion less than projected for 2008–09 and $5.13 billion less than anticipated for 2010–11. Thus, there was a structural deficit built into the budget from the property tax relief of $9.16 billion for 2008–09 and $9.95 billion for 2010–11. For 2012–13, the deficit from tax relief was projected to be $9.84 billion.

The initial response of state leaders to the impending fiscal shortfall was a call for immediate spending cuts in the current fiscal year. In January 2010, the governor, lieutenant governor, and Speaker of the House asked all state agencies and institutions of higher education to plan to reduce spending by 10 percent in fiscal year 2010 and 5 percent for fiscal year 2011. In December 2010, there was an additional 2.5 percent cut in spending. State leaders also drew upon the Economic Stabilization Fund (the Rainy Day Fund). Under a supplemental appropriations bill in 2011, the 2011 budget deficit thus was closed, $1.2 billion coming from reduced spending and $3.2 billion coming from the Rainy Day Fund (see Table 11.7).

But the bigger problem lay with the multibillion-dollar shortfall for the next biennium. Legislators had to agree exactly on what the deficit was, finally concluding that it was approximately $22.6 billion. How was this to be addressed? Conservative Republicans led by Governor Perry and Tea Party supporters rejected

TABLE 11.7

Legislative Response to the 2011 Budgetary Shortfall during the 2011 Session

Reduce spending during the 2010–11 biennium	$1.2 billion
Tap Economic Stabilization Fund (Rainy Day Fund)	3.2 billion

SOURCES: Legislative Budget Board, *Fiscal Size-Up, 2012–13*, January 2012.

the idea that new taxes might be a solution. Instead they looked to spending cuts, payment deferments, and various "revenue enhancements" that would bring the budget back into balance. It took a special session of the legislature in June 2011 to finally pass the bill that brought the budget for 2012–13 back into balance. There were a few financial tricks used to balance the budget. For example, some taxpayers were required to speed up payments of various sales, alcohol, and motor fuel taxes so that the revenues would be received during this biennium rather than the next. The transfer of motor fuel tax receipts from the General Revenue Fund to the State Highway Fund was delayed, keeping money in this biennium. Payments to school districts for August 2013 were also deferred to September 2013, pushing another set of expenditures into the next biennium. Such budgetary sleights of hand can be done only once. But the hope was that the worst of the crisis would have passed by the time that these tactics became an issue in a future biennium.

The most important initiatives taken up to address the budget shortfall were spending cuts. Entitlement funding to public schools in the state was cut by $4 billion for the 2012–13 biennium. In addition, five months of the two-year Medicaid budget, approximately $4.3 billion, was not funded. On the face of it, one might think that a partially unfunded Medicaid proposal would not pass constitutional muster. But key legislators and the comptroller agreed to cover these unfunded Medicaid expenditures with either unexpected revenues or the remaining $7 billion in the Rainy Day Fund. They also agreed that this would meet the balanced budget requirement. Medicaid also underwent $1.8 billion in "cost containment savings." Ultimately, a total of $5 billion in new revenues was put into place along with $17.6 billion in cuts in expenditures (Table 11.8).

On paper at least, the budget deficit had been addressed and political leaders had met their constitutional duties to balance the budget. Sales tax receipts began to recover from the depths of the recession throughout 2011 and into 2012. In June 2012, Comptroller Susan Combs reported that sales tax receipts were up 7 percent over the previous year and had increased every month for 12 months. The Texas economy was outperforming that of much of the nation, but not enough to cover a projected $4 billion budget shortfall for the 2012–13 biennium. There were also a number of school financing lawsuits in court that could potentially cost the state over $4 billion. In addition, state leaders had to figure out how to cover the onetime school payment delay and the Medicaid underfunding in the 2012–13 budget. But the biggest threat to a balanced budget did not lie in school funding or even in sales tax receipts. President Obama's federal reforms to health care present new short-term and long-term spending commitments that could drench the Texas state budget with red ink.

TABLE 11.8

Legislative Response to the 2012–13 Biennium Deficit

REVENUE SOLUTIONS

Increased recurring revenues	$0.7 billion
Created one-time revenues	1.4 billion
Improved revenue estimate and other revenue	1.9 billion
Made some funding contingent on improved revenue collection	1.0 billion
Subtotal	5.0 billion

SPENDING SOLUTIONS

Reduced entitlement funding to local schools	$4.0 billion
Deferred 8/2013 payment to school districts until 9/2013	2.3 billion
Medicaid cost containment	1.8 billion
Underfunded Medicaid for 5 months in 2012	4.3 billion
Reduced in other spending in 2012–13	5.2 billion
Subtotal	17.6 billion
Total	**$22.6 billion**

SOURCES: Legislative Budget Board, *Fiscal Size-Up, 2012–13*, January 2012. p. 3

● Thinking Critically about Public Finance in Texas

Public finance in Texas will continue to be a troubling issue for political leaders in Texas. Although revenue from the sales tax appears to have recovered at least in part, few policy makers feel confident that the state economy is freed of the effects of the Great Recession or that it is about to launch into a new boom period. Property values and income from property taxes may be recovering from the worst of the downturn, but state and local political leaders must remain cautious in their projections about the future. There is simply too much uncertainty in the national and international economies. Texas's economy is tied inextricably to the booms and busts of the U.S. economy as well as the world economy. State budgetary policy is ultimately dependent upon the successful implementation of a national recovery policy that works. Few leaders in the state are confident about the current direction of national economic policy. A looming national deficit with no solution in sight may lead to calls in Washington to push more responsibilities (and costs) onto the backs of the states, further exacerbating the state's budgetary problems.

Four factors will continue to dominate public finance in Texas over the next few bienniums. First, the structural deficit brought on by the 2006 property tax reductions will continue until a new source of revenue is found or expenditures are slashed. Second, there will be increased demands from the federal government for paying for expanded federal initiatives in health care. We will discuss this in detail in the next chapter. Third, increased population will lead to increased demands upon state agencies for services ranging from health care to roads, to water, and to public education. All other things being equal, a larger population demands more from government, and that costs money. Fourth, there is a growing antigovernment feeling among portions of the population in Texas that state government is too big already. For Tea Partyers and other conservative Republicans, "no new taxes" is a successful mantra for winning office. Whether it will be a successful one for legislating and leading is another question. Navigating a passage between the Scylla of intensifying demands for expanded services and the Charybdis of "no new taxes" may be the most difficult problem legislators face in the foreseeable future.

What Is the Budget?

■ **Explain the purpose of the state budget and what is typically included (pp. 313–14)**

Texas is required to operate within a balanced budget. The budget can be considered in light of five revenue streams: the General Revenues Fund Budget, the General Revenue–Dedicated Funds Budget, the Federal Funds budget, the Other Funds Budget, and the All Funds Budget.

Key Terms

General Revenues Fund budget (p. 313)

General Revenue–Dedicated Funds budget (p. 313)

Federal Funds budget (p. 313)

Other Funds budget (p. 313)

All Funds budget (p. 313)

Practice Quiz

1. The Texas Constitution requires that the Texas budget must be *(p. 313)*
   a) balanced.
   b) approved by the governor's cabinet.
   c) funded only from sales taxes.
   d) approved by the governor, the legislature, and the state treasurer.
   e) funded only from federal grants.

2. Federal expenditures primarily affect the state budget in two areas *(p. 314)*
   a) energy and law enforcement.
   b) health-human services and education.
   c) business development and highways.
   d) interstate highways and airports.
   e) Medicare and transportation.

Spending and Revenue in Texas

■ **Describe the general pattern of state spending in Texas and where state revenue comes from (pp. 314–24)**

Texas spends less than the national average in a variety of policy areas, including education and highway spending. Although Texas does not have an income tax, it has one of the highest sales taxes in the nation. However, the per capita revenue from those sales taxes is among the lowest in the nation. Property taxes in Texas are among the highest in the nation. Among other important state taxes are the Natural Gas Production Tax and the Oil Production and Regulation Tax. Although a controversial issue in the past, a state income tax has little support either in the legislature or in the population as a whole. Texas also has on average fewer state employees per capita than other states.

Key Terms

regressive (p. 320)

progressive (p. 322)

matching funds (p. 322)

3. Texas has the reputation for being *(p. 314)*
   a) a low-service, low-tax state.
   b) a high-service, high-tax state.
   c) a low-service, high-tax state.
   d) a high-service, low-tax state.
   e) an average-service, average-tax state.

4. The proportion of state employees to the population in Texas is *(p. 315)*
   a) far below the national average.
   b) far above the national average.
   c) right at the national average.
   d) exactly the same as in California.
   e) greater than in New York.

5. One major revenue source for Texas is the sales tax, which is *(pp. 315–16)*
   a) 8.25 percent for state government and 2.25 percent for local government.
   b) 4.25 percent for state government and 2 percent for local government.
   c) 6.25 percent for state government and 2 percent for local government.

d) 5 percent for state government and 1.25 percent for local government.
e) none of the above.

6. A Texas personal income tax *(p. 322)*
   a) used to exist but was repealed because of new taxes on oil production.
   b) would have to be approved by the voters, and the revenues from it would have to support public education.

c) would have to be passed through a Constitutional amendment.
d) could only be imposed on incomes greater than $250,000 per year.
e) would be unlikely to raise much revenue.

> Ⓢ **Practice Online**
> "Exploring Texas Politics" exercise: *Tax Policy*

State Funds

■ **Describe how the money in the budget is organized into specific funds (pp. 324–27)**

Money flows into and out of a variety of over 400 different funds controlled by the state. Among the most important are the General Revenue Fund, the Permanent School Fund, the State Highway Fund, and the Economic Stabilization Fund (the Rainy Day Fund). The existence of these funds makes budgeting a complicated process.

Key Terms

General Revenue Fund (p. 324)

Permanent School Fund (PSF) (p. 325)

State Highway Fund (p. 325)

Economic Stabilization Fund (ESF, or the Rainy Day Fund) (p. 325)

Permanent University Trust Fund (PUF) (p. 325)

Higher Education Fund (HEF) (p. 327)

National Research University Fund (NRUF) (p. 327)

Practice Quiz

7. The Rainy Day Fund *(p. 325)*
   a) provides funds for flood victims.
   b) was designed to provide funding for the state during times of financial distress.
   c) contains only a small amount of state funds.
   d) is used to promote oil and gas development.
   e) can only be spent by the Texas Comptroller.

8. The National Research University Fund *(p. 327)*
   a) pays for university-level research at all state universities.
   b) provides the funding for the University of Texas at Austin.
   c) funds Texas universities seeking national prominence as research institutions.
   d) only provides funds to universities with Nobel Prize winners.
   e) will not provide funds if more than 20 percent of students fail to graduate in four years.

The Texas Constitution and the Budget

■ **Outline the constitutional provisions that affect how the state budget is made (pp. 327–30)**

There are many constitutional restrictions on the budget, including the requirement of a biennial budget, a pay-as you-go limit, a welfare spending limit, a limit on the growth of some appropriations, rules on the spending of funds by state agencies, and limitations on debt payable from general revenue fund. These restrictions play important roles in shaping the budget policy-making process.

Key Terms

Article III, Section 49a (p. 329)

appropriations (p. 329)

debt service (p. 330)

Practice Quiz

9. Which of the following is *not* a constitutional constraint on the budgetary process in Texas? *(pp. 329–30)*
   a) the annual budget
   b) a welfare spending limit
   c) a pay-as-you-go limit
   d) a limitation on the debt payable from the General Revenue Fund
   e) All are constitutional limits

10. What is meant by "the budget-execution authority"? *(p. 330)*
    a) the power to execute the laws of the land
    b) the legislature's power to establish rules for the expenditure of funds by state agencies
    c) the governor's power to veto the budget
    d) the LBB's power to create the budget for the Judiciary in Texas
    e) none of the above

The Budgetary Process

 Identify the major steps and players in making the state budget (pp. 330–33)

In theory, Texas has a dual budget system with budgeting shared by the governor and the legislature. In reality, the budget is the responsibility of the legislature. There are a series of steps that the budget must go through to be passed by the legislature. Among the most important is the requirement that the Texas Comptroller certify the budget as being balanced.

Practice Quiz

11. Who is the chief planning officer of the state of Texas? *(p. 330)*
    a) the lieutenant governor
    b) the Speaker of the House
    c) the comptroller
    d) the governor
    e) the state treasurer

12. The principal job of the Legislative Budget Board is *(p. 330)*
    a) to keep track of the expenses of the executive.
    b) to monitor the operations of the House.
    c) to raise taxes.
    d) to recommend appropriations for all agencies of state government.
    e) to conduct audits of state expenditures

 Practice Online
Video exercise: *Balancing the Budget*

Budget Crises in Twenty-First-Century Texas

 Analyze major budget crises in Texas (pp. 333–37)

Texas has experienced a number of budgetary crises in the early years of the twenty-first century. Budgetary problems were exacerbated by property tax reforms and the Great Recession, which led to serious declines in revenue while the demands for services were increasing.

Practice Quiz

13. What factors lie behind the budget crisis of 2011? *(pp. 334–35)*
    a) the Great Recession and property tax reform
    b) declining oil and gas prices
    c) a burdensome income tax being implemented for the first time
    d) bipartisan government
    e) Obamacare

14. What solution was put into place to address the budget crisis of 2011? *(p. 336)*
    a) instituting a state income tax
    b) speeding up the payments of various taxes on alcohol and motor fuels
    c) increasing the state sales tax
    d) allocating more money to elementary and secondary education
    e) increasing gasoline taxes

The Religious Viewpoints Antidiscrimination Act required Texas school districts to protect religious speech on campus, allowing students to express their faith in public. These students at Grapevine High School sang along with a Christian band at an event organized by the Christian organization Students Standing Strong.

Public Policy in Texas

WHAT GOVERNMENT DOES AND WHY IT MATTERS Like other states, Texas is involved in a broad range of public-policy initiatives. Some of these activities, such as criminal corrections or public education, are largely state responsibilities. Although the national government may contribute some funds and regulate various aspects of these public-policy areas, they remain for the most part the duty and responsibility of the state of Texas. Other public-policy areas, however, have involved considerable intermingling of state and federal government responsibilities. The balance of power between the state and federal governments in these areas has shifted over time.

Throughout the first decade of the twenty-first century, state policy makers in Texas waded through a variety of policy problems, including tax reform, educational testing, and criminal incarceration. Republican domination of both houses of the state legislature and the executive offices in the state ensured that a new conservative agenda would dominate policy debates across a variety of issues. Perhaps nothing captured this ideological orientation in public policy better than a new law that was passed during the 2007 session of the state legislature: the Religious Viewpoints Antidiscrimination Act.[1]

The law, which many claimed simply codified existing constitutional rulings by the federal courts, required Texas school districts to adopt a number of policies that would protect religious speech on campus. School districts were ordered to develop a neutral method for choosing student speakers at school events and graduation ceremonies, to ensure that religious-oriented clubs had the same access to school facilities as secular-oriented clubs, and to protect students who wished to express their religious beliefs in classroom assignments. The legislation did more than just give students permission to express their religious views in public schools; it also mandated the creation of a "limited public forum" for student speakers at public events that wouldn't discriminate against expressions of faith.

Social conservatives were ecstatic about the Religious Viewpoints Antidiscrimination Act, claiming that, at last, individual religious expression would be protected in the schools. Professional educators were somewhat hesitant in their praise for the bill, citing concerns about how the bill would be implemented and what it might mean for members of religious minorities. One commentator wrote for a law review that under the act "a student would be free to ask his or her fellow students to join in prayer to accept Jesus Christ as their personal savior so that they might have eternal life. Or a student would be free to tell his or her fellow students that Jesus was not God's son or that the Bible is a book of myths. Alternatively, a student might talk about why Catholics or Mormons are not Christians."[2] Far from solving the problems of religious discrimination, the act may unintentionally introduce religious bias and controversy into the classroom.

The Religious Viewpoints Antidiscrimination Act brings out two important truths about public policy in Texas. First, what goes on in Austin matters. The state legislature plays a major role in defining how public policy is conducted in the state. Second, public policy involves more than just introducing a bill in the legislature, passing it, and getting it signed. Laws also must be implemented. Implementation of policy by state agencies such as school boards is where the rubber meets the road in political life.

This chapter explores public policy making in Texas across a variety of leading issue areas including public education, welfare, Medicaid, and water. We will provide an overview of the problems confronting policy makers in these key areas and explain how political choices have shaped and continue to shape policy making in each case. We will also consider the current debates that are driving public policy in these areas.

chaptergoals

- Describe the major issues that have shaped education policy in Texas (pages 345–51)

- Describe the state's role in addressing poverty and how it is affected by national policies (pages 352–58)

- Explain why Medicaid in particular and health care policy in general have been so controversial in Texas (pages 358–68)

- Consider the growing importance of policies related to water supplies in Texas (pages 368–73)

Education Policy

Describe the major issues that have shaped education policy in Texas

The debate over public education in Texas extends back to the break with Mexico.[3] One of the indictments of the Mexican regime contained in the Texas Declaration of Independence was that the government had failed to establish a public system of education. Later, the Constitution of the Republic of Texas required a public system of education, but a bill actually establishing a public school system did not pass the legislature until 1854.

Public education was to be financed with a special school fund that would use $2 million of the $10 million given to Texas by the U.S. government on Texas's admission to the Union to settle outstanding land claims in parts of what are now New Mexico, Colorado, and Oklahoma. Unfortunately, the fund was used for a variety of other purposes in the following years, including the purchase of railroad stock and the building of prisons. When Democrats returned to power following Reconstruction, an effort was made to protect the fund and commit its use solely to education. Under the Constitution of 1876, the Special School Fund became the Permanent School Fund, and restrictions were placed on how the money could be used and invested.[4] The Constitution of 1876 also had provisions to support public education through one-quarter of the occupation tax, a $1 poll tax, and local taxation.

Throughout much of the late nineteenth and early twentieth centuries, public education remained largely a local affair. Schools were funded by local taxes, and decisions such as what to teach and how long the school year would be were made at the local level. Many of the school systems were chronically short of funds, facing such problems as a shortage of supplies and textbooks, inadequate facilities, and poorly trained teachers. In 1949 the state legislature tried to address some of these problems by passing the **Gilmer-Aikin Laws**, under which school districts were consolidated into 2,900 administrative units, state equalization funding was provided to supplement local taxes, teacher salaries were raised, and a minimum school year was established. In addition, the laws established the Texas Education Agency (TEA), originally known as the State Department of Education, to supervise public education in the state.

The Gilmer-Aikin Laws also established bureaucratic institutions responsible for public education in the state. Previously, public education had been run by a state board of education, whose nine members were appointed by the governor for six-year terms, and an elected state superintendent of public instruction. This was replaced by an elected 21-member board. The State Board of Education became the policy-making body for public education in the state, selecting budgets, establishing regulations for school accreditation, executing contracts for the purchase of textbooks, and investing in the Permanent School Fund. The board also had the power to appoint a commissioner of education, subject to confirmation by the Texas Senate. The commissioner of education served a four-year term and became the chief executive officer for the TEA. The TEA was responsible for setting standards for public schools, for supervising the public schools of the state, and for handling federal funds related to public education. For the next 50 years, educational policy in the state would work through the institutional framework established by the Gilmer-Aikin Laws.[5]

Since 1949, the State Board of Education has undergone occasional restructuring. Membership was expanded to 24 in 1973 and to 27 in 1981. Following a special legislative session, the board became a 15-member appointed body in 1984. But in 1988, it reverted to an elected body composed of 15 members serving four-year terms.

Gilmer-Aikin Laws education reform legislation passed in 1949 that supplemented local funding of education with public monies, raised teachers' salaries, mandated a minimum length for the school year, and provided for more state supervision of public education

Three issues have played a major role in shaping educational policy over the last 50 years: desegregation, equity in funding, and the search for educational excellence.

Desegregation

Few issues have troubled educational policy in Texas as much as desegregation. Segregation of the races was provided for under the Texas Constitution of 1876. In *Plessy v. Ferguson* (1896), the U.S. Supreme Court upheld the validity of state-imposed racial segregation through the now-infamous "separate but equal" doctrine. In Texas, as elsewhere across the South, segregated schools may have been separate, but they were far from equal. In the 1920s and '30s, for example, the length of the school term for black schools was only about four days shorter than that for white schools, but Texas spent an average of $3.39 less per student (about one-third less) on the education of African American students than on white students.[6]

The U.S. Supreme Court overturned *Plessy v. Ferguson* in the 1954 case *Brown v. Board of Education*, ruling that state-imposed segregation in schools violated the equal protection clause of the Fourteenth Amendment. School districts were ordered to desegregate their school systems "with all deliberate speed." In some cases, "all deliberate speed" was rapid. The San Antonio school district, for example, became one of the first school districts in the nation to comply with the Supreme Court's order. Other school districts in the state, such as Houston's, were much slower in implementing the Court's desegregation ruling.

The desegregation of public schools was hampered further by political opposition at both the local and state levels. In 1957 the Texas state legislature passed laws encouraging school districts to resist federally ordered desegregation, although then-governor Price Daniel Sr. chose to ignore such laws.[7] By the late 1960s, legally segregated schools were largely a thing of the past. Nevertheless, de facto segregation remained a problem, particularly in urban areas with large minority populations. As in many other urban areas across the country, a large number of middle- and upper-income whites in Texas abandoned urban public school systems for suburban public schools or private schools.

Equity in the Public School System

Federal court cases such as *Brown v. Board of Education* played a major role in shaping educational policy regarding the desegregation of schools. Two other important court cases have affected education policy and politics in Texas over the last 30 years: *San Antonio v. Rodríguez* and *Edgewood ISD v. Kirby*.

San Antonio v. Rodríguez *San Antonio v. Rodríguez* was a landmark case involving the constitutionality of using property taxes to fund public schools.[8] At the heart of the case lay the question of the equitable funding of public schools. Lawyers for Rodríguez and seven other children in the poor Edgewood independent school district (ISD) in the San Antonio area argued that the current system of financing public schools in Texas was unfair. The Edgewood school district had one of the highest property tax rates in the country, but could raise only $37 per pupil. Meanwhile the neighboring school district of Alamo Heights was able to raise $413 per pupil with a much lower property tax rate. The difference was that the value of the property subject to taxation in Alamo Heights far exceeded that in Edgewood. Equalizing educational funding would require Edgewood to tax at the rate of $5.76 per $100 of property value, while Alamo Heights could tax at a rate of $0.68 per $100 of property value.

A three-judge federal district court was impaneled to hear the case in January 1969. The district court initially delayed action, giving the 1971 Texas legislature time to address the funding issue. When the legislature failed to act during its regular session, the court took action. On December 23, 1971, it ruled that the Texas school finance system was unconstitutional under the **equal protection clause** of the Fourteenth Amendment to the U.S. Constitution. However, on appeal to the U.S. Supreme Court, the decision was overturned. On March 21, 1973, the Supreme Court ruled 5–4 that states such as Texas were not required to subsidize poorer school districts under the equal protection clause of the U. S. Constitution. The question of equity in public school funding would have to be addressed later in terms of Texas's state constitution and in Texas courts.

equal protection clause provision in the Fourteenth Amendment of the U.S. Constitution guaranteeing citizens the "equal protection of the laws"; this clause has been the basis for the civil rights of African Americans, women, and other groups

Edgewood ISD v. Kirby The second landmark case involving the financing of public schools was *Edgewood ISD v. Kirby*. Unlike *Rodriguez*, *Edgewood* considered whether the system of funding public schools through local property taxes fulfilled the Texas State Constitution's provisions on education. Much of the litigation over the next few years would center on Article VII, Section 1, of the 1876 Constitution, which read:

> A general diffusion of knowledge being essential to the preservation of the liberties and rights of the people, it shall be the duty of the Legislature of the State to establish and make suitable provision for the support and maintenance of an efficient system of free public schools.

A key constitutional issue would be exactly what constituted an "efficient system of free public schools."

On behalf of the Edgewood ISD, the Mexican American Legal Defense and Education Fund (MALDEF) sued William Kirby, the State Commissioner of Education, on May 23, 1984. Initially, only eight districts were represented in the case. By the time the case was finally decided, 67 other school districts had joined the original plaintiffs. The plaintiffs argued that the state's reliance on local property taxes to fund public education discriminated against poor children by denying

The Edgewood *cases challenged the property tax–based funding system that made for inferior facilities and impoverished resources for schools in poor districts (such as the one shown here), while schools in wealthy districts thrived.*

them equal opportunities in education. One month after the original case was filed, the legislature passed House Bill 72, a modest reform measure that increased state aid to poor districts. In 1985 plaintiffs filed an amended lawsuit, arguing that the legislature's action was far from satisfactory.

The amended case was heard early in 1987 by a state district judge, who ruled on April 29, 1987, in favor of the plaintiffs. He found the state's system for financing public education unconstitutional, violating both the "equal protection" (Article I, Section 3) and "efficient system" (Article VII, Section 1) clauses of the Texas Constitution. The judge called for the institution of a new system of public school funding by September 1989.

In a 2–1 vote, a state appeals court reversed this decision in December 1988, finding that the funding system was constitutional. Appealing this decision to the Texas Supreme Court, plaintiffs finally won on July 5, 1989. In a 9–0 decision, the Texas Supreme Court held that the funding system was, indeed, in violation of the state constitution. The court held that education was a fundamental right under the Texas Constitution and that the "glaring disparities" between rich and poor schools violated the efficiency clause of the constitution. In its ruling, the court did not demand "absolute equality" in per pupil spending. But it did require a standard of "substantially equal access to similar revenues per pupil at similar levels of tax effort."[9] It ordered the legislature to implement an equitable system by the 1990–91 school year.

The Texas Supreme Court's ruling touched off a political firestorm that swept through Texas politics throughout the early 1990s. The legislature failed to pass appropriate legislation in four special sessions called to address the funding problem. Finally, on June 1, 1990, a special judge known as a master, who was appointed by the Texas Supreme Court, announced an equity financing plan that would be implemented if the legislature failed to develop one of its own. Essentially, the plan called for wealthy school districts to transfer funds to poorer districts in order to equalize funds available to all public schools across the state. The so-called Robin Hood plan finally shook the legislature into action. During a sixth special session, the legislature passed Senate Bill 1 (SB 1), which, among other things, implemented funding adjustments to further assist poor school districts. Significantly, the bill did not restrict the ability of wealthier districts to enrich themselves through their higher property tax bases.

The new system of funding was found to be unconstitutional by a state district court in a case that came to be known as *Edgewood II*. The state supreme court upheld the lower court ruling, arguing that SB 1 failed to restructure the overall funding system. The court was particularly critical of the ability of wealthy school systems to accumulate funds outside the system and hinted that a solution might lie in the creation of consolidated countywide tax bases. The legislature responded by passing Senate Bill 351 (SB 351), creating 188 "county education districts," which would equalize wealth across districts by broadening the tax base. Property taxes funding schools were to be collected by both the county education district and the local school district.

This time wealthier districts challenged the legislative initiatives to settle the equity problem in public schools. In January 1992, the state supreme court held 7–2 in *Edgewood III* that SB 351 violated two constitutional provisions. First, it had failed to get the required local voter approval of school property tax levies (Article VII, Section 3). Second, it had violated Article VII, Sections 1–3, which had prohibited a state property tax since 1980. Interestingly, the court did not rule on the nature of the tax itself or whether it adequately addressed the equity question. The state was given until June 1993 to devise a new system for funding public education that was equitable and constitutional.

The legislature met in special session and during regular session in an attempt to meet the court-imposed deadline. A constitutional amendment to allow for a statewide property tax was put before the voters on May 1, 1993, and soundly defeated. The legislature responded by quickly passing Senate Bill 7 (SB 7). The key difference between SB 7 and earlier attempts to address the equity issue was its equalization and recapture provisions. Seeking to redress the imbalance between wealthier and poorer districts, the bill set a $280,000 cap on the per student taxable property value base in all districts. Districts with property values exceeding this limit had to choose one of a variety of methods to reduce their taxable wealth. Among these methods were consolidating with a poorer district, ceding property tax base to a poorer district, writing a check to the state, partnering with a poorer district, or consolidating with one or more other districts.

SB 7 was challenged in *Edgewood IV* but was upheld as being constitutional by the state supreme court. The court noted that additional work was still needed on equalizing and improving school facilities across the state. Unfortunately, not enough was done in a timely manner to address the problem. In November 2005, the Texas Supreme Court upheld a lower court ruling that the school districts lacked "meaningful discretion" in setting local maintenance and operation tax rates. In the court's opinion, too many districts were being forced to set tax rates at the maximum $1.50 per $100 valuation. Essentially, this meant that the school system was being financed by an unconstitutional state property tax. The court gave the legislature until June 1, 2006, to address the matter or it would enjoin the state from distributing funding to the public school system.

One means of encouraging educational excellence has been to allow students to transfer from low-performing to high-performing schools, thus promoting competition among the schools and allowing parents more choices.

It took three special sessions of the state legislature to craft a compromise and finally put constitutional concerns over the financing of public schools brought on by Robin Hood to rest. The final proposal cut property taxes by a third and replaced lost revenues with money raised statewide by an expanded business tax and a new $1-per-pack tax on cigarettes. General revenue monies are now used to address some of the inequities of the property tax system.[10] Unfortunately, the compromise may have generated as many problems as it solved. As was noted in Chapter 11's discussion of the budgetary crisis of 2011, policy makers had woefully overestimated the revenue that would be generated by the new business taxes. A large portion of the long-term budget deficit facing the state in the upcoming 2013 legislative session can be directly attributed to the compromise put into place to resolve the constitutional problem of financing public education. Ironically, the compromise over funding public education was a primary factor responsible for the large cutbacks in public school funding across the state beginning in 2012.

The struggle to rework the funding mechanism for public education was only one dimension of educational policy in Texas in the 1980s and '90s. Concerns over the quality of education in the state and how best to promote educational excellence will continue to define educational policy in the early twenty-first century.

Educational Excellence and Accountability in Texas

The equity issue in public education had been touched off by litigation. Only when forced by the courts to rethink how schools were being funded was the legislature finally willing to act. A different set of factors has driven the debate over educational excellence and accountability.

The issue of education reform came to a head in the early 1980s in Texas. The Texas debate was actually part of a larger national debate over the state of education in the United States.[11] A 1983 report by the National Commission on Excellence in Education, *A Nation at Risk*, identified a number of crises that were beginning to grip the nation's educational system. Test scores were declining and functional illiteracy was on the rise. Students were simply not equipped with the intellectual skills required in the modern world. If steps were not taken soon to reform education in the United States, the report argued, the nation was at risk of falling behind other countries in the rapidly changing world of international competition.[12]

Educational reform was put on the state agenda when, at the end of the 1983 regular session, the legislature established the Select Committee on Public Education (SCOPE). SCOPE was created as a 22-member committee to which the governor would have only five appointments.[13] The remaining seats were filled by appointments made by the House and Senate leadership and by three members of the State Board of Education. The intent of the legislature in creating SCOPE was not only to figure out how to fund pay raises for teachers, but also to evaluate the entire system of public education in the state.

One of the most important decisions made by Governor White was appointing the Dallas businessman Ross Perot to chair the committee. Perot had supported White's opponent in the 1982 gubernatorial race. It was felt that his participation in the process would help broaden support for the committee across party lines as well as bring in needed support from the business community. At the time of his selection, however, few knew how important Perot would be to the process of educational reform. To the surprise of many, Perot took an active role in SCOPE, mobilizing the committee in private and public to take on what he considered abuses in the public education system.

Perot was particularly scornful of athletic programs and what he considered the misplaced priorities of the existing educational system. In the end, SCOPE presented 140 recommendations for reforming the Texas education system in its final report on April 19, 1984. Among the most controversial of the proposed reforms was "no pass, no play." Students who failed to earn a passing grade of 70 would be unable to participate in any extracurricular activities for the next grading period of six weeks. But "no pass, no play" was only the tip of the iceberg. Other reform proposals set new standards for students' attendance and performance; annual school performance reports and tighter accreditation standards, with schools that did not meet these higher standards losing state funds; a longer school year—from 175 to 180 days; and a professional career ladder for teachers, tying pay raises to performance.[14]

In early July 1984, many of the reform proposals were put into place in a 266-page education reform bill, along with the necessary accompanying tax increases.

The so-called Perot reforms were but the first round in the debate over excellence and accountability in the public school system. A second round opened during the 1995 legislative session. There were some important differences in the reform package finally signed by Republican governor George W. Bush. The Perot reforms had generally centralized control over education policy in the state. The Bush reforms, in contrast, gave more discretion to local school districts to achieve the educational goals the state was mandating. Some of the reforms put through were symbolic. The controversial "no pass, no play" rule was relaxed, cutting the period of nonparticipation from six to three weeks and lifting a ban on practicing while on scholastic probation. But other changes were more substantive. Local control of public schools was increased by limiting the power of the TEA. Local voters were empowered to adopt home charters that could free their school districts from many state requirements, including class-size caps at lower grades. The 1995 reforms also enabled students, under certain circumstances, to transfer from low-performing schools to high-performing schools in their districts, thus promoting competition among the schools by holding them accountable for the performance of their students.[15]

Education Policy in Perspective

It is difficult to judge whether the reforms instituted in the 1980s and '90s have improved the overall equity and excellence of public education in Texas. Recent statistics suggest that the state still has a long way to go in turning its public school system into one of the best in the nation. Despite the efforts of recent administrations to raise them, teacher salaries and overall state and local spending on public education remained low compared with those in other states. In 2009 the high school graduation rate in Texas was 80.6 percent (ranging from 73.5 percent for Latinos to 93.5 percent for Asians/Pacific Islanders), ranking the state 36th in the nation. In 2010 the average SAT scores in Texas were 481 in reading and 504 in math, compared with a national average of 1017 for the two tests together.[16] These scores represented a slight but ongoing fall in Texas test scores in the first decade of the twenty-first century.

Although the dropout rate in grades 7 through 12 has been declining since the 1990s, it is still high among minorities. At the same time, scores on standardized tests such as the TAAS (Texas Assessment of Academic Skills) test improved across the state, sparking calls for the development of new assessment tests to hold teachers and schools accountable. The TAKS (Texas Assessment of Knowledge and Skills) test replaced TAAS in 2003 and expanded the number of subjects assessed from grades 3 through 11. Despite such efforts to increase oversight and accountability in the classroom, concerns were mounting that too much time was spent "teaching to the test." Reforms passed during the 2007 legislative session limited TAKS to grades 3 through 8. In high school TAKS was replaced by new subject tests given at the end of a course.[17]

One of the ways that the 2011 legislature balanced the budget without raising taxes was by making severe cuts in elementary and secondary education funding. The cuts jeopardized many of the reform initiatives of the previous 20 years. Whether the cuts will be reduced or expanded in coming legislative sessions will be determined by the overall economic health of the state and the political commitments of the state's leaders. Reforming education with a concern for equity and excellence will continue to be a major policy issue in the state for many years to come.

● Welfare Policy

Describe the state's role in addressing poverty and how it is affected by national policies

One long-term policy issue has been how to provide for the basic needs of poor people in Texas. This issue raises fundamental questions about the state's role in helping people in poverty and the extent to which national policies determine the state's response to the needs of poor people.

Poverty in Texas

Poverty has never been a popular subject in Texas. The idea that some individuals have trouble taking care of themselves or meeting the basic needs of their families seems to fly in the face of Texas's individualistic culture. In light of the booming Texas economy of the late 1990s, many may have hoped that the poverty problem would go away. It hasn't. Between 1990 and 1999, the percentage of Texans living in poverty fell from 15.9 percent to 15.0 percent but rose again in 2008 to 15.8 percent. According to the U.S. Census Bureau, 4,143,077 people in Texas lived at or below the poverty line in 2009. In November 2010, a total of 3,498,992 people were enrolled in Medicaid, the federally financed, state-operated program providing medical services to low-income people.[18] Poverty remains one of the most intractable problems facing the state.

Policy makers define poverty in very specific terms. Poverty is the condition under which individuals or families do not have the resources to meet their basic needs, including food, shelter, health care, transportation, and clothing. The U.S.

The Texas Department of Public Welfare was established in 1939 during the New Deal. This photo shows farmers receiving support from the government at the time.

Department of Health and Human Services developed a "poverty index" in 1964. This index was revised in 1969 and 1980. The index calculates the consumption requirements of families based on their size and composition. The poverty index is adjusted every year to account for the rate of inflation. Although there is considerable controversy as to whether it adequately measures the minimal needs of a family, the poverty index is the generally accepted standard against which poverty is measured.

In 2011 the federal poverty guideline was $10,890 a year for one person and $3,820 a year for each additional person in the family. Almost one out of four Latinos and African Americans in Texas are poor. Slightly more than 12 percent of persons over 65 years of age in Texas are poor compared to 9.9 percent in the nation as a whole. Poverty among children, especially young children, is much higher than in the United States as a whole. Fifty-eight percent of poor families in Texas have a worker at the head of the family. More than one in four Texans (26.6 percent) are at 150 percent of the poverty level or less, and 36.5 percent are at 200 percent of the poverty level or less. One hundred fifty percent of the poverty level is $26,400 a year for a family of three, and 200 percent of the federal poverty level is $35,200 a year for a family of three.

Texas uses these federal poverty guidelines to determine eligibility for a variety of social programs. For example, a family of three is eligible for reduced-price school meals if the family is at no more than 185 percent of the poverty level. A family of three is eligible for free school meals if the family is at no more than 130 percent of the poverty level, and eligible for food stamps if the family is at no more than 130 percent of the poverty level.[19]

Welfare in Texas, 1935–96

The origins of modern welfare policy lie in President Franklin Delano Roosevelt's **New Deal**.[20] Prior to the 1930s, welfare was considered to be a state and local responsibility. The Great Depression overwhelmed many state and local welfare arrangements, causing the federal government to expand its role in addressing the needs of the poor and the unemployed. The Social Security Act of 1935 transformed the way in which welfare policy was implemented in the United States. Along with two social insurance programs (Old Age Insurance and Unemployment Insurance), the Social Security Act established a number of state-federal public assistance programs: Aid for Dependent Children (ADC, later **Aid to Families with Dependent Children** or **AFDC**), Old Age Assistance (OAA), and Aid for the Blind (AB). States administered and determined the benefit levels for these programs. In exchange for federal assistance in funding, state programs had to meet certain minimum federal guidelines.

The Department of Public Welfare was established in Texas in 1939 to run the state's various public assistance programs. It was to be supervised by a state board of welfare, composed of three members appointed by the governor for six-year terms. The board appointed an executive director who, in turn, was the chief administrative officer of the department.[21]

Through the early 1960s, the basic strategy adopted by welfare policy makers in Texas was to minimize the cost to the state while maximizing federal dollars. Some programs were expanded during these years. In 1950, ADC became AFDC as mothers were included in the program. Other new social-service programs were also added. Much of the initiative for the expansion of welfare came from the federal

New Deal President Franklin Delano Roosevelt's 1930s programs to stimulate the national economy and provide relief to victims of the Great Depression.

Aid to Families with Dependent Children (AFDC) a federally and state financed program for children living with parents or relatives who fell below state standards of need. Replaced in 1996 by TANF.

Medicaid a federal and state program financing medical services to low-income people.

Supplemental Security Income (SSI) a national welfare program passed in 1972 that provides assistance to low-income elderly or disabled individuals; replaced the federal-state programs that had offered assistance to the blind, the permanently and totally disabled, and the aged

In 2012, 3.6 million Texans participated in the food stamps program (now called SNAP), which allows low-income people to buy groceries with a special debit card. SNAP benefits are paid by the federal government, but the state and federal governments share administrative costs.

government. One of the major issues in Texas was the problem of the constitutional ceiling on welfare spending. This had to be raised from $35 million in 1945 to $52 million in 1961, and again to $60 million in 1963.[22]

Welfare policy in Texas was transformed fundamentally in the 1960s. Federal court decisions between 1968 and 1971 effectively ended a series of policies such as bans on men in the houses of welfare recipients and residency requirements, both of which had been used by states to keep welfare rolls low. In 1965, Congress established **Medicaid**, a state-federal program to finance health care for the poor. President Lyndon Johnson's "War on Poverty" also expanded the number of social service programs available to the poor. Increasingly, it was argued, the solution to alleviating poverty was through expanded federal control over welfare programs.

In 1965 the Department of Public Welfare was authorized to work with the federal government's new antipoverty programs. The welfare ceiling was raised to $80 million in 1969. Among the welfare programs administered by the department were four public assistance programs: AFDC, Aid for the Blind, Aid to the Permanently and Totally Disabled, and Old Age Assistance. The latter three programs were taken over by the federal government in 1972 in the form of the new national **Supplemental Security Income (SSI)** program to provide assistance to individuals in need who have disabilities or are aged. Along with these programs, the department ran the Texas Medical Assistance Program (Medicaid), the national food stamp program, and a series of social-service programs.

In 1977 the Department of Public Welfare became the Department of Human Resources. It was renamed again in 1985 as the Texas Department of Human Services and then to the Health and Human Services Commission in 2003. The name reflected an ongoing desire on the part of policy makers to think of the agency less as a welfare agency and more as a service agency to the poor. By 1980, the department was reorganized to focus on the major client groups it served: families with children and aged and disabled people. In 1981 the constitutional ceiling on welfare spending was replaced with a more flexible standard. Instead of a flat cap of $80 million, welfare expenditures could not exceed 1 percent of the total state budget. In 1989 the state board of welfare was expanded from three to six members.[23]

Between 1967 and 1973, participation rates and welfare expenditures in Texas exploded. The number of children on AFDC during this time rose from 79,914 to 325,244, while the number of families on AFDC went from 23,509 to 120,254. Rates leveled off in the late 1970s, but they began to push upward again in the 1980s. Liberal attempts to reform welfare by nationalizing AFDC (turning the state-federal program into a national program like SSI) failed throughout the 1970s. Conservative attempts to compel welfare recipients to participate in job-training programs, such as the Work Incentive Program of 1967, had limited success. A frustrating political stalemate set in. Few were happy with welfare policy as then conducted. But no consensus had emerged as to what would be a better alternative. Meanwhile, welfare rolls expanded and expenditures continued to increase in both Texas and the nation.

The Idea of Dependency and Welfare Reform in the 1990s

By the mid-1980s, a new critique of welfare programs had begun to emerge. At its heart lay the idea that the well-intentioned policies of the 1960s had back-fired, creating a dysfunctional underclass of people dependent on welfare. Welfare programs such as AFDC may have helped people financially in the short run, but in the long run they had robbed people of the character traits and the moral values that would enable them to succeed in a market economy.[24] Observers believed that the skyrocketing rate of children born to poor, unwed mothers was in part the result of a perverse set of incentives created by welfare programs. Under the existing welfare system, at least to a point the more children you had, the higher the welfare check. Because some states did not provide welfare to families with fathers in the home, fathers were actually being encouraged to abandon their families so that they might qualify for welfare. According to critics, the poor needed encouragement and proper incentives to become independent workers rather than a permanent source of income from the state.

At the national level, the deadlock over welfare reform was broken with the passage of the Family Support Act in 1988. In the attempt to stem the rising tide of illegitimacy rates and single-parent families among the poor, the act mandated two-parent coverage for all state AFDC programs. It also established a number of new "workfare" programs whose goals were to get people off welfare and into the workforce. New standards were also developed requiring parents to participate in these workfare programs or lose their benefits.[25]

Much hyperbole surrounded the passage of the Family Support Act. Although the act did break new ground in formulating programs to help people make the transition from welfare to work, it also was an important expansion of the existing AFDC system. Far from declining, welfare roll expansion was unabated in the early 1990s. In Texas, this expansion was especially rapid. By 1994, an average 786,400 people were receiving AFDC in Texas. Total federal and state expenditures rose from $188.3 million in 1984 to $544.9 million in 1994. Food stamp costs also rose rapidly during this period, from $664.9 million to $2.2 billion. But AFDC and food stamps were only part of the problem. Medicaid was escalating at a rate of more than 20 percent a year. During the 1994–95 biennium, $18.6 billion in state and federal funds was being spent on Medicaid. Texas's share was 13 percent of the state budget, or $6.7 billion. Escalating costs of AFDC, food stamps, and Medicaid provided the backdrop to the welfare reforms that would be put into place by Texas policy makers in 1995.

Growing discontent over welfare policy across the country encouraged many states to seek waivers from federal regulations so that they too might experiment with welfare reform.[26] Some states sought to modify AFDC rules to eliminate some of the perverse incentive structures in the welfare system. Other states set caps on benefits and how long one could continue to receive welfare. Welfare became a state issue during the 1994 elections. As governor of Texas, George W. Bush echoed the ideas of conservative critics of the welfare system, arguing that the existing system was robbing people of their independence. Among the changes that he called for were

- strengthening child-support procedures and penalties
- imposing a two-year limit on benefits for recipients able to work
- requiring individuals receiving welfare to accept a state-sponsored job if after two years they were unable to find work
- creating new child-care and job-training programs

- requiring unwed mothers to live with their parents or grandparents
- moving family support systems from the state to the local level

Data released by the comptroller's office lent support to the Bush contention that there were serious problems with the existing system of welfare in Texas. Over one-quarter of all welfare recipients in 1993 were "long-term" recipients who had remained on the rolls for five years or more. The publication of *A Partnership for Independence: Welfare Reform in Texas*, by the office of the comptroller, John Sharp, a Democrat, helped to set the legislative agenda for the debate over welfare policy. Agreeing with other critics across the nation who were unhappy with the current state of welfare policy, the report documented how welfare often failed to help those most in need or to encourage those dependent on welfare to become independent of government largesse. Among the report's 100 proposals were many of the reforms that had been put into place by conservative reformers in other states or by the Bush gubernatorial administration.

A bipartisan legislative coalition ultimately supported major welfare reform in Texas. On May 26, 1995, the vote on House Bill 1863 was 128 to 9 in the House and 30 to 1 in the Senate. The law provided a number of "carrot and stick" incentives that sought to mold the character of welfare recipients in positive ways and wean them off welfare. Among the carrots were expanded education and job-training programs, as well as a select number of pilot studies involving transitional child care and medical benefits. Among the sticks were a limitation on benefits to 36 months, alimony for spouses who couldn't support themselves, and the institution of a five-year ban on reapplying for benefits once benefits ran out. To implement the state reforms, Texas secured a waiver from the federal government that freed the state from various federal regulations regarding welfare programs. In granting the waivers to Texas and other states, the Clinton administration hoped to stimulate innovative reforms that might be duplicated elsewhere.

Texas was ahead of the welfare reform curve in 1995. In 1996, President Bill Clinton signed into law the most important reform in federal welfare policy since the New Deal. The Personal Responsibility and Work Opportunity Reconciliation Act essentially rethought the assumptions that had guided the expansion of welfare programs for 60 years. Under the legislation, AFDC, JOBS (a work-related training program), and the Emergency Assistance Program were combined into one block grant entitled **Temporary Assistance for Needy Families (TANF)**. As with the welfare reforms instituted in Texas and in other states across the country, the primary purpose of TANF was to make families self-sufficient by ending the cycle of dependency on government benefits. States such as Texas were given great flexibility in setting benefit levels, eligibility requirements, and other program details.

Today in Texas, TANF provides temporary financial assistance to families with needy children when one or both of the parents are missing or disabled.[27] The TANF program provides a one-time $1,000 payment to individuals in certain crisis situations. To qualify, a recipient's income must be below 17 percent of the poverty income limit based on family size. In addition, the combined equity of the family may not exceed $2,000 ($3,000 for the elderly and disabled). People participating in TANF receive a monthly assistance payment based on the size of their family. They cannot receive benefits for more than 36 months. They are also eligible for Medicaid benefits, food stamps, and child day-care services. Unless legally exempt, recipients are also required to participate in an employment services program.

Temporary Assistance for Needy Families (TANF) a welfare program passed in 1996 to provide temporary assistance to families with needy children; replacing the AFDC program, TANF sought to make poor families self-sufficient and to give states greater flexibility in setting benefit levels, eligibility requirements, and other program details

Evaluating Welfare Reform

The welfare reforms in Texas will probably be evaluated along two dimensions. First, they will be measured in terms of the number of people receiving welfare assistance from the state. Success will be determined by the degree to which the reforms help lower the number of welfare recipients in Texas. If the reforms do not decrease the welfare rolls, they likely will be considered a failure. A second measure of success will be the degree to which the reforms help take people off welfare and move them into the workforce as productive, independent members of society.

Judged by changes in the number of people on welfare, the reforms appear to be a success. The average monthly number of people on welfare in Texas rose from a little more than half a million in 1989 to a peak of more than three-quarters of a million in 1994 but then began to fall in 1995. Time limits and work requirements were put into place by the state legislature in 1995, one year before similar measures were passed nationally by the U.S. Congress. The decline in the number of people on welfare continued over the next decade, falling to 155,895 people in 2006 and to 103,110 in 2011.[28]

By the second measure—the number of people moving from welfare to work—preliminary indications are that the welfare reforms of 1995 are more mixed in their success. A 2006 study by the Center for Public Priorities in Austin found that caseloads on TANF may have fallen, but child poverty was on the rise. Moreover, there were indications that people leaving the welfare rolls were not necessarily transitioning to work. Such problems were likely exacerbated by the economic downturn of the Great Recession that began in 2008.[29] Welfare reform in the 1990s took place under conditions of a booming economy and a rising demand for all types of labor. Jobs seemed to be available for people who were willing and able to work. But how will the new welfare policies respond to the economic problems of the early years of the twenty-first century? Now that labor markets have tightened and jobs are difficult to find, will Texas policy makers be satisfied with the

Though poverty in Texas afflicts many different social groups, Latinos currently make up the majority of Texans living below the poverty line. The border counties in west Texas are by far the poorest in the state.

welfare reforms in place? How far will unemployment be allowed to go before policy makers demand that we reconsider the incentive structure created to get people off the public dole? These are questions that policy makers concerned with welfare reform will have to consider one day. Only then will we be able to have an exact evaluation of the welfare reforms of the mid-1990s.

● Medicaid and Health Care Policy

> **Explain why Medicaid in particular and health care policy in general have been so controversial in Texas**

Medicaid, which provides for the health care of poor people, is an especially costly program for the state. The program's costs have risen more quickly than the rate of inflation, which makes Medicaid increasingly burdensome for the state budget. Funding Medicaid is a major issue in the broader debate over the state and national governments' roles in providing health care, as we will see in this section.

Medicaid

Medicaid is a state-federal program that was established under the Social Security Amendments of 1965 as Title XIX of the Social Security Act. The Social Security Act requires that Texas and other states follow certain principles and meet certain standards if they are to receive federal funds. First, Medicaid services must be available on a statewide basis. Second, the same level of service must be available to all clients throughout the state. Children are entitled to a broader range of services than adults. Third, participants must be allowed to use any health provider who meets program standards. (Providers, of course, must be willing to accept Medicaid recipients.) Fourth, the amount, duration, and scope of medical services must be "sufficiently reasonable." Exactly what this constitutes is a problem and Medicaid reimbursement rates tend to be much lower than those provided for under conventional private insurance plans. While Texas may limit the services provided to adult clients, it may not arbitrarily deny services for specific conditions or illnesses.[30]

Federal law also allows states to be granted waivers from these principles to create programs directed toward particular clients. In this approach, federal Medicaid policy mirrors the initiatives in welfare policy by providing states more freedom of action in developing programs to serve clients. For example, Texas has been granted the authority to enroll clients in managed care programs. In traditional fee-for-service programs a doctor or a hospital provides a service directly to the patient and is paid a fee for that service. In the managed care organization (MCO) model, programs such as health maintenance organizations or doctor-hospital networks act as an intermediary between the patient and the doctor, and negotiate discounted fees for medical services. In addition, MCOs reimburse their member health care providers with a monthly payment, which is known as a capitation payment because it has a limit or "cap" based on medical expenses calculated for the average patient. Another model is the Primary Care Case Management (PCCM) program, which is a noncapitated program enabling Medicaid recipients to receive medical home services from a primary care provider. As a noncapitated plan, there is no average dollar amount per patient per month set by the state to pay for the cost of health care service. Primary care providers receive fee-for-service reimbursement and a small monthly management fee directly from the state. Begun as a pilot program in 1993, the PCCM program now serves Medicaid clients in 202 mostly rural counties.

Managed care programs in Texas Medicaid have been growing in popularity since the early 1990s and became an essential part of cost containment measures instituted by the legislature over the next 20 years. In 1994, 2.9 percent of Texas Medicaid recipients were in state-sponsored managed care programs. By 2004, this participation had risen to 41.44 percent. By 2009, almost 71 percent of Medicaid recipients were in managed care programs.[31]

In addition to the PCCM program, there are several other significant managed care initiatives operating under the Medicaid program.

- The STAR (State of Texas Access Reform) program begun in 1994 operates in major urban areas of Texas, including Dallas, Houston, El Paso, Lubbock, San Antonio, Fort Worth, Austin, and the southeast region of Texas. The STAR program is primarily targeted at nondisabled children, low-income families, and pregnant women.

- STAR+PLUS is an integrated program that provides acute and long-term medical services for individuals on SSI. STAR+PLUS began as a fully capitated managed care program in the Harris County area in 1998, and was expanded to include Bexar, Nueces, and Travis counties in 2007, and Dallas and Tarrant counties in 2011.

- NorthSTAR was established in 1999 to integrate publicly funded programs in the Dallas region directed toward mental health and chemical dependency services for the indigent and the poor. Directed by the Department of State Health Services and the Texas Commission on Alcohol and Drug Abuse, NorthSTAR is the first program in Texas to provide service programs and financial assets into an integrated system of care.

- Begun in 2008, STAR Health is a statewide program aimed at providing health care services to children in foster and kinship care. Among other benefits, STAR Health participants receive medical, dental, and vision care, along with unlimited prescriptions.

Medicaid Participation The initial goal of Medicaid in 1965 was to pay the medical bills of low-income individuals on public assistance. Over the last five decades, Medicaid has grown from a narrowly defined program targeting people on public assistance to a large, complex insurance program serving a variety of special groups. In the late 1980s and early 1990s, Medicaid was expanded to include older adults not fully covered by Medicare (a federal medical insurance program funded through payroll taxes for persons 65 years of age and older), people with disabilities, and pregnant women. Individuals participating in TANF and SSI automatically qualify for Medicaid, as do others who meet these other criteria.[32]

A variety of factors can affect an individual's eligibility to participate in Medicaid. People can go on and off Medicaid given their changing eligibility status. For example, eligibility can change when a parent or caregiver has a change in income or when a child is born. Eligibility also can change when a child reaches a certain age. For these reasons, there is significant fluctuation in Medicaid enrollment from month to month. However, one fact is strikingly clear: participation rates have gone up significantly in the first decade of the twenty-first century. Between 2001 and 2009, the average monthly Medicaid enrollment in Texas rose from 1.87 million people to 3.1 million.

It is important to note that the increase in participation is not caused by a rise in participation through Texas's principal public assistance program, the TANF program. As monthly caseloads grew between 2001 and 2009 for Medicaid, the number of those eligible through the TANF actually decreased from approximately 500,000 to less than 350,000 in 2009. Although Medicaid and public assistance are still joined together, the close link between them that existed at the founding of Medicaid has largely been severed.

In 2009, 55 percent of the Medicaid population was female and more than 65 percent were children. Children, however, accounted for only 32 percent of the overall cash expended by Medicaid in Texas. Fifty-eight percent of expenditures went to care of aged and disabled beneficiaries who constituted only 30 percent of the beneficiary population. Nondisabled adult beneficiaries constituted 9 percent of the Medicaid population and received 10 percent of the expenditures. Figure 12.1 shows 2009 participants by age group. In 2009, 54 percent of Medicaid recipients were Latino, 23 percent were Caucasian, and 18 percent were African American.

Administration and Financing of Medicaid in Texas In Texas, Medicaid is administered through the Texas Health and Human Services Commission. At the federal level, the Centers for Medicare and Medicaid in the Department of Health and Human Services monitor Texas's Medicaid program and establish basic ser-

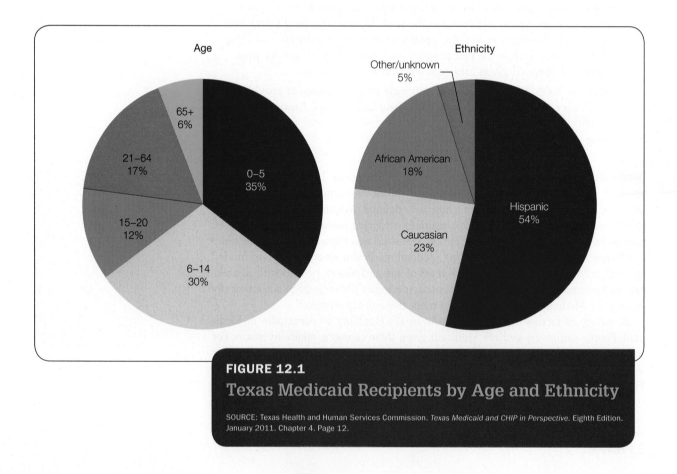

FIGURE 12.1

Texas Medicaid Recipients by Age and Ethnicity

SOURCE: Texas Health and Human Services Commission. *Texas Medicaid and CHIP in Perspective.* Eighth Edition. January 2011. Chapter 4. Page 12.

vices, delivery, quality, funding, and eligibility standards. Through Medicaid, Texas and the federal government together pay for a variety of health care services for a number of low-income populations. The acute health care services paid for include physician bills, inpatient care in a hospital and outpatient care, and pharmacy, lab, and x-ray services. Medicaid also provides for selected long-term and support services including home- and community-based services for the disabled, home-health and personal care, and nursing services (Figure 12.2).

The federal portion of the program is determined every year by comparing average state per capita income to the average national per capita income. Each state thus has its own FMAP (the federal medical assistance percentage). Poorer states receive more federal assistance for the program than richer states. In 2011 the FMAP for Texas was 60.56 percent, which means that 39.44 percent of all Medicaid expenditures were state funded.

A related program to Medicaid is the Children's Health Insurance Program (CHIP), which provides coverage for children in families with incomes too high to qualify for Medicaid. Established in 1997 under Title XXI of the Social Security Act, CHIP is administered like Medicaid through the Centers for Medicare and Medicaid Services in the U.S. Department of Health and Human Services. The 2010 federal allocation to Texas for CHIP was more than $925 million. The average monthly caseload for CHIP was 28,300 in 2000 and rose to more than 503,000 in 2009.

Medicaid and CHIP expenditures have become an increasing part of both the national and state budgets. In 1996 the total Medicaid budget of both federal and state dollars was $8.2 billion. By 2009, this had risen to $22.8 billion. By 2009, federal expenditures on Medicaid and CHIP encompassed 7 percent of the $3.5 trillion federal budget.[33] Figure 12.3 shows the average increases in Medicaid spending between 1990 and 2010. Figure 12.4 shows the distribution of Medicaid payments across various enrollment groups.

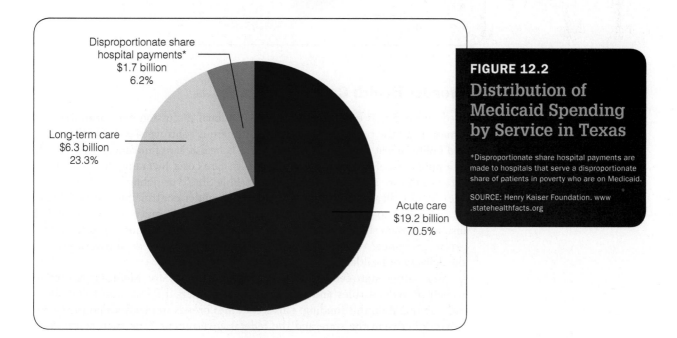

Disproportionate share
hospital payments*
$1.7 billion
6.2%

Long-term care
$6.3 billion
23.3%

Acute care
$19.2 billion
70.5%

FIGURE 12.2

Distribution of Medicaid Spending by Service in Texas

*Disproportionate share hospital payments are made to hospitals that serve a disproportionate share of patients in poverty who are on Medicaid.

SOURCE: Henry Kaiser Foundation. www .statehealthfacts.org

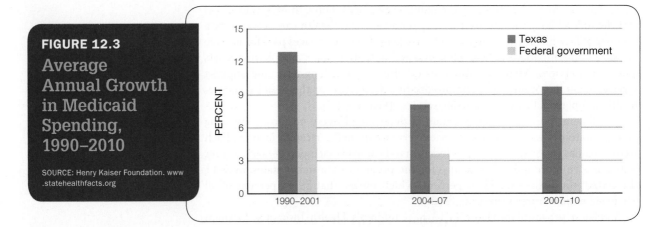

FIGURE 12.3

Average Annual Growth in Medicaid Spending, 1990–2010

SOURCE: Henry Kaiser Foundation. www.statehealthfacts.org

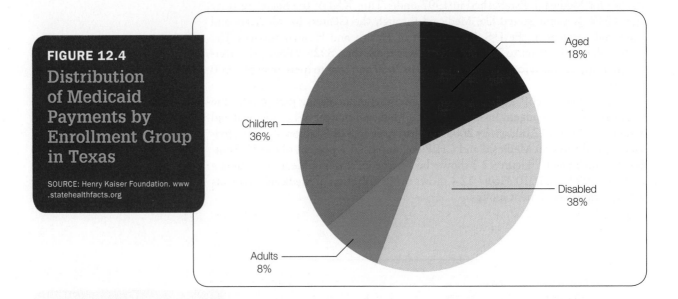

FIGURE 12.4

Distribution of Medicaid Payments by Enrollment Group in Texas

SOURCE: Henry Kaiser Foundation. www.statehealthfacts.org

Broader Health Care Issues in Texas

Medicaid policy is embedded in a larger national discussion over health care in America and the proper way to fund it. Numerous controversies divide the public and politicians at all levels of government. Is health care fundamentally a private or a public issue? How can exploding health care costs, including the costs of private health care insurance like Blue Cross/Blue Shield or public health care insurance like Medicare and Medicaid, be brought under control? Should individuals be compelled to purchase health care insurance? How much and what kind of insurance? Who should foot the bill for individuals who cannot afford to pay for private insurance? What is the proper role for the state and federal governments in the delivery of health care across the nation?

As in other state-federal programs, federal money for Medicaid is accompanied by federal rules and regulations with which the state must comply in order to maintain this funding. This sometimes breeds tremendous political controversy between the state and the federal government. One such controversy broke out in early 2012 over provisions relating to Texas's Medicaid Women's Health Program.[34]

The Medicaid Women's Health Program in Texas serves more than 100,000 women and is funded by $35 million from federal funds and $7 million from state funds. Through subsidized clinics located across the state, the program helps pay for birth control, health screening, and family exams for a select group of women on Medicaid. Planned Parenthood offers these services as well as abortion services at its various clinics across the state. Conservatives in Texas, including Governor Perry, were unhappy with any state monies being used to subsidize groups supporting abortion and moved to cut program funds from going to these clinics. But federal regulations clearly state that patients in the program, not state officials, decide where money from the program is spent.

By March 2012, an impasse had been reached. On one side were Governor Perry and the Republican-dominated state legislature, who ordered an end to Medicaid funding of Planned Parenthood clinics. On the other side were the federal government and supporters of Planned Parenthood, who insisted on strictly following federal rules and guidelines. Interestingly, some moderate Republicans, like Senator Kay Bailey Hutcheson, broke with the governor and backed Planned Parenthood in the dispute. By early March 2012 all federal funding of the Texas Women's Health Program had been pulled. Governor Perry claimed that he would find new funding for the program at the state level that would exclude Planned Parenthood.

In early May 2012, the issue became even more complicated. Eight Planned Parenthood clinics that did not provide abortion services sued the state, claiming their rights to freedom of speech and freedom of association had been violated. A federal appeals court ruled on August 22, 2012 that Texas could ban Planned Parenthood from receiving funds. Texas Solicitor General Jonathan Mitchell reiterated the state's opposition to providing taxpayer money "to entities that affiliate with abortion-promoting entities."[35] The conflict over the funding and administration of the Texas Women's Health Program signals the emergence of a new set of conflicts over Medicaid in Texas and a new round in the debate over the relationship between the national and the state government in the federal system.

Cost, however, is the single most important issue confronting policy makers regarding Medicaid in Texas. Now encompassing more than 25 percent of state expenditures, Medicaid in Texas as in other states threatens to overwhelm the budget. In the spring of 2012, Texas comptroller Susan Combs began referring to Medicaid as "The Big Red," the program that was going to push an otherwise healthy state budget into the red. By 2023, she claimed, "Big Red is going to be over a third of state spending."[36] Medicaid expenditures, many mandated by the federal government, would begin to crowd out other forms of spending from the state budget.

Policy makers are forever looking for ways to make the program less costly. Two strategies have predominated over the past 20 years: first, to bring more efficiency into the program by expanding managed care initiatives across the state, and second, to institute cost controls and cutbacks to providers. Both efforts have had limited success, and at the same time have sparked concern over the quality of care being offered to Medicaid participants across the state. As cost containment efforts intensify, Texas policy makers inside and outside the legislature will be compelled to increase their monitoring of the delivery of the program.

As in the nation as a whole, the problem of the uninsured lies at the heart of the debate over Medicaid and health care in Texas. In 2012 a Gallup survey found that

The Texas Sonogram Law

In 2011, the Texas legislature passed a new law requiring doctors who perform abortions to provide a sonogram to women before implementing the procedure. Abortion laws are among the most politically contentious social policies, and the Texas law garnered national attention. Because Texas is a conservative state, supporters of the sonogram policy were able to get it passed in the legislature and signed into law by Governor Rick Perry, who at the time was preparing his 2012 run for president. Opponents of the new law immediately challenged it in court, arguing that it is unconstitutional given the U.S. Supreme Court's rulings in abortion cases since the landmark *Roe v. Wade* in 1973.

The law requires doctors to provide with the sonogram "a simultaneous verbal explanation of the results of the live, real-time sonogram images, including a medical description of the dimensions of the embryo or fetus, the presence of cardiac activity, and the presence of arms, legs, external members, and internal organs." Doctors are also required to make the fetus's heartbeat audible to the woman. Although the law does not require vaginal sonograms, which entail an invasive procedure of inserting a probe into the pregnant woman's vagina, according to medical experts some cases would require this type of sonogram. Pregnant women affected by the law may choose not to view the sonogram, listen to the doctor's explanations, or listen to the heartbeat. However, doctors who refuse to comply with the law are subject to losing their licenses to practice medicine. Doctors are not required to perform the sonogram procedure for women who were impregnated as a result of rape or incest.

Proponents of Texas's new law argue that because abortion involves a nascent human life, efforts to make women think twice about going forward with the procedure should be implemented. They argue that women can still go forward with a legal abortion if they so choose, but they should have full and complete information about the consequences of the decision they are making. They also argue that the procedure is constitutional because it does not prevent women from having abortions; it only makes them go through an additional step. The Court, they argue, has already upheld waiting periods and parental consent laws for abortion. Supporters of the sonogram law believe that the state has a compelling interest to protect the lives of what they consider to be human beings in the earliest stages of development.

Opponents of the new law argue that abortion is a constitutional right that has been protected by the Supreme Court. They argue that the state is making it more difficult for women to exercise this constitutionally protected right. The law also makes women come into a medical office twice—once for the sonogram and again for the abortion after the 24-hour waiting period. They cite the Court's argument that any abortion laws cannot place an undue burden on women who choose to obtain an abortion. In particular, they argue that vaginal ultrasounds invade a woman's privacy, as they necessarily involve an

invasive procedure that women should not be required to endure. They also argue that the law violates doctors' First Amendment rights because it requires them to make statements and perform activities that are not medically necessary and that some women may not want.

Opponents sought a court ruling to delay the implementation of the law, but in February 2012, a federal district court judge refused to delay the law, deciding that the U.S. Court of Appeals for the Fifth Circuit, which includes Texas, had already ruled that the law was constitutional. While the U.S. Supreme Court can decide to hear the case if it chooses, as of late 2012, it had not agreed to do so, which meant that the law would remain in effect for the foreseeable future. Because the law strikes at the heart of the contentious debate of when life begins and whether abortions should be legal, this issue will no doubt continue to be debated all over the state and nation.

critical thinking questions

1. What are the trade-offs of this piece of legislation? Does it balance the rights of women and the interests of the state to protect fetuses?

2. Are there any possible compromises to this issue? If so, what would they look like?

for the fourth consecutive year Texas led the nation in the percentage of its population that lacked health care insurance. The Texas rate of 27.6 percent uninsured is 4 points higher than that of the next state, Mississippi at 23.5 percent. This compares with an overall national rate of 17.1 percent. Several factors were identified as contributing to this high rate: Texas has a large uninsured Latino population, a large number of people employed in low-income jobs that don't offer health insurance, a state insurance system that either does not insure preexisting conditions or only insures those conditions at high cost, and health insurance rates that are largely unregulated and cost more than the national average.[37]

Efforts to grapple with the problem of uninsured individuals go back to the New Deal in the 1930s. Although the Social Security Act of 1935 originally instituted a social security program along with various assistance programs for the poor, elderly, and disabled, provisions for health care insurance were notably missing. Efforts to push through a national health insurance program failed during the Truman administration in the late 1940s and the Clinton administration in the 1990s. The passage of Medicare for older Americans and Medicaid for the poor in 1965 provided health coverage for two groups of people but left the vast majority of the working population to private coverage or no coverage at all. Failing to pass a comprehensive health care package that would cover everyone in the United States, Congress settled on an incremental approach, one that over the years gradually expanded coverage to uninsured Americans.

The Affordable Care Act

In March 2010, Congress passed two bills, the Patient Protection and Affordable Care Act and the Health Care and Reconciliation Act of 2010, which together became known as the Affordable Care Act (ACA), often referred to as Obamacare. The passage of the ACA transformed the debate over health care policy in the United States. Passed on a largely party line vote by Congress, the legislation requires individuals not covered by existing plans to pursue health insurance or pay a penalty. Along with this "individual mandate," as the mandatory coverage came to be called, the act also increased coverage for preexisting conditions and expanded medical insurance to an estimated 30 million people.[38]

When fully implemented, the ACA is expected to bring significant change to the health insurance market in Texas as well as to Texas's Medicaid program.[39] Among the most important changes are the following:

- The ACA requires Texas to establish a Health Benefit Exchange where individuals will get assistance in accessing affordable health insurance. If Texas fails to establish one by January 1, 2014, one will be established for the state by the federal government.
- The Texas Medicaid program must be expanded to include the roughly one-quarter of the population that is currently uninsured.

Initial estimates in 2012 projected that under the ACA, insurance coverage in Texas will rise to 91 percent, with almost 40 percent of the remaining uninsured being undocumented workers. The expansion of Medicaid in Texas will be funded through a complicated set of subsidies based on family income. For the first three years of the expansion (2014–16), the federal government will cover all costs for newly eligible participants in Medicaid and CHIP. Thereafter, the percentage will slowly decline, committing Texas to a larger portion of the funding. The long-term effect of Obamacare for Texas will be a budgetary one. Increased expenditures on Medicaid and health care in Texas are all but inevitable.

The ACA sparked a national controversy that played itself out over the next two years. A majority of the states and a number of private individuals and groups challenged the constitutionality of the act in court, focusing on the mandatory coverage provisions. For three days in March 2012, the U.S. Supreme Court held oral argument on the case, *National Federation of Independent Business v. Sebelius*. A complicated decision was delivered by a divided Court on June 28, 2012. Four liberal justices believed that most features of the ACA were constitutional. Four conservative justices countered that they were not. Representing the decisive vote, Chief Justice Roberts rejected the idea that people could be mandated or forced to buy insurance under Congress's power to regulate commerce, but he nevertheless concluded that a tax penalizing people who did not get medical insurance met constitutional muster. Regarding the expansion of Medicaid, he supported a conservative position, arguing that states could not be bullied into expanding medical insurance coverage for poorer segments of the population. For federalism to thrive, Chief Justice Roberts wrote that states had to have a meaningful and real choice as to whether or not they participated in federally sponsored programs.

The complicated U.S. Supreme Court decision opened the door for a new round of political posturing around the health care issue in Texas. In early July 2012, Governor Perry announced that Texas might refuse to participate in the expanded Medicaid program, giving up millions of federal dollars for not having to incur new financial responsibilities at the state level. The final decision would be up to the legislature in the 2013 session. Perry also decided that the state would not go into the business of designing an insurance exchange in the state. Texas would let the federal government sell federally designed insurance policies in the state on its own.

As if things weren't complicated enough in the emerging discussion over what to do about Medicaid and health care coverage for the poor in Texas, a 2012 survey was released by the Texas Medical Association that found only 31 percent of Texas doctors were accepting new patients who relied on Medicaid for insurance coverage, down from 42 percent in 2012 and 67 percent in 2000. Low payment and excessive red tape were cited as the reasons for the declining acceptance of Medicaid as a form of medical insurance.[40] Further complicating matters, officials from the Texas Health and Human Services Commission released a new estimate of the costs of the ACA in Texas based upon new, more conservative assumptions about how quickly newly eligible people might apply to participate in the program. The new estimates were 42 percent less than the original ones. In July 2012, state officials believed that if Texas opted into the new ACA Medicaid programs, by 2023 the state would spend $15.6 billion of state money and bring in $100.1 billion of federal money. Despite these new projections, neither the Health and Human Services commissioner Tom Suehs nor Governor Perry believed that Texas should opt into the new ACA programs. Before Texas should participate in an expanded program, they believed the act should be "fixed" by Congress.[41]

Medicaid in Texas stands at a crossroad entering the 2013 legislative session. The ACA will go into effect, but it is unclear what that will mean for poorer Texans. Individuals will have to buy a health insurance package or pay a penalty on their federal income tax. Federal exchanges will be offering health insurance, but not with the assistance of Texas. The failure to opt into the expanded federal programs under ACA will mean a sizable portion of the poor population will continue to not have health insurance coverage, including undocumented workers whose health care was not addressed under the ACA. Texas's rejection of an expanded

What Are the Trade-Offs in Texas Public Policy?

The contemporary Texas government tends to pass conservative policies. The figures below show this in comparison to other states. Texas collects the lowest share of taxes of any state. But when government lacks revenue, it cannot spend money to address social problems, such as providing health insurance to those who cannot afford it.

State Taxes (as a percentage of gross state product)

Sixth lowest state taxes
7.9%

6.3% ⚫⚫⚫⚫⚫ 12.2%

Percent Uninsured

Highest % uninsured
24.6%

5.6% ⚫⚫⚫⚫⚫ 24.6%

State Taxation Compared to Percent Uninsured

	TAXES	UNINSURED		TAXES	UNINSURED		TAXES	UNINSURED
AK	6.3%	18.0%	VA	9.1%	14.1%	NC	9.8%	17.0%
NV	7.5%	21.3%	GA	9.1%	19.4%	NE	9.8%	13.3%
SD	7.6%	13.0%	FL	9.2%	20.8%	AR	9.9%	18.7%
TN	7.6%	14.7%	KY	9.3%	14.9%	IL	10.0%	14.8%
WY	7.8%	17.3%	WA	9.3%	13.8%	MD	10.0%	13.1%
TX	7.9%	24.6%	ID	9.4%	19.2%	MA	10.0%	5.6%
NH	8.0%	10.3%	WV	9.4%	13.5%	PA	10.1%	11.0%
SC	8.1%	20.6%	ND	9.5%	13.1%	ME	10.1%	9.4%
LA	8.2%	20.0%	IN	9.5%	13.4%	VT	10.2%	9.5%
NM	8.4%	21.6%	IA	9.5%	12.3%	MN	10.3%	9.8%
AL	8.5%	15.4%	DE	9.6%	11.3%	CA	10.6%	19.4%
CO	8.6%	13.0%	HI	9.6%	7.7%	RI	10.7%	11.4%
AZ	8.7%	19.1%	MI	9.7%	13.0%	WI	11.0%	9.4%
OK	8.7%	17.0%	UT	9.7%	13.6%	CT	12.0%	11.0%
MT	8.7%	18.1%	KS	9.7%	12.7%	NY	12.1%	15.0%
MS	8.7%	21.1%	OH	9.7%	13.7%	NJ	12.2%	15.4%
MO	9.0%	14.0%	OR	9.8%	16.2%			

SOURCES: Tax Data from the Tax Foundation, State and Local Tax Burdens: All States, One Year, 1977–2009, http://taxfoundation.org/article/state-and-local-tax-burdens-all-states-one-year-1977-2009. Health Insurance Data from the American Community Survey, U.S. Census Bureau. Health Insurance Coverage Status by State for All People: 2010. www.census.gov/hhes/www/cpstables/032011/health/toc.htm (accessed 12/13/12).

for critical analysis

1. How does the political and government structure of Texas contribute to conservative policy outcomes such as low taxes and lower spending on social programs?

2. What are the benefits of having such a low tax rate in the state? Do the benefits of a low tax rate outweigh the problems in your opinion?

Medicaid program may be a wedge issue that conservative Republicans inside and outside the state use to mount a campaign challenging federal initiatives after the fall 2012 presidential elections. One thing is clear: few individuals are willing to argue that Texas has solved the problem of providing health care to the poor. In a report released by the federal Agency for Health Research and Quality in July 2012, Texas ranked dead last in health care services and delivery.[42]

● Water Policy

Consider the growing importance of policies related to water supplies in Texas

Water is the life blood of Texas. Access to plentiful water supplies over the past 100 years has been a necessary condition for a thriving economy and an expanding urban population in Texas. Approximately 59 percent of the water used in Texas comes from aquifers (underground pools of water), the vast majority of which (60 percent) is used in irrigation, particularly in the arid Panhandle region (Figure 12.5). The remainder comes from surface sources, including rivers and reservoirs. Twenty-seven percent of the state's water use is in municipal areas. Individual cities rely on various amounts of aquifer and surface water, but overall, aquifers are the source for more than one-third of the water consumed by metropolitan areas.

Texas's water consumption is projected to increase by 82 percent, from about 18 million acre-feet per year in 2010 to about 22 million acre-feet per year in 2060.[43] An acre-foot is a volume measurement used by water planners. It com-

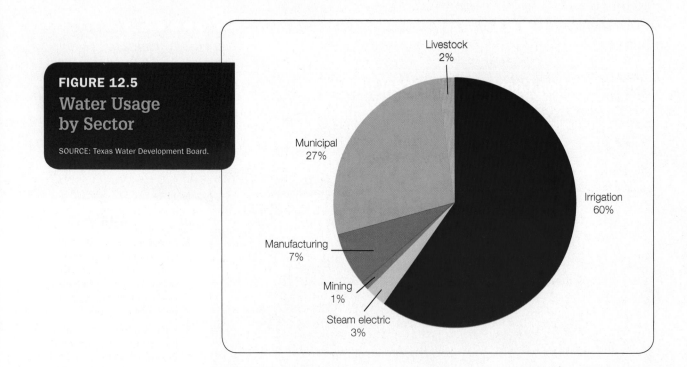

FIGURE 12.5
Water Usage by Sector

SOURCE: Texas Water Development Board.

Livestock 2%

Municipal 27%

Manufacturing 7%

Mining 1%

Steam electric 3%

Irrigation 60%

prises an acre of area (66 feet x 660 feet, one foot deep).[44] At the same time, existing supplies under current systems of production and conservation are expected to decrease by 10 percent, largely as a result of the depletion of the Ogallala Aquifer in the Texas Panhandle and reduced reliance on the Gulf Coast Aquifer. By 2060, experts project that an additional 8.3 million acre-feet per year will be needed for the state to continue to thrive.

Formulating a coherent water policy in Texas to address these and other issues is difficult for many reasons. As noted in Chapter 1, Texas is a large state with a diverse climate. The water-related issues along the Gulf Coast in southeast Texas near Houston, which is subtropical and humid, are quite different from those in the high plains Panhandle, which is semi-arid savanna, or in the El Paso desert. For example, along the southeastern border with Louisiana, average annual rainfall is more than 80 inches per year, while near El Paso it is only 10 inches per year.[45] There are 15 major river basins and 8 coastal basins across the state, as well as 9 major and 21 minor aquifers.

Water policy is further complicated by the fact that various regions of the state have experienced periodic severe droughts and devastating floods. Throughout the twentieth century, reservoirs have been built to more effectively distribute water during times of shortage and to control flooding. In 1913, when the Texas Board of Water Engineers was established, there were only eight major reservoirs in the state. By 1950, the number of major reservoirs had grown to 53. Today there are 188.[46]

Water Law in Texas

Underlying water policy in Texas is a complicated system of private property rights derived from three sources: Spanish law, traditional English common law, and statutory law. Texas law recognizes several legal classes of water rights for surface water and groundwater that are governed by different rules. Historically, these variations in the law have made the forging of water policy an arduous and at times a politically charged matter.

In 1967 the law covering surface water and relatively well-defined underground streams was markedly clarified when the state legislature passed the Water Rights Adjudication Act. This legislation essentially merged the various water rights doctrines dating back to the nineteenth century into a unified water permit system. It requires individuals seeking water rights to file a claim with the Texas Commission on Environmental Quality (originally called the Texas Water Commission) before using the water. A complex administrative and judicial process was put into place that essentially grants water rights holders certificates of adjudicated water rights. The ability of the state to control and manage surface water use thus was greatly expanded by the 1967 act.[47]

Groundwater law, that is, law regarding water flowing, or "percolating," underground, differs significantly from surface water law.[48] In *Houston and the Central Railroad Company v. East* (1904), the Texas Supreme Court adopted a strict common law notion of property law for percolating underground water called the "law of capture." This standard is also found in Texas oil and gas law. Essentially, the law says that the first person to "capture" the water by pumping it out of the ground and using it owns the water. Landowners have the right to capture as much groundwater that is under their property as they wish without regard to the interests of other property owners whose land may also lie on top of the pool of underground water. The rule of capture in water property rights has one important consequence for the development of underground water resources in the state. It encourages landowners to take as much water as possible from groundwater sources without considering the needs of other consumers. The law of capture can work against conservation efforts of private individuals who are trying to protect the water under their lands. It can also undercut efforts of planning authorities to develop a water plan for a particular area that takes into account the short-term and long-term availability of water as well as the competing uses for available water.

Finding a balance between the law of capture and the need to plan has troubled policy makers for much of the last 60 years. *Houston and the Texas Central Railroad v. East* was reaffirmed by the Texas Supreme Court in 1955. In their ruling, the court stated that "percolating waters are regarded as the property of the owner of the surface who may, in the absence of malice, intercept, impede and appropriate such waters while they are on their premises, and make whatever use of them they please, regardless of the fact that use cuts off the flow of such waters to adjoining land and deprives the adjoining owner of their use." Nevertheless, the court also came to accept the state's authority to regulate groundwater. In 1949 the state legislature passed the Texas Groundwater Act, which created water districts to manage groundwater supply.

Today there are 99 groundwater districts in Texas with varying powers. The smallest district is the Red Sands Groundwater Conservation District in Hidalgo County, covering 31 square miles. The largest is the High Plains Underground Water District, covering 12,000 square miles over the Ogallala Aquifer. Generally, the groundwater districts are able to develop regulations to protect the water supply provided by groundwater sources, including rules that may restrict pumping, require well permits, delineate well-spacing, and establish rates of water usage. The rules and regulations generated by these groundwater districts, however, can come into direct conflict with the law of capture, as we will see later.[49]

Planning Authorities and Water Policy

The history of water planning in Texas stretches back to the early twentieth century. A constitutional amendment in 1904 paved the way for the development of various agencies and authorities concerned with water planning. Among the most important innovations put into place by the state legislature in the early 1900s were drainage districts (1905); conservation and reclamation districts, later referred to as river authorities (1917); and water and control improvement districts (1925).

In 1913 the Texas legislature established the Texas Board of Water Engineers, a three-member commission appointed by the governor to serve six-year terms. Among the responsibilities of the board were the organization of irrigation and water supply districts, the approval of bonds for such districts, the issuance of permits for storing and diverting water, and the development of plans for storing and using floodwater. Additional duties later assigned to the board included groundwater policy, such as designating groundwater aquifers (1949), authorizing underground water conservation districts (1949), conducting studies related to water problems, and approving projects such as those sponsored by the U.S. Army Corps of Engineers (1956). By 1956, there were 84 full-time workers in the agency.[50]

From 1950 to 1956, Texas experienced its worst drought in history. Every major urban area experienced the effect of the drought, many turning to emergency supplies and to rationing. In 1957 the drought was ended by heavy rains that resulted in the massive flooding of every major river and tributary in the state. Two hundred fifty-three of Texas's counties were declared disaster areas. Estimates were that the drought had cost the state hundreds of millions of dollars. Damages from flooding were calculated to cost another $120 million. Calls for a more permanent planning and policy agency to direct and coordinate water policy came from all over the state.[51]

To address these problems, a number of new agencies were established and, in later years, reestablished with different responsibilities. The Board of Engineers was renamed the Texas Water Commission in 1962 and given responsibilities for water planning. In 1965 the responsibilities for water planning were transferred to the newly created Texas Water Development Board (TWDB). At the same time, the Texas Water Commission was renamed the Texas Water Rights Commission (TWRC). In 1977 the three major state water agencies (the TWDB, the TWRC, and the Water Quality Board) were combined into the Texas Department of Water Resources, whose job was to develop Texas's water resources, maintain the quality of water, and assure an equitable distribution of water rights. Sunset legislation in 1985 reorganized this single agency into two new agencies: a new Texas Water Commission and a new version of the Texas Water Development Board. Today, the TWDB is the state's primary water planning and financing agency. Enforcement of the state's environmental regulations regarding water is the job of the Texas Commission on Environmental Quality, an agency that resulted from the 1993 consolidation of the Texas Water Commission with the Texas Air Control Board.[52]

The TWDB is composed of a six-member board serving six-year terms with overlapping membership. Each member comes from a different part of the state. Since 1997, when the legislature passed an omnibus water planning law, the TWDB has had a number of important responsibilities, including the following:

- Supporting the development of 16 regional water plans
- Developing a state water plan every five years

Recent droughts in Texas have made water policy an increasingly pressing issue.

- Providing financial assistance to local governments for (1) water supply and waste management projects, (2) flood protection and control projects, (3) agricultural water conservation projects, and (4) the creation of groundwater districts

- Administering the Texas Water Bank, which facilitates the transfer, sale, and lease of water and water rights throughout the state

- Administering the Texas Water Trust, where water rights are held for environmental flow maintenance purposes

- Data collection for the state's freshwater needs[53]

A number of strategies for meeting the short- and long-term water needs in the state were articulated in the 2012 State Water Plan. Two elements of the plan stand out. First, there is a notable focus on the importance of conservation. Policy makers agree that in the future water must be used more efficiently in Texas. One of the most important policies is a conservation strategy throughout all regions that seeks a more efficient use of current water supplies. Second, there is an emphasis on the importance of expanding and developing available surface water throughout Texas. The plan calls for the building of 26 new major reservoirs by 2060, each with a storage capacity of at least 5,000 acre-feet. Most of the proposed reservoirs would be along the Interstate Highway 35 corridor, where rainfall and runoff are more plentiful than in the western part of the state.[54] Another surface water recommendation is to build new pipeline infrastructure from existing sources to new points of use. Proposed construction includes a pipeline from Lake Palestine to Dallas and from Tarrant Regional Water District Lakes to Fort Worth. Such projects represent an important shift in existing water policy in some planning areas, as they shift the focus of water policy from flood control or hydroelectric power generation to the provision of water.

Groundwater strategies include the expansion of production by drilling more wells or building treatment plants for water quality. Conservation efforts also play a major part in groundwater initiatives, as some of the aquifers are experiencing overuse. The TWDB estimates that total groundwater supplies available to Texans will decline by 30 percent between 2010 and 2060. The Ogallala Aquifer (which runs from the Texas high plains up through western Kansas and into Nebraska) and the Edwards Aquifer (which runs along the Balcones fault line near San Antonio) are estimated to decline by 50 percent by 2060.

The total capital needs of funding these future initiatives proposed by regional water planning groups are estimated to be $53 billion, along with annual operating and maintenance costs. But cost is not the only challenge facing water policy makers. Some environmental groups in the state are opposed to the further expansion of the state reservoir system, arguing that the costs to the ecosystem of the state far outweigh the advantages provided by more water. On the other hand, some property owners, particularly in west Texas, are opposed to any new conservation restrictions or penalties put upon them by the state. Texas water law itself may be one of the most intractable problems that water planners may have to face in coming years.

On February 24, 2012, the Texas Supreme Court ruled on the case *The Edwards Aquifer Authority v. Burrell Day and Joel McDaniel*, which has important implications for future attempts to regulate water usage in Texas, particularly in those areas that rely heavily upon aquifers. The case involved two farmers who had applied to the Edwards Aquifer Authority for permission to pump 700 acre-feet per year of water to irrigate their 350-acre ranch in Van Ormy, a small town south of San Antonio. The farmers argued that they had rights to water from the aquifer based upon their ownership of land above it. Maintaining that the farmers were unable to prove "historical use" of water from the aquifer, the authority granted them a permit for pumping only 14 acre-feet.

Writing for the 9–0 court majority, Justice Hecht ruled that using "historical use" as a criterion for granting a permit to pump water was a departure from the Texas Water Code. "Unquestionably," Hecht wrote, "the state is empowered to regulate groundwater production . . . [but] groundwater in place is owned by the landowner on the basis of oil and gas law."[55] Texas regulatory authorities thus had the power to reasonably regulate the use of water drawn from an aquifer in the public interest, but they may have to pay property owners with a stake in that water any damages that are incurred by the regulation. The Texas Supreme Court returned the case to the district court to determine whether the farmer's private property in the aquifer's water had been wrongfully seized by the state, and if so, whether the Edwards Aquifer Authority must pay a penalty to the farmers for the taking of their property.

The ruling sparked a firestorm of controversy among interested parties. Landowners celebrated the decision as vindication of their ownership of water under their lands. In contrast, state planning authorities and environmentalists were aghast at the implications that the case could have for their attempts to efficiently allocate and conserve water in Texas. The Texas Supreme Court's ruling raised an important question regarding water policy in Texas: Which policy-making body would dominate water policy in the foreseeable future in Texas? Would it be the courts working through judicial interpretations of the applicability of water property law? Or would it be the regulatory bodies whose job was to plan and to allocate water based upon their assessment of available water supplies and the competing needs for water? Developing regulatory rules for the use of aquifer water that both protect property rights and promote the public interest through reasonable and efficient regulations will be a challenge facing these policy makers in years to come.

● Thinking Critically about Public Policy in Texas

In this chapter, we examined various aspects of public-policy making in Texas. We focused particular attention on the complex issues that have driven policy making in public education, welfare, health care, and water policy. Looking at these matters with a critical eye demands that we pay attention to a number of key political questions: Who benefits by a particular public policy? Who pays for the policy? What ideas are used to justify or legitimate a particular program? How do particular public policies evolve and change over time to address new problems? How do they alter the relationship between individual citizens and the government that represents them in Austin?

In earlier chapters, we saw how the high-tech revolution transformed Texas's economy in the 1980s and '90s. We also traced how social and political changes have restructured the political party system in the state and the increasing power of the Republican Party. In this chapter, we have seen how many of these shifts resulted in important changes in public policy in the twentieth and twenty-first centuries. These policy changes are occurring as the Texas political economy moves from an oil, cattle, and cotton economy into an era of computers, high technology, and globalization. We can't be sure exactly where public policy in Texas will go in the next decade. We can be sure that new solutions will be required in the areas of welfare, education, health care, and water policy as the Texas political system tries to meet the challenges and opportunities of the twenty-first century.

study guide

Ⓢ **Practice online with:** Chapter 12 Diagnostic Quiz ▪ Chapter 12 Key Term Flashcards

Education Policy

■ **Describe the major issues that have shaped education policy in Texas (pp. 345–51)**

One of the most important functions of state government is providing and funding public education. Under the Gilmer-Aikin Laws, Texas extended its control over financing and administering public education through local school districts. As in many southern states, segregation of public schools was a major problem that was not dealt with until federal courts forced Texas to desegregate in the 1950s and '60s. Equity in the funding of public education remains a major issue in Texas. State courts continue to play an important role in addressing the equity issue. Concerns over excellence and accountability in public education persist today.

Key Terms

Gilmer-Aikin Laws (p. 345)

equal protection clause (p. 347)

Practice Quiz

1. The Gilmer-Aikin Laws *(p. 345)*
   a) regulate schools in the Gilmer-Aikin ISD.
   b) were major educational reforms passed in 1949.
   c) established an office of elected State Superintendent of Public Education.
   d) allowed for homeschooling of children.
   e) required that money raised from the poll tax be spent on public education.

2. State courts tried to address the issue of equity in the funding of public schools *(pp. 346–48)*
   a) in the case of *Edgewood ISD v. Kirby*.
   b) in the case of *Brown v. Board of Education*.
   c) in the case of *San Antonio v. Rodriguez*.
   d) by appointing Ross Perot to recommend changes the property tax in Texas.
   e) by abolishing the office of the State Board of Education.

3. Among the reforms in public education in Texas to improve the quality of education was *(p. 350)*
   a) No Pass–No Play
   b) No Play–No Pass
   c) shorter school year
   d) more flexible standards for accrediting schools
   e) tying teacher pay raises to student grades

Welfare Policy

■ **Describe the state's role in addressing poverty and how it is affected by national policies (pp. 352–58)**

Texas has large numbers of people living in poverty who have received governmental assistance since the New Deal when the Social Security Act of 1935 was passed. Texas's most important welfare program was AFDC. President Lyndon Johnson's War on Poverty expanded social welfare programs for the poor in the 1960s. But compared to other states, welfare benefits remained low in Texas. Concerns over the problem of welfare dependency led to major reforms at the national level in 1996 when AFDC was replaced with TANF. Since these reforms, welfare rolls have declined, although poverty has remained a chronic problem among a significant portion of the Texas population.

Key Terms

New Deal (p. 353)

Aid to Families with Dependent Children (AFDC) (p. 353)

Medicaid (p. 354)

Supplemental Security Income (SSI) (p. 354)

Temporary Assistance for Needy Families (TANF) (p. 356)

Practice Quiz

4. Poverty in Texas *(p. 353)*
   a) is almost nonexistent due to the welfare reforms of the 1990s.
   b) is at a level above the national average.
   c) is at a level below the national average.
   d) was largely eliminated by the Social Security Act of 1935.
   e) was largely eliminated by Lyndon Johnson's "War on Poverty."

5. The welfare reforms of the 1990s *(pp. 355–56)*
   a) resulted from a belief that the welfare policies of the 1960s had failed.
   b) led to a 36-month limitation on welfare benefits in Texas.
   c) led to a five-year ban on reapplying for benefits once benefits ran out.
   d) expanded education and job-training programs.
   e) all of the above

6. Two presidents who had major roles in welfare policy are *(pp. 353–54)*
   a) Franklin Delano Roosevelt and Lyndon B. Johnson
   b) Dwight Eisenhower and Herbert Hoover
   c) Harry Truman and John F. Kennedy
   d) Woodrow Wilson and Franklin Delano Roosevelt
   e) Lyndon B. Johnson and George H. W. Bush

Medicaid and Health Care Policy

■ **Explain why Medicaid in particular and health care policy in general have been so controversial in Texas (pp. 358–68)**

One major welfare program that has become increasingly costly is Medicaid, a state-federal program providing the financing of health care for the poor. Reforms instituted under the Obama administration have significantly expanded health care coverage for the poor. But as of 2012, it was unclear if Texas will participate in that expansion. The rising cost of Medicaid is seen by many conservatives to be a growing threat to the financial integrity of the state's budget.

Practice Quiz

7. Which of the following statements is *true* about Medicaid in Texas? *(p. 358)*
   a) Medicaid is a program that was part of the New Deal.
   b) Texas policy makers make all the major decisions regarding the principles and standards directing Medicaid in Texas. There is no federal oversight.
   c) Texas can apply for a waiver with the federal government, enabling it to create programs directed toward particular clients.

   d) Medicaid employs doctors and nurses as members of the Department of Health and Human Services hired to provide medical care to the poor.
   e) Medicaid is funded entirely by the state.

8. Managed care programs *(p. 359)*
   a) are not found in the Texas Medicaid program.
   b) provide medical care to an increasing number of Medicaid clients in Texas.
   c) provide medical care to a small number of Medicaid clients in Texas.
   d) provide direct fee-for-service care for Medicaid recipients.
   e) have declined in popularity since the 1990s.

9. The Affordable Care Act *(p. 365)*
   a) was part of the War on Poverty.
   b) merged Medicare and Medicaid into a single program.
   c) will increase health insurance coverage to millions of Texans.
   d) was declared unconstitutional by the Texas Supreme Court.
   e) originated in the Texas Legislature.

Water Policy

■ **Consider the growing importance of policies related to water supplies in Texas (pp. 368–73)**

A looming threat to Texas's further economic development is access to freshwater. Over the next 50 years, water consumption is expected to vastly increase while existing supplies may decrease. Current water law in Texas adds complexity to the development of rational water policies for the state.

Practice Quiz

10. Which of the following is *true*? *(p. 369)*
    a) Texas water consumption will decrease as the population expands.
    b) The idea of planning for future water provision has been rejected by the Texas state legislature as being too socialistic.
    c) Water law in Texas distinguishes between surface water and ground water.
    d) Providing water in Texas is primarily a federal responsibility.
    e) Current state water policies do not emphasize conservation.

11. The rule of capture concerns *(p. 369)*
    a) property rights in underground percolating water.
    b) the right of the state to regulate rivers and estuaries.

    c) political control of the legislature by a particular policy interest.
    d) the Corps of Engineers' various attempts to direct the flow of the Rio Grande River.
    e) the federal government's ability to override Texas water laws.

12. Which of the following is *true*? *(p. 370)*
    a) The Texas Supreme Court rejects the idea that the state can regulate *surface* water.
    b) Texas is empowered by the state constitution to seize without compensation an individual's right to use underground water.
    c) Aquifers provide a negligible supply of water to Texas.
    d) Attempts to regulate groundwater access frequently come into conflict with property rights.
    e) The Water Rights Adjudication Act of 1967 prohibits the state from regulating surface water permits.

Ⓢ **Practice Online**
Video exercise: *Water Policy in Texas*

Recent scandals involving the Dallas County constables—including the high number of traffic tickets issued and the high number of cars impounded by constables—have raised questions about local government in Texas.

Local Government in Texas

13

WHAT GOVERNMENT DOES AND WHY IT MATTERS Local government is generally praised for being closer to the people it serves and, therefore, being more responsive to those people than the state or national government can be. The problem is that sometimes local governmental officials work in relative obscurity, avoiding media and public scrutiny. This means that if they abuse their power, their behavior often takes longer to come to light. One example has been a recent scandal involving two of the five constables in Dallas County. Traditionally in Texas, the office of constable has been an elective office with limited duties. Constables have served civil court papers and have provided bailiffs for justices of the peace. However, some constables, such as those in Dallas County, transformed their offices into full-fledged police departments. Dallas County constables, for example, developed a traffic enforcement role. In Dallas County, in 1995, no deputy constable positions were devoted to traffic enforcement; in 2010, 76 deputy constables in that county handled traffic enforcement. Constables also formed heavily armed, tactical units. They patrolled high-crime areas, shut down drug houses, arrested parents who were behind on child support, and cracked down on drug dealers selling "cheese" heroin to students. County commissioners not only approved some of the expanded activities of constables, but also implemented new legal strategies to expand their law enforcement functions. Since constables are elected officials, they are not subject to much oversight and instead function as law enforcement fiefdoms in larger counties in Texas.

In two constables' precincts in Dallas County, there have been problems with vehicles being impounded. These constables have impounded thousands of vehicles without requiring that the towing companies account for what happened to the vehicles. Subsequent investigations of the two constables have also identified issues such as complaints that deputy constables have been forced to work on unpaid security details and to sell raffle tickets to raise money for constables' re-election campaigns.[1] These problems, going on for years, have only recently caused county commissioners to reconsider the expanded role of constables.

Sadly, it is not only the office of constable that shows problems at the local governmental level. Recent scandals in Dallas involving city council members show still other disturbing aspects of local government in Texas. Former mayor pro tempore Don Hill and a number of associates were accused of taking bribes from low-income housing developers in exchange for political support for their projects. The corruption probe first became public in 2005, but did not result in convictions until toward the end of 2009. Hill was convicted of selling his votes in a bribery and extortion scheme that involved pressuring low-income housing developers for kickbacks.[2]

The cases of the constables and Don Hill show that while local government provides many of the services people depend on, the fact that few people pay close attention to local government means there is room for abuses of power and action that go against the interests of the public. In this chapter, we will take a closer look at the main features of local government in Texas.

chaptergoals

- Explain the importance of county government in Texas (pages 381–88)

- Describe the major types of city government in Texas (pages 388–95)

- Examine the role of special districts in Texas government (pages 395–401)

● County Government in Texas

Local government institutions play a major role in Texas. There are roughly 4,835 general-purpose local governments, an average of 19.1 per county. Of these, 254 were county governments and 1,221 were municipal governments. There were also 3,373 special purpose governments, including 1,082 public school systems and 2,291 special district governments.[3] Local government is everywhere in Texas, providing water, electricity, and sewer services, as well as police protection and public education.

All but two states have governmental units known as counties (or parishes), but Texas has 254 counties, more than any other state.[4] County government in Texas is primarily a way of governing rural areas. Because Texas is so vast, with huge areas that are sparsely populated, county government remains an important aspect of local government. As was discussed in previous chapters, the Texas Constitution places numerous restrictions on government, and numerous provisions of the constitution place restrictions on counties. Indeed, in Texas, counties have very constricted governmental powers. Unlike city governments, county governments usually do not have powers to legislate. Because they lack much of the power of self-government, they often function primarily as an administrative arm of the state government.

Texas counties have their origins in the "municipality," which was the local governmental unit under Spanish and Mexican rule. These municipalities were large and included settlements and surrounding rural territories. In 1835, Texas was divided into 3 departments and 23 municipalities. With the Republic of 1836, the 23 municipalities became counties. By the time Texas became a state in 1845, there were 36 counties, and when Texas entered the Confederacy in 1861, there were 122 counties. The number of counties increased steadily until 1921, when the 254th county was created. The underlying goal of the proliferation of counties was that any citizen could travel to the county seat—on horseback, of course—and return home in a day. Given the sparse population of west Texas, in particular, that initial plan for county organization was eventually rejected, but it does show that Texans believed that the local center of government, the county seat, should be accessible to the people.[5]

Numerous County Offices: Checks and Balances or Built-In Problems?

As with the state government, one of the characteristics of county government in Texas is a multiplicity of elected governmental officials. Some argue that the large number of public officials at the county level is desirable because it creates a strong system of checks and balances, allowing no one official to dominate county government.[6] However, that system of checks and balances comes at a high price. There are problems of coordination of governmental activity, much as at the state level. One of the most important bodies of county elected officials is the **county commissioners court**, which is the main governing unit in the county. Although the commissioners court is not really a judicial court, it may have gotten its name from the Republic of Texas Constitution (1836–45), in which the county governing unit consisted of the chief justice of the county court and the justices of the peace within the county.[7]

county commissioners court
the main governing body of each county; has the authority to set the county tax rate and budget

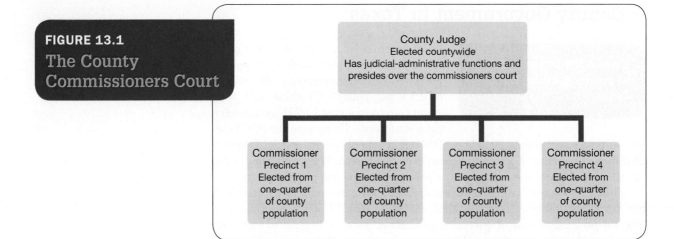

FIGURE 13.1
The County Commissioners Court

County Judge
Elected countywide
Has judicial-administrative functions and
presides over the commissioners court

Commissioner
Precinct 1
Elected from
one-quarter
of county
population

Commissioner
Precinct 2
Elected from
one-quarter
of county
population

Commissioner
Precinct 3
Elected from
one-quarter
of county
population

Commissioner
Precinct 4
Elected from
one-quarter
of county
population

county judge the person in each of Texas's 254 counties who presides over the constitutional county court and county commissioners court, with responsibility for the administration of county government; some county judges carry out judicial responsibilities

county commissioner government official (four per county) on the county commissioners court whose main duty is the construction and maintenance of roads and bridges

The current structure of the county commissioners court, shown in Figure 13.1, consists of a **county judge** and four commissioners. The county judge is elected countywide and serves for four years. He or she presides over the meetings of the commissioners court and has administrative powers as well as judicial powers in rural counties. In those counties, the county judge hears minor criminal cases and handles some civil matters such as probate matters. In larger counties, the county judge is an administrator only, with the judicial duties of the office removed by the creation of judgeships, such as probate judgeships and county court-at-law judgeships.

Each commissioners court also has four **county commissioners**; each of these officials is elected from a precinct that encompasses roughly one-fourth the population of the county. In the late 1960s, one of the great issues in constitutional law involved the issue of malapportionment, the allegation that election districts did not represent equal population groupings. The malapportionment of Texas's county commissioners courts became an important case before the U.S. Supreme Court because those precincts tended to be drawn to represent fairly equal land areas rather than equal population groupings. In *Avery v. Midland County* (1968), the U.S. Supreme Court held that the principle of "one person, one vote" applies to commissioners courts just as it applies to legislative districts. The result was that commissioners precincts must now be drawn to reflect equal population groupings within counties.[8]

The main duty of county commissioners is the construction and maintenance of roads and bridges; usually each commissioner provides for roadwork within his or her precinct. That aspect of a commissioner's work is, of course, very important to rural residents; it can be politically controversial and has sometimes been tinged with corruption.[9]

The commissioners court also sets the county tax rate and the county budget. Related to its taxing and budgeting powers is its power to make contracts and pay bills. Perhaps the most important expenditure of most county commissioners courts, other than road and bridge expenditures, is the cost of building and maintaining county jails. Indigent health care can be a significant cost for counties as well, along with, in some cases, fire protection and sanitation. Some counties also have costs associated with the maintenance of libraries and hospitals and costs for

TABLE 13.1

Countywide and Precinct-Level Elected Officials

COUNTYWIDE OFFICIALS	PRECINCT-LEVEL OFFICIALS
County judge	County commissioners
Possibly county court-at-law judges, possibly probate judges, and district judges	Justices of the peace
County and district attorney or criminal district attorney	Constables
Sheriff	
County and district clerk or district clerk	
Possibly county treasurer	
Tax assessor-collector	
Possibly county surveyor	

emergency welfare expenditures, such as those brought on by natural disasters or fires. The commissioners court can appoint certain county officials, and it can hire personnel as well as fill vacancies in county offices. It also administers elections in the county.

However, as noted earlier, there are numerous elected officials in Texas counties, each with an independent power base. It seems nearly inevitable that tensions would develop between the budgetary powers of the commissioners courts and the needs and desires of other elected county officials.

As Table 13.1 shows, other officeholders are elected at the county level and still others at the precinct level of the county. There is some variation in the numbers of officeholders, depending on the county. For example, larger counties will have more justices of the peace and more **constables** than smaller ones. In some counties, constables serve legal papers, while in others, as discussed in the introduction to this chapter, constables also have a law-enforcement role with the authority to patrol, give tickets, and make arrests. Some counties use constables to check on truants from school, having found a niche area that others in law enforcement do not seem to want.

constable precinct-level county official involved with serving legal papers and, in some counties, enforcing the law

Larger counties may have probate judges, numerous district judges, and county court-at-law judges. Smaller counties may not have probate judges or even county court-at-law judges. Some of the smaller counties may share district judges and district attorneys with other counties. Laws setting up different offices often vary from county to county as well. As a result, some counties have county attorneys and district attorneys; others have criminal district attorneys that combine the county attorney and district attorney offices. Some counties have county clerks and district clerks; smaller counties may combine the offices in one person. Some counties have county treasurers; others do not have such an office.

Are Some Counties Too Small?

The reason for the variation in offices is not simply that laws were passed at different times, thus sacrificing uniformity among counties. It is also the case that Texas is a large, diverse state with great variation among its counties. The result is

The county commissioners court is the main governing unit at the county level, with control over the county budget and projects such as road construction. Here, Denton County Commissioner Andy Eads appears with Texas Motor Speedway president Eddie Gossage at the groundbreaking for a highway extension near the speedway.

great variation in the numbers of government officials, the duties of officials, and the services provided by the different county governments. Brewster County has a population of only 9,232, but it covers a territory of 6,193 square miles, about the size of Connecticut and Rhode Island combined. Rockwall County, in contrast, has only 149 square miles and a population of 78,337. Although Harris County has a population of 4,092,059, Loving County has a population of only 82; yet Loving County covers a huge land area—nearly 677 square miles.[10] Most residents of Loving County work for the Loving County government. The fact that the county government is the major employer in the county may be the main justification for Loving County's continuing existence as a governmental unit—although people with taxable property may also prefer the Loving County tax structure to that of another governmental unit.[11]

A small population may create a sense of community and closeness to local government, but it can place a terrific strain on county resources when unusual events occur.

One of the medium-size Texas counties is Jasper County in east Texas, which has a population of 35,710. Jasper County had huge costs as a result of the capital murder trials of three men accused in the 1998 dragging death of James Byrd Jr. Two of the three men were sentenced to death; the third got life in prison. Costs associated with the trial came to over $1.02 million. The result was such a strain on the $10 million annual county budget that the county was forced to increase property taxes by 6.7 percent over two years to pay for the trial. Only a massive flood in the county in the late 1970s had come close to creating a financial burden similar to that of the trial.

Jasper County is not the only county struggling with a huge financial burden from capital murder trials. The basic cost of prosecuting a capital case averages $200,000 to $300,000, and that does not include the costs of indigent-defense lawyers, appeals, and trial transcripts.

The burden of the capital case on Jasper County convinced Texas lawmakers to expand a program to assist counties in paying the "extraordinary costs" of prosecuting capital murder cases. That aid program was motivated by a fear that underpopulated counties would pursue lesser charges than those carrying the death penalty to avoid incurring financial hardship. One of the sponsors of the legislation, for example, said that he had often heard concerns expressed over the cost pressures of capital trials from officials in the 17 rural counties he represented.

Polk County in east Texas (population about 45,413) estimated that it had unanticipated costs of $200,000 when the U.S. Supreme Court overturned the sentence of Johnny Paul Penry, who was convicted in the stabbing death of a woman in 1979, and sent the case back for another trial. Even with $100,000 in aid from the state to help pay the bill, the costs of one trial tremendously burdened Polk County.[12] An even more severe situation faced

The county commissioners court is also responsible for constructing and maintaining bridges, such as this one near Houston.

tiny Franklin County (population 10,605) in 2007, when it needed to come up with a minimum of $250,000 for a murder trial.[13] Since capital murder cases were so rare in the county, the commissioners had no money at all budgeted for such a purpose. For small counties such as Polk and Franklin, expenses like these require either major cuts in other budget items or tax increases.

One hundred sixty Texas counties have populations of fewer than 30,000, and 137 of those counties have populations of fewer than 20,000. One recent study confirmed fears that Texas has wide variations in its counties' application of capital punishment, in part because of the costs of death penalty cases to smaller counties. Between 1976, when the U.S. Supreme Court reinstated capital punishment, and July 2011, Texas sent just over 1,060 inmates to death row. Only four of the state's most heavily populated counties—Harris, Bexar, Dallas, and Tarrant—accounted for 534 of these death sentences. By itself, Harris County, the county with the largest population, accounted for 280, or 28 percent, of the death sentences. In contrast, 135 Texas counties with relatively small populations have not sent an inmate to death row in the last three decades.[14]

Counties exist as they do for a variety of reasons. The original goal of making county seats easily accessible by horseback is, of course, no longer pertinent. Other reasons are political. For example, wealthy landowners may have urged the legislature to create counties so that they could control county government and hence the amount of property taxes they might pay. Still, we must wonder if so many small counties are needed. The Jasper County situation suggests that even moderate-size counties by Texas standards may be too small to function adequately in unusual situations.

The Functions of County Government

What, then, are the main functions of Texas county government? Table 13.2 lists them. Like most other aspects of county government in Texas, these five primary functions are performed with great variation among the counties.

County road and bridge construction and maintenance have traditionally been such important functions of the commissioners court that often county commissioners are called "road commissioners." County commissioners maintain more than one-half of the roads in the state.[15] There are roughly 134,000 miles of rural roadways and 17,000 rural bridges in Texas. Maintenance of these roads and bridges is

TABLE 13.2

Primary Functions of County Government

- Construction and maintenance of roads and bridges
- Law enforcement
- Dispute resolution
- Record-keeping
- Social services

a major cost for county government.[16] For example, a twenty-foot asphalt road for lightweight traffic costs a county $45,000 per mile to resurface; a road for heavy trucks costs about $100,000 per mile.[17] Although a 1947 law allowed counties to place the road system under the authority of a county engineer, in most counties roads and bridges remain one of the most important responsibilities of the commissioners.

Law enforcement is another important responsibility of county government. This job is undertaken by constables and by the sheriff. The sheriff is the chief law-enforcement officer within county government. In rural counties with few city police departments, the sheriff may be the major law-enforcement official in the county. In addition to law enforcement and the provision of deputies for the district and county courts, sheriffs are responsible for the county jail. In many counties, operating a county jail is an expensive and major undertaking. On August 1, 2011, for example, Harris County was guarding and supervising 9,009 inmates in its county jail, Dallas County had 6,462 inmates in its jail, and Tarrant County had 3,519. On the other hand, 19 counties had no jails. Glasscock County had room for 12 inmates in its jail but had no inmates; Trinity County had room for 7 inmates but had only 1 inmate. Real County had a jail capacity of 3 and had no inmates, and Terrell County had a capacity of 8 and had no inmates.[18]

Although the law-enforcement budget is approved by the county commissioners court, sheriffs often have considerable influence in county government and develop their own law enforcement styles. The sheriff of Smith County, for example, has not only a SWAT team but also two armored personnel carriers, each of which weighs 13 tons, moves on tracks at up to 40 miles per hour, and is capable of climbing 60-degree grades and floating.[19]

County attorneys and **district attorneys** also perform a law-enforcement role by prosecuting criminal cases. Usually, the district attorneys prosecute the more serious criminal cases in the district courts, whereas the county attorneys prosecute

county attorney county official who prosecutes lesser criminal cases in the county court

district attorney public official who prosecutes the more serious criminal cases in the district court

County governments are important for law enforcement. Here, a captain from the McLennan County sheriff's office discusses the procedures for a protest with Cindy Sheehan. After Sheehan's son died in Iraq, she and her supporters demonstrated against the Iraq War outside President Bush's Texas ranch.

In rural parts of Texas, county courts are where civil and criminal cases are heard. This photo shows the Jasper County Courthouse during the capital murder case of the men accused of the 1998 dragging death of James Byrd Jr.

the lesser criminal cases in the county courts. In more urban counties, the offices of county attorney and district attorney may be combined into one office that is usually called the office of criminal district attorney.

Record-keeping is an important function of county government. **County clerks** keep vital statistics for the county and issue licenses; they maintain records for the commissioners court and the county courts. Most important, the county clerk is responsible for records relating to property transactions. Sometimes the county clerk maintains election and voting records. If there is a **district clerk**, he or she maintains records for the district courts, though in small counties this office is combined with the office of the county clerk. Tax records are maintained by the **county tax assessor-collector**, who also collects taxes, though in the smaller counties the sheriff often performs this job. Although constitutional amendments have eliminated the office of county treasurer in many counties, where the office does exist, the treasurer is responsible for receiving and expending county funds. The **county auditor** now does much of the work of the county treasurer. There are now about 200 county auditors in Texas. Auditors are not elected; they are appointed by the county's district judges. Not only do they audit the county's funds, but in large counties they will often prepare the county budget for the commissioners court.

Counties also have an important role in dispute resolution through their court system. Civil law is a way to resolve disputes between people, and the justice of the peace court and the county and district courts deal with large numbers of civil disputes as well as criminal matters. County and district attorneys may also represent the interests of the county or state in disputes that involve governmental interests.

Finally, counties may perform a social service function. The social services provided vary from county to county. However, the most important social services involve emergency welfare assistance to individuals. This may include the

county clerk public official who is the main record-keeper of the county

district clerk public official who is the main record-keeper of the district court

county tax assessor-collector public official who maintains the county tax records and collects the taxes owed to the county

county auditor public official, appointed by the district judges, who receives and disburses county funds; in large counties, this official also prepares the county budget

provision of food, housing, rental assistance, or shelter to needy individuals. Larger counties have health departments to work on the prevention and control of communicable diseases. Some counties operate mental health services. Some counties provide parks, airports, fire protection, and sanitation facilities. One of the most important social services provided by counties is indigent health care.

County Government in Perspective

County government occupies an important role in Texas local government, although the powers of county government are greatly restricted by the Texas Legislature. One of the most notable features of Texas counties is their great variation in geographical size, population, and even in county offices, duties of county officials, and services provided by county government. Additionally, like state government, county government has a large number of elected county officials. Although this may limit the power of any one county official, it also produces disagreement, conflict, and difficulty in accomplishing objectives.

Many of Texas's counties are very small, possibly too small to meet the needs of Texans in the twenty-first century, although there is no serious effort to change the current structure of counties. Counties perform important and often expensive functions. Some of those functions of county government and the costs associated with them—for example, road and bridge construction and maintenance, jail construction and operation, and indigent health care—are likely to increase significantly in the future.

TABLE 13.3

Municipal Governments in Texas, 2010

SIZE	NUMBER
100,000 or more	28
50,000–99,999	30
10,000–49,999	157
5,000–9,999	115
Fewer than 5,000	891
Total	1,221

SOURCE: Calculated from www .texasalmanac.com/topics/ government/government.

home-rule charter the rules under which a city operates

● City Government in Texas

Describe the major types of city government in Texas

As of 2010, there were 1,221 municipal governments in Texas, ranging in size from 27 residents in Corral City to nearly 2.1 million in Houston (see Table 13.3). Like county governments, municipal governments are creations of the state of Texas. In the early years of the Republic of Texas, the Texas Congress was responsible for enacting laws that incorporated cities. The number of urban areas grew in the state in the late nineteenth and early twentieth centuries, making the management of local affairs a growing burden on the state legislature. In 1912, the legislature passed the Home-Rule Charter Amendments that enabled cities of more than 5,000 inhabitants to adopt home-rule charters with a majority vote of qualified voters.

Home-rule charters essentially lay down the rules under which a city will operate.[20] They provide for the form of government that operates in the city and specify the number of members serving on the city's governing body. They also may grant the governing body the power to annex land adjacent to the city as well as to set property tax rates up to $2.50 per $100 valuation. Home-rule cities are also constitutionally authorized to borrow money in ways not available to smaller municipal entities. Home-rule charters must be consistent with the state constitution and any other relevant statutory provisions. For example, the state has mandated that most city elections take place on a date provided by the Texas Election Code. City elections must be conducted under the general guidelines set by the state. Nevertheless, home rule in Texas has delegated enormous power to local city governments. According to a report by the Advisory Commission on Intergovernmental

TABLE 13.4

The Largest Home-Rule Cities, 2010

NAME	POPULATION	FORM OF GOVERNMENT	FIRST CHARTER	PRESENT FORM ADOPTED
Houston	2,099,451	Mayor-council	1905	1994
San Antonio	1,327,407	Council-manager	1914	1951
Dallas	1,197,816	Council-manager	1889	1907
Austin	790,390	Council-manager	1919	1994
Fort Worth	741,206	Council-manager	1924	1985
El Paso	649,121	Mayor-council	1873	1907
Arlington	365,438	Council-manager	1920	1990
Corpus Christi	305,215	Council-manager	1926	1993
Plano	259,841	Council-manager	1961	1993
Laredo	236,091	Council-manager	1848	1911

SOURCES: Compiled from *Texas Almanac 2006–2007* (Dallas: *Dallas Morning News*, 2006), 340–64; *Texas Almanac 2008–2009* (Dallas: *Dallas Morning News*, 2008), 8; Texas State Data Center; www.citypopulation.de/USA-Texas .html; City Charter of the City of Laredo as Amended (2010).

Relations, the Texas Constitution leaves cities more "home rule" than does any other state. There are now 335 home-rule cities in Texas.[21] Table 13.4 lists the 10 largest of these.

Cities and towns of fewer than 5,000 people are chartered by general statute, as was the case for all cities and towns prior to the 1912 home-rule amendments. These "general-law" cities and towns may act or organize themselves only as explicitly permitted by statutory law passed by the state legislature. The constitution also limits what they can do. For example, general-law cities may levy, assess, and collect taxes as authorized by statute. But the constitution sets a maximum property tax rate of $1.50 per $100 valuation, compared with $2.50 per $100 valuation for home-rule cities.

Politics at the local level is often politics at its most basic. Unlike in presidential elections, in which the issues may well involve questions of war and peace, or state elections, which may involve issues such as whether a state should have an income tax, in local elections the most pressing issue may well be potholes in the city streets. Although pothole repair may not seem earthshaking in the hierarchy of political concerns, it is exactly such an issue that most directly and routinely affects most people's lives, and thus it becomes a prime issue for discussion among candidates. As mundane as such concerns are, these are the fundamental issues in most local elections because they reflect the needs and expectations that residents have of local government.

Forms of Government in Texas Cities

Texas home-rule cities have had three major forms of city government: the mayor-council form, the commissioner form, and the council-manager form. The **mayor-council form of government** is the oldest. It consists of an elected mayor and city

mayor-council form of government a form of city government in which the mayor is the chief executive and the city council is the legislative body; in the *strong mayor-council* variation, the mayor's powers enable him or her to control executive departments and the agenda of the city council; in the *weak mayor-council* variation, the mayor's power is more limited

at-large election an election in which officials are selected by voters of the entire geographical area, rather than from smaller districts within that area

single-member district an electorate that is allowed to elect only one representative for each district

council. The mayor is elected from the city in an **at-large election**. The council may be elected either at-large or from a series of **single-member districts**, or a mixture of the two. In the mayor-council form of government, the mayor is the chief executive officer of the city. He or she presides over council meetings and has a variety of appointment powers. The city council, meanwhile, serves as the legislative body in the city, passing local laws and watching over the executive departments.

There have been both strong mayor–council systems and weak ones, depending on the powers given to the mayor by the city charter or state statute. In the *strong mayor-council* variation, various executive powers, such as appointive and removal powers to boards and departments or veto powers, are concentrated in the office of mayor. These powers enable the mayor to establish effective control over various executive departments in the city and to control the legislative agenda of the city council. In the *weak mayor-council* variation, these executive powers are much more limited, fragmenting power between the mayor and other elected or appointed officials.

In the 1990s, the mayor-council form of government was the dominant form of government in most of the incorporated cities in Texas, particularly among general-law cities. However, among home-rule cities the mayor-council government was not popular. According to a 1995 survey of 284 home-rule cities conducted by the *Texas Almanac*, only 31 had adopted the mayor-council form of government.

commissioner form of government a form of city government in which the city is run by a small group of elected commissioners who act in both legislative and executive capacities

A second form of city government found in Texas is the **commissioner form of government**.[22] Under the commissioner system, the city is run by a small commission, composed of between five and seven members generally elected at-large. The commission acts in both a legislative and an executive capacity. As a group, commissioners enact laws for the city. Each commissioner is in charge of one of a variety of departments. One commissioner is also designated as the mayor to preside at meetings.

The commission plan was developed as a response to the devastating hurricane that hit Galveston in 1900, claiming an estimated 6,000 lives. It reflected a desire to bring good business practices to city government that would somehow escape

The commissioner form of government was developed as a response to the devastating hurricane that hit Galveston in 1900.

the squabbles and inefficiency of traditional local government found in the mayor-council form. The commission plan was adopted by Houston in 1905 and by a number of other Texas cities in 1907, including Dallas, Fort Worth, and El Paso. Republicans and Democratic Progressives across the country supported the plan and other reform principles often integrated with it, including nonpartisan elections, merit selection of employees, and such direct democracy techniques as the initiative, referendum, and recall. At its peak in 1918, the commission form was used by approximately 500 cities across the country and 75 cities in Texas. Following World War I, the number of commission-form cities decreased. By 2000, no city in Texas had a pure commission form of government, although 26 still claimed to have some variation of a commission-manager form of government.[23] In practice, none of the "commissioners" in these cities exercised executive control over specific city departments as envisioned in the original commission system. Instead, they functioned more like council members under the council-manager form of city government.[24]

The third form of city government found in Texas is the **council-manager form of government**.[25] As originally envisioned, a city council elected in at-large elections was to be the policy-making body. Council members generally received little or no pay and were intended to be publicly motivated citizens interested in serving the public good, rather than professional politicians. A mayor was selected from among the council members. The city manager was to be a professional public manager who served as the chief executive and administrative official in the city. As in the commissioner form of government, the goal of the council-manager form of government was twofold: to free local government from the seamier side of politics and to bring administrative expertise to local government.

In 1913, Amarillo was the first city to abandon the commissioner form of government for the council-manager system. In 1914, Taylor and Denton followed suit. By 1947, there were 47 council-manager systems in Texas. By the mid-1990s, 251 of the home-rule cities had council-manager systems. Across the United States, it has become the most popular form of government for cities of over 10,000 residents.

Today, council-manager systems vary across the state in a number of ways. The desire for professional administration of local government remains high. Most city managers have graduate degrees and are paid high salaries like other executive officers in the private sector. But a desire for more political accountability through traditional democratic processes has introduced some changes. The growing ethnic and racial diversity of some Texas cities has forced many political leaders to question the wisdom of freeing local government too much from democratic controls. In most cities, mayors now are elected at large from the population as a whole, rather than only from the council. Many cities also elect council members from single-member districts rather than only from at-large districts. Many see at-large districts as undercutting minority representation by diluting minority votes. Only when Dallas moved from an at-large council to a council elected from single-member districts in 1991 did minorities come to play a major role in the decision-making processes of city government. But most cities and towns under the council-manager system continue to view local political offices as part-time jobs. Mayoral and council salaries remain low. A few cities, such as Austin, offer considerably higher salaries. The demand for more democratic accountability in local government will likely continue to lead to more changes in the council-manager system of government across Texas. Balancing an efficient city government run by professionals with democratic political processes will continue to be a problem as Texas's metropolitan areas grow and diversify in the early twenty-first century.

council-manager form of government a form of city government in which public policies are developed by the city council and executive and administrative functions are assigned to a professional city manager

A Tale of Three Cities

Houston is the largest city in Texas, with nearly 2.1 million people. It has a strong mayor-council form of government. There are 16 elected officials in the city serving concurrent two-year terms, including a mayor, a controller, and 14 council members. The mayor serves as the chief executive official in the city and is the city's chief administrator and official representative. Much of the mayor's power stems from the authority to appoint department heads and people serving on advisory boards, subject to council approval. The mayor also presides over the city council with voting privileges. The 14-member council is a legislative body composed of five at-large seats and nine single-member district seats.

Unlike in most other cities, the city controller in Houston is an elected official.[26] The city controller, currently Ronald Green, is the city's chief financial officer. Besides investing city funds, conducting internal audits of city departments, and operating the city's financial management system, the controller is also responsible for certifying the availability of funds for city council initiatives. In the end, the office of the controller is both a professional position and a political position. Not surprisingly, the controller often comes into conflict with the mayor and the council over important policy issues.

Although local politics in Houston is nominally nonpartisan, in recent years it has taken on a partisan flavor. Houston's current mayor is Annise Parker, who serves as executive officer of the city. She is a well-known Democrat and is also a lesbian who supports gay marriage. Her call for legalizing gay marriage and her proclamation that Valentine's Day was Freedom to Marry Day have led to a political outcry among social conservatives including Republican leaders who claim that she is putting her personal political agenda ahead of the interests of Houston. Parker barely escaped a runoff in her election campaign in November 2011, and two incumbent city council members were defeated by opponents of gay marriage. Even after the election, the partisan furor over gay marriage has not died down in Houston.

Annise Parker is the current mayor of Houston. She previously served as a member of the city council and as city controller.

Recently, San Antonio has overtaken Dallas as the second largest city in Texas. San Antonio has a council-manager form of government. The council is composed of members elected from 10 single-member districts on a nonpartisan basis. The mayor, currently Julián Castro, is the eleventh member of the council and is selected at large. All members of the council serve for two-year terms and receive largely honorific salaries. The mayor's salary is a paltry $3,000 per year in addition to payment as a council member; other council members are paid $20 per meeting, not to exceed $1,040 per year. Members are subject to recall if 10 percent of the qualified voters in a district sign a petition of recall and a recall election is successful. The city charter also provides for initiatives and referendums that emerge from the voters.

The city manager in San Antonio serves at the pleasure of the council as the chief executive and administrative official in the city. He or she has wide-ranging appointment and removal authority over officers and employees in the administrative service of the city. The current city manager is Sheryl Sculley. Prior to becoming city manager, she was assistant city manager of Phoenix. She supervises the activities of all city departments, a budget of $2 billion, and 12,000 employees.

San Antonio mayor Julián Castro, elected in 2009, previously served as a member of the city council.

Dallas also operates under a council-manager form of government. For years, city politics had been dominated by the white business community. At-large nonpartisan elections tended to elect a council that was relatively united in its understanding of the problems facing the city and its vision of where the city should go. A bitter struggle in the late 1980s and early 1990s over rewriting the city charter divided the city along racial lines. The new charter, which went into effect in 1991, called for a 14-member council elected from single-member districts and a mayor elected at large. Members are limited to serving four 2-year terms consecutively. Under the new charter, membership on the council was transformed as a significant number of African Americans and Hispanics were elected to the council.

As in other council-manager systems, the power of the mayor in Dallas is weak. The mayor—currently Mike Rawlings—presides over council meetings, creates council committees, and appoints members, chairs, and co-chairs. In many ways, however, the mayor is only first among equals on the council. The council as a whole is the legislative body for the city, approving budgets, determining the tax rate, and appointing key public officials, including the city manager, city attorney, city auditor, city secretary, municipal court judges, and various citizen boards and commissions. The city manager serves at the will of the council and is removable by a two-thirds vote of the council. As in San Antonio, the city manager's powers in Dallas are great. As the chief administrative officer, the city manager has the power to appoint and remove all heads of departments and subordinate officers and employees in the city, subject to civil service provisions. Despite the attempt to remove the city manager from the pressures of political life in Dallas, recent city managers have found themselves forced to accommodate the reality of an increasingly politicized city council. The political pressures

Mayor Mike Rawlings of Dallas was elected in 2011. He was previously the CEO of Pizza Hut.

Choosing City Council Members

City councils are the legislative bodies for municipalities in Texas. They are tasked with making laws that affect the residents of their city. These include zoning laws, such as the rules about what kinds of establishments can be in a particular neighborhood. They also make laws regulating the health and safety of their city's citizens, including ordinances dealing with texting while driving or smoking in public places, for example.

The number of city council members varies by city and the types of districts they represent also vary. How a city elects council members—whether in at-large districts or from specific single-member districts—can affect representation and policy decisions.

Some cities employ an at-large system of electing city council members. In these cities, each city council member is elected by the whole city, similar to way the mayor is chosen. Other cities use single-member districts, such that city council members represent different parts of the city rather than the city as a whole. Many cities have a hybrid system with some at large members and others elected via a single member district system. Each city decides how they would like to elect their city councils and any changes must be approved by voter approval of an amendment to the city charter (the city "constitution"). In Texas and other states subject to certain requirements of the Voting Rights Act, these changes must also be approved by the U.S. Department of Justice to make sure that the voting power of minorities is not diluted.

Social science research seems to suggest that minorities fare better under a system of single-member districts, although this may not necessarily be the case in all cities. This research presupposes that minority populations are concentrated in certain areas of the city, which makes it easier to draw districts ensuring a majority of minority voters. It is also important to consider

that minority groups may not form coalitions with other minority groups. For example, African Americans and Latinos might have distinct interests in some localities.

Consider the recent debate in Austin about the proposal to change the city's at-large method of electing members to one that incorporates a single-member

district system. Austin currently elects six city council members, all using the at-large approach. Mayor Lee Leffingwell has proposed a hybrid system that would entail six members elected from single-member districts, two elected at-large, and the mayor elected at-large. He argues that this will ensure an effective balance of the representation of all parts of the city.

Which system is best for the representation of the city's residents? Advocates of the at-large approach argue that city council members must represent the interests of the city as a whole and not their narrow neighborhood interests. They also argue that single-member district sytems are more divisive, with city council members only advocating for their district's specific interests without concern for the city as a whole. Supporters of at-large elections also suggest that minority representation on the city council is already strong

in Austin because of a "gentlemen's agreement" that ensures that an African American and Latino candidate is represented on the city council. They point to research that shows that female candidates are more likely to win in cities with at-large districts.

Advocates of switching to single-member districts argue that it would enhance minority representation and make sure that all parts of the city are represented. Because Austin does not have a majority of minorities in the city population, it is more difficult to elect minorities in citywide, at-large elections. However, if single-member districts were created, several districts could be created to ensure that African Americans and Latinos are represented. In Austin, critics of the at-large system point out that no city council members are from South Austin, so that area of the city is unrepresented.

critical thinking questions

1. What are the trade-offs of at-large versus single-member districts for city council elections?

2. Is the hybrid approach the best way to compromise on the conflict between advocates of each approach?

emerging from Dallas's single-member district council may ultimately compel the city to reexamine the wisdom of retaining a council-manager system. As Dallas learned in the 1990s, efficient government and democratic governance are not as easy to balance as advocates of the council-manager system once thought.

One illustration of the push for change is that in 2001–02, each of the three major candidates for mayor suggested that the structure of city government needs reexamining. One of the mayoral candidates publicly commented on the need for more power to be in the hands of the mayor. A city council member argued that council members have so little power to set spending priorities or influence city staff that individual citizens do not see city government as a way to influence their lives. There has even been some discussion of the value of partisan elections in city races.

● Special Districts

Examine the role of special districts in Texas government

A **special district** is a unit of government that performs a single service in a limited geographic area. These governments solve problems that cross borders of existing units of government. Special districts can be created to serve an entire county, part of a county, all of two or more counties, or parts of two or more counties. The number of special districts has increased dramatically in the last 50 years. In the United States, the number increased by 400 percent.[27] In Texas, the number increased by more than 600 percent.[28] By the year 2002, there were more special districts than any other form of local government.

Districts can be created to do almost anything that is legal. Some districts are formed to provide hospital care, others to furnish pure water to cities that, in turn, sell it to their residents. Mosquito control, navigation, flood control, sanitation, drainage, and law enforcement are a few more examples of services provided by special district government.

special district a unit of local government that performs a single service, such as education or sanitation, within a limited geographic area

Types of Special Districts

There are two types of special districts in Texas. The first is the **school district**, which consists of independent school districts in the state. These districts offer public education from pre-kindergarten through twelfth grade. Almost all school districts offer the full range of educational opportunities; however, some small, rural schools provide education only through the eighth grade. Others limit their programs to the sixth grade, and still others end with the fourth grade. Those with limited offerings contract with nearby districts to complete the education of their students.

The second classification of special districts is the **nonschool special district**. Everything except the school districts is included in this category. Municipal utility districts, economic development corporations, hospital districts, and fire-prevention districts are the most common examples.

school district a specific type of special district that provides public education in a designated area

nonschool special district any special district other than a school district; examples include municipal utility districts (MUDs) and hospital districts

School Districts

Every inch of land in Texas is part of a school district, and the state contains slightly more than 1,000 school districts. Some districts in east and west Texas cover an entire county. In metropolitan counties, there may be a dozen or more districts.

Each is governed by an elected board of trustees composed of five to nine members. The board employs a superintendent to oversee the daily operation of the district. On the recommendation of the superintendent, the trustees

- set overall policy for the school district
- adopt the budget for the district
- set the tax rate for the district (The maximum tax rate for a district is $1.04 for each $100 the property is worth. A rate higher than $1.04 requires voter approval.)
- select textbooks for classroom use
- hire principals, faculty, and support staff
- set the school calendar
- determine salaries and benefits for employees

Educating millions of students is a daunting task. By localizing public education, the state places much of the burden on the local school districts. This allows local residents to participate in governing the school districts. Unfortunately, few people vote in the elections to select members of the board of trustees. Even fewer individuals attend meetings of the school board.

Nonschool Special Districts

municipal utility district (MUD)
a special district that offers services such as electricity, water, sewage, and sanitation outside the city limits

Municipal Utility Districts Municipal utility districts (MUDs) offer electricity, water, sewer, and sanitation services outside the city limits. These governments might offer all utility services or only one or two, depending on the needs of the special district. Though located throughout Texas, the vast majority are found in the Houston greater metropolitan area.

MUDs can be a financial blessing for developers. Entrepreneurs who build housing additions outside the city limits must furnish utilities to the homes they build, but few developers can afford to do this over a long period of time.

Banks and finance companies, legislators, and land developers maintain a warm and snug relationship with each other. Banks and finance companies willingly lend land developers millions of dollars to establish residential subdivisions, build new homes, and run water and sewer services to these houses. When a few houses are sold, the developer asks the residents to establish a MUD. Enabling the legislation is seldom a problem because of the close relationship between developers and local legislators.

Once the MUD is up and running, the board of directors sets a tax rate and determines how much to charge residents for its services. One of its first activities is to borrow money by issuing bonds. The bond proceeds are used to purchase the utilities from the developer, often at a premium. Using the proceeds from the sale of the utilities, the developer is able to repay loans. By establishing the MUD, residents agree to pay a property tax to retire the bonded indebtedness. In addition to the property tax, residents pay a monthly fee for the water, sewer, and sanitation services.

Flood-Control Districts Flooding is seldom confined to a single county, and a flood-control district can be created to solve a multicounty flood-control problem.

Community College Districts Community college districts are classified as nonschool special districts because they do not offer public education from prekindergarten through grade twelve. Community colleges offer postsecondary

Who Represents Texans at the Local Level?

Texas has many local governments, and as a result Texans have many elected representatives in different local governments. The charts show all of the local elected officials for two places in the state—the West Campus neighborhood in Austin and the Woodcreek neighborhood in North Harris County. Between county, city, school district, and community college district officials, Texans have many, many people serving them in local government.

AUSTIN—WEST CAMPUS AREA

COUNTY

County Judge, Sam Biscoe
County Commissioner, Precinct 2, Sarah Eckhardt
District Attorney, Rosemary Lehmberg
County Attorney, David Escamilla
County Sheriff, Greg Hamilton
County Tax Assessor-Collector, Bruce Elfant
District Clerk, Amalia Rodriguez-Mendoza
County Clerk, Dana DeBeauvoir
County Treasurer, Dolores Ortega Carter
County Constable, Precinct 5, Carlos Lopez
Justice of the Peace, Precinct 5, Herb Evans

CITY

Mayor, Lee Leffingwell
Council, Place 1, Chris Riley
Council, Place 2, Mike Martinez
Council, Place 3, Kathie Tovo

CITY (continued)

Council, Place 4, Laura Morrison
Council, Place 5, Bill Spelman
Council, Place 6, Sheryl Cole

SCHOOL DISTRICT: AUSTIN ISD

District 5, Mark Williams

COMMUNITY COLLEGE DISTRICT: AUSTIN COMMUNITY COLLEGE

Place 1, Tim Mahoney
Place 2, John-Michael Cortez
Place 3, Nan McRaven
Place 4, Jeffrey Richard
Place 5, Victor Villareal
Place 6, Guadalupe Sosa
Place 7, Barbara Mink
Place 8, James McGuffie
Place 9, Allen Kaplan

NORTH HARRIS COUNTY—WOODCREEK AREA

COUNTY

County Judge, Ed Emmett
County Commissioner, Precinct 4, Jack Cagle
District Attorney, Patricia Lyons
County Attorney, Vince Ryan
County Sheriff, Adrian Garcia
County Tax Assessor-Collector, Mike Sullivan
District Clerk, Chris Daniel
County Clerk, Stan Stanart
County Treasurer, Orlando Sanchez
County Constable, Precinct 4, Ron Hickman
Justice of the Peace, Precinct 4, Place 1, J. Kent Adams
Justice of the Peace, Precinct 4, Place 2, Tom Lawrence
School Trustee, Position 2, Angie Chesnut
School Trustee, At Large, Position 7, Jim Henley
School Trustee, Position 5, Debra Kerner
School Trustee, Position 3, Michael Wolfe

SCHOOL DISTRICT: ALDINE ISD

Board, Position 1, Rick Ogden
Board, Position 2, Marine Jones
Board, Position 3, Rose Avalos
Board, Position 4, Merlin Griffs
Board, Position 5, Steve Mead
Board, Position 6, Alton Smith
Board, Position 7, Violet Garcia

COMMUNITY COLLEGE DISTRICT: LONE STAR COLLEGE SYSTEM

Board, Position 1, David Holsey
Board, Position 2, Thomas Forestier
Board, Position 3, Stephanie Marquard
Board, Position 4, Robert Adam
Board, Position 5, David Vogt
Board, Position 6, Bob Wolfe
Board, Position 7, Linda Good
Board, Position 8, Randy Bates
Board, Position 9, Priscilla Kelley

for critical analysis

1. Why would there be so many local elected officials? What are the advantages of having many elected officials? How does this system promote democratic values?

2. Think of your own local school board. Do you know the elected officials who serve on it? How many people in your community do you think know all their local elected officials? If people do not know who is in office, can they evaluate the job their officials are doing at election time?

academic and vocational programs. They are governed by an elected board of regents. Residents of the district pay a property tax to the district. In return, residents pay lower tuition. The board employs a president or chancellor, who operates the college on a daily basis. The regents set policy on the recommendation of the president or chancellor. Among the regents' responsibilities are to

- set overall policy for the district
- set the tax rate
- set the cost of tuition and fees
- build new buildings and repair older ones
- hire teachers, counselors, administrators, and nonprofessional staff
- set the school calendar
- determine salaries and benefits for employees

Creating a Special District Special districts are created by voters of the area to be served. Creating a special district requires

- a petition signed by the residents of the area to be served, requesting the legislature to authorize an election to create a special district
- enabling legislation in the form of a law that authorizes a special election to create the district
- a majority positive vote of those voting in the special election

Governing a Special District Most special districts are governed by boards elected by the voters of the district. The board of a school district is called the board of trustees, the governing board of a community college is often called the board of regents, and the governing boards of other special districts are known as boards of directors. Each board is the policy-making group for its district. The directors set the tax rate and establish rules and policy for the operation of the district. The district employs an individual who runs the district on a day-to-day basis.

property tax a tax based on an assessment of the value of one's property, which is used to fund the services provided by local governments, such as education

user fee a fee paid for public goods and services, such as water or sewage service

Revenues **Property taxes** are the primary source of revenue for special districts. This was not always the case. In 1949, school districts received 80 percent of their income from the state, and the school district furnished 20 percent of necessary funds, primarily from property taxes. Today, property taxes comprise as much as 90 percent of revenues for some districts. The second largest source of income is **user fees**. State and federal aid furnish the remainder of special district funding.

Property tax rates and actual user fees are set by governing boards. User fees are raised from providing goods and services. Water districts, for example, sell water, sewer, and possibly sanitation services.

Hospital districts set fees for room occupancy, medicine dispensed, use of surgical suites, X-rays taken and evaluated, nursing and laboratory service, and myriad other charges. The board of trustees of a school district sets the local property rate for taxes, which fund pre-kindergarten through twelfth grade education. Tuition paid by in-district and out-of-district students, building fees, student fees, and technology and lab fees are determined by the board of regents of a community college district.

Hidden Governments Everyone in Texas lives in at least one special district, their school district. Most people live in several, have the opportunity to vote for people to represent them on the governing board of each district, and pay property taxes to these agencies of government. Yet few people are aware these agencies exist, thus their reputation as "**hidden governments**."

Special districts provide needed services in specific geographic areas. Existing governments may lack authority to provide the service or the necessary funds to finance the project. In theory, special districts are an example of democracy at work. Districts are created by a vote of the residents of the area to be served, and the districts' governing boards are elected by the voters. Board meetings, at which decisions on policy, taxing, and fees are made, are open for attendance by any interested residents. However, fewer than 10 percent of eligible voters cast ballots in special district elections, and fewer than 1 percent of district residents ever attend a board meeting.

Problems with Special Districts There is a potential for abuse in the creation of special districts. Many special districts were originally authorized by the Texas Legislature to develop the economies of poor, rural counties. More recently, however, developers of large tracts of land began creating these districts to place the burden of developing the property's infrastructure on future owners of the property. In order to comply with the law, all the developers must do is create the district and hold an election where at least one short-term resident must vote. These short-term residents then approve bonds in the millions of dollars that must be paid for with the taxation of future homes and property owners. In the 1980s, this kind of special district creation in Harris County led to defaults on bond issues after a housing bust.

The creation of special districts by developers has sometimes been controversial. Recent investigations have charged developers with abusing the process in order to circumvent inconvenient laws and to give the developers greater control over taxes and other government functions in the district.

hidden government a term that refers to special districts of which many citizens are unaware

In 2001, a major investigation of special districts created by developers in Dallas found unusual and questionable practices. Some developers drew district boundaries to exclude existing residents of an area. The developers then moved people into rent-free mobile homes shortly before the special district election. These newly established "residents" were the only ones eligible to vote in the election. After the election, the voters for the new district would often move away after approving large bond sales for the construction of roads, water lines, and sewers. Future homeowners in the area were then expected to pay for the bonds with property taxes on their homes. The investigation found that sometimes a single voter—and always fewer than 10 voters—approved the bonded indebtedness that helped the developers create an infrastructure for their properties. In the Lantana subdivision near Flower Mound, for example, a family of three voted to authorize $277 million in bond sales by two water districts. That bond proposition rivals the biggest bond proposals by the city of Dallas.[29]

Similar schemes have been especially prevalent in Travis, Harris, and Denton counties. In 2006, developers in Denton County housed six people at below-market rents on property to be developed. These temporary residents were thus eligible to vote in a special tax-district election that would affect the taxation of thousands of future homeowners.[30]

In 2010, two voters in the Four Seasons Ranch Municipal Utility District No. 1 approved $292.5 million in bonds, including $138.5 million in bonds for water, sewer, and storm sewer systems and $154 million in roads. Recent special district elections near the Four Seasons Ranch district in Denton and Collin Counties have authorized close to $1 billion dollars in public debt.[31]

The pervasiveness of these government bodies is shown by one study of Texas special districts that address water issues. The study found that about 1,000 MUDs were engaged in supplying water; 48 special districts existed to deal with water drainage issues; 66 special districts existed solely to supply fresh water. Others had these purposes: 91 to conserve groundwater, 25 for irrigation, 46 to improve levees, 42 to manage municipal water, 26 to deal with navigation, 31 to deal with rivers. Fifty-five special utility districts dealt with general water issues; 221 were water control and improvement districts; and 18 were water improvement districts. Of course, this hodgepodge of special districts dealing with all aspects of water makes a coherent approach to statewide water policy virtually impossible.[32]

Special districts are among the least-studied areas of Texas politics, but their use as an instrument of private gain and their use by developers as a way to minimize their financial risks suggest the need for much greater scrutiny. Of course, developers may defend this system as a way to improve property and enhance the tax base of communities. On the other hand, the extent of enlistment of governmental taxing powers with little public scrutiny or accountability is disturbing. And if the huge bond issues floated by these entities default, thousands of people could suffer the financial consequences.

Councils of Government (COGs)

One of the greatest problems facing local governments in Texas today is coordination across legal boundaries. The Regional Planning Act of 1965 initially provided for the creation of regional **councils of government (COGs)** to promote coordination and planning across all local governments in a particular region. There are 24 regional councils in Texas today, each with its own bylaws or articles of agreement. The governing body of a regional council must consist of at least two-thirds of

council of government (COG) a regional planning board composed of local elected officials and some private citizens from the same area

local elected officials of cities and counties, and may include citizen members and representatives of other groups.

The basic responsibilities of regional councils include planning for the economic development of an area, helping local governments carry out regional projects, contracting with local governments to provide certain services, and reviewing applications for state and federal financial assistance. Originally, COGs focused considerable attention on meeting federal mandates for water and sewer provision, open space, and housing planning. More recently, activities have focused on comprehensive planning and service delivery in such policy areas as aging, employment and training, criminal justice, economic development, environmental quality, and transportation.[33]

● Thinking Critically about Local Government

In this chapter, we have investigated the role of local government in Texas government and politics. In many ways, local government affects the average citizen's life much more than either the federal or the state government. Sadly, local government may not be functioning as well as we might hope. Part of the problem may lie in the conflicting demands we have come to place on it. On the one hand, Texans want local government of all kinds to provide an efficient delivery of services to all in a fair and equitable manner. On the other hand, Texans also want to keep local government under some sort of democratic control. But what sort of local controls are the best? The demands of efficiency and democracy are not easily balanced. The social, political, and economic changes of the last 20 years may spark a rethinking of local government in Texas for the first time since the early decades of the twentieth century.

study guide

⑤ Practice online with: Chapter 13 Diagnostic Quiz ▪ Chapter 13 Key Term Flashcards

County Government in Texas

■ Explain the importance of county government in Texas (pp. 381–88)

There are more counties in Texas than in any other state. County governance in Texas affects the lives of everyday Texans in ways ranging from hospital care to trash pickup.

Key Terms

county commissioners court (p. 381)

county judge (p. 382)

county commissioner (p. 382)

constable (p. 383)

county attorney (p. 386)

district attorney (p. 386)

county clerk (p. 387)

district clerk (p. 387)

county tax assessor-collector (p. 387)

county auditor (p. 387)

Practice Quiz

1. Which of the following is *not* a type of local government found in Texas? *(p. 381)*
   a) city
   b) council of government
   c) county
   d) special district
   e) parish

2. The basic governing body of a county is known as *(p. 381)*
   a) a council of government.
   b) a county council.
   c) a city-manager government.
   d) a county commissioners court.
   e) a county governing committee.

3. How many counties are there in Texas? *(p. 381)*
   a) 25
   b) 56
   c) 110
   d) 254
   e) 500

4. All county commissioners' precincts must be equal in population according to *(p. 382)*
   a) Article I of the Texas Constitution.
   b) the Civil Rights Act of 1964.
   c) the Voting Rights Act of 1975.
   d) *Avery v. Midland County.*
   e) *Marbury v. Madison.*

5. A county judge *(p. 382)*
   a) only hears appellate cases from JP courts.
   b) is an appointive position from the governor.
   c) presides over the constitutional county court and the county commissioner's court.
   d) implements all the decisions of the Supreme Court affecting the county.
   e) judges juvenile cases.

6. Which county officials are responsible for the jail and the safety of the prisoners? *(p. 386)*
   a) sheriff
   b) county council
   c) county commissioners court
   d) council of mayors
   e) city manager

Practice Online
"Exploring Texas Politics" exercise: *County Tax Rates*

City Government in Texas

 Describe the major types of city government in Texas (pp. 388–95)

Municipalities in Texas vary in terms of how they are governed. Some cities have strong mayors who run the city, while other cities have weak mayors where the day-to-day running of the city is delegated to city managers. Mayors and city councils often decide issues which directly affect the lives of everyday people.

Key Terms

home-rule charter (p. 388)

mayor-council form of government (p. 389)

at-large election (p. 390)

single-member district (p. 390)

commissioner form of government (p. 390)

council-manager form of government (p. 391)

Practice Quiz

7. To adopt a home-rule charter, a city must have a minimum population of *(p. 388)*
   a) 201.
   b) 5,000.
   c) 10,000.
   d) 50,000.
   e) There is no minimum.

8. The two legal classifications of Texas cities are *(pp. 388–89)*
   a) local and regional.
   b) general law and home rule.
   c) tax and nontax.
   d) charter and noncharter.
   e) big and small.

9. The form of city government that allows the mayor to establish control over most of the city's government is called the *(p. 389)*
   a) commissioner form of city government.
   b) council-manager form of city government.
   c) council of government form of city government.
   d) strong mayor–council form of city government.
   e) none of the above.

10. A city controller *(p. 392)*
    a) works directly for the governor.
    b) controls and manages the election in a city.
    c) is a city's chief elected official who presides over the city council.
    d) is independent of all political control in a small statutory city.
    e) is a city's chief financial officer.

 Practice Online
Interactive simulation: *Models of City Government*

Special Districts

Examine the role of special districts in Texas government (pp. 395–401)

Special districts often span different cities and counties. They are tasked with operating such things as school districts or water utility districts. They have the authority to levy property taxes to fund the operation of services essential to the lives of many residents.

Key Terms

special district (p. 395)

school district (p. 395)

nonschool special district (p. 395)

municipal utility district (MUD) (p. 396)

property tax (p. 398)

user fee (p. 398)

hidden government (p. 399)

council of government (COG) (p. 400)

Practice Quiz

11. Which local government provides a single service not provided by any other local government? *(p. 395)*
    a) special district
    b) council of government
    c) police district
    d) city
    e) county

12. What are the two types of special districts found in Texas? *(p. 395)*
    a) school and nonschool
    b) home rule and general law
    c) tax and nontax
    d) statutory and constitutional
    e) none of the above.

13. A special district *(p. 395)*
    a) must be limited to under 150,000 people.
    b) covers the entire state to provide a particular service.

c) is a unit of local government that provides a special service to a limited geographic area.

d) temporarily combines two congressional districts.

e) none of the above.

14. A MUD *(p. 396)*

a) serves the needs of developers.

b) is generally opposed by banks and real estate developers as being too expensive.

c) provides ambulance service inside a city's geographic limits.

d) delegates the setting of tax rates in a particular geographic area to the state legislature.

e) provides funding for special districts.

15. Comprehensive planning and service delivery in a specific geographic area is the function of a *(pp. 400–401)*

a) special district.

b) council of government.

c) city.

d) county.

e) town.

Recommended Websites

Individual State Descriptions
www.census.gov

Texas Association of Counties
www.county.org

Texas Local Government Code
www.statutes.legis.state.tx.us/

U.S. Census Bureau, State and County QuickFacts
http://quickfacts.census.gov/qfd/

glossary

action by the governor the final step in the legislative process, during which the governor signs, vetoes, or refuses to sign a bill

agricultural commissioner elected state official who is primarily responsible for enforcing agricultural laws

Aid to Families with Dependent Children (AFDC) a federally and state financed program for children living with parents or relatives who fell below state standards of need. Replaced in 1996 by TANF.

All Funds budget the budget that aggregates all monies flowing into the state treasury and all state spending

answer the presentation of a defendant's defense against an allegation in a civil case

appointment the power of the chief executive, whether the president of the United States or the governor of a state, to appoint persons to office

appropriations authorization by the legislature to a government agency or body to spend up to a particular amount of money

Article III, Section 49a portion of the Texas Constitution that requires the state to maintain a balanced budget

at-large election an election in which officials are selected by voters of the entire geographical area, rather than from smaller districts within that area

attorney general elected state official who serves as the state's chief civil lawyer

bail payment of money to the state as an assurance that an accused person who is released from jail pending trial will appear for trial; if the accused does not appear, the bail is forfeited

bench trial a trial held without a jury and before only a judge

beyond a reasonable doubt the legal standard in criminal cases, which requires the prosecution to prove that a reasonable doubt of innocence does not exist

bicameral having a legislative assembly composed of two chambers or houses

biennial occurring every two years

bill a proposed law that has been sponsored by a member of the legislature and submitted to the clerk of the House or Senate

block grants federal grants that allow states considerable discretion in how the funds are spent

Blue Dog Democrats another name for conservative Democrats, mostly from the South

bundling the interest-group practice of combining campaign contributions from several sources into one larger contribution from the group, so as to increase the group's impact on the candidate

bureaucracy the complex structure of offices, tasks, rules, and principles of organization that are employed by all large-scale institutions to coordinate the work of their personnel

capital case a criminal case in which the death penalty is a possible punishment

civil law a branch of law that deals with disputes, usually between private individuals over relationships, obligation, and responsibility

closed primary a primary election in which only registered members of a particular political party can vote

coercive federalism federal governmental efforts to accomplish national policy goals by preempting state power, forcing states to change their policies, and forcing the expenditure of money by states without compensation by the national government

commissioner form of government a form of city government in which the city is run by a small group of elected commissioners who act in both legislative and executive capacities

complaint the presentation of a grievance by the plaintiff in a civil case

comptroller elected state official who directs the collection of taxes and other revenues

concurrent resolution a resolution of interest to both chambers of the legislature and which must pass both the House and Senate and generally be signed by the governor

Confederacy the Confederate States of America, those southern states that seceded from the United States in late 1860 and 1861 and argued that the power of the states was more important than the power of the central government

conference committee a joint committee created to work out a compromise on House and Senate versions of a piece of legislation

consideration by standing committee the third step in the legislative process, during which a bill is killed, amended, or heard by a standing committee

constable precinct-level county official involved with serving legal papers and, in some counties, enforcing the law

constituent a person living in the district from which an official is elected

constitution the legal structure of a government, which establishes its power and authority as well as the limits on that power

contingent fee a fee paid to the lawyer in a civil case and which is contingent on winning the case

cooperative federalism a type of federalism existing since the New Deal era in which grants-in-aid have been used to encourage states and localities (without commanding them) to pursue nationally defined goals. Also known as "intergovernmental cooperation"

council of government (COG) a regional planning board composed of local elected officials and some private citizens from the same area

council-manager form of government a form of city government in which public policies are developed by the city council and executive and administrative functions are assigned to a professional city manager

county attorney county official who prosecutes lesser criminal cases in the county court

county auditor public official, appointed by the district judges, who receives and disburses county funds; in large counties, this official also prepares the county budget

county chair the county party official who heads the county executive committee

county clerk public official who is the main record-keeper of the county

county commissioner government official (four per county) on the county commissioners court whose main duty is the construction and maintenance of roads and bridges

county commissioners court the main governing body of each county; has the authority to set the county tax rate and budget

county convention a meeting held by a political party following its precinct conventions, for the purpose of electing delegates to its state convention

county courts the courts that exist in some counties that are presided over by county judges

county executive committee the party group, made up of a party's county chair and precinct chairs, that is responsible for running a county's primary elections and planning county conventions

county judge the person in each of Texas's 254 counties who presides over the constitutional county court and the county commissioners court, with responsibility for the administration of county government; some county judges carry out judicial responsibilities

county tax assessor-collector public official who maintains the county tax records and collects the taxes owed to the county

courts of appeals the 14 intermediate-level appellate courts that hear appeals from district and county courts to determine whether the decisions of these lower courts followed legal principles and court procedures

criminal law the branch of law that regulates the conduct of individuals, defines crimes, and specifies punishment for criminal acts

debt service money spent by the state to pay off debt; includes interest and principal payments

directive and supervisory power the legislature's power over the executive branch; for example, the legislature determines the size of appropriations for state agencies

district attorney public official who prosecutes the more serious criminal cases in the district court

district clerk public official who is the main record-keeper of the district court

district courts the major trial courts in Texas, which usually have general jurisdiction over a broad range of civil and criminal cases

Dixiecrats conservative Democrats who abandoned the national Democratic Party in the 1948 presidential election

dual federalism the system of government that prevailed in the United States from 1789 to 1937, in which most fundamental governmental powers were strictly separated between the federal and state governments

Duverger's Law the observation that in a single-member district system of electing representatives, a two-party system will emerge

early registration the requirement that a voter register long before the general election; in effect in Texas until 1971

early voting a procedure that allows voters to cast ballots during the two-week period before the regularly scheduled election date

Economic Stabilization Fund (ESF) established by constitutional amendment in 1988 to provide funds for the state during times of financial stress, commonly known as the *Rainy Day Fund*

electoral power the legislature's mandated role in counting returns in the elections for governor and lieutenant governor

elite a small group of people that dominates the political process

en banc referring to an appellate hearing with all judges participating

Equal protection clause provision in the Fourteenth Amendment of the U.S. Constitution guaranteeing citizens the "equal protection of the laws"; this clause has been the basis for the civil rights of African Americans, women, and other groups

executive budget the state budget prepared and submitted by the governor to the legislature, which indicates the governor's spending priorities. The executive budget is overshadowed in terms of importance by the legislative budget

Federal Funds budget a state budget that includes all grants, payments, or reimbursements received from the federal government by state agencies and institutions

federalism a system of government in which power is divided, by a constitution, between a central government and regional governments

felony a serious criminal offense, punishable by a prison sentence or a fine. A capital felony is punishable by death.

filibuster a tactic used by members of the Senate to prevent action on legislation they oppose by continuously holding the floor and speaking until the majority backs down. Once given the floor, senators have unlimited time to speak, and it requires a vote of three-fifths of the Senate to end a filibuster

floor action the fourth step in the legislative process, during which a bill referred by a standing committee is scheduled for floor debate by the Calendars Committee

general bill a bill that applies to all people and/or property in the state

general election the election in which voters cast ballots to select public officials

General Revenue–Dedicated Funds budget a budget composed of funds for dedicated revenues that target money for specific purposes

General Revenues Fund budget a budget for a nondedicated revenue account that functions as the state's primary operating fund

General Revenues Fund the state's primary operating fund

Gilmer-Aikin Laws education reform legislation passed in 1949 that supplemented local funding of education with public monies, raised teachers' salaries, mandated a minimum length for the school year, and provided for more state supervision of public education

grand jury jury that determines whether sufficient evidence is available to justify a trial; grand juries do not rule on the accused's guilt or innocence

Grange a militant farmers' movement of the late nineteenth century that fought for improved conditions for farmers

hidden government a term that refers to special districts of which many citizens are unaware

Higher Education Fund (HEF) a state higher education fund for universities not having access to PUF monies

home-rule charter the rules under which a city operates

impeachment under the Texas Constitution, the formal charge by the House of Representatives that leads to trial in the Senate and possible removal of a state official

indictment a written statement issued by a grand jury that charges a suspect with a crime and states that a trial is warranted

individualistic political culture the belief that government should limit its role to providing order in society, so that citizens can pursue their economic self-interests

interest group an organization established to influence the government's programs and policies

introduction the first step in the legislative process, during which a member of the legislature gets an idea for a bill and files a copy of it with the clerk of the House or secretary of the Senate

investigative power the power, exercised by the House, the Senate, or both chambers jointly, to investigate problems facing the state

issue advocacy independent spending by individuals or interest groups on a campaign issue but not directly tied to a particular candidate

Jaybird Party after the white primary was ruled unconstitutional, this offshoot Democratic party pre-selected candidates for the Democratic primary and prohibited African Americans from participating

joint resolution a resolution, commonly a proposed amendment to the Texas Constitution or ratification of an amendment to the U.S. Constitution, that must pass both the House and Senate but which does not require the governor's signature

Judicial Campaign Fairness Act a judicial reform under which campaign contributions are limited by the amount that a judicial candidate can receive from donors

judicial power the power of the House to impeach and of the Senate to convict members of the executive and judicial branches of state government

justice of the peace courts local trial courts with limited jurisdiction over small claims and very minor criminal misdemeanors

La Raza Unida Party political party formed in Texas in order to bring attention to the concerns of Mexican Americans

land commissioner elected state official who is the manager of most publicly owned lands

layer-cake federalism a way of describing the system of dual federalism where there is no interaction between the levels of government

legislative budget the state budget that is prepared and submitted by the Legislative Budget Board (LBB) and that is fully considered by the House and Senate

lieutenant governor the second-highest elected official in the state and president of the state Senate

limited government a principle of constitutional government; a government whose powers are defined and limited by a constitution

line-item veto the power of the executive to veto specific provisions (lines) of an appropriations bill passed by the legislature

lobbyist an individual employed by an interest group who tries to influence governmental decisions on behalf of that group

local bill a bill affecting only units of local government, such as a city, county, or special district

marble-cake federalism a way of describing cooperative federalism where there is interaction between the levels of government

matching funds federal monies going to a state based on state spending for a program

mayor-council form of government a form of city government in which the mayor is the chief executive and the city council is the legislative body; in the *strong mayor-council* variation, the mayor's powers enable him or her to control executive departments and the agenda of the city council; in the *weak mayor-council* variation, the mayor's power is more limited

Medicaid a federal and state program financing medical services to low-income people.

merit selection a judicial reform under which judges would be nominated by a blue-ribbon committee, appointed by the governor, and, after a brief period in office, would run in a retention election

misdemeanor a minor criminal offense, usually punishable by a small fine or a short jail sentence

moralistic political culture the belief that government should be active in promoting the public good and that citizens should participate in politics and civic activities to ensure that good

motor voter law a national act, passed in 1993, that requires states to allow people to register to vote when applying for a driver's license

municipal courts local trial courts with limited jurisdiction over violations of city ordinances and very minor criminal misdemeanors; municipal courts are located in each of Texas's incorporated cities and towns

municipal utility district (MUD) a special district that offers services such as electricity, water, sewage, and sanitation outside the city limits

National Research University Fund (NRUF) established in 2009 to provide funding to universities seeking to achieve national prominence as research institutions

necessary and proper clause Article I, Section 8, of the U.S. Constitution; it provides Congress with the authority to make all laws "necessary and proper" to carry out its powers

New Deal President Franklin Delano Roosevelt's 1930s programs to stimulate the national economy and provide relief to victims of the Great Depression.

New Federalism attempts by Presidents Nixon and Reagan to return power to the states through block grants

Nineteenth Amendment ratified in 1919, amendment guaranteeing women the right to vote

nonschool special district any special district other than a school district; examples include municipal utility districts (MUDs) and hospital districts

North American Free Trade Agreement (NAFTA) trade treaty among the United States, Canada, and Mexico to lower and eliminate tariffs among the three countries

Occupy movement political movement aimed at limiting the influence of Wall Street and big corporations in American politics. Created following government bailouts in 2008

one-person, one-vote principle the principle that all districts should have roughly equal populations

open primary a primary election in which any registered voter can participate in the contest, regardless of party affiliation

ordinance a regulation enacted by a city government

Other Funds budget a budget consisting of all other funds flowing into the state treasury that are not included in other state budgets. This includes the Texas Highway Fund, various trust funds operated by the state, and certain revenues held for local higher education accounts.

parole the conditional release of an offender who has served some prison time, under specified rules and under the supervision of a parole officer

partisan polarization the degree to which Republicans have become more conservative and Democrats have become more liberal

patronage the resources available to higher officials, usually opportunities to make partisan appointments to offices and to confer grants, licenses, or special favors to supporters

per diem daily payment to a public official engaged in state business

Permanent School Fund (PSF) fund created in 1854, which provides monies for primary and secondary schools

Permanent University Trust Fund (PUF) established in 1876 and funded from the proceeds from land owned by the state; monies go to various universities in the UT and Texas A&M systems

pigeonholing a step in the legislative process during which a bill is killed by the chair of the standing committee to which it was referred, as a result of his or her setting the bill aside and not bringing it before the committee

plea bargain negotiated agreement in a criminal case in which a defendant agrees to plead guilty in return for the state's agreement to reduce the severity of the criminal charge or prison sentence the defendant is facing

plural executive an executive branch in which power is fragmented because the election of statewide officeholders is independent of the election of the governor

political action committee (PAC) a private group that raises and distributes funds for use in election campaigns

political culture broadly shared values, beliefs, and attitudes about how the government should function and politics should operate. American political culture emphasizes the values of liberty, equality, and democracy

political economy the complex interrelations between politics and the economy, as well as their effect on one another

political socialization the introduction of individuals into the political culture; learning the underlying beliefs and values on which the political system is based

poll tax a state-imposed tax on voters as a prerequisite for voting. Poll taxes were rendered unconstitutional in national elections by the Twenty-Fourth Amendment, and in state elections by the Supreme Court in 1966

post-adjournment veto a veto of a bill that occurs after the legislature adjourns, thus preventing the legislature from overriding it

precinct the most basic level of political organization at the local level

precinct chair the local party official, elected in the party's primary election, who heads the precinct convention and serves on the party's county executive committee

precinct convention a meeting held by a political party to select delegates for the county convention and to submit resolutions to the party's state platform; precinct conventions are held on the day of the party's primary election and are open to anyone who voted in that election

preclearance provision under Section 5 of the Voting Rights Act of 1965 requiring any changes to election procedures or district lines to be approved by the U.S. Department of Justice or the U.S. district court for the District of Columbia

preponderance of the evidence the standard of proof in a civil jury case, by which the plaintiff must show that the defendant is more likely than not the cause of the harm suffered by the plaintiff

presidential Republicanism a voting pattern in which conservatives vote Democratic for state offices but Republican for presidential candidates

primary election a ballot vote in which citizens select a party's nominee for the general election

probation punishment where an offender is not imprisoned but remains in the community under specified rules and under the supervision of a probation officer

progressive tax a type of tax where the tax burden falls more heavily on upper income individuals

property tax a tax based on an assessment of the value of one's property, which is used to fund the services provided by local governments, such as education

proportional representation a multi-member district system that allows each political party representation in proportion to its percentage of the total vote

provincialism a narrow, limited, and self-interested view of the world

Radical Republicans a bloc of Republicans in the U.S. Congress who pushed through the adoption of black suffrage as well as an extended period of military occupation of the South following the Civil War

reapportionment process that takes place every 10 years to determine how many congressional seats each state will receive, depending on population shifts

recognition The power to control floor debate by recognizing who can speak before the House and Senate

redistricting the process of redrawing election districts and redistributing legislative representatives in the Texas House, Texas Senate, and U.S. House. This usually happens every 10 years to reflect shifts in population or in response to legal challenges in existing districts

referral the second step in the legislative process, during which a bill is assigned to the appropriate standing committee by the Speaker (for House bills) or the lieutenant governor (for Senate bills)

regressive tax a type of tax where the tax burden falls more heavily on lower-income individuals

regular session the 140-day period during which the Texas Legislature meets to consider and pass bills; occurs only in odd-numbered years

republican government a representative democracy, a system of government in which power is derived from the people

resolution an expression of opinion on an issue by a legislative body

retention election an election in which voters decide whether to keep an incumbent in office by voting "yes" or "no" to retain the incumbent and where there is no opposing candidate

runoff primary a second primary election held between the two candidates who received the most votes in the first primary election if no candidate in the first primary election had received a majority

school district a specific type of special district that provides public education in a designated area

secretary of state state official, appointed by the governor, whose primary responsibility is administering elections

senatorial courtesy the practice whereby the president, before formally nominating a person for a federal judgeship, seeks the indication that senators from the candidate's own state support the nomination; in Texas, the practice whereby the governor seeks the indication that the senator from the candidate's home supports the nomination

separation of powers the division of governmental power among several institutions that must cooperate in decision making

Shivercrat movement a movement led by the Texas governor Allan Shivers during the 1950s in which conservative Democrats in Texas supported Republican candidate Dwight Eisenhower for the presidency because many of those conservative Democrats believed that the national Democratic Party had become too liberal

simple resolution a resolution that concerns only the Texas House or Senate, such as the adoption of a rule or the appointment of an employee, and which does not require the governor's signature

single-member district an electorate that is allowed to elect only one representative for each district

sovereign possessing supreme political authority within a geographic area

Speaker the chief presiding officer of the House of Representatives. The Speaker is the most important party and House leader, and can influence the legislative agenda, the fate of individual pieces of legislation, and members' positions within the House

special bill a bill that gives an individual or corporation a special exemption from state law

special district a unit of local government that performs a single service, such as education or sanitation, within a limited geographic area

special election an election that is not held on a regularly scheduled basis; in Texas, a special election is called to fill a vacancy in office, to give approval for the state government to borrow money, or to ratify amendments to the Texas Constitution

special session a legislative session called by the governor that addresses an agenda set by him or her and that lasts no longer than 30 days

standing committee a permanent committee with the power to propose and write legislation that covers a particular subject, such as finance or agriculture

state chair and **vice chair** the top two state-level leaders in the party

state convention a party meeting held every two years for the purpose of nominating candidates for statewide office, adopting a platform, electing the party's leadership, and in presidential election years selecting delegates for the national convention and choosing presidential electors

state executive committee the committee responsible for governing a party's activities throughout the state

State Highway Fund fund that supports the construction, maintenance, policing of roadways, and acquires rights of way; funded through a variety of taxes such as motor vehicle registration fees, the federal highway fund, and the sales tax on motor lubricants

statutory county courts at law courts that tend to hear less serious cases than those heard by district courts

statutory probate courts specialized courts whose jurisdiction is limited to probate and guardianship matters

suffrage term referring to the right to vote

Sunset Advisory Commission (SAC) a commission created in 1975 for the purpose of reviewing the effectiveness of state agencies

Supplemental Security Income (SSI) a national welfare program passed in 1972 that provides assistance to low-income elderly or disabled individuals; replaced the federal-state programs that had offered assistance to the blind, the permanently and totally disabled, and the aged

supremacy clause Article VI of the U.S. Constitution, which states that the Constitution and laws passed by the national government and all treaties are the supreme law of the land and superior to all laws adopted by any state or any subdivision

Tea Party movement created after Barack Obama's election, a political movement that advocates lower government spending, lower taxes, and limited government

Temporary Assistance for Needy Families (TANF) a welfare program passed in 1996 to provide temporary assistance to families with needy children; replacing the AFDC program, TANF sought to make poor families self-sufficient and to give states greater flexibility in setting benefit levels, eligibility requirements, and other program details

Texas Court of Criminal Appeals the highest criminal court in Texas; consists of nine justices and has final state appellate authority over criminal cases

Texas Supreme Court the highest civil court in Texas; consists of nine justices and has final state appellate authority over civil cases

"three strikes" provision a law that allows persons convicted of three felonies (or in some cases two felonies) to be sentenced to life imprisonment

traditionalistic political culture the belief that government should be dominated by political elites and guided by tradition

unicameral comprising one body or house, as in a one-house legislature

urbanization the process by which people move from rural areas to cities

user fee a fee paid for public goods and services, such as water or sewage service

veto the governor's power to turn down legislation; can be overridden by a two-thirds vote of both the House and Senate

Voting Rights Act of 1965 important legislation passed in order to ensure that African Americans would be guaranteed the right to vote. Renewed several times since 1965, the act also prevents the dilution of minority voting strength

white primary primary election in which only white voters are eligible to participate

endnotes

Chapter 1

1. Alan Rosenthal, "On Analyzing States," in *The Political Life of the American States*, ed. Alan Rosenthal and Maureen Moakley (New York: Praeger, 1984), pp. 11–2.
2. Daniel Elazar, *American Federalism: A View from the States*, 2nd ed. (New York: Crowell, 1971), pp. 84–126. See also John Kincaid, "Introduction," in *Political Culture, Public Policy and the American States*, ed. John Kincaid (Philadelphia: Center for the Study of Federalism, Institute for the Study of Human Issues, 1982), pp. 1–24.
3. Rosenthal, "On Analyzing States," p. 13.
4. U.S. Census Bureau, 2010 Census.
5. The following is drawn from Dallas Morning News, *Texas Almanac 2000–2001* (Dallas: Dallas Morning News, 1999), pp. 55–8.
6. American Ground Water Trust, "What Have We Done to the Ogallala Aquifer," The American Well Owner (2002).
7. See Joseph A. Schumpeter, *Capitalism, Socialism, and Democracy*, 3rd ed. (New York: Harper & Brothers, 1950), chap. 6.
8. The following is drawn from Karen Gerhardt Britton, Fred C. Elliott, and E. A. Miller, "Cotton Culture," *Handbook of Texas Online*.
9. See Dallas Morning News, *Texas Almanac 2000–2001*, p. 51.
10. Dallas Morning News, *Texas Almanac 2000–2001*, p. 567–8.
11. See "Ranching" in *Handbook of Texas Online*.
12. U.S. Department of Agriculture, National Agricultural Statistics Service, "Texas Upland Cotton Production Estimated at 8.05 Million Bales," News Release, December 10, 2010.
13. The following is drawn from Mary G. Ramos, "Oil and Texas: A Cultural History," Dallas Morning News, *Texas Almanac 2000–2001*, pp. 29–35; and Roger M. Olien, "Oil and Gas Industry," *Handbook of Texas Online*.
14. Ramos, "Oil and Texas," p. 31.
15. Olien, "Oil and Gas Industry."
16. Texas State Comptroller, "Where the Money Comes From: Texas Budget Source," August 2, 2011.
17. Financial Statements and Independent Auditors' Report Permanent, University Fund, Years Ended August 31, 2010 and 2009.
18. The following is drawn from Anthony Champagne and Edward J. Harpham, "The Changing Political Economy of Texas," in *Texas Politics: A Reader*, 2nd ed., ed. Anthony Champagne and Edward J. Harpham (New York: W.W. Norton, 1998), pp. 4–6. Production figures are drawn from Dallas Morning News, *Texas Almanac 1994–95* (Dallas: Belo, 1993); John Sharp, *Forces of Change: Shaping the Future of Texas* (Austin: Texas Comptroller of Public Accounts, 1993).
19. Texas State Comptroller, "Texas Gross State Product Detail—Calendar Years 1990–2040."
20. Texas Wide Open for Business, "Overview of the Texas Economy."
21. Anil Kumar, "Did NAFTA Spur Texas Exports?" *Southwest Economy* 2 (March–April 2006), www.dallasfed.org/research/swe/2006/swe0602b.html (accessed 3/28/08); U.S. Department of Labor Employment & Training Administration, "Trade Adjustment Assistance: Number of Certified Workers by State"; Robert E. Scott, "Heading South: U.S.-Mexico Trade and Job Displacement after NAFTA," Economic Policy Institute (May 3, 2011).
22. U.S. Census Bureau. "State Exports for Texas" and "State Imports for Texas." See also Texas Economy Online Report from the Office of the Governor, "Overview of the Texas Economy."
23. Daniel Gross, "Lone Star: Why Texas Is Doing So Much Better Than the Rest of the Nation," *Slate*, April 19, 2010, www.slate.com/id/2250999 (accessed 7/7/10).
24. Bruce Wright, "Weathering the Storm," *Fiscal Notes*, March 2009; D'Ann Petersen and Laila Assanie, "Texas Dodges Worst of Foreclosure Wars," Federal Reserve of Dallas.

25. Federal Reserve Bank of Dallas, Texas Leading Economic Indicators, May 2010. See also Texas Wide Open for Business, "Overview of the Texas Economy."

26. See "Estimated Population by Year for Texas, 1980–94."

27. Office of the State Demographer, "Changing Demographics in Texas," presented at the 2011 Texas Labor Management Conference, June 22, 2011, San Antonio, Texas.

28. See Arnoldo De León, "Mexican Americans," *Handbook of Texas Online.*

29. U.S. Census Bureau, 2010 Census; Sharon R. Ennis, Merarys Rios-Vargis, and Nora G. Albert. "The Hispanic Population: 2010," *2010 Census Briefs*, May 2011.

30. Data provided by the National Association of Latino Elected and Appointed Officials (NALEO).

31. See W. Marvin Dulaney, "African Americans," *Handbook of Texas Online*; Chandler Davidson, "African Americans and Politics," *Handbook of Texas Online.*

32. U.S. Census Bureau, "Texas."

33. Bruce H. Webster Jr. and Alemayehu Bishaw, "Income, Earnings, and Poverty Data from the 2006 American Community Survey" (American Community Survey Reports, U.S. Census Bureau, August 2007); U.S. Census Bureau, Poverty 2007 and 2008 American Community Surveys (September 2009); U.S. Census Bureau, *Texas Quick Facts: 2009.*

34. The following is based on David G. McComb, "Urbanization," *Handbook of Texas Online.*

35. The following is drawn from David G. McComb, "Houston, Texas," *Handbook of Texas Online.*

36. Estimates are drawn from the U.S. Census Bureau, American Community Survey 2006–2008.

37. The following is drawn from Jackie McElhaney and Michael V. Hazel, "Dallas, Texas," *Handbook of Texas Online.*

38. The following is drawn from Janet Schmelzer, "Fort Worth, Texas," *Handbook of Texas Online.*

39. The following is drawn from T. R. Fehrenbach, "San Antonio, Texas," *Handbook of Texas Online.*

40. Estimates are drawn from the U.S. Census Bureau, American Community Survey 2006–2008.

Chapter 2

1. Rick Perry, *Fed Up! Our Fight to Save America from Washington* (New York: Little, Brown, 2010), p. 5.

2. Perry, *Fed Up!*

3. Perry, *Fed Up!* pp. 6, 43–50, 137–46.

4. Perry, *Fed Up!* p. 32.

5. Perry, *Fed Up!* p. 41.

6. Perry, *Fed Up!* pp. 41–42.

7. Perry, *Fed Up!* pp. 42–43.

8. Perry, *Fed Up!* p. 44.

9. Perry, *Fed Up!* p. 185.

10. Morton Grozdins, *The American System*, ed. Daniel J. Elazar (Chicago: Rand McNally, 1966).

11. Grozdins, *American System.*

12. See Benjamin Ginsberg, Theodore J. Lowi, Margaret Weir, Caroline J. Tolbert, Anthony Champagne, and Edward J. Harpham, *We the People: An Introduction to American Politics*, 9th Texas ed. (New York: W.W. Norton, 2013), pp. 74–111 and William T. Bianco and David T. Canon, *American Politics Today*, 3rd ed. (New York: W.W. Norton, 2013), pp. 68–109.

13. Ginsberg et al., *We the People*, pp. 74–111; Bianco and Canon, *American Politics Today*, pp. 68–109.

14. Ben Guttery, *Representing Texas* (Charleston, SC: BookSurge, 2008), p. 2.

15. James W. Riddlesperger Jr. and Anthony Champagne, *Lone Star Leaders* (Fort Worth: TCU Press, 2011), pp. 8–15.

16. Charles E. Neu, "House, Edward Mandell," *Handbook of Texas Online* (Texas State Historical Association).

17. Evan Anders, "Gregory, Thomas Watt" and Seymour V. Connor, "Burleson, Albert Sidney," *Handbook of Texas Online* (Texas State Historical Association); "Thomas W. Gregory (1914–1919): Attorney General," Miller Center, University of Virginia, www.millercenter.org/president/wilson/essays/cabinet/467 (accessed 8/30/12).

18. John W. Payne Jr., "Houston, David Franklin," *Handbook of Texas Online* (Texas State Historical Association).

19. Dewey W. Grantham Jr., "Texas Congressional Leaders and the New Freedom, 1913–1917," *Southwestern Historical Quarterly* 53 (July 1949): 35.

20. Grantham, "Texas Congressional Leaders," p. 35.

21. Grantham, "Texas Congressional Leaders," p. 37.

22. Riddlesperger and Champagne, *Lone Star Leaders*, pp. 17–23.

23. Riddlesperger and Champagne, *Lone Star Leaders*, pp. 24–31.

24. *Hammer v. Dagenhart*, 247 U.S. 251 (1918).

25. *United States v. E.C. Knight Co.*, 156 U.S. 1 (1895).

26. The classic case is *Lochner v. New York*, 198 U.S. 45 (1905).

27. The Supremacy Clause is in Article VI, Section 2 of the Constitution. It states: "This Constitution, and the Laws of the United States which shall be made in Pursuance thereof; and all Treaties made, or which shall be made, under the Authority of the United States, shall be the supreme Law of the Land; and the judges in every State shall be bound thereby, any Thing in the Constitution or Laws of any State to the Contrary notwithstanding."

28. James Chace, *1912: Wilson, Roosevelt, Taft & Debs—The Election That Changed the Country* (New York: Simon & Schuster, 2004), pp. 96–97.

29. Quoted in Anthony Champagne, Douglas B. Harris, James W. Riddlesperger Jr. and Garrison Nelson, *The Austin-Boston Connection* (College Station: Texas A&M University Press, 2009), p. 75.

30. Republicans in the post-Reconstruction period in Texas were very rare until the Reagan era. See generally Guttery, *Representing Texas.*

31. Lionel V. Patenaude, "Jones, Jesse Holman," *Handbook of Texas Online* (Texas State Historical Association).

32. Riddlesperger and Champagne, *Lone Star Leaders*, pp. 32–38; Anthony Champagne, *Congressman Sam Rayburn* (New Brunswick, NJ: Rutgers University Press, 1984).

33. Riddlesperger and Champagne, *Lone Star Leaders*, p. 23.

34. *Wickard v. Filburn*, 317 U.S. 111 (1942).

35. *Katzenbach v. McClung*, 379 U.S. 294 (1964).

36. *West Coast Hotel Company v. Parrish*, 300 U.S. 379 (1937).

37. *Ferguson v. Skrupa*, 372 U.S. 726 (1963).

38. Champagne, *Congressman Sam Rayburn*, pp. 151–5.

39. Champagne, *Congressman Sam Rayburn*, pp. 151–5.

40. For example, Robert Caro, *Means of Ascent* (New York: Alfred A. Knopf, 1990), pp. 74–75.

41. Riddlesperger and Champagne, *Lone Star Leaders*, pp. 63–70, 95–104.

42. Riddlesperger and Champagne, *Lone Star Leaders*, pp. 44, 47, 52.

43. Riddlesperger and Champagne, *Lone Star Leaders*, pp. 28–29, 31.

44. Champagne, *Congressman Sam Rayburn*, pp. 148–51.

45. See generally, Robert Caro, *The Passage of Power* (New York: Alfred A. Knopf, 2012).

46. Riddlesperger and Champagne, *Lone Star Leaders*, pp. 197–202.

47. *United States. v. Lopez*, 514 U.S. 549 (1995).

48. *Gonzales v. Raich*, 545 U.S. 1 (2005).

49. *Printz v. United States*, 521 U.S. 898 (1997).

50. *South Dakota v. Dole*, 483 U.S. 203 (1987).

51. Ibid., pp. 217–18. Please replace ibid, with the author and title of this work.

52. Teddy Davis, "Texas Titans Battle for GOP Nod in Governor's Race," *ABC News*, March 2, 2010.

53. Davis, "Texas Titans Battle."

54. Isadora Vail, "Protesters Gather at Hutchison's Austin Office," *Statesman.com*, December 21, 2009.

55. Neal Barton, "Tea Party vs. John Cornyn," *KETK*, September 7, 2010.

56. Sam Stein, "Booed, Called Traitor and 'The Problem' at Tea Party Protest," *Huffington Post*, updated May 25, 2011, www.huffingtonpost.com/2009/07/06/cornyn-booed-called-trait_n_226110.html (accessed 9/13/12).

57. Brendan Steinhauser, "Republican Senator John Cornyn Boo'd at Austin Tea Party," *Freedom Works*, July 5, 2009.

58. Chris Tomlinson, "Conservative Groups That Backed Tea Party Challenger in Ind. Shift Focus to Texas Senate Race," *Republic* (Columbus, Indiana), May 9, 2012.

59. "Joe Straus Texas Tea Party Public Enemy No. 1," *Tea Party 911.com*, January 23, 2012.

60. Gromer Jeffers Jr., "Carona's Fundraiser for West Raises Eyebrows in Dallas," *The Dallas Morning News*, May 15, 2012, www.dallasnews.com/news/politics/headlines/20120515-caronas-fundraiser-for-west-raises-eyebrows-in-dallas.ece (accessed 9/13/12).

61. Michael E. Young, "North Texas Water Needs Could Cost Billions in Coming Years," *The Dallas Morning News*, June 9, 2012, www.dallasnews.com/news/state/headlines/20120609-north-texas-water-needs-could-cost-billions-in-coming-years.ece (accessed 9/13/12).

62. "Editorial: The Texas GOP's New Stance on Immigration," *The Dallas Morning News*, June 12, 2012, www.dallasnews.com/opinion/latest-columns/20120612-editorial-the-texas-gops-new-stance-on-immigration.ece (accessed 9/13/12).

Chapter 3

1. The following is drawn from Proposition 10, Deleting Constitutional References to County Office of Inspector of Hides and Animals, www.hro.house.state.tx.us/focus prop80–10.pdf (accessed 3/31/08); Eric Aasen, "Round 'Em Up: Hide Inspectors Abolished," *Dallas Morning News*, November 8, 2007; John Council, "Richmond Lawyer Has Personal Stake in Hide Inspector Position," *Texas Lawyer*, November 2, 2007; Mark Lisheron, "Prop. 10 Would Abolish Office That No One Holds," *Austin American-Statesman*, October 15, 2007.

2. See Dick Smith, "Inspector of Hides and Animals," *Handbook of Texas Online*.

3. Donald E. Chipman, "Spanish Texas," *Handbook of Texas Online*; Donald E. Chipman, *Spanish Texas, 1519–1821* (Austin: University of Texas Press, 1992).

4. S. S. McKay, "Constitution of 1824," *Handbook of Texas Online*.

5. S. S. McKay, "Constitution of Coahuila and Texas," *Handbook of Texas Online*.

6. See Ralph W. Steen, "Convention of 1836," *Handbook of Texas Online*.

7. The following is drawn from Joe E. Ericson, "Constitution of the Republic of Texas," *Handbook of Texas Online*.

8. Randolph B. Campbell, "Slavery," *Handbook of Texas Online*.

9. For a brief summary of the war, see Eugene C. Barker and James W. Pohl, "Texas Revolution," *Handbook of Texas Online*.

10. S. S. McKay, "Constitution of 1845," *Handbook of Texas Online*.

11. The Texas Ordinance of Secession (February 2, 1861).

12. See Walter L. Buenger, "Secession Convention," *Handbook of Texas Online*; Walter L. Buenger, *Secession and the Union in Texas* (Austin: University of Texas Press, 1984).

13. See Claude Elliott, "Constitutional Convention of 1866," *Handbook of Texas Online*; S. McKay, "Constitution of 1866," *Handbook of Texas Online*; Charles W. Ramsdell, *Reconstruction in Texas* (New York: Columbia University Press, 1970).

14. See S. S. McKay, "Constitution of 1869," *Handbook of Texas Online*; Ramsdell, *Reconstruction in Texas*.

15. See John Walker Mauer, "Constitution Proposed in 1874," *Handbook of Texas Online*; John Walker Mauer, "State Constitutions in a Time of Crisis: The Case of the Texas Constitution of 1876," 68 *Texas Law Review* (June 1990), 1615–46.

16. For a further discussion, see George D. Braden et al., *The Constitution of the State of Texas: An Annotated and Comparative Analysis* (Austin: University of Texas Press, 1977), pp. 707–10.

17. See Sam Kinch Jr., "Sharpstown Stock-Fraud Scandal," *Handbook of Texas Online*; Charles Deaton, *The Year They Threw the Rascals Out* (Austin: Shoal Creek, 1973).

18. CBSDFW.com, "Texas Voters Approve 7 Constitutional Amendments," November 9, 2011.

19. Angela Shah, "Both Sides Claim Victory in Approval of Lawsuit Caps," *Dallas Morning News*, September 15, 2003, pp. 1A, 10A.

20. Terry Maxon, "Prop. 12 Battle Was Costliest Yet," *Dallas Morning News*, January 19, 2004, p. 2D.

21. John Council, "Power and the Prize," *Texas Lawyer*, June 16, 2003, pp. 1, 22.

Chapter 4

1. Jeffrey M. Jones, "Special Report: Many States Shift Democratic during 2005," Gallup, January 23, 2006, www.gallup.com/poll/21004/Special-Report-Many-States-Shift-Democratic-During-2005.aspx (accessed 4/7/08).

2. Use of party affiliation as an ideological cue is discussed in Philip L. Dubois, *From Ballot to Bench* (Austin: University of Texas Press, 1980).

3. University of Texas/*Texas Tribune*, "Texas Statewide Survey," May 7–13, 2012, www.laits.utexas.edu/txp_media/html/poll/files/201205-summary.pdf (accessed 11/28/12).

4. University of Texas/*Texas Tribune*, "Texas Statewide Survey."

5. Quoted in Chandler Davidson, *Race and Class in Texas Politics* (Princeton, NJ: Princeton University Press, 1990), p. 198.

6. Davidson, *Race and Class in Texas Politics*, pp. 24–25.

7. Jones, "Special Report: Many States Shift Democratic during 2005."

8. Pew Research Center for the People and the Press, "Fewer Voters Identify as Republicans," March 20, 2008.

9. Jeffrey M. Jones, "Party ID: Despite GOP Gains, Most States Remain Blue," Gallup Politics, February 1, 2010, www.gallup.com/poll/125450/party-affiliation-despite-gop-gains-states-remain-blue.aspx (accessed 11/29/12).

10. James R. Soukup, Clifton McClesky, and Harry Holloway, *Party and Factional Division in Texas* (Austin: University of Texas Press, 1964), p. 22.

11. Robert T. Garrett, "2 Major GOP Donors Show Rift in Party," *Dallas Morning News*, February 3, 2006, p. 2A.

12. Robert T. Garrett, "PAC's Late Aid Altered Races," *Dallas Morning News*, March 10, 2006, pp. 1A, 16A.

13. Dante Chinni and James Gimpel, *Our Patchwork Nation* (New York: Gotham, 2011).

14. Terri Langford, "District Judge Fends Off Democratic Rival's Challenge," *Dallas Morning News*, November 9, 2000.

15. Anthony Champagne and Greg Thielemann, "Awareness of Trial Court Judges," *Judicature* 75 (1991): 271–2.

16. Anthony Champagne, "The Selection and Retention of Judges in Texas," *Southwestern Law Journal* 40 (1986): 80.

17. The lone Democratic survivor, Ron Chapman, became an appellate judge. Democratic judges who did not switch to the Republican Party were defeated.

18. Langford, "District Judge Fends off Democratic Rival's Challenge."

19. Joe Holley, "Are Texas' Hispanics Ready to Go Democrat?" *Houston Chronicle*, April 3, 2010.

20. In 1994, it was estimated that there were between 420,000 and 460,000 illegal immigrants in Texas. Many of those illegal immigrants were Hispanic. See Leon F. Bouvier and John L. Martin, "Shaping Texas: The Effects of Immigration, 1970–2020," Center for Immigration Studies, April 1995, www.cis.org/articles/1995/texas.html (accessed 4/7/08). The Federation for American Immigration Reform cites the Immigration and Naturalization Service for a January 2000 estimate that there were 1,041,000 illegal immigrants then in Texas. See their report, "Texas: Illegal Aliens," www.fairus.org/site/PageServier?pagename=research_researchable (accessed 4/7/08). An April 2006 study by the Pew Hispanic Center estimated that between 1.4 and 1.6 million unauthorized individuals were living in Texas. Pew Hispanic Center, "Estimates of the Unauthorized Migrant Population for States Based on the March 2006 CPS, Fact Sheet: April 26, 2006," http://pewhispanic.org/files/factsheets/17.pdf (accessed 4/7/08).

Chapter 5

1. Texas Secretary of State, "Turnout and Voter Registration Figures, 1970–Current," www.sos.state.tx/elections/historical/70-92.shtml (accessed 4/7/08). Dallas and Harris counties have more voting precincts than are found in the entire state of New Hampshire.

2. Wayne Slater, "Strayhorn Gets Democratic Cash," *Dallas Morning News*, January 26, 2006, pp. 1A, 17A.

3. Pete Slover, "Independents' Day Is a Bid for the Ballot," *Dallas Morning News*, March 8, 2006, p. 14A.

4. Sam Acheson, *Joe Bailey: The Last Democrat* (New York: Macmillan, 1932), p. 354.

5. Joe Robert Baulch, "James B. Wells: State Economic and Political Leader" (Ph.D. dissertation, Texas Tech University, 1974), pp. 358–9.

6. Sue Tolleson-Rinehart and Jeanie R. Stanley, *Claytie and the Lady* (Austin: University of Texas Press, 1994), pp. 18–19.

7. O. Douglas Weeks, "The Texas-Mexican and the Politics of South Texas 34," *American Political Science Review* (1930): 625–6; Anthony Champagne, "John Nance Garner," in *Masters of the House*, ed. Roger H. Davidson, Susan Webb Hammond, and Raymond W. Smock (Boulder, CO: Westview, 1998), pp. 145–80.

8. *United States v. Texas*, 384 U.S. 155 (1966).

9. *Beare v. Smith*, 321 F. Supp. 1100 (1971).

10. *Kramer v. Union Free School District No. 15*, 395 U.S. 621 (1969); *Hill v. Stone*, 421 U.S. 289 (1975).

11. *Dunn v. Blumstein*, 405 U.S. 330 (1972).

12. *Newberry v. United States*, 256 U.S. 232 (1921).

13. *Nixon v. Herndon*, 273 U.S. 536 (1927).

14. *Nixon v. Condon*, 286 U.S. 73 (1932).

15. *Grovey v. Townsend*, 295 U.S. 45 (1935).

16. *Smith v. Allwright*, 321 U.S. 649 (1944).

17. *Terry v. Adams*, 345 U.S. 461 (1953).

18. Gary Scharrer, "Holder Issues Challenge to Texas on Voter Rights," chron.com, December 13, 2011.

19. National Conference of State Legislatures, "State Requirements for Voter ID."

20. Texas Secretary of State, "Turnout and Voter Registration Figures, 1970–Current."

21. The motor voter law is a federal statute that requires states to allow voter registration when individuals apply for or renew their driver's licenses.

22. Texas Secretary of State, "Turnout and Voter Registration Figures, 1970–Current."

23. Thomas R. Patterson, *The American Democracy* (New York: McGraw-Hill, 1999), p. 188.

24. Daniel Elazar, *American Federalism: A View from the States*, 2nd ed. (New York: Crowell, 1971).

25. Donald R. Kinder and Lynn M. Sanders, *Divided by Color: Racial Politics and Democratic Ideals*.

26. University of Texas/*Texas Tribune*, "Texas Statewide Survey," February 1–7, 2010, www.laits.utexas.edu (accessed 12/18/12).

27. University of Texas/*Texas Tribune*, "Texas Statewide Survey," June 11–22, 2009, www.laits.utexas.edu (accessed 12/18/12).

28. University of Texas/*Texas Tribune*, "Texas Statewide Survey," May 14–20, 2010, www.laits.utexas.edu (accessed 12/18/12).

29. University of Texas/*Texas Tribune*, "Texas Statewide Survey," May 14–20, 2010, www.laits.utexas.edu (accessed 12/18/12).

30. University of Texas/*Texas Tribune*, "Texas Statewide Survey," May 11–18, 2011, www.laits.utexas.edu (accessed 12/18/12).

31. For this classic in campaign mistakes, see the October 2002 issue of *Texas Monthly* magazine. An example of the negative impact of the ad can be found in a front-page article, Wayne Slater and Pete Slover, "Dewhurst Campaign Ad: The Flag Is Ours, but What's with the German Officer?" *Dallas Morning News*, October 26, 2001.

32. Candidates in Texas Supreme Court races are affected by "friends and neighbors" voting, whereby voters tend to cast ballots for candidates from their home county or from neighboring counties. See Gregory Thielemann, "Local Advantage in Campaign Financing: Friends, Neighbors, and Their Money in Texas Supreme Court Elections," *Journal of Politics* 55 (1993): 472–8.

33. Roy A. Schotland, "Campaign Finance in Judicial Elections," *Loyola of Los Angeles Law Review* (2001), 1508–12.

Chapter 6

1. *Kelo v. City of New London*, 545 U.S. 469 (2005).

2. James W. Lamare, *Texas Politics: Economics, Power and Policy*, 3rd ed. (St. Paul: West, 1988), p. 82.

3. Kenneth R. Mladenka and Kim Quaile Hill, *Texas Government: Politics and Economics* (Belmont, CA: Wadsworth, 1986), pp. 80–2.

4. Governor Rick Perry's schedule, September 15, 2010.

5. Jason Embry, "The Most Powerful Group in Texas Politics Has Wentworth in Its Sights," *Statesman.com*, December 7, 2011.

6. Texans for Public Justice, "Power Surge: TXU's Patronage Grid Plugs All but Seven Lawmakers," *Lobby Watch*, March 1, 2007.

7. Matt Stiles, "Lobbyist Gives 'Shocking' Gift to Lawmaker," *Texas Tribune*, February 15, 2010.

8. Steve McGonigle, "For Perry, Big Game Means Big Business—Trucking Lobby Paid for Governor's Private Jet to Rose Bowl," *Dallas Morning News*, December 12, 2006.

9. Matt Stiles and Chris Chang, "Texas Lobbying Directory Details Spending, Clients," *Texas Tribune*, March 15, 2011.

10. Emily Ramshaw and Marcus Funk, "For Some Dallas-Area Legislators, Donations Fund the Good Life," *Dallas Morning News*, February 1, 2009.

11. Ross Ramsey, "Legislature Is a Training Ground for Lobbyists," *Texas Tribune*, June 10, 2010.

12. Ramsey, "Legislature Is a Training Ground."

13. Texas for Public Justice, "Ten New Lawmaker Retreads Merge into the 2009 Lobby," *Lobby Watch*, May 20, 2009.

14. "Rick Perry's Former Staffers Made Millions as Lobbyists," *Huffington Post*, December 19, 2011.

15. "Rick Perry's Former Staffers."

16. Ramsey, "Legislature Is a Training Ground."

17. Texans for Public Justice, "Texas Revolvers: Public Officials Recast as Hired Guns" (1999).

18. Texas Ethics Commission.

19. Texans for Public Justice, "Austin's Oldest Profession" (2012).

20. Texans for Public Justice, "Austin's Oldest Profession."

21. Texans for Public Justice, "Austin's Oldest Profession."
22. Texans for Public Justice, "Special-Interests Spend Up to $180 Million on Lobby Services in 1999 Legislative Session," May 24, 1999.
23. Texans for Public Justice, "Money in Politex" (2008).
24. Anthony Champagne, "Campaign Contributions in Texas Supreme Court Races," *Crime, Law & Social Change* 17 (1992): 91–106.
25. Texans for Public Justice, "Texans for Lawsuit Reform Sustains Pricey Primary Hits," *Lobby Watch*, March 5, 2010; Julian Aguilar, "Primary Color: HD-43," *Texas Tribune*, February 26, 2010.
26. Embry, "Most Powerful Group."
27. National Institute on Money in State Politics.
28. Kristen Mack, "New Lawmakers Learn to Juggle Hectic Lives; Everybody—Lobbyists, Family—Wants a Moment of Their Time," *Houston Chronicle*, February 6, 2005, p. 1B.
29. Texans for Public Justice, "Texans for Lawsuit Reform."
30. Embry, "Most Powerful Group." John W. Gonazalez, "Campbell Upsets Wentworth for Texas Senate," *San Antonio Express-News*, August 1, 2012.
31. Texans for Public Justice, "Operation Vouchsafe: Dr. Leininger Injects $5 Million into Election; Many Candidates Fail on His Life Support," *Lobby Watch*, n.d.
32. Emily Ramshaw, "Fighting for Fair Warning—Man Who Lost Wife, Kids in Blaze Seeks Visual Smoke Alarms for Deaf," *Dallas Morning News*, April 17, 2009; "Tragedy Leads to Improved Fire Safety in Texas," National Association of the Deaf, July 1, 2009.

Chapter 7

1. The preceding is drawn from S. C. Gwynne, "Tom Craddick: How Did Tom Craddick Become the Most Powerful Speaker Ever—and the Most Powerful Texan Today? Let Us Count the Ways," *Texas Monthly*, February 2005; R. G. Ratcliffe and Gary Scharrer, "Craddick Safe as Session Ends, but '08 Race Is Ahead," *Houston Chronicle*, May 28, 2007; Dan Collins, "Chaos in Texas House over Speaker Fight," CBSNEWS, May 26, 2007; Karen Brooks and Christy Hoppe, "Craddick Quits House Speaker's Race; Straus Poised to Take Over," *Dallas Morning News*, January 5, 2009; Karen Brooks, "GOP Bloc Backs Joe Straus to Topple House Speaker Tom Craddick," *Dallas Morning News*, January 3, 2009.
2. "Senate Gives Tentative OK to Guns on Campuses," *Dallas Morning News*, May 20, 2009.
3. "Texas Bill to Allow Guns on Campus Rejected for Violating Constitutional Requirement," *Security Director News*, June 7, 2011.
4. Ann Marie Kilday, "Equal Measure," *Dallas Morning News*, May 24, 2001, p. 31A.
5. Anthony Champagne and Rick Collis, "Texas," in *The Political Life of the American States*, ed. Alan Rosenthal and Maureen Moakley (New York: Praeger, 1984), p. 138.
6. Ross Ramsey, "Will Texas Lawmakers Cut Their Own Benefits?," *Texas Tribune*, March 11, 2011.
7. Ramsey, "Will Texas Lawmakers Cut."
8. "State Rep. Joe Driver of Garland Double-Billed for Travel," *Dallas Morning News*, August 16, 2010; "Garland Republican Joe Driver Pleads Guilty to Double-Dipping on Travel Reimbursements," *Dallas Morning News*, November 22, 2011.
9. Kelley Shannon, "Doctor Twice Honored by the Texas Legislature Registered as Sex Offender," *Sulphur Springs News-Telegram*, June 22, 2007, p. 1.
10. Frank M. Stewart, "Impeachment in Texas," *American Political Science Review* 24, no. 3 (August 1930): 652–8; George D. Braden et al., *The Constitution of the State Texas: An Annotated and Comparative Analysis* (Austin: University of Texas Press, 1977), 707–18.
11. Legislative Reference Library of Texas, "Bill Statistics."
12. Lisa Falkenberg, "Texas Lawmakers Scramble to Finish Last-Minute Bills," *Dallas Morning News*, March 10, 2001, p. 38A.
13. Office of Governor Rick Perry, "Press Release," June 19, 2009.
14. Mike Ward, "Perry Vetoes Texting while Driving Ban, 22 Other Bills," *Statesman.com*, June 17, 2011.
15. Karen Brooks, "Craddick's Win May Cost Him," *Dallas Morning News*, May 27, 2007, p. 1.
16. Karen Brooks, "In 1877, Lawmakers Ran Republican Out of the Chair," *Dallas Morning News*, May 27, 2007, p. 26A.
17. John W. Gonzalez, "Texas Legislature; Jobs Well Done; Laney, Lauded for Maintaining Order and Fairness, Ends 3rd Term as Speaker," *Houston Chronicle*, June 6, 1999, p. State 1.
18. Vince Leibowitz, "Texas Senate Republicans Trying to Dump Two-Thirds Voting Rule," *Capitol Annex*, January 14, 2009.
19. Terrence Stutz, "Texas Senate at Odds over Voter ID Legislation, Two-Thirds Rule," *Dallas Morning News*, January 14, 2009.
20. *Baker v. Carr*, 369 U.S. 186 (1962); *Reynolds v. Sims*, 377 U.S. 533 (1964).
21. *Wesberry v. Sanders*, 376 U.S. 1 (1964).
22. Sam Attlesey, "Panel OKs Map Favoring GOP," *Dallas Morning News*, December 7, 2001.
23. The preceding is drawn from Sam Attlesey, "Taking Stock of the Fallout from Redistricting," *Dallas Morning News*, December 11, 2001; Terrance Stutz, "GOP Expecting to Grab the House," *Dallas Morning News*, January 3, 2002; Sam Attlesey, "Before Election, House Democrats Seeing Losses," *Dallas Morning News*, December 11, 2001.
24. Medill School of Journalism, "On the Docket: *League of United Latin American Citizens, Travis County, Jackson, Eddie and GI Forum of Texas v. Perry, Rick (Texas Gov.).*"
25. State Appellants' Brief in the Supreme Court of the United States, *LULAC v. Perry*.
26. Medill School of Journalism, "On the Docket."
27. Appellants' Brief on the Merits, *LULAC v. Perry*.

28. See, generally, Steve Bickerstaff, *Lines in the Sand: Congressional Redistricting in Texas and the Downfall of Tom DeLay* (Austin: University of Texas Press, 2007).

Chapter 8

1. The next two paragraphs rely on James C. McKinley Jr., "Re-elected Texas Governor Sounding Like a Candidate," *New York Times*, November 5, 2010, p. A18.
2. See the discussion of gubernatorial power in Cheryl D. Young and John J. Hindera, "The Texas Governor: Weak or Strong?" in *Texas Politics: A Reader*, ed. Anthony Champagne and Edward J. Harpham (New York: W.W. Norton, 1998), p. 53.
3. Sam Kinch, in *Government by Consent—Texas, A Telecourse* (Dallas: Dallas County Community College District, 1990).
4. Brian McCall, *The Power of the Texas Governor: Connally to Bush* (Austin: University of Texas Press, 2009).
5. McCall, *Power of the Texas Governor*, p. 120.
6. Christy Hoppe and Robert T. Garrett, "How Deep Does Governor Dig into Issues?," *Dallas Morning News*, November 27, 2011, pp. 1, 30A.
7. Kinch, *Government*.
8. Polly Ross Hughes, "Farewell to a Yalie, Howdy to an Aggie," *Houston Chronicle*, December 14, 2000, p. 1A.
9. Hughes, "Farewell to a Yalie," p. 26A.
10. George Kuempel, "The Tab Texas Taxpayers Are Picking up for Security Protection," *Dallas Morning News*, February 2, 2000, p. 25A.
11. William P. Hobby, in *Government by Consent—Texas, A Telecourse* (Dallas: Dallas County Community College District, 1990).
12. Christy Hoppe, "Lt. Gov. Rick Perry, Honoring the Economic Generators of Texas Tourism," *Dallas Morning News*, February 28, 2000, p. 13A.
13. Hoppe, "Lt. Gov. Rick Perry."
14. Hoppe and Garrett, "How Deep Does Governor Dig," p. 30A.
15. Steve McGonigle and James Drew, "Perry Stocks State Boards with Allies," *Dallas Morning News*, December 4, 2011, pp. 1, 32A.
16. Young and Hindera, "Texas Governor: Weak or Strong?," p. 62.
17. Legislative Reference Library of Texas, "Bill Statistics."
18. Richard Whittaker, "Gov. Perry's Ham-Fisted Veto Pen Strikes Again," *Austin Chronicle*, June 22, 2007.
19. Office of Governor Rick Perry, "Governor Perry Signs State Budget That Reduces GR by $1.6 Billion," Press Release, June 19, 2009.
20. Texas Legislative Library, Special Sessions of the Texas Legislature (2010).
21. Young and Hindera, "Texas Governor: Weak or Strong?," p. 61.
22. Young and Hindera, "Texas Governor: Weak or Strong?," p. 61.

23. The above discussion was taken from Jim Yardley, "Public Lives: This Texan, Too, Has a Lot Riding on Bush's Campaign," *New York Times*, October 7, 2000, p. 9; Kathy Walt, "Texas Legislature; Jobs Well Done; Senators Give Perry High Marks after Starting out with Low Expectation," *Houston Chronicle*, June 6, 1999, p. State 1.
24. Jim Yardley, "Public Lives: A Power in Texas Governing Finds Fault in Texas Politics," *New York Times*, June 9, 2001, p. A7.
25. Much of this material on the attorney general's office is taken from the website of the Attorney General of Texas Greg Abbott.
26. Much of this material on the Texas General Land Office is taken from the website of the Texas General Land Office.
27. Christy Hoppe, "Perry's Appointees Give Him Unprecedented Hold on Texas—Longest-Serving Governor Spreads Pro-Business View," *Dallas Morning News*, December 19, 2008.
28. Christy Hoppe, "Perry Ousts Officials before Arson Hearing—He's Assailed as New Chair Delays Session on Flawed Case That Led to Execution," *Dallas Morning News*, October 1, 2009.
29. William McKenzie, "Rich Perry's Curious Ways—Governor's Strongman Tactics Are Hard to Comprehend amid a Heated Campaign, Says William McKenzie," *Dallas Morning News*, October 20, 2009.
30. Terrence Stutz, "Senate Rejects Perry Appointee to Parole Board—Activist Faulted on Credentials; Governor Stands by Nominee," *Dallas Morning News*, May 14, 2009.
31. Texas Department of Insurance, "Texas Department of Insurance History."
32. Bill Peacock, "Policy Perspective: Is the Free Market Working for the Texas Homeowners' Insurance Market?" Texas Public Policy Foundation, February 28, 2006.
33. Terrence Stutz, "State Farm Stiff-Arming Regulators," *Dallas Morning News*, April 14, 2010; Terrence Stutz, "State Farm Near Top in Rates," *Dallas Morning News*, September 7, 2011, p. 1.
34. Terrence Stutz, "Legal Tactics Stall Insurance Reform," DallasNews.com, September 16, 2007.
35. Russell Shorto, "How Christian Were the Founders?" *New York Times*, February 14, 2010; Terrence Stutz, "Debate Continues over Social Studies," *Dallas Morning News*, March 11, 2010.
36. Morgan Smith, "Texas State Board of Education Races Could Get Ugly," *Texas Tribune*, November 7, 2011.

Chapter 9

1. Ralph Blumenthal, "Texas Judge Draws Outcry for Allowing an Execution," *New York Times*, October 25, 2007; Christy Hoppe, "Criminal Appeals Court Creates Emergency Filing System," *DallasNews.com*, November 6, 2007; "Texas Judge Fosters Tough-on-Crime Reputation,"

MSNBC, October 23, 2007; State Commission on Judicial Conduct, Special Master's Findings of Fact, In Re: Honorable Sharon Keller, Presiding Judge of the Texas Court of Criminal Appeals, January 20, 2010.

2. Texas Office of Court Administration, "Activity Report for Justice Courts, September 1, 2009 to August 31, 2010."

3. Barbara Kirby, "Neighborhood Justice: Campaign Funding and Texas Justice of the Peace Courts," paper presented at the annual meeting of the Southern Political Science Association, New Orleans, Louisiana, January 3, 2007.

4. Ed Housewright, "Emotional Issues, Historical Pedigree," *Dallas Morning News*, April 9, 2001, p. 10A.

5. Texas Office of Court Administration, "Activity Report for Municipal Courts, September 1, 2008 to August 31, 2009."

6. Texas Office of Court Administration, "Activity Report for Municipal Courts, September 1, 2009 to August 31, 2010."

7. Steve Thompson, "Toughen Up, City Officials Tell Judges," *Dallas Morning News*, August 2, 2012, pp. 1B, 7B.

8. Thomas Petzinger Jr., *Oil and Honor: The Texaco-Pennzoil Wars* (New York: Putnam, 1987).

9. Task Force on Indigent Defense, "Evidence for the Feasibility of Public Defender Offices in Texas."

10. Mary Alice Robbins, "West Texas Plans Public Defender Office for Capital Cases," *Texas Lawyer*, August 20, 2007, pp. 1, 19; "New Public Defender for Capital Cases," *Tex Part Blog*, October 16, 2007.

11. Ken Anderson, *Crime in Texas* (Austin: University of Texas Press, 1997), p. 40.

12. Anderson, *Crime in Texas*, 44. Nationally, 95 percent of felonies are plea-bargained.

13. Of the 79 judicial appointments made by Governor William Clements, only 6 were either African American or Hispanic. In contrast, one-third of Governor Ann Richards's judicial appointees were minorities. See Michael Totty, "Is This Any Way to Choose a Judge?" *Wall Street Journal*, August 3, 1994, pp. T1, T4.

14. Texas Office of Court Administration, "Profile of Appellate and Trial Judges as of September 1, 2009."

15. Anthony Champagne, "The Selection and Retention of Judges in Texas," 40 *Southwestern Law Journal* (1986), 78–79.

16. Texans for Public Justice, "Payola Justice: How Texas Supreme Court Justices Raise Money from Court Litigants."

17. Texans for Public Justice, "Judging Texas Justice in the Court of Opinion."

18. L. Douglas Kiel, Carole Funk, and Anthony Champagne, "Two-Party Competition and Trial Court Elections in Texas," 77 *Judicature* (1994), 291.

19. Linda Campbell, " 'H' as in Herasimchuk," *Fort Worth Star-Telegram*, December 6, 2001.

20. Mary Flood and Brian Rogers, "Why Some Harris County Judges Lost Not Entirely Clear," *Houston Chronicle*, November 6, 2008.

21. Eden Stiffman and Tristan Hallman, "Did Name Cost Justice in Race?" *Dallas Morning News*, August 2, 2012, p. 9A.

22. Elliott Slotnik, "Gender, Affirmative Action, and Recruitment to the Federal Bench," 14 *Golden Gate University Law Review* (1984), 524.

23. Texas Office of Court Administration, "Profile of Appellate and Trial Judges as of March 1, 2011."

24. Barbara L. Graham, "Toward an Understanding of Judicial Diversity in American Courts," 10 *Michigan Journal of Race and Law* (2004), 178.

25. One report is that 90 percent of African American voters and 60 to 79 percent of Hispanic voters vote Democratic. See Ronald W. Chapman, "Judicial Roulette: Alternatives to Single-Member Districts as a Legal and Political Solution to Voting-Rights Challenges to At-Large Judicial Elections," 48 *SMU Law Review* (1995), 182.

26. The trial court opinion was unpublished.

27. *League of United Latin American Citizens v. Clements*, 902 F2d 293 (1990), and *League of United Latin American Citizens v. Clements*, 914 F2d 620 (1990).

28. *Houston Lawyers' Association v. Attorney General of Texas*, 501 U.S. 419 (1991).

29. *League of United Latin American Citizens Council v. Clements*, 999 F2d 831 (1993).

30. A discussion of the Bullock plan and the politics surrounding it is in Anthony Champagne, "Judicial Selection in Texas," *Texas Politics: A Reader*, 2nd ed., ed. Anthony Champagne and Edward J. Harpham (New York: W.W. Norton, 1998), pp. 99–103.

31. Susan Carbon and Larry Berkson, *Judicial Retention Elections in the United States* (Chicago: American Judicature Society, 1980), p. 21.

32. A discussion of these general systems of selection is found in Champagne, "Judicial Selection in Texas," pp. 88–104.

33. Daniel Becker and Malia Reddick, *Judicial Selection Reform: Examples from Six States* (Chicago: American Judicature Society, 2003), pp. 1–10.

34. Phil Hardberger, "Juries under Siege," 30 *St. Mary's Law Journal* (1998), 6–7.

35. "High Court Voting Patterns," *Texas Lawyer*, September 6, 1999, p. 5.

36. David A. Anderson, "Judicial Tort Reform in Texas," 26 *Review of Litigation* (2007), 7.

37. Lynne Liberato and Kent Rutter, "Reasons for Reversals in the Texas Courts of Appeals," *Houston Law Review* (2012), 993–1018.

38. "Disciplinary Actions," *Texas Bar Journal*, April 2012, p. 331.

39. John McCormack, "Barratry Suit Names Corpus Lawyers," *San Antonio Express News*, December 9, 2011.

40. McCormack, "Barratry Suit."

41. Isiah Carey, "Lawyer Filed Reynolds Barratry Complaint," *myfoxhouston.com*, April 25, 2012.

42. Data from the American Bar Association.

43. The material on the State Commission on Judicial Conduct is taken from the Staff Report of the Sunset

Advisory Commission, "State Commission on Judicial Conduct," March 2012.

Chapter 10

1. This material is from Brandi Grissom, "In Deposition, Morton Prosecutor Can't Recall Details," *Texas Tribune*, November 30, 2011; Brandi Grissom, "A Tough Prosecutor Finds His Certitude Shaken by a Prisoner's Exoneration," *Texas Tribune*, November 18, 2011; Brandi Grissom and Benjamin Hasson, "Michael Morton: A Timeline," *Texas Tribune*, November 18, 2011.
2. Fred Dahr, "Crimes and Punishment in Texas State Court," www.texasdefenselaw.com; Texas Criminal Defense Lawyer, "Texas Criminal Laws & Penalties," www.mytexasdefenselawyer.com.
3. Texas Board of Pardons and Paroles, www.tdcj.state.tx.us/bpp/.
4. Information is from the Texas Association of Counties. The term *district attorney* will be used to encompass district attorneys, county attorneys, and criminal district attorneys.
5. Robert S. DuBoise and Kathleen Catania, "The Longest Sentence in Texas History," *The Prosecutor* (March–April 2009).
6. Valerie Wigglesworth, "Collin County District Judge Suzanne Wooten Found Guilty of Bribery," *Dallasnews.com*, November 22, 2011.
7. Jennifer Emily, "DA Seeks to Have Judge Indicted," *Dallas Morning News*, February 8, 2012, pp. 1B, 7B; Jennifer Emily, "DA Raises Stakes in Judge Inquiry," *Dallas Morning News*, February 9, 2012, pp. 1B, 6B.
8. Brian Rogers, "Grand Jury Won't Indict DA's Office, but Issues Strong Rebuke," *Houston Chronicle*, February 1, 2012.
9. Texas Department of Criminal Justice, "Fiscal Year 2010 Statistical Report."
10. Texas Legislative Budget Board, "Criminal Justice Uniform Cost Report Fiscal Years 2008–2010" (January 2011), p. 316; Texas Department of Criminal Justice, www.tdcj.state.tx.us.
11. Harry Mika and Lawrence J. Redlinger, "Crime and Correction," in *Texas at the Crossroads*, ed. Anthony Champagne and Edward J. Harpham (College Station: Texas A&M University Press, 1987), pp. 245–6.
12. Mika and Redlinger, "Crime and Correction," pp. 245–6.
13. *Ruiz v. Estelle*, 503 F. Supp. 1265 (1980).
14. Mika and Redlinger, "Crime and Correction," p. 247.
15. Texas Department of Criminal Justice, "Texas Board of Criminal Justice," www.tdcj.state.tx.us/tbcj/index.html (accessed 8/30/12).
16. See Associated Texans against Crime, "Annual Report" (1998); Texas Department of Criminal Justice, "Fiscal Year 2011 Operating Budget and Fiscal Years 2010–2013 Legislative Appropriations Request" (August 16, 2010).
17. Marc A. Levin, "2009–2010 Legislators Guide to the Issues" (November 2008), p. 1.
18. See Associated Texans against Crime, "Annual Report" (1998).
19. Texas Department of Criminal Justice, "Fiscal Year 2010 Statistical Report"; Mika and Redlinger, "Crime and Correction," p. 245.
20. Texas Department of Criminal Justice, "Fiscal Year 2010 Statistical Report." See Associated Texans against Crime, "Annual Report" (1998).
21. Texas Department of Criminal Justice, "Fiscal Year 2006 Statistical Summary" (December 2006).
22. Texas Department of Criminal Justice, "Fiscal Year 2010 Statistical Reports."
23. Texas State Historical Association, *Texas Almanac 2010–2011* (2010), p. 482.
24. Mika and Redlinger, "Crime and Correction," p. 245.
25. U.S. Department of Justice, "Bureau of Justice Statistics Bulletin: Prisoners in 2009" (December 2010), p. 24.
26. Scott Morgan and Kathleen O'Leary Morgan, eds., *Crime State Rankings 2009* (Washington, DC: CQ Press, 2009), p. xxi.
27. Texas Department of Criminal Justice, "Fiscal Year 2010 Statistical Report."
28. Texas State Historical Association, *Texas Almanac 2010–2011*, p. 482.
29. Bill Jeffreys, "Death, Simplified," *Texas Lawyer*, October 23, 2000, p. 1.
30. Pete Slover, "Attorney's Inexperience No Barrier," *Dallas Morning News*, September 11, 2000, p. 12A.
31. The data are from the Death Penalty Information Center.
32. Texas Department of Criminal Justice, "Death Row Information."
33. Mike Ward, "Cost of Executions Skyrocketing in Texas, Other States," *Statesman.com*, February 24, 2012.
34. Texas Department of Criminal Justice, "Death Row Information."
35. Texas Department of Criminal Justice, "Death Row Information."
36. Texas Department of Criminal Justice, "Executions, December 7, 1982 through March 16, 2010"; Texas Department of Criminal Justice, "Gender and Racial Statistics of Death Row Offenders"; *McClesky v. Kemp*, 481 U.S. 279 (1987).
37. Erica C. Barnett, "No Sunshine on Clemency," *Austin Chronicle*, January 1, 1999.
38. "Gov. Perry Commutes Sentences of Man Scheduled to Die Thursday," ABC13, August 30, 2007.
39. David McCord, "What's Messing with Texas Death Sentences?" 43 *Texas Tech Law Review* (2011), 601–12.
40. The Innocence Project of Texas, "Facts on Post-Conviction DNA Exonerations."
41. "DNA Proving to Cut Both Ways on Death Penalty," *Dallas Morning News*, January 14, 2006, p. 10A.
42. The Innocence Project of Texas, "Texas Exonerations."
43. Radley Balke, "The 250th DNA Exoneration," *Reason*, February 4, 2010.

44. Steve McGonigle, "Righting Wrongs," *Dallas Morning News*, January 22, 2007, p. 1; Jennifer Emily, "DA: Man Didn't Do '82 Rape," *Dallas Morning News*, September 17, 2007, p. 1B.

45. Mike Ware, "Dallas County Conviction Integrity Unit and the Importance of Getting It Right the First Time," 56 *New York Law School Law Review* (2011–2012), 1034–50.

46. Michael Hall, "Why Can't Steven Phillips Get a DNA Test?" *Texas Monthly*, January 2006.

47. Jeff Blackburn, "Dog Scent Lineups: A Junk Science Injustice," a special report by the Innocence Project of Texas (September 21, 2009).

48. David Grann, "Trial by Fire," *New Yorker*, September 7, 2009.

49. Jeff Carleton, "Cameron Todd Willingham: Texas Governor Dismisses 3 Commission Members Just 48 Hours before Arson Review," *Huffington Post*, September 30, 2009.

50. Allan Turner, "Abbott Ruling Limits Probe of Arson Case," *Houston Chronicle*, July 29, 2011.

51. See Nate Blakeslee, *Tulia: Race, Cocaine, and Corruption in a Small Texas Town* (New York: Public Affairs, 2005).

52. Paul Duggan, " 'Sheetrock Scandal' Hits Dallas Police," *Washington Post*, January 18, 2002, p. 12.

53. Pamela Colloff, "Innocence Lost," *Texas Monthly*, October 2010; Pamela Colloff, "Innocence Found," *Texas Monthly*, January 2011.

54. "Texas and Mississippi: Reducing Prison Population, Saving Money, and Reducing Recidivism," *ABA Criminal Justice Section Parole & Probation*, www2.americanbar.org/sections/criminaljustice/CR203800/Public Documents/paroleandprobationsuccess.pdf (accessed 8/30/12).

Chapter 11

1. See Jeannie Kever, "As Texas Public College Tuition Rises, Legislators Feel the Heat," *Houston Chronicle*, July 10, 2008; Texas Higher Education Coordinating Board, "Tuition Set-Aside-House Bill 3013, 78th Texas Legislature," *Overview*, February 2010.

2. See Texas Legislative Budget Board Staff, *Financing Higher Education in Texas: Legislative Primer*, as submitted to the 82nd Texas Legislature, January 2011; Texas Higher Education Board, "Tuition Deregulation," *Overview*, March 2011.

3. See Reeve Hamilton, "Texplainer: How Can I Get a $10,000 Degree?" *Texas Tribune*, March 29, 2012.

4. See Minjae Park, "UT Regents Back Some Tuition Hikes, New Med Schools," *Texas Tribune*, May 3, 2012. See also Reeve Hamilton and Morgan Smith, "UT's Reform-Minded Chairman at the Center of Controversy," *The Texas Tribune*, May 18, 2012.

5. See Texas Legislative Budget Board, *Texas Facts 2012* (Austin: State of Texas), p. 42.

6. See Texas Legislative Budget Board, *Fiscal Size-Up: 2012–13 Biennium* (Austin: State of Texas, 2012), p. 58.

7. See Texas Legislative Budget Board, *Fiscal Size-Up: 2012–13*, p. 59.

8. See Texas Legislative Budget Board, *Fiscal Size-Up: 2012–13*, p. 60.

9. See data provided by the Federation of Tax Administrators at www.taxadmin.org and Texas Public Policy Foundation at www.texasbudgetsource.com. Other ranking information is available from Lisele Zavala, Revenue Estimate Division, Texas Comptroller of Public Accounts. See also tax burden rankings provided by the Tax Foundation at www.taxfoundation.org.

10. The preceding data on Texas are from the Tax Foundation at www.taxfoundation.org.

11. The following explanations and data on the various taxes in Texas are based upon Texas Legislative Budget Board, *Fiscal Size-Up: 2012–13*, "Revenue Sources and Outlook," pp. 29–32.

12. See Texas Legislative Budget Board, *Fiscal Size-Up: 2012–13*, p. 31.

13. See Carl David et al., Institute on Taxation and Economic Policy, *Who Pays? A Distributional Analysis of the Tax Systems in All 50 States*, 3rd ed. (Washington, DC, November 2009), p. 4.

14. See Carl David et al., Institute on Taxation and Economic Policy, *Who Pays?* See also Susan Combs, *Tax Exemptions and Tax Incidence: A Report to the Governor and the 82nd Texas Legislature* (Austin: Texas Comptroller of Public Accounts, February 2011), pp. 41–2.

15. See Clay Robinson, "Bullock Paints a Grim Picture/Says Income Tax Needed to Avert Financial Crisis," *Houston Chronicle*, March 12, 1991; Clay Robinson, "Bullock Plan May Open Door to Tax Battle," *Houston Chronicle*, March 2, 1993.

16. See Senate Research Center, *Budget 101: A Guide to the Budget Process in Texas*, pp. 34–5.

17. Texas Lottery Commission, "Demographic Survey of Texas Lottery Players 2009" (December 1, 2009). See Office of the Texas Comptroller, "Window on State Government, Revenue by Source for Fiscal Year 2011," www.window.state.tx.us/taxbud/revenue.html. See also Texas Lottery Commission, "Demographic Survey of Texas Lottery Players 2009," p. 11.

18. See James LeBas, "Who Wants to Be a Billionaire? Texas Spending Tobacco Money on Health Care, Endowments," Texas Comptroller of Public Accounts, *Fiscal Notes* (January 2000); Texas House of Representatives, House Research Organization, "State Finance Report No. 82-3" (March 11, 2011). The income projections are from Texas Legislative Budget Board, *Fiscal Size-Up: 2012–13*, p. 13.

19. See Michael E. McClellan, "Permanent School Fund," *Handbook of Texas Online*. See also Texas Educational Agency, "Texas Permanent School Fund, Comprehensive

Annual Financial Report, Fiscal Year Ending August 31, 2011."

20. See Texas Legislative Budget Board, *Fiscal Size-Up: 2012–13*, p. 452.

21. See Susan Combs, Texas Comptroller of Public Accounts, "Rainy Day Fund 101," *Fiscal Notes*, February 2011.

22. See Texas Higher Education Coordinating Board, "Overview: Permanent University Fund (PUF)" Higher Education Fund (HEF), (December 2012).

23. See Texas Higher Education Coordinating Board, "National Research University Fund Eligibility: A Report to the Comptroller and the Texas Legislature" (February 2012).

24. See Legislative Budget Board, *Texas Fact Books 2012*, p. 27.

25. The following is drawn from Senate Research Center, *Budget 101*, p. 29.

26. See Texas Legislative Budget Board, *Fiscal Size-Up: 2012–13*, p. 24; Texas Bond Review Board, "2011 Annual Report: Fiscal Year Ended August 31, 2011."

27. See Senate Research Center, *Budget 101*, pp. 24–5.

28. See Senate Research Center, *Budget 101*, p. 28.

29. See the discussion in Senate Research Center, *Budget 101*, p. 28.

30. See the discussion in Senate Research Center, *Budget 101*, pp. 34–5.

31. See Bernard L. Weinstein, "Taxes in Texas," in *Texas Politics: A Reader*, ed. Anthony Champagne and Edward J. Harpham (New York: W.W. Norton, 1998), chap. 12.

32. The following discussion is drawn from Texas Legislative Budget Board, *Fiscal Size-Up:. 2012–13*; Texas Legislative Budgeting Board, *Texas Fact Book* (Austin: State of Texas, 2012). The data for the following are drawn from Texas Legislative Budgeting Board, *Fiscal Size-Up: 2012–13*; Robert T. Garrett, "Tension Rises over Future Cuts," *Dallas Morning News*, February 24, 2012, p. A1; Dave Montgomery and Anna M. Tinsley, "Texas Budget with $15 Billion in Cuts Clears Legislature," *Fort Worth Star-Telegram*, May 28, 2011; Ross Ramsey, "The End Game: Special Session Wraps Up Today," *Texas Tribune*, June 29, 2011. See also Robert T. Garrett, "Many Texas Politicians, Including Perry and White, Talk Little of $21 Billion Budget Gap," *Dallas Morning News*, September 12, 2010; Robert T. Garrett, "Budget Likely to Cut Deep," *Dallas Morning News*, October 24, 2010; Emily Ramshaw, "Legislators Consider Medicaid Withdrawal," *Texas Tribune*, November 7, 2010. See also Dave Montgomery and Anna M. Tinsley, "Texas Budget with $15 Billion in Cuts Clears Legislature, *Fort Worth Star–Telegram*, May 28, 2011; Eugenio Aleman and Tyler B. Kruse, "Texas Budget: 2012–2013 Biennium," Wells Fargo Securities, June 24, 2011.

33. For a discussion of the factors lying behind the financial collapse and federal responses to it, see Simon Johnson and James Kwak, *13 Banks: The Wall Street Takeover and the Next Financial Meltdown* (New York: Pantheon Books, 2010); Roger Lowenstein, *The End of Wall Street*

(New York: Penguin Press, 2010); David Wessel, *In Fed We Trust: Ben Bernanke's War on the Great Panic* (New York: Crown Business, 2009). See Texas Comptroller of Public Accounts, *Window on State Government*, May 2012 State Sales Tax Collections to General Revenue.

34. This discussion relies heavily upon Dick Lavine, "How to Fill the Hole in the Texas Revenue System," Center for Public Policy Priorities, February 2012.

Chapter 12

1. The following is drawn from Brandon Formby, "Schools Wrestling with Policies under New Religious Liberties Act," *Dallas Morning News*, August 27, 2007; Jenny Lacoste-Caputo, "Law on Religion in School Spurs Fear," *San Antonio Express-News*, July 25, 2007; Kelly Coghlan, "Religion Gets Equal Treatment," *Dallas Morning News*, September 6, 2007; Karen Brooks, "One State under God," *Dallas Morning News*, April 22, 2007; Wendy Gragg, "New State Law on Religious Expression in Schools Draws Mixed Reactions," *Waco Tribune-Herald*, August 9, 2007. The text of HB 3678 is available at www.capitol.state .tx.us/tlodocs/80R/billtext/html/HB03678F.htm (accessed 4/21/08).

2. See Texas Association of School Boards, "Legal Notes: An Open Mike." The quotation is from Melissa Rogers, "The Texas Religious Viewpoints Antidiscrimination Act and the Establishment Clause," 42 *University of California Davis Law Review* (2009), 939, 991–2.

3. For a discussion of the history of public education in Texas from which the following is drawn, see Max Berger and Lee Wilborn, "Education," *Texas Handbook Online*, www.tshaonline.org/handbook/online/articles/EE/khel. html (accessed 4/21/08); Dallas Morning News, "Public Schools," *Texas Almanac 2000–2001*, Millennium Edition (Dallas: Dallas Morning News, 1999), 533–4.

4. See Lewis B. Cooper, *The Permanent School Fund of Texas* (Fort Worth: Texas State Teachers Association, 1934); Michael E. McClellan, "Permanent School Fund," *Handbook of Texas Online*, www.tshaonline.org/hand book/ online/articles/PP/khpl.html (accessed 4/21/08).

5. See Oscar Mauzy, "Gilmer-Aikin Laws," *Handbook of Texas Online*, www.tshaonline.org/handbook/online/ articles/GG/mlgl.html (accessed 4/21/08); Dick Smith and Richard Allen Burns, "Texas Education Agency," *Handbook of Texas Online*, www.tshaonline.org/handbook/ online/articles/TT/met2.html (accessed 4/21/08); Berger and Wilborn, "Education."

6. See Anna Victoria Wilson, "Education for African Americans," *Handbook of Texas Online*, www.tshaonline .org/handbook/online/articles/EE/kde2.html (accessed 4/21/08).

7. Arnoldo De León and Robert A. Calvert, "Segregation," *Handbook of Texas Online*, www.tshaonline.org/handbook/ online/articles/SS/pksl.html (accessed 4/21/08).

8. The following discussion of the *Rodríguez* and *Edgewood* cases is drawn from Texas Legislative Budget Board Staff, "Financing Public Education in Texas: Kindergarten through Grade 12," *Legislative Handbook* (February 1999); Berger and Wilborn, "Education"; Cynthia E. Orozco, *"Rodríguez v. San Antonio ISD,"* *Handbook of Texas Online*, www.tshaonline.org/handbook/online/articles/RR/jrrht.html (accessed 4/21/08); Teresa Palomo Acosta, *"Edgewood ISD v. Kirby,"* *Handbook of Texas Online*, www.tshaonline.org/handbook/online/articles/EE/jre2.html (accessed 4/21/08).

9. See Texas Legislative Budget Board Staff, "Financing Public Education in Texas: Kindergarten through Grade 12," pp. 26–7.

10. See Texas House of Representatives, House Research Organization, "Focus Report: Schools and Taxes" (May 25, 2007), www.house.state.tx.us/featured/schools&taxes79–13.pdf (accessed 4/21/08); Jason Embry, "Session Ends with Property Tax Cut," *Austin American-Statesman*, May 26, 2006.

11. See Clark D. Thomas, "Education Reform in Texas," in *Texas Politics*, ed. Anthony Champagne and Edward J. Harpham (New York: W.W. Norton, 1998), pp. 213–32.

12. National Commission on Excellence in Education, *A Nation at Risk: The Imperative for Educational Reform* (Washington, D.C.: Department of Education, 1983).

13. See Thomas, "Education Reform in Texas," p. 218.

14. See Thomas, "Education Reform in Texas," p. 221.

15. See Thomas, "Education Reform in Texas," p. 231; *Dallas Morning News*, "Public Schools," *Texas Almanac 2000–2001*, Millennium Edition (Dallas: Dallas Morning News, 1999), 533. See also Terrence Stutz, "State's List Cites Sub-par Schools in Transfer Plan," *Dallas Morning News*, December 24, 1999, p. 1.

16. Commonwealth Foundation, *Texas Fact Book* (2009), p. 19; College Board, "Mean 2009 SAT Scores by State"; College Board, "2009 College-Bound Seniors Total Group Profile Report" (2009), p. 3. See also Texas Education Agency, "College Admissions Testing of Graduating Seniors in Texas High Schools, Class of 2010" (October 2011) and Texas Education Agency, *2010 Comprehensive Annual Report on Texas Public Schools.* (Austin: 2010).

17. See Joshua Benton, "Legislators Left Unanswered Questions on New State Tests," *Dallas Morning News*, June 11, 2007, p. B1. See also Terrence Stutz, "Failing Tests, Passing Grades," *Dallas Morning News*, March 8, 2012, p. A1.

18. Data from U.S. Bureau of the Census and Texas Health and Human Services Commission.

19. Center for Public Policy Priorities, "Policy Point, Policy 101" (Austin: September 2009).

20. The following is drawn from Edward J. Harpham, "Welfare Reform and the New Paternalism in Texas," in *Texas Politics*, ed. Champagne and Harpham, pp. 233–49.

21. See Vivian Elizabeth Smyrl, "Texas Department of Human Services," *Handbook of Texas Online*, www .tshaonline.org/handbook/online/articles/TT/mct6.html (accessed 4/23/08).

22. Harpham, "Welfare Reform and the New Paternalism in Texas," 238.

23. See Smyrl, "Texas Department of Human Services."

24. See Charles Murray, *Losing Ground* (New York: Basic Books, 1984).

25. For a discussion of these programs, see Lawrence Mead, *The New Politics of Poverty: The Nonworking Poor in America* (New York: Basic Books, 1992).

26. The following paragraphs are drawn from Harpham, "Welfare Reform and the New Paternalism in Texas," pp. 244–7.

27. See Texas Health and Human Services Commission, "Temporary Assistance for Needy Families (TANF): Frequently Asked Questions," www.hhsc.state.tx.us/programs/TexasWorks/TANF-FAQ.html (accessed 4/23/08).

28. See Texas Workforce Investment Council, "Issues in Welfare to Work: A State of the Workforce Report on State Issues Arising from TANF Reauthorization" (December 2006), p. 11, www.governor.state.tx.us/divisions/twic/files/wfwissues.pdf (accessed 4/23/08); Texas Health and Human Services Commission, "Texas TANF and SNAP Enrollment Statistics" (March 2010), www.hhsc.state.tx.us (accessed 4/23/10). See also Texas Health and Human Services Commission, TANF Statistics, www.hhsc.state.tx.us/research/TANF-Statewide.asp.

29. Center for Public Policy Priorities, "TANF at 10: Has Welfare Reform Been a Success in Texas?" August 22, 2006.

30. Texas Health and Human Services Commission, *Texas Medicaid and CHIP in Perspective: Eighth Edition* (January 2011), pp. 2–7. Medicaid data in this chapter are taken from Texas Health and Human Services Commission, *Texas Medicaid and CHIP in Perspective: Eighth Edition* (January 2011). See also the data for Texas on the Henry Kaiser Family Foundation website, www.statehealthfacts.org.

31. See Texas Health and Human Services Commission, *Texas Medicaid*, pp. 6–13.

32. In 2011 there were three distinct FMAPs calculated for Texas: the basic FMAP (60.56%); the Enhanced FMAP (72.39%), which is used for the CHIP program federal match; and the American Reinvestment and Recovery Act Enhanced FMAP (66.46%).

33. See Texas Health and Human Services Commission, *Texas Medicaid*, p. 7.2.

34. See Louis Radnofsky, "Texas Medicaid Funds Cut Over Planned Parenthood," *Wall Street Journal*, March 15, 2012; Emily Ramshaw and Thanh Tan, "The Storm Over Women's Health Care Had Been Brewing," *Texas Tribune*, March 23, 2012; Wade Goodwyn, "As Texas Cuts Funds, Planned Parenthood Fights Back," www.npr.com, May 7, 2012; Amanda Peterson Beadle, Thinkprogress.org, March 16, 2012; Sean Walsh, "Hutcheson Backs Planned Parenthood in Funding Dispute," *Dallas Morning News*, March 22, 2012.

35. Moni Basu, "Court Rules Texas Can Ban Planned Parenthood from Health Program." CNN U.S. (articles.cnn.com) August 22, 2012; "Judge Says Texas Not Allowed to Cut Funds to Planned Parenthood," May 4, 2012, www.foxnews.com.

36. See Nancy Flake, "Combs: Texas in Great Shape, but Watch out for Medicaid," *Cyprus Creek Mirror*, May 2, 2012. See also Kristie Avery, "Comptroller Warns of Medicaid Costs," *Texas Gazette*, www.susancombs.com/media/comptroller-warns-medicaid-costs.

37. *The Dallas Morning News*, "Texas Leads Again in Lack of Health Coverage," March 2012, p. 3a.

38. In the Senate, 58 Democrats and 2 Independents voted for the Patient Protection and Affordable Care Act. All 39 Republicans in the Senate were opposed. In the House of Representatives, the final vote was 219 to 212. All supporters of the bill were Democrats, with 34 Democrats and 178 Republicans opposing the bill.

39. See Texas Health and Human Services Commission, *Texas Medicaid*, chap. 3, for a further discussion of the impact of federal health care reforms on Texas.

40. "Fewer Texas Doctors Taking Medicaid Patients," *Dallas Morning News*, July 9, 2012.

41. Robert T. Garrett, "State Slashes Health Law Estimate," *Dallas Morning News*, July 13, 2012.

42. "Federal Scorecard Ranks Texas Last in Health Care," *Dallas Morning News*, July 6, 2012.

43. Peter G. George, Robert E. Mace, and Rima Petrossian, *Aquifers of Texas*, "Texas Development Board, Report 380" July 2011.

44. An acre-foot is equal to 325,851.43 U.S. gallons. Planners typically assume that a suburban family will consume an acre-foot of water a year.

45. Texas Water Development Board, *Water for Texas 2012 State Water Plan* (January 2012), p. xii.

46. See Texas Water Development Board, *Water for Texas 2012*, pp. 17–18.

47. See Otis W. Templer, "Water Law," *Handbook of Texas Online*; Otis W. Templer, "Water Rights Issues. Texas Water Rights Law: East Meets West," *Journal of Contemporary Water Research and Education* 85 (Spring 1991). The following is drawn largely from Templer, "Water Law" and "Texas Water Rights." See also Terry L. Hadley, "Texas Water Commission," *Handbook of Texas Online*; Laurie E. Jasinski, "Texas Water Development Board," *Handbook of Texas Online*; Texas Water Development Board, "Water for Texas," Executive Summary and chap. 1. See also Texas Water Development Board, *A Texan's Guide to Water and Water Rights Marketing*; Ronald Kaiser, *Handbook of Texas Water Law: Problems and Need* Water Monograph No.87-1 (College Station: Texas Water Resources Institute, Texas A&M University, 1987). We also thank Benedict Voit for his useful summary of water policy issues. See Benedict Voit, "Texas Water Policy for the 21st Century," unpublished paper, University of Texas at Dallas, April 10, 2008.

48. The following is drawn largely from Templer, "Water Law" and "Texas Water Rights." See also Terry L. Hadley, "Texas Water Commission," *Handbook of Texas Online*; Laurie E. Jasinski, "Texas Water Development Board," *Handbook of Texas Online*; Texas Water Development Board, "Water for Texas," Executive Summary and chap. 1. I also thank Benedict Voit for his useful summary of water policy issues. See Benedict Voit, "Texas Water Policy for the 21st Century," unpublished paper, University of Texas at Dallas, April 10, 2008.

49. See Texas Water Development Board, *A Texan's Guide to Water*.

50. See Laurie E. Jasinski, "Board of Water Engineers," *Handbook of Texas Online*; Texas Water Development Board, *Water for Texas 2012*, chap. 1.

51. Texas Water Development Board, *Water for Texas 2012*, pp. 15–6.

52. See the historical timeline regarding environmental policy at the Texas Commission on Environmental Quality website, www.tceq.texas.gov.

53. See Texas Water Development Board, "About the Texas Water Development Board," www.txdb.texas.gov.

54. Texas Water Development Board, *Water for Texas 2012*, p. 190.

55. See Kate Galbraith, "Texas Supreme Court Rules for Landowners in Water Case," *Texas Tribune*, February 24, 2012. See also Forrest Wilder, "The Texas Supreme Court Turns Water into a Landmark Groundwater Decision," *Texas Observer*, February 24, 2012; Chuck Lindell, "Supreme Court Delivers Major Water Ruling on Water Regulation," *Austin American Statesman*, February 24, 2012.

Chapter 13

1. This discussion of the office of constable is taken from Ed Timms and Kevin Krause, "Constables' Tickets Collect Funds, Critics," *Dallas Morning News*, October 25, 2009; Kevin Krause, "Commissioners OK Hiring Own Lawyer," *Dallas Morning News*, September 30, 2009; Kevin Krause, "Towed Cars Remain on Road to Nowhere," *Dallas Morning News*, September 18, 2009; Ed Timms and Kevin Krause, "Constables' Mission Has Changed," *Dallas Morning News*, October 26, 2009.

2. This discussion of the Hill corruption case is from Gromer Jeffers Jr., "Political Star Tainted by Liabilities—Dallas: Hill's Successes Slowed by Sanctions, FBI Investigation," *Dallas Morning News*, July 23, 2005; Jason Trahan, "Hill's Trial Opens Today—Third Corruption Case Involving a Councilman Is Wide in Scope," *Dallas Morning News*, June 29, 2009; Jason Trahan and Diane Jennings, "Three Sentenced in 'Betrayal of Our City,'" *Dallas Morning News*, February 27, 2010.

3. Dallas Morning News, *Texas Almanac 2009–2010* (Dallas: Dallas Morning News, 2008), p. 500; U.S. Census Bureau, *Lists & Structure of Government*; www.texasalmanac

.com/topics/government. Different sources provide varying numbers regarding municipal governments in Texas.

4. The two states that don't use counties as units of local government are Connecticut and Rhode Island. See Richard L. Cole and Delbert A. Taebel, *Texas: Politics and Public Policy* (Fort Worth: Harcourt Brace Jovanovich, 1987), p. 151.

5. Texas Association of Counties, "About Counties: County Government."

6. Texas Association of Counties, "About Counties."

7. Cole and Taebel, *Texas Politics and Public Policy*, p. 152.

8. *Avery v. Midland County*, 390 U.S. 474 (1968).

9. Anthony Champagne and Rick Collis, "Texas," in *The Political Life of the American States*, ed. Alan Rosenthal and Maureen Moakley (Washington, DC: CQ Press, 1984), p. 140.

10. Texas State Data Center.

11. Brenda Rodriguez, "Loving and Losing in West Texas," *Dallas Morning News*, March 14, 2001, p. 21A.

12. Russell Gold, "Counties Struggle with High Cost of Prosecuting Death-Penalty Cases," *Wall Street Journal*, January 9, 2002, p. B1.

13. "Capital Trial Could Be Costly for Franklin Co.," *Sulphur Springs News-Telegram*, June 27, 2007, p. 4.

14. Adam M. Gershowitz, "Statewide Capital Punishment: The Case for Eliminating Counties' Role in the Death Penalty," 63 *Vanderbilt Law Review* (2010), 8–9.

15. Cole and Taebel, *Texas: Politics and Public Policy*, p. 155.

16. Lawrence M. Crane, Nat Pinnoi, and Stephen W. Fuller, "Private Demand for Publicly Provided Goods: A Case Study of Rural Roads in Texas," *TAMRC Contemporary Market Issues Report No. CI-1-92* (1992).

17. Texas Association of Counties, "Debate Goes Back and Forth, Just Like Overweight Trucks," www.county.org/resources/library/county-mag/county/124/bridge debate.html.

18. Texas Commission on Jail Standards, "Abbreviated Population Report," August 1, 2011.

19. "Knock! Knock! Smith County Sheriff's Office Goes Armored," *County Magazine*, July–August 1997.

20. Article XI, Section 5, of the Texas Constitution is concerned with home rule. For a further discussion of home rule in Texas, see Terrell Blodgett, *Texas Home Rule Charters* (Austin: Texas Municipal League, 1994); Terrell Blodgett, "Home Rule Charters," *Handbook of Texas Online*, www.tshaonline.org/handbook/online/articles/HH/mvhek.html (accessed 4/17/08).

21. Correspondence with Terrell Blodgett, Wednesday, February 3, 2000; *Texas Almanac 2009–2010*, 500–10.

22. The following is drawn from Bradley R. Rice, "Commission Form of City Government," *Handbook of Texas Online*.

23. Dallas Morning News, *Texas Almanac 1996–97* (Dallas: Dallas Morning News, 1995), p. 513.

24. Correspondence with Terrell Blodgett, Wednesday, February 3, 2000.

25. For a further discussion, see Terrell Blodgett, "Council-Manager Form of City Government," *Handbook of Texas Online*; Blodgett, *Texas Home Rule Charters*.

26. For a history of the Office of Controller in Houston, see "Office History."

27. Jack C. Plano and Milton Greenberg, *The American Political Dictionary*, 10th ed. (Fort Worth: Harcourt, Brace, 1997).

28. *Texas Almanac and State Industrial Guide, 2000–2001* (Dallas: Dallas Morning News, I.P 1999), p. 533; *Statistical Abstract of the United States* (Washington, DC: Bureau of the Census, 1998), p. 496.

29. Brooks Egerton and Reese Dunklin, "Government by Developer," *Dallas Morning News*, June 10, 2001, p. 1A.

30. Peggy Heinkel-Wolfe, "Developers Still Using Renters to Create Special Tax Districts," *Dallas Morning News*, November 1, 2006, p. 1B.

31. Peggy Heinkel-Wolfe, "Bonds Approved with Blessing of 2 Voters," *Dallas Morning News*, November 22, 2010, p. B6.

32. Sara C. Galvan, "Wrestling with MUDs to Pin Down the Truth about Special Districts," 75 *Fordham Law Review* (2007), 3041–80.

33. See Texas Association of Regional Councils, "About TARC."

answer key

Chapter 1
1. b
2. a
3. c
4. b
5. b
6. d
7. c
8. a
9. e
10. c
11. b
12. c
13. a
14. a

Chapter 2
1. c
2. c
3. a
4. a
5. c
6. c
7. e
8. b
9. a
10. b
11. e
12. e
13. a
14. e
15. b

Chapter 3
1. a
2. c
3. d

4. c
5. e
6. d
7. a
8. d
9. d
10. c
11. a
12. a
13. d
14. d
15. d

Chapter 4
1. b
2. b
3. a
4. b
5. a
6. a
7. a
8. d
9. c
10. b
11. b
12. a

Chapter 5
1. c
2. c
3. d
4. e
5. c
6. c
7. a
8. a
9. a

10. c
11. b
12. b
13. a
14. d
15. c

Chapter 6
1. b
2. e
3. e
4. e
5. a
6. e
7. a
8. d
9. e
10. c
11. c
12. e
13. b
14. d
15. a

Chapter 7
1. a
2. a
3. d
4. b
5. c
6. b
7. d
8. d
9. c
10. a
11. d
12. a

13. d
14. a

Chapter 8
1. d
2. e
3. e
4. b
5. d
6. a
7. a
8. b
9. b
10. b
11. e
12. a
13. c
14. a
15. e

Chapter 9
1. c
2. c
3. c
4. b
5. b
6. a
7. e
8. d
9. e
10. e
11 e
12 a
13. a
14. a
15. c

Chapter 10
1. a
2. b
3. c
4. c
5. d
6. c
7. e
8. a
9. b
10. e
11. c
12. e
13. a

Chapter 11
1. a
2. b
3. a
4. a
5. c
6. b
7. b
8. c
9. a
10. b
11. d
12. d
13. a
14. b

Chapter 12
1. b
2. a
3. a
4. b

5. e
6. a
7. c
8. b
9. c
10. c
11. a
12. d

Chapter 13
1. b
2. d
3. d

4. d
5. c
6. a
7. b
8. b
9. d
10. e
11. a
12. a
13. c
14. a
15. b

credits

Chapter 1: Page 2: Bo Zaunders/Corbis; p. 7: Karl Stolleis/Getty Images; p. 10: Ted Spiegel/Corbis; p. 11: Joseph Scherschel/Time & Life Pictures/Getty Images; p. 14: Bettmann/Corbis; p. Mike Stone/Reuters/Newscom; p. 17: Jason Janik/Bloomberg via Getty Images; p. 19: Bettmann/Corbis; p. 20: Marjorie Kamys Cotera/Daemmrich Photography; p. 22: Petri (Fredich Richard) Collection, di_01468, The Dolph Briscoe Center for American History, The University of Texas at Austin; p. 23: AP Photo; p. 25: AP Photo; p. 31: Robert W. Ginn/Alamy; p. 34: Jensen Walker/Getty Images. **Chapter 2:** Page 38: Bob Daemmrich/Alamy; p. 41: Superstock; p. 46: Courtesy Sam Houston Memorial Museum; p. 48: MCT via Getty Images; p. 50 (both): Library of Congress; p.54 (left): Time & Life Pictures/Getty Images; (right): Popperfoto/Getty Images; p. 56: AP Photo; p. 58: Richard Ellis/Getty Images; p. 60: AP Photo; p. 61: AP Photo; p. 62: Steve Taylor. **Chapter 3:** Page 68: Lana Sundman/Alamy; p. 73: Library of Congress; p. 75: Courtesy Texas State Library and Archives Commission; p. 77: Library of Congress; p. 78: Courtesy Terry Jeanson, TexasEscapes.com; p. 82: Courtesy Texas State Library and Archives Commission; p. 92: Courtesy Bob Taylor; p. 93: AP Photo; p. 96: Harry Lynch/Raleigh News & Observer/MCT via Getty Images; p. 97: AP Photo. **Chapter 4:** Page 104: Courtesy Mark Bauer; pgs: 07-108: AP Photo; p. 113; Courtesy David K. Stall; p. 114: ZUMA Press, Inc./Alamy; p. 115; Erich Schlegel/Dallas Morning News/Corbis; p. 119: Al Fenn/Time Life Pictures/Getty Images; p. 126: AP Photo. **Chapter 5:** Page 132: AP Photo; p. 137: Adam Lotia; p. 139: Time & Life Pictures/Getty Images; p. 143: AP Photo; p. 145: AP Photo; p. 152: Jeff Newman/ZUMA Press/Newscom; p. 156: Tom Reel/San Antonio Express News/ZUMA Press/Newscom. **Chapter 6:** Page 160: AP Photo; p. 163: Larry Kolvoord/American Statesman/World Picture Network; p. 166: Photo by Lisa Provence; p. 168: Courtesy www.empowertexans.com; p. 174: Bob Daemmrich/Bob Daemmrich Photography, Inc./Corbis; p. 176: AP Photo. **Chapter 7:** Page 180: Kyle Woods/Texas House of Representatives; p. 183: Chris Howes/Wild Places Photography/Alamy; p. 184: AP Photo; p. 188: David Coleman/Alamy; p. 195: Bob Daemmrich; p. 196: Courtesy Office of the Governor Rick Perry; p. 198: Bob Daemmrich; p. 199: AP Photo; p. 200: AP Photo; p. 202: Laura Skelding, Austin American-Statesman/World Picture Network; p. 204: AP Photo; p. 206: AP Photo. **Chapter 8:** Page 212: AP Photo; p. 216: David Woo KRT/Newscom; p. 219: AP Photo; p. 222: AP Photo; p. 224: Mark Wilson/Getty Images; p. 229: AP Photo; p. 231: AP Photo; p. 233: AP Photo; p. 236: AP Photo; p. 239: AP Photo; p. 241: AP Photo. **Chapter 9:** Page 246: Darren Greenwood/Getty Images; p. 249: Courtesy Texas Supreme Court; p. 251: Courtesy Texas Court of Criminal Appeals; p. 253: AP Photo; p. 256: AP Photo; p. 257: Sargent: © 2001 & 2002 The Austin American Statesman. Reprinted with permission of Universal Press Syndicate. All rights reserved; p. 258: Courtesy Rebeca Martinez; p. 260: Courtesy Keith Hampton for Judge Campaign; p. 267: Bob Daemmrich/Corbis. **Chapter 10:** Page 278: AP Photo; p. 282: Paul Moseley/Fort Worth Star-Telegram/MCT via Getty Images; p. 284: Steve Snodgrass. January 2012. Bonding Service sign. http://creativecommons.org/licenses/by/2.0/deed.en; p. 285: AP Photo; p. 287: Courtesy Rosemary Lehmberg and GNI Strategies; p. 289: AP Photo; p. 295: Courtesy Roo Reynolds (rooreynolds.com); p. 297: AP Photo; p. 300: Reuters/Landov; p. 304: Robert Nickelsberg/Getty Image. **Chapter 11:** Page 310: Marjorie Kamys Cotera/Daemmrich Photos/The Image Works; p. 316: AP Photo; p. 319: AP Photo; p. 324: AP Photo; p. 326: Rodolfo Gonzalez/Austin-American Statesman. **Chapter 12:** Page 342: Paul Moselley/KRT/Newscom; p. 347: AP Photo; p. 349: AP Photo; p. 352: Corbis; p. 354: Picture Contact BV/Alamy; p. 357: Robert Nickelsberg/Getty Images; p. 364: AP Photo; p. 371: Mike Stone/Reuters/Landov. **Chapter 13:** Page 378: David Woo/Dallas Morning News; p. 384: Tom Pennington/Getty Images for Texas Motor Speedway; p. 385: David Lawrence/Corbis; p. 386: AP Photo; p. 387: AP Photo; p. 390: North Wind Picture Archive; p. 392: Courtesy of the Office of Mayor Annise Parker; p. 393 (top): AP Photo; (bottom): Jason Janik; p. 394: Courtesy Lacy Lakeview City Council; p. 399: Charles O'Rear/Corbis.

index

Page numbers in *italics* refer to figures, illustrations, and tables.

corporate franchise tax, 319
Corpus Christi, 27, *389*
Corral City, 388
corruption, 380
cotton industry, *10*, 10–11, 12, 31
council-manager form of government, 391, 392–93, 395
councils of government (COGs), 400–401
country roads, maintenance and construction of, 385–86
county attorneys, 286, 386
county auditors, 387
county chairs, 111
county clerks, 387
county commissioners, 382, *383*, 385
county commissioners court, 381–83, *382*, 384, 385
county convention, 112
county courts, 252
county executive committee, 111
county government, 381–88, *397*
    functions of, *385*, 385–88
    numerous county offices and, 381–83, *382*, *383*
    size/population of counties and, 383–85
county judges, 252, 382
county-level courts, *250*
county tax assessor-collectors, 387
court-appointed lawyers, 255
court of appeals, *250*, 251, 252
court of criminal appeals, 123, *250*, 251, *251*, 252, 256, 258, 262, 273, 296, 299
courts
    influence on legislative agenda, 198–99
    structure of, 249, *249*, *250*, 251, 251–53
    see also Supreme Court, U.S.; Texas judiciary; Texas Supreme Court
Craddick, Tom, 181, 200, *200*, 205, 207
Creager, R. B., 118
crime
    classification of, *281*, 281–83
    property, 292
    punishing, *281*, 282–83, 285
    violent, 292, 293, 294
criminal cases, 255

criminal justice system
    district attorneys and, 286–88, *287*
    integrity of, 299–304, 305
        death penalty and wrongful convictions, 299
        Graves case and, 303–4
        problems with police procedures and evidence, 299–301
        Tulia drug arrests and, 302–3
        Willingham case and, 301–2
    process after arrest, 283–88
        arraignment and posting bail, 283–84, *284*
        as creating criminals, 285–86
        grand jury indictment, 284
        pretrial hearings, 284–85, *285*
        trial and sentencing, 285
    reforms, 304–5
    in Texas *vs.* in other states, *291*
    see also death penalty; prison system
criminal law, 254
crop-lien system, 10–11
Cruz, Ted, 59, 110, 111, 117, 132, *132*, 133–34, 264
Culberson, Charles A., 48, *218*
culture, political. *See* political culture

D
Dallas
    city government in, 391, 393, 395
    immigrants in, *34*
    in Metroplex, 31–32
    municipal judges in, 253
    population of, 27, *30*, 31, 60, *389*
    scandal involving city council members, 380
    special districts in, 400
Dallas County
    courts in, 251, 253
    death sentences and, 296
    judicial elections in, 266
    political parties in, 125, 126–27
    prisoners in, 386
    race, ethnicity, and, *30*
    scandal involving constables in, 378, 379–80
Dallas–Fort Worth International Airport, 18

Dallas–Fort Worth metropolitan area, 31–32
Dallas Police Department, 305
Daniel, Price, 217
Daniel, Price, Sr., 346
Davis, Edmund J., 81, 83, 117, 234
death penalty, 247–48, *291*, 296–99, 305, 385
    appeals, 296, 297
    governor and, 226, 298
    minorities and, 298
    racial and ethnic variations in, 148
    wrongful convictions and, 299
debt service, 330
Declaration of Independence, Texas, 74–76, *75*, 87, 345
defendants, 255
DeLay, Tom, 55, *63*, 123, 206
Democratic Party, 4, 106, 107, 125–26, 128–29, *129*
    African Americans and, 105, 106, 108, 110, 111, 127, 140–41, 148, 157
    conflicts within, 118–19, 124
    conservative Democrats and, 81, 119–20, 123
    contemporary, 109, 110–11
    control of Texas legislature, 6, 50, 117
    funds raised in 2010, *155*
    Latinos and, 105, 106, 108, 109, 111, 127, 129, 148, 157
    New Deal and, 53
    redistricting and, 149, 205–7
    in Texas House, 105, *120*, *205*
    Texas judges in, 260, 262, 263, 959
    see also political parties
Denton, 31, 60, 391
Denton County, 400
Department of Agriculture, 232
Department of Human Resources, 354
Department of Justice, 143.204–5
Department of Parks and Wildlife, 236, *236*
Department of Public Safety, 143, 219, 224
Department of Public Welfare, 352, 353, 354
Department of Transportation, 23, 161, 162

incumbents, 154, 156, 173–74, *174*
indentured servants, 126
independent candidates, 137–38
Indiana toll road, 161
indictments, 255
indigent criminal defendants, 255
individualistic political culture, 5
inheritance tax, 320
Innocence Project, 300, 302
Inspector of Hides and Animals, Office of the, 69–70
Institute on Taxation and Economic Policy, 322
Insurance, Texas Department of, 237–38
insurance companies, 237–38
insurance occupation taxes, 320
interest groups, 161–76
    definition of, 163
    "8F Crowd" and, 163, 164
    incumbents and, 173–74
    influence on legislature, 199
    interests unrepresented by, 170, 172–73
    judges and, 249, 269
    policy makers and, 164–65, 166–67, 169–70
    political action committees and, 172–75
    types of, 165–66
Interior Lowlands, 8, *8*
interstate commerce, 52, 55–56, 57
Interstate Highway System, 13, *13*, 125
introduction in legislative process, definition of, 191
investigative powers, 190
Ireland, John, *218*
irrigation, 368
Irving, 31
issue advocacy, 172

J
Jackson, Andrew, 41
James, Craig, 133
Jasper County, 384
Jasper County Courthouse, *387*
Jaybird Party, 140–41
Jefferson, Thomas, 75–76
Jefferson, Wallace, 127
Jefferson County, 296
Jim Crow laws, 5
JOBS, 356

Johnson, Andrew, 79
Johnson, Gary, 114, *114*
Johnson, Lyndon B., *54*, 58, *63*, 113
    civil rights and, 53, 54, 141
    factional battles and, 120, 124
    Great Society and, 43
    New Deal and, 51, 53, 54
    swearing in of, 264
    voting rights and, 141
    War on Poverty, 354
Joint Committee on Prison Reform, 289
joint resolutions, 190
Jones, Anson, 77
Jones, Elizabeth Ames, 174
Jones, Jesse, 51, 64, 163
Jones, Mark, 123
Jones, Marvin, 51
Jordan, Barbara, 25
judges
    federal, 249
    in Texas, 87, 246, 249, *249*, 251, *251*, 252
        alternative selection system for, 266–68, 273
        appointment by governor, *257*, 257–59, *259*
        civil court *vs.* criminal court, 257
        county, 252, 382
        courts of appeals, 251
        discipline of, 271–72
        district, 251–52
        election of, 257, 258, 259–62, *261*, 263, 266–68, 273–74
        justice of the peace, 252–53
        names of, 262, 264
        removal of, 257
        statutory probate court, 252
judicial branch. *See* Texas judiciary
Judicial Campaign Fairness Act, 268
judicial politics, 256–68
    alternative selection system and, 266–68, 273
    highly partisan elections and, 259–62, *261*, 273
    initial appointment of judges by governor, *257*, 257–59, *259*
    minority representation and, *264*, 264–66
    name game and, 262, 264

judicial powers
    of Texas governor, 225–26
    of Texas legislators, 191
Junell, Rob, 92
juries
    felony, 285
    grand, 255, 284
    women on, *98*
Justice, Department of
    redistricting and, 204–5
    voter identification law and, 143
justice of the peace courts, *250*, 252–53

K
Keffer, Jim, 168
Keller, Sharon, 247, 248, 260, 299
Kelo v. City of New London, 162
Kennedy, Edward, 239
Kennedy, John F., 113, 264
Kentucky, 5
Kerrigan, Patricia, 262
Kerry, John, 146
Kinch, Sam, 217
Kinder, Donald, 148
King Ranch, *11*
Kirby, William, 347
Kirk, Ron, 110, 127, 133
Kitchin, Claude, 49
Klotz Associates, 161
Koons, Don, 260

L
labor unions, 6
land commissioner, 231, *231*
Laney, Pete, 220
Lanham, S. W. T., *218*
Lara, José Bernardo Gutiérrez de, 72
La Raza Unida Party, 113, 115
Laredo, *389*
Latinos
    bilingual education and, 149
    death penalty and, 148
    on death row in Texas, 298
    DREAM Act and, 149
    election of 2008 and, 147
    health insurance and, 365
    high school graduation rate for, 351
    as Medicaid recipients, 360, *360*
    party affiliations of, 105–6, 108, 109, 111, 113, 115, 127–28, 129, 148, 157

Roosevelt, Franklin Delano, 117
court-packing plan of, 51, 53
election of 1932, 51
New Deal and, 40, 42–43, 51,
53, 64, 353
Roosevelt, Theodore, 49, 114
Ross, Lawrence S., *218*
Ruiz, David, *289*
Ruiz v. Estelle, 289, 290
runoff primary elections, 135, 157
rural areas, 125
see also county government
Russia, 49

S
SAC (Sunset Advisory
Commission), 240
Sadler, Paul, 134
sales taxes, 61, 315–16
same-sex marriage, 93, *95*, 96, 97,
98, 148–49, 392
San Antonio, 32, 392
Anglo influence on, 27–28
cotton industry and, 10
Democratic Party and, 111
population of, 27, *30*, 32, *389*
Spanish influence on, 27
San Antonio Railroad, 32
San Antonio school district, 346
San Antonio v. Rodriguez, 346–47
Sanchez, Tony, 127–28, 154, 217
Sanders, Lynn, 148
Sandlin, Max, 123
San Jacinto, Battle of, 76
Santa Anna, 76
Santorum, Rick, 110
SAT scores, 351
Sayers, Joseph D., *218*
school desegregation, 346
school districts
funding for, 68, 346–50
as special districts, 395–96
schools, public. *See* public schools
school segregation, 25, 82
Schumpeter, Joseph, 9
SCOPE (Select Committee on
Public Education), 350
Sculley, Sheryl, 392
Second Amendment, 56
secretary of state, 228–29
Securities and Exchange
Commission, 90
segregation, 23, 25, 30, 46, 82

Select Committee on Public
Education (SCOPE), 350
Senate, U.S., 134
first Texans elected to, 46
impeachment and, 88
see also Congress, U.S.
Senate Bill 1, 348
Senate Bill 7, 349
Senate Bill 351, 348–49
Senate Criminal Justice
Committee, 235
Senate Finance Committee, 230, 331
senatorial courtesy, 223
sentencing, 285
separation of powers, 85
Sephra Burks Law, 175
SES (socioeconomic status), 145
Seventeenth Amendment, 40, 48
Shapiro, Florence, 167
Shapleigh, Eliot, 193
sharecropping system, 10–11
Sharp, John, 127, 356
Sharpstown State Bank, 89–90, *92*
Sheehan, Cindy, *386*
Sheppard, Morris, 48, 51
Sheppard-Towner Act, 48
sheriffs, 386, *386*
Sherman Anti-Trust Act, 49
Shivercrat movement, 53, 118
Shivers, Allan, 53, 118, *119*, 124,
215–16, 217, 226
Sibley, David, 169
Sid W. Richardson Foundation, 16
Sierra Club, 166
simple resolutions, 190
single-member districts, 116,
203, 390
Sixteenth Amendment, 39–40
slavery, 42, 80
in Texas, 20, 24, 76, 78, 79
traditionalistic political culture
and, 5
Smith, Preston, 90, 235
Smith County, 97, 386
Smith v. Allwright, 25, 140
smoke alarms, 175
SNAP, 354
socialization, political, 109
social media, 154
social policy. *See* public policy
Social Security, 43
Social Security Act, 43, 353, 358,
361, 365

social service functions of Texas
counties, 387–88
socioeconomic status (SES), 145
Solomon, Burt, 182
sonogram law, 364
South Carolina, 41
South Dakota, 56–57, 322
South Dakota v. Dole, 56–57
Southland Corporation, 142
sovereign, definition of, 41
Soviet Union, 54
Spain, 72–73
Spanish Texas, 72–73
Speaker of the House (Texas), 108,
108, 181–82, 193, 195,
200, *200*, 201, 203, 207,
241, 331
Speaker of the House (U.S.), *63*
special bills, 189
special districts, 395–96, 398–401
nonschool, 395, 396, 398–400
problems with, 399–400
school districts, 395–96
special elections, 136
special purpose governments, 381
Special School Fund, 345
special sessions of Texas legislature,
187, 189, 225
spending in Texas, trends in,
314–15, *315*
Spindletop, 12
SSI (Supplemental Security
Income) program, 354
standardized test scores, 351
standing committees, 191, 193,
194, 203
Staples, Todd, *155*
STAR Health, 359
STAR+PLUS, 359
STAR (State of Texas Access
Reform) program, 359
State Bar of Texas, 270
State Board of Education, 87, 215,
226, 238–40, *239*, 345, 350
state chair, definition of, 112
State Commission on Judicial
Conduct, 247, 271
state conventions, 112
State Depository Board, 234
state executive committee, 112
State Farm, 237–38
state government
dual federalism and, *42*, 42–43

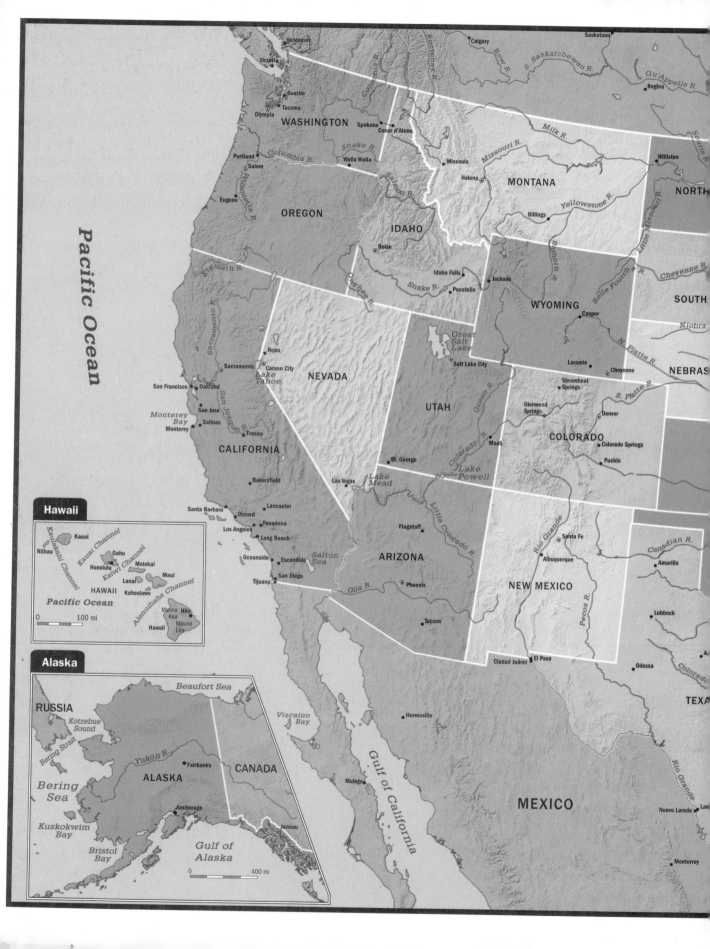

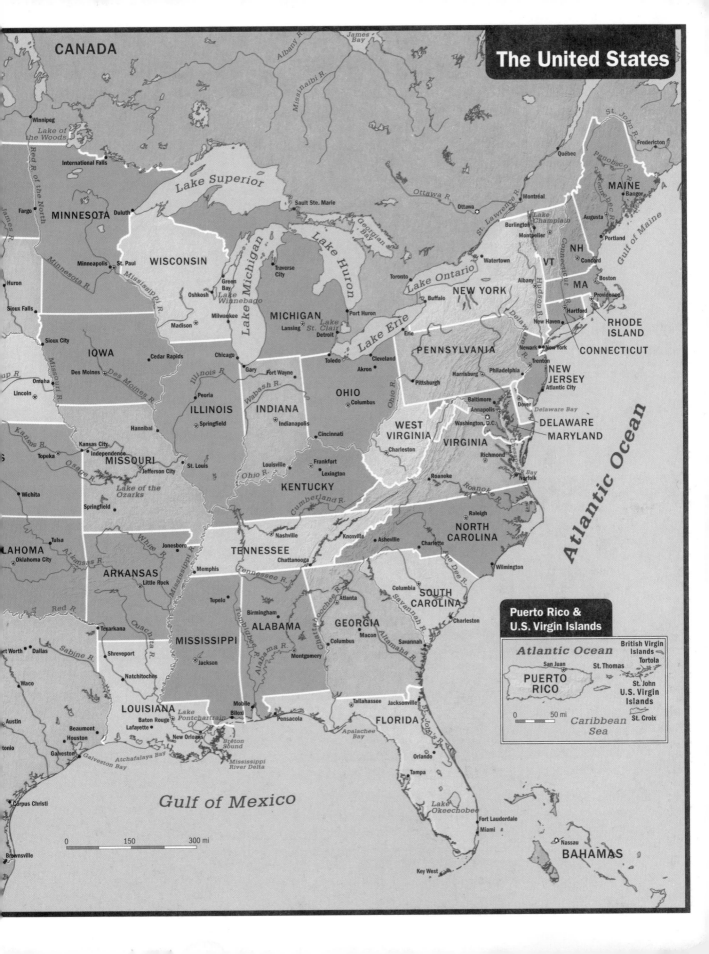